# Essays in Southern Economic Development

Edited by
Melvin L. Greenhut
and W. Tate Whitman

THE UNIVERSITY OF NORTH CAROLINA PRESS · CHAPEL HILL

*Copyright © 1964 by The University of North Carolina Press*

*Library of Congress Catalog Card Number 64-13551*

*Printed by the Seeman Printery, Durham, North Carolina*

*Manufactured in the United States of America*

338.0975
G 83 e
Cop. 2

Map & Geog.

# Preface

This volume consists of papers which grew out of research projects supported in part or whole by the Inter-University Committee for Economic Research on the South. The Committee was established in 1958 and now consists of: James Buchanan, University of Virginia; Alan Cartter, American Council on Education; Frank de Vyver, Duke University; Melvin Greenhut, Florida State University; Maurice Lee, The University of North Carolina at Chapel Hill; John McFerrin, University of Florida; James McKie, Vanderbilt University; Howard Schaller, Indiana University; Ernst Swanson, North Carolina State of The University of North Carolina at Raleigh; and W. Tate Whitman, Emory University. During a considerable part of its existence, the Committee included B. U. Ratchford and William Nicholls as members.

The Committee received a Ford Foundation grant in 1958 for the purpose of encouraging research on Southern economic development. Under this grant, it sponsored several conferences in the past and is planning two during the year 1964. In addition, the Committee has provided funds to various professors throughout the nation to assist them in research projects concerned with the Southern economy. Several studies supported by grants from the Committee have resulted in articles published in professional journals and in books.

The present collection of essays comprises papers which the editors of this book believe are representative as well as of great value to scholars interested in a region's economic development. Materials published elsewhere as a separate volume, and most papers published in journals before the beginning of the editorial processing of this book, were automatically excluded from consideration. Still other papers proposed for consideration are not included here because of either their high specialization and/or a subject matter content which falls outside the basic interest areas of most economists.

It is because the papers included in this collection actually are not part of any basic plan of study on Southern economic development, but rather are essentially the outgrowth of the *individual* interests of their authors, that a classification of them or an impelling division of the book has been veritably impossible. What has been done in this respect is simply to group together papers which used common methods of analysis or were concerned with somewhat related themes. This grouping was done in the belief that some division, even though rough, would aid readers in finding material of special interest. Because no clear-cut division of subject matter or methodology exists, we have not titled the different parts of the book. In partial substitution, we have presented brief introductions to the papers in each part of the book. Readers who wish to know in advance the main objectives and findings of a paper may thereby gain a bird's-eye view. For reasons related to the general background of the book, we encouraged each writer to use whatever style he most preferred rather than to follow a designated format. Manifestly, the present volume is simply a collection of diverse essays, each concerned with some phase of the economic development of the South.

December 20, 1963                                   The Editors

# Contents

# List of Charts

# List of Figures

# List of Maps

# List of Tables

Chapter

## VI. Trends in Population and Employment in the South, 1930–60

### Appendix Tables

## VII. Income in the South Since 1929

**XIII. The Postwar Corps of Engineers Program in Ten Southern States: An Evaluation of Economic Efficiency**

# Essays in Southern Economic Development

# PART ONE

## Introductory Summary

The initial paper, by Clarence H. Danhof, surveys the literature which deals with the broad problem posed by the South's seemingly bounteous resources and the less than satisfactory results the region derives from their use. His survey reveals four views of "basic approaches to a more satisfactory economic order" for the South. One view "looked backward to an organization reaffirming traditional values; another concentrated on incremental improvements in the position of the farmers." A third view, not inconsistent with the first two, was that "disaffected Southerners should migrate out of the region." The fourth "looked towards industrial development within the region as a solution to its problems."

The fourth position, Danhof feels, was the most significant, and provided the most extensive analysis and prescription. Therefore, the bulk of his article is concerned with the problem of industrial development—causes for the lack of it and programs for its achievement.

Danhof notes that in much of the literature prior to the end of World War II a "conspiracy thesis" was accepted as the explanation of the South's economic problems. Although he finds no direct critique of the thesis, he summarizes the analyses and evaluations which appeared following World War II of each of the major specific charges—tariffs, railroad rates, monopoly, and absentee ownership. The author concludes that: "the colonial-imperialistic thesis of conspiracy must be considered an unfortunate episode—a resurgence of a crude sectionalism—that diverted the attention of some of the South's ablest men from constructive approaches to the region's problems."

The final portion of the paper is devoted to the economic situation and writings of the post-World War II period. Danhof views the study by Calvin B. Hoover and B. U. Ratchford entitled *Economic Resources and Policies of the South* (1951), which took the fundamental position "that Southern economic growth was dependent upon a national economy operating at high levels of unemployment," as a major "turning point in the analysis of Southern economic problems." The thorough survey of the literature of this period bears him out.

The next article in Part One is by C. Addison Hickman; it deals with the exercise of the entrepreneurial function in the South. This paper is divided into two sections: the first is "concerned with establishing an approach to the functions of entrepreneurship," and the second "attempts to utilize the approaches developed . . . toward gaining greater understanding of the entrepreneurial function in the South."

The first section sketches the traditional concept of the entrepreneurial function. Here the author describes some contemporary concepts which attempt to redefine the entrepreneurial function in the light of present-day business organization structures, and the economic, political, and social environment within which the firm operates. He examines aspects of the internal and external environment of the firm, in particular those which assume relevance in terms of the redefined entrepreneurial function. The reader will find in this part of the paper the venturer or leader, the therapist, balance wheel, or unifier, and the all-purpose entrepreneur.

The second section, dealing specifically with the entrepreneurial function in the South, seeks to shed light "upon how that function, as it exists in the South, compares in character and in quantitative terms to the function in the United States as a whole." The analysis proceeds through an investigation of the internal and external environments and their implications for entrepreneurship in the South. Finally, reference is made to forces that may bring the South, and perhaps Southern entrepreneurship, into closer conformity with the remainder of the country.

Following the paper on general aspects of entrepreneurship in the South, James Hund and Harding Young present the results of their study on "Negro Entrepreneurship in Southern Economic Development." Through investigation of the background, development, and present status of Negro entrepreneurship in the South, they attempt to answer such questions as: Will the southern Negro be ready to move into the mainstream of the region's economic life when the opportunity appears? If he is, what form will the participation take—expansion of Negro business parallel with white or an amalgam of business efforts without regard to racial identity? Emphasis is placed on culture, social mores, and other factors found to affect the growth of Negro entrepreneurship.

The study provides a review of the existing relevant literature and information obtained from interviews with Negro businessmen representing a cross-section of types of business enterprises in selected Southern cities. The findings cover past and current barriers to the development and growth of Negro business, and include examples of sizable and important units owned and operated by Negroes, and the origins of these units. Most Negro entrepreneurs in the South have had advanced education. Some have been educators. A good many have obtained business experience in rather unusual ways. Motivation has often been the "uplift" of the race rather than profits, though the latter have been necessary to the former. Much business opportunity for Negroes has, as we know, sprung from the practices of segregation which provided an isolated market. Integration is seen by most of those interviewed, however, as more an opportunity than a threat to business success. (Incidentally, operators of small retail stores and service establishments were not interviewed.)

Young and Hund conclude that although Negro-owned and -operated enterprises will continue to exist, the long-range future of Negro business does not lie in this direction, but in integration of the work forces in both white and Negro enterprises. This is beginning to occur, even in the South. When the pattern develops more fully, the authors feel that the future of potential Negro entrepreneurs possessing a solid background of education and experience stemming from a gradual elimination of discrimination will be bright. The current contribution of Negro entrepreneurs is found to be in "the constant modification of structures, situations, or ideas in a continuing process of interaction."

The last paper included in Part One is by George Macesich. In it, the hypothesis is made and tested that Southern bankers have a higher "liquidity preference" than do bankers elsewhere in the country and hence are not helping to foster the industrial development of the South as much as they could. Macesich's findings fail to confirm this hypothesis. He suggests, accordingly, the following implications for Southern development:

(1) Member banks of the Fifth and Sixth Federal Reserve Districts do not appear to be derelict in performing their principal function of lending money to business. In fact, their performance appears to be better than that of member banks in many other districts in the country.

(2) Member banks are not serving in the first instance as a vehicle for the transfer of resources out of the region, which conclusion he derives from the comparatively smaller proportion of their assets held in U.S. Government Securities. Masesich observes that loans may also be made on a national market and, when they are, no difference exists between the drainage effects on loans and those on investments in governments. He points out, however, that the majority of business loans, on balance, are made in local markets.

(3) Southern bankers appear to be less "conservative" in their financial outlook than their counterparts elsewhere.

We might summarize Macesich's findings by noting that Southern bankers may, in fact, be more active in promoting this region's economic development than is generally true of banking elsewhere in the United States.

# I

## Four Decades of Thought on the South's Economic Problems*

*Clarence H. Danhof*

Southerners have perennially been impressed by the resources of their region and frustrated by the results that have followed from their use. The broad problem so posed has generated a literature which, both in size and in diversity of view as to objectives, diagnoses, and prognoses, exceeds that of any other region of the United States. The sheer mass of this literature as well as its diversity reflect a broad participation in a debate that began a century and a quarter ago. The participants have included journalists; men of public affairs; and academicians, particularly sociologists, historians, literati, and, increasingly in the last two decades, economists. In the years since 1920, the period of interest here, the large majority have been Southerners, though numerous non-Southerners have also contributed their observations. Though many Southerners have claimed to speak for the South, or sought to do so by offering their ideas as rallying points, no single spokesman has articulated a position that can be accepted as Southern doctrine on its special economic problems.[1] Many value positions, analyses, and policy proposals have been rejected as untrue, unworkable, or undesirable, though elements of such ideas frequently

* This study has been completed while the author was serving as a member of the Senior Staff, The Brookings Institution. The views expressed in this study are those of the author and do not purport to represent the views of the other staff members, officers, or trustees of the Brookings Institution. The author is indebted to Stephen L. McDonald for his comments made when an earlier draft of this study was prepared for the Second Annual Conference of the Inter-University Committee for Economic Research on the South.

1. That very great diversity exists also in Southern politics is pointed out in V. O. Key's classic study, *Southern Politics in State and Nation* (New York, 1949), esp. p. 504.

are to be found in the more recent literature as part of an unconscious intellectual heritage. Widely accepted objectives and related policies have, however, emerged from the slow and laborious process of public discussion. This body of thought constitutes the current generally accepted position, recognizes the areas sensitive to action, and identifies unresolved problems of Southern economic change.

This literature has arisen in response to the need for interpreting the significance to the South of the vigorous growth of the North's economy. Before 1840, the two regions were not markedly dissimilar in productivity per worker or in the nature of productive activity.[2] Thereafter, the growth of non-agricultural economic pursuits in the North was so rapid that active concern developed in the 1850's in the South over the region's changing relationships to the national economy. Though Southern per capita incomes in 1860 compared favorably with incomes in the North, the distinguished Southern editor, J. B. D. De Bow, foresaw the increasing divergence and urged Southerners to follow the methods of the North, particularly of Massachusetts, if the South wished to have power and wealth.[3] Numerous conventions were called to consider the issue but no program resulted; the small commercial classes of the South could not arouse in the dominant planter groups an interest in exploring the possibilities of manufacturing. De Bow nevertheless inaugurated a concern with the South's economy and its economic policies that has continued to the present time.

The Civil War interrupted the debate. A substantial manufacturing effort was stimulated by the war but was not maintained. Instead, the war provided a facile explanation for the deficiencies of the Southern economy, an apologia that persisted for more than three-quarters of a century with little support from objective analysis.[4]

2. Richard A. Easterlin, "Interregional Differences in Per Capita Income, Population and Total Income 1840–1950," *Trends in The American Economy in the Nineteenth Century,* National Bureau of Economic Research (Princeton, 1960), pp. 97–105.

3. Cited in Joseph Dorfman, *The Economic Mind in American Civilization 1606-1865* (New York, 1946), II, 906, 947. De Bow's review also published numerous apologia for an agrarian anti-industrial society.

4. Uncritical views of the causal relationship between the Civil War, particularly the destruction of capital involved, and the South's subsequent economic lag are nearly universal in the literature. A straightforward statement of the common view is James L. Sellers' "Economic Incidence of the Civil War in the South," *Mississippi Valley Historical Review,* XIV (1927–28), 178–91. For critical comment on this thesis see Ralph Andreano (ed.), *The Economic Impact of the American Civil War* (Cambridge, 1962), particularly the editor's introduction; Joe A. Martin, "Some Myths of Southern Economic Growth: A Study of

In the years immediately following the war, Southerners were pre-occupied with re-establishing the institutional basis of their society, particularly that of their agricultural economy. They succeeded with remarkable rapidity; the South's income from its staple crops reached a new peak in 1870, and production in physical terms reached new highs soon after. The bright prospects were diminished by the economically depressed years after 1870, but the postwar commitment to agricultural staples for international as well as national markets was too complete. Like other economic setbacks, the depressed cotton markets of the 1870's failed to stimulate any broad interest in change; in the opinion of most, cotton and tobacco remained the fundamental source of Southern wealth.

From 1880 to 1920, Southern per capita incomes changed little, whereas incomes rose steadily in the North as urban-based industry increasingly became dominant.[5] In the South, some manufacturing appeared, particularly in the textile and tobacco industries. The industrialization experienced by the South during the half-century prior to 1920 was the product of a group of Southern advocates of a New South pursuing a policy of aggressive imitation of the Northern system and welcoming Northern assistance and participation.[6] Though modestly successful, the advocates of this New South were of limited influence. The movement during these years was not of a magnitude capable of providing employment for those who might wish to escape the low returns of staple agriculture.

The last years of World War I were a brief period of considerable prosperity. "To simple men, glorying in good crops, the old way of life was restored."[7] But instead of establishing a trend, world markets for the South's staples collapsed after the war, and the South entered upon a depression while the rest of the nation moved forward. The deeper significance of the South's agricultural depression was not immediately apparent. Southern spokesmen were slow to understand its significance while "Southern farmers had never come to under-

Comparative Growth Rates in the Manufacturing Economy of the Eleven South-Eastern States," *Journal of Farm Economics,* XXXVIII (1956), 1363–74.

5. Contemporary awareness of these trends was based on general impressions rather than on quantitative data. Quantitative measures have become available with the publication of Everett S. Lee, Ann R. Miller, Carol Brainderd and Richard A. Easterlin, *Population Redistribution and Economic Growth, United States, 1870–1950,* ed. Simon S. Kuznets and Dorothy S. Thomas (Philadelphia, 1957), I, 703 ff.

6. Francis B. Simkins, *The South, Old and New; a History, 1820–1947* (New York, 1947), pp. 243 ff.

7. Thomas D. Clark, *The Emerging South* (New York, 1961), p. 12.

stand the meaning of statistics as applied to their future."[8] It slowly became apparent that the end of an era had arrived. With that realization, what had been a desultory debate was transformed into a vigorous and wide-ranging search for solutions to the South's economic problems.

Prior to 1920, Southerners, with few important exceptions, acted as if they believed themselves to be free to determine the terms of their rapprochement with the rest of the nation. That sense of freedom rested upon the position of the region's agricultural staples in world markets. Any such regional independence had disappeared in the post-World War I collapse of those international markets. The resulting, greatly increased dependence of the South's economy on that of the nation was only slowly recognized.[9] A rebuilding of the historic relationship was to be rendered impossible by a series of events that were external to the region but which had revolutionary impacts upon the South. World War I had temporarily accelerated industrialization in the South, disturbing traditional relationships more deeply than any events occurring since 1880. Of more lasting effect were the events that followed: the Great Depression; some of the policies of the federal government originating in the New Deal period; World War II; the subsequent high levels of economic activity; and the revolution in the South's technology centering on the automobile and, specifically in agriculture, on the tractor.

After 1920, the proposition that the Old South was a viable system in a modern world was no longer tenable.. In the South's cities and towns, labor unrest, accumulating during the war years, was followed by a build-up of union activity to culminate in a series of strikes marred by violence. Both agriculture and industrialization in the South gave cause for Southerners everywhere to engage in sober reassessments of the region's values and objectives, problems and policies.[10]

8. *Ibid.*, p. 13.

9. Jonathan Daniels in 1938 made the significant observation that "for most Southerners there is no choice between the Southern way and the alien way, they must take what they can get." *A Southerner Discovers the South* (New York, 1938), p. 117.    Howard Odum and Rupert Vance in their numerous writings held much the same position.    The Agrarians, discussed below, on the other hand necessarily assumed that a free choice was possible.    See also Donald Davidson, *The Attack on Leviathan* (Chapel Hill, 1938), p. 325.

10. As shared by the authors, almost all Southerners, of the articles that comprise *The Coming of Industry to the South*, the January, 1931, issue of *The Annals of the American Academy of Political and Social Science*.    Also such volumes as C. T. Murchison, *King Cotton is Sick* (Chapel Hill, 1930).

The forty years following 1920 were characterized by the search for a new rationale of the old system, for the causes of the South's predicament, for a new system, or for methods of accelerating the emergence of the New South that had been proclaimed several generations earlier. In the debate, the South, like the nation in dealing with recovery, grasped at a wide variety of ideas of all degrees of realism and feasibility.

Dissatisfaction with the operation of the South's economy was directed to many of its aspects and expressed in a variety of ways. In broad terms the problem was that of the relatively low incomes which characterized virtually all segments of the South's population. The income problem was, however, most acute for the region's farm population, which received much the lowest incomes in the United States and which was also a very large part of the region's population. Those incomes were low even in the prosperous years of World War I. The collapse of world markets for farm products after the war, though affecting all of the nation's farmers, struck most harshly in the South. The problems of this large farm population were central in most analyses of the South's economy.

The Great Depression accentuated the problems of the 1920's as urban employment opportunities disappeared and for a few years stimulated a reverse migration as migrants returned from the cities to the farms they had left. That movement proved no escape—poverty on the farm was as real as in the cities. With the development of federal programs to administer relief to the urban unemployed, a migration to urban centers once again was established, motivated in part at least by the minimum standards established by relief authorities, which were higher than those attainable on many Southern farms.

To the problems of economic depression were added those of technological change. The tractor was adopted in Southern agriculture much more slowly than elsewhere, but its effects in farm employment were drastic. Among its impacts were the consolidation of tenant holdings into operational units of large acreages and the substitution of a wage system for the old share-cropping system, with the end result of a forced displacement of the farming population. This tendency was greatly stimulated by the appearance of the mechanical cotton picker, while other innovations were to contribute to replacing the old system of cotton cultivation with one requiring far less labor. Simultaneously, the technological problems long associated with cattle-grazing in the South were solved to an important degree, greatly stimulating that industry at the expense of row crops. The growth of pulp-wood using industries, also based on technological change, similarly opened the way for a new productive use of land. All three developments promised higher labor incomes from land use but with necessary changes in the man-land ratio that greatly reduced the labor force necessary to produce the food and fiber that the market would accept at remunerative prices.

## The Search for Solutions

Four basic approaches to a more satisfactory economic order appear in the literature over this period. All four approaches attracted proponents over the four decades, though emphasis shifted with changing circumstances as the nation moved from deep economic depression to the high levels of economic activity of the war and postwar years. One group looked backward to an organization reaffirming traditional values; another concentrated on incremental improvements in the position of farmers. Both positions were consistent with a third view that disaffected Southerners should migrate out of the region. The first two positions were more or less vigorously espoused and the third was accepted as necessary, but a fourth approach was the most significant. This looked towards industrial development within the region as the solution to its problems.

### The Revival of Agrarianism

One position passively accepted the fact of low farm-incomes from marketed products, and urged a curtailment in those commercial relations and a return to self-sufficient agriculture. This position rested upon a deep and long-standing Southern commitment to the fundamental importance of agriculture and the virtues of rural life, with a parallel distrust of industrialism and urbanism.[11] Such views were expressed throughout the nation as the Great Depression spread

11. The values encompassed in the phrase, "agricultural fundamentalism" were widely held earlier in the nation's history. While persisting everywhere, these values remained more deeply held and more directly influential on everyday attitudes in the South than elsewhere; they were expressed in extreme form by the Agrarians. The depression-induced revival of these values was widespread, vigorously expressed in O. E. Baker, Ralph Borsodi, and M. L. Wilson, *Agriculture in Modern Life* (New York, 1939), particularly Part II. See also Joe R. Motheral, "The Family Farm and the Three Traditions," *Journal of Farm Economics*, XXXIII (1951), 514–29; Gilbert C. Fite, "The Historical Development of Agricultural Fundamentalism in the Nineteenth Century," *Journal of Farm Economics, Proceedings*, XLIV (1962), 1203–11.

but were most vigorously enunciated in the South. In the two decades following 1920, there was widespread pessimism regarding the future of industrialism or of the South's ability to move in that direction.[12] T. J. Cauley declared in 1935 that "farming had failed utterly in the matter of making money in the South in recent years, but it may still be capable of making a living for the people."[13]

The possible necessity of a return to self-sufficiency became in the hands of others a virtue. Blending their romantic views of Southern history and culture, a group of academicians known as the Southern Agrarians expounded the virtues and indeed the imperatives of a new agrarianism by which the South might neutralize Northern influences, isolate itself from the evils of urbanized industrialism, and retain its own cultural heritage. Though their theories varied in details and methods of accomplishment, the objective was a society based on numerous small but independent farmers who would "secure the state" and who would be supported by numerous small and independent business firms, competitive but responsible by reason of owner-management of property. Some of the Agrarians envisaged this new society as protected from Northern corporations as well as from the federal government in some manner as by regional tariffs.[14]

The Southern Agrarians may be viewed as the between-wars version of the Southern radical right or possibly as Utopians, whose views were rooted in the ideas of economists and social philosophers who had been concerned with a simpler world.[15] Though agricultural

12. The experience of some Southern states clearly supported pessimism regarding the future of industrialism. In Arkansas, Florida, Kentucky, Louisiana, and Mississippi, there were actually fewer jobs in industry in 1939 than in 1909. Vernon W. Ruttan, "Industrial Progress and Rural Stagnation in the New South," *Social Forces*, XXXIV (1955), 115.

13. In *Problems of the Cotton Economy*, Proceedings of the Southern Social Science Research Council (Dallas, 1936), p. 17. See also Cauley's *Agrarianism* (Chapel Hill, 1935).

14. The major statements are Twelve Southerners, *I'll Take My Stand: The South and the Agrarian Tradition* (New York, 1930) and Herbert Agar and Allen Tate (ed.), *Who Owns America? A New Declaration of Independence* (Boston, 1936).

15. For contemporary critiques see Rupert B. Vance, "Is Agrarianism for Farmers?," *Southern Review*, I (1935), 42–45; Thomas J. Pressly, "Agrarianism: An Autopsy," *Sewanee Review*, XLIX (1941), 145–63; Marian D. Irish, "Proposed Roads to the New South: Chapel Hill Planners vs. Nashville Agrarians," *Sewanee Review*, XLIX (1941), 1–27; W. J. Cash, *The Mind of the South* (New York, 1954), pp. 378–83. More recent appraisals include Idus A. Newby, "The Southern Agrarians: A View after Thirty Years," *Agricultural History*, XXXVII (1963), 143–55; William Nicholls, *Southern Tradition and Regional Progress* (Chapel Hill, 1960), esp. pp. 27–34.

fundamentalism and loyalty to traditional Southern values remained strong, the Agrarian's "vision of what the good life can be" was not widely shared. Pessimistic and backward-looking, the Agrarians stood aside from the main course of the debate, which was both optimistic in assuming that the nation could accomplish economic recovery and forward-looking in that the values that motivated most men rested upon a revival of the productivity of the nation's industrial economy.

## The Modernization of Agriculture

A second position also focused on agriculture but sought to improve the welfare of the farm population by strengthening the markets for their products. This group sought the intervention of the federal government in those markets through export bounties or price supports.[16] It sought also to increase the productivity of agriculture by applying superior techniques and better conservation practices and by reforms in the institutional structure of agriculture as in land tenure, financial and marketing institutions.[17] These objectives were shared with farm groups throughout the nation and were pursued by political alliances to form national coalitions.

Success in securing federal support of prices of farm products served to stabilize Southern farm income at somewhat higher levels, but did not and has not changed the relatively low level of those incomes. Federal credit programs and support for cooperative marketing arrangements have similarly alleviated the problem but have offered no major step toward solution. Efforts to settle families on small farms, on the other hand, have tended to accentuate the problems of low productivity and incomes.[18] The developments in farm technology greatly reduced labor requirements. Since the demand for the South's staple products was inelastic, a marked accentuation of the population problem followed upon the modernization of agricultural technology.[19]

Immediately after the war, the prospects facing the South's agri-

16. A brief authoritative account is that of Chester C. Davis, "The Development of Agricultural Policy Since the End of the World War," U.S. Department of Agriculture, *Yearbook, 1940* (Washington, 1941), pp. 297–326.

17. For an introduction to an extensive literature, see Broadus Mitchell, *Depression Decade, From New Era through New Deal, 1929–41* ("The Economic History of the United States," Vol. IX [New York, 1947]), pp. 421–24.

18. For a protest against the efforts to promote small farm settlements, see Robert W. Harrison, "Land Improvement vs. Land Settlement for the Southeast," *Southern Economic Journal*, XII (1945), 23–38.

19. James H. Street, *The New Revolution in the Cotton Economy* (Chapel Hill, 1957).

cultural population appeared "dreary." The war-stimulated acceleration in the adoption of technological changes was marked by wide
variations between farms in the acceptance of such changes. Farms
which adopted the new techniques tended to have good land-capital-
labor relationships and yielded incomes which, if not satisfactory compared with urban incomes, nevertheless permitted sound financing
and continued growth. They were to be distinguished from the low-
income farms that had not made such adjustments, most of which
were not likely to be able to do so. In 1949, it was estimated that
seventy percent of the nation's one million low-income full-time
farmers were located in the South. These had been "largely by-passed
by the movement of the decade to enlarge farm size and increase
productivity per acre."[20]

The possibility that the postwar federal farm programs might
introduce rigidities in the movement of the Southern farm population
was considered and discounted.[21] Programs looking towards improving the position of farmers have been beneficial to those in the best
position to take advantage of them by applying this newer technology,
but have accentuated employment problems for the large remaining
farm population. Earle L. Rauber urged that the key to the problem
of low agricultural incomes lay not in agriculture but in the national
economy as a whole: "In a demand for labor in the nation's industries
and at such wages that the excess of the population will be drained
off," or "better still, [in a] sufficient industrial expansion in the South
to absorb the surplus rural population."[22]

### Out-Migration

A third position constituted a passive reliance upon the fact
that migration has been the historic method by which Americans,
including many Southerners, have made their individual adjustments
to changing opportunities. Southerners have long migrated out of the
region in numbers which show a fluctuating, though strongly upward,
trend. Given the limits on the land available, off-the-farm migration

20. Testimony of Walter W. Wilcox and W. E. Hendrix in: *Underemployment
of Rural Families,* Joint Committee on the Economic Report, Subcommittee on
Low-Income Families, 81 Cong. 1 sess. (Washington, 1949).

21. E. L. Baum and Earl O. Heady, "Some Effects of Selected Policy Programs
on Agricultural Labor Mobility in the South," *Southern Economic Journal,* XXV
(January, 1959), 327–37.

22. Arthur C. Bunce, William H. Fisher, and Earle L. Rauber, *Agricultural
Adjustments and Income,* Postwar Economic Studies, Board of Governors of the
Federal Reserve System (Washington, 1945), pp. 64–65.

was essential to maintenance of existing income levels while the slow growth of Southern industrial employment opportunities forced the migrants to industrial centers outside the region.

This out-migration served to mitigate the South's economic problem but appeared on the historical record to offer no prospects that reliance was to be placed upon such movement as a solution to income problems. The historic expansion of the non-agricultural labor force of the North had been based to a large degree first upon foreign immigration and then upon the entry of women into a wide variety of employments supplemented by Southern migrants.[23] Limited demands by Northern industry and immobility of Southern rural population limited out-migration as a solution. As mechanization became more extensive, Northern employment opportunities for labor of the experience and skills possessed by the typical Southern migrant tended to become fewer. Though out-migration from the South continued to be large, it accounted for little more than the South's differential birth rate.[24] The population resident in the South has grown almost at the national rate, and out-migration has served only as a mild alleviation of the region's economic problems. The volume of out-migration which could find employment opportunities outside the region was never sufficiently large to have an important effect upon the economy of the region, and there appeared to be little prospect that it might eventually become larger.[25] Viewing the matter from the point of view of the local sources of migrants, W. H. Nicholls pointed out that there were counties in the Piedmont which had had large-scale out-migration for more than a century and which continued to be characterized by large numbers of low-income families.[26]

Aside from the inadequacy of the volume of out-migration that led some to reject it as a reliable solution and to urge a more active approach, there were also other objections. "The truth of the matter is," said Rupert Vance, "that the South is not competent under its present economy to rear and educate and send out the Nation's popu-

23. Ann Ratner Miller, "Components of Labor Force Growth," *Journal of Economic History*, XXII (1962), 47–58.

24. Victor R. Fuchs and Richard Perlman, "Recent Trends in Southern Wage Differentials," *Review of Economics and Statistics*, XLII (1960), 299.

25. Dale E. Hathaway, "Migration from Agriculture: The Historical Record and its Meaning," *American Economic Review*, L (1960), 379–91; *Labor Mobility and Population in Agriculture*, Iowa State University Center for Agricultural and Economic Adjustment (Ames, 1960).

26. William H. Nicholls, *The South's Low Income Rural Problem and Rural Development Programs*, National Planning Association (Washington, 1959); the same author, *Southern Tradition and Regional Progress*, pp. 12–13 ff.

lation reserves. Not only is the region too poor, but such a process means a constant drain on its resources. Whatever may be the net worth of the region's human exports, it is safe to estimate that to rear and educate a child to adulthood costs family, community and State some $2,000 to $5,000 per person." This, Vance suggested, was too high a price to pay to protect the incomes of those remaining. The solution was further development of the South's economy, which, "by increasing the variety and range of occupational opportunities, will raise the level of living and training, will reduce the differential birth rate, and will keep more of the South's human and material capital at home to participate in its own development."[27]  The fact that a large part of the region's resources invested in training its youth was lost with their departure upon reaching the productive ages impaired the region's ability to raise its income level. This vicious circle could be escaped only by industrialization within the South.[28]

There was also the objection that out-migration might be selective of the very people that were needed to give leadership to the South. Out-migration might be selective in respect to racial groups; to the intrinsically more or less able; to those more or less highly trained; and in other ways. There can be no question that many Southerners welcomed the out-migration of Negroes. Some, however, protested against such migration on the ground that the region needed the labor, and particularly the ability and training, of those most likely to migrate.[29]

27. Rupert B. Vance, *All These People* (Chapel Hill, 1945), p. 278.

28. David Cushman Coyle estimated in 1937 that the cost to the rural South of rearing migrants to the city amounted to some $36 billion dollars over a ten-year period. ("The South's Unbalanced Budget," *The Virginia Quarterly Review,* XIII [1937], 192–208.)

Such estimates continue to be made. A 1959 estimate places the cost to rear and educate a young person to the age of economic productivity at $10,000. "Tennessee, in effect, has exported to other states a staggering $2,280 million investment in productive manpower over the past eight years." (*Unemployment Problems,* Hearings before the Special Committee on Unemployment Problems, U.S. Senate, 86 Cong., 1 sess., pursuant to S. Res. 196, Part 5 [Washington, 1960], p. 2102.)

Another recent estimate places the cost of rearing a youth to age 18 or high school graduation at $20,000. The author observes that "costly as it might appear on the surface, to the sending community, it is a lower financial and social burden for it than would result from the damming up of this outflow of redundant population." Marvin J. Taves, "Consequences of Population Loss," in *Labor Mobility and Population in Agriculture,* p. 117.

29. The protest is implicit in the work of Odum and Vance. Jonathan Daniels is very explicit in writing, regarding the small role played by Negroes in the South's industrialization, that "Not even now can the South spare the labor of its Negroes." "Men at a Corner," *Virginia Quarterly Review,* XXXI (1955), 222.

Attention to the possible selectivity of out-migration has not been primarily concerned with the matter of race but has been directed chiefly to the possibility that the out-migrants might include disproportionately large numbers of the more able and energetic individuals in the Southern population. The publication of Wilson Gee's pioneer study, "The Drag of Talent Out of the South,"[30] confirmed the vague awareness that significant numbers of the South's native sons had achieved distinguished careers and had made significant contributions outside the region. It seemed possible that the out-migrants were a group with superior abilities, and it followed that the remaining population might be suffering from a deterioration of its inherent capacities. Odum asserted that "migration exerts a selective drag on the talent of the region. . . . This selection of the most able and energetic doubtless extends all the way down the social scale."[31]

The possibility that out-migration was selective was to John Van Sickle an argument for industrialization as the only way by which the region could hope to retain a larger share of the leadership material upon which its reconstruction depended. Van Sickle felt that the massive out-migration "has probably not yet affected the biological quality of the population." The migrants, however, included "those possessing better than average health and education." The out-migration "has been due in part to the direct pressure of poverty, but also in part to the absence of a sufficiently broad range of choices for the varied tastes and talents of the millions of young people growing up in the area."[32]

There is abundance of evidence that Southern out-migrants have achieved distinction in most of the recognized fields and also that such national distinction is much less frequently achieved in the South.[33] It is difficult to argue that Southern out-migrants have achieved distinction out of proportion to their numbers, particularly if allowance is made for the fact that national centers draw some as mature men because of their achievements in the South. In the latter

30. "The Drag of Talent Out of the South," *Social Forces*, XV (March, 1937), 343–46.

31. Howard Odum, *Southern Regions of the United States* (Chapel Hill, 1936), p. 471.

32. John V. Van Sickle, *Planning for the South* (Nashville, 1943), p. 99.

33. H. L. Geisert, "The Trend of Interregional Migration of Talent, The Southeast, 1899-1936," *Social Forces*, XVIII (October, 1939), 41–47. On businessmen, W. Lloyd Warner and James C. Abegglen, *Occupational Mobility in American Business and Industry* (Minneapolis, 1955), is the most detailed study. See also Clarence H. Danhof, "Business Leadership in the South," *The Journal of Business*, XXIX (April, 1956), 130–37.

cases, their talents have served their native region and their departure to national centers represents merely a facet of the integrated nature of the economy.

That migration out of the South has been selective of the more productive age groups as well as of the more highly educated has been amply demonstrated. Four generalized hypotheses regarding the nature of migration selectivity as it relates to inherent abilities have attracted attention. They are that:

1. Rural out-migrants are selected from the superior elements in the parent population;
2. Rural out-migrants constitute the inferior elements;
3. Rural out-migrants include the extremes, consisting of both inferior and superior elements;
4. Rural out-migrants are a random selection of the parent population.

There appears to be some evidence to support each of these hypotheses. D. S. Thomas concludes that it is probable that "selection does operate positively, negatively and randomly, at different times, depending on a variety of factors that have not been adequately investigated."[34]

These possibilities apply not only to the out-migrants from a given area but also to the in-migrants an area receives. In the case of the South it is possible to argue, as do Calvin Hoover and B. U. Ratchford, that the out-migrant whites were less well educated than the in-migrants and that the selective process was thus in some rough balance.[35] This may be true for the region as a whole. However, few in-migrants moved into the areas which were the major source of out-migrants. The considerable migration within the South and the migrants coming from outside the region tended strongly to con-

34. Dorothy S. Thomas, "Selective Migration," *Milbank Memorial Fund Quarterly*, XVI (October, 1948), 403–7.
The question of the selectivity of migration has also been raised with regard to farming in general. The inconclusive nature of knowledge on the issue is suggested in a review of the literature by Paul R. Johnson, "Effects of Off Farm Migration of Managers on Managerial Resources in Agriculture," *Journal of Farm Economics*, XLIV (1962), p. 1463.
35. Calvin B. Hoover and B. U. Ratchford, *Economic Resources and Policies of the South* (New York, 1951), pp. 37–39. See George L. Wilbur and James Suh Bang, "Some Characteristics of Mississippi Migrants," in *Unemployment Problems*, Hearings before the Special Committee on Unemployment Problems, U.S. Senate, 86 Cong., 1 sess., pursuant to S. Res. 196, Part 5 (Washington, 1960), pp. 2164–66, and literature there cited.

verge upon the same urban centers. It is therefore possible that some rural areas have suffered from adverse selectivity. In the case of the region's urban centers, it is highly doubtful that a selective process of an unfavorable nature has been operating; the opposite seems more likely.

There is reason to assume that inherent ability is very widely diffused throughout the population and reason to believe that a large proportion of that inherent ability remains undeveloped in the nation.[36] Such failure to develop human capabilities is substantially greater in the South, and in both the Southern white and colored populations, than in the rest of the United States. To the degree that the Southern educational system fails, relatively, in developing the capabilities of its population, no comparison with other populations is possible. The most reasonable assumption to be made regarding the inherent abilities of the South's urban population would seem to be that they do not differ in any way that can be accurately measured from the distribution of such abilities to be found elsewhere.

It should be noted, however, that the South has failed to benefit from two forms of selective migration. The Northeast in recent years has suffered even greater losses than the South by the out-migration of men who attained eminence outside their native states. Such migrants went chiefly to the Middle States and to the Midwest, rather than the South. The South was also unattractive to foreign in-migrants. Vance observes that "one of the handicaps of the Southeast was its failure to secure a proportionate share of the distinguished men of foreign birth."[37] That observation might well be extended to include all foreign immigrants. Such migrants made important contributions where they settled, not only in producing eminent men but also in forcing upon the indigenous population a restructuring of values and broadened horizons.[38]

### Industrialization

The re-examination of the South's economic problems and the considerations of the alternatives before it as described to this

36. As analyzed in such studies as Dael Wolfle, *America's Resources of Specialized Talent* (New York, 1954); Eli Ginzberg, *Human Resources: The Wealth of a Nation* (New York, 1958); Charles C. Cole, Jr., *Encouraging Scientific Talent* (New York, 1956), as well as the 1947 and 1957 Presidential Commission Reports.

37. *All These People,* p. 455.

38. Thomas H. Carroll, testimony before the U.S. Senate Immigration Committee Joint Hearings on S. J. Res. 64 and H. J. Res. 168, 66th Cong., 1st sess. (Washington, 1939), 152–55.

point led back to the objective of increased industrialization. The expansion of non-agricultural employment opportunities, specifically in manufacturing, had been pursued by small but increasing numbers of Southerners over a century and a quarter. Success had come slowly but was nevertheless substantial in at least some Southeastern states. World War I had provided a brief stimulus, but the South had not participated in any adequate measure in the boom of the 1920's. There followed a collapse of the industrial system which cast a shadow over the nation's productive organization and over the South's desire to be a larger part of it.

It was this failure of the nation's economic system that gave the Southern Agrarians an invitation to question the soundness and desirability of the system, to attack Southerners who had urged or participated in industrialization, and to offer an alternative to the South's continued and growing participation in it. The Agrarian movement, however, failed to attract a significant following and disappeared as an organized effort with the revival of the national economy. Since agricultural reform programs had a selective impact to the relative disadvantage of the low-income population, and since out-migration was a course of action too limited in accomplishment or potential, the final result was a considerable strengthening of the move towards industrialization.

The increased interest in sources of non-agricultural employment within the region intensified the long-standing problem of accelerating the rate of the desired industrialization. In the search for ways and means of facilitating the growth of non-agricultural sources of employment, Southerners sought to understand their position, to identify barriers, and to devise new methods of promoting the region's growth, particularly by enlisting the aid of the federal government.

## The South's Strategy for Industrialization

The pattern of the South's conscious approach to industrialization was established from the beginning of interest in industry before the Civil War and revived in the 1880's. The initiative was typically Southern as local groups organized to carry out an industrial project, accumulated equity capital, established a plant, and undertook operations on a small scale. Capitals were supplemented by commercial credits from Northern suppliers. Occasionally such indigenous entrepreneurs found it desirable to employ Northern technical and managerial skills. In textiles, and in other industries as well, the sales function frequently was turned over to Northern institutions.[39]

Since the equity capital available was typically too small to meet the exigencies of business or to support expansion, larger sources were sought in the North. Both the problems of exploiting expansion opportunities as well as the problems of financial stringencies tended to bring such firms under the control of outside interests who supplied needed capital. Many a Southern firm owed its continued existence to the willingness of Northern interests to share in or to assume risks that local capital could or would not meet.

The panic of 1873 had demonstrated to many Southerners the limitations of indigenous efforts to establish industry. The solution took the form of increased emphasis by more communities on promotional activities. Groups of Northern interests viewed at first hand the advantages of textile manufacturing in the Carolinas, Georgia, and Virginia.[40] A number of industrial expositions were held in the 1880's to demonstrate the region's potentialities to all who could be interested. Most Southern communities were confident that they had some resource of industrial significance, and all had more than adequate supplies of labor employed at very low levels of productivity who would find even low hourly wages more attractive than the income possible from full-time agriculture. What was lacking were adequate numbers of men with some managerial ability, with access to capital, and with knowledge of products, markets, and the requisite technological processes. The South's approach to industrialization was then to seek to import going business firms, with the expectation that they would supply whatever was needed to generate employment opportunities for local labor. There was nothing unique about the approach; it was typical of town and city building throughout the nation.[41] What was characteristic was the almost complete concen-

---

39. Jack Blicksilver, *Cotton Manufacturing in the Southeast, An Historical Analysis* (Georgia State College of Business Administration, Studies in Business and Economics, Bulletin No. 5 [Atlanta, 1959]), Pt. I. See also Broadus Mitchell, *The Industrial Revolution in the South* (Baltimore, 1930); Vance, *All These People*, Chap. XIX.

40. Simkins, *The South Old and New.*

41. Considering the importance attached to it, this phenomenon has been neglected by scholars. Among the few studies relating to the South are Robert E. Lowry, "Municipal Subsidies to Industries in Tennessee," *Southern Economic Journal*, VII (1941), 317–29; George I. Whitlatch, "State and Local Industrial Development Programs," Institute on Regional Development of the Southeast, *The University of Tennessee Record*, Extension Series, Vol. XXVI (1950); Ernest J. Hopkins, *The Louisville Industrial Foundation, A Study in Community Capitaliza-*

tration of Southern hopes and efforts on attracting employers by publicizing the advantages possessed by a community or a state. Such promotions were frequently accompanied by some forms of inducement, publicized or covert.

Southern entrepreneurs emerged in a few industries and achieved some regional and even national dominance. The pursuit of industrialization, however, continued to be based on the importation of employers. The approach enjoyed some success, though the supply of employers who were foot-loose and susceptible to relocation in the South was never large and the competition was vigorous. The agricultural depression which set in in 1920 brought intensification of these efforts. With the establishment of the BAWI plan by Mississippi in 1930, state governments increasingly undertook to aid local communities in their promotional efforts.[42]

As the South struggled with its problems, now deepened by its agricultural depression, the nation's economy collapsed into the Great Depression, and the New Deal began its search for the keys to recovery. That search exposed the inadequacies of existing sources of data that measured economic and social conditions and trends. President Hoover's Commission on Unemployment had produced *Recent Economic Changes* in 1929, inaugurating the development of socioeconomic measurements and analyses on a scale incomparably greater than anything that had preceded.[43] As the nation sought to analyze its problems and to establish policies and programs looking toward a more effective economic organization, some Southerners looked for-

*tion of Local Industries,* Federal Reserve Bank of Atlanta (1945); Paul Barnett, "An Analysis of State Industrial Development Programs in the Thirteen Southern States," *University of Tennessee Record,* Vol. XLVII (1944); and the same author, "Industrial Development in Tennessee: Present Status and Suggested Program," *University of Tennessee Record,* Vol. XLIV (1941). A brief, critical account of the Chamber of Commerce movement in the South may be found in Vance, *Human Geography of the South,* pp. 485–89.

There is some historical material in *Financing Small Business,* Hearings before a Subcommittee of the Committee on Banking and Currency, U.S. Senate, 85 Cong., 2 sess. (Washington, 1958). Donald R. Gilmore, *Developing the Little Economies,* Committee on Economic Development (New York, 1960), contains considerable current information.

A critical appraisal, old but still useful, is C. S. Logsdon, "Some Comments upon the Effectiveness of State and Local Area Development Programs," *Southern Economic Journal,* XV (1949), 303–10.

42. Ernest J. Hopkins, *Mississippi's BAWI Plan, An Experiment in Industrial Subsidization,* Federal Reserve Bank of Atlanta (Atlanta, 1944).

43. *Recent Economic Changes in the United States,* National Bureau of Economic Research (New York, 1929). Among the pioneer studies relating to the South was Clarence Heer, *Income and Wages in the South* (Chapel Hill, 1930).

ward to benefiting accordingly, while others pursued programs aimed at the region's special problems.

In the South, a variety of private and quasi-private organizations had appeared concerned with analysis of the problems of the region and in making recommendations for their solution. Comprehensive, organized research on the problems of the region was begun at the University of North Carolina about 1925, and found support in 1930 with the establishment of the Southern Regional Committee of the Social Science Research Council. Over the next fifteen years, the Committee's activities were directed to an intensive inventorying of Southern resources and identification of Southern deficiencies, economic and sociological, these findings constituting a body of information more complete than that existing for any other region.[44] In its analytical work, the North Carolina group developed a philosophical approach which distinguished strongly between sectionalism and regionalism and which saw a solution to Southern problems through governmental action.

Resource inventorying was encouraged by the work of the National Resources Board, and almost all the Southern states established state planning boards, as was also the case elsewhere in the nation. The functions they undertook were to measure the characteristics of the population and of resources, to evaluate assets, identify problems, and recommend action to their governments.[45] In the South, the Tennessee Valley Authority came to serve as the great example of what might be done.[46] Though some disagreed, Vance expressed a view popular in the South when he argued that the region lacked "the large incomes necessary to develop its own resources," with the result that incomes in the region "remain low because resources are appropriated at low prices by outside interests. By virtue of this condition, the Southeast is favorable to government financing and stands to benefit when its resources are developed by a public agency like the TVA rather than by outside holding companies."[47]

44. Richard A. Harvill, "The Economy of the South," *Journal of Political Economy,* XLVIII (February, 1940), 61.

45. Albert Lepawsky, *State Planning and Economic Development in the South,* (National Planning Association Committee of the South, Report No. 4 [1949]), pp. 14–19.

46. The literature is immense, but see Philip Selznick, *TVA and the Grass Roots* (Berkeley, 1949).

47. Vance, *All These People,* pp. 265–66. But Van Sickle took the position that "planning in the United States should give precedence to measures that increase the geographical mobility of men. In addition, if it is to be consistent with the free enterprise system it should make liberal use of private initiative

A number of other organizations contributed to the analysis and action. Business interests in 1932 organized the Southern States Industrial Council, which, though generally conservative, was nevertheless more liberal on labor issues than many Southern employers.[48] A Southern Policy Committee was formed in 1933 to bring political, business, and academic figures together as a source of policy statements on Southern issues.[49] A Southern Association of Science and Industry was organized in 1941. As the Southern Research Institute, after 1944, it served as a center for research in areas of interest to industry.[50]

Of significance also was the formation in 1937 of the Southeastern Governors' Conference. The Conference's formal program for a "Decade of Progress," adopted in 1940, dealt in such generalities as to be of little significance.[51] Its principal concern was with cooperative action to enhance the South's economy and its primary program was that of attracting industry to the region.[52] It may have been instrumental in changing the character of the competition between the states since the developmental literature changed in character from publicizing the cheapness and docility of Southern labor to an emphasis on "the natural advantages of the region."[53] The Conference may also have been a factor in withholding the support of state government administrations from those employers and employer organizations that fought the application of the Fair Labor Standards Act in the South. The Conference took a major role in seeking to remove what were believed to be barriers to Southern growth, such as discriminatory railroad rates, and formally urged the federal administration to

and private motivations, of which the most potent is the profit motive." ("Regional Aspects of the Problem of Full Employment at Fair Wages," *Southern Economic Journal*, XIII [1946], 37.) And Donald Davidson held the TVA to be an example of regional imperialism. In his view, it should be administered by the region concerned, with the help of Federal appropriations: "As it stands the T.V.A. is an irresponsible projection of a planned, functional society into the midst of one of the most thoroughly democratic parts of the United States." In Agar and Tate (ed.), *Who Owns America?*, p. 125.

48. Manning J. Dauer, "Recent Southern Political Thought," *Journal of Politics*, X (May, 1948), 330.

49. Virginius Dabney, *Below the Potomac* (New York, 1942), p. 309. See the Committee's *Southern Policy Papers*, Atlanta, 1936–37.

50. Dauer, *loc. cit.*

51. Dabney, *op. cit.*, 390–410.

52. H. C. Nixon, "The Southern Governors' Conference as a Pressure Group," *Journal of Politics*, VI (August, 1944), 338–45.

53. Marian D. Irish, "The Proletarian South," *Journal of Politics*, II (August, 1940), 250.

decentralize the awarding of defense and war contracts. More recently, it founded the Southern Regional Council on Education as a device to meet some of the South's problems in higher education.[54]

The development of the Southern Governors' Conference as an agency dealing directly with the tasks of attracting new employers as the source of regional economic development mirrored the changes brought on by the war. In particular, it reflected the decline in national interest in planning involving governmental finance of projects of the TVA type. The private planners such as the North Carolina group and the state planning agencies typically provided information about the region and the states as units. They effectively demonstrated needs but failed to supply the kind of information required by private employers considering a new plant location. Information on the characteristics of specific labor markets, on raw material supplies and costs, and similar detailed data required by prospective business firms did not appear in their materials. While recognizing broad deficiencies, the planners ignored the frequently minor barriers which prevented the establishment of plants to utilize local resources.

In the 1940's, the state planning organizations changed their functions (and frequently their names) to become economic development agencies.[55] As such, they continued to collect and analyze data but in local rather than in state terms; their aggressive publicity campaigns emphasized assets rather than deficiencies. Their special contribution, however, was that of bringing together prospective employers and local groups, private and governmental, thereby serving as a channel towards greater mutual understanding so that the requirements of a business firm might be supplied by local governmental action, while local groups might better appreciate what was involved in an association with a specific industrial project.

### Accelerating Industrialization

The development of the governmental and academic activities described supported the South's strategy for industrialization. Those institutions and that strategy may or may not have accelerated the establishment of industry in the South but in either case the pace

54. Marian D. Irish, "Recent Political Thought in the South," *American Political Science Review*, XLVI (March, 1952), 130; cf. Irish, "Foreign Policy and the South," *Journal of Politics*, X (May, 1948), 314.

55. Albert Lepawsky, "Governmental Planning in the South," *Journal of Politics*, X (August, 1948), 551, 562–64. A brief analysis of this shift in long perspective is in E. Long Norton, "Businessman's Stake in Regional Planning," *Harvard Business Review*, XXXVI (1958), 136–44.

of change was far from adequate to the region's needs for more non-agricultural employment opportunities. The need supported faith in the possibilities. In addition to its labor supply, which seemed obviously more than adequate, many Southerners acted from a conviction that the region had abundant resources which were unquestionably able to support greater industrialization. Attention turned then to efforts to identify those causes of the slow pace of industrialization that were external to the South and to remove them by federal action if necessary. Partially related to and partially independent of those efforts were the efforts of others who placed some hopes in advancing Southern industrialization by means of a federal policy to force the decentralization of industry.

### Decentralizing Industry

The problem of urban unemployment aroused some interest in the nation in the dispersal of industry so that, among other reasons, larger numbers of the population might have an opportunity to engage in part-time food production.[56] Federal sponsorship of a program of decentralization of industry had been recommended to President Hoover by his Committee on Industrial Decentralization and Housing. President Roosevelt had suggested the desirability of industrial decentralization as one of the justifications for the Tennessee Valley Authority. Some of the resettlement programs of the New Deal included some decentralization features, rationalized as providing wage-earners with the security of part-time farming as a defense against industrial unemployment.

There was, however, little agreement as to the objectives of a sponsored program of decentralization. One concept included reducing the existing urban conglomerations and diffusing industry more broadly around such centers. Another concept comprised dispersing industry more or less evenly over the national landscape. To the South, any federal program to promote the geographic dispersion of industry was appealing as a source of more employment within its boundaries.[57]

56. David Cushman Coyle, "Decentralize Industry," *Virginia Quarterly Review*, XI (1935), 321–28. See also John P. Ferris, "Industry's Stake in Decentralization," *American Economic Review, Proceedings*, XXV (March, 1936), 172–73.

57. For an account of Federal activities, see Carter Goodrich, *Migration and Economic Opportunity* (Philadelphia, 1936), pp. 618–59. For some other views of economists, see J. H. Willets, "Decentralization of Population and Industry," *American Economic Review, Proceedings*, XXV (1935), 171–73; Daniel B.

The general interest in decentralization stimulated a major study of the need for population redistribution. In the report of the study's conclusions in 1936, Carter Goodrich recommended that the federal government make no efforts to disperse industry, on the grounds that "without great migratory movements we cannot possibly redress our sectional inequalities or use our human and material resources to best advantage. It should therefore be a cardinal point of social policy to encourage mobility, to give it surer purpose and direction."[58]

Much of the study was devoted to the South's problems. Goodrich saw the South's future as resting upon a decreasing rate of population growth, an increasing utilization of regional resources, and a redistribution of part of the population.[59] Despite the predictions current at the time that the nation's population was soon to become static, it was assumed that the South's population would continue to grow.

With regard to the possibility of increasing employment by more intensive utilization of the region's resources, Goodrich observed that the South had "gained its new industries by underbidding and undercutting industries already established in the East," and that those gains had been principally in "light industry, notably textiles, where the lower costs of production, possible through cheap labor drawn from agriculture, enabled the Piedmont to attract part of the industry from New England." Goodrich suggested that "[t]he South may expect a continued industrialization, calculated to keep pace with its markets. But it is too much to expect the process of industrialization to continue at the pre-depression rate or to absorb the entire 'surplus' population of the region."[60]

There were some other factors. Although Goodrich thought that low-cost TVA power should attract light industry and might aid in encouraging development of the chemical industries, the effect would be felt more "in raising incomes of skilled and selected groups than in providing a large amount of employment." In the same vein, Goodrich suggested that forestry, concentrating on pulpwood, offered possi-

---

Creamer, *Is Industry Decentralizing?* (Study of Population Redistribution, Bulletin III [Philadelphia, 1935]).

On subsistence homesteads see: L. B. Tate, "Possibilities and Limitations of Subsistence Homesteads," *Journal of Farm Economics,* XVI (1934), 530–33; M. L. Wilson, "The Place of Subsistence Homesteads in our National Economy," *Journal of Farm Economics,* XVI (1934), 73–87; W. E. Zeuch, "The Subsistence Homestead Program from the Point of View of an Economist," *Journal of Farm Economics,* XVII (1935), 710–19.

58. *Migration and Economic Opportunity,* p. 162.
59. *Ibid.,* p. 672.
60. *Ibid.,* p. 158.

bilities of raising incomes but "would provide less employment for the population than agriculture now furnishes in a given area."[61] Rural rehabilitation programs can at best provide for only a small part of the rural population. Goodrich concluded that "migration remains the area's sole immediate resource to soften the blow of lost markets or lift it from stabilized poverty in case of a return of pre-depression conditions."[62]

The National Resources Planning Board endorsed the Goodrich conclusions. It reported that there was "little support for a belief that opportunities for part-time or full-time industrial employed can be widely distributed geographically in the near future. The records both of past migration and of industrial expansion show that workers have usually moved to the factory, rather than the factory to the worker."[63]

While this position no doubt was acceptable to some Southerners and welcomed by the Agrarians, it was anathema to those who had come to look upon industrialization as the only hope of the region. The federal government's sponsorship of TVA had been regarded as tangible evidence of a federal policy looking to the decentralization of industry. Throughout the South, groups were busily engaged seeking to claim support for more federal action of that general type. If prospects for such aid were now much reduced, much more serious was the implied prediction that the region's long pursuit of more industrialization was not likely to provide a solution to its problems. Though the importance of out-migration as a protection of per capita incomes was recognized, fundamental objections were raised against the complete reliance upon it that was being suggested.

Southerners dissented from Goodrich's interpretation of the historical record. J. J. Spengler held that manufacturing expansion constituted the principal correction of the current occupational and regional maldistribution of population, and he predicted considerable growth in the South.[64] John Van Sickle, pointing out that the Goodrich conclusions were based on rigidities operating in the economy, held that the strength of those rigidities had been overestimated, as was demonstrated by the rate at which capital was invested in Southern manufacturing in the late 1930's. Van Sickle interpreted that flow of

61. *Ibid.*, p. 160.
62. *Ibid.*, p. 162.
63. National Resources Committee, *The Problems of a Changing Population* (Washington, 1938), p. 72.
64. Joseph J. Spengler, "Regional Differences and the Future of Manufacturing in America," *Southern Economic Journal*, VII (April, 1949), 475–93.

capital as suggesting the beginnings of a new trend in the Southeast's share of wage employment.[65]

Meanwhile, the Southern Regional Committee working at Chapel Hill published its first major study a short time before Goodrich's work appeared. In *Southern Regions of the United States,* Howard Odum supplied an inventory of the South's problems and an appraisal of its capacity for development. Odum took the view that the region must itself build on its own physical and cultural resources. "More industry," Odum declared, "seems essential to any sort of regional balance."[66] A few years later another member of the Chapel Hill group, Rupert Vance, was more specific. Noting that the South's pursuit of a larger participation in the nation's industrialization "had been put on the defensive," he defended that continuing interest on the grounds that despite out-migration, the region's "differential fertility continues to replace" the out-migrants faster than Southern agriculture and industry can absorb them.[67]

Efforts to secure federal assistance during World War II were directed towards securing for the South a fair share of government production contracts. Proposals that the federal government establish decentralization policies received little further attention until World War II was approaching its end. The fact that the federal government might be in a position to carry out policies which, relating to reconverting the economy to peacetime, could promote a selective decentralization of industry aroused considerable interest. All such efforts were rejected by President Truman. The reconversion program submitted and accepted by the Congress was neutral as between regions.[68] The significance to the South of the re-emergence of decentralization as a policy dictated by military requirements is dealt with in a subsequent section.

## The Obstacles to Rapid Industrialization

In 1936 Howard Odum, in the *Southern Regions of the United States,* after describing the South's resources in an optimistic vein, turned to an appraisal of the technology applied to their development. That technology he found deficient not in what it included but in its incomplete range. He observed, as had many others before, that: "Un-

65. John V. Van Sickle, *Planning for the South,* pp. 97–98, 104.
66. Howard Odum, *Southern Regions,* pp. 51, 221.
67. *All These People,* p. 277.
68. "Outline of Plans Made for the Reconversion Period," Message from the President of the United States, September 6, 1945, 79 Cong., 1 sess. House Document No. 282 (Washington, 1945).

til recently, the South was a furnisher of raw materials to the manufacturing regions, essentially colonial in its economy."[69] A few years later he removed the qualification. Observing that New York was the economic center of the national economy and that other metropoles, towns, and villages arranged themselves into series ranks, he concluded that "some regions are still in the status of colonial economy. . . . The southern region has traditionally filled this role within the United States, and partly because of that fact, seems destined to continue doing so for some time."[70]

Odum saw the "colonial type" deficiency in applied technology as producing an imbalance. "The South's proportion of national manufacturing . . . is still far below its ratio of people and resources." One of the chief causes for this "uneven technology" was "the South's very contracted access to capital, expressing itself in a differential in rates of interest." That differential required that a Southern capital-using enterprise have a higher return than a similar operation in the North. "Accordingly most sorts of manufacture involving elaborate technologies have avoided the South because, as a rule, the elaborate technology is expressed in expensive and elaborate plants." Odum explained further that, like debtor countries, the South, because of the inequality of incomes, tended to import luxuries which resulted in debt and an inability to "enlarge its capital."[71]

The word "colonial," as Odum used it, was probably intended to convey what Colin Clark defined in the now familiar terms of primary as contrasted with secondary production. In this sense "colonial" merely describes an economy primarily concerned with producing, and preliminary fabrication of, raw materials. The word does carry with it the notion of dependence, although it is a dependency in a specialized structure, all elements of which are more or less equally dependent upon each other. Nor does it necessarily carry with it the idea of lower levels of productivity, although in fact primary economics tend to have lower levels of living than do those engaged in more advanced productive activities. In this usage Odum was correct; the South was, and continues in large measure to be, an economy engaged somewhat more largely in primary production. So used, the term "colonial" has a limited connotation. The word came to have a much stronger significance.

69. P. 353.
70. Howard Odum and H. E. Moore, *American Regionalism, A Cultural-Historical Approach to National Integration* (New York, 1938), p. 361.
71. *Southern Regions,* pp. 354–55, 367.

In June, 1938, President Franklin D. Roosevelt called a Conference on Economic Conditions in the South. In his letter to the Conference, the President expressed his conviction that the South presented the nation with its Number-1 economic problem.[72] The report of the Conference was prepared by a staff of Southerners and reviewed by the Conference members, who were also all Southerners. The report appears to have drawn heavily from Odum's work as well as from data gathered by the Temporary National Economic Committee. Although it made no explicit reference to the South as suffering from a colonial status, it made some observations that went well beyond the Odum analysis in suggesting subservience and exploitation. The report stated, for example, that:

Lacking capital of its own, the South has been forced to borrow from outside financiers, who have reaped a rich harvest in the form of interest and dividends. At the same time it has had to hand over the control of much of its business and industry to investors from wealthier sections.

After pointing out the high cost of credit in the South, the report continues:

Faced with these handicaps, the South has had to look beyond its boundaries for the financing of virtually all of its large industries and many of its small ones. This has turned policy-making powers over to outside managements whose other interests often lead them to exercise their authority against the South's best advantage. For example, many such companies buy most of their goods outside of the South, and often their sales policies are dictated in the interest of allied corporations in other sections of the country.[73]

Another result of the South's dependence on outside sources of capital was its effect upon state and local government revenues:

So much of the profit from southern industries goes to outside financiers in the form of dividends and interest, that State income taxes would produce a meager yield in comparison with similar levies elsewhere. State taxation does not reach dividends which flow to corporation stockholders and management in other States; and as a result, these people do not pay their share of the cost of southern schools and other institutions.

The efforts of southern communities to increase their revenues and to spread their tax burden more fairly have been impeded by the

72. *Report to the President on the Economic Conditions of the South*, National Emergency Committee (Washington, 1938), p. 1.
73. *Ibid.*, pp. 53–54.

vigorous opposition of interests outside the region which control much of the South's wealth. Moreover, tax revision efforts have been hampered in some sections by the fear that their industries would move to neighboring communities which would tax them more lightly—or even grant them tax exemption for long periods.[74]

Turning to natural resources, the report stated that:

Because of the poverty in which the South was left after the War between the States, and because of the high cost of credit since that time, a very large share of the natural resources of the South is owned in other regions. To the extent that this is true, the South is exposed to a double danger. On the one hand, it is possible for a monopolistic corporation in another region of the country to purchase and leave unused resources in the South which otherwise might be developed in competition with the monopoly. On the other hand, the large absentee ownership of the South's natural resources and the South's industry makes it possible for residents elsewhere to influence greatly the manner in which the South is developed and to subordinate that development to other interests outside the South.[75]

After enumerating Southern industries which were wholly or almost completely controlled outside the region (almost all public utilities, all the major railroad systems, the transmission of and distribution of natural gas, the richest deposits of iron ore, coal and limestone, most of the rich deposits of bauxite, zinc ores, sulphur, many of the largest cotton and rayon mills), the survey observes that:

For mining its mineral wealth and shipping it away in a raw or semi-finished form, the South frequently receives nothing but the low wages of unskilled and semiskilled labor. The wages for manufacturing this natural wealth into finished products often do not go to southerners, but to workers in other areas; and the profits likewise usually go to financial institutions in other regions. When a southerner buys the finished product, on the other hand, the price he pays includes all the wasteful cross-hauling involved in the present system.[76]

Further handicaps to the South were the freight-rate differentials and the tariff:

The present interterritorial freight rates which apply on movements into other areas of many southern manufactured and semifinished goods, and some agricultural products and raw materials, handicap the

74. *Ibid.*, p. 23.
75. *Ibid.*, p. 55.
76. *Ibid.*, p. 58.

development of industry in the South. This disadvantage works a hardship particularly with regard to shipments into the important northeastern territory. This region, containing 51 percent of the Nation's population, is the greatest consuming area. The southeastern manufacturer sending goods across the boundary into this region is at a relative disadvantage of approximately 39% in the charges which he has to pay as compared with the rates for similar shipments entirely within the eastern rate territory. The southwestern manufacturer, with a 75 percent relative disadvantage, is even worse off. Such a disadvantage applies to the southern shipper, even when, distance considered, he is entirely justified on economic grounds in competing with producers within the eastern territory. In effect, this difference in freight rates creates a man-made wall to replace the natural barrier long since overcome by modern railroad engineering. . . .

An equally serious deterrent to the South's economic development has been the nation's traditional high tariff policy. The South has been forced for generations to sell its agricultural products in an unprotected world market, and to buy its manufactured goods at prices supported by high tariffs. The South, in fact, has been caught in a vise that has kept it from moving along with the main stream of American economic life. On the one hand, the freight rates have hampered its industry; on the other hand, our high tariff has subsidized industry in other sections of the country at the expense of the South. Penalized for being rural, and handicapped in its efforts to industrialize, the economic life of the South has been squeezed to a point where the purchasing power of the southern people does not provide an adequate market for its own industries nor an attractive market for those of the rest of the country.

Moreover, by curtailing imports, the tariff has reduced the ability of foreign countries to buy American cotton and other agricultural exports. America's trade restrictions, without sufficient expansion of our domestic markets for southern products, have hurt the South more than any other region.[77]

The National Emergency Committee report contained no new information. The issues on which it took positions were matters on which there were wide differences of opinion in the South. The dark picture it presented conformed with the depression-spawned school of realism—in fiction and fact—which at the time dominated the nation in general and the South in particular. The report was, then, a curious episode in the depression-stimulated concern with economic-political-social problems. It aroused resentment in conservative anti-New Deal circles in the South, while Liberals felt it was poorly timed, if at all

77. *Ibid.*, p. 60.

necessary.[78]   The report did lead some liberal Southern groups to call a Conference for Human Welfare to consider what action might be taken, but such groups already existed and were in no particular need of the type of publicity provided by Mr. Mellet's pamphlet.[79] The Southerners who signed their names to the report apparently did not meet again as a group.

In the longer run, two results may be distinguished.  One was to stimulate, and to call public attention to, the work under way, which was to include numerous appraisals of the data underlined in the report.  The other result was that the report supplied ammunition for an upsurge of sectionalism which was to see some of the South's distinguished liberals allied with some of its most notorious demagogues.

The NEC report suggested strongly that the South was being exploited and extended an implied invitation to seek the use of Federal power to secure remedies.  The evidence suggested that the South's ills could be ascribed to discriminatory freight-rates, the tariff, monopoly and absentee ownership, all imposed upon the South by interests outside her borders.  Colonialism was thereby given a political rather than a purely economic content.  For those who found useful an explanation of the South's economic problems that was external to herself, colonialism was synonymous with imperialism.  The data supplied by Vance, Odum, and others, as supplemented and publicized by the NEC report, provided the opportunity.  Odum's pursuit of a constructive regionalism was now converted into a renewed sectionalism of a peculiarly vitriolic character.[80]

### A Touch of Paranoia

These issues had long been part of the stock-in-trade of Southern demagogues and had received some emphasis from Southern figures who cannot justly be so labeled.  Some decades earlier, the railroads had been a central target of the populists in the South as they were also in the North.  The tariff issue was, of course, the hardy perennial of disputes between the nation's regions.  These, together with attacks on absentee corporations and on monopolies, were favorite campaign material of such demagogues as Jeff Davis of Arkan-

78. For comment on reaction to the report, see W. J. Cash, *op. cit.*, p. 422; Dabney, *Below the Potomac*, p. 60; Dauer, *op. cit.*, "Southern Political . . . ," 337–38; Irish, *Journ. of Pol.*, X, "The Proletarian South," *Journ. of Pol.*, II, 252.

79. Dauer, *op. cit.*, p. 338; Irish, *loc. cit.*

80. For an appraisal of the conversion of regionalism into sectionalism, see Howard Odum and Katharine Jocher, "In Search of the Regional Balance of America," *Social Forces*, XXIII (March, 1945).

sas, James K. Vardaman and Theodore C. Bilbo of Mississippi, Cole L. Blease of South Carolina, Huey Long of Louisiana, Eugene Talmadge of Georgia, "Alfalfa Bill" Murray of Oklahoma, and similar "panderers to the pride and prejudices of their white constituents."[81] The group of intellectuals who constituted the Southern Agrarians had pointed to these problems in support of the argument that it was necessary for the South to seek to develop a society quite different from that of the North.   What was more significant was the fact that men of sounder judgment, strong critics of demagogic politicians, were led to criticize those Southern political figures who had refused to participate in these attacks.   Those who exercised such restraint were charged with being "agents of the business interests that had tightened their hold on Southern economic life," and therefore "guaranteeing the protection of Northern imperialist interests in the region."[82] John Nance Garner, Carter Glass, Walter F. George, and James F. Byrnes were among those who were held to "speak for the Northern corporate and industrial wealth which has enslaved their own people."[83]   It did not follow that their loyalty to the South was necessarily questioned, however, since their subservience to Northern interests might be explained by the fact that they represented a subordinate part of a great capitalistic country.[84]

The tariff, discriminatory railroad rates, monopoly, and absentee ownership of southern resources and industrial operations by large corporations were the principal targets.   In each case the South was forced to accept policies developed and applied from outside the region.   There were differences in emphasis, but each or all these together could be looked upon as tools utilized to prevent the region from reaching its goals of either greater agricultural prosperity or of greater industrialization.   Sectional conflict, which some held to be inevitable, resulted in a conspiracy, deliberate or fortuitous, on the part of the North, the large national corporations, or some financial groups, with the help of the federal government, to thwart the South.[85]   Ex-

81. Simkins, *South Old and New*, p. 438.
82. Benjamin B. Kendrick, "The Colonial Status of the South," *Journal of Southern History*, VIII (February, 1942), 19.
83. Allan A. Michie and Frank Ryhlick, *Dixie Demagogues* (New York, 1939), pp. 8–9.
84. Simkins, *op. cit.*, pp. 445–46.
85. The sophisticated view of the exploitative conspiracy was expressed by Donald Davidson: "I do not argue that it represents some deliberate highly wrought conspiracy against the South but rather that it is in the nature of an urban industrialized society to behave thus towards whatever stands in its path." *Attack on Leviathan*, p. 317. See also William B. Hesseltine, "Regions, Classes

posure of the conspiracy and neutralization of its weapons would permit the region, given the great confidence of the South in its resources, to move along the path it wished to follow.

The tariff was, of course, an old sore. Writing in 1934, Peter Molyneaux reminded the South that the first suggestion by Southerners that "the time had come to calculate the value of the Union" had occurred with the passage of the 1824 tariff. He argued that the poverty of the South was not a product of the tenant and crop lien system but was a result of the fact that the region bought most of its manufactured goods from the North and East, while devoting its own energies to the production of export commodities. It was because the ultimate returns from their products are measured in terms of a domestic price level, maintained by a high tariff system, while the prices of their products are adjusted to a world price level, that the South's poverty has persisted, and it is that poverty in turn which has prevented the checking in any degree of the progressive impoverishment of the mass of cotton farmers.[86] "The outlook for the cotton states," he held, "will be determined very largely by whether the United States follows a policy of international economic co-operation, on the one hand, or a policy of narrow economic nationalism on the other."[87]

Molyneaux demanded that this "ancient wrong" be righted. "To say today that the national welfare requires the maintenance of the high-tariff policy is equivalent to saying that the national welfare requires the irreparable submersion, economically and socially, of the greater part of the population of a whole region of the country. . . . A continuance of the high-tariff policy must henceforth be more injurious to the cotton South than it has ever been in the past."[88] A Southern economist, M. D. Anderson, agreed, asserting that "The high protective tariff on manufactured articles . . . has the double effect of cutting off the South from some certain markets for its cotton, and at the same time raises the price the South has to pay for manufactured articles it purchases from the North."[89]

The issue of equitable railroad freight rates was one which peren-

---

and Sections in American History," *Journal of Land and Public Utility Economics,* XX (February, 1944), 35–44.

86. Peter Molyneaux, *What Economic Nationalism Means to the South* (Foreign Policy Association World Affairs Pamphlets, No. 4 [New York, 1934]), p. 19.

87. *Ibid.,* p. 20.

88. *Ibid.,* p. 24.

89. M. D. Anderson, "Problems of the Cotton Economy," *Proceedings of the Southern Social Science Research Council* (New Orleans, March 8 and 9, 1935), p. 72. Comments of this type are frequent. Cf. Dabney, *op. cit.,* p. 9.

nially attracted attention throughout the nation as well as in the South and was a problem to which Congress had addressed itself frequently. The claim that the South suffered regional discrimination under the existing rate structure arose in 1937 when J. Haden Allredge, an economist for the TVA, completed an elaborate analysis of the territorial rate structure. In transmitting a copy of the report to President Roosevelt, Harcourt Morgan, Chairman of the TVA, wrote that the existing territorial freight rate structure constituted a barrier which tended "to retard substantially the commercial and economic development of the Tennessee River drainage basin and adjoining areas in the South."[90] That charge became the basis for the agitation over the following two decades over territorial freight rates, a charge that was quickly incorporated in the conspiracy thesis.

Jonathan Daniels, writing in 1938, declared that New England prosperity seems to be based on the freight differential and the tariff: "imperial advantages which New England took as its loot after the Civil War." There was, he continues, "some sort of bargain then, now dimly seen. The Negroes were sold down the river again after emancipation, and the price paid was a fixed economic differentiation, which left the whole South in slavery to New England instead of some of the South in slavery to other Southerners."[91]

Interviewing Southern public officials, Daniels quotes Governor Bibb Graves of Alabama as holding that "the United States is divided into empires on the one hand and satrapies on the other by the freight rate differential." Others, Daniels found, referred to the freight rate differential as if it were the product of an invisible conspiracy. In Daniels's view, there was an historical explanation for the higher rates south of the Ohio, but he suspected that both the Northern and Southern railways were controlled by the same banks. "Was it possible," he asked, "that the great railroad investment north of the wall must be protected at all costs, that the migration of manufacture to the South must be watched lest Northern traffic be threatened?" And must then, the Interstate Commerce Commission, "acting in the public interest, take no action that would threaten this section? Was it, in sum, possible that the course of economic history had made the stability of the American system depend upon that region and simultaneously, was it to the advantage of finance capital that it remain so?" Daniels concludes that it may be "that the cruelest aspects of conquest were not

90. *The Interterritorial Freight Rate Problem in the United States.* H. R. Doc. No. 264, 75 Cong., 1 sess. (1937).

91. Daniels, *Southerner Discovers the South*, p. 345.

involved in Reconstruction in the South but in the use of national power to entrench sectional advantage elsewhere over the South."[92]

Ellis Arnall, then Governor of Georgia, was a leader active in the campaign for revision of railroad rates. He demanded the "abandonment of a colonial policy toward the Southern and Western States," declaring that this exploitation was "more wasteful than that practiced by the most greedy of European powers in Africa or the Pacific." "Only exploitation," he asserted, "can account for the enormous waste of human and natural resources. Why were not these people engaged in more intelligent farm operations, planting crops that would not loot the earth of the stored richness that they were obligated as men to leave as a legacy to their children's children? Why were not any of them engaged in industrial employments?"[93] Arnall complained further that federal grants-in-aid programs to the aged, to highways, to dependent children, to public health and to vocational rehabilitation were deliberately intended to maintain colonialism, since they were predicated upon an ability to match federal funds with the result that Southern states must levy crippling taxation or provide inadequate services.

Less pugnaciously, Hodding Carter told millions of readers that before the South can conquer its bigotry, its people must be better educated and better paid. A higher income level in the South would eliminate most of the frictional competition among the submarginal whites and Negroes. Before these things can be accomplished, Carter asserted, "the South must be freed from the economic despotism imposed by the North."[94]

Men like Arnall occupied themselves also in seeking to attract new industries, branch plants of large corporations being attractive prospects. But others saw the South's problems epitomized in the absentee ownership that was concomitant. M. D. Anderson felt strongly on the matter. "Another factor to be reckoned," he said, "is the financial control of the national banking mechanism by Northern and Eastern interests. By means of this control, the rich resources of the South, other than cotton (petroleum for instance) are bought at relatively low prices by concerns operating under Northern control and owner-

92. *Ibid.*, pp. 264, 268.
93. Ellis G. Arnall, *The Shore Dimly Seen* (Philadelphia, 1946), pp. 143, 165–7. See also pp. 130, 151, 268.
94. Hodding Carter, "Chips on Our Shoulder Down South," *Readers' Digest*, L (January, 1947), 126. The article appeared in a longer version in the *Saturday Evening Post*, November 2, 1946. See also Carter's "Southerners Look at the South," *New York Times Magazine*, July 7, 1946, p. 9.

ship, and the products are sold back to the South and to other regions at a stiff profit, impoverishing the people who might have developed these resources to their own advantage if they had had financial control."[95]

The distinguished Southern historian, Walter Prescott Webb, joined in the attack, declaring that "whereas the South and West have within their boundaries most of the natural wealth of America," the North "has gathered practically all the economic fruits of a nation's industry and labor."[96] This, Webb held, had been accomplished by the two hundred largest Northern corporations supported by the federal government by a variety of devices. Among these were the tariff and the federal patent policy, which operated as a government subsidy to the North. Taking his cue from the widespread interest at the time in the concentration of power in large corporations, Webb urged reforming the structure of the nation's business organization by repealing that part of the 14th Amendment to the federal Constitution which protected the corporation as a legal person.

Assistance came also from an influential Northern source as Thurman Arnold adapted his crusade against monopoly to aid in the exposure of the exploitation conspiracy and at the same time invited Southern support for his efforts. Arnold argued that the relationship between the industrial East and the South and West had developed along colonial lines with the East functioning as the Mother country. The East had garnered to itself the raw materials of the other two regions and exploited them by selling them "manufactured necessities at artificially controlled prices." Since the East was the principal source of both the capital and organization applied in the development of the South, it controlled that development "in the way which would contribute the most to its domination." In the process "the competitive energy of the South and West has been stifled." As a result, local independent capital disappeared and local independent enterprise has

95. Anderson, *loc. cit.*

96. Walter P. Webb, *Divided We Stand, the Crisis of a Frontierless Democracy* (New York, 1937). In more recent writings, Webb has abandoned this position and taken a much more conciliatory and optimistic view. See "The South and the Golden Slippers," *Texas Quarterly*, I (1958), 1–13; and "The South's Call to Greatness: Challenge to All Southerners," *Texas Business Review*, October, 1959, p. 1.

The exploitation view, however, has become imbedded in the writings of historians on the South: see C. Vann Woodward, *Origins of the New South, 1877–1913*, Vol. IX of *A History of the South* (Baton Rouge and Austin, 1951), Chap. XI; and Henry B. Parkes, *The American Experience* (New York, 1947), p. 291; Emory Q. Hawk, *Economic History of the South* (New York, 1934), pp. 529–30.

constantly been handicapped, with the farmer the chief victim.  This was accomplished through the "age-old principle of colonial empires": tightly organized cartels which controlled supply, transportation, and distribution "in such a way as to put new competing enterprise in the colonies under a continuing handicap."[97]

Monopoly was not viewed primarily as a source of injury to the South because of the higher prices that might prevail on Southern purchases.  The Justice Department was not accused of dealing with Southern instances of monopoly in any way differently from the manner with which it dealt with monopoly elsewhere; in fact, monopolies would tend to be national in scope and to have nation-wide effects. The problem was the possibility that monopolistic control over Southern resources might result in rates of resource utilization lower than would be the case under competitive conditions.  There were suspicions and charges that such was the situation in the Birmingham coal and iron industry.[98]  That industry had not expanded in accord with the rosy prospects held out when the United States Steel Corporation entered the area.[99]

George Stocking supplied data supporting the view that the Birmingham steel plants enjoyed the lowest costs in the nation's steel industry on some basic products.  The growth of the Birmingham industry did not reflect such advantages.  The basing point pricing system, Stocking held, placed Southern steel fabricators at a disadvantage in supplying their "natural market" and restricted the size of that market while the United States Steel Corporation "subordinated the management of its southern properties to the combined interests of its national operations."[100]

Meanwhile the nation had entered upon World War II.  The changes that might be brought about were not foreseen; instead, the possibility that the South would suffer damage through loss of foreign markets without participating in production of war materiel gave support to the imperialistic thesis.  Frank L. Barton, one of the few economists who supported this point of view, pointed out that orders for

97. Speech, August 22, 1951, in Hot Springs, Arkansas.  The theme is elaborated in Thurman Arnold, *Democracy and Free Enterprise* (Norman, 1942).

98. George R. Leighton described Birmingham as an exploited colony of the East in "Birmingham, Alabama," *Harper's* CLXXV (August, 1937), 225–42.

99. On that optimism see Edward Mims, *The Advancing South* (New York, 1926), pp. 94–5.

100. George W. Stocking, *Basing Point Pricing and Regional Development; a Case Study of the Iron and Steel Industry* (Chapel Hill, 1952), pp. 74, 111, 143, 155.

war production were not going to the Southern states in significant volume, partly because Southern firms were handicapped by high freight rates in bidding on war contracts.  Admitting that heavy industrial capacity simply did not exist in the Southeast, that the freight-rate structure alone should not be blamed for the present lack of industrial development in the South and West, and that those residing in the South must shoulder part of the blame, he asserted that "it seems that the freight-rate structure is a manifestation of a fundamental situation in the national economy—a part of the design in the national economic pattern."[101]   That design, Barton felt, was well described in Thurman Arnold's exposition.

The South was soon to be assured by the Chairman of the War Production Board that it was the nation's Opportunity No. 1,[102] and the region did participate heavily, though somewhat belatedly, in the war effort.[103]   Though that participation had great impact, the imperialistic theme persisted.  A Southern historian observed that "it was the task of outside capital to direct Southern manpower and resources toward performing their share in the war effort."[104]  Purchases by Northern interests of Southern-owned textile mills proved that absentee ownership was still much in evidence.  A Northern journalist labeled Texas—the Southern state which enjoyed the greatest industrial expansion during the war—"New York's most valuable foreign possession."  During the war, it was held, monopoly strengthened its hold everywhere, so that "the South will continue to ship out huge sums in interests and profits."[105]

In 1947 Wendell Berge, then Assistant U. S. Attorney General, assured the Southern Economic Association that: "Absentee ownership and control of Southern industry and economic assets are still very much in the picture.  They represent, basically, the major economic problems of the South."  Though railroad rates remained a problem,

101. Frank L. Barton, "The Freight-Rate Structure and the Distribution of Defense Contracts," *Southern Economic Journal,* VIII (October, 1942), 122–33. That the South lacked skilled labor and that most defense orders would consequently go elsewhere was recognized in a study of the South's needs for a large quantity of better-balanced industry: Harriet L. Herring, *Southern Industry and Regional Development* (Chapel Hill, 1940), esp. p. 79.

102. Donald M. Nelson, "The South's Economic Opportunity," *American Mercury,* LIX (October, 1944), 423.

103. For a broad review of the effects of World War II see Frank E. Smith, "The Changing South," *Virginia Quarterly Review,* XXXI (1955), 276–91.

104. Simkins, *op. cit.,* p. 485.

105. Avrahm G. Mezerik, "Southern Boom, Cotton Bust," *The Nation,* CLXIII (November 9, 1946), 524.  The argument is elaborated in his *Revolt of the South and West* (New York, 1946).

the South, he held, must be especially concerned with monopoly because it "has many new industrial capacities which will be a target for monopolies seeking to extend their control." The total cost of such monopolies, Berge said, is incalculable, "but it has been estimated that the price paid by the South for the existence of just one monopoly, that in commercial fertilizers, was great enough to have provided a college education for every high school graduate of the southern states." He added ominously that "at the present time, such factors as the control of technology, of research, and of 'know-how' are far more likely to be the basis of monopoly power. Where these are not sufficient, the whole array of ingenious devices may be employed to substitute monopoly power for the free play of competition in the market."[106]

Acceptance of the exploitation doctrine logically called for compensation of some kind, and the approach of the end of World War II provided the opportunity to make such demands. Adherents of the conspiracy thesis were not the only proponents of federal reconversion policies that would discriminate regionally in the lifting of wartime priorities and in disposal of war plants—but they pressed their proposals most vigorously. Spokesman for such a policy in the U. S. Congress was not a Southerner but Senator Pat McCarran of Nevada. As Chairman of a Special Committee to Investigate Industrial Decentralization, Senator McCarran submitted a report which asserted that "Our major industries have fought a desperate and ruthless battle, subverting our whole transportation system to their purpose, to deny the West and South the industries they can support and to which they have every right." To redress the alleged wrongs, McCarran proposed a program for the South as follows:

1. Immediately the World War ends, production, particularly of chemical products, textiles, clothing, ammunition, and shells should be shifted to this area.

2. Government-owned plants and war surpluses should be so disposed of as to allow maximum encouragement to new industries in this area.

3. Through federal aid, research and technological assistance should be provided so as to encourage more indigenous operation and ownership of local industries. Changes in freight rates must be pressed immediately to make it possible for new industries to meet competi-

---

106. Wendell Berge, "Monopoly and the South," *Southern Economic Journal,* XIII (April, 1947), 360–69. See also Berge's *Economic Freedom for the West* (Lincoln, Neb., 1945).

tive prices on the Nation's markets. Precautions must be taken not to sacrifice the raw-materials producers in this region, as well as the seventeen Western states, to the policy being pressed in industrial circles to make this Nation primarily an exporter of producer's goods and a large-scale importer of raw materials.[107]

McCarran's efforts aroused little support in the Congress, and with that failure ended significant efforts to carry the conspiracy thesis to its logical conclusion. The thesis nevertheless continued to have adherents. One of the most vigorous and unqualifiedly defiant assertions of this point of view appeared in 1952 and components of the doctrine continue to appear in the literature.[108]

### Evaluation of the Conspiracy Approach

The claim that a conspiracy exists is a common reaction to a difficult and possibly disagreeable problem. This approach is attractive because it absolves of responsibility and offers a solution through identifying the culprits, bringing them to justice, and levying compensation through political or legal action. The alternative of accepting full responsibility for the problem is unpleasant and may appear to impose an impossible burden. As in the present instance, conspiracy explanations typically rest upon assumptions regarding the relative importance of the factors involved in a situation, with emphasis being placed on those which support the charge while others are ignored. A conspiracy thesis also rests typically upon overly simplified concepts of economic, political, and social relationships and upon naive concepts of the constraints which operate upon those who seem to personify power and influence. These are characteristics of the conspiracy approach that render any specific reply difficult, if not futile.

No social scientists undertook a direct critique of the conspiracy thesis. Each of the specific charges was, however, analyzed and evaluated effectively, if somewhat belatedly, over the five years immediately following the war.[109] A comprehensive analysis which repre-

107. *A Graphic Guide to Decentralization and Some Simple Facts on Reconversion*, Special Committee to Investigate Industrial Centralization, Pat McCarran, Chairman, U.S. Senate, 79 Cong., 2 sess. (1944), Sen. Doc. Vol. 5, No. 75.

108. Francis B. Simkins, "The South," in Merrill Jensen (ed.), *Regionalism in America* (Madison, 1952). The colonial-conspiracy point of view is applied in an attack on the policies of the nation's philanthropic foundations in Carl M. Rosenquist, "Academic Colonialism," *Southwestern Social Science Quarterly*, XXXV (1954), 3–10.

109. It is useful to recall Frederick C. Mills' observation that "one of the serious disabilities from which the social sciences suffer arises from their failure to give

sented a broad consensus of most economists on the issues was made by Calvin Hoover and Benjamin U. Ratchford, another by the Committee on the Southwest Economy.[110]

*The tariff.*—The tariff has been the hardy perennial of conflict between the North and South. Southern views, however, had long since become increasingly divided, particularly as industry became important. There were two opposed positions with many variations in between.

One was the traditional position which looked upon the South as an exporter of raw materials to world markets and which objected to any restraint upon its freedom to sell in such markets as well as its freedom to buy manufactured goods. Free trade in world markets guaranteed protection against Eastern monopolies. This point of view was based on a commitment to an agrarian society and made no provision for the South's industrial development.

A second position not only made no objection to tariffs but favored them as a source of protection of established interests or as a method for promoting more rapid industrialization. William Hicks as early as the 1870's argued that through protectionism the South could achieve equality with New England.[111]

William J. Robertson in more recent years held a similar position, suggesting that "the South demand a protective tariff that would be designed to benefit the nation as a whole."[112] An increasing number of textile manufacturers took positions favorable to the tariff as the industry encountered stronger competition from world producers. Sugar and cattle interests also tended to be pro-tariff.

Whatever the effect of the tariff on the South's historic economic position, in the 1930's the region was far from united on the issue. The world situation had, moreover, become exceedingly complex, with tariffs merely one of a wide variety of interferences with world trade. In Cordell Hull, the South had a strong advocate of its traditional point of view in a position of high responsibility. By that date it was

---

prompt and effective quietus to useless, meaningless, even to false theories." In Introduction to Alfred C. Neal, *Industrial Concentration and Price Flexibility* (Washington, 1942), p. vii.

110. Hoover and Ratchford, *Economic Resources;* "The Southwest" (Report of the Committee on the Southwest Economy to the President's Council of Economic Advisors, Washington, 1952). "The Southwest" includes an analysis and the critical appraisal of the notion of colonialism as applied to the region. (Chap. IX, pp. 6–8.)

111. Dorfman, *Economic Mind,* III, 11.

112. William J. Robertson, *The Changing South* (New York, 1937), p. 272.

clear that the tariff was a national question that reflected differences in industry groupings rather than sectional interests.[113]   In the 1940's, the South's dependence on foreign trade in agricultural products declined further while the operation of agricultural price support programs operated very much to the region's advantage, since her farm products were sold in world markets at prices that represented a substantial subsidy.   Meanwhile, the region's interest in foreign markets for manufactured products continued to increase while Southern manufacturers were increasingly concerned with competition from abroad. The tariff argument as used by the conspiracy school was then obsolescent, and the fact that it was employed is open to the interpretation that it was conceived of not so much as an economic issue as an identification with internationalism which "served to set limits to the South's integration into American culture."[114]

*Railroad rates.*—Although the charges of railroad-rate discrimination suggest that there had been a long neglect of harmful abuses, such was not the case.   The Southern rate structure had developed out of the needs of the shippers in the region and, like rate structures elsewhere, was under more or less continuous review either by shipper negotiation with the railroads or by action of the Interstate Commerce Commission.[115]   No charges of discrimination were made regarding the commodity rates under which much the larger volume of traffic moved.   The charges were made by public officials rather than by shippers and were directed towards class rates which accounted for a minor part of freight movement.   With regard to these rates, the Interstate Commerce Commission found that inter-territorial inequities did exist.   Appropriate changes were ordered in an action which was upheld by the Supreme Court.

The significance of this adjustment as it related to Southern economic development was probably slight.   Reviewing the evidence as presented in the Southern Governors' and related cases, Hoover and Ratchford conclude that "high freight rates are not now, and never were, a major barrier to the economic development of the South."[116]

113. Hoover and Ratchford, *op. cit.*, Chap. xvii; Irish, "Foreign Policy and the South," *Journal of Politics*, X (May, 1948), 306.

114. Paul Seabury, *The Waning of Southern Internationalism*, Center of International Studies (Princeton, 1957), p. 14.

115. David M. Potter, "The Historical Development of Eastern-Southern Freight Rate Relationships," *Law and Contemporary Problems*, XII (1947), 416–48.   William H. Joubert, *Southern Freight Rates in Transition* (Gainesville, 1949) supplies a useful account and bibliography of the freight rate controversy.

116. *Op. cit.*, p. 78.

"The difference in rates has not been presented in its true perspective and its importance has been greatly exaggerated since most traffic moved by commodity rates while the charges were directed at class rates."[117] Furthermore, as Milton Heath pointed out, some of the differentials that existed might have been advantageous to Southern producers, a fact that explained why Southern shippers did not give significant support to the Southern Governors.[118]

*Monopoly.*—The sweeping charges made regarding the effects of monopoly on the South found few adherents. Albert S. Keister denied Arnold's charges that the Northern monopolies were throttling the South. He pointed to the acceleration of industrialization, which was "proceeding much more rapidly during the past generation than that of the country at large," and added, "Nor is local independent capital disappearing in the South, if one may judge by bank deposits. . . . These evidences of capital increased between 1930 and 1940 more rapidly in the South than in the nation at large."[119]

More specific was the question of monopoly as presented by the steel industry. The basing point system of pricing in that industry was under critical attack for reasons much broader than the South's interest. With the abolition of that pricing system by the Federal Trade Commission, there were expectations that activity in the iron and steel industries in the Birmingham area would be stimulated.[120] That no appreciable gain followed stimulated another study of the Southern iron and steel industry. That study observes that while "policies have not always been those that would stimulate the greatest development," the "slow development of metal-using industries and the markets for steel in the South cannot be charged too heavily to the policies of the big iron and steel companies." "It must be emphasized that substantial progress has been made in the Southern industry and that the United States Steel Corporation and other steel makers have had an important place in that record of progress."[121]

117. *Ibid.*, p. 79.
118. Milton S. Heath, "The Uniform Class Rate Decision and Its Implications for Southern Economic Development," *Southern Economic Journal*, XIII (January, 1946), 213–37. The political significance of differences of opinion within the South are dealt with in Robert A. Lively, *The South in Action: A Sectional Crusade Against Freight Rate Discrimination* (Chapel Hill, 1949).
119. Albert S. Keister, review of Thurman Arnold's *Democracy and Free Enterprise*, in *Southern Economic Journal*, IX (1942), 157–58.
120. Harry D. Bonham, "Prospect of Heavy Industry in the South," *Southern Economic Journal*, XIV (1947), 395–403.
121. H. H. Chapman and others, *The Iron and Steel Industries of the South* (University, Alabama, 1953), p. 389.

*Absentee Ownership.*—The South's concern with the organization and practices of business, specifically with monopoly and absentee ownership, was a facet of a larger group of dissatisfactions with big business which were widely expressed throughout the Nation.[122] The basic source of concern was the fact that the emergence of very large business corporations appeared to have changed the structure of the American economic order, which no longer conformed to the abstract ideal of an economy of small owner-managed firms operating competitively. The depression had exposed the system as very vulnerable to financial difficulties and to instability in employment. Serious doubts were being cast upon the basic justification for very large firms—their superior efficiency. Moreover, the apparent ability of the very large firms to escape the pressure of competition raised problems with regard to the responsibility with which their great power was exercised, problems accentuated by the separation of ownership from management.[123] To the South, the facts of very large size and the consequent concentration of power seemed, or were suspected of being, particularly serious since the region was dependent upon decisions made outside the region.

There could be no denial that there was much absentee ownership of Southern resources, that much of such ownership had been welcomed, and that many agencies were seeking to increase it. It has been the South's experience that its business adventures outside of agriculture and commerce tended to fall under the control of firms headquartered outside the region. After the Civil War, the region's railroads were partially rebuilt by local interests with local and governmental funds, but the task of extending the lines and consolidating them into systems was assumed by railroad interests from outside the region. The South's early industrialization—the cotton mill movement of the 1880's—originated in local enterprise applying local risk capital. It too, though in lesser degree, came under the control of Northern companies. Much the same has been true in such developments as in the iron and steel, furniture, rayon and synthetic fibers, petroleum and other industries. Instances of Southern industrialists controlling firms

122. J. D. Glover, *The Attack on Big Business,* Harvard University Graduate School of Business Administration (Boston, 1954) surveys the criticism of "big business and indeed of industrial civilization" without referring to the literature emanating from the South.

123. A. A. Berle and Gardner C. Means, *The Modern Corporation and Private Property* (New York, 1933) and subsequent writings by Berle, most recently *The American Economic Republic* (New York, 1963). See also "The Southwest," Chap. ii, 16–17.

which have achieved national dominance of their industries exist but have been limited, cigarettes and soft drinks being the major examples. Even such Southern contributions to technological advance as the production of pulpwood from Southern pine were not applied until Northern sources of capital and management undertook to do so.

Given the great gap which was a result of the South's persistent agrarianism, the region had developed only a relatively small group of men who were cognizant of modern technologies, alert to markets and marketing institutions, possessed of managerial competencies, and with access to capital resources. Though Southerners frequently did assume the initiative, what the South had to offer in raw material, untrained labor, and modest markets it could not supplement with adequate managerial and financial resources. Though other methods of solving its problems were not ruled out, the South chose to emphasize the one most readily available to it: the acceleration of industrialization by importing the wherewithal to bring it about.

John B. McFerrin provided an appraisal of the net effects on the South of this process. He argued that Southern corporations did and should continue to go outside the region for their capital requirements. The complaint that they thereby lost some control and that income was drained out of the region by payment of interest and dividends, he dismissed by pointing out that "the income would not be there . . . if the original capital had not been imported."[124]  The suggestion, implicit in the objections to absentee ownership, that, if the South had been able to generate more capital, as out of retained profits, it would have prospered more rapidly is exceedingly dubious. Given a national market, capital will flow where the opportunities are most attractive.

The fact is that the Southerners most directly involved operated from the assumption that what chance the South had of accelerating its growth rested on its ability to attract capital to provide the foundations of a more productive economy. The problem was not only that the region lacked capital but also and perhaps principally that the region lacked men with the ability to command the capital available in the nation.[125]  To obtain the employment it desired, the South, historically and contemporaneously, had to join the rest of the nation in accepting corporate organization, absentee ownership, and, what was

124. John B. McFerrin, "Resources for Financing Industry in the South," *Southern Economic Journal*, XIV (1947), 61; cf. Hoover and Ratchford, *op. cit.*, pp. 28–29.

125. Particular attention to this problem was given in "The Southwest," Chap. ii, p. 23.  See also William H. Baughn, "Capital Formation and Entrepreneurship in the South," *Southern Economic Journal*, XVI (1949), 161–69.

perhaps a more immediate source of annoyance, outside management of its plants. The attacks on monopoly and on absentee ownership were then, in part, an expression of values held by some Southerners in conflict with those held elsewhere in the nation. In the words of one of the Agrarians, the South wanted an economy with a wide distribution of tangible capital properties—a kind of economy which the region could understand. Many non-agrarians appeared to agree.

Their view implied a preference for the local employer, possibly paternalistic, as in the textile towns—though that relationship found its fair share of critics in the South itself. It was also naive in that it failed to recognize that, in the American experience, industry tended to become large scale, and large-scale industry over time typically and inevitably became an absentee-owned operation. That separation posed issues of policy, but they were national problems and did not explain the difference between the South's economic development and that of the rest of the nation.[126]

If large corporate organizations presented problems, they also presented opportunities that escaped the nostalgia of the Agrarians, critics of industrialism such as Webb, and others. Milton Heath called attention to such opportunities when he wrote: "I do not fear for the future of free productive enterprise within the corporate structure. But there is need for a new doctrine of liberalism which comprehends the greatly expanded potential of the corporate organization for both production and consumption and which integrates the aims and possibilities of free activity in both spheres."[127]

The colonial-imperialistic thesis of conspiracy must be considered an unfortunate episode—a resurgence of a crude sectionalism—that diverted the attention of some of the South's ablest men from constructive approaches to the region's problems. It was attractive to some who held the liberal belief that a more nearly perfect mobility of factors would solve the South's difficulties. It was also attractive to some who found in it an escape from the burdens they carried. The conspiracy thesis shifted those burdens to others, and carried with it claims for compensation to be secured from the federal government.

That the thesis dealt with significant matters is obvious, but they were national problems and their relationship to the South's economic retardation highly doubtful. While the South's legitimate claims were

126. See W. Lloyd Warner, *The Corporation in the Emergent American Society* (New York, 1962).
127. Milton S. Heath, "Freedom, Economics and Corporate Organization," *Southern Economic Journal*, XXIV (1958), 251–58.

recognized, as in the rate cases, there is no evidence that such changes were of any significance to its growth. Though it did not always eschew the charges and demands of the exploitation school, the main stream of thought and action continued to press for solutions along the well-established lines of promoting new industry and approving out-migration.

## The Immediate Postwar Years

The most obvious impact of World War II upon the South was a growth in per capita income sufficiently great to reduce significantly the gap between average per capita incomes in the region and in the nation. Those gains, rising from the nation's need for the South's human and natural resources in the war effort, took the form of rapid industrialization, out-migration, and disproportionately large federal disbursements for military purposes in the South and to Southerners. Almost as obvious was the fact that its war experience drew the South more fully into the national society than had been the case at any earlier time. Rupert Vance made the point when he suggested that the region adopt as its goal "the Nation's Future for the South."[128] That future now lay unquestionably with industrialization, and the problem that was to occupy most attention was that of accelerating the volume of employment in industry.

If accelerated industrialization was now an unquestioned long-range objective, there were the immediate problems of holding the war-time gains and moving forward from what was still a very low base. The South gained no special concessions in reconversion policy, but the early postwar period was one that saw developments of more fundamental significance. Most important was the reaction of the Congress to the general consensus that adequate provision must be made to deal with fluctuations in economic activity. That problem was dealt with by the passage of the Employment Act of 1946, which established the Council of Economic Advisers and the Joint Economic Committee of the Congress. The responsibilities assumed in the Employment Act included not only the maintenance of conditions conducive to the promotion of maximum employment production and purchasing power in the nation but also in "any considerable portion thereof." This broadening of the federal government's activities in

128. *All These People*, Chap. xxxii. A useful appraisal of the effects of World War II on the South is Frank E. Smith, "The Changing South," *Virginia Quarterly Review*, XXXI (1955), 276–91.

UNIVERSITY OF
ILLINOIS LIBRARY

promoting internal economic growth was to be considerably expanded in subsequent years, significantly changing the environment within which the South might pursue its objectives.

In addition to the tasks of converting to peacetime conditions, the South faced the special problems of a technological revolution based on the now perfected mechanical cotton picker and related mechanical and chemical cultivation equipment. The anticipated rapid postwar adoption of these techniques promised serious dislocation effects upon the region's agricultural population. Anxiety over such problems led the U. S. House Committee on Agriculture, under the leadership of Congressman Frank Pace, to plan hearings on the economic problems of the Cotton Belt. An elaborate and well-documented presentation was made at the Hearings held in 1947.[129]

The Congressional Committee was presented with a program which, the authors said, was "designed to set free the free enterprise system." "It is a program designed to meet the needs of the South by eliminating the handicaps that it now bears—handicaps that, if not eliminated, will almost certainly become so urgent that enormous pressures will develop in favor of large-scale Federal direction of economic activities. The choice is thus not a free one. Either aggressive steps will be begun, or economic difficulties will necessitate even more comprehensive action."[130]

The forces causing low incomes and living standards in the cotton South were identified as: 1. the low productivity of manpower in Southern agriculture; 2. the exceptionally high rate of natural increase of the Southern farm population; 3. the past and continuing high rate of soil erosion and soil depletion; 4. lack of capital; 5. educational deficiencies; 6. health deficiencies; 7. lack of skills for non-farm pursuits; 8. the South's infant industry status; 9. inadequate local market demand; 10. adjustments required by increased rate of farm mechanization.[131]

The recommendations of the Committee were to "involve collaboration between individuals, groups and government at federal, state and local levels" in a program that would:

1. Provide financial assistance to small business through loan insurance,

129. *Study of Agricultural and Economic Problems of the Cotton Belt*, Special Subcommittee on Cotton of the House Committee on Agriculture, Hearings, 80 Cong., 1 sess. (July 8–9, 1947).
130. *Ibid.*, p. 581.
131. *Ibid.*, p. 560.

2. Carry on research and promote the application of research to business enterprises,

3. Promote a transportation policy that will stimulate a more diversified and a more highly finished type of industry throughout the Southern states. Two suggested measures were the greater use of class rates, based as far as possible on cost principles and coordination of expansion in transportation both within itself and with other branches of the Southern economy.

4. Eliminate monopolistic practices that hold back Southern production. The committee regarded monopolies as so peculiarly detrimental to the South that it recommended a long-range study of the problem by competent public or private agencies.

5. Eliminate interstate trade barriers, and work for the elimination of restrictions in other regions on the use of Southern products (e.g. margarine),

6. Promote use of the large surplus war plants in the South by small business through plans such as multiple tenancy,

7. Provide minimum standards of welfare and promote wage agreements that reflect the full contribution of workers to production, through adequate minimum wage standards and through the responsible exercise of collective bargaining,

8. Maintain a substantially federally financed investment program designed—

(a) to encourage industrial expansion or other readjustments that will increase productivity,

(b) to maintain and improve both human and natural resources through Federal aid, particularly for education, health, and conservation; and

(c) to moderate fluctuations in the level of economic activity.[132]

The Committee emphasized its proposal for a federally financed investment program. On the basis of detailed estimates of investment requirements, it was concluded that it "was clearly impossible for the region to secure from internal savings the millions of dollars that can profitably be invested in industrial expansion, in soil conservation, and in other improvements." Since industry in the South was in an "infant" status, it was necessary to recognize that "in the opening stages of new industry, there occur serious but short-lived difficulties that often threaten survival. Yet the South's industrial development has

132. *Ibid.*, p. 558.

had to go forward within the largest free trade area in the world and one in which its industries, from the start, have had to compete with well-established enterprises elsewhere in the country." Moreover, local markets were inadequate. "Inadequate market demand is both a reflection and a cause of low incomes in the South. Limited demand in the South has led to caution in business expansion there and has retarded business development."[133]

The three-pronged public investment program was therefore held to be "one of the most important of the recommendations made." The Committee explained that:

The first type of public investment is intended to stimulate enterprises where they are most productive. It would help workers shift from present unproductive jobs and locations to those where they can do better, relieving them of some of the costs involved that otherwise would hold them back. It would provide for public improvements that are necessary in many southern communities if private industrial expansion is to take place. And it would include direct investments in enterprises that would not be developed adequately by private capital of which TVA, with its numerous direct and indirect benefits to business and to the region as a whole, is the outstanding example.

The second is aimed at human resources, health and education, housing, old age, medical care, etc., but also includes soil protection, clearing and draining of lands not now in use, improvement of forest resources, development of wildlife lands, etc.

The third type is important to industrialization of the South since investment of private capital simply does not take place in periods of severe recession.[134]

This program represented a transitory stage of thought. Those proposals that were reminiscent of the views of the conspiracy school received little, if any, attention. But the study included also proposals intended to provide an environment facilitating economic growth in the nation including the South. While the Cotton Belt study resulted in no immediate legislation, many of the suggested actions were in some form enacted into law over the succeeding fifteen years.

### The Committee of the South

With the return to peace, individual scholars and organized groups increased their efforts to analyze the region's problems and to

133. *Ibid.*, p. 557.

134. *Ibid.*, p. 558.

suggest programs to further its objectives. Most important among the organized groups was the establishment by the National Planning Association of a Committee of the South to "seek ways of expanding employment, production, markets and economic opportunity in the South." Its membership represented business, academic, and governmental interests predominantly from the South but including also many non-Southerners.[135] The committee's research staff, under Calvin B. Hoover as director, undertook a substantial research program. The most important result was Calvin B. Hoover's and B. U. Ratchford's *Economic Resources and Policies of the South,* published in 1951.[136]

The Hoover and Ratchford study marks a turning point in the analysis of Southern economic problems. Each of the issues which had agitated earlier writers—issues including those that were the foundation of the exploitation point of view—was examined. As has been noted, many were pushed aside as superficial, as unimportant, or as having no causal significance. The fundamental position taken was that Southern economic growth was dependent upon a national economy operating at high levels of employment. Much of the volume is devoted to an appraisal of the region's human and natural resources. The frequently reiterated claim that Southern natural resources were abundant though relatively underdeveloped was examined with care. It was concluded that many of the claimed resources were marginal or sub-marginal by market standards, particularly in the case of minerals. Other resources called for the application of conservation policies. The overall view of the South's resource base was cautious and restrained. "Low per capita income in the South," they said, "stems from a low ratio of natural and capital resources to population." Regarding human resources, the report pointed out that "the low status of the population in education and in training for industrial production accentuates the poor ratio of natural and capital resources but the

135. The organization, financing, procedures, and research program of the NPA Committee of the South is described in "Problems in the Study of Economic Growth" (Universities-National Bureau of Economic Research, 1949), pp. 217–25.

136. In 1949 the Council of Economic Advisers, in pursuance of its responsibilities under section 4 (e) 2 of the Employment Act, arranged with the National Planning Association Committee of the South for a report on the relationship of Federal policies to the economic needs of the region. The result was published as a Report of the Joint Committee on the Economic Report on *The Impact of Federal Policies on the Economy of the South,* 81 Cong., 1 sess. (Washington, 1949). Prepared by Hoover and Ratchford, it constituted a briefer, preliminary statement of the positions taken in *Economic Resources and Policies.*

low level of educational opportunity likewise reflects low per capita wealth and income."[137]

The South's need for more industry was regarded as obvious, but the region's interest was in greater selectivity so that the number of industries characterized by higher worker productivities could be increased. The dependence of the region upon industrialization based on attracting employers was mildly protested: "The need for more entrepreneurs who can recognize and develop profit opportunities in the South is probably more important than the need for capital."[138]

Federal action of appropriate types was necessary and desirable. Federal fiscal policies should be such as to encourage growth of the industry nationally. Taxation, which deprived firms of retained earnings for expansion, "the principal source of funds and the main driving force for industrial development," should be reduced or eliminated. Direct federal action was desirable in the allocation of defense industries to the South. The federal government should also provide financial aid for research centers and graduate technical schools in which the region could share.

While the South's problems must be dealt with by the federal government, this must be done within the framework of a modified free enterprise society. The South cannot expect special treatment, but federal policies can and should be such as to encourage the region's growth, particularly in the agricultural and fiscal areas. Agricultural policies should be such as to encourage the reorganization of Southern agriculture, especially by stimulating the trend under way to increased productivity through larger, more highly mechanized farms.

The Hoover and Ratchford study performed an exceedingly useful service in placing Southern resources in perspective, in interring topics that had claimed far more attention than they merited, in directing attention to the critical importance of national prosperity to Southern growth, and in recognizing that federal developmental programs directed specifically to the South were neither desirable nor likely to be obtained. In so doing, a sound foundation was laid for further analytical efforts. A deeper understanding of the region's problems and of the processes of growth was necessary if policies and programs by which the South might accelerate its participation in the nation's increasingly complex society were to be improved or developed. Other studies of the Committee of the South contributed to that end.

137. *Economy of the South*, p. 53.
138. *Ibid.*, p. 47.

## The Determinants of Industry Location

A second study of the Committee of the South provided the first large-scale survey of the factors underlying the growth of industry in the South by means of in-migrant industrial employers. In *Why Industry Moves South*, Glenn McLaughlin and Stefan Robock concluded that Southern industrialization was occurring in large part through the location within the region of branch plants of national concerns.[139] This growth was taking place largely because of the intrinsic advantages of Southern location, of which markets was an important element. It was further concluded that local subsidization of industry had played a small part, that such inducements in many cases had been unnecessary, and that some communities had been hurt rather than benefited by attracting an industry that required a subsidy.

The McLaughlin and Robock study stimulated a large volume of further investigation. While the South could expect to continue to attract such plants, given high national levels of employment and continued expansion of its own markets, the rate of growth that prevailed was far from adequate to absorb the region's labor force. In fact, industrialization in the South, though rapid in terms of the region's historic base, was occurring at national rates of growth with the result that the South's share of the nation's manufacturing employment remained a low and constant share of the nation's.[140] It was also true that Southern states and cities were competing with each other and with industry-hungry areas elsewhere in the nation for the available supply of firms seeking new plant locations. Numerous efforts were made, and continue to be made, to identify the factors that operate in location decision-making across a broader spectrum and also more specifically and in more detail than did McLaughlin and Robock.[141] Frequently intended to provide guides to public officials

139. Glenn E. McLaughlin and Stefan Robock, *Why Industry Moves South* (National Planning Association Committee of the South, Report No. 3 [1949]).

140. Victor R. Fuchs, *Changes in the Location of Manufacturing in the United States Since 1929* (New Haven, 1962), pp. 23–25 ff.

141. Among many, Joe S. Floyd, *The Effect of Taxation on Industrial Location* (Chapel Hill, 1952); James E. Chapman and William H. Wells, *Factors in Industrial Location in Atlanta, 1946–55*, Research Paper No. 8, Georgia State College of Business Administration; Business Executives Research Committee, *Factors Affecting Industrial Location in the Southwest*, University of Oklahoma (Norman, 1954); *Industrial Development in the TVA Area during 1958*, Tennessee Valley Authority (Chattanooga, 1959). The subject continues to be an area of conflicting views, e.g., Melvin L. Greenhut, "An Explanation of Industrial Development in Underdeveloped Areas of the United States," *Land Economics*, XXXVI (1960), 371–79.

charged with securing new industry, the literature in part also supplies appraisals critical of industrial promotion programs which employ subsidies to attract employers.[142]

## Federal Regulation of Wages

An issue neglected by the conspiracy school and discussed at length but inconclusively by Hoover and Ratchford relates to the differences in wage rates, specifically in manufacturing industry, between the South and the rest of the nation.[143] The issue was of concern to many who believed that not only were the lower costs of labor in the South the region's chief attraction to outside industry but also that higher wages elsewhere stimulated out-migration. While reduction in the wage differential would occur and be welcomed as industrial employment increased, any reduction in the differential by legislation might be viewed as tending to reduce the South's rate of industrialization and to add to the problems of reducing the agricultural labor force. The passage of the Fair Labor Standards Act in 1938 and its subsequent Amendments and, to a lesser extent, the Public Contracts Act of 1936 have been viewed by some as serious threats to the South's continuing growth.

On the other hand, the low wages paid in the South and the conditions that followed also caused concern, not only to Eastern competitive employers but also within the South.[144] Demands for action to improve the conditions of Southern workers and for protection against those employers who came South for cheap labor had been made from time to time.[145] Virginius Dabney, for example, complained of the "carpetbaggers of industry from the north coming south to take up fantastic inducements which were offered without discriminating between those who paid fair wages and those who did not."[146] During the bottom of the depression, Southern industry joined in the quest to establish a floor beneath which competitors

142. The literature is critically reviewed in John E. Moes, *Local Subsidies for Industry* (Chapel Hill, 1962).

143. See James M. Buchanan's review of Hoover and Ratchford's *Economic Resources and Policies of the South*, in *Journal of Political Economy*, LX (1952), 81–82.

144. See John F. Kennedy, "New England and the South: The Struggle for Industry," *Atlantic Monthly*, CXCIII (January, 1954), 32–36.

145. Charles W. Pipkin, *Social Legislation in the South* (Southern Policy Papers, No. 3 [1936]); Robin Hood, *Industrial Social Security in the South* (Southern Policy Papers, No. 5 [1936]).

146. *Below the Potomac*, p. 91.

could not drive wage rates.[147] However, the Fair Labor Standards legislation was strongly opposed by all but a small minority of Southern employers in the affected industries and by all Southern Congressmen. In their general view, the legislation was "outright discrimination against the South to offset its natural advantages in the matter of climate and proximity to raw material."[148]

The war-induced boom in employment absorbed the immediate impact of the 1938 Act, but there was much concern over the long-run effect. The problems associated with the wage-differential attracted considerable attention from economists. Van Sickle led the defense of the wage differential, arguing that the fixing of minimum wages was an unfortunate departure from liberalism that introduced rigidities which would reduce the mobility of labor and the ability of the South to attract industry. "From the point of view of the agrarian South this law deserves to be classed with the protective tariff and the freight rate structure as an additional protective barrier thrown around the 'industrial quadrilateral,' as an additional obstacle to diversification."[149] The Act, he held, should be amended "to make mandatory either regional differentials or differentials according to accurately determined community cost-of-living studies."

Others held opposite views. Richard Lester found that during the war Southern industry had adjusted to the narrowing of the North-South differential without the dire consequences that had been predicted. Many of the grounds for the differential had been disappearing or had less economic validity than they had had in past decades; their disappearance could help improve living standards in the South. "Assuming the desirability of northward migration of labor," Lester argued that "there is still a question of the importance of South-North wage differences in such migration compared with other factors like job opportunities, living conditions, and social advantages. One must bear in mind that wage differentials in labor-market areas within the South are greater than the true South-North differential in most industries."[150]

147. H. M. Douty, *Wage and Hour Legislation for the South* (Southern Policy Papers, No. 9 [1937]), p. 8.
148. Irish, "The Proletarian South," *Journ. of Pol.*, II, 252.
149. *Planning*, pp. 189, 191; also the same author's "Regional Aspects of the Problem of Full Employment at Fair Wages," *Southern Economic Journal*, XIII (July, 1946), 45.
150. Richard A. Lester, "Southern Wage Differentials: Developments, Analysis, and Implications," *Southern Economic Journal*, XIV (April, 1947), 391–94; see also the same author's "Trends in Southern Wage Differentials Since 1890,"

Vance argued to similar conclusions: "If Southern industry and labor are to gain access to national markets, they must in the long run be equal in efficiency and productivity to any in the Nation. . . . Southern firms on the margin of bankruptcy cannot long be saved from the consequences of mismanagement by recourse to the payment of substandard wages. . . . Higher standards . . . offer industry its one hope of disposing of its product in mass markets once the war boom has passed. It is doubtful if the Southeast or any other region can present legitimate claims to stand in the way of the development of a national minimum wage"; and he urged that the coverage of minimum-wage legislation be extended.[151]

The application of the 1938 minimum and the subsequent increases have each occurred under conditions of a buoyant national economy characterized by upward price level movements. Whatever impact the minimum wages so established may have had upon Southern employment and the South's wage differential as an attraction to new industry has consequently been obscured. Some have held that there have been no lasting effects.[152] Others have argued that negative results on Southern employment have followed, apparent or not.[153] Marshall Colberg in a recent study concludes that "basically the national minimum wage as applied to manufacturing, at least, is a device for waging regional warfare."[154] The recent increase of the legal minimum wage and particularly the broadening of coverage may well stimulate greater concern in this area.

## Industry Dispersal

A new movement looking towards the decentralization of industry originated not in the South but within the federal government in response to the vulnerability of large aggregations of the nation's industry to nuclear warfare, augmented by the needs for additional productive capacity as the Korean war created increased military re-

---

*Southern Economic Journal,* XI (April, 1945), 317–44; Hoover and Ratchford, *op. cit.,* Chap. xvi.

151. *All These People,* p. 485.

152. Victor R. Fuchs and Richard Perlman, "Recent Trends in Southern Wage Differentials," *Review of Economics and Statistics,* XLII (1960), 297.

153. The position of George Stigler, "The Economics of Minimum Wage Legislation," *American Economic Review,* XXXVI (1946), 358–65.

154. Marshall Colberg, "Minimum Wage Effects on Florida's Economic Development," *Journal of Law and Economics,* III (October, 1960), 106, 117. W. H. Nicholls expresses some doubts. Cf. *Southern Tradition and Regional Progress,* p. 169.

quirements in the face of a near fully employed economy. Although Congress considered the matter, action was taken by the federal executive agencies in the form of two directives calling upon procurement agencies to place contracts to the largest degree possible in areas which the Department of Labor found to possess a surplus of labor. All other things, including price, being equal, suppliers in such labor surplus areas are given preference in the award of federal contracts.[155]

Compared with earlier interest in federal action to decentralize industry, the current policy has attracted little regional attention. Such effects as can be discerned seem to be principally in the participation of small business in federal procurement. Federal military procurement contracts in the decade of the fifties and since have tended to concentrate in Southern New England and in California. Any favorable effects on the South as a result of dispersal policies have been slight, if not negligible.[156] On the other hand, the South has benefited in some degree from federal expenditure in the research and development areas. Such expenditures in the South have been very large relative to the narrow base of regional effort in this area.

### Changing Directions in Analysis

The South has made substantial progress since World War II in building the institutional structure of a modern society. While the growth of per capita incomes in the region has somewhat exceeded the national rate, the gain has been at very low levels and the income gap remains very substantial. Agricultural overpopulation remains a serious problem, and much of that population seems to be characterized by a high degree of immobility.[157] Though industrialization has proceeded at impressive rates, the fact remains that the South's share of the nation's manufacturing employment continues to be about 15 percent of the nation's, far below its proportion of the nation's population. New industrial employment has not grown with sufficient rapid-

155. For an account of the development and nature of these policies, see Conley H. Dillon, "Channeling Government Contracts into Depressed Areas," *The Western Political Quarterly*, XVI (1963), 279–93.

156. Charles E. Marberry, "Government Defense Industrial Activity in Relation to the South," *Southern Economic Journal*, XXIV (1958), 458–70; Maurice Fulton, "Plant Location–1965," *Harvard Business Review*, XXXIII (March–April, 1955), 40–50.

157. The characteristics and significance of immobility emerge most strikingly in studies of smaller areas over a period of time. See Anthony M. Tang, *Economic Development in the Southern Piedmont, 1860–1950* (Chapel Hill, 1958) and other writings by Tang and William H. Nicholls.

ity to meet the needs of the region's labor force, has not provided the desired stimulus to incomes, has been insufficient to absorb the products of the improving educational system, and has to a large degree excluded the Negro population migrating out of agriculture.[158]

Over this period, the nation's economy has on the whole provided a dynamic environment. The federal government has and is stimulating technological change by very large expenditures on research and development. In addition, the federal government has supplied institutional machinery such as the Small Business Investment Act, the Area Redevelopment Act, and related legislation intended to be of assistance in accelerating growth through changes in the environment of private business.[159] It is significant that the programs of the federal government are directed to economic groupings, the geographic nexus being the concept of the labor market.[160] The old prohibition against federal action which discriminated between regions is thereby circumvented. At the same time, the approach obscures the differences in the problems of areas seeking to climb from a low base and areas seeking to recover a position that was at some time in the past relatively high.

Southern state governments have also acted to increase the activities of their development agencies and to provide machinery to facilitate the growth of business firms and particularly to aid in meeting financial

158. Rupert B. Vance, "The Urban Breakthrough in the South," *Virginia Quarterly Review*, XXXI (1955), 223–32; Donald Dewey, "Negro Employment in Southern Industry," *Journal of Political Economy*, XL (1952), 270–93. Eli Ginzberg, *The Negro Potential* (New York, 1954), pp. 156, 229–30. The Committee of the South sponsored a series of studies of Negro employment in industry: *Selected Studies of Negro Employment in the South*, Report No. 6 (Washington, 1953–54).

The cost of discriminatory participation in industrialization is dealt with in Gary S. Becker, *The Economics of Discrimination* (Chicago, 1957). See also Anthony M. Tang, "Economic Development and Changing Consequences of Race Discrimination in Southern Agriculture," *Journal of Farm Economics*, XLI (1959), 1113–26.

159. A useful review of recently inaugurated federal programs is *Federal Programs of Assistance to Labor Surplus Areas*, A Report of the Interdepartmental Committee to Coordinate Federal Urban Area Assistance Programs, U.S. Department of Commerce (Washington, 1960).

160. The labor market approach would also seem to require changes in the traditional concepts of the region. The current high level of interest in the methodology of regionalism (as in the *Proceedings of the Regional Science Association*) may be expected to reflect the statutory establishment of the labor market as the unit of analysis. For an example of such reaction see Selz C. Mayo, "Organizing for Growth and Development: The Area Approach," in *Conference on Area Development*, University of Georgia (Athens, 1962), 154–170.

problems.[161] Efforts of state governments as well as private groups to accelerate industrialization continue to be based on securing industrial employers from outside: "Almost every conversation, speech or report is predicated on the fact that new industry must be brought in from the outside instead of being organized at home."[162] This is not to say that the sources of indigenous business firms—a highly educated enterprising native population—are neglected, but such long-run considerations receive little attention in discussions of the need for industrialization.

The persistence of the South's economic problem has invited not only a continuing process of measurement and assessment but also has stimulated more penetrating analyses of the nature of the changes that are taking place and that are required.[163] The cautions expressed by Hoover and Ratchford with regard to the long-run effect of encouraging low-wage industries have proved well taken.[164] Intensive analysis of the composition of state incomes by Frank Hanna confirmed opinions expressed earlier that the industry-mix of the region compared unfavorably with that of the non-South: that is to say, a large proportion of Southern industry was of the type characterized by low productivities and low wages.[165] Edgar Dunn approached the problem in terms of slow, stable, and rapidly growing industries, finding that the industries of the South are characteristically of the slow-growth type.[166]

161. Joe S. Floyd and Luther H. Hodges, Jr., *Financing Industrial Growth: Private and Public Sources of Long Term Capital for Industry.* Research Paper No. 10. School of Business Administration, University of North Carolina (Chapel Hill, 1962).
While sources of capital for growth are frequently an important problem, the facile assumption that capital is a, or perhaps the, critical factor can no longer be accepted without question. Other factors are almost certainly more important. See Charles T. Taylor, "The South's Capital Needs and Resources, Public and Private," in *Economic Development—Raising the Income and Productivity of the South,* Proceedings of the 1961 Annual Southern Regional Conference of the Council of State Governments (Mobile, 1961).
162. T. D. Clark, *The Emerging South,* p. 276.
163. In the areas of economic measurement and the assessment of financial problems, important work is being done by the research staffs of the Federal Reserve Banks of Dallas, Richmond, and particularly Atlanta. Bureaus of Business Research of the state universities in the region are also making significant contributions.
164. *Economic Resources and Policies of the South,* pp. 364–67. See also Jesse Markham, "Some Comments upon the North-South Differential," *Southern Economic Journal,* XVI (1950), p. 280.
165. Frank A. Hanna, *State Income Differentials, 1919–1954* (Durham, 1959).
166. Edgar S. Dunn, *Recent Southern Economic Development as Revealed by the Changing Structure of Employment* (Gainesville, 1962).

Closely related are the conclusions reached by Stephen McDonald. "In recent years, there really is no significant association between manufacturing employment and per capita income." McDonald suggests that the growth of manufacturing employment may be overrated as a source of equilibrating increases in the South's per capita incomes. "Where cheap labor and low taxes, as opposed to raw materials availability, are the chief inducements, the South may tend to attract low-value-added non-progressive manufacturing industries that contribute little—even detract from—the South's economic progress relative to the rest of the country." McDonald is somewhat more specific than others have been in questioning the wisdom of continuing industrialization programs that try "to imitate the occupational structures of other regions by inducing manufacturing activities, if necessary, under terms of subsidization. . . . In the long run, it may simply mould southern industry to the old economic conformations of the South rather than alter it in the interest of more rapid progress and earlier income parity." To continue its growth, changes in the South more fundamental than those that have occurred seem necessary. McDonald suggests hopefully that, if full employment levels in the national economy continue and if the momentum of Southern income growth can be maintained, "it may, within another decade or so, fatally weaken those cultural peculiarities that have tended to perpetuate the South's chronic condition of excessive labor resources, meanwhile helping produce an occupational structure best suited to the South's own regional assets."[167]

In William Nicholls' view, "except where the South has rich sources of raw materials not readily available elsewhere . . . success in attracting these more desirable industries depends primarily upon its developing a labor force with or capable of acquiring the necessary industrial skills and upon its having urban communities which are good places in which to live."[168]

Aside from doubts that past policies directed to industrialization should be continued, there is also room for doubt that reliance upon the importation of industrial firms can be continued with as much effect as has been achieved in the past. It may be that the movement to locate in the South to serve its markets will slow down as those markets are adequately supplied. Given the present technology, the labor

167. Unemployment Problems, p. 2201. See also McDonald's, "On the South's Recent Economic Development," *Southern Economic Journal,* XXVIII (1961), p. 39.
168. Nicholls, *Southern Tradition and Regional Progress,* p. 100.

requirements of Southern resources that have been brought into use in recent decades may stabilize at or near present levels of employment. Furthermore, employment in the nation's manufacturing industries has been declining in relation to total employment. Employers interested in labor of relatively low skills are likely to be fewer in the future than in the past, while supplies of low-skilled labor exist in numerous areas outside the South. Widely scattered about the nation are "depressed areas," eager to secure a solution to their immediate needs for employment. They are following the South's long-time strategy in seeking to entice a relatively small number of foot-loose employers. As more of such areas enter the competition for available employers, it is increasingly clear that this approach cannot provide satisfactory solutions.

These considerations suggest that industrialization as it has been carried out in the past is no longer a way in which the region can hope to claim its part in the Nation's future. The Nation's future is on the technological frontiers. There exists a very strong tendency, historically and contemporaneously, that the locality in which technological developments occur is the locality which will enjoy the fullest benefit of the product. New England has resuscitated itself in this manner, and the West Coast is enjoying rapid change on a similar foundation.

In the South, the economic progress that has been accomplished does not appear to provide a broad base for accelerated growth. The reason, William Nicholls argues, is that the South's progress has occurred in spite of strongly inhibiting social, political, psychological, and philosophical elements in its cultural heritage. These are identified as: 1) the persistence of agrarian values; 2) the rigidity of the social structure; 3) the undemocratic nature of the political structure; 4) the weakness of social responsibility, and 5) conformity of thought and behavior. These values, Nicholls argues, are inconsistent with the high rate of industrialization which continues to be necessary if the region's excess of rural population is to be corrected.[169] It is clear that successful participation in a modern economy built around a core of industrialization cannot be accomplished by imposing a layer of industrial activity upon the traditional society, particularly when efforts are also made to inhibit change in that society.[170]

169. Nicholls, *op. cit.*, 15.
170. The literature on the nature and characteristics of the South's traditional society is superabundant. For an effort to analyze those contemporary characteristics comparatively, see John Gillin, "National and Regional Cultural Values in the United States," *Social Forces*, XXXIV (1955), 107–13.

The history of thought on the problems of the underdeveloped countries is significant and relevant. Within a decade, analysis of the problems of growth in the less developed societies moved from a pre-occupation with capital to concern with the political structure, the educational process, and the underlying value systems of these societies. These subjects have not been neglected in analysis of the South's problems.[171] They have rarely, however, been considered as integral parts of policies looking towards economic growth. Economic activity is not something apart but is an integral part of a social system and reflects the values, attitudes, and human relationships of that system. This fact is particularly significant when the borrowing region is a part of a nation which is stimulating continuing technological change at rates approaching the capabilities of its population.

The recommendations of Hoover and Ratchford, and many others, that the federal government provide assistance for research and for higher education have been provided in substantial and increasing degree. In so doing, the Federal government has made a large contribution to the solution of the South's dilemma of supporting more effective educational and research efforts from a low-income base. The South's share of that assistance is not, however, automatic, but is determined in an important degree by the capacity of the region's colleges and universities, research organizations, and business interests to take advantage of opportunity. The region's participation in these programs has so far been modest.[172] The degree to which the South possesses those capabilities that can contribute to the building of the

171. E.g., Ernst Swanson and John Griffing, *Public Education in the South Today and Tomorrow* (Chapel Hill, 1955); Patrick McGauley and Edward D. Ball (eds.), *Southern Schools: Progress and Problems* (Nashville, 1959), and The Commission on Goals for Higher Education in the South, *Within Our Reach* (Atlanta, 1961).

172. A recent colloquy in a Congressional Committee is revealing. The discussants were a Southern Congressman and an official of the National Institutes of Health, also a Southerner. The subject was a program to stimulate research capabilities and the specific question sought an explanation for the low number and value of research grants made to Southern universities. The NIH official reported that investigation had shown that the rejection rates for grant applications from Southern institutions were identical with the national rejection rates. The explanation for the low level of grants was then: "It was the asking power that was not there." The significance of that fact may also be left in his words: "If they do not have this kind of research environment in their graduate training, it raises serious questions, I think, about the adequacy of these educational programs, and whether you are not losing an opportunity to reach some people who could make a research contribution in the future." *Health Research and Training*, Hearings of the Subcommittee of the Committee on Government Operations, House, 87 Cong., 1 sess. (Washington, August 1, 1961), 48–49.

new technology measures the region's future. It is useful to recall that Vance argued for industrialization not only or even primarily to provide jobs for the unemployed. Industrialization was to him a base upon which a new society might be built.

It is not that the less complex economies are concerned simply with the employment and wage payments afforded by manufacturing. The proportions employed in manufacturing in a complex economy are not especially large nor are industrial wages always the highest. It is the complexity and diversity of a rich economy that the more backward States desire, and the development of manufacturing appears the first logical step to the development of such an economy. No one has determined the precise ratio of auxiliary services needed by manufacturing, but they include many in the higher levels of professional and technical services as well as in clerical, trade, transportation and others in the distributive groups. Compared with the range of specialized occupations and skills found in New York, the occupational structure of a State like Mississippi borders on the primitive.[173]

The national economy has provided over the past twenty years the favorable conditions without which Southern progress was scarcely possible but which also invite greater gains than have been achieved. The Nation may well provide in the near future an even more stimulating environment. The South's capacity to take advantage of such opportunities will determine whether the continuity of its economic problems can be broken.

That capacity includes not only the ability to imitate but also an ability to contribute to the Nation's objectives and thereby to its own. Such abilities inhere in human capacities and in organization. Both are a product of social policy expressed actively or passively. They rest on the existence and effective operation of what has been called the quinary group of industries; that is, those activities that result in the refinement and extension of human capacities, that are devoted to the cultivation of behavior to which men are not accustomed, that have the function of engendering social and economic development. These are industries that follow predominantly from public investment and are also the industries which in the current situation offer the highest multiplier of any form of investment.[174] It will be through

173. *All These People*, p. 476.
174. Nelson S. N. Foote and Paul K. Hatt, "Social Mobility and Economic Advancement," *American Economic Review, Proceedings*, XLII (1952), 364–65. See also Forest G. Hill, "The South's Role and Opportunity in Prospective National Growth," William M. Murray, "Research and Technology in the South," and George L. Simpson, Jr., "The South, The National Society and Industrial

more and more effective education and research that the South must raise the capabilities and thereby the "bidding power" of its people.

The forty years covered in this review have witnessed substantial and basic progress in the South in building a more diverse economy, in creating a more favorable environment, and in enhancing the capabilities of its basic resource—its people. There has been much uncertainty and hesitancy, much conflict of values and doubt as to some procedures, some pursuit of false objectives, much preoccupation with problem areas that proved to be of little or only superficial significance, and excessive devotion to immediate but inadequate objectives. Meanwhile the nation has also changed so that some of the objectives and procedures of twenty years ago are now obsolescent. Throughout, it has remained true that the economy of the South has evolved as the capabilities of its citizens to respond to their environment have been enhanced. That experience suggests that persistent adherence to the fundamental task of upgrading human capabilities is the region's best guarantee of continued growth.

Growth," in *Economic Development—Raising the Income and Productivity of the South*, pp. 16–21, 54–59, 67–70.

# II

## The Entrepreneurial Function:
## The South as a Case Study*

*By C. Addison Hickman*

This paper is about the entrepreneurial function; specifically, it deals with the exercise of that function in the South. This essay is designed to suggest an approach and to provide a point of departure rather than to produce either a tightly constructed model or a systematic application of such a model. The two major objectives around which the paper is organized are: 1) to construct a conceptual frame of reference which may prove useful in examining entrepreneurship in a particular place and time, such as the South in the 1960's; and 2) to place, in suggestive and tentative fashion, the South within that frame.

Part I is thus concerned with establishing an approach to the functions of entrepreneurship. This approach is derived largely, although not wholly, from contemporary sources. It is assumed that present American scholarly theories of entrepreneurial functions mirror with reasonable faithfulness some of the actual functions of entrepreneurship in the contemporary United States.

Part II attempts to utilize the approaches developed in Part I toward gaining greater understanding of the entrepreneurial function in the South. This section not only will tap the relatively limited body of work dealing explicitly with Southern entrepreneurship, but

* I wish to acknowledge a specific debt to two persons who have given unstinting assistance. Mr. Girish Trivedi participated in the search of the literature that helped to make possible the first half of the paper, and he was a source of continuing support during the final weeks preceding the completion of the Conference draft. Mr. David Baumgartner has been helpful in the subsequent revision of the paper, especially through his tough-minded and critical evaluation of the Conference draft.

also will relate what seem to be relevant aspects of the Southern economic, political, and social structure to entrepreneurship.

## Part I: Approaches to Entrepreneurship

Part I has three sections. The first section attempts to sketch, in brief and cursory fashion, a little of the abortive history of the traditional concept of entrepreneurship. The second section describes some contemporary concepts, largely of American origin, which attempt to redefine the entrepreneurial function in the light of the modern business organization and the economic, political, and social environment in which the firm is now placed. The third section attempts to examine certain aspects of the internal and external environment of the firm which assume relevance in terms of the redefined entrepreneurial function.

### Traditional Concepts of the Entrepreneurial Function

There has been paradoxically little attention paid to the nature of the entrepreneurial function. During most of the past two centuries, during which time business enterprise has played a leading role, the entrepreneurial function has been either ignored, described only in fragments, or related meaningfully merely to a particular time and place. The term "entrepreneur" was introduced to the literature by Cantillon in the eighteenth century. His entrepreneur, usually a farmer or merchant and a risk-bearer, purchases goods at a certain price to sell them again at an uncertain price because he cannot know the extent of the demand. Cantillon's entrepreneur is essentially a functionary of the market structure, but as Schumpeter has observed, he is nevertheless involved in the functions of direction and speculation that "do enter somehow into entrepreneurial activity."[1]

There have been varying explanations for the spasmodic and half-hearted attention paid to the entrepreneur since Cantillon first attempted to popularize the term. N. S. B. Gras believes that this conceptual void stems from the disposition in economic analysis "to stress the physical."[2] He states that this tendency was given strong

1. Joseph A. Schumpeter, "Economic Theory and Entrepreneurial History," in *Change and the Entrepreneur,* Research Center in Entrepreneurial History (Cambridge: Harvard University Press, 1949), p. 64.

2. N. S. B. Gras, "Capitalism—Concepts and History," in *Enterprise and Secular Change,* eds. Frederic C. Lane and Jelle C. Riemersma (Homewood: Richard D. Irwin, 1953), p. 68. This article was originally published in *Bulletin of the Business History Society,* 16: 21–34 (1942).

early support and impetus by the Physiocrats, with their emphasis upon land as the sole productive factor. Land, labor, and capital, being physical and tangible, have received far more emphasis than entrepreneurship.

Another explanation for the persistent neglect of entrepreneurship in economic analysis is that this function has been so much in evidence in the actual economy that it has been taken for granted. Arthur H. Cole made this point in 1946, before the recent upsurge of interest in entrepreneurship, when he stated that interest in economic history has tended to center on the new and novel, while "the restless, innovating businessman could be taken for granted, a wholly familiar figure, even as, a hundred years ago, McCulloch thought that free trade was a self-evident truth."[3]

John E. Sawyer elaborates this explanation, noting that ". . . this relative absence of analysis did not reflect any absence of entrepreneurs, vigorously and visibly performing their tasks . . . The explanation seems to fall rather at the opposite pole: in the abundant presence of classical individual entrepreneurs performing their role so 'naturally' amidst the institutions of their time that their existence and function could be—and was—assumed to be universal. Analysis rarely concerns itself with the obvious; and so, here, a highly specialized performance in a given time and place was taken as a given, a constant in human affairs requiring little scrutiny."[4] These assumptions, Sawyer adds, were not particularly crippling in nineteenth-century England. It was only with wider horizons of time and place that entrepreneurship could be seen to be not only complex but also not necessarily to be taken for granted.

Still another answer that has been suggested as to why the entrepreneurial function was so long neglected is the nature of nineteenth-century methodology in economics. Cole claims that Ricardo is the villain of the piece, diverting attention to long-run conditions, static analysis, and the deductive method, away from the short-run, repetitive forces productive of change.[5] Cole adds that Ricardo also failed to follow up the suggestion of Cantillon and Say that the entrepreneur

3. Arthur H. Cole, "Approach to the Study of Entrepreneurship," in *Enterprise and Secular Change*, p. 182. This article was originally published in the *Journal of Economic History*, 6, supplement: 1–15. This is essentially the Presidential address of the 1946 annual meeting of the Economic History Association.

4. John E. Sawyer, "Entrepreneurial Studies: Perspective and Directions, 1948–58," *Business History Review*, 32:435 (Winter, 1958).

5. Cole, *op. cit.*, pp. 182–83.

should be distinguished from the other agents of production. Rather, asserts Cole, Ricardo treats economic principles and ignores business leaders as agents of change. Say, although not emphasizing adventure and innovation, does stress the entrepreneur as a crucial economic agent who unites and employs the factors of production, who pays the factors, and who reaps profits.[6] Ricardo represents in this matter, in Cole's judgment, an influential retrogression from Say's level of sophistication.

Finally, a somewhat parallel explanation for the long-time relative unconcern with entrepreneurship is the suggestion that the entire economic system was long believed to be impersonal and to function automatically. Thomas C. Cochran writes, ". . . in classical English economic theory the concept of the entrepreneur became lost in the study of the operation of impersonal forces. When the term re-emerged in the writings of John Stuart Mill and Alfred Marshall, at the time when the professional, noncapitalist, manager was gaining importance in the real world of business, the emphasis ironically was put not on him but only on the man risking capital for productive purposes. Because of this restricted English meaning, and the continuing pre-occupation of economic theorists with aggregates, the concept of entrepreneurship was little used."[7]

In the twentieth century there has been at least a limited resurgence of interest in entrepreneurship. Much of this new concern and the resultant redefinition of the entrepreneurial function date back perhaps a decade, although Berle and Means, Gordon and others had done earlier path-breaking work that was to suggest new directions in examining entrepreneurship. These more recent developments will be sketched in the next section of this paper.

Suffice it to note at this juncture, however, that there have been at least two other major conceptions of entrepreneurship, both appearing in the inter-war period, that have left a strong imprint on current thinking. One of these conceptions, of course, was that of F. H. Knight, who has focused attention within economic theory upon the role of the entrepreneur as the bearer of uncertainty and the insurer of risk. This has been a respected and influential contribution to the understanding of one of the traditional functions of entrepre-

---

6. *Ibid.*, p. 183. Cole quotes from Say's *Catechism of Political Economy* (London, 1816), pp. 28–29, and from Say's *Treatise on Political Economy* (London, 1821), I, 104.

7. Thomas C. Cochran, *Railroad Leaders, 1845–1890: The Business Mind in Action* (Cambridge: Harvard University Press, 1953), p. 8.

neurship. It has not, however, given rise to much further work along these lines nor has it been especially appropriate to an era marked by the large corporation, the professional manager, the separation of ownership and control, and the diffusion of the entrepreneurial function.

The other important concept that still wields great influence is Schumpeter's innovating entrepreneur. This is also a valid and significant concept, of great appeal in a "programmed" and managerial age, but perhaps of somewhat limited contemporary applicability. Although economics is in debt to this concept, modifications continue to be made, and the concept has come to be regarded either as depicting an ideal type or as descriptive of a somewhat special case.

Clarence H. Danhof, utilizing Schumpeter's concept of innovating entrepreneurship, has nevertheless constructed a typology which does materially stretch Schumpeter's concept.[8] Danhof suggests four types of entrepreneurship: innovating, imitative, "Fabian," and drone.

When Schumpeter's concept is applied to the current world-wide scene, in which underdeveloped countries are seeking rapid economic growth, to restrict the entrepreneurial function to genuine innovation becomes especially difficult. When a technology is "adapted" to a country in a radically different stage of development, with a divergent culture and political order, is this adaptation or is it innovation?

Students of nineteenth-century United States economic history, such as Cochran,[9] W. Paul Strassman,[10] and others, have also insisted that Schumpeter's innovating entrepreneur was often less in evidence than was the cautious, careful, reluctant risk-bearer.

The entrepreneurial historians, many of whom were colleagues or students of Schumpeter's, freely acknowledge the stimulation which he gave to interest in the entrepreneur and agree that the innovating aspect of entrepreneurship should not be minimized. They do suggest, however, that work must now go beyond this point. One of the fullest statements on this matter made by a member of this group is by Sawyer.[11] Noting that Schumpeter was deeply rooted in Conti-

8. Clarence H. Danhof, "Observations on Entrepreneurship in Agriculture," in *Change and the Entrepreneur*, pp. 23–24.

9. Cochran, *op. cit.*

10. W. Paul Strassmann, *Risk and Technological Innovation: American Manufacturing Methods during the Nineteenth Century* (Ithaca: Cornell University Press, 1959).

11. Sawyer, *op. cit.*, pp. 436–38. The quotes immediately following are also from these pages.

nental traditions and remained deeply committed to their values, he suggests that this may account in part for the dramatic form which Schumpeter gave to the entrepreneurial role and to his emphasis on its historic novelty. Sawyer states, "The heroic entrepreneur became and remained the heart of his system, the ultimate dynamic of the process, the 'pivot on which everything turns'—and the figure and fiction that fascinated him to the end. While subsequent inquiry has departed from his conception, as we shall see, there can be little dispute about his part in placing the question squarely before modern economics and giving momentum to its historical investigation."

Sawyer poses a paradox: Schumpeter, who gave such thrust and importance to the entrepreneurial role, so identified and circumscribed it that he almost closed the door to further investigation of its actually diffused and varied set of functions. First, Schumpeter identified with vitality and concreteness *the* entrepreneurial function with a particular set of agents in a particular place and era. Despite refinements, his conception was appropriate to the innovating giants, the bearers of great visions and risks, the Fuggers or Rothschilds. But Sawyer asserts, "Schumpeter's sun was an arbitrary shaft, however. It shone only on the few who were exercising a striking role in a striking way at a striking time. It was, he insisted, a limited and localized phenomenon. With the passing of that era, clouds such as had earlier obscured the question might have again descended and veiled anew the presence of the several functions in varied guises."

The second way in which Schumpeter inadvertently almost closed off the study of entrepreneurship was in what Sawyer terms "the excessive clarity of his argument." His definition is so sharp and categorical, the force of illustration which accompanies it is so strong, that the concept is pressed beyond the real world of the twentieth century. Thus ". . . the categorical differentiation between innovation and adaptation, between entrepreneur and manager, between creative and imitative are distinctions that must yield to the relentless erosion of degree. Similarly, any effort to fix the locus of the dynamics of economic processes in a single historic form or a single economic actor cannot weather the tests of time and comparative observation." A double paradox in the history of entrepreneurial studies thus emerges: ". . . a function little recognized in nineteenth-century economics when in full flower, might have been reinterred by the very insight that did most to unearth it in the twentieth."

Contemporary Concepts of the Entrepreneurial Function

Although Schumpeter's innovating entrepreneur and Knight's bearer of uncertainty continue to loom large in the literature of economics, new concepts of entrepreneurship are now gaining increasing support. These concepts tend to reflect the growth of the large corporation, the increasingly complex internal organization of the firm, and the ramified economic, political, and social environment in which the present-day firm operates. The newer concepts reflect not only a reexamination of the theory of the firm but also scholarship in industrial organization, managerial economics, management science, organization theory, entrepreneurial history, and other contemporary "disciplines in embryo."

In a sense, much of the contemporary emphasis upon the managerial and environmental context of entrepreneurship was foreshadowed by Alfred Marshall. As early as 1890, Marshall wrote: "The task of directing production so that a given effort may be most effective in supplying human wants is so difficult under the complex conditions of modern life, that it has to be broken up and given unto the hands of a specialized body of employers, or to use a more general term, of businessmen, who 'adventure' or 'undertake' its risks, who bring together the capital and the labour required for the work, who arrange or 'engineer' its general plan, and who superintend its minor details."[12]

The Marshallian concept is more nearly relevant to the conditions of twentieth-century economic life than were most of the earlier visions of the entrepreneurial function. Yet it has been claimed by Frederick H. Harbison and Charles A. Myers that even this concept was limited in at least two respects.[13] First, Marshall assumes for purposes of abstraction that the qualities of entrepreneurship are found in one person, rather than in a hierarchy of individuals such as those functioning in the contemporary corporation. Second, Marshall seems to envisage the businessman as performing in a relatively passive manner and adapting to fixed external conditions, rather than also leading, influencing, and modifying that external environment.

Marshall furnished a bridge, however, from nineteenth-century concepts of entrepreneurship to those now in vogue. As Sawyer notes,

12. Alfred Marshall, *Principles of Economics* (1st. ed.; London: Macmillan, 1890), I, 354–55. Virtually the same statement is in the eighth ed., p. 293.
13. Frederick H. Harbison and Charles A. Myers, *Management in the Industrial World* (New York: McGraw-Hill, 1959), pp. 9–10.

Marshall was not alone in moving in this direction.[14] Sombart, Weber, and others also approached entrepreneurial motivation and behavior from a new and broader vantage point.

In the contemporary era, a host of concepts of entrepreneurship and the entrepreneurial function are evolving in the wake of these early foreshadowings of an organization-oriented, environmentally-conditioned approach. Some of these concepts seem, on the surface, to stress the traditional notions of venturesomeness and leadership, but even here the new society is mirrored. Still other contemporary concepts of entrepreneurship also grope for relatively simple explanations but again within the complex modern setting. Certain other concepts of entrepreneurship are openly eclectic and include a vast range of activities under the entrepreneurial function. Finally, two approaches make a frontal attempt to redefine entrepreneurship in complex contemporary terms. The entrepreneurial historians, with their emphasis upon the complexity, variability, and cultural relativity of entrepreneurship, have furnished one of these approaches. The organization theorists, and those attempting to apply organization theory, have furnished the other. In the pages immediately to follow, this spectrum of redefinitions will be sketched.

### The Venturer or Leader

Even those current definitions of entrepreneurship which tend to retain an emphasis upon venturesomeness or that accent leadership tend increasingly to include these aspects of the function within the context of the organization and its economic and social environment.

Edith Penrose defines enterprise in these terms: ". . . for our purposes it can usefully be treated as a psychological predisposition on the part of individuals to take a chance in the hope of gain, and, in particular, to commit effort and resources to speculative activity."[15] The decision of a firm to investigate the prospective profitability of expansion is a basic 'enterprising' decision, because it is based not so much upon sober calculations as upon a willingness to make some calculations.

In making such decisions, Miss Penrose notes, a sharp distinction must be made between entrepreneurial competence and managerial

14. Sawyer, *op. cit.*, p. 436.
15. Edith Tilton Penrose, *The Theory of the Growth of the Firm* (New York: John Wiley and Sons, 1959), p. 33. The quote immediately following is from p. 41.

competence, necessary though the latter may be. Distinctive qualities of entrepreneurial services include versatility, ingenuity, ambition, and, of course, judgment—qualities perhaps not unsuitable to Schumpeter's innovating entrepreneur as well.

Yet Miss Penrose concludes, as a preface to much of the remainder of her study:

To a large extent, however, the problem of entrepreneurial judgment involves more than a combination of imagination, 'good sense,' self-confidence, and other personal qualities. It is closely related to the organization of information-gathering and consulting facilities within a firm, and it leads into the whole question of the effects of risk and uncertainty on, and of the role of expectations in, the growth of firms. These aspects of the matter can be made an integral part of the analysis of the growth process, because the 'expectations' of a firm— the way in which it interprets its 'environment'—are as much a function of the internal resources and operations of a firm as of the personal qualities of the entrepreneur.

The "leader" is presumably also a figure of at least potentially heroic proportions who could be venturesome, creative, and innovating. Yet contemporary studies of leadership place increasing emphasis on the persuasive and coordinating aspects of the role and especially upon the relationship between the leader and the organization.

Philip Selznick argues that the executive becomes a statesman as he moves from administrative management to institutional leadership.[16] This shift in role involves viewing the organization as an institution, which is more than an organization with its formal system of rules and objectives. An institution is ". . . more nearly a natural product of social needs and pressures—a responsive, adaptive organism. Institutionalization is a *process*. It is something that happens to an organization over time, reflecting the organization's own distinctive history, the people who have been in it, the groups it embodies and the way it has adapted to its environment. Of special importance: the degree of institutionalization depends on how much leeway there is for personal and group interaction. To institutionalize is to *infuse with value* beyond the technical requirements of the task at hand."

Derived from this general point of view is a concept of leadership which is directly related to the broader organization experience of

16. Philip Selznick, *Leadership in Administration: A Sociological Interpretation* (Evanston: Row, Peterson, 1957), as abstracted in *The Executive*, 2:8–10 (July, 1958). The quotes immediately following are also from these pages.

which it is a phase. "The leader is an agent of institutionalization, offering a guiding hand to a process that would otherwise occur more haphazardly. He is primarily an expert in the promotion and protection of values." These comments, although relevant to leadership per se, may also be applied to leadership within the economy.

Alex Bavelas links leadership even more explicitly to the organization when he distinguishes between leadership as a personal quality and leadership as an organizational function. Bavelas notes, "The first refers to a special combination of personal characteristics; the second refers to the distribution throughout the organization of decision-making powers. The first leads us to look at the qualities and abilities of individuals; the second leads us to look at the patterns of power and authority in organizations."[17] Early studies of leadership, he adds, dealt almost entirely with personal qualities; contemporary studies are focusing with increasing frequency upon the function. This parallels, perhaps, the recent shift in emphasis from the entrepreneur as a person to preoccupation with the entrepreneurial function or entrepreneurship.

Under the organizational function concept of leadership, one does not ask about an organization, "Who is the leader?" but rather, "How are the leadership functions distributed in this organization?" Bavelas concludes, "This new emphasis has not eliminated the role of personal leadership, but it has significantly redefined it. Under normal conditions of operation, leadership in the modern organization consists not so much in the making of decisions personally as it does of maintaining the operational effectiveness of the decision-making systems which comprise the management of the organization." Thus, the stereotype of the leader who consults mostly himself is out of date, replaced by a newer stereotype of the "thoughtful executive discussing in committee the information supplied by a staff of experts." Bavelas observes, ". . . it may be that the brilliant innovator, in the role of manager, is rapidly becoming as much an organizational embarrassment as he is an asset."

### The Therapist, Balance Wheel, or Unifier

Many other contemporary concepts of entrepreneurship lack much concern with venturesomeness or leadership per se. In these

17. Alex Bavelas, "Leadership: Man and Function," *Administrative Science Quarterly*, 4:491–98 (March, 1960). The quotes immediately following are also from these pages.

concepts, the entrepreneurial function is tied in from the outset to the assumption of a large business enterprise, probably a corporation, operating in a complex environment. Thus, although these concepts are not eclectic in the sense of explicitly encompassing all of the functions that are involved in such a setting, their nominally single-factor explanations do reflect a new pattern of organization, a new environment, a new "climate."

Some views of entrepreneurship now stress the maintenance of organizational health. Chris Argyris has contended that emphasis should be shifted from executive development per se toward "the process of increasing the healthy development of the total organization. If one does not deeply respect the health of an organization, one will always be hesitant in developing a philosophy (and practice) to optimize organizational health."[18] How, then, should a going organization begin to establish the processes that lead to health? Argyris suggests that the first step is for the company to define what its concept of organizational health is to include; the second step is to translate this concept into actual behavior so that it can be practiced; the third step is to develop criteria to measure and evaluate the state of the company. Because health is the primary concern of the organization, its creation and maintenance must be a principal function of the executive, the management, the entrepreneur—whatever one's label for those with final and ultimate responsibility and authority.

Interestingly, a major executive has placed similar stress on organizational health as a primary concern. Crawford H. Greenewalt has suggested that growth has been overemphasized in recent years and asserts, "We look [at du Pont] to the health of business as being more important than growth—if one has to make a choice."[19] To illustrate his concept of health, Greenewalt uses this analogy: ". . . you might liken a healthy business to a barrel that is set to catch rain water. When it rains new developments, the level of the barrel increases. On the other hand, you have to have a drain at the bottom to take out those things that have become marginal and constitute a drain on the resources of your management. Only if you have that drain at the bottom will the contents of your barrel remain fresh and healthy.

18. Chris Argyris, "Organizational Health and Executive Development," *Advanced Management*, 24:8–11 (December, 1959), as abstracted in *The Executive*, 3:23 (January, 1960).

19. Statement by Crawford H. Greenewalt, New York, September 7, 1961, as published in booklet entitled *Transcript New York Society of Financial Analysts Meeting with Representatives of Management of E. I. du Pont de Nemours and Company*, p. 13. The quote immediately following is from p. 15.

The freshness of the contents of the barrel is really what counts for us. The size of the barrel will take care of itself."

It is not far from this concept of organizational health to the concept of maintenance of organizational balance as a primary function of the executive or entrepreneur. L. F. Urwick poses this conundrum: "Because foresight is required the leader has always to be doing two apparently incompatible things. He has to encourage his administrators to promote order, to maintain established routines. At the same time he has to protect from their wrath the originals, the inventors, the crazy people to whom order is anathema and an established routine a challenge to change it, because it is from this lunatic fringe that he is most likely to derive something original. They may have a large litter of illegitimate ideas on the way; they usually do. It is the leader's job to arrange to have them drowned or otherwise disposed of and to comfort the bereaved parent."[20]

Balance also has other requirements, of course. Marshall E. Dimock states, "Administration is often unbelievably complex; everything blends together, all being related. If the administrator concentrates upon one area to the neglect of others, the machine will become deranged."[21] Dimock, unlike many who stress the managerial group or hierarchy, sees this balance as being ". . . brought about by the integration of all parts under one person and by the progress of all parts at the same rate." In fact, Dimock goes on to argue, "Balanced individuals are also needed. Individuality is our secret weapon; team leadership cannot be substituted for it."

It is perhaps the concept of the entrepreneurial function as that of unifying or coordinating that best epitomizes this new emphasis upon the organization and its environmental context. Sir Noel Frederick Hall states, "The higher executive is fundamentally the unifier. The team—that is, a carefully composed amalgam of different but complementary specialists—has to be unified."[22] Hall also observes

20. L. F. Urwick, *Leadership in the Twentieth Century* (London: Pitman, 1957), p. 46.

21. Marshall E. Dimock, *A Philosophy of Administration: Toward Creative Growth* (New York: Harper and Brothers, 1958), as abstracted in *The Executive,* 2:6–7 (December, 1958). The quotes immediately following are also from these pages.

22. Sir Noel Frederick Hall, "The Higher Executive—Developing the Whole Man," in *The Making of Higher Executives: The Modern Challenges* (New York: School of Commerce, Accounts, and Finance of New York University, 1958), pp. 1–29, as abstracted in *The Executive,* 2:4 (December, 1958).

that it is from individuals who have undergone the process of specialization, so necessary for the operation of the firm, that the synthesizers and coordinators must be drawn.

The entrepreneur as the unifier receives additional support from Greenewalt, whose not inconsistent concern with organizational health was earlier cited. Greenewalt concludes: "The best that I can offer is to say that the basic requirement of executive capacity is the ability to create a harmonious whole out of what the academic world calls dissimilar disciplines. This is a fancy way of saying that an executive is good when he can make a smoothly functioning team out of people with the many different skills required in the operation of a modern business. His most important function is to reconcile, to coordinate, to compromise, and to appraise the various viewpoints and talents under his direction to the end that each individual contributes his full measure to the business at hand."[23]

The concept of the entrepreneurial function as essentially that of a coordinator was formulated earlier in Robert A. Gordon's classic, *Business Leadership in the Large Corporation*. Gordon sees the management function as divided into two major areas, direction and coordination. Direction, involving the making of decisions, may be spread throughout management and shared with outside interests. Coordination, the more important function of corporate leadership, includes ". . . some decision-making: establishing broad objectives, initiating and approving changes in key personnel and in management organization, approving decisions on various matters in terms of the approver's interpretation of broad objectives, approving decisions on specific matters to avoid conflicts with other decisions."[24] Gordon also notes that this function includes the exercise of personal leadership, and especially the mere possession of authority, which gives cohesion to, and maintains, organization. He also adds that the essential coordination is "the residual coordination that applies to the enterprise as a whole and must therefore be exercised at the apex of the organizational pyramid. By its very nature, this is not a function which can be delegated in the way that making specific decisions can be."[25]

23. Crawford H. Greenewalt, *The Uncommon Man* (New York: McGraw-Hill, 1959), p. 64.

24. Robert A. Gordon, *Business Leadership in the Large Corporation* (Washington: Brookings Institution, 1945), p. 53. This passage is also quoted in Harbison and Myers, *op. cit.*, p. 12.

25. *Ibid.*, p. 53 in Gordon, p. 13 in Harbison and Myers.

## The All-Purpose Entrepreneur

Another manifestation of the increasing complexity of entrepreneurship and of its new institutional setting is the growing tendency to define the entrepreneurial function in eclectic and all-encompassing terms.

G. Heberton Evans, Jr., after pressing for a broad definition of entrepreneurship, one not restricted to the innovating function, finally concludes: ". . . the entrepreneur in each firm is the person or group of persons who has (or assumes) the task of determining the *kind of business to be operated.*"[26] Evans acknowledges that at first glance this may seem to involve too many aspects to be useful for defining or locating entrepreneurship, but he argues that the answer to what kind of business a particular firm is operating really involves only a small number of matters. The answer will relate not to management-labor relations, the proper level of liquid resources, etc., but rather to ". . . the nature of the goods and services offered, the size of operations, and the clientele catered to." Evans also states that his study of company histories reassures him as to the feasibility of locating in most firms those who are really responsible for such decisions. Even thus defined, however, the function of determining the "kind of business to be operated" remains broad and inclusive.

Other current definitions are more avowedly eclectic. Stephen Enke first defines the entrepreneurial function in negative or residual terms: ". . . all productive contributions that are not routine human effort, do not involve the use of indestructible natural resources, and do not entail the provisions of capital funds."[27] Affirmatively, the entrepreneurial function includes undertaking, originating, combining factors, risk-taking, and "perhaps more besides." Enke insists that entrepreneurship involves doing several of these things, not merely just one of them. He acknowledges, however, that in the modern corporate context entrepreneurship is diffused and that "it is invalid to suppose that *one* man will always and necessarily perform *all* the entrepreneurial functions and *none* of the functions of the *other* three productive factors."

26. G. Heberton Evans, Jr., "A Century of Entrepreneurship in the United States: With Emphasis upon Large Manufacturing Concerns c. 1850–1957," in *The Entrepreneur*, papers presented at the annual Conference of the Economic History Society, at Cambridge, England, April, 1957, p. 50. The quote immediately following is from pp. 50–51.

27. Stephen Enke, *Intermediate Economic Theory* (New York: Prentice-Hall, 1950), p. 454. The quotes immediately following are taken from p. 456.

A more colloquial version of this eclectic concept of entrepreneurship is given by John S. Gambs and Sidney Wertimer, Jr.: *"Entrepreneurship,* which refers to the special productive service of the policymaking person or board of any business establishment; to the special contribution of the big boss—his judgment; ability to combine land, labor, and capital in the most fruitful proportions; labor-management skill; inside knowledge; market information; lucky hunches; sixth sense about business affairs; good contacts with persons informed on business and political matters; discretion; poker face; ability to pick good lieutenants; aplomb when testifying before legislative committees; and the like."[28]

Indeed, this all-embracing nature of the entrepreneurial function, the disagreement as to which specific functions are crucial, and the diffusion of the function throughout the organization have led many to become disenchanted with the very concept of the entrepreneur. Thus some have suggested, as does James H. Stauss, that the *firm* is the entrepreneur, and that this concept will prove more fruitful than trying to determine the locus or nature of the entrepreneurial function through individual functionaries.[29]  Stauss insists that this approach does not involve substituting one elusive entity, the firm, for another, the entrepreneur. He adds, "With respect to the proposition that the firm is the entrepreneur, it must be set forth at the beginning that the entity known subsequently as *the firm* is taken as a real institution. As such the firm *exists* apart from the individuals who compose its decision-making organization but it *does not function* apart from them. Thus the entity is not a fiction; it is a fact." Although the fruitfulness of such a conceptual short-cut is perhaps moot, the implications of the suggestion as a reflection of the growing complexity, ramifications, and elusive nature of entrepreneurship are clear enough.

### The Entrepreneur in History and Society

The entrepreneurial historians have done much to redefine entrepreneurship in contemporary, environment-oriented terms consistent with the dominance of organizations.  Arthur H. Cole, a leader of this group, attempted such a redefinition as early as 1946: "Entrepreneurship may be defined in simplest terms as the utilization by one productive factor of the other productive factors for the creation of

28. John S. Gambs and Sidney Wertimer, Jr., *Economics and Man* (Homewood: Richard D. Irwin, 1959), p. 55.
29. James H. Stauss, "The Entrepreneur: The Firm," *Journal of Political Economy,* 52:112–27 (June, 1944). The quote immediately following is from p. 112.

economic goods. But such a definition means little until we have answered a barrage of questions: Why? How? Through what institutions and instrumentalities? With what concessions to the prevailing political and social environment?"[30] Cole then describes entrepreneurship in these terms: ". . . the integrated sequence of actions, taken by individuals or by groups operating for individual business units, in a world characterized by a large measure of uncertainty, such action being modified in greater or less degree by contemporary economic and social forces."

In his *Business Enterprise in its Social Setting*, published some thirteen years later, Cole amplified this definition. Cole states: "Here I shall have in mind the purposeful activity (including an integrated sequence of decisions) of an individual or group of associated individuals, undertaken to initiate, maintain, or aggrandize a profit-oriented business unit for the production or distribution of economic goods and services."[31] He adds, "The aggregate of individuals which together and cooperatively develop the decisions might perhaps be denominated the 'entrepreneurial team.' It is really a team in the senses (a) that each person or officer plays a particular position or represents a particular aspect of the total enterprise, and (b) that each person or officer is in some measure a complement of the others as far as the total purposes of the unit are concerned." Cole further suggests that ". . . it should be specified that this entrepreneurial activity proceeds in relationship to the situation internal to the unit itself, the social group that really constitutes the unit, and to the economic, political, and social circumstances—institutions, practices, and ideas which surround the unit."

There have been some interesting and divergent reactions to Cole's very inclusive concept. W. T. Easterbrook, in reviewing Cole's book, holds that this definition, by embracing routine as well as innovational performance, blurs the entrepreneurial function. Easterbrook concedes that it may be well to drop the figure of the 'heroic' entrepreneur, but he states ". . . there is much to be said for limiting the function to its creative, shaping aspects, less in terms of major achievements or acts of synthesis than in the constant modification of structures, situations or ideas in a continuing process of interaction."[32]

30. Cole, *op. cit.*, pp. 183–84. The quote immediately following is from p. 184.
31. Arthur H. Cole, *Business Enterprise in its Social Setting* (Cambridge: Harvard University Press, 1959), p. 7. The quotes immediately following are from pp. 7, 8.
32. W. T. Easterbrook, review of Cole's *Business Enterprise in its Social Setting*, in *Business History Review*, 34:122 (Spring, 1960).

Kenneth E. Boulding, contrariwise, suggests that Cole has not gone quite far enough and has not been able to bring himself to "liberate" the concept of the entrepreneur from "the shackles of economics." "Surely," Boulding states, "the concept of the role creator, the organizer, is perfectly general, and the founders of sects, lodges, states, armies, and gangs can as readily be considered entrepreneurs as the founders of firms."[33]

Sawyer credits Cole with providing a base and an impetus for a stream of studies that have helped to redefine our conception of entrepreneurial functions on broader and more useful lines. Sawyer asserts that these explorations, largely by the entrepreneurial historians, have ". . . established the concept, not of a unique figure tied to one era and place, but rather of a many-sided variable of complex determination, to be analyzed for its presence or absence in various forms and degrees in any economy that moves."[34]

Sawyer, in reviewing the work associated with the Research Center in Entrepreneurial History, concludes that several new currents of thought have clearly emerged. These include: 1) a shift in emphasis from the person to the function, and with it a more comprehensive conception of that function; 2) the spreading of attention from the few (the spectacular individual entrepreneur) to the many (large numbers of less conspicuous decision-makers widely diffused through an economy); 3) a new focus, "once attention moves from the unique act to a range of behavior," upon the problem of cause as falling within the domain of systematic inquiry. The language changes from such terms as "the will to command," "men of force and intellect," or "the mysteries of isolated personalities," and the function becomes instead ". . . a study of characteristic patterns, a fit subject for comparative social analysis in all its causes and its consequences." Sawyer adds that although the entrepreneurial giants were supposedly men who would break through anyway, whether as heroes or pirates, regardless of environment, "no one has made any parallel claim to immunity to environmental influences on behalf of the many."

### Organization and the Entrepreneur

Somewhat parallel to the work of the entrepreneurial historians, although along more formal lines, has been the work of the organization theorists, notably Herbert Simon and his associates, and those

33. K. E. Boulding, review of Cole's *Business Enterprise in its Social Setting*, in *Administrative Science Quarterly*, 4:362 (December, 1959).

34. Sawyer, *op. cit.*, p. 439. The paraphrases and quotes immediately following are from pp. 439–42.

who have applied organization theory. In many ways the most fruitful of these organization-oriented descriptions of the entrepreneurial function has been that of Andreas Papandreou.[35]  His model, featuring the "peak coordinator," makes systematic application of organization theory to the theory of the firm, and it also lends itself to empirical application.

Papandreou is not especially fond of the term "entrepreneur," which he believes to have been colored by ideological usage, and he utilizes instead the term "peak coordinator." He also places emphasis on the function of peak coordination rather than upon the person or persons performing it. This function ". . . has been defined as the supply of conscious and authoritative coordination at the apex of the organizational structure.  Coordination, in turn, is conceived as the deliberate provision of communications which 'integrate' the strategies of the cooperating participants in order to produce the system of actions which we have named *organization*."[36]

Papandreou discusses both the process of coordination *within* the firm as an organization and the process of influence *upon* the firm from the outside. In the latter connection, Papandreou adds, "This is just another way of saying that the firm is a component of a much broader cooperative system which, in its informal aspects, becomes coextensive with what we call society."[37]  These external influences involve not only the other "interest groups" and the force of the market itself, but also the mores, folklore, customs, institutions, social ideas, and myths of the society.

Howard R. Bowen has made essentially the same point when he raises the question, Where does power over the firm reside?[38]  He states that there are at least two valid approaches to this question. One approach holds that the power of decision in a firm rests ultimately with those who actually hold authority, whether these be stockholders, "top management," or whoever may actually possess it. Bowen labels the holders of effective authority and hence of power "the command" of the firm. Many decisions are also made, of course, at lower levels. The other approach to power over a firm is that such power ". . . is

35. Andreas G. Papandreou, "Some Basic Problems in the Theory of the Firm," in *A Survey of Contemporary Economics,* II (Homewood: Richard D. Irwin, 1952), 183–219.

36. *Ibid.,* p. 213.

37. *Ibid.,* p. 192.

38. Howard R. Bowen, *The Business Enterprise as a Subject for Research* (New York: Social Science Research Council, 1955), pp. 24–27. The quotes immediately following are also from these pages.

diffused among all those who influence the actions of the firm by delegation, persuasion, rewards, money charges, threats, regulation, or other sanctions." Power would thus rest not only with the command but with competitors, bankers, employees, labor unions, government, suppliers, customers, etc. There are thus many power centers, not one.

These approaches are not necessarily mutually exclusive. It is possible to assume, as Bowen ultimately does, that power is vested in the command and yet to acknowledge that this exercise of power is heavily influenced by the actions and power of others. The command thus becomes the instrument through which these other sources of power make themselves felt.

### The Internal and External Environment of Entrepreneurship

The conceptual framework established by Papandreou, Bowen, and others suggests the desirability at this juncture of a brief exploration of the internal and external environment within which the entrepreneurial function must be performed. This investigation may then disclose a useful bridge between our study of the general entrepreneurial function and our analysis of that function as it apparently exists in the South.

#### The Internal Environment

The story of what has happened to the size and complexity of the American business firm, especially the large American corporation, is a familiar one. Likewise, the separation of ownership and control; the development of a managerial hierarchy or bureaucracy; the professionalization of management; and the diffusion of decision-making, and perhaps even authority, are treated in a vast and growing literature.

Not quite so familiar, perhaps, is the beginning of attempts to examine the internal environment of the business firm from the vantage point of disciplines other than economics or management. These attempts have gone well beyond a beginning in the case of those interested in organization theory. Simon, his Carnegie Institute of Technology associates, and others in this constellation have gone far in re-examining the firm as an organization and in reformulating the theory of the firm.

Attention is also beginning to be paid in disciplines such as political science and sociology to this complex internal environment of the firm. Robert A. Dahl, for example, has made a preliminary study of the business firm as a political order.[39] Focusing upon the internal government of the firm, which he states has been largely ignored by the political scientists, he reviews the work of Drucker, Gordon, Berle, and others as constituting the embryo of a needed new body of knowledge. Dahl suggests that the bureaucratic aspects of the firm may also provide an avenue of approach, adding that the study of bureaucracy may prove to be really a special case of organization theory. Dahl concludes that the techniques developed by political scientists in studying community "power-structures" might be carried over almost intact to studies of the internal government of business firms.

Meanwhile, the internal workings of the business firm are becoming the object of increasing attention by sociologists and by entrepreneurial historians using sociological concepts and techniques. Paul F. Lazarsfeld, for example, has made a companion study to that of Dahl's and includes in it his essay, "The Businessman's Role."[40] The "role" approach has been used by several of the entrepreneurial historians, both in establishing conceptual frameworks and in case-studies. Leland H. Jenks,[41] Cochran,[42] Cole,[43] and several others have begun to make fruitful use of this approach.

Perhaps the most detailed description of the internal environment of the firm is given by Bowen.[44] He believes that a firm is, to a large extent and over extended periods of time, a prisoner of its own history. It develops certain characteristics, resulting from past decisions and actions, which cannot be swiftly changed. These characteristics constitute a kind of culture within the enterprise. This culture impinges on the behavior of the firm in a fashion analogous to the way in which culture generally influences human behavior. There is also an external culture, but more of that later.

39. Robert A. Dahl, "Business and Politics: A Critical Appraisal of Political Science," in *Social Science Research on Business: Product and Potential* (New York: Columbia University Press, 1959), pp. 5–12.

40. Paul F. Lazarsfeld, "Sociological Reflections on Business: Consumers and Managers," in *Social Science Research on Business: Product and Potential,* pp. 141–46.

41. See Leland H. Jenks, "Role Structure of Entrepreneurial Personality," in *Change and the Entrepreneur,* pp. 108-52.

42. See Thomas C. Cochran, "Role and Sanction in American Entrepreneurial History," in *Change and the Entrepreneur,* pp. 153–75.

43. See Cole, *Business Enterprise in its Social Setting,* Chapter iii, "The Elements in a Positive View: The Entrepreneur and His Organization."

44. Bowen, *op. cit.,* pp. 33–34. The list immediately following is also taken from these pages.

Among the characteristics of the firm that constitute its internal culture are these:

1. Internal organization of the firm (formal and informal)
    a. Identity of the command and its position in the organization
    b. Definition of roles and location of detailed responsibilities
    c. Communication system
        (1) Within the firm
        (2) From outside the firm
    d. Control of operations
2. Decision-making process within the firm
    a. Functioning of the command in decision making
    b. Degree of participation in central decisions by subordinate personnel
    c. Location of internal sources of advice and centers of influence —internal politics
    d. Delegation: degree of autonomy of subsidiary persons and divisions
    e. Relationships with outside advisers
3. Present components, characteristics, and obligations of the firm
    a. Sunk capital investment of the firm, which has determined its present size, products, location, composition of assets, methods of production, facilities for research, etc.
    b. Present capital structure
    c. Established marketing and purchasing channels and areas
    d. Unexpired contracts, vested interests that have been created, and expectations which the firm has aroused and which it would be unjust to disappoint
    e. Established reputation of the firm with customers, workers, suppliers, public officials, the local community, and the general public
    f. Characteristics of the present personnel as individuals: their unique cultural origins, experiences, personalities, motives, values, attitudes, intelligence, mental and physical skills, inventiveness, habits, morale, perception, interpretations, expectations
        (1) Members of the command
        (2) Other personnel
    g. Characteristics of the present personnel as a group or as subgroups: the traditions, behavior patterns, symbols, values, attitudes, and roles which have come to be accepted throughout all or parts of the organization
4. Over-all results of operations
    a. Profitability
    b. Security of the firm
    c. Rate of growth

## Implications of the Internal Environment

The growing size, complexity, and "culture" of the business firm, especially of the large corporation, have certain implications for the shaping of the entrepreneurial function. Some of these implications relate to the character of the function, the way in which it is performed, and its diffusion among many levels of functionaries. Other implications, however, have to do with the quantitative aspect of entrepreneurship: specifically, the demand on the part of the firm (and the economy) for entrepreneurial talent.

The implications of the large, complex, and diversified business unit for the nature and locus of the entrepreneurial function have been thoroughly explored in a considerable literature. The separation of ownership and control and the resultant creation of a large, powerful, self-perpetuating managerial group has been well charted by Berle and Means and many since.[45] This development not only has tended to center attention upon management as the group performing the entrepreneurial function, but has also diminished the former emphasis upon ownership and risk-bearing as major parts of that function.

A further outgrowth of this development is the growing emphasis upon the professionalization of leadership within the firm.[46] This development has had profound implications for the goals of the firm; the internal structure of authority and communication; the relative emphasis upon coordination, balance and unity as against boldness, venturesomeness, etc.; and even the relations between the corporation and its external environment.

The emergence of the business firm as a large aggregate of persons, operating through a complex organization, has also placed new emphasis upon communication and persuasion as primary functions of the executive. Mabel Newcomer concludes ". . . the executive function is no longer wielded by dictators. It requires leaders who can cooperate and persuade."[47] Herrymon Maurer concurs: "Dictatorship and dissension alike rob a large company of the basic element of any business decision—broad experience. Only a group of men can provide

45. See Adolf A. Berle, Jr. and Gardiner C. Means, *The Modern Corporation and Private Property* (New York: Macmillan, 1932); Gordon, *op. cit.*; and Mabel Newcomer, *The Big Business Executive* (New York: Columbia University Press, 1955).

46. See especially Gordon, *op. cit.*, and Newcomer, *op. cit.*, as well as the work of C. Wright Mills.

47. Newcomer, *ibid.*, p. 23.

the experience—and judgment—needed by a committee complex in organization, gigantic in size."[48]   Maurer adds, "Hence committees."

This recurring theme of the necessity of group management, of decentralization, and of heavy reliance upon the committee or board appears in much of the current literature in and about corporate management.   Standard Oil of New Jersey, Du Pont, General Motors, General Electric, and many other major corporations have urged the necessity and wisdom of this kind of dispersion or diffusion of entrepreneurial authority and function.   Frank Abrams, of Standard Oil of New Jersey, explained, "It stands to reason that if you get five men together and one man is wrong, the mistake is going to be picked up. Or if one man has a good idea, the others will contribute to it and develop it."[49]   Du Pont is, of course, an especially articulate and confirmed advocate of this approach, the entire organization structure being capped by an executive committee.[50]   Du Pont asserts: "The management of enterprise today is a multiple effort drawing its strength from the diversity of the group involved."[51]

This dispersion or diffusion of function has led Alfred W. Stonier and Douglas C. Hague to suggest that the theory of the firm, although still useful, is no longer descriptive.   They note that ". . . the largest and most important companies today are not run by *an* entrepreneur . . . Modern industry cannot point easily and equivocally to *the* entrepreneur."[52]   They continue, "How then can there be a managerial function?   One could give a paradoxical answer.   Perhaps it is that the theory is right but the facts are wrong.   This explanation may seem unscientific.   It may be held that the duty of a theory is to explain real concrete facts.   If the facts differ it is the theory which is at fault. But is this necessarily so?   The analysis of the entrepreneurial function is perfectly reasonable and internally consistent.   Its only real fault is that it is about a hundred years out of date as far as large businesses are concerned, though there are still thousands of small

48. Herrymon Maurer, *Great Enterprise* (New York: Macmillan, 1955), p. 209.
49. Quoted in Thomas C. Cochran, *The American Business System: A Historical Perspective, 1900–1955* (Cambridge: Harvard University Press, 1957), p. 137.
50. For a description of this system, see William H. Mylander, "Management by Executive Committee," *Harvard Business Review*, 33:51–58 (May–June, 1955).
51. *The Story of Management* (Wilmington: E. I. du Pont de Nemours & Co., 1961), p. 8.
52. Alfred W. Stonier and Douglas C. Hague, *A Textbook of Economic Theory* (New York: Longmans, Green, 1953), p. 323. The quotes immediately following are taken from pp. 323–24.

one-man firms. It is the development of joint-stock companies which spoils the picture." Stonier and Hague add wistfully, "Yet the theory did apply once," and ". . . it applies still to other facts and other times."

There is another implication for entrepreneurship involved in the new internal structure and environment of the firm and in the economic and technological conditions which have helped to produce the large corporation. There seems to be a relation between the size and complexity of the firm and the quantity of entrepreneurial talent demanded. Harbison and Myers have explored this relationship and advance certain propositions concerning the use of management as an economic resource.[53] These propositions, which will be useful in commenting upon the demand for entrepreneurial talent in the South, include:

First: "Enterprises differ both in the size and complexity of their activities, and the more complex the organization the greater is the intensity of use of managerial resources."

Second: "The larger the market and the more complicated the market structures and mechanisms, the greater is the intensity of use of managerial resources."

Third: "Industries requiring large capital investment appear to require a correspondingly heavy investment in high-talent managerial resources. Or put in a different way, large expenditures for equipment and machinery are likely to be quite unproductive unless there is a corresponding investment in the technical, professional, and managerial manpower to make them effective."

Fourth: "Innovations of all kinds require very heavy investment in high-level managerial resources."

### The External Environment

The external environment of the firm includes, ultimately, the entire society. Hence no attempt will be made at this juncture to sketch all of the ramified relationships that might exist between a firm and the industry, economy, society, culture and political order of which it is a part. This is the domain of much of the literature of social science and of many writings on modern America.

There has been a renewed interest in recent years, however, in aspects of these relationships that have special relevance to the study of entrepreneurship. Studies have now been made, for example, con-

53. Harbison and Myers, *op. cit.*, pp. 21–39. The four propositions quoted below are found on pp. 21, 22–23, 24, 26.

cerning investment in education as investment in entrepreneurship and growth. A number of contemporary writers have also focused upon the "organizational revolution," the interaction of interest groups and pressure blocs (such as the corporation, the government, and labor unions), the alleged (and denied) countervailing power of these blocs, and the effect of public opinion and public consensus.[54]

In recent years, at least two writers have attempted to make explicit lists of some of the external forces (facilitating, restraining, or shaping) that bear upon the business firm and the entrepreneur. These lists provide a useful checklist if one is to describe the external environment existing for a firm in a particular culture, economy, or region.

Joseph D. Coppock states that although it might be thought that the declining power of stockholders over the firm's action has left the management with a free hand, this is not the case. There are many forces which exercise control over the firm in varying degrees. These include the following for the corporation (modifications for non-corporate enterprise could readily be made):[55]

Owners: stockholders
Management: officers, directors
Suppliers (of labor power, things or use of things, funds)
    Households
    Other firms
    Governments
    Miscellaneous organizations
Customers
    Households
    Other firms
    Governments
    Miscellaneous organizations
Rivals
    Firms in the same industry
    Firms in other industries
Governments (protective and regulatory, in general, but also often one or more of above categories)
    National (directly and through international organizations)
    State
    Local

54. See, for example, the recent books by J. K. Galbraith, K. E. Boulding, David E. Lilienthal, A. A. Berle, Sumner Slichter, Max Lerner, Arthur H. Cole, and many others.

55. The following list is quoted from Joseph D. Coppock, *Economics of the Business Firm* (New York: McGraw-Hill, 1959), p. 8.

Coppock agrees that power of immediate and direct decision almost always rests with the management, but pressures from sources such as these will affect decisions. The sources and extent of non-management control will vary from firm to firm, he adds.

Bowen, whose checklist of the internal conditions or culture of the firm we have noted, has made a comparable outline of the principal external influences surrounding and impinging upon the firm:[56]

1. Cost conditions
   a. Physical conditions of production
   b. Existing technical knowledge and its availability to the firm or to other firms
   c. Conditions, including availability, prices, and terms of sale, in markets in which the firm is a buyer, borrower, or renter of:
      (1) Labor
      (2) Land and natural resources
      (3) Materials and supplies
      (4) Capital
2. Demand conditions
   a. Conditions, including extent, elasticity, and steadiness of demand, in markets in which the firm is a seller
   b. Extent of competition and potential competition and behavior of competitors
      (1) Firms in the same industry
      (2) Firms in other industries
3. Governmental controls
   a. Governmental regulations and influence
   b. Taxation
4. Informal social pressures deriving from accepted traditions, practices, values, and definitions of roles
   a. Local community
   b. Business community
   c. General social milieu
5. Influence or pressures exerted by other firms, e.g., bankers, suppliers, customers

These environmental influences become fully effective, Bowen asserts, through decisions of the command—decisions which may be active, passive, or involuntary. Thus it is not merely the objective conditions in the environment that matter but also how the business command perceives these conditions and appraises their significance.

56. The following list is quoted from Bowen, *op. cit.*, pp 31–32.

*Implications of the External Environment*

It is apparent, of course, that just as the internal environment of the firm can help to shape both the qualitative and quantitative aspects of the entrepreneurial function, so also can the outside environment in which the firm operates. As the firm ceases to be a free-wheeling entity and becomes a part of an environment that presses in on it from all sides, the relative importance of certain of the entrepreneurial functions—such as innovation, perhaps—may decline relative to such other functions as achieving stability, balance, unity, or coordination. It is also possible, however, that a permissive, encouraging outside environment, such as that existing in a state or region eager to attract or develop industry, might encourage a more nearly traditional type of entrepreneurship.

An obvious additional effect of the contemporary external environment of the firm is to extend further the diffusion of entrepreneurial function and authority. As Coppock and Bowen point out, the entrepreneur may indeed continue to make the key decisions and be the source of formal authority within the firm, but this does not make him a free agent or allow him to escape *de facto* sharing of his function. Thus, with the entrepreneurial function diffused within the firm and with a comparable *de facto* diffusion involving forces outside the firm, a major change in the locus of the entrepreneurial function has obviously taken place.

It is also possible, of course, that the external environment of the firm will appreciably influence the supply of entrepreneurship. The degree of urbanization, the mobility of the population, the extent and quality of education, family attitudes, political patterns and social mores and values may all produce a greater or lesser flow of potential entrepreneurs.

## Part II: The Entrepreneurial Function in the South

This section of the paper will attempt to examine the entrepreneurial function in the South in the light of the general approach formulated in the latter portion of Part I. In the process, it is hoped some incidental light may be cast upon how that function as it exists in the South compares in character and in quantitative terms to the function in the United States as a whole.

Part II contains three sections. The first section will examine the internal environment or conditions of the firm in the South and will suggest some implications concerning the nature of the entrepreneurial function and the demand for entrepreneurial talent. The second section will make a parallel exploratory search of the external environment of the Southern business firm and will also search for implications regarding entrepreneurship and the supply of entrepreneurial talent. Finally, in the concluding section of Part II, the paper will make passing reference to certain forces that may bring the South and perhaps Southern entrepreneurship into greater conformity with the remainder of the country.

In Part II, two limiting decisions have been made at the outset. First, the focus will be upon non-farm entrepreneurship. Significant changes are indeed occurring in the agricultural domain, but these are beyond the confines of this paper. Second, this Part will content itself with generalizing about the South, with only incidental and passing references to the doubtless very striking contrasts that might be found from sub-region to sub-region, state to state, or even from one part of a state to another. Because Part II pretends to be no more than a suggestive application of a general frame of reference, such detailed applications are not attempted.

## The Internal Environment of the Entrepreneur in the South

This section of Part II will concern itself with certain obvious aspects of the size, composition, and structure of the business firm, especially the industrial firm, in the South. These aspects are selected as relevant to the nature and extent of the Southern entrepreneurial function.

### Size and Character of Firms

Most of the traditional leading industries of the South tend to be organized in relatively small or modest-size firms. These firms have conducted, by national standards, relatively simple operations and have not carried diversification very far. Although many sell in national markets, some of these do not compete broadly in these markets and still others market primarily on a regional basis. These traditional industries also tend to be labor-intensive rather than capital-intensive, and they are often known as low-wage industries. It is against this background that change is taking place, although perhaps not as rapidly as is sometimes supposed.

Thus, Stefan H. Robock's study of a few years ago, after noting that recent industrial gains in the Southeast have partly resulted from rapid expansion in durable goods and non-traditional regional industries, nevertheless concludes that manufacturing remains predominantly non-durable and continues to be heavily concentrated in the traditional textile, lumber, food, and apparel industries.[57] In 1947, for example, these four industries accounted for over three-fifths of the manufacturing production workers in the Southeast.

In recent years, the relative importance of these industries has been declining, while newer, more complex, more capital-intensive, higher-wage industries have been gaining. B. U. Ratchford wrote in 1954 that this trend was to be expected as the area develops industrially. He generalizes, "The first industries developed are those which perform the simpler and more elementary processes and which require comparatively little capital investment and little or no skill on the part of workers. But the demand for the products of such industries is comparatively inelastic as incomes rise. If industrialization continues the area must turn to the more intricate and complex industrial operations which require larger investment outlays and demand higher skills for the workers. The demand for the products of these industries is usually much more elastic with respect to income and there is room for greater expansion as incomes rise. It would seem that the South is now in transition from the first and simplest stage of industrial development to the second and more complex stage."[58]

Seeming to confirm such analyses, some of the newer, capital-intensive industries continue to expand in the South. The Federal Reserve Bank of Atlanta reported in 1960 that, according to the National Industrial Conference Board, the chemicals and allied products industry, one of the District's growth industries, has an average capital investment per worker of $17,000.[59] Capital investment per worker in the textile industry requires $8,000. In the District, value added per worker for the former industry averaged $14,000 in 1957; for the latter, $4,500. This would seem to suggest that Ratchford's rather comforting prognosis is being fulfilled.

Yet, despite declines in employment in textiles and lumber manufacturing over the 1947–1958 period, the Atlanta Bank concludes that for its District states as a group, ". . . there was surprisingly little change in the ranking of the most important industries by employment. The first four industries in 1947—textiles, lumber, food processing, and

57. Stefan H. Robock, "Industrialization and Economic Progress in the Southeast," *Southern Economic Journal*, 20:314–15 (April, 1954).

58. B. U. Ratchford, "Patterns of Economic Development," *Southern Economic Journal*, 20:221–22 (January, 1954).

59. *Monthly Review*, Federal Reserve Bank of Atlanta, February, 1960.

apparel—were still the first four in 1958. Textiles, with over 170 thousand employees in 1958, maintained the number one position, while the other three traded positions."[60] Thus, perhaps the earlier generalizations based on the pre-eminence of the traditional industries are not yet wholly invalid.

The 1961 Southern Governors' Conference seems to reflect knowledge on the part of Southern political leaders that industrial progress remains less than wholly satisfactory, and that low-wage, labor-intensive industries loom too large.[61] Governors Ernest Vandiver of Georgia, Farris Bryant of Florida, and Bert T. Combs of Kentucky, comprising the conference committee on industrial development, are reported to have suggested to their colleagues that the South should be more selective in looking for new plants. The committee's report stated that the reason the annual per capita income of Southern workers in manufacturing is $800 below that of workers in the non-South is the region's historic reliance on industries in which wages are at the bottom of the list. The three governors singled out apparel, leather, and textiles as low-wage industries and contrasted them with machinery, transportation equipment, and chemicals, along with paper, petroleum, and coal. The report suggested, "Therefore, our future industrial development offers other opportunities to further strengthen the region's economic position through the selection of industries which offer our people a more substantial wage."

A 1961 study by Stephen L. McDonald suggests that the South is not of one piece in this regard.[62] In some Southern states, industry is attracted primarily by non-human resources—oil and gas, sulphur, salt, water, timberland, etc. These industries tend to be characterized by high value added, mechanization, and skilled labor at high wages, with limited employment. Other Southern states, in contrast, seem to rely on the traditional low-wage, labor-intensive industries. These industries, it is argued, have less economic impact than the number employed would suggest. This study concludes that industrialization, per se, may be over-emphasized as a source of Southern economic progress. Texas, Louisiana, and Florida, relatively high-growth states, are cited as evidence of what can be done by non-manufacturing activities based on distinctive regional assets ranging from oil and gas to tourism.

60. *Monthly Review*, Federal Reserve Bank of Atlanta, June, 1960.
61. *New York Times*, October 1, 1961. The quote immediately following is also taken from this account.
62. Stephen L. McDonald, "On the South's Recent Economic Development," *Southern Economic Journal*, 28:39 (July, 1961).

It should also be noted that these traditional Southern industries have not been notable for research outlays or innovation, a significant factor (according to Harbison and Myers) in demand for entrepreneurship. Clifford D. Clark and Bernard M. Olsen concluded after an intensive study of technological change in the textile industry: ". . . the degree of technical change experienced by the six textile firms studied, and probably by the entire basic textile industry, has not been as great as the long term rate of change in other industries. Reasons for the disparity are probably due to such diverse causes as the low income elasticity of demand for textile products and the market conditions of textile machinery manufacturers."[63]

### Outside Capital and Branch Plants

It is well known, of course, that a good deal of capital has come into the South from the rest of the United States. The precise amount and relative importance of this "foreign" capital has been disputed, but its movement has been substantial. During the post-World War II period, with most Southern states working hard to attract new industry, often in the form of branch plants of non-Southern firms, this movement has continued.

A 1949 study by the National Planning Association's Committee of the South noted that in 1939, 18.5 percent of all manufacturing establishments in the United States were branch plants, providing about 65 percent of the total value of manufactured products.[64] In the Southeastern region, 27.2 percent of manufacturing establishments were branch plants, providing about 70.5 percent of the region's total value of manufactured products. The Committee asserted that this predominance of branch plants continues to apply to new facilities constructed since 1939.

Calvin B. Hoover and B. U. Ratchford estimated in 1951 that ". . . most, if not all, the large southern plants in such fields as tobacco, rayon, paper and pulp, and petroleum are owned by large national companies which have their headquarters outside the region. The same is true of the railroads and often of the public utilities. We do not know what proportion of the stocks of such companies are owned

63. Clifford D. Clark and Bernard M. Olsen, "Technological Change in the Textile Industry," Southern Economic Journal, 26:133 (October, 1959).

64. Glenn E. McLaughlin and Stefan Robock, Why Industry Moves South, NPA Committee of the South, Report No. 3 (Washington: National Planning Association, 1949), pp. 13–14.

by southerners, although in most cases we would be safe in assuming that it was quite a small minority."[65]

Robock's study, three years later, runs along similar lines.[66] He concludes that in the traditional fields of textiles, lumber products, apparel, shoes, and food processing, much of the expansion has been by "locally-owned" firms. In other important fields, notably chemicals, primary metals, transportation equipment, rubber products, pulp and paper, machinery, etc., branch plants have prevailed. This pattern is in contrast to New England, where a high proportion of new plant expansion has been regionally inspired and regionally owned.

## Implications of the Internal Environment

Even the foregoing rather brief and cursory exploration of certain aspects of the internal environment of the Southern firm, especially in the leading traditional industries, does suggest some implications for the entrepreneurial function in the South.

Some of these implications have to do with the nature of the function. Many of these firms being relatively small, simple, and undiversified the problems of coordination, balance and unification would presumably not loom so large as in a very large and complex company.

There are other implications relative to the locus of the function. To the extent that these firms still remain in the traditional mold, the separation of ownership from control, the professionalization of management, the decentralization of management, and the growth of decision by committee have not yet made their full appearance. Thus the entrepreneurial function is presumably more nearly in one piece and in one set of hands than would be the case in very large firms.

Finally, there are clear implications for the quantity of entrepreneurial talent needed. Harbison and Myers, it may be recalled, advanced certain propositions which involved the use of management as an economic resource. They suggested that the intensity of use of managerial resources will vary directly with increases in the size and complexity of the organization, the size and complexity of the market structures and mechanisms, the relative amount of capital used, and the extent of innovation.[67] The bigger and more complex the firm and its markets, the more capital-intensive it is, and the more it innovates, then the more it requires top-level managerial or entrepreneurial

65. Calvin B. Hoover and B. U. Ratchford, *Economic Resources and Policies of the South* (New York: Macmillan, 1951), p. 193.
66. Robock, *op. cit.,* pp. 316–17.
67. Harbison and Myers, *op. cit.,* pp. 21–39.

talent. The smaller and simpler the firm and its markets, the less capital-intensive it is, and the less it innovates, then the smaller the amount of top-level managerial or entrepreneurial services it needs. By these standards, it is obvious, much of Southern industry still places relatively little strain on the demand for entrepreneurship.

Likewise, the fact that non-Southern capital remains of such importance and that so many of the newer industrial establishments are branch plants may have had a similar effect on the demand for Southern entrepreneurship. True, some of these branch plants have brought with them the latest technology and provide a demonstration effect. They may also be somewhat larger and more capital-intensive than in the general Southern pattern. Yet they are likely also to bring with them key personnel, perhaps involved in mid-passage in career rotation, rather than to rely upon Southern entrepreneurship. The previously cited study by the NPA Committee of the South also notes that efforts by promoters of Southern economic development have often tended to induce outside companies to build new plants in the South rather than to aid local entrepreneurs.[68]

The sheer fact that there is also less industrialization in the South —that the region has not yet "caught up"—has also had a depressing effect upon the demand for Southern entrepreneurship. Southern industrialization has been in forms and fields not conducive to intensive use of entrepreneurial talent, and there has simply not been enough industrialization of any sort to offset this drag.

### The External Environment of the Entrepreneur in the South

The South is a multi-cultured, rapidly-changing area whose total environment—economic, social, and political—can scarcely be detailed here. Yet certain aspects of the environment in which Southern entrepreneurship functions seem relevant at this juncture. These aspects will be described separately, and the net effect of these parts of the environment upon the function of the Southern entrepreneur and the supply of Southern entrepreneurial talent will then be briefly assessed.

### Out-Migration

One of the facts about the environment in which the Southern entrepreneur is working is that heavy net out-migration of population continues. Ratchford, describing the 1930–50 period, notes that this

68. McLaughlin and Robock, *op. cit.*, p. 14.

out-migration was sharply reduced, presumably by a blockage of employment opportunities in the urban-industrial North, during the 1930's.[69] This was the only decade in this century that the South had a higher rate of population growth than the non-South. World War II, however, with its enormous demand for labor, spurred a resumption of mass out-migration, and two and a half million people moved out to the North and West. As a result, the South's population during that decade grew at a rate slightly below that of the non-South.

The Federal Reserve Bank of Atlanta, reporting on population trends in its deep-South region during the 1950's, notes a continuance of out-migration for most of the District.[70] Over-all, the District had an 18 percent increase in population, as contrasted to 17 percent for the nation—this despite the high rate of natural increase in the District. In each District state except Florida, more people left than came in, and in these states the net population growth was only 8 percent. These out-migration losses during the 1950's ranged from fifty thousand people in Louisiana to almost a half million in Mississippi.[71] One million six hundred thousand more people moved into Florida than left, however, and as a result the District did have a net gain from migration.

The net effect of this out-migration upon economic development, specifically upon entrepreneurship, may be a bit mixed. This population movement may lead to a long-run improvement in the allocation of resources in the South, perhaps away from a labor-intensive economy with extensive under-employment and toward a more capital-intensive pattern. This is by no means certain, of course, because labor is also a resource and the capital must be forthcoming. Meanwhile, the drain in population reduces in some measure the potential supply of entrepreneurs, especially as part of that migration consists of Southern college graduates with scientific and technical training.

### Degree of Urbanization

The South has been traditionally a rural or at least a non-urban region. This generalization is subject to all sorts of sub-regional exceptions, and it is of course now modified by a rapid increase in general Southern urbanization. Nevertheless, this historic non-urban pattern, with its accompanying social structure, attitudes, and political implications, has long loomed large in the South.

69. Ratchford, *op. cit.*, p. 224.
70. *Monthly Review*, Federal Reserve Bank of Atlanta, February, 1960.
71. *Monthly Review*, Federal Reserve Bank of Atlanta, April, 1961.

In 1930, Ratchford notes, only a third of the Southern population was urban; by 1950 the figure had risen to almost half (47 percent.)[72] Another fourth of the population by 1950 was rural non-farm, with only about one-fourth of the population on the farm. During the 1930–50 period, urban population increased by 81 percent; rural non-farm, by 46 percent; and the rural farm population declined by 28 percent. Even so, it should be noted, the South remains more rural, farm or non-farm, in its population structure than does most of the rest of the country.

As Robock observes, most of the recent industrial growth in the traditional industries of the South, as well as in such newer industries as chemicals, has been outside of metropolitan areas and rather widely dispersed throughout the region. During the 1939–47 period, only Atlanta (26th), Birmingham (28th), and New Orleans (35th) ranked among the fifty most rapidly expanding major industrial concentrations.[73] The Atlanta Federal Reserve Bank reports that during the 50's, in its District, there was heavy out-migration from the rural counties, and any population explosion that occurred was in the metropolitan areas.[74] The urban population of the District rose by 50 percent during the 1950–60 decade, contrasted with a national average gain of less than 30 percent.[75] Even so, the Bank notes, many urban areas in the District showed little net gain through in-migration. The Birmingham, Knoxville, Chattanooga, and Gadsden metropolitan areas contributed more people to other areas than they could attract. Only one-third of the District counties with urban populations had a net gain through migration in that decade.

Clarence Danhof notes, however, that even the new urbanism will not necessarily be conducive to the emergence of business leadership or entrepreneurship.[76] He observes that the correlation in the South between degree of urbanization and the production of business leaders has been weak and erratic. Danhof adds, however, that both urbanization and the consequent need for business leadership are relatively recent phenomena and that there may now be developing within the new urban community the requisite business leadership. In any event, there does seem to be ". . . a broad and basic relationship be-

72. Ratchford, op. cit., p. 224.
73. Robock, op. cit., p. 315.
74. Monthly Review, Federal Reserve Bank of Atlanta, February, 1960.
75. Monthly Review, Federal Reserve Bank of Atlanta, April, 1961.
76. Clarence Danhof, "Business Leadership in the South," The Journal of Business, 29:135–36 (April, 1956). The quotes immediately following are from p. 136.

tween urbanization and the emergence of business leadership." Whether increasing urbanization stimulates leadership, or whether leadership stimulates industrialization and the other foundations of urbanism, cannot readily be determined ". . . so long as the complex reciprocal forces which operate defy disentanglement."

W. Lloyd Warner and James C. Abegglen, who have made a national study of big business leaders in America and of occupational mobility, conclude that urbanization is closely associated with appearance of business leadership. Using 1900 as the key year (the average birth year of our top business leaders as of 1955), they find that half of the population lived in rural areas and towns of 2,500 or less in 1900, but only a fourth of present business leaders were born there.[77]

Warner and Abegglen also concluded that the larger the community, the greater the probability of membership in the business elite. There is, however, some variation by region. The smaller communities, with populations under 25,000, generally produce a smaller proportion of business leaders than would be expected from their total populations. The North, Midwest, and West do not differ markedly in this respect, but ". . . in the South these communities are underrepresented to a marked degree."[78]

### Occupational Mobility

The predominantly rural pattern that has historically characterized the South has already been noted. This pattern, together with the nature of traditional industries in the South, has had a marked effect upon occupational mobility. As here used, this term refers to "vertical mobility" over time and not merely to job changes.

Warner and Abegglen relate the region of birth to occupational mobility and the makeup of the business elite: ". . . the rate of social mobility is highest for sons of Midwestern businessmen and lowest for sons of Southern laborers; the sons of Midwestern businessmen are members of the business elite in nearly 7 times their proportions in the population, while the representation of sons of Southern farmers is less than one-fifth the expected proportion."[79] Warner and Abegglen also find that sons of businessmen are highly represented in the business elite everywhere, but much less so in the South and West than elsewhere in the country. Sons of professional men in these areas

77. W. Lloyd Warner and James C. Abegglen, *Big Business Leaders in America* (New York: Harper & Brothers, 1955), p. 186.

78. *Ibid.*, p. 187.

79. *Ibid.*, p. 183–84.

also have a lower than usual representation. These facts may reflect the tendency of men with these backgrounds to go into government, law, military services, and other non-business activities.

### Educational Opportunities

There is also an obvious connection between the educational opportunities available in a society or in a region and the quantity and character of entrepreneurship. Education as an investment in economic growth is beginning to receive increasing recognition and support. Warner and Abegglen, in their study of the backgrounds of business leadership, title one chapter "The Royal Road: Higher Education."[80] It is true, of course, that higher education is today increasingly relevant to aspirations for leadership in business. It is also true, however, that the entire educational system, from top to bottom, is relevant to economic growth, the provision of necessary scientific and technical talent, and the ultimate supply and character of entrepreneurship.

It is striking that although the South makes a very considerable effort in terms of percent of personal income devoted to education, the results in terms of average per-pupil expenditures are not impressive. The states of the South are usually among the national leaders in terms of such effort but tend to be near the bottom in terms of per-pupil expenditure results.

In a 1961 Southern Regional Education Board study, "Goals for Higher Education in the South," the conclusion was reached that the South had fallen further behind the nation in the percentage of the tax dollar spent for higher education.[81] Thus if the issue is confined to tax revenue rather than personal income, and to higher education, even the effort made by the South appears open to some question.

According to the Board study, ten years ago 5.24 percent of the general revenue of the sixteen states it includes as Southern was devoted to higher education, as against a national figure of 5.29 percent. Now the national average has risen to 6.47 percent, but the region's average has reached only 5.57 percent. Thirty-nine percent of the nation's college-age youth go to college, compared with 29 percent in the South. Utilizing other measures, the Board study comes up with roughly similar findings. Thus it is apparent that the relative

80. *Ibid.*, Chapter iii.
81. *New York Times* News Service, report published in *St. Louis Post-Dispatch*, November 19, 1961.

inadequacy of educational opportunity, although it has been confronted with resolution in many parts of the South, continues.

### Racial Composition

One of the environmental factors persistently affecting the entrepreneurial function in the South is the racial make-up of the region's population and the economy, social structure, and attitudes built in part upon this racial composition. The existence of two racial communities, living adjacent to each other but in large measure apart from each other, with divergent levels of educational opportunity, occupational mobility, and per capita incomes, has been a pervasive influence. This has been stressed by Nicholls, Danhof, and others.

The effects are ramified and often subtle. Certainly the entrepreneurial function assumes somewhat different aspects in such a setting, if only because a different set of alternatives, constraints, and pressures confront the entrepreneur. It is perhaps even more evident that this existence of a dual society drastically constricts opportunities for entrepreneurship on the part of Negroes in the South. To be sure, entrepreneurship is possible within the separated Negro business community and Negro market, notably in such cities as Atlanta. Even so, entrepreneurship in the broader economic community of the South is blocked for the Negro. Danhof notes that although Negroes in 1900 constituted 29 percent of the population of the South (thus implying that a large proportion of Southern entrepreneurs today might nominally be expected to be Negro), very few are actually listed among the business leaders in *Who's Who in Commerce and Industry*.[82] Significantly, none were identified among the names associated with Southern states.

This problem may be "solved" for the Negro, but not necessarily for the South, by the persistent and heavy out-migration of Negroes. Ratchford notes that for the 1930–50 period, the South's population rose by nearly eight million.[83] For every increase of one in the Negro population, the white population increased by ten. For the 1940–50 decade, the ratio was thirty to one. This occurred despite high Negro natural growth rates. The out-migration was heavy and remains so, as recent reports indicate. During this same decade, between 1950 and 1960, the net out-migration of Negroes was especially heavy.[84]

82. Danhof, *op. cit.*, p. 134.
83. Ratchford, *op. cit.*, p. 224.
84. UPI Wire, published in *St. Louis Post-Dispatch*, December 28, 1961. Source: the Census Bureau.

About 1,500,000 Negroes left the region, two-thirds going in nearly equal numbers to the Northeastern and North Central states. The rest moved farther west. Mississippi lost 323,000 Negroes. Other Southern states having heavy losses of Negroes were Alabama, South Carolina, North Carolina, and Georgia, each of which lost more than 200,000.

### Social Structure, Values, and Attitudes

Warner and Abegglen, in their general study of business leadership, note that the Southern states have lagged in producing business leaders.[85] This lag is attributed partly to the general lag in Southern industrialization and economic development, as well as to a generally lower standard of education and to the exclusion of Negroes from entrepreneurial ranks. Considerable importance is also attached, however, to certain traditional occupational preferences that seem to mirror the larger Southern culture and social structure. Thus there may " . . . be a tendency for young men of higher status backgrounds and advanced formal education to enter other than business careers. For example, recruitment by the armed forces has generally been high in the South; tradition, military schools, and economic conditions may well combine to lead potential Southern leadership into military careers. Politics may offer a similar opportunity in contrast to other sectors of the country." Warner and Abegglen add, however, that ". . . changes in the industrial development of the South coupled with a breakdown of the area's traditional isolation from the rest of the country, might well lead to an increase in Southern representation in the business elite in the future."

There is no doubt that the South is indeed changing. Ratchford, who believes that the South is moving into a more advanced stage of industrialization, asserts: "Partly because of developments in education, transportation, and communication, the South has come more and more to accept the ideas and values of the rest of the United States which give high priority to 'progress' and tend to identify change with progress, especially when the change is based upon scientific principles. Also, as a people we have developed a stronger demand for the conveniences and gadgets of an industrialized, urbanized society and that has raised our propensity to seek material advance."[86]

85. Warner and Abegglen, op. cit., pp. 180–81. The quotes immediately following are from p. 180.
86. Ratchford, op. cit., p. 228.

William H. Nicholls, however, is apparently not quite this confident of the South's capacity and tolerance for change, arguing rather that the South has not yet made the crucial choice it must make: the choice between tradition and progress. At a memorable Presidential Address before the Southern Economic Association annual meetings, and in subsequent journal articles and book, Nicholls explores this choice with great thoroughness. He argues that the South has been drifting, reluctantly or perhaps unawares, toward Progress, but that this drift may be too slow. He concurs that Southerners probably do want more industrialization but he adds that " . . . few Southerners have yet faced up to the question as to whether they want industrialization badly enough to give up firmly held Southern traditions which are inconsistent with it."[87]

In what is perhaps the heart of his paper, the section on "Tradition as a Barrier to Progress," Nicholls explores the nature of these traditions.[88] He lists five constituent elements of this tradition: (1) the dominance of agrarian values, (2) the rigidity of the social structure, (3) the undemocratic political structure, (4) the weakness of social responsibility, and (5) conformity of thought and behavior. Each of these elements in the Southern tradition, he argues, has had a pervasive and largely negative effect upon economic growth and progress.

### Implications of the External Environment

Although this sketch of the external environment in which Southern entrepreneurship is placed is obviously only fragmentary and suggestive, it may serve to show some of the implications of this environment for both the nature of the function and the supply of the functionary. In each part of this section, some of these implications have been noted. Suffice it at this juncture to briefly recapitulate and perhaps to extend the analysis a bit.

Several of these aspects of the external environment in the South influence the character of the entrepreneurial function and the freedom of those performing the function. In some ways, this is a permissive, encouraging atmosphere, especially in this era of aggressive attempts to induce industries to locate in the region. The generally favorable attitudes of state and local governments, and the large infusions of income made by the federal government, may have given

87. This account of Nicholl's position is taken from his paper, "Southern Tradition and Regional Economic Progress," *Southern Economic Journal*, 26:187–98 (January, 1960). This quote is from p. 193.
88. *Ibid.*, pp. 191–93.

the Southern entrepreneur a good deal of help. Likewise, the less-developed state of labor organization has limited the power of this competing claimant to entrepreneurial authority.

Yet in other subtle, indirect, long-run ways, this environment may place constrictions upon freedom of action and decision that are not present to the same degree elsewhere in the country. This is perhaps particularly true of the somewhat traditional aspect of the culture and of the rigidities in the social and economic structure, especially as these involve race. Defensiveness and rigidity in one sector of a society's life may readily inhibit change in other sectors.

These aspects of the external environment also have an appreciable influence upon the available supply of entrepreneurial talent. Restrictive influence upon the supply of entrepreneurship has been evident throughout, whether the restriction is imposed by a loss of potential entrepreneurs through out-migration, by the lack of the urbanization conducive to development of entrepreneurship, by limited occupational mobility, by inadequate educational opportunities, by the maintenance of a racially-based dual society, or by a tradition-influenced culture and social structure.

There is abundant evidence that, whether through these supply factors or through limitations upon the demand for entrepreneurship (as discussed earlier), the quantity of entrepreneurship in the South has contrasted markedly with that of the non-South. Danhof has done the principal work on this disparity, although Warner and Abegglen come to a similar conclusion. It is also clear from these two studies that many of the entrepreneurs whom the South does produce move out of the region in order to perform this function.

### Future Trends in the Southern Entrepreneurial Function

It is apparent from the analysis in Part II of this paper that the entrepreneurial function in the South may differ from that function as it is found in the country as a whole. There also seems to be considerable evidence that the extent of internal or external diffusion or sharing of that function may differ as between the South and non-South. Finally, there is still more evidence that the internal and external environment of the firm is such in the South that both the demand for, and the supply of, entrepreneurship is curtailed.

The question remains: Will these differences grow smaller over time, and will be the character, diffusion, and extent of entrepreneurship in the South come to be closer to national norms? Or are these differences deeply rooted in the Southern economic, social, and political order and, as such, resistant to change?

Many believe that the South is already coming to be less of a distinct region and more nearly an integrated part of a homogenized American economy and culture. This trend, it is claimed, will inevitably continue. We have noted that Ratchford believes that the South has begun to move out of the early stages of industrialization and will follow the familiar pattern found in the industrially more advanced areas.

Harbison and Myers, seeking an internationally applicable concept of management, make some observations that might also be applied to a region less industrially advanced than its surrounding economy. They state:

The general direction of management development in all advancing industrial societies is the same. In the end, management as a resource, as a system of authority, and as a class is likely to be similar in significant aspects in an advanced socialist economy, an advanced market economy, or an advanced totalitarian economy. The initial push to start the economy on the road to industrialism may be made by widely differing groups such as an existing dynastic elite in a feudal society, a rising class of proprietary capitalists in a market economy, a colonial administration, a socialist government, or a communist regime. But they all steer toward modern industrialism. And modern industrialism has a uniform prescription for management.[89]

Harbison and Myers freely concede, however, that the pace of the drive toward industrialism may be accelerated or retarded by certain factors affecting management development—such as tenacious patrimonial or political managements.

Others argue, without resort to this sort of model, that the South is simply too deeply tied into the United States economy to remain very divergent. This approach stresses such connections as: (1) the increasing reliance of the South upon national markets and hence upon national employment and income levels; (2) the reliance of the South upon rising levels of non-South employment in order to absorb those who migrate out of the South; (3) continued capital movements into the South, including branch plants of national corporations; (4) very large outlays by the federal government, including huge military installations, that have been virtually as important as has industrialization in increasing income levels in the South.

89. Harbison and Myers, *op. cit.*, pp. 121–22.

Yet we are reminded by Nicholls that the fundamental decision as to whether the South is willing to pay the price of economic progress may not yet have been made. Lloyd Saville, in his study of sectionalism in the U.S. and in Italy, finds that sectionalism is decreasing between New England (one of his two U.S. regions) and the Southeast (the other U.S. region).[90] Yet he feels that present trends will not ultimately produce complete equality in the United States. Saville suggests that education may be the only practical answer: "When there is a rapid population growth in the backward area, the volume of funds available for investment in the area from domestic and foreign markets is not large enough to bring about equality in standard of living with other areas. Education, however, offers the promise of facilitating the troublesome transition from an agricultural society to an industrial one not only by enabling the individual to produce more by the efficient utilization of individual initiative, but also to realize for himself the economic alternatives available to him in an industrial society."

Interestingly, Harbison and Myers come to virtually the same conclusion. They claim that the generation and development of managerial resources may be encouraged or checked by the investments made in education and by the extent to which higher education is oriented toward the needs of an industrial society. Barriers to entry into the managerial hierarchy must be lowered. They conclude: "The second half of the twentieth century, even more than the first half, will be an era of technical and managerial brain power in the service of an industrial society."[91]

90. Lloyd Saville, "Sectional Developments in Italy and the United States," *Southern Economic Journal*, 23:39–53 (July, 1956). The quote immediately following is from p. 50.
91. Harbison and Myers, *op. cit.*, pp. 132–33.

# III

# Negro Entrepreneurship in
# Southern Economic Development

*By Harding B. Young and James M. Hund*

Ten years after the end of World War II and ninety years after the end of the War Between the States, Negroes could not be found in the upper levels of the nation's business leadership. In any comparison of North and South in terms of contribution to such leadership, it was recommended that the Negro population be excluded.[1] Yet various segments of the public press have recently commented, often flamboyantly, on the aggregations of Negro wealth, Negro society, and the accomplishments of individual Negroes in many endeavors.[2] The easy assumption is that any marked accomplishments must have occurred in the North, because the stifling effects of segregation would certainly have prevented such from being realized in the South. Most of the scholarly studies of Negroes in business appeared a decade ago or more.[3]

1. Clarence Danhof, "Business Leadership in the South," *Southern Economic Journal*, April, 1956, p. 134.
2. For example, see Bill Davidson, "Our Negro Aristocracy," *Saturday Evening Post*, January 13, 1962; article on the Negro market in *Time*, February 9, 1962; and a similar item in the *New York Times*, July 1, 1962. An earlier article was "Negro Businessmen in New Orleans," *Fortune*, November, 1949.
3. Robert H. Kinzer and Edward Sagarin, *The Negro in American Business* (New York: Greenberg, 1950); W. Hardin Hughes, *The Negro in Our Economy* (Atlanta: Southern Regional Council, 1951); Arnold Rose, *The Negro in America* (New York: Harper and Bros., 1948); or Joseph A. Pierce, *Negro Business and Business Education* (New York: Harper and Bros., 1947). A more recent study is Louis H. Schuster, Edgar G. Epps, and Vivian W. Henderson, *Business Enterprises of Negroes in Tennessee* (Tennessee Agricultural and Industrial State University, 1961). An excellent study of broader scope, but limited to New Orleans, is Daniel C. Thompson, *The Negro Leadership Class* (Englewood Cliffs, N.J.: Prentice-Hall, 1963).

It is appropriate, then, to review from several aspects the status of Negro entrepreneurship and to hazard some predictions for the future. Accordingly, in what follows there are offered first some notions on the dimensions of this phenomenon and the past and present barriers to its development. A description of the fields of Negro entrepreneurship in the South is then presented. Finally, in the light of the changes which have occurred, some conclusions will be drawn about the form and future course of Southern Negro entrepreneurship. In carrying out this effort there has been an attempt "to grasp the economic significance of certain aspects . . . of business enterprise conceived as social phenomena, and . . . to view these elements as in a state of constant change." In other words, emphasis is on merging "some aspects of the supposedly distinct disciplines of business administration, economics, sociology, and history."[4]

"From the very moment of emancipation, Negro leaders urged the free men to have faith in business and property as an escape from poverty and as the road to the achievement of economic independence."[5] To a great extent this has been a will-o'-the-wisp because of the barriers which have prevented achieving the objectives of such exhortation. In a bitter, though realistic, vein, Franklin Frazier has dubbed this "Negro Business: A Social Myth."[6] He notes that "it has always been claimed that despite the oppression of the Negro in the South, there was a compensatory fact, namely, that the South offered an opportunity for the development of Negro business. Nor has the belief in the myth been affected by the fact that the attempts of Negro businessmen to establish industrial undertakings have constantly resulted in failures."[7] If one defines "industrial undertakings" as manufacturing, mining, or large-scale distribution, one can find but few outstanding successes, but not so much on account of failure as for lack of enterprises in these fields. A broader definition will find notable exceptions to Frazier's sweeping generalizations, and it is these which are the principal concern of this paper.

Even though many of the problems associated with Negro entrepreneurship are matters of slow change and are intimately entwined with the social progress of the Negro in the United States, it is not possible here to recapitulate a century or more of this progress. Yet

4. Arthur H. Cole, *Business Enterprise in Its Social Setting* (Cambridge: Harvard University Press, 1959), p. 7.

5. Kinzer and Sagarin, *op. cit.*, p. 53.

6. Franklin E. Frazier, *Black Bourgeoisie* (Glencoe: The Free Press, 1957), title to Chapt. vii.

7. *Ibid.*, pp. 163–64.

the conditions under which Northern white entrepreneurship and its counterpart in the South have arisen are quite different, though undoubtedly some close parallels might be found historically in first- and second-generation national and ethnic groups. Cole has, for example, noted the importance of non-economic stimuli and motivations among businessmen as being universal in character. Achievement "can be regarded as an expression of the almost universal human desire for prestige."[8] "Whatever the immediate motivations, those potent in business seem related to one or another of the psychological incentives of search for security, prestige, power, and social service."[9] In spite of this emphasis on prestige as a universal, it will be pointed out in some detail below that the relative importance of this motivation in the Negro community is quite different from what it is in the white. Exceptions of this kind call for some historical perspective on, and a current evaluation of, the factors which have both encouraged and retarded the growth and development of Southern Negro entrepreneurship. This is the task of the next section.

### Entrepreneurship: Requirements and Barriers

Entrepreneurship is not an economic phenomenon which autonomously springs into being like Minerva from the head of Zeus. Its seeds may exist in dormant condition, but require a beneficent climate for germination and development to full flower. In his excellent introduction and background to Southern entrepreneurship, Professor Hickman notes the degree to which environment will appreciably affect the supply of entrepreneurship. Some relevant factors are: "the degree of urbanization, the mobility of the population, the extent and quality of education, family attitudes, political patterns and social mores and values. . . ."[10] It is because of, or in spite of, such factors that entrepreneurship occurs. These factors, and others such as markets, financing, experience, and communication, are examined in this section as contributing to or retarding the development of Negro entrepreneurship in the South. The following section presents examples of the kinds of Negro business enterprises which have arisen in response to the combination of forces stemming from the several conditioning factors.

For purposes of this discussion, a relevant definition of entrepre-

8. Cole, *op. cit.*, p. 104.
9. *Ibid.*, p. 16
10. C. A. Hickman, "The Entrepreneurial Function: The South as a Case Study" (in this volume, p. 95).

neurship must be chosen from the many which have been suggested in the literature. Just as in defining leadership, a choice must be made between a reliance on personal effectiveness or organizational behavior. One is tempted to choose the former and mold a definition around those who have demonstrated the strength of character and ability to pierce through the several barriers to be discussed rather than around those who might be deemed "peak coordinators" or maintainers of efficient decision-making systems. Yet Danhof, concentrating on personal effectiveness, claims that "an individual may be characterized by entrepreneurial activity only if he is primarily concerned with changes in the formula of production of an enter-prize over which he has full control,"[11] This is too restrictive for a discussion of Negro entrepreneurship. Cole, focusing on organization-al behavior, offers an all-encompassing definition: "purposeful activity of an individual or group of associated individuals, undertaken to initiate, maintain, or aggrandize a profit-oriented business unit for the production or distribution of economic goods and services."[12] One of Cole's reviewers agrees that "It may be well to drop the figure of the 'heroic' entrepreneur, but there is much to be said for limiting the function to its creative, shaping aspects, less in terms of major achievements or acts of synthesis than in the constant modification of structures, situations or ideas in a continuing process of interac-tion."[13] It will be seen that these suggestions have particular applica-bility to Negro entrepreneurship where neither the qualities and functions of a Thomas A. Edison nor an Alfred P. Sloan are to be found. For the South as a whole, Hickman found the entrepreneurial function less complex. He points out that coordination, balance, and unification have been needed only recently, entrepreneurship being more nearly in one set of hands, undiffused, than would be the case in a very large firm.[14] This is true of most Negro enterprises, yet the situation is often more complex because of the combination of social and economic motives behind Negro entrepreneurship. It is perhaps time to note just how the several factors presented above have shaped this phenomenon, viewed first in some historical perspec-tive and then in the forms they assume today.

11. Clarence Danhof, *Change and the Entrepreneur,* Research Center in Entre-preneurial History, Harvard University (Cambridge: Harvard University Press, 1949), p. 21.

12. Cole, *op. cit.,* p. 7.

13. W. T. Easterbrook, review of Cole's *Business Enterprise in Its Social Set-ting,* in *Business History Review,* Spring, 1960, p. 122.

14. Hickman, *op. cit.,* p. 90.

"Know-How"

Entrepreneurship and craftsmanship are certainly not coextensive, but many craftsmen have been found in the entrepreneurial ranks, particularly if craftsmanship is broadened to include invention.[15] Where a Lee deForest and a Preston Tucker could fail, a Thomas Edison and a Henry Ford could succeed brilliantly. Immediately after the Civil War, the Negro had a virtual monopoly on labor in the Southern plantation economy because white people had generally eschewed it. "Negroes were to a large extent the craftsmen and the mechanics . . . for even skilled labor was degraded. The whites had often been denied the opportunity of acquiring training since so many masters had preferred to work with slaves."[16] It is true that these skills were employed in plantation work in an agricultural economy, but in terms of being equipped for the coming transition to a more urbanized and industrialized economy and culture, the Negro had an edge. Of course, the things which he sorely lacked were the other two of the triad of economic factors, land and capital.[17] In the shrinkage of economic values which accompanied the collapse of the Confederacy, his white brother was not much better off in terms of capital accumulation. Even though the Negro possessed the rudiments of industrial skills on the eve of expansion of the non-agricultural economy, existing cultural mores and values did not point to business as the place for the Negro to seek fulfillment. "In these men just released from slavery three ambitions seemed to dominate: a desire to learn Greek and Latin; to hold public office; to become preachers."[18] During Reconstruction the second of these was possible in the South, and is becoming possible again today. The first was sublimated into general academic work, and the third persists. Several other professions have over the years been added to the list.

If economic inflation rather than deflation had followed in the years after the Civil War, the lot of the Negro might have been somewhat easier, but as the agricultural economy became less able

15. Hughes, *Negro in Our Economy*, p. 3, notes that "the records of the U.S. Patent Office at Washington show approximately five thousand patents credited to Negroes."

16. Rose, *Negro in America*, pp. 101–2.

17. Charles S. Johnson, *The Negro in American Civilization* (New York: Henry Holt and Co., 1930), p. 102, does point out, however, that "individual Negroes were skilled traders in money long before the Civil War."

18. Roi Ottley, *Black Odyssey* (New York: Charles Scribner's Sons, 1948), p. 187.

to support both Negroes and whites, prompting migration to the cities, economic competition for jobs became severe. Even though the Negro had the skills, he was also a minority group which could be easily distinguished. Not only were Negroes driven out of old jobs, but they were not given the opportunity to try for the new ones opening up. Jim Crow legislation came during the 1890's, the pressures of deflation continued, and political representation for the Southern Negro became a thing of the past. "During this development, defensive beliefs were constantly growing among whites in the South that the Negro was inefficient, unreliable, and incompetent to work with machines. It was true that fewer and fewer young Negroes could keep up with skills when they were not allowed to experience the better working conditions and the new techniques or get training."[19]

The legacy of these attitudes and practices lingers today in the difficulty Negroes with basic abilities and some financial resources have in securing experience which can serve as a firm basis for entrepreneurship. One Negro banker remarked in an interview that mastery over the separate business functions at both the operating and managerial levels calls for a balanced combination of formal education and on-the-job training which is seldom found among Negro businessmen. Far too often Negroes who wish to engage in given business enterprises can cite no prior experience in the line of business they plan to enter. They do not seem to realize the importance of know-how. Aside from the larger amount of capital needed to enter manufacturing, and the requisite access to markets, there was the feeling expressed by many who were interviewed that the Negro will enter manufacturing only after he better understands the corporate form of enterprise and has had more training in management.

Herein lies one of the central problems of the Negro businessman. First, he has had no tradition in business. Only in a few instances has he had the opportunity to learn from his father, or has taken the opportunity when presented.[20] Until very recently he has been denied the opportunity to work at the managerial level in a white enterprise in the North or South to gain the necessary on-the-job

19. Rose, *op. cit.,* p. 102.
20. Thompson, *Negro Leadership,* p. 130, notes that in New Orleans "the children of these founders [of Negro business enterprises] usually attend college and prepare for professional careers."

experience.[21] Education can sometimes be a partial substitute for experience. How has the Negro fared in this regard?

## Education

Some Negroes have managed to gain experience or know-how in a particular chosen field and have been motivated to enterpreneurship. For them one barrier has been the lack of other qualified personnel with which to staff an expanding enterprise. It is true that many business ventures have been initiated by Negroes with the hope of offering, as an important ancillary benefit, other than menial employment to members of the race. Yet a nucleus of qualified people is essential. The fact is that the image of business in the minds of those fortunate enough to pursue college work has held little attraction. Forty-five years ago Thomas I. Brown noted that "but a small percentage of college-bred Negroes seem to enter business."[22] This continues to be true today, as corroborated by those interviewed. The view was expressed that far too few Negro college graduates enter business; even where available, business education has not been in great demand. It has only been in the past ten to fifteen years that departments of business administration have been added to Negro colleges and universities. Where they exist, many suffer from lack of teachers qualified in both training and experience, though there are some notable exceptions. It has therefore been difficult to provide a flow of appropriately educated people for the would-be entrepreneurs to hire. The training programs of the insurance companies mentioned below are evidence of this.

Several reasons for the reluctance to enter business were offered. Most important was the belief that the professions have been more

21. Caroline Bird, "More Room at the Top: Company Experiences in Employing Negroes in Professional and Management Jobs," *Management Review*, March, 1963, p. 14, reports that ". . . relatively few Negroes are yet to be found in the general line management of large-scale enterprises. Those who have high-level jobs with big manufacturing companies are usually scientists, engineers, accountants, and other technical specialists working singly or invisibly, or they are likely to be salesmen, personnel interviewers, and industrial and public relations specialists retained especially to deal with Negro employees and customers. Employment of Negro executives in management jobs outside of the above categories is largely concentrated in big-city department stores, defense manufacturers, and to a somewhat lesser extent, big-city savings banks." Thus she found Negroes supervising mixed work groups at the Lockheed plant in Georgia, more fully reported in *Business Week*, April 13, 1963.

22. Thomas I. Brown, ed., *Economic Cooperation among the Negroes of Georgia* (Atlanta University Publications No. 19 [Atlanta: Atlanta University Press, 1917]), p. 11.

attractive because of the economic security and prestige afforded. The average Negro would rather risk his nest egg or line of credit on dental equipment than on a business venture. Since he is at the bottom of the economic ladder, his chances of making a comeback from failure are not considered good. The prestige accorded the image of the successful Negro in legitimate business is hardly worth the risks. Of those college-trained Negroes who have entered business in any substantial way, the highest percentage have been in the general area of finance—banks, insurance companies, mortgage companies, and savings and loan associations. This probably accounts for the large measure of success which has been achieved in these fields of enterprise. The authors' research confirmed Pierce's observation that "on the average, the enterprises operated by persons who took business education in college have been established longer, employ more persons, and have larger volumes of business than those operated by persons with no business education."[23]

Even in the general area of finance, respondents reported their inability to recruit and retain persons adequately prepared for the highly complex business structure. This problem is further magnified by the fact that Negro business firms find themselves in competition with white firms which are increasingly employing top-quality Negro help. One man stated that part of the solution here is for Negroes to hire whites (or reverse integration, one might call it). Some evidence of this approach is appearing, although it involves some readjustment in attitudes toward one of the basic purposes for Negro business, the provision of jobs for Negroes above the unskilled and semi-skilled levels.

Finally, it must be assumed that in the large migrations of Negroes to the North, beginning in 1900, but particularly in the past twenty years, much of the South's potential Negro entrepreneurship has been lost. Any numerical estimate is of course impossible, but it is not hard to imagine that those Negroes with ambition for business success who did not have the advantage of higher education would move. One could add to this group those who had no available access to business opportunity through marriage or family connections.[24] The

23. Pierce, *Negro Business*, p. 203.
24. This should not be overemphasized. According to Kinzer and Sagarin, *op. cit.*, p. 17, "the difference between North and South, as far as business opportunities are concerned, frequently becomes one of etiquette and superficialities. The doors of northern industries are open, but the invisible sentry of discrimination stands guard, and entry is not forbidden, but successful passage

calculated chance for success has been important, and receptive markets have raised appreciably the chance.

## Restricted Markets and the Chance for Success

Trying to make a virtue out of a necessity, leaders like Marcus Garvey declared that Negroes must become independent of white capital and white employers.[25] Booker T. Washington also encouraged the development of Negro business, bringing about the National Negro Business League in 1900 to encourage such activity. "The dominant direction of this interest has been more racial than economic. Attention has been centered more upon Negro business for Negro patronage than upon this business as a purely economic venture for profit."[26] This was necessarily so, since it is hard to conceive of building an enterprise devoted to the production of goods and services which could survive catering to the Negro ten percent of the population unevenly scattered over the land. Business had to be local in nature, serving concentrated centers of Negro population. The market was and is restricted in two ways. First, it is racially restricted; second, it is restricted as to income.

Negro customers, who constitute the great bulk of the patronage of Negro businesses, are members of the poorest racial group in America. Although there has been a marked increase in the level of Negro income, there is still a sizable gap, in figures for the nation, of over two thousand dollars between white and Negro median wage incomes. In the South this disparity is even greater. For example, in the state of Georgia the median white family income in 1960 was $5,027 as compared to $2,188 for the non-white family. Interviews revealed that while Negro businesses in the South depend mainly upon Negro patronage, such establishments are not sharing significantly in the increases in Negro purchasing power which have occurred except in areas left to Negro businessmen by patterns of segregation, law, and custom. These patterns affect both sides of the market, buying and selling. Negro businesses not dependent on segregation find they are in keen competition with those of whites in many lines. Retail trade has been the prime example, but now one or more white insurance

---

is rare." A decade ago, Donald Dewey stated that "at present the social cost of the southern employment pattern lies mostly in the export of Negro ability." "Negro Employment in Southern Industry," *Journal of Political Economy,* August, 1952, p. 289.

25. Ottley, *op. cit.,* p. 238.
26. Johnson, *op. cit.,* p. 101.

companies in the South are considering employing Negro salesmen to work the Negro market. This looms in special significance when it is recalled that at one time white companies would not insure the lives of Negroes at all. Such competition has been increasing as attention is called more and more to the growth of Negro purchasing power. A counter-penetration on a national scale has not been accomplished by Negro firms, though cosmetics seems to offer a possible exception.

The president of one Negro insurance company related that because of custom, Negro firms do not insure lives of whites, and employment is restricted to Negroes. Such organizations are caught in this situation and therefore give white companies an advantage. It has been pointed out that this is changing, but with few exceptions the market for Negro business firms has been limited to less than ten percent of the population and about five percent of the income. Job discrimination together with a lower level of training and skill have kept the Negro's income low.

At low-income levels one customarily finds little or no accumulated savings and a high propensity to consume. Of necessity, purchasers at these levels avail themselves of credit when it is extended. Negro businesses as a whole are under-capitalized and therefore unable to grant credit and at the same time try to carry a wide variety of goods to meet competition of white firms.[27] As a result the Negro housewife avoids the colored grocer as well as the chain store. Often the Negro family goes to a cheap clothing store to purchase on credit rather than to get good values. When the Negro furniture dealer is unable to extend credit, he finds it difficult to compete with the white retailer who experiences no trouble in having his paper picked up by the local bank.

Even in those cases where some business success was realized, it was not always tolerated by the surrounding community. It is reported, for example, that "in many towns any sign of marked progress by a Negro business house [was] taken as a notice that that business should be crippled or destroyed. Hence, in a certain town . . . it is said to [have been] customary for the white city fathers to revoke the license or charter of any Negro business which does well. . . . If the Negro proprietor is making money, he dare not let it appear so."[28]

This necessity to operate in a somewhat furtive manner has carried

27. For examples see Thompson, *op. cit.*, p. 129.
28. Brown, *op. cit.*, p. 18.

over today and is at least partly accountable for the unattractiveness of so many Negro places of business and for the lack of adequate business records.  The latter also stems, of course, from lack of training in business procedures and a desire to avoid the scrutiny of the tax collector, who will most certainly be white and a possible source of information which could lead to retaliation.  This is probably unwarranted today.

E. E. Hagen has pointed to the rise of business leaders from among disadvantaged groups at various times and places under conditions where success in business could compensate for discrimination against entering the high-prestige professions.  Elaborating on this theme, McClelland injects the provisos that the minority group be predominantly middle class and reasonably high in his dimension of "n Achievement."[29]  These conditions have not generally existed for American Negroes.  The high-prestige professions have been open, though often only in terms of service to the race, while only a small segment of the minority group has attained middle class status.  It is success in business which has been most difficult to attain.

Given a background of slavery, rejection, and segregation, it is surprising that any seeds of entrepreneurship could find soil suitable for germination, particularly in the South.  Much of Negro business supports the hypothesis that innovation will be slow or non-existent when stress on the organization, or the difference between the level of aspiration and the level of achievement, is great.  Frustration or desperation have often been the result where aspirations have far exceeded achievements, personal or organizational.[30]  Such outcomes of entrepreneurial efforts have hardly served to enhance the image of Negro business.

## Financing

Even for those Negroes who have succeeded in meeting the requirements of education and/or experience, and who feel they can make money in a restricted market, the problem of financing remains if anything but the smallest of enterprises is to be undertaken.  There is probably more wealth in the Negro community than is commonly assumed, but it is not often concentrated in what one views as the

29. David C. McClelland, *The Achieving Society* (Princeton, N.J.: D. Van Nostrand Co., Inc., 1961), p. 280.
30. James G. March and Herbert A. Simon, *Organizations* (New York: John Wiley and Sons, 1958), p. 184.

usual channels to be tapped for equity money or loans. This may be due to the historical fact of Negro bank failures and a consequent unwillingness to entrust one's funds to a Negro financial institution. The failure of the much-heralded Freedmens Bank after the Civil War, and the other failures of Negro financial institutions, have dimmed the faith of Negroes in economic units the white economy regards as essential to the growth of business enterprise.

As might be expected, those interviewed in the study reported financing as their most serious obstacle to business growth and expansion. It would seem that there has been little change in this regard during the last twenty years. Pierce noted this in his work as he attributed the chief difficulties in organizing a Negro business or in promoting its expansion and growth to the lack of adequate capital and hard-to-get or inaccessible credit.[31]

The difficulties faced by Negro businessmen seeking bank credit stem from several factors: prejudice of the white bank officials; the lines of business in which Negroes engage; the adequacy of records kept in a large percentage of businesses; lack of financial sophistication by many Negro businessmen; and finally, the marginal position of many businesses.

Evidence of the first factor was often found during the course of the study, though it was impossible to validate by actual check. For example, in one large city a distributor of consumer products said that he has found it extremely difficult to get a business loan from a white institution and so has worked to get a Negro-sponsored commercial bank in that city. In his words, "Banks do the bulk of lending on financial statements and on character. Negroes have no character so far as white banks are concerned. The more collateral over the loan, the better." He cited an attempt to borrow $2,000 with good financial statements. The borrower had to pledge $3,000 in gilt-edged securities. At the same time another bank over eight hundred miles away was willing to make the loan on the strength of the same financial statements.

In another Southern city a Negro bank official said that prior to 1949 a Negro could hardly get a legitimate business loan, usurious rates being the rule for Negroes. If one were obtained, it carried balloon payment provisions rendering it almost impossible to repay. Banks have been more interested in guarantees by whites than in the applicant's business ability, according to some of those interviewed.

31. Pierce, *op. cit.*, p. 18.

This would seem to confirm what Pierce found in his study: "Southern mores, generally, require endorsement by whites as a definition of the character of Negroes. . . . Frequently this means that Negroes are not investigated for their business competence as whites might be."[32]

The president of one of the larger Negro-sponsored banks related another side of this story. He said that very often unsuccessful business operators attribute their poor showing to a lack of sufficient capital and the inability to obtain a bank loan when these may not be the real causes of their difficulty. To use his words: "We might as well observe that the charge of discrimination because of race is often incorrectly raised when some Negroes are unable to obtain desired credit assistance for their business operations. Actually, the credit may be denied for perfectly sound reasons which have no immediate relation to the applicant's racial identity." Capital, he maintained, is constantly looking for profitable avenues of use in both large and small business. It is the responsibility of the borrower to demonstrate his capacity to make profitable use of capital. In the opinion of this bank official, a firm intention to liquidate indebtedness on schedule coupled with the preparation of regular, accurate financial statements is the best approach to securing financial assistance.

In this connection the proprietors of a large restaurant and lounge said that they have never experienced difficulty in securing money, and that long ago they learned the importance of good record-keeping. A Negro educator, also a businessman of some note, told the authors that many businessmen keep records sufficient for tax purposes, but that these are often not adequate to make business decisions or serve as means of control. Accordingly, they will then be wanting as support for a loan application. This partially explains the reticence of white banking institutions to make loans to Negro businesses. The Negro institutions, on the other hand, are often more conservative in their loan policies, but at the same time have been willing to work with selected businesses so that the necessary records could be developed to present a clear financial picture.

Another bank president emphasized the average Negro businessman's unwillingness to put all his effort and capital into his business. He may invest instead in some "broken down real estate," hoping thus to be a landlord rather than ploughing back earnings into the business. There is also the natural inclination to expand personal consumption at the expense of reasonable retention of earnings. "The rule is sacrifice"

32. *Ibid.*, p. 89.

to get capital formation, and this conservative, self-reliant attitude does not enjoy high popularity, according to this banker.

An additional aspect of the problem of financing, according to some respondents, is the information held by credit agencies about Negroes. This is, they contend, often incomplete and inaccurate. Because of the lack of communication, for example, of the kind afforded by Chambers of Commerce, Rotary Clubs, and other civic and business groups, credit agencies rely on figures only when white references are not presented. It is felt that the merchants' bureaus rate all Negro customers as sub-standard and therefore charge higher rates—15 percent instead of 8 percent.

The greatest barrier is the need for equity capital, a problem of all business, and particularly small business. Here the Negro businessman faces a dilemma. The small Negro banks, just like other banks, cannot supply venture capital which is sorely needed to enable the Negro businessman to break out of the service type of establishments into manufacturing, which contributes so much more in terms of value added and employment. On the other hand, Negroes, because of the low level of incomes and consequent inability to save large amounts of capital to build up their enterprises, have been unable (and, as has been pointed out, unwilling) to rely on internal financing. It seemed to the authors that there exists in some quarters an unawareness of sources of capital which might be tapped, such as the Small Business Administration, to which some have successfully applied. There was also some lack of sophistication concerning the proper balance in a capital structure for different kinds of business.

Since the urgent need is for equity financing which banks cannot provide, the Negro businessman may well turn to greater use of the corporate form of business. Many corporations which do exist are closed and in some instances are still family organizations. There is some evidence that cooperation and a pooling of equity funds is taking place. Possessing but little capital as individuals, it is incumbent for those with entrepreneurial instincts to get these individuals to pool their resources. As can be seen, a requisite for such pooling is the existence of a spirit of mutual trust.

## Mutual Trust

If wider use of the corporate form of business is to serve the potential Negro entrepreneur by providing a pooling of capital funds, it must be preceded by growing willingness to participate in risky ventures. Because of their disadvantaged position, Negroes have often been relieved of what they had by members of both races. The stereotypes of Amos and Andy and the Kingfish, though repugnant to a race trying to better itself, are nonetheless easy to identify today. This lack of mutual trust, coupled with wariness in dealings with whites, has been a serious obstacle to the development of Negro enterprise.

In a biting commentary the Reverend Gholson has declared that "much of the wealth which he [the Negro] has acquired has been literally stolen from him by unscrupulous and designing individuals who felt a kind of divine mandate to live by the sweat of another's brow. Having a better knowledge of economic trends, and enjoying a better economic position, they could do this not only with impunity but with public approval."[33]  Such experience stirred in the Negro a deep distrust of the white man in business. This was added to the psychological set carried forward from the days of slavery when Negroes were divided into "house" and "field." The former usually had more privileges and more education and were naturally exposed to the culture of the day. They also gained favors by acting as a sort of spy system on their less fortunate fellows, so that even within the Negro race in the South there was no natural development of solidarity and mutual trust.[34]  Centers of Negro business in the South visited by the authors exhibited both extremes of this dimension, which helps historically to account in a major way for the success or lack of success of Negro entrepreneurship.

The extreme of distrust or individualism was found in New Orleans. "Coming down through the years since slavery Negroes have been successfully brainwashed not to trust each other" is the way it was expressed by a long-time resident of that city. He listed different racial backgrounds and cultures which characterize New Orleans and an absence of leadership as reasons for the lack of real entrepreneurship among Negroes there. With a Negro population of a quarter million, New Orleans has no Negro savings and loan association or commercial bank. Three attempts have been made to organize a commercial bank. Once, the state banking commission would not grant approval; and since then it has been impossible to raise the

---

33. Edward Gholson, *The Negro Looks into the South* (Boston: Chapman and Grimes, Inc., 1947), p. 12.

34. The failure of Negroes to develop cooperatives was attributed to the fact that "envy and jealousy continue to work mightily against coordination of effort among colored people." Brown, *op. cit.*, p. 10.

$300,000 necessary for a federal charter. At the same time there are some eighteen small industrial-type insurance companies in the one city, each with its own family interest. According to one respondent, this variety of backgrounds will make it extremely difficult to effect mergers necessary to avert failures which must certainly occur attendant on the swing away from industrial to ordinary insurance.

## Communication

Granted the ingredients of education and know-how joined to adequate financing, directed toward viable market objectives, and reinforced with a spirit of mutual trust, successful entrepreneurship outside "the rackets" still requires what Cole had called "a beneficent climate of social opinion, a changing climate, to be sure, but one that does not discourage the flotation of new enterprises."[35] Relegation of Negro business to a position out of the mainstream serving only in those areas where white businessmen did not choose to serve could hardly be regarded as a climate favorable to entrepreneurship. With the focus of business in general changing from community, to industry, and then to nation, most Negroes were perforce limited to community, though exceptions to this can be found.

The beginning of modern economies as we know them today was tied to the emergence of markets and trade following the feudal period. The years following the Civil War are comparable for the South. The general trend to commercial development and the spread of communication media and the lifeblood they gave to commerce were largely missing for the Negro. He could not join trade associations or local Chambers of Commerce where information of the marketplace was exchanged, and trade publications seldom were directed to his problems in business. This is the rule even now. Various professional organizations pertaining to one of the functional fields of business are generally closed to his membership.

One businessman who engages in manufacturing said that the lack of communication constitutes a part of his trouble in obtaining financing and access to markets. He maintained that the Negro bank is not familiar with his kind of manufacturing business and the white bankers do not know him. "One way to open up the channel of communication and thereby permit the Negro to learn some know-how of business would be to integrate the Chamber of Commerce," says this manufacturer. Thompson has described this situation with particular

35. Cole, *op. cit.*, p. 77.

reference to New Orleans: "There is no Negro member of the New Orleans Chamber of Commerce, the powerful Young Men's Business Club, Rotary, or any other organization where economic trends, opportunities, and planning are discussed by experts. This, coupled with the fact that the Negro Business League in New Orleans has always been anemic, means that the individual Negro businessman has few, if any, opportunities to benefit from the thinking and experience of other businessmen."[36]

Of course it would be ridiculous to contend that there are no points of contact between the white and Negro business communities in any given situation. But on the Negro side they are often limited to a few persons of prominence such as the barbers who were the founders of the two large life insurance companies or the president of the multiple-line casualty company who gained his experience working with whites. There have been others who for one reason or another served as communication links between the two communities and were sometimes dubbed "Uncle Toms" for their efforts. In failing to wave the black flag and thus destroy his effectiveness, Dixie's only Negro legislator in a century, Senator Johnson of Atlanta, is beginning to have this reputation.[37]

One can see, then, that for the Southern Negro the usually assumed requirements for the rise of entrepreneurship have often been lacking or present only in diluted form. Some of these, it might be added, were missing for the white man too, notably tolerance for any breakdown in the social structure or acceptance of change.[38] The combination of a rural economy and an orientation to European customs and values when considering a career left but little acceptance for money-making or a social structure built on obvious accumulation of property and conspicuous consumption rather than on land. Incentives for white men to engage in entrepreneurship in the South were weaker than in the North, and artificial barriers have made entrepreneurship appear even less appealing to the Negro.

Yet in spite of the difficulties, past and present, recited in this section, Negro entrepreneurship has occurred in the South. It has performed several important functions beyond the merely economic, though in terms of employment offered and markets served it has not

36. Thompson, *op. cit.*, p. 131.
37. *Wall Street Journal*, July 12, 1963.
38. One of the best treatments of this theme is William H. Nicholls' *Southern Tradition and Regional Progress* (Chapel Hill: University of North Carolina Press, 1960).

made important contributions. It is the task of the following section
to describe specific enterprises in a cross section of Negro business.

## Southern Negro Entrepreneurship Today

### Financial Institutions

The greatest entrepreneurial activity demonstrated by Negro
businessmen has been in the area of financial institutions. Here the
authors noted the most complete preparation for the entrepreneurial
role and the most astute leadership. These institutions include insurance companies, banks, and savings and loan associations.

#### *Insurance Companies*

Negro insurance companies visited by the authors ranged from
the special assessment type with assets of $1,500,000 to the largest
life company with present assets close to $77,000,000 and $337,000,000
insurance in force. A composite statement of member firms of the
National Insurance Association, Inc., based on forty-one companies
submitting the full statistical report as of September 1, 1961, shows
total assets of over $300,000,000. At present it is estimated that the
fifty-one N.I.A. companies have total admitted assets of close to $320,-
000,000 and total insurance in force of $1,900,000,000. Three major
Southern institutions included in this association were visited—North
Carolina Mutual, Durham, North Carolina; Atlanta Life, Atlanta,
Georgia; and Universal Life, Memphis, Tennessee. Figures from company records indicate changes in assets and life insurance in force as
follows:

Assets and Insurance in Force of Three Southern Life
Insurance Companies Visited

| Name of Company | ASSETS | | | |
|---|---|---|---|---|
| | Dec. 31, 1960 | Dec. 31, 1951 | Increase | Percent |
| North Carolina Mutual | $67,600,990 | $33,558,781 | $34,042,209 | 101.44 |
| Atlanta Life | 53,663,900 | 26,622,571 | 27,011,329 | 101.46 |
| Universal Life | 18,749,310 | 9,284,149 | 9,465,161 | 101.94 |
| | LIFE INSURANCE IN FORCE | | | |
| North Carolina Mutual | $277,186,658 | $164,540,211 | $112,646,447 | 68.46 |
| Atlanta Life | 176,192,665 | 145,721,897 | 30,470,768 | 20.91 |
| Universal Life | 116,220,219 | 73,594,999 | 42,625,220 | 57.91 |

These statistics indicate the growth of these life companies over a decade. However, the figures should be interpreted in the light of changes which have taken place in the Negro market over the last twenty years. Population has doubled since World War II, and income has increased more than 50 percent since 1950 and has more than tripled since 1940. There are more and more Negroes moving from lower to upper levels of income. At the same time their life expectancy is sixty-four years, over 40 percent greater than twenty years ago.[39]

The most notable example of entrepreneurship in life insurance is that of North Carolina Mutual. The Penrose definition of enterprise ". . . as a psychological predisposition on the part of individuals to take a chance in the hope of gain, and in particular, to commit effort and resources to speculative activity," does not characterize the motivation of the founders of this company.[40] A definite need existed, as most white companies simply refused to insure the lives of Negroes. Those which did offer insurance would not consider individual applications, and considered all Negroes as substandard risks justifying higher premiums. With the expenses of final illness and burial sapping small financial resources, the hat was often passed at the cemetery. Two persons in the city of Durham who were always called on for assistance were John Merrick, who operated a barber shop for whites, and a young Negro physician. To provide a systematic and organized approach to aid, they set out to organize an insurance company. These men had no knowledge of, or experience in, life insurance, although they did have some familiarity with fraternal organizations. Joining the two was C. C. Spaulding, bringing to the position of general manager his experience as a grocer.

During the company's early years trained personnel were not available, and trial and error was often the method. Establishing confidence in a financial institution owned, managed, and staffed by Negroes was a pioneering job. But the regulatory authorities approved the operation and claims were paid. Word of this spread, and the company was on its way to becoming the 185th largest among more than 1,400 in the United States. Employment is offered currently to 1,200 Negroes in more than 50 job categories such as those of executive, technician, lawyer, investment specialist, manager, programmer,

39. *1962 Statistical Abstract of the U.S.* and *1960 Census of Population, U.S. Summary, General Social and Economic Characteristics,* U.S. Department of Commerce, Bureau of the Census.
40. As quoted by Hickman, *op. cit.*, p. 76.

and salesman. Equipment and other facilities are all modern, including the latest in electronic data processing. The firm is at present engaged in building a new home office on the famous Duke four acres in Durham.

One of the major problems faced by the company through the years has been obtaining and retaining qualified personnel. One response has been home-office and regional schools in agency management and life-insurance selling. In addition, office personnel have been given special courses, and appropriate persons have been enrolled in leading schools in insurance.

Growth of the company can be attributed to various factors: improved training of the home office and field staff; new lines of insurance coverage; improved economic status of the Negro stemming from improved job opportunities for him; and merger with other companies. The company's image has continually strengthened, and as income and life expectancy of the Negro have increased, so has his demand for ordinary insurance to replace the weekly premium type.

The second largest Negro-owned life insurance company is located in Atlanta. It is a stock company, founded by another barber who catered to the white trade. Professor Hickman in his descriptions of entrepreneurship spoke of the eclectic concept of Gambs and Wertheimer, which includes ". . . good contacts with persons informed on business and political matters; discretion . . . ability to pick good lieutenants . . ." as characteristics of the true entrepreneur.[41] Such a description fits the founder of this company. It was in barbering that Mr. Herndon made many acquaintances with people of influence in the community who helped him. He was approached by a group of Negro ministers who had been administering a benevolent society which they wished him to take over. In 1905 the Atlanta Mutual Benefit Association was formed. It was a weekly premium operation, but by 1927 it was writing ordinary insurance too.

Influenced by the failure of Standard Life in Atlanta, Atlanta Life has striven to make safety its prime objective. Operating through sixty offices in eleven states, it employs close to 1,700 people in the field; and a career training course is now peopled almost entirely by college graduates. The administrative officers are highly competent in their specialties.

In Memphis, Tennessee, is another example of entrepreneurship in life insurance, headed by a man holding degrees from Fisk, the Uni-

41. Hickman, op. cit., p. 83.

versity of Michigan, and New York University. He is also president of the Tri-State Bank of that city. Unlike other Negro entrepreneurs, he has a business background furnished by his father, who was the founder. The latter had been active in business in Mississippi and moved to Memphis to form Universal Life. In 1958 the company purchased Excelsior Life of Dallas, and in 1961, it took up 83 percent of the stock of Louisiana Life of New Orleans. The company employs 122 persons in its home office and 650 in the field. Supplying money for mortgages on Negro housing projects, it has serviced hundreds of borrowers and lent millions of dollars, two-thirds of it federally insured.

As with other life companies, the major problem is finding the qualified personnel so essential to efficient operations. The president's approach is to locate young men with potential within his organization and to pay for their training in a leading institution such as Harvard or the University of Michigan. Life Office Management Training Programs are also used. Of note was this man's comment that Negro businesses suffer from trying to operate exclusively with Negro personnel.

Although these three enterprises are soundly managed and make profits, one can easily detect the persistence of uplift motives. Each company takes pride in the fact that it has contributed to better housing. "Because of the Negro financial institutions," the president of one company said, "you will find that Negroes are better housed in Durham, Atlanta, and Memphis than anywhere in the world." Not only does the Negro financial institution make mortgage loans, it calls to the attention of the white community the fact that the Negro is a good risk for a home mortgage. In addition to home development, one executive reported certain funds allocated for small churches, widows, or young men just starting careers. An example was cited of a young mechanic who had made application for a five-year $18,000 loan to finance a truck service station and small restaurant. Although the amount requested was larger than the company usually lends to an individual, it was approved because the officers felt this young man was deserving of help he might not otherwise be able to obtain.

In contrast to the vigorous life companies just described, the authors found in New Orleans eighteen small family-owned companies selling industrial insurance. One company executive talked at length about the problems of entrepreneurship in that city and about the insurance business in particular. With the trend to ordinary life one would wonder whether such companies can continue to survive, much less grow.

An interesting example of fraternal insurance is in a Southwestern city where a small burial society has grown to a membership of 25,000 and assets of $1.5 million. Insurance in force amounts to $20 million and over $100,000 in claims is paid yearly. Since this city has not had until recently a commercial bank, and only a small savings and loan, sources of funds such as this have played an important role in financing some Negro enterprises at reasonable rates of interest.

Negroes have also entered the casualty, fire, and fidelity insurance fields. Two examples will be offered. The entrepreneur behind the growth of the first company is a graduate of Morehouse College who started as an insurance agent. When his company was sold to a white firm, he developed some of his own brokerage connections and was later able to establish his own company. Deciding to try for some large accounts, he formed an alliance with the oldest established firm in the city. By serving as a subagent for them, he was able to learn the techniques and practices of the industry. By 1947, premium volume was over $300,000, and was thought to be sufficient to start the company referred to above. The president of the local commercial bank was consulted, along with other Negroes in the professions and business. Capital of $200,000 was raised in thirty days to meet the state requirement. Here is an example of the importance of mutual trust.

By 1958, the executives of the company saw that they should follow the trend to become a multiple-line firm. The public took up a stock issue of $300,000 rather quickly, and they are now the only multiple-line Negro company operating in the United States. Operations are carried on in four states, and resources are $1 million with an annual policy volume of over $800,000.

The president attributes his success to a number of factors. First, the support and cooperation received from the local bank aided immeasurably. This support went beyond providing financial entrepreneurship; it served to provide customers through its contacts in the business community. Because these people are in the service business, any prosperous Negro businessman is a potential customer for them all. Second, nearby Negro educational institutions were of indirect and direct benefit. Some of their professors have business interests and have brought their students into the businesses with them. The institutions have also provided a flow of educated trainees. Finally, the business climate, while not frankly encouraging to the growth of Negro enterprise, has not been repressive. There has even been the desire to have some Negro business succeed to prove lack of repression.

The rise of fraternal orders among Negroes created the need to provide bonding for those who were handling funds and who could not get coverage from existing companies. The firm visited in the fidelity insurance field was organized with the assistance of Negroes in the life insurance field. A stock company with $50,000 capital and $25,000 surplus was formed. The stock was distributed locally to organizations and individuals. The major problems have centered around this undercapitalization. By requirement, not more than ten percent could be committed to any one risk, which created a limit of about $7,000. As economic growth required larger amounts of insurance, the limitation kept the firm's volume low. While the firm can now write up to $27,000 on one risk, it cannot do business in other states because of limited capital. In fact, it had to withdraw from one state where it had been operating.

The president feels that the prospect of increasing capital is almost nil, since profits are restricted by insurance rates and most of the income is from premiums and not investments. With the trend away from fidelity into multiple-line firms, this company is now in the process of merging with a fire insurance firm in the city to make a multiple-line company with a minimum capital of $750,000. It will, in time, become a subsidiary of a Negro life insurance company. With consummation of the merger the president believes the company will be better able to compete in the developing situation where patronage will be on the basis of service and not on race.

### Commercial Banks

"The Negro banking industry has long been a source both of race pride and race difficulty. The banker . . . symbolizes the successful businessman of the community, and the race, anxious to demonstrate the extent of its success in the business world, has looked hopefully upon its banking efforts."[42] While there have been failures, beginning with the famous Freedmen's Savings Bank, a bank for Negroes managed by whites, the experience has not been unlike that of white banks. Reasons for these failures are those common to all types of banks: speculation, over-capitalization, stock manipulation, mismanagement, and misappropriation.

42. Kinzer and Sagarin, *op. cit.*, p. 102.

According to what the authors found in three commercial banks visited, such reasons for failure are not likely to characterize them. The president of each is well educated, knowledgable in financial matters, and surrounded with competent executives. Generally conservative practices seem to prevail.

As in the case of insurance, Negro banking has aimed at satisfying a definite need—to provide a range of credit assistance to Negroes. An important side effect has been to force a reconsideration of loan policies in white banks which welcome Negro depositors but are generally not interested in extending loan services. There has been no real competition from white banks for Negro business loans; a survey of major Atlanta banks revealed but few Negro business loans on their books.

In most instances the same people who were founders of the insurance companies were also instrumental in starting the banks. In some cases the banks were created as depositories for the insurance companies. This connection helped to win public confidence, lack of which was a problem inherited from early failures.

Despite marked progress and growth, the fact is that Negro banking today is still an extremely small part of the American banking industry and can service only a small proportion of American Negroes. For example, the ten Negro banks in 1960 had combined resources of $53 million, which is about the size of the Bank of Georgia alone, and only one thirty-third of one percent of total assets of all banks in the United States. But an individual bank such as Citizens Trust in Atlanta today has more assets than all Negro banks combined had in 1933. The past twenty years have seen extraordinary growth. In 1940, the eight commercial banks owned and operated by Negroes had total assets of only $5 million. Over the same twenty-year period, the total assets of all U.S. commercial banks went from $68 billion to almost $200 billion. The problem has been in founding new institutions. If the premise is accepted that no business community can achieve its full business potential without adequate banking facilities, it is easily seen that the Negro business community has suffered from this situation.[43] On the other hand, bank growth is based on the number and strength of business customers. One might ask which will come first in the Negro community.

43. These figures taken from H. Naylor Fitzhugh, ed., *Problems and Opportunities Confronting Negroes in the Field of Business* (Washington: U.S. Department of Commerce, 1962), p. 74.

The newest entrepreneurial attempt in banking was found in Houston, Texas. There a young Harvard Business School graduate and professor at Texas Southern University has sparked the organization of a commercial bank. Local Negroes of means, and a number of persons from the white educational community, have assisted. With a broad base of community support, the $500,000 initial capital was quickly oversubscribed. The building is almost finished, and even those who had opposed the idea have bought stock.[44]

Houston had no Negro commercial bank, and Negroes found it difficult to obtain financing. One aspect of the problem as expressed by the new bank's president is a lack of communication between the white and Negro business communities. He recognized that while race is a factor, large banks deal with large customers, and it happens that most Negro business is small. In his opinion, the business interests of Houston's 250,000 Negroes cannot reach their full potential without adequate banking facilities, which until recently have been lacking. Although the primary motivation behind establishing the bank was to provide working capital financing, it is not intended to serve Negroes alone. Rather, it will cater to the total financial needs of the racially mixed area where it is located. Many of the local businessmen are stockholders and will naturally take their business to the new bank.

Again, the barrier to organization of the enterprise has been locating persons with training and experience in banking. Negro banks in other cities can ill afford to release some of their trained employees in whom they have made a heavy investment. The problem is made all the more acute by the fact that Negroes have not been in responsible managerial positions in banks other than those operated by Negroes. The number of Negro savings and loan associations has grown faster than the number of commercial banks, and some people might be recruited from them.

### Savings and Loan Associations

The increasing significance of the savings and loan association in Negro financial circles is fairly apparent because of the enormity of the Negro housing problem. There are approximately forty-five savings and loan associations in the United States with assets totaling about $300 million. According to the Department of Commerce, in 1947 there were only twenty-five with combined assets of $9–$10 mil-

44. The Wall Street Journal, Oct. 25, 1962, p. 1.

lion. Besides demonstrable need, there are other reasons accounting for this growth. First, the recent success of Negro-managed financial institutions has led to increased confidence in them, and good management has justified this confidence. The increase in the level of Negro income generally has made home ownership a more feasible solution to housing pressures. Regulation has contributed to success. Being federally chartered, these associations are required to hold membership in, and are supervised by, the Federal Home Loan Bank System and the Federal Savings and Loan Insurance Corporation. Furthermore, since charters are from the federal level, possible discrimination at the state level is by-passed. Federal examinations have been welcomed by the Negro savings and loan executives as instilling confidence and assuring proper operation.

Three associations were visited. An outstanding example is an association which began operating with $1,500 of the original $15,000 permanent capital subscribed by the board of directors, composed of fifteen of the city's leading Negro business and professional men. Since the granting of a federal charter a decade ago, shareholders have received $700,000 in dividends; and loans have been made in the metropolitan area of over $12 million. Many whites are counted among the 5,000 shareholders, indicating public confidence. In 1963, a branch office was opened in another part of the city, and by the end of that year assets amounted to over $10 million. Loans of $8.6 million were distributed as follows: 39.4 percent for home purchases, 29.2 percent for refinancing, 26.8 percent for home construction, and the remaining 4.6 percent for other purposes.

Another example is an association located in a smaller city, but with equivalent resources and 30 percent of deposits coming from whites in the area. The president of the company, a native of Atlanta and a graduate of Atlanta University, started work as an agent for an insurance company in his home city. He moved to take over management of the association in 1935, and attributes much of its success to the coordination and cooperation between the local bank and insurance company. There is some competition from white banks and savings and loan associations in this city, but it is not bitter because the profit potential is not great. They do not take up each other's paper. He noted, however, that the white banks' reaction to the Negro-managed savings and loan company has progressed from curiosity to concern to competition.

One of the most remarkable examples of entrepreneurship was

found in a large Southern city where Negro business revolves around one family. Interests include: a life insurance company with over $50 million of insurance in force; a federal savings and loan association with assets of $5 million accumulated in three and one-half years; a chain of funeral homes throughout the state valued at $250,000; a cemetery worth $200,000; apartment houses containing more than seventy units; a realty and investment company with assets over $300,000; a business college which trains personnel to run these far-flung enterprises; and a modern motel and restaurant. Recently completed is a million-dollar building which houses some of these enterprises. Employment is afforded over 360 persons with an annual payroll of close to $800,000. These business interests are reputed to serve over two-thirds of the Negro population of the state.

In contrast to many of the examples cited so far, the president and founder of this "empire" had little formal education. Furthermore, he has catered to a totally segregated clientele. His accomplishments could not be duplicated today. For him a strong motivating force has been a fervent desire to provide employment for Negroes, seeing economic strength as one avenue to improve the Negro's position in the South.

### Non-Financial Enterprises

The preceding section attests to the success of Negro entrepreneurship in banking and insurance, where Negroes have moved to fill the needs created by the general unwillingness of white institutions to trust Negroes in financial matters. Any Negro-business census performed today in selected Southern cities along the lines of Pierce's study of twenty years ago would still reveal the great bulk of such business to encompass very small concerns in retail trade and services, employing from two to ten people, with assets and gross annual sales of less than $20,000.[45] Such establishments, located mostly in neighborhood areas, make up about 94 percent of total Negro businesses, with financial institutions comprising another 4 percent. Only 2 percent of total establishments thus remain to include such activities as printing and publishing, manufacturing and distribution, or construction and real estate. It is in these areas where evidence of entrepreneurship can be found.

One might at once ask why there is so little business success out-

45. Fitzhugh, *op. cit.,* pp. 20–29.

side the general area of finance. In 1917, Brown noted that "corporate business success of any appreciable proportions calls for individuals with liberal intellectual culture, efficient business training, and keen business sense."[46] These he found lacking among Negroes, a situation which has not changed greatly in the intervening forty-five years. Frazier has complained that in past studies of Negro business there has been failure to state the basic reason for the lack of business success. In his view, it is the "fundamental sociological fact that the Negro lacks a business tradition. . . . Neither the tradition of the gentleman nor his peasant heritage had provided the Negro with this outlook on the world."[47] Even if a tradition and training roughly comparable to that possessed by whites be assumed, the size and distribution of the market served would remain a problem. The patterns of segregation, in both the North and the South, would still preclude a market penetration sufficient to support businesses which could make important contributions to economic development in terms of value added, sales, or any other measure which might be chosen. White firms are paying increased attention to the so-called Negro market.[48] There is a definite disadvantage in dealing with a theoretical ten percent of the population which is in the lower-income brackets. It is not so apparent in the retail and service industries where patrons are concentrated. It would be immediately encountered in manufacturing for a racial segment of the national market.[49] "Where Negro business cannot base its appeal on convenience of locality, or on custom and law, but on competition, the Negro-owned store obtains practically none of the white trade, but also obtains only a fraction of the available Negro trade."[50] Nationwide competition in the general market is even more difficult.

46. Brown, *op. cit.*, p. 11.
47. Frazier, *op. cit.*, p. 165.
48. Recent references may be found in *Business Week*, May 26, 1962, p. 76; in *Time*, February 9, 1962, p. 80; the *New York Times*, July 1, 1962, p. 1F; and a special staff report prepared by Jack L. Cooper of the Federal Reserve Bank of Atlanta entitled "The Negro Market: Reality or Illusion?"
49. There is little empirical evidence to demonstrate that Negro consumption patterns differ markedly from white, aside from some specialized cosmetics.
50. Kinzer and Sagarin, *op. cit.*, pp. 9–10. This is pointed up in the effects of the boycott of white establishments during desegregation campaigns. Some store owners in downtown Albany, Ga., reported a 40 percent decline in sales, some of this undoubtedly due to whites avoiding areas of racial disturbance. This same report also noted an increase in business in Negro stores to such an extent as to encourage further investment by Negroes in these businesses. *Wall Street Journal*, Sept. 6, 1962, p. 1.

*Manufacturing and Distribution*

In spite of the barriers to success just recounted, examples of Negro entrepreneurship in manufacturing and distribution were found by the researchers. Probably one of the most interesting demonstrations of self-help can be found in Clinton, N.C., an area seriously affected by the unemployment or underemployment typical of so many Southern towns in agricultural areas. A sewing company was organized in 1961 and is operating in two modern plants turning out children's clothing. A Negro physician and other leading Negroes of the town were the organizers, abetted by local support of a stock issue now held 60 percent by whites and 40 percent by Negroes. Over one hundred girls are employed in the production work, and active day-to-day management is in the hands of a Northern white man familiar with the business. Money has been borrowed from the local white savings and loan association, and the employees have a stock purchase plan. The marketing problem is minimized, since the firm acts as a subcontractor and does not have to compete in the primary market.

Some Negro manufacturing has been centered around the so-called Negro market. The best-known example is cosmetics, particularly hair preparations. Two firms were visited which differed in some respects. The owner of one came out of the rice paddies of Louisiana and managed to secure an education as a pharmacist. On weekends, he packed his mixtures in a car and sold them house-to-house on plantations. His next step was to attract agents to sell the products while he devoted his time to manufacturing. The operation at present is relatively small, carried on in outdated premises. The machinery seems modern, but the packaging is not. Most of the quarter-million in annual sales goes to Louisiana, Texas, and Mississippi, though there are active accounts in Cleveland, St. Louis, and Chicago, and on the West Coast. Distribution is principally through chain stores. Though some of the products would likely be used only by Negroes, a major portion of the line is in general use, and the owner estimates that 40 percent of his sales go to whites.

The other firm is thirty-five years old, but much more modern in appearance, in terms of both product line and place of business. The present owner is a son of the founder, who had also invested in a newspaper, an insurance company, and a construction firm. This man had gone to Fisk and then to Columbia University, where he had learned about preparing mixtures basic to cosmetics. His son, the present owner, had also gone to college, but was not prepared for business management. He admitted to the authors that he had made mistakes and thus was learning the hard way—through experience. He made an interesting comment to the effect that the average white man has seen and known a businessman; the average Negro has not. In locating his new factory and office out of the Negro business district, and in hiring white salesmen, he has tried to break out of the category of "Negro businessman," which for him implies severe limitations.

The two principal problems faced by this young entrepreneur are staffing and finance. He admits that he is a one-man organization with no depth in the executive ranks. The ready-made Negro executive is just not available for hire, some of the best having already been hired by white firms trying to exploit the Negro market. Even he had been offered the job of sales manager for the Negro market for a large Northern cosmetics firm.[51] He refused the offer, not wishing to have his activities circumscribed in this way. As he now operates, he competes on a national basis with the giants of the industry. In many places where his products are sold, however, it is not known by the dealers and their clientele that they come from a Negro firm.

To compete on a national basis requires substantial capital, not only for manufacturing facilities extensive enough to handle volume orders at low cost, but for money to carry a large inventory of raw materials and shipments in transit. The short-term commercial loans needed to carry the latter two items would not be difficult for a white firm with similar markets to secure. Two things make it difficult for a Negro firm. First, white institutions in the South have not been interested in Negro loans, even though they are familiar with the financing of enterprises engaged in manufacturing and wholesale distribution. Second, the Negro institutions are, on the other hand, often unfamiliar with these lines of business and are accordingly cautious about accepting such risks. This cosmetics firm has therefore been financed in a piecemeal fashion, borrowing from banks, friends, family, or the Small Business Administration. Here is a business, then, suffering from certain handicaps while trying to clear the barriers of segregation and to meet the full force of competition from established white businesses.[52]

51. Harvey C. Russell, vice-president (special markets) of Pepsi-Cola Co., is one of the best known examples of Negro executives with white firms.
52. Other Negro manufacturing enterprises embracing brooms, mattresses,

The researchers also visited firms engaged in the distribution of cosmetic products. Though originally designed for a racial market, the product lines now have general appeal, as pointed out above. In one city, this type of business is carried on by a college graduate who has also earned a degree at Oxford University and taught at Fisk University. His time has been divided between his business and civic activities. While serving as president of the Negro business association, he was active in organizing the first Negro commercial bank in his city. The distributorship now has eight offices, fifteen salaried people, and about three hundred commission salesmen are employed.

A strong motivating force behind the entrepreneurial activities of this man has been the desire to create jobs for Negro students coming out of college. While a professor, he wanted to prove to himself that this could be done. Many students are currently employed, and one college graduate earns $12,000 per year with the organization. In turning from the teaching profession, this man started working as a "troubleshooter" for the manufacturer of his present line of products. He wanted to learn the business from the ground up—not only sales but also administration. In time, he asked for a distributorship, managed to borrow some money, and settled in a growing Southern city. The eight offices were opened in eight years. Capital has been a perennial problem in spite of the demonstrable success of the business. Lack of Negro-operated banking facilities has been a factor, and was a spur to this entrepreneur's activity in bringing these into being.

This enterprise does not cater exclusively to the Negro market; two white salesmen are employed to sell to the white dealers. Integration can only help this business, as even more of the general market can then be tapped. There are still potential customers of both manufacturers and distributors of these products who will not purchase from a Negro firm, and various measures are taken to hide this identity. Employing white salesmen to call on white accounts is one. "Forced identity" is also avoided by using a "blind" Fifth Avenue address on advertising and promotional literature.

Another firm in cosmetics distribution has from 1,500 to 2,000 retail stores as customers in a three-state area in the Deep South. It is in the form of a partnership. One man has supplied most of the

plastic apparel, shirts, shoes, and meat products have existed or are at present in operation, but these were not visited. For one report see *Wall Street Journal,* May 4, 1962, p. 1.

money, the other the know-how gained from experience as a pharmacist in a Northern city. The latter started out in sheet-metal work and drafting, but found discrimination in the North in that line. He turned to pharmacy school and with this education was able to secure employment, first with a small drug chain and then with a very large one. Moving back to the South in 1961, he rejoined the firm and has been responsible for a major increase in the volume of business done. Experience with the large drug chain equipped him to activate and then enlarge a training program for the commission salesmen, who now number about twenty.

Operations differ from the firm described above in that retail drug stores and beauty shops are an important part of the business in the large city where the firm is located. Another important difference lies in the attitude toward dependence on a racial market. The retail and service activities located in the Negro neighborhoods obviously focus attention on the racial aspects of the business, but racial loyalty is also viewed as some insulation from the full force of competition. Added to this is the greater availability of educated employees. All are high school graduates, and a few have had some higher education. To a degree, this may represent underemployment of certain talents, but with other avenues of employment closed to those who do not prepare for the professions within the segregated community, these opportunities appear attractive and can be financially rewarding.[53] In sum, the present orientation of both the firms in cosmetics distribution is toward the Negro customer, but, in the case of the first, integration is welcomed as an opportunity for business expansion rather than as a precursor of stiff competition.

In the general area of distribution, another example is a firm which holds a franchise from one of the large tire manufacturers. The principal in this firm is a college graduate possessing a master's degree who had at one time been the principal of a school. His firm is now enjoying gross sales of nearly a quarter-million dollars per year and is about to undergo expansion into another district. When he asked for his own franchise in the upper-class Negro district, know-how had to be joined to capital. The latter was obtained by privately selling an issue of stock which brought in $26,000. The business was started on a cash basis, but as it grew, credit was extended. This

53. The element of underemployment is pointed up in "A Statement on the Economic Costs of Racial Discrimination in Employment" presented to the Joint Economic Committee of the Congress in September 1962 by the Council of Economic Advisers.

required more capital, and bonds bearing a six-percent coupon were sold and later converted into others bearing seven percent when some difficulty was encountered meeting interest payments. The tire manufacturer extended a line of credit, and friends of the owner granted further loans. Recently the company has been approved for a SBA loan. Almost all avenues of finance have thus been exploited.

On the strength of the franchise with the national tire firm, even local white banks have extended credit; so this entrepreneur does not now regard financing as a major problem. He admitted to paying some very high interest rates at certain junctures in the history of the business, but was inclined to regard this as a problem of all small business. Perhaps this opinion is colored by the fact that his franchise lends his business an image of legitimacy in the eyes of the white business community not enjoyed by other Negro businesses of equal stature. For him, the major problems seem to be getting and retaining competent personnel and the development of an understanding by the community in general that a Negro business can be successful, well-run, dependable in its dealings with the public, and a contributor to the welfare of the community.

This section can be concluded by briefly mentioning some occupations in which success has been almost wholly dependent on the maintenance of segregation. These are undertaking, food service, and innkeeping. The first has undoubtedly been the most profitable. This is because of the heavy emphasis placed on a decent burial, one often far beyond what the deceased's income level would warrant. However, the many burial societies, often originally connected with fraternal orders, and other forms of insurance provide a firm base on which this industry can operate. The authors found in several instances that operation of a funeral parlor or a casket business was the first in a series of business enterprises, and that the owners of such establishments serve as private sources of capital for other would-be entrepreneurs in the community.

Eating and drinking places, along with cleaning-and-pressing "clubs," have long been the most numerous of small businesses operated by Negroes. The great majority of the former are uninviting. However, two places visited in the research rival comparable white establishments. One was started by two brothers, one of whom had had relevant experience. Together they had two-thirds of the money needed to get into business, and were able to borrow the remainder from the local Negro bank. In 1959 new modern premises were occupied. When a white bank proved "slow" to provide financing, a Negro bank made 67 percent of the construction costs available. Expansion has followed, and plans have been made to go into inn-keeping and possibly other businesses.

### Construction and Real Estate

Nowhere is the Negro's need more desperate than in the field of housing.[54] Expansion in the South, as in the North, has been direct-ly tied to patterns of segregation in many ways which will not be enlarged upon here. Suffice it to say that "segregated money" for home mortgages and the opportunities for profit from real estate specula-tion have made home ownership for the Negro a much more expensive item in his market basket than it is for whites similarly situated. The growth of Negro financial institutions gives promise of substantial improvement over abuses of the past. Even large white insurance companies are beginning to remove racial restrictions on the mortgages they will buy. Added to this is the executive order on discrimination in housing. The president of an Atlanta savings and loan company stated that "for both economic and social reasons, we don't make loans to colored people moving into all-white or transitional neighbor-hoods. We owe it to our stockholders not to risk their money on such properties. We also have to consider impairment of the value of the mortgages we already hold in those areas."[55] If existing white institu-tions will not finance the expansion of available housing for Negroes, then Negro institutions must do it or new housing must be built.

The effective approach to desegregating money seems to be through competition. Wherever one finds a Negro financial complex, one finds comparable white institutions making loans to Negroes. Upon the organization of a Negro commercial bank in Houston, white lenders in that city conceded that the bank would affect them. "We're not admitting it publicly, but we're beginning to make an effort to show our Negro customers that we're interested in lending to them," said the vice president of a white savings and loan association. "In the past we haven't been interested in making mortgage loans to Negroes."[56]

Adequate financing is the essential prerequisite of construction activity. Some has been accomplished by Negroes in selected South-

54. Note the article "Race and Residence" in the *Wall Street Journal,* Aug. 13, 1962, p. 1.
55. *Wall Street Journal,* Oct. 25, 1962, p. 1.
56. *Ibid.*

ern cities, though all the concerns visited will not be discussed. One gentleman, now retired, produced $4–$5 million in construction in one city, and had at one time a payroll of $1,500 per week. His parents were born slaves but had college educations, and he went to Hampton Institute, where he came under the influence of Booker T. Washington. After World War I, he worked in Philadelphia as a laborer and later as a construction superintendent, and thus acquired experience. Returning to the South in 1921, he worked hard and received financing from a Northern life insurance company. He stated that, during the Depression in his city, no Negroes who owned homes lost them. Even granting the qualifying assumption that Negro home-ownership was limited at that time to the relatively well-to-do, it is still a notable record. It is evidence of the place which Negroes accord home-ownership in their scale of values, and the consequent strength of the desire to repay, one of the principal factors upon which a lender depends.

One active construction firm is operated by two men both of whom have college educations. One graduated from Tuskegee Institute, the other from the University of Chicago. They formed a partnership in order to be able to bid on large contracts such as college buildings and housing projects. The Tuskegee graduate gained his experience with a New York firm following World War II and then returned South to go into business for himself. After ten years, he joined the Chicago graduate, who had been teaching mechanical drawing in high school.

For this firm, the major problems are again the familiar ones of financing and staffing. The former is minimized in the financial climate in which they operate; the local Negro financial institutions have taken $25 million in mortgages over the past ten years. Insurance companies will not lend on unimproved property, and so obtaining construction loans and making the required bonds are the financial hurdles. The greatest need is for qualified employees. There are reportedly fewer skilled Negro carpenters, cement finishers, and brick masons than there were some years ago. One contributing factor is the progress of unionization in the South. Many unions have been segregation-minded, and one author writing a decade ago stated that "a really successful organizational drive would write finis to Negro prospects in southern manufacturing for many years to come."[57] The partners feel that insufficient emphasis is placed on vocational educa-

57. Dewey, "Negro Employment," *Jour. of Pol. Ec.*, Aug., 1952, p. 290.

tion in the Negro high schools. Only two schools in their city offer mechanical training. However, as Dewey pointed out: "So long as individual Negroes cannot gain admission into white work groups, vocational training is both wasteful and a cruel hoax, unless it takes the form of providing Negro work groups to particular employers."[58] The firm under discussion is encouraging the first Negroes to enter the state technical institute and offers them jobs during the vacation periods. There are only two or three registered Negro architects in this same city, but the company was hoping to hire one, in addition to a structural engineer and an estimator. With the addition of these skills, they will be fully qualified to bid on city jobs. Recently a large multiple-housing project, a part of urban renewal, was awarded to the firm in competitive bidding.

More in real estate management than in construction are two other firms visited. One has entrepreneured a development of thirty-two individual homes built mostly with Negro labor by Negro contractors. It has also purchased, and is providing the management for, a housing project of 267 units valued at $1,250,000 in a neighboring city. The other firm is active in developing a shopping center and building residences. With favorable Negro financing as a start, the single-unit development was financed by working through the FHA and local institutions. The other project was handled by borrowing enough to purchase the equity with the property as security for a mortgage on the remainder. Both firms are, however, one-man shows, though some younger help is being developed.

In one city, the problem is not so much availability of money as it is a flow of qualified borrowers. The people have low salaries and wages, and the relative certainty of continuous employment must stand behind home purchase. Urban renewal is currently underway in many places in the South, particularly where slum conditions have existed in Negro areas. It will have both favorable and unfavorable results as far as individual businesses are concerned. Some small, underfinanced units will probably not reopen, while other new ones will emerge. In any event, it is an opportunity for local Negro finance and know-how to demonstrate their capabilities and resourcefulness.[59]

The developer in the other city who was interviewed reported less favorable financing for real estate development. A native of New

58. *Ibid.*, p. 292.
59. It has been recently announced, for example, that the Citizens Trust Co. of Atlanta will develop a multiple-story office building, parking garage, and other facilities in a block of urban renewal property in Atlanta.

York who attended two institutions of higher learning, he has succeeded in borrowing a substantial sum from a local white bank, a success attributable partly to his political connections. He reports the local Negro bank as too conservative. There is a ready market for homes in the $9,000 to $10,000 price range. Whites are not particularly interested in Negro risks, often preferring to have Negroes continue renting from them. In an attempt to counter these rather typical attitudes, this developer worked with Negroes to point up the necessity of meeting obligations on time, since many delinquencies were for lateness rather than failure to pay. He also investigated the credit of many with the intention of helping them qualify for VA and FHA loans. He talked with the local FHA representative and managed to prove that Negroes could qualify, and will pay on their homes. One of the local savings and loan associations was requested to check its Negro contracts, and a low percentage of foreclosures was found.

In spite of this progress, the interviewee was not very optimistic about the future of purely Negro entrepreneurship in his city. There is not enough cooperative spirit among local Negroes, perhaps because of the failure of some fraternal orders and poor leadership in the past. Integration of Negroes into white firms was seen as a more likely method of "hatching" men with entrepreneurial instincts than a strictly Negro business structure.

### Newspapers and Printing

The service trades of printing and publishing have afforded the last area of entrepreneurial activity to be discussed. Principals or employees in five newspapers in four cities were interviewed, as were owners of two printing establishments in two cities. These establishments are small, but one of them, doing an annual volume of $100,000, is the third largest of the fifteen print shops in the city where it is located. It was started by two men who had studied at Hampton Institute and another who had been a journeyman printer for a newspaper in a neighboring city where all three had once been employed. Printing was begun to supplement a newspaper business which was failing because the children of the former owner had no experience or taste for the business. They wished to sell and were willing to be paid from the receipts of the new owners as they came in. The newspaper ceased publication and the printing business was expanded.

Again, financing was the initial problem. The three had no collateral, the business was at low ebb, and only small sums from individuals could be obtained. Hiring has been selective, three people have been trained, and eleven qualified people are now employed. Expansion of the business into other commercial lines is under way, and there is no dependence on a single customer or type of work. The owners view progressing integration not as a threat, but as a help, since a larger market would be opened to them.

The other printing concern was started in 1921. The present owner, a graduate of Bishop College, taught at the local Negro university and operated a print shop to do the university's work. By 1953, with the help of an RFC loan after World War II, the firm had expanded its operations so as to require his full attention. There has been constant reinvestment of earnings. The Negro community provides only about 25 percent of the business volume, mostly church bulletins, an undependable source of business. With sales volume running at less than $40,000 per year, and with the obvious requirement of competition with better-established white firms, growth of this enterprise seems limited. At one time the owner considered a stock issue, to be sold principally to customers, but the idea was abandoned.

One of the most interesting people interviewed was the retired owner of a weekly paper in a large Southern city. He started out in an insurance company and put out a house organ which became a weekly paper when he left the insurance business. Thus in 1924 a Negro paper made its first appearance since Reconstruction. The white papers would not carry news about Negroes except that concerned with their crimes. There was, and is, a need for a place where Negro social, fraternal, school, church, and athletic news can be adequately covered, and not just in the sensational way it is often handled in both the Negro and white press. Only recently have white papers in the South begun to devote any space to such news.

A recognized *raison d'etre* of the Negro press is protest. This was the theme of the publisher of another paper begun in 1924 as a partnership and later purchased by one of the partners for less than $500. Having hired the printers and trained the office staff, he now employs twelve people. With circulation running about 23,000, it is estimated that 100,000 people see the paper. It perhaps wields more influence than any other Negro paper in the state.

Competition from Negro counterparts has been the spur even in newspaper publishing. Some white papers are now printing Negro news, particularly sports, though they have not yet gone to protest editorials nor to publishing pictures of Negro "society" figures. In one city, there are two Negro papers, one of quite recent origin, the other dating back to before the Depression, when it was founded by a graduate of the Harvard Law School. With money built up from his law practice, he established a chain of six papers in the state. Currently, sixty-five people in two cities are employed to contribute to issuing the paper twice a week for statewide distribution.

The other paper in this same city is owned by a former employee of the first paper who built up some capital and decided to reenter the business. The decision was based on two factors. He felt, first, that there was need for a fresh editorial policy, and, second, he proposed to use a less expensive printing process. Unable to obtain backing from white financial sources, he turned to individual Negroes of wealth in the community, who helped him launch the new enterprise. It will be interesting to see if both papers can survive the competition.

In this section, the objective has been to fill in with some richness of detail and illustrations of entrepreneurship the discussion on requirements and barriers presented earlier. It is to be hoped that now the motives, beginnings, and sometimes tortuous paths which have led to success in various industries in several locations can be appreciated. Evidence of the competitive struggle for industrial development is constantly before us. One could hardly have expected the Negro to keep pace, and his accomplishments are therefore all the more remarkable. In the concluding section, there will be an opportunity to point out some recent developments, to appraise Negro entrepreneurship in the South, and to make some predictions of its future course.

### Negro Entrepreneurship in the South: Retrospect and Prospect

Race and segregation have created a sharp cleavage between white and Negro business communities. However, Southern Negro entrepreneurship cannot be regarded as an independent phenomenon. Both communities have been handicapped by the dislocations associated with the imperative transition from an impoverished agricultural economy to the increased income levels promised by industrialization. Almost all research on the Southern economy emphasizes the many areas in which the South lags behind the national average, particularly when the measures are on a per capita basis. It can be no secret that the present pattern of industrialization is not calculated to remedy these disparities, since the nation's future is on the technological frontiers, and these are only beginning to appear in the South. Manufacturing in the South is mostly in non-durables such as textiles, lumber, food, and apparel; the demand for these products is comparatively income-inelastic.[60] These are the fields in which local firms have engaged. The measurements of the Southern economy are further depressed by the inclusion of large numbers of educationally and economically depressed Negroes. Southern Negro entrepreneurship is certainly unequal to the task of greatly improving the economic status of any significant percentage of these people, but the preceding sections have pointed to the contributions made.

In spite of attempts to prove otherwise, the fact remains that the Negro is largely imitative of the community in which he lives, in terms of both culture and economic activity.[61] Considering the traditional attitudes towards business careers in the South, in both white and Negro communities, it is not surprising that Negroes with sufficient background and education have not been attracted to business in large numbers. Hickman surmised that the entrepreneurial function carried on by whites might be different in the Southern setting "if only because a different set of alternatives, constraints, and pressures confront the entrepreneur. It is perhaps even more evident that this existence of a dual society drastically constricts opportunities for entrepreneurship on the part of Negroes in the South. To be sure, entrepreneurship is possible within the separated Negro business community and Negro market . . . [but] entrepreneurship in the broader economic community of the South is blocked for the Negro."[62] One of the tasks of this paper has been to examine these statements.

On the surface they seem to be justifiable generalizations, and space has been devoted to elaborating on the latter one. At the same time, the burden of the research was to seek out and investigate not only those examples which indicate that entrepreneurship has been successful "in the separate community and market," but those which serve to break down the notion that "entrepreneurship in the broader economic community is blocked." True it is that many barriers remain, but a breakdown is occurring. The summer of 1963 witnessed some swift moves in this direction.[63]

60. Hickman, *op. cit.*, p. 97.
61. For a recent treatment of this theme see "The Ivy League Negro," *Esquire,* August 1963.
62. Hickman, *op. cit.*, p. 106.
63. *The Wall Street Journal* on June 6, 13, 19 and July 3, 1963, had lead articles with the following titles: "Desegregated Jobs," "Jobs for Negroes," "Federal Racial Push," and "Negroes Wanted." On June 15 and 22, 1963,

At this point one may well ask the question: What has been the contribution of Southern Negro entrepreneurship, and in what directions do further developments lie? Certainly the greatest contribution has been the amelioration of some of the conditions under which the Negro people have lived over the years. The "social service" motive has been strongly behind the financial enterprises, for example. It is true that these avenues of opportunity were open because comparable white institutions generally refused to offer such services to Negroes. Yet the availability of financing, corporate or personal, for reasonable risks at reasonable rates has been a major factor in permitting segments of the Negro community to progress in accord with their capabilities. Insurance has not only removed the fear of being buried in a potter's field, but has made possible investment in projects calculated to add to the betterment of widely scattered Negro communities. Thrift has been encouraged in a people whose natural propensity to consume is very high, and has made available funds for housing, churches, private recreational facilities, and the setting-up in practice of the various kinds of young Negro professionals so badly needed.

For budding and growing business enterprises, good, sound advice has often accompanied the lending of funds, though in certain areas, such as manufacturing, the Negro financial institutions are less well prepared. One banker told the authors that often the notion held by the prospective borrower of what comprises a reasonable business opportunity is naive. To put it simply: "Everyone's got to eat" does not automatically mean that a restaurant in a given location will succeed. The bankers have impressed on their clients the need for reinvestment and for resisting the natural urge to make a little money, put it in a piece of property, and become a landlord. With housing pressures for both businesses and families severe, owning property seems like the royal road to economic independence. Almost without exception, the Negro businesses of any substance visited by the researchers were the result of heavy reinvestment and other conservative financial policies, usually coupled with abstemious habits on the part of the entrepreneurs themselves.

One of the most direct contributions of the financial institutions has been to afford employment opportunities to well-educated men and women who would otherwise have added to the substantial

---

*Business Week* had the following articles: "Negroes Push Harder for Construction Jobs," and "Crashing Gates to Better Jobs." Improved job opportunities are a first step to the acquisition of know-how, one of the important requirements for entrepreneurship.

amount of underemployment which exists in this racial group, not only in the South, but in the nation as a whole.[64] Not only is employment offered, but the young Negro is given an image of what it means to succeed in business and is thereby encouraged to go into it instead of one of the professions. This is not to imply that the professions are overcrowded. Quite the contrary. Not only are more doctors and dentists needed, but, for business to flourish, lawyers and certified public accountants are prime requisites. The point is that Negro businessmen can provide employment opportunities pending integration and the gradual elimination of discrimination in employment. This asset will assist in halting the migration of the better qualified from the South and thus build up a large cadre of modestly trained people who can serve as a way of moving the Negro into the mainstream. This was one of the themes of the National Conference on Small Business sponsored in Washington in 1961 by the U.S. Department of Commerce.[65]

The once-held position that the economic salvation of the Negro lay in the development of his own business empire was either naive or deliberately misleading, though the Black Muslims seem entirely willing to go that way. Small business of the personal service types can prosper, as has been depicted above, and add a good deal to the communities touched by its payrolls and employment. Occasionally, as in cosmetics, Negro business can deal with the national market with marked success while not depending wholly on its racial components. Yet the stock of capital, in the wider sense of the term, is insufficient to warrant prediction of rapid acceleration in the growth of Negro business. On the other hand, there may be a sizable expansion in the number of Negro entrepreneurs. Is this a paradox?

The "stock of capital" referred to includes not only financial resources, but also such things as appropriately educated graduates of both colleges and secondary schools, a fund of generally held knowhow in the skilled trades, ancillary services connected with law and accountancy, and more widely distributed abilities in the field of sales. To this must be added sufficient mutual trust to permit larger aggregations of capital and the corporate form of business, and a culture which recognizes, respects, and rewards legitimate business success.

64. It is estimated that "If non-whites had the same educational levels as whites and if the economy fully utilized their education, GNP today might be perhaps 3.2 percent higher. This amounts to about $17 billion at today's levels of GNP." Report to the Joint Economic Committee, *op. cit.*

65. H. Naylor Fitzhugh, ed., *Problems and Opportunities Confronting Negroes in the Field of Business* (Washington, D.C.: U.S. Department of Commerce, 1962).

Recent evidence of progress is seen in Washington, D.C., where the city's wealthier Negroes are being pressed by leaders "to invest in Negro businesses and back what would be the first Negro-owned savings and loan association there." In Detroit the Group on Advanced Leadership requires members to put up ten dollars each for a "redevelopment corporation" to spur "capital formation among Negroes."[66] Too many enterprises have been family affairs in the Negro community, and management has often deteriorated when passed to the second or third generation. Cole notes that "biological and social forces are antagonistic to the family enterprise." In Europe, the family buys out the disgruntled and the spendthrift; and management is not allowed to deteriorate.[67] Closely held family business has, for example, been common in New Orleans, and nothing very remarkable has developed there in terms of either business enterprise or leadership.[68]

Granted that the total amount of capital, so defined, is lacking, it does not follow that it may not be sufficiently concentrated in some persons or places to encourage the rise of entrepreneurs. After all, they have emerged in the past under less favorable circumstances generally than exist today. The word "generally" is important, as the one major circumstance which is for many kinds of businesses less favorable today is the breakdown of segregation and discrimination, both of which have individual applicability. Integration in today's context means that publicly available facilities will be open to all who can pay the price or qualify as citizens. The Negro has been barred from patronizing many kinds of businesses by his color rather than his income level, and has thus been forced to take his trade to comparable establishments in the segregated community. Since many of these businesses do not hold to the standards of like enterprises in the white community, they are in truth supported by segregation, since many of their customers would gladly trade elsewhere. These units will be forced to upgrade or fail. Were integration an accomplished fact today, it would be easier to predict the latter.

Discrimination has in most respects been an unfortunate burden for the Negro. However, several interviewees presented a new facet of this practice. It often handily serves as the universal justification for failure. Though many times it accounts for lack of training and thus indirectly for failure, it is used to cover other sins, usually of

66. *The Wall Street Journal,* May 17, 1963, p. 1.
67. Cole, *op. cit.,* p. 58.
68. Corroborated by Thompson, *op. cit., passim.*

omission. For many it is a justification for never making the effort, since, it is argued, potential success would be thwarted by discrimination. As this barrier is removed, the Negro will have to stand up to the general level of competition in the marketplace, though current demands by some activist organizations are hardly in this spirit. If his opportunities for education and then for jobs are unhampered by artificial barriers, he will then have to face the truth of his capabilities and accomplishments. Speaking to the graduating class at Morris Brown College in Atlanta in June 1963, Harry Golden reminded his hearers that "the ghetto is a fortress as much as it was a prison." When all people are dealt with by universalistic criteria, a Negro can be denied a job or fired from one if he does not measure up to these criteria. Integration will also muffle criticism of Negro businesses which hire whites and thus depart from a strict policy of racial loyalty. Unfortunately this day is hardly on the horizon, but the march towards it is accelerating. Removal of the psychological "protection" of both segregation and discrimination will not be a completely unmixed blessing, particularly during the period of transition.

Yet this is a situation in which increasing numbers of Negro entrepreneurs can emerge. One has only to look back to the specific examples detailed above. The great majority of the successful men there depicted had either or both of the two important ingredients for entrepreneurship: advanced education and experience in the chosen field. Some have themselves been educators or professionally trained men. Much of the strength of the business community in Atlanta, for example, is attributable over the years to the existence of the Atlanta University complex, with its several undergraduate colleges and professional schools. In many instances, the acquisition of know-how has occurred in the North. This is particularly true in construction, since the chance for the Negro to work at skilled trades in this industry has been almost non-existent in the South. With technical schools such as Georgia Institute of Technology opening its doors to Negroes, and with the increased opportunity to receive training in white businesses, Negroes in the South will more easily lay claim to the requisites of entrepreneurship. If Negroes have under former conditions succeeded as entrepreneurs in markets not wholly protected by segregation, improved conditions should presage a marked growth in their numbers.

This bright day is at present only a hoped-for goal, and many things must be done before it becomes a reality. High on such a list are improvements in the education available to Negroes. Certainly progressing integration will not mean the end of the Negro colleges and institutes of the South. In the past, with certain exceptions such as Hampton and Tuskegee, or programs of business education at places such as North Carolina College or Atlanta University, Negro higher education has been heavy on either the academic or pre-professional program. Since but few Negroes were encouraged to go into business, preparation typically offered has been for occupations of high status, such as public-school teaching, medicine, dentistry, or the ministry. Saville expresses the opinion that "education . . . offers the promise of facilitating the troublesome transition from an agricultural society to an industrial . . . only by enabling the individual to produce more by the efficient utilization of individual initiative, . , . [and] to realize for himself the economic alternatives available to him in an industrial society."[69] This will require a reorientation and reorganization of the curricula of many Negro educational institutions.

At the small business conference referred to above, the opinion was voiced that business and education may be growing further apart. With the mass of the teachers coming from the academically oriented programs of the Negro colleges, it is understandable that the average Negro high school student knows very little about what business is like. Many substantial Negro concerns are now offering scholarship aid to encourage young people of promise to enter upon business careers, and they must receive proper counseling in the high schools.

Beyond the level of formal education and specific training or experience in a chosen field lie the many "extra-curricular" contacts so necessary to becoming part of the business community. Most local Chambers of Commerce do not welcome Negro members, and Southern regional associations within a specialty such as banking or accountancy have the same policies. The substitute Negro groups are out of the mainstream, their educational value is meager, and valuable business contacts are necessarily foregone.

Harry Golden, in the same context alluded to above, remarked that the free exchange of ideas in an open society has been the foundation of all civilized progress. In a more practical vein, contracts are often closed verbally at luncheon in private clubs, and business opportunities and deals discussed on the golf course. Acquisition of

69. Lloyd Saville, "Sectional Developments in Italy and the United States," *The Southern Economic Journal*, XXIII (July 1956), 50. In this connection "At Howard University alone, recruiters from more than 100 companies have made campus recruiting visits in the past several months." Caroline Bird, *op. cit.*, p. 15.

civil rights will not secure admittance to these business scenes. Southern Negro businessmen often do participate in national conventions, but this is no substitute for contact with local figures. Yet there are hopeful signs that even some of these barriers are being softened, if not broken. This is at least a move toward the "beneficent climate of social opinion" so strongly emphasized by Cole.

Most of the emphasis has been on the more noble motives behind Negro entrepreneurship, but the scarcity of contacts between the two communities, combined with the lack of mutual trust, has the potential of putting power in the hands of relatively few in any given Negro community. If these few are possessed of more pedestrian motives, exploitation can be the result. If, for example, regular channels are not open to secure funds, those few Negroes of wealth can exact a high toll for their assistance, particularly if the borrower, perhaps through lack of trust, wishes to retain full control of his enterprise. More contacts with the total business community fostering a high level of sophistication in business, coupled with the development of mutual trust, would reduce dependence on these few persons and, in so doing, dilute the possibilities for exploitation where they exist.

The removal of "reverse discrimination," or a "Negroes only" policy, in Negro businesses will be an additional avenue of contact with the total business community. If the Negro entrepreneur is to cease being identified by his color, he must integrate his enterprises and become just another businessman. Many already recognize this. Mr. L. D. Milton, president of Citizens Trust of Atlanta, has observed that "the more successful Negroes become in the operation of businesses, the stiffer becomes the competition which they must face from other firms—competition for both customers and employees." The Negro must thus become as universalistic in his approach to economic resources as the white man tackling the same business.

Finally, then, one finds the present generation of Negro entrepreneurs fairly well characterized by the definition chosen earlier. They have not been heroic innovators, effecting major changes in the formulae of production. They are even accused by some of their younger colleagues of having stood still and "locked up security." Yet they have been agents of change in a period of transition, a period of social and economic change in the South. Increasing numbers will make contributions in the future. The burden will be great, but past performance gives promise of success.

# IV

# "Liquidity Preference"— A Southern Banking Tradition?*

*By George Macesich*

The purpose of this paper is to examine the empirical consistency of the hypothesis that Southern bankers are impeding the region's development because of their conservative predilection, which manifests itself in a comparatively high "liquidity preference." For purposes of this study the South is defined as the Fifth and Sixth Federal Reserve Districts. Southern bankers are represented by member banks in these two districts, and the period selected for analysis is 1950–60.

Section I discusses the hypothesis and its implications. Section II tests the empirical consistency of the hypothesis. Section III discusses a number of implications for Southern development.

## I. The Hypothesis and Its Implications

In a recent attempt to ascertain the empirical validity of the hypothesis that there exists a significant variation in interest rates between centers and peripheries of economic development, it was discovered that the hypothesis is not supported by data for member banks in the Sixth Federal Reserve District.[1] The analysis indicated that there is not a statistically significant variation between earning ratios of member banks located in the centers and those located in

* I am indebted to Marshall R. Colberg and Richard G. Cornell for useful comments and suggestions and to the Computer Center, Florida State University, for a number of computations.

1. George Macesich, "Interest Rates in the Periphery and in the Center of Economic Development," *Southern Economic Journal*, October, 1961, pp. 138–47.

the peripheries of economic development in the Sixth Federal Reserve District. A statistically significant variation in earning ratios does occur between member banks when they are classified by deposit size. The smaller banks have significantly higher earning ratios than larger banks.

These results suggest that "imperfections" of the capital markets are not as important in explaining the deficiency in capital investment as is sometimes argued. There are, however, some important exceptions to the apparent free access to the funds market especially among new and small businesses. These businesses must rely primarily upon local sources of funds.

If, as it seems indicated, the South has fairly good access to the capital markets in the United States so far, at least, as the banking system is concerned, why is not any deficiency in capital investment soon corrected by a greater inflow of funds toward the area? One hypothesis advanced by some students is that the South's demand for capital funds is relatively weak.[2] In this view, the South's ability to attract and retain funds depends primarily on the area's demand for capital funds. The most important factors determining the strength of this demand are the quality and quantity of the South's managerial efficiency, the labor supply, the size and efficiency of the character of the technology utilized, and the nature of its natural resources.

It seems reasonable to postulate that the size of bank assets tends to be geared roughly to many factors, including the magnitude of the loan market. The composition of bank assets, however, reflects attitudes of bank officials, including what might be called their "liquidity preference." The Southern banker may prefer the safety and convenience of greater liquidity to the income he will lose through this attitude. Moreover, such an attitude may be reinforced by a desire to preserve "Southern tradition" and its agricultural mores. The new "industrial upstarts" would be prevented from upsetting the existing status quo, if only because Southern bankers allocate and hold a smaller proportion of their assets in the form of loans. These bankers, however, in substituting leisure for profits would be derelict in carrying out the principal function of commercial banking—namely, the "production" of loans. If this hypothesis is correct, then, all other things being equal, Southern bankers share much of the responsibility for impeding the South's economic development.

2. Charles T. Taylor, "The South's Capital and Credit Needs," (Paper presented at the Twenty-eighth Southern Economic Association, November 21–22, 1958).

Liquidity in a bank and elsewhere may be defined as the possession of those assets which can be converted into cash easily, quickly,
and without significant loss. Although technically fully liquid, a bank's
cash assets only imperfectly describe its "liquidity preference." Cash,
deposits with correspondent banks and Federal Reserve banks, and
cash items in the process of collection are its *primary reserves* and
represent working balances used in day-to-day operation of the bank.
It is thus only to a very limited extent that cash assets per se can
be counted among its liquid assets. Commercial banking students
consider the so-called *secondary reserve* of short-term, readily marketable, high-quality assets as the real source of a bank's liquidity. In
effect, these secondary reserves represent its planned liquidity in the
sense that a bank can control the quantity it holds of such assets.

Very few assets meet banking requirements for secondary reserves.
Short maturity, ready marketability, and high quality are tests passed
by short-term U.S. Government securities. These securities, in fact,
constitute the vast preponderance of secondary reserves of the banking system, although other readily marketable short-term securities of
prime quality are also included in the secondary reserves of many
banks. At times, even the loans made to some very high-quality borrowers are counted by banks as constituting their secondary reserves.

For purposes of this paper I shall consider holdings of U.S. Government securities by banks as an indicator of their liquidity preference;
cash asset holdings, though important, are not nearly so accurate an
indicator of liquidity preference as these securities, for reasons discussed above. According to the hypothesis to be tested, we should expect to observe that Southern bankers hold a comparatively larger
proportion of their assets in the form of U.S. Government securities
than banks elsewhere in the country. At the same time, we should
expect to observe that Southern bankers allocate a comparatively
smaller proportion of their total assets to loans.

## II. Empirical Consistency of the Hypothesis

### A. Data and Statistical Tests

In order to test the empirical consistency of the hypothesis
that Southern bankers have a relatively higher "liquidity preference,"
Operating Ratios of member banks in the several Federal Reserve
Districts are employed. Published by the several Federal Reserve
Banks, these data are available by deposit classification of member
banks for the several operating ratios including "Distribution of Assets"

**Table 1.** Federal Reserve Districts and Bank Cities*

| Federal Reserve District | Federal Reserve Bank City |
|---|---|
| First District | Boston, Mass. |
| Second District | New York, N. Y. |
| Third District | Philadelphia, Pa. |
| Fourth District | Cleveland, Ohio |
| Fifth District | Richmond, Va. |
| Sixth District | Atlanta, Ga. |
| Seventh District | Chicago, Ill. |
| Eighth District | St. Louis, Mo. |
| Ninth District | Minneapolis, Minn. |
| Tenth District | Kanas City, Mo. |
| Eleventh District | Dallas, Texas |
| Twelfth District | San Francisco, Calif. |

* Source: *Federal Reserve Bulletin*, July 1956, p. 792.

as a percentage of total assets. The asset category consists of cash, U.S. Government securities, other securities, loans, and real estate assets. The several Federal Reserve Districts are presented in Table I.

For the eleven-year period 1950–60, availability of comparable data by deposit bank size limited the study to Federal Reserve Districts Two through Eleven. Member banks in each of these Districts were divided as nearly as possible into five deposit-size categories. In millions of dollars, the sizes considered were 0.5 to 1, 1 to 2, 2 to 5, 5 to 10, and 10 to 25. These were designated bank sizes one through five respectively.

The statistical analysis is in the form of an analysis of variance involving the following four classifications: year, District, bank size, and asset category. This method of analysis appears to be the most appropriate for the purposes of this paper. The statistical object is to see if the tests of the various possible interactions with the distribution of assets among the asset categories are significantly different from zero. The results are expected to shed light on preferences of banks for the several categories of assets.

In order to examine these preferences among Southern bankers, tests are made between Districts Five and Six and the rest of the country as well as within these two subdivisions of the area studied. These three sets of comparisons, which when taken together give a comparison among all the Federal Reserve Districts, are studied separately as well as together when interactions with bank size in addition to asset distribution are computed. The same is also done in computing interactions between District, bank size, and asset distribution classifications. In the analysis of variance presented in Table 2, the symbols DA, $D_1A$, $D_2A$, $D_3A$ represent respectively asset distribution among all Districts; between Districts Five and Six as opposed to Districts Two to Four and Seven to Eleven; between Districts Five and Six; and among Districts Two to Four and Seven to Eleven.[3]

Similarly, comparisons of asset distribution among banks are computed for three subcategories of bank sizes as well as all bank-size categories. Higher-order interactions involving bank size are, however, computed only among all bank-size categories. As presented in Table 2, BA represents variation in asset distribution among all five bank-size categories; $B_1A$ among first three bank sizes; $B_2A$ among last two bank sizes; $B_3A$ between first three bank-size and last two bank-size categories.

Interaction of time in years and asset distribution is also computed for two breakdowns among the years in the study, but higher-order interactions involving time are not. In Table 2, TA represents variation among all eleven years; $T_1A$ stands for variation attributable to a linear progression; $T_2A$, for variation which cannot be accounted for by a linear progression over time.

F-tests are conducted relative to the mean square for the third order DBTA (District, Bank size, Time, Asset category) interaction. The tests of significance for computed F-ratios are on the one-percent significance level so as to take into account the possibility of lack of

3. The proportions in the various asset categories varied from low proportions such as 0.001 to proportions close to 0.50. In order to render the analysis of variance more reliable, stabilization of the random variation inherent in the data is achieved by transforming all of the observed proportions by means of the sin

$$\sin^{-1} \sqrt{p}$$

function, where $p$ is an observed proportion. Expressed in radians, these transforms are used in the analysis of variance calculations.

The analysis of variance is further complicated by the absence of data on some bank-size categories in a number of Districts. The absence consists of sixty-five sets of data where each set consists of five proportions describing an asset distribution. These missing values are replaced by averages for the year, District, and bank-size combinations involved where these average data are computed from the 2,425 transforms of observed proportions which are available. The analysis of variance calculations is carried out using these estimated values for the categories for which no data are available as well as the transforms of observed proportions. Although such a procedure is biased, it appears to be the best one available for handling these data. As a consequence, the total degrees of freedom in the analysis of variance table are reduced from 2,749 to 2,424 to compensate for the use of these estimates in the place of the missing data. And, of course, a corresponding reduction resulted in the error degrees of freedom which are taken to equal 1,115 instead of 1,440.

**Table 2.** Analysis of Variance*

| Source | | Degrees of Freedom | Mean Square | F-Ratio | |
|---|---|---|---|---|---|
| TA | | 40 | 0.029657 | 111.49 | |
| | $T_1A$ | 4 | 0.281924 | | 1059.86 |
| | $T_2A$ | 36 | 0.001627 | | 6.12 |
| DA | | 36 | 0.048053 | 180.65 | |
| | $D_1A$ | 4 | 0.045372 | | 170.57 |
| | $D_2A$ | 4 | 0.021801 | | 81.96 |
| | $D_3A$ | 28 | 0.052186 | | 196.19 |
| BA | | 16 | 0.039029 | 146.73 | |
| | $B_1A$ | 8 | 0.035860 | | 134.81 |
| | $B_2A$ | 4 | 0.004935 | | 18.55 |
| | $B_3A$ | 4 | 0.079460 | | 298.72 |
| TDA | | 360 | 0.000774 | 2.91 | |
| | $TD_1A$ | 40 | 0.000629 | | 2.36 |
| | $TD_2A$ | 40 | 0.000250 | | 0.94 |
| | $TD_3A$ | 280 | 0.000870 | | 3.27 |
| TBA | | 160 | 0.001003 | 3.77 | |
| DBA | | 144 | 0.003909 | 14.70 | |
| | $D_1BA$ | 16 | 0.004123 | | 15.50 |
| | $D_2BA$ | 16 | 0.006824 | | 25.65 |
| | $D_3BA$ | 112 | 0.003462 | | 13.02 |
| ERROR-TDBA | | 1115 | 0.000266 | | |

* Note:

DA = Variation in asset distribution among all Districts taken together.

$D_1A$ = Variation in asset distribution in Districts 5 and 6 as opposed to Districts 2–4 and 7–11.

$D_2A$ = Variation in asset distribution in District 5 as opposed to District 6.

$D_3A$ = Variation in asset distribution among Districts 2–4 and 7–11.

BA = Variation in asset distribution among all five bank-size categories.

$B_1A$ = Variation in asset distribution among first three bank sizes.

$B_2A$ = Variation in asset distribution among last two bank sizes.

$B_3A$ = Variation in asset distribution between first three and last two bank sizes.

TA = Variation in asset distribution among all eleven years of study.

$T_1A$ = Portion of Variation attributable to a linear progression over the time of study.

$T_2A$ = Variation in asset distribution which cannot be accounted for by linear progression over time.

independence or of failure of other assumptions required for the analysis of variance to hold exactly.

### B. Test Results

All of the F-ratios calculated and presented in Table 2 except the one for $TD_2A$ (Time, District Five as opposed to Six, Asset distribution), are significant at the one-percent probability level of significance. It is also clear from the evidence summarized in the table that some of the differences in asset distribution are much greater than others. For example, the mean square for $T_1A$ is 0.281924 while that for $T_2A$ is only 0.001627. This indicates that the changes in asset distributions are mostly linear in pattern over the time period under study even though this linear pattern varies among the asset categories. Such a result is of course expected. If the proportion invested in one asset category increased linearly over the period, a similar decline would be expected in other asset categories.

Regarding the relationship between time and asset distribution, the evidence summarized in Table 3 is helpful. Average percentages of assets for all Districts and bank sizes are listed by year for each asset category. These averages are computed by calculating arithmetic means on the transformed scale used in the analysis of variance with the estimated missing values included in the computations. These means are then transformed back to the percentage scale to give the averages summarized in Table 3.

**Table 3.** Average Percentage Distribution of Assets by Year 1950–60 for Federal Reserve Districts 2–11 and Bank Sizes 1–5

| | ASSET CATEGORIES | | | | |
|---|---|---|---|---|---|
| Year | Goverment Securities | Other Securities | Loans | Cash | Real Estate |
| 1950 | 39.6 | 7.2 | 29.1 | 22.6 | 0.71 |
| 1951 | 37.2 | 7.3 | 30.2 | 23.9 | 0.72 |
| 1952 | 36.1 | 7.3 | 30.8 | 24.3 | 0.74 |
| 1953 | 36.0 | 7.4 | 31.9 | 23.2 | 0.79 |
| 1954 | 35.0 | 7.5 | 33.0 | 23.0 | 0.80 |
| 1955 | 34.8 | 7.8 | 34.0 | 21.8 | 0.85 |
| 1956 | 33.6 | 8.1 | 35.5 | 21.1 | 0.91 |
| 1957 | 33.5 | 8.3 | 35.5 | 21.1 | 0.97 |
| 1958 | 32.1 | 8.9 | 36.6 | 20.7 | 1.02 |
| 1959 | 32.1 | 9.1 | 37.3 | 19.8 | 1.04 |
| 1960 | 31.2 | 8.8 | 38.6 | 19.6 | 1.09 |

The evidence contained in the table suggests a steady decline over the eleven-year period 1950–60 in the average proportion of bank assets invested in Government securities. Except for a drop in 1960 relative to 1959 and 1958, there is an upward trend in the proportion of assets invested in other securities. The pattern for cash assets is upward until after 1952 and then is generally downward. The evidence suggests, on the other hand, a steady upward trend in the percentage of assets invested in loans and real estate. To judge from these data for the period 1950–60, member banks in Districts Two to Eleven shifted away from such liquid assets as cash and government securities to loans and real estate assets which are relatively less liquid.

Analysis of variance presented in Table 2 shows that the mean square and resulting F-ratio for DA (District, Asset distribution) is very large, indicating a highly significant difference in asset distribution among the several Districts tested. As to the various Districts, $D_1A$ and $D_3A$ have similar mean squares while the mean square for $D_2A$ is smaller though highly significant.

The large mean squares for DA, $D_1A$, $D_2A$, and $D_3A$ indicate that the asset distributions among Federal Reserve Districts differ from each other by a highly significant amount regardless of whether the comparison is made among Districts Two to Eleven, among Districts Two to Four and Seven to Eleven, between Districts Five and Six or between Districts Two to Four and Seven to Eleven taken together and Districts Five and Six taken together. The evidence thus indicates that every District in the country differs in the asset distribution of its member banks.

**Table 4.** Average Percentage Distribution of Assets by Federal Reserve Districts for Years 1950–60 and Bank Sizes 1–5

| Federal Reserve District | Asset Categories | | | | |
|---|---|---|---|---|---|
| | Government Securities | Other Securities | Loans | Cash | Real Estate |
| 2 | 35.2 | 9.1 | 35.3 | 19.3 | 0.98 |
| 3 | 35.4 | 8.8 | 36.6 | 17.6 | 1.02 |
| 4 | 35.9 | 8.4 | 35.6 | 18.8 | 0.88 |
| 5 | 33.9 | 7.0 | 35.9 | 22.1 | 1.18 |
| 6 | 32.2 | 7.3 | 32.8 | 25.7 | 1.03 |
| 7 | 38.2 | 7.7 | 31.8 | 20.5 | 0.72 |
| 8 | 37.6 | 7.7 | 30.6 | 22.8 | 0.70 |
| 9 | 36.7 | 8.4 | 33.6 | 19.6 | 0.76 |
| 10 | 33.8 | 7.6 | 33.0 | 24.4 | 0.56 |
| 11 | 28.3 | 7.7 | 33.1 | 29.3 | 0.98 |

In order to examine more closely the differences in asset distribution among the several Districts, the average percentage distribution of assets for each District is computed and presented in Table 4. The averages are taken over all years and bank-size categories and computed in the same manner as those in Table 3. Estimates presented in Table 4 indicate that member banks in Districts Five (Richmond), Six (Atlanta), and Eleven (Dallas) invested a smaller proportion of their assets in Government and other securities than did member banks in other Districts. Moreover, member banks in Districts Five and Six invested a higher proportion of their assets in real estate than did member banks in other Districts.

Analysis of variance for differences among bank sizes indicates that asset distribution differs significantly at the one-percent probability level among the five bank-size categories considered. Moreover, since the mean squares for $B_3A$ and $B_1A$ are much larger than the mean square for $B_2A$, the difference in asset distribution for bank sizes one through three as opposed to bank-size categories four and five and the differences among the asset categories within bank sizes 1–3 were greater than the differences between the asset distributions for bank sizes four and five. Indeed, the $B_2A$ mean square is much smaller than all the other mean squares for first-order interactions, indicating similar asset distributions for bank sizes four and five. Moreover, the mean square obtained for $B_3A$ is larger than any obtained when the interactions of Districts with asset distribution are compared, so that bank size seems to be somewhat more important as a determinant of asset distribution than does location.

The average percentage distribution of assets by bank size is presented in Table 5. These averages include data on all Districts throughout the eleven-year period of study. They are computed in the same manner as those presented in Tables 3 and 4. Data in Table 5 indicate that the larger the bank size, the greater the con-

**Table 5.** Average Percentage Distribution of Assets by Bank Size for Federal Reserve Districts 2–11 and for Years 1950–60

| Bank Size Category[a] | ASSET CATEGORIES | | | | |
|---|---|---|---|---|---|
| | Government Securities | Other Securities | Loans | Cash | Real Estate |
| 1 = small | 32.9 | 6.0 | 35.1 | 24.1 | 0.74 |
| 2 | 35.1 | 6.8 | 33.8 | 23.0 | 0.73 |
| 3 | 35.2 | 8.7 | 33.5 | 21.1 | 0.86 |
| 4 | 35.2 | 9.6 | 32.8 | 20.9 | 0.95 |
| 5 = large | 34.8 | 9.0 | 33.9 | 20.5 | 1.11 |

[a] Bank Size Category:
    1 = $0.5 to $1 million in deposits;
    2 = $1 to $2 million in deposits;
    3 = $2 to $5 million in deposits;
    4 = $5 to $10 million in deposits;
    5 = $10 to $25 million in deposits.

centration of assets in real estate and the smaller the proportion of cash assets. There is also a trend throughout the first four bank sizes for the proportion of assets in other securities to go up and in loans to go down as bank size increases.

Finally, the mean squares for the TDA, TBA, and DBA second-order interactions, although significantly greater than the mean square for the third-order interaction TDBA which is used as an error term, are much smaller in general than the first-order interactions. These higher-order interactions, therefore, do not seem nearly so important for the understanding of differences in asset distribution as the interactions with time, location, and bank size, taken separately, with the distribution of assets. Location and bank size interact more in their effect on asset distribution than location and time or bank size and time, since the mean square for DBA is quite a bit larger than those for TDA or TBA. This is also true for such division of TDA and DBA into interactions involving $D_1$, $D_2$ and $D_3$.

### III. Implications for Southern Development

Results summarized in this study and their inconsistency with the hypothesis that Southern bankers tend to have a higher "liquidity preference" than bankers elsewhere in the country have several implications for Southern development. First, these results indicate that, insofar as member banks in the South are concerned, they do not appear to be derelict in performing commercial banking's principal function, which is the production of loans. In fact, their performance on this score appears to be better than that of member banks in many other Districts in the country.

Second, the comparatively small proportion of their assets held in U.S. Government securities indicates that member banks in the South are not serving as a vehicle for the transfer of resources out of the region. Investment in U.S. Government securities is made on a national market and thus tends to draw resources out of a region. It is, of course, true that loans can also be made on the national market, but the majority of loans are, on balance, made in local market areas.

Third, the evidence suggests that Southern bankers tend to be less "conservative" in their financial outlook than their colleagues elsewhere. We should, accordingly, expect to see them actively promoting economic development in the South. The Southern banker apparently has little desire to stop the wheels of progress for the sake of a mystical tradition.

Although suggestive, the results reported in this study are by no means conclusive. At least one limitation of the study should be kept carefully in mind. Non-member banks are not considered in the analysis.

# PART TWO

## Introductory Summary

James Henderson's paper deals with general interregional growth factors. He observes that different patterns of population growth and employment have taken place regionally throughout the United States and in particular notes a correspondence between non-agricultural employment growth and that of urban population. He describes the migration process in the South and projects it forward. His paper concludes with a discussion of implications of recent developments for regional growth analysis.

Henderson employs an exponential (growth) function as the basis for his population and migration model. He finds that the South is an urbanizing rural area which experienced a rural out-migration rate substantially above the national rate, with large numbers moving into Southern cities. Moreover, he finds a mass exodus of non-whites from the South, in which regard he refers to New York, Pennsylvania, Massachusetts and the District of Columbia as "mature-urban areas for white, but frontier areas for non-whites."

The projections by Henderson center on declining rates, with respect to both rural population decrease and urban population increase. The forecasted rise in total population will approach the national rate. "The structure and performance of the South . . . will more closely approach that of the nation as a whole."

Henderson examines employment growth-rates, and studies weight and rate effects. The rapid Southern growth in non-agricultural employment combines with decreasing specialization among the regions of the United States as developments of interest to the author. On the basis of his study, he suggests that population shifts (i.e., migration of people to jobs at particular locations) should be more a part of location theory than it has been in the past.

The paper of John L. Fulmer on "Trends in Population and Employment in the South Since 1930 and Their Economic Significance" is divided into four parts.

Part I deals with population trends. Overall, the South has gained slightly more than the rest of the nation since 1930. However, he finds that this relative gain was concentrated entirely in the 1930–40 decade. Since 1940, the South's gains have been substantially less than that of the nation. Individually, the states ranged from those with rapid growth—Florida, Texas, Virginia, and Louisiana—to those with very low annual rates of growth or even declines during one or more decades of the period—Mississippi, West Virginia, and Arkansas.

Part II examines employment trends and finds that although the region as a whole had an upward trend in yearly rates of employment growth, the rate of increase for the entire period was 16 percent below the rate for the rest of the nation and 17 points under the rate of population growth.

In the interpretation of the economic significance of these changes in Part III of his paper, the growth in population is seen to have two favorable economic effects: one is a direct impact which was rather small; and the other, for which no measure exists, is the effect of population growth upon business expectations. The change in the population-to-employment ratio is regarded, unfortunately, as an increase in "population pressure."

The final section of the paper is devoted to the rise in cities as a development force in the South. Here the impact of cities and their significance for the future development is explored. Not only have the city complexes accounted for most of the recent growth, but they are seen to have an efficiency in economic processes which are capable of generating economic growth.

Professor Frank Hanna's paper on "Income in the South since 1929" reports on the changes in total and per capita personal income since 1929 and seeks to determine their economic significance. An examination of data for the states which he includes in the South points to a need not only for study of the area as an entity but for attention to be given to the behavior patterns of one or more individual states within the South.

The bulk of the paper is devoted to setting forth the changes which have occurred not only in total and per capita income but in income components (labor, property, proprietors' income, and transfer payments) and in major sources (farm, federal government disbursements, state and local government disbursements, and private non-farm income). Special attention is given to changes in the South in income from manufacturing.

The final sections of the paper are devoted to demographic factors and an analysis of distributions of income by size in the South and in the rest of the United States.

The fourth paper in Part Two of the book is by Bernard Olsen and Gerald Garb. The authors employ factor analysis in the belief that it is effective as a tool for analyzing the relationships among large numbers of variables. In the case of their own subject matter interest, they claim it to be an aid in understanding (and deriving) the growth characteristics of regions.

One region studied by Olsen and Garb is the South, composed of the thirteen states usually designated as "the South"; the other region studied consists of ten high-income states drawn from the remainder of the nation. They employed this classification rather than one which might be derived from factor analysis in order to avoid circular reasoning.

Five factors emerged from their analyses. Factor One was labeled "urbanization," because the associated characteristics indicated a pattern of urban living. The second factor in the non-South area seemed to reflect the suburban development of recent years, and was designated "suburbanization." Factor Two in the South was tentatively identified as a "capitalization" factor, where capital was defined in the broadest sense to include human capabilities. The third factor suggested the industrial origins of income for each region. The fourth factor in both regions was taken to represent the presence of a lower-income group of unskilled labor. Factor Five, like Factor Two, was different in the two regions, indicating the presence of low-wage industry in the South, and identified in the other region as small-business commercial activity. Each of the emergent factors is examined in detail, and reasons are given for the association of characteristics.

The authors claim that factor differences offer explanations of the different growth rates of the two regions, and contend that their study demonstrates the usefulness of the technique.

The paper by Werner Hochwald concludes Part Two of the book. It, too, employs factor analysis, though just as a final tool and not as the only one. Using references to other writers, Hochwald notes the downward proportionality shift in selected decentralizing industries and the general continuance of low income in the South. He finds little explanatory material from the typical statistics on Southern development, and, accordingly, turns his attention to interregional income flows.

According to Hochwald, income from Southern exports was used primarily for investment abroad or for the import of luxury goods. Manifestly, regional development requires frugality and domestic investment, for, even under economic base theory, the development of residentiary industries to supply demands stemming from the export base is necessary. Hochwald goes on to note that location coefficients point to a substantial concentration in cotton, tobacco, coal, lumber, and textiles. More generally, and with some recent improvement noted, the author refers to the net outflow on personal-capital account against a net inflow on business-capital account as evidence of the regional cultural-industrial lag.

The factor analysis leads Hochwald to emphasize the importance of construction and manufacturing in accounting for the variations by regions of demographic, resource, and economic data. He finds income per capita and expenditures for education as vital forces behind differential growth. In general, his findings support the hypothesis that the South has been an export economy, low in developing its market and high in manufacturing, albeit with a low rank in growth and welfare. A factor analysis comparison between 1940 and 1960 shows generally a worsening status for the South, at least with respect to tertiary industries.

# V

## Some General Aspects of Recent Regional Development*

*By James M. Henderson*

### Introduction

A number of significant changes has occurred in the regional
distributions of population and employment within the United States
in recent years. There have been marked declines in the importance
of agriculture and mining as sources of employment. There was a
net movement of more than nine million persons from rural to urban
areas during the 1950–60 decade. Many persons moved across state
lines. The various states and regions in the United States experienced
quite different patterns in terms of population and employment increase. The loosening of locational ties to resources resulted in a high
degree of foot-looseness on the part of the American population. The
effects of these nation-wide movements were considerable in the
South.[1] The South accounted for roughly 60 percent of the nation's
rural out-migration. As a result, its total population grew slowly, but
its urban population boomed.

Non-agricultural employment growth generally followed urban
population growth. The composition of total non-agricultural employment in the nation as a whole shifted substantially, with governments
and service-type industries becoming increasingly important as employers. Similar shifts occurred in nearly every state. As a net result

* The author's views concerning migration and employment analyses have
been influenced by his work with Larry A. Sjaastad and R. Stephen Rodd respectively.

1. The South as defined here contains the states of Alabama, Arkansas, Georgia,
Kentucky, Louisiana, Mississippi, North Carolina, Oklahoma, South Carolina,
Tennessee, Texas, Virginia, and West Virginia.

of recent employment changes, regional specialization has declined, and the various regions within the United States have generally become more alike.

The second section of this paper contains a description of the migration process and the massive rural-to-urban movement during the 1950–60 decade. Southern migration and population growth are projected into the future in the third section in order to gain insight regarding the potential for future urban growth in the South. The growth of non-agricultural employment and tendencies toward regional equalization are covered in the following two sections. A final section contains a discussion of some of the implications of recent developments for regional growth analysis.

## Migration and Population Growth

### Migration Estimates

Large-scale movements of people have been one of the most important regional developments in recent years. Millions have left farms and other rural areas to move to cities. Many others have moved from one city to another, often from one state to another.

Attention is here directed to net migration—i.e., the number of in-migrants minus the number of out-migrants. State-wide estimates for the 1950–60 decade have been prepared by the Bureau of the Census.[2] The "residual method" was used whereby net migration equals 1960 population less 1950 population less the excess of births over deaths during the decade. A negative figure indicates net out-migration and a positive figure indicates net in-migration.

Migration estimates were made for each of the states of the conterminous United States and the District of Columbia for four population components: (1) urban white, (2) urban non-white, (3) rural white, and (4) rural non-white. Net migration for each of the groups within a state was calculated as the difference between the group's 1960 population and its 1950 population times a natural increase factor:

$$(1) \qquad M_{ij} = P_{60,ij} - P_{50,ij} e^{10\lambda_{ij}} \quad (i=1, \ldots, 49), (j=1, \ldots, 4)$$

where $M_{ij}$ is decennial net migration for group $j$ in state $i$, the $P$'s are the group's 1950 and 1960 population levels, $e = 2.71828 \ldots$ is the base of the system of natural logarithms, and $\lambda_{ij}$ is a continuous annual rate of natural increase.

2. *Current Population Reports*, Series P-23, No. 7 (November, 1962).

Census rates of natural increase for the United States as a whole were 1.44 and 2.34 percent per year for whites and non-whites respectively.[3] These rates served as an initial base for the computations using Equation (1). The same rate was used for the urban and rural components for each racial class. The initial migration estimates for the four groups in a state were summed and compared with the state's Census control total. The natural increase rates were then increased or decreased proportionately to force the component sum to the control total.

Net migration can also be expressed as a rate times population. In continuous terms:

$$(2) \quad M_{ij} = r_{ij} P_{50,ij} \int_{t=0}^{t=10} e^{\mu_{ij}t} dt \quad (i=1, \ldots, 49), \ (j=1, \ldots, 4)$$

where $r_{ij}$ is a group's continuous annual migration rate, and $\mu_{ij}$ is its continuous actual annual population growth rate.[4] Equation (2) was solved for the $r_{ij}$ since the values of its other components were known:

$$r_{ij} = \frac{M_{ij}\mu_{ij}}{P_{60,ij} - P_{50,ij}} \quad (i=1, \ldots, 49), \ (j=1, \ldots, 4).$$

Each rate carries the same sign as the corresponding migration estimate.

### Rural-Urban Patterns

State estimates of net migration for total, urban, and rural populations are presented together with migration rates in Table 1. Estimates are also presented for the conterminous United States and a thirteen-state South. Total net migration for the United States largely represents foreign immigration.

Out-migration from rural areas was almost universal; only Florida, Connecticut, Nevada, New Hampshire, and New York experienced rural in-migration. More than nine million people on net moved from farms, towns, and other rural areas to cities; this represented an over-all rural out-migration of 1.69 percent per year. As a result of natural increase, the absolute decline of rural population was limited to approximately one-half million. The corresponding annual net urban in-migration rate was smaller, 1.07 percent per year, because

3. These percentages must be divided by 100 to be used in Equation (1).

4. The rate $\mu_{ij}$ is calculated by solving $P_{60,ij} = P_{50,ij}e^{10\mu_{ij}}$. It can be verified that $\mu_{ij} = \lambda_{ij} + r_{ij}$.

**Table 1.** Total, Urban, and Rural Migration: 1950–60

| | Migration (Thousands of Persons) | | | Migration Rates (Percents per Year) | | |
|---|---|---|---|---|---|---|
| | Total | Urban | Rural | Total | Urban | Rural |
| United States | 2,621 | 11,733 | −9,112 | .16 | 1.07 | −1.69 |
| South | −3,247 | 2,607 | −5,854 | −.75 | 1.20 | −2.73 |
| Alabama | −368 | 166 | −534 | −1.16 | 1.07 | −3.35 |
| Arkansas | −422 | 17 | 450 | −2.34 | .25 | −3.93 |
| Georgia | −214 | 260 | −474 | −.58 | 1.40 | −2.60 |
| Kentucky | −390 | 67 | −457 | −1.30 | .56 | −2.58 |
| Louisiana | −50 | 223 | −272 | −.17 | 1.27 | −2.26 |
| Mississippi | −434 | 77 | −511 | −1.99 | 1.09 | −3.49 |
| North Carolina | −328 | 133 | −461 | −.76 | .84 | −1.69 |
| Oklahoma | −219 | 147 | −365 | −.96 | 1.13 | −3.75 |
| South Carolina | −222 | 21 | −242 | −.99 | .23 | −1.77 |
| Tennessee | −273 | 138 | −410 | −.80 | .83 | −2.32 |
| Texas | 114 | 1,133 | −1,019 | .13 | 1.91 | −3.88 |
| Virginia | 15 | 320 | −306 | .04 | 1.72 | −1.74 |
| West Virginia | −447 | −94 | −353 | −2.31 | −1.34 | −2.87 |
| Florida | 1,617 | 1,451 | 166 | 4.30 | 5.52 | 1.49 |
| Arizona | 330 | 412 | −83 | 3.30 | 6.30 | −2.48 |
| California | 3,145 | 3,364 | −219 | 2.42 | 3.10 | −1.05 |
| Colorado | 164 | 279 | −115 | 1.07 | 2.67 | −2.41 |
| Connecticut | 234 | 197 | 37 | 1.04 | 1.12 | .75 |
| Delaware | 64 | 53 | 11 | 1.69 | 2.17 | .84 |
| Dist. of Columbia | −158 | −158 | a | −2.02 | −2.02 | a |
| Idaho | −40 | 11 | −51 | −.64 | .39 | −1.49 |
| Illinois | 124 | 383 | −259 | .13 | .52 | −1.33 |
| Indiana | 63 | 139 | −75 | .15 | .53 | −.45 |
| Iowa | −228 | 30 | −258 | −.85 | .22 | −1.93 |
| Kansas | −44 | 153 | −197 | −.22 | 1.33 | −2.24 |
| Maine | −66 | −37 | −29 | −.70 | −.77 | −.63 |
| Maryland | 320 | 326 | −6 | 1.18 | 1.70 | −.08 |
| Massachusetts | −93 | −120 | 27 | −.19 | −.29 | .34 |
| Michigan | 156 | 288 | −132 | .22 | .57 | −.67 |
| Minnesota | −97 | 189 | −285 | −.30 | 1.01 | −2.16 |
| Missouri | −130 | 120 | −250 | −.32 | .45 | −1.69 |
| Montana | −25 | 30 | −55 | −.40 | 1.01 | −1.65 |
| Nebraska | −117 | 40 | −158 | −.86 | .59 | −2.34 |
| Nevada | 86 | 84 | 2 | 3.97 | 6.04 | .28 |
| New Hampshire | 13 | 12 | 1 | .22 | .35 | .05 |
| New Jersey | 577 | 614 | −37 | 1.06 | 1.29 | −.55 |
| New Mexico | 52 | 160 | −108 | .65 | 3.41 | −3.25 |
| New York | 210 | 152 | 58 | .13 | .11 | .25 |
| North Dakota | −105 | 22 | −127 | −1.68 | 1.14 | −2.94 |
| Ohio | 409 | 560 | −152 | .46 | .89 | −.61 |
| Oregon | 16 | 146 | −130 | .10 | 1.53 | −1.90 |
| Pennsylvania | −475 | −235 | −240 | −.44 | −.30 | −.76 |
| Rhode Island | −26 | −5 | −22 | −.32 | −.06 | −1.80 |
| South Dakota | −94 | 7 | −101 | −1.41 | .28 | −2.38 |
| Utah | 10 | 83 | −72 | .13 | 1.50 | −3.14 |
| Vermont | −38 | −6 | −32 | −.99 | −.45 | −1.31 |
| Washington | 88 | 186 | −98 | .34 | 1.08 | −1.09 |
| Wisconsin | −53 | 186 | −239 | −.14 | .83 | −1.66 |
| Wyoming | −20 | 11 | −31 | −.64 | .69 | −2.16 |

a The District of Columbia has no rural population.

the urban population base was larger. Migration plus natural increase resulted in an urban population increase of more than twenty-eight million.

Many states and regions of the United States can be placed within three general categories: (1) mature-urban, (2) urbanizing-rural, and (3) frontier.[5] Mature-urban states experienced both total and urban out-migration. Their cities were unable to retain their own natural increase. These areas are generally the older industrial or service centers. Pennsylvania, Massachusetts, Rhode Island, and Maine are in the mature-urban group.

The District of Columbia is a special case. Its net out-migrants appear to have moved to residential areas in surrounding states. Net movements from other mature-urban areas appear to be predominantly to the frontier areas, often over relatively long distances.

The South and most Midwest states are urbanizing-rural areas. They contain relatively large rural populations, and are characterized by the coincidence of rural out-migration and urban in-migration. Their rural out-migrants serve as a basis for urban expansion. They do not appear to draw substantial numbers of net urban in-migrants from beyond their own and adjoining states.[6] Urban growth generally is not sufficient to absorb all of the rural out-migrants of an urbanizing-rural area. Hence, net total out-migration is the usual case.

Frontier areas are experiencing high rates of urban and total in-migration. Their urban growth cannot be explained by their rural out-migration. They are drawing the total in-migrants from mature-urban and urbanizing-rural areas. Florida, with a total net in-migration of 4.3 percent per year, is in this category. Arizona, California, and Nevada also had total in-migration rates in excess of 2 percent per year.

### The Southern Experience

Florida is a frontier area. The nearby Southern states constitute an urbanizing-rural area. Rural-to-urban movements were very pronounced. The South possessed 41 percent of the nation's rural population in 1950 and experienced a rural out-migration rate of 2.73 percent per year, which was substantially above the national

5. A few states and regions cannot be classified unambiguously into these categories.

6. State lines do not necessarily provide the boundaries for such regions. For example, more of Arkansas' rural out-migrants appear to have moved to urban areas in Texas and Louisiana than urban areas in Arkansas.

rate of 1.69 percent. Each of the thirteen Southern states experienced a rural out-migration rate equal to or above the national rate. The South consequently contributed more than 60 percent of the nation's rural out-migrants. Texas had more than 1,000,000. Alabama, Arkansas, Georgia, Kentucky, Mississippi, North Carolina, and Tennessee each had more than 400,000.

Large numbers of rural out-migrants moved to Southern cities. The South experienced a net urban in-migration of 2,600,000. Its urban in-migration rate of 1.2 percent per year exceeded the national rate of 1.07. Excepting West Virginia, each of the Southern states experienced net urban in-migration. Urban in-migration, however, was not sufficiently large to offset rural out-migration in eleven of the thirteen Southern states, and the South as a whole experienced a net total out-migration of more than 3,000,000 people to other parts of the country. On net, the South was able to retain 44.5 percent of its rural out-migrants as urban in-migrants.

**Table 2.** Southern Rural Migration by Race: 1950–60

| | Migration (Thousands of Persons) | | Migration Rates (Percents per Year) | |
|---|---|---|---|---|
| | White | Non-White | White | Non-White |
| South | −3,955 | −1,899 | −2.40 | −4.00 |
| Alabama | −315 | −219 | −2.82 | −4.60 |
| Arkansas | −326 | −124 | −3.63 | −5.01 |
| Georgia | −241 | −233 | −1.86 | −4.44 |
| Kentucky | −428 | −29 | −2.52 | −4.12 |
| Louisiana | −115 | −157 | −1.47 | −3.76 |
| Mississippi | −203 | −307 | −2.63 | −4.46 |
| North Carolina | −254 | −206 | −1.26 | −2.92 |
| Oklahoma | −326 | −39 | −3.70 | −4.23 |
| South Carolina | −42 | −201 | −.52 | −3.53 |
| Tennessee | −344 | −67 | −2.16 | −3.75 |
| Texas | −848 | −171 | −3.70 | −5.15 |
| Virginia | −194 | −112 | −1.42 | −2.84 |
| West Virginia | −318 | −34 | −2.72 | −6.02 |
| Florida | 210 | −44 | 2.32 | −2.09 |

## Migration by Race

Table 2 contains rural migration estimates for Southern whites and non-whites. Non-whites accounted for almost one-third of rural out-migration from the South. They left the Southern rural areas at much more rapid rates than whites. The non-white out-migration rate exceeded the corresponding white rate in every Southern state. The

**Table 3.** Urban Net Migration by Race: 1950–60

| | MIGRATION (Thousands of Persons) | | MIGRATION RATES (Percents per Year) | |
|---|---|---|---|---|
| | White | Non-White | White | Non-White |
| United States | 9,745 | 1,988 | .96 | 1.67 |
| South | 2,602 | 5 | 1.54 | .03 |
| Alabama | 189 | −23 | 1.80 | −.46 |
| Arkansas | 29 | −11 | .53 | −.71 |
| Georgia | 255 | 5 | 1.99 | .08 |
| Kentucky | 76 | −9 | .71 | −.64 |
| Louisiana | 181 | 42 | 1.50 | .77 |
| Mississippi | 82 | −5 | 1.84 | −.18 |
| North Carolina | 147 | −14 | 1.26 | −.35 |
| Oklahoma | 133 | 14 | 1.13 | 1.16 |
| South Carolina | 49 | −29 | .80 | −1.12 |
| Tennessee | 145 | −8 | 1.14 | −.20 |
| Texas | 1,077 | 56 | 2.08 | .75 |
| Virginia | 317 | 4 | 2.14 | .10 |
| West Virginia | −78 | −16 | −1.19 | −3.50 |
| Florida | 1,285 | 166 | 6.11 | 3.16 |
| Arizona | 397 | 15 | 6.39 | 4.56 |
| California | 2,984 | 380 | 2.98 | 4.58 |
| Colorado | 266 | 13 | 2.63 | 3.94 |
| Connecticut | 157 | 40 | .93 | 5.31 |
| Delaware | 48 | 5 | 2.27 | 1.47 |
| Dist. of Columbia | −224 | 66 | −5.26 | 1.90 |
| Idaho | 10 | 1 | .37 | 2.83 |
| Illinois | 147 | 236 | .22 | 2.85 |
| Indiana | 94 | 45 | .39 | 2.12 |
| Iowa | 22 | 8 | .16 | 3.86 |
| Kansas | 149 | 4 | 1.39 | .49 |
| Maine | −39 | 1 | −.80 | 6.30 |
| Maryland | 282 | 45 | 1.78 | 1.34 |
| Massachusetts | −146 | 26 | −.36 | 2.82 |
| Michigan | 173 | 115 | .38 | 2.07 |
| Minnesota | 181 | 7 | .99 | 3.19 |
| Missouri | 80 | 40 | .34 | 1.30 |
| Montana | 29 | 1 | .98 | 3.80 |
| Nebraska | 35 | 5 | .53 | 2.03 |
| Nevada | 76 | 8 | 5.83 | 9.29 |
| New Hampshire | 11 | 1 | .32 | 8.52 |
| New Jersey | 483 | 131 | 1.10 | 3.51 |
| New Mexico | 155 | 5 | 3.42 | 3.10 |
| New York | −173 | 325 | −.14 | 2.78 |
| North Dakota | 22 | 0 | 1.13 | 1.26 |
| Ohio | 428 | 132 | .75 | 2.16 |
| Oregon | 139 | 7 | 1.49 | 3.25 |
| Pennsylvania | −329 | 94 | −.47 | 1.33 |
| Rhode Island | −7 | 3 | −.11 | 1.65 |
| South Dakota | 6 | 1 | .25 | 2.21 |
| Utah | 82 | 1 | 1.51 | .66 |
| Vermont | −7 | 0 | −.45 | 2.34 |
| Washington | 168 | 18 | 1.01 | 3.18 |
| Wisconsin | 146 | 39 | .67 | 7.72 |
| Wyoming | 11 | 0 | .71 | −.14 |

over-all non-white rate, 4 percent per year for the South, is sub-stantially above the rate for whites, 2.4 percent. Florida provides an interesting case. It experienced rural in-migration of whites and rural out-migration of non-whites.

White and non-white migration estimates for urban areas are listed in Table 3. The racial character of urban in-migration in the South is just opposite from that of rural out-migration. Excepting Oklahoma, the white-urban migration rate exceeds the corresponding non-white rate in every Southern state. Eight of the Southern states experienced urban out-migration by non-whites.

The 44.5 percent urban retention rate for the South separates into two very dissimilar components: a rate of 65.8 percent for whites and one of 0.3 percent for non-whites. An estimated 1.4 million whites and 1.9 million non-whites left the South during the 1950's.

Non-white urban in-migration outside of the South further empha-sizes the mass exodus of non-whites from the South. Non-white urban migration rates are positive for all but one state outside of the South, and exceed white urban migration rates in twenty-eight of the thirty-five states. The District of Columbia, Massachusetts, New York, and Pennsylvania are mature-urban areas for whites, but frontier areas for non-whites.

The mass exodus of non-whites from the South represents a move-ment in search of social and political as well as economic opportunity. It cannot be explained by economic variables alone. The conse-quences of this movement for the economic development of the South and other portions of the nation are many.

## The Southern Migration Potential

### Rural Population and Migration

Rural out-migration from the Southern states during the past decade was sufficiently large to result in an absolute decline in the region's rural population. A continuation of current rates would eventually drive rural population toward zero, but it might be a long time before this happened. The South's current rural-to-urban migra-tion is here extrapolated forward in order to gain an insight into the size of the potential for future urban growth and the potential speed of rural depopulation. These extrapolations are limited to the thirteen-state South.

Assume that observed rural migration and natural increase rates remain unchanged for each racial group in each of the thirteen states.

The rural population for racial group $j$ in state $i$ at time $t$, denoted by $R_{ij}(t)$, is

(3) $R_{ij}(t) = R_{ij}(0)e^{(r_{ij}+\lambda_{ij})t}$      $(i=1, \ldots, 13)$, $(j=3,4)$

where $r_{ij}$ and $\lambda_{ij}$ are annual migration and natural increase rates respectively as defined above. For convenience, 1960 corresponds to $t = 0$, 1970 to $t = 10$, and so on. The rural migration rates, $r_{ij}$, are generally negative. The rural population of group $j$ in state $i$ will decline over time and eventually approach zero if $(r_{ij} + \lambda_{ij}) < 0$, i.e., if its out-migration rate exceeds its natural increase rate in absolute value. The 1950–60 rates satisfy this condition for the non-white rural populations in all thirteen states and for the white rural populations in all of the South except Louisiana, North Carolina, South Carolina, and Virginia.

The level of rural migration for group $j$ over the period from $t = t_1$ through $t = t_2$ is

(4) $M_{ij} = \dfrac{r_{ij}[R_{ij}(t_2) - R_{ij}(t_1)]}{r_{ij}+\lambda_{ij}}$      $(i=1, \ldots, 13)$, $(j=3,4)$

and is easily calculated once rural populations have been derived.

### Urban Population and Migration

The South is assumed to retain as urban in-migrants the same proportion of its rural out-migrants as it retained during 1950–60:

(5) $X_j = -\rho_j \sum\limits_{i=1}^{13} M_{i,j+2}$      $(j=1,2)$

where $X_j$ is the net urban in-migration for group $j$ for the South as a whole, and the $\rho_j$ are the 1950–60 retention rates. No attempt was made to calculate levels for individual states.

Urban in-migration for the period $t = t_1$ through $t = t_2$ can also be expressed as

(6) $X_j = \dfrac{r_j[U_j(t_2) - U_j(t_1)]}{\lambda_j+\mu_j}$      $(j=1,2)$

where the $\lambda_j$ are constant urban natural increase rates derived from 1950-60 data, and the $r_j$ are the average urban in-migration rates for the South over the period under analysis.

Total urban population at $t = t_2$ is

(7) $U_j(t_2) = U_j(t_1)e^{(\lambda_j+r_j)(t_2-t_1)}$      $(j=1,2)$.

**Table 4.**  Population and Migration Projections for the South: 1970–2020

| Year | POPULATION | | | MIGRATION | |
|---|---|---|---|---|---|
| | Thousands of Persons | Percent Increase | Percent of Total | Thousands of Persons | Percent Rate |
| | | | Rural | | |
| 1960 | 20,522 | −.89 | 44.9 | −5,878 | −2.98 |
| 1970 | 18,946 | −.80 | 37.1 | −5,181 | −2.63 |
| 1980 | 17,655 | −.71 | 30.6 | −4,619 | −2.53 |
| 1990 | 16,609 | −.61 | 25.2 | −4,150 | −2.42 |
| 2000 | 15,773 | −.52 | 20.9 | −3,758 | −2.32 |
| 2010 | 15,119 | −.42 | 17.3 | −3,431 | −2.22 |
| 2020 | 14,626 | −.33 | 14.4 | −3,157 | −2.12 |
| | | | Urban | | |
| 1960 | 25,188 | 3.07 | 55.1 | 2,632 | .88 |
| 1970 | 32,145 | 2.43 | 62.9 | 2,334 | .82 |
| 1980 | 40,081 | 2.20 | 69.4 | 2,105 | .59 |
| 1990 | 49,225 | 2.05 | 74.8 | 1,913 | .43 |
| 2000 | 59,849 | 1.94 | 79.1 | 1,753 | .32 |
| 2010 | 72,272 | 1.88 | 82.7 | 1,620 | .25 |
| 2020 | 86,874 | 1.83 | 85.6 | 1,509 | .19 |
| | | | Total | | |
| 1960 | 45,711 | 1.10 | 100.0 | −3,247 | −.67 |
| 1970 | 51,091 | 1.11 | 100.0 | −2,847 | −.59 |
| 1980 | 57,736 | 1.22 | 100.0 | −2,514 | −.46 |
| 1990 | 65,835 | 1.31 | 100.0 | −2,237 | −.36 |
| 2000 | 75,622 | 1.39 | 100.0 | −2,005 | −.28 |
| 2010 | 87,391 | 1.45 | 100.0 | −1,811 | −.22 |
| 2020 | 101,500 | 1.50 | 100.0 | −1,648 | −.17 |

Equations (6) and (7) comprise two sets of two equations each in two variables: $U_j(t_2)$ and $r_j$. These were solved by an iterative method.

### Future Population and Migration Levels

The extrapolation results at ten-year intervals through the year 2020 are given in Table 4. The percent increases and percent rates are average annual rates for the appropriate decades. These figures show a large potential for future rural out-migration from the South despite a continuing decline of rural population. Current rates imply rural out-migration in excess of three million per decade well into the twenty-first Century.

The data in Table 4 exhibit a number of interesting properties: (1) Rural population will decline at a declining rate.[7] Rates are assumed constant for each group in each state. The groups with the higher rates of decline will constitute decreasing proportions of total rural population, and thus the aggregate rate will become smaller. (2) Urban population will increase at a declining rate. Urban in-migration declines in absolute number with rural out-migration. In addition, total urban population is increasing. Hence, the rate of growth beyond natural increase declines. (3) Total population will increase at an increasing rate. The absolute magnitude of population loss through non-retained rural out-migrants will become smaller and the population base larger. Total population increase will approach natural increase.

### Questionable Assumptions

The extrapolations given in Table 4 are not intended as accurate predictions of the South's future population levels. A number of the parameters assumed constant for these projections will undoubtedly change over time. White–non-white differentials may decline with social and political advances. The use of the same increase rates for rural and urban populations probably results in an underestimate of rural growth and an overestimate of urban growth. Many as yet unforeseeable changes will serve to alter the competitive position of the South and thus change retention rates.

Basic patterns, however, appear inalterable. Migration and retention rates can change within wide bounds without affecting their directions. The South will continue to generate large numbers of rural out-migrants who will serve as the basis for above-average urban growth within the region. This movement will continue on a large scale for many years. The structure and performance of the South, however, will more closely approach that of the nation as a whole.

## Growth of Non-Agricultural Employment

### Growth and Composition

Total employment in the South increased at an annual rate of 0.59 percent during 1950–60, contrasted with a national increase of 1.13 percent. The South's slower total employment growth is a con-

7. Since white rural populations are increasing slightly in four states, a point will eventually be reached at which their increases will dominate and the rural population of the region as a whole will increase. This point, however, is not reached in the sixty-year projections, and, therefore, is of little interest.

## Table 5. Non-Agricultural Employment: 1950 and 1962*

| | EMPLOYMENT (THOUSANDS) | | | | PERCENT PER YEAR GROWTH: 1950-62 | |
| | United States | | South | | | |
| | 1950 | 1962 | 1950 | 1962 | United States | South |
|---|---|---|---|---|---|---|
| Total | 44,942.3 | 55,123.6 | 9,098.4 | 11,753.3 | 1.70 | 2.13 |
| Mining and Oil | 902.6 | 649.4 | 432.1 | 341.0 | −2.74 | −1.97 |
| Manufacturing | 15,248.2 | 16,783.7 | 2,608.1 | 3,259.4 | .80 | 1.86 |
| Construction | 2,343.6 | 2,817.3 | 536.3 | 692.8 | 1.53 | 2.13 |
| Transport. Comm. and Public Utilities | 4,041.5 | 3,879.9 | 854.0 | 843.2 | −.34 | −.11 |
| Trade | 9,412.6 | 11,502.4 | 1,990.8 | 2,502.4 | 1.67 | 1.91 |
| Finance, Insurance and Real Estate | 1,843.7 | 2,793.4 | 292.2 | 518.4 | 3.46 | 4.78 |
| Services and Misc. | 5,115.6 | 7,724.4 | 1,004.4 | 1,469.8 | 3.43 | 3.17 |
| Governments | 6,034.5 | 8,973.1 | 1,380.5 | 2,126.3 | 3.31 | 3.60 |

* Source: Bureau of Labor Statistics, *Employment and Earnings Statistics for States and Areas: 1939-62*, Bulletin No. 1370 (1963).

comitance of its slower total population growth. The South and the nation each experienced a decline of agricultural employment and an increase of non-agricultural employment. During 1950–60, the South's agricultural employment declined 6.29 percent per year and the nation's declined 4.82. This section is devoted to a consideration of the growth patterns for non-agricultural employment.

Non-agricultural employment levels for eight major divisions for 1950 and 1962 are given in Table 5. The composition of total employment changed dramatically. There was a nation-wide increase in the importance of service and service types of industries. National employment in finance, insurance, and real estate; in services and miscellaneous; and in governments each grew at approximately twice the national aggregate rate. By 1962, governments represented more than 16 percent of total non-agricultural employment. State and local government employment grew much more rapidly than federal. More than two million new jobs were created by state and local governments. At the other end of the scale, employment in mining and transportation industries declined in absolute amount. Manufacturing, once thought to be the bulwark of economic growth, experienced an employment growth rate less than half the national aggregate rate. The South experienced the same general changes in employment composition as the nation as a whole.

**Table 6.** Non-Agricultural Employment Growth Rates and Differentials: 1950–62* (Average Percents Per Year)

|  | Growth Rate | Differential | Weight Part | Rate Part |
|---|---|---|---|---|
| South | 2.13 | .43 | −.05 | .48 |
| Alabama | 2.03 | .33 | −.06 | .39 |
| Arkansas | 2.36 | .66 | .11 | .55 |
| Georgia | 2.56 | .86 | .05 | .81 |
| Kentucky | 1.54 | −.16 | −.26 | .10 |
| Louisiana | 1.85 | .15 | −.01 | .16 |
| Mississippi | 2.58 | .88 | .20 | .68 |
| North Carolina | 2.49 | .79 | −.05 | .84 |
| Oklahoma | 1.94 | .24 | .00 | .24 |
| South Carolina | 2.29 | .59 | −.05 | .64 |
| Tennessee | 1.99 | .29 | .07 | .22 |
| Texas | 2.65 | .95 | .00 | .95 |
| Virginia | 2.45 | .75 | .05 | .70 |
| West Virginia | −1.35 | −3.05 | −.86 | −2.19 |
| Florida | 5.62 | 3.92 | .33 | 3.59 |
| Arizona | 6.75 | 5.05 | .15 | 4.90 |
| California | 4.04 | 2.34 | .21 | 2.13 |
| Colorado | 3.56 | 1.86 | .19 | 1.67 |
| Connecticut | 1.78 | .08 | −.09 | .17 |
| Delaware | 2.07 | .37 | −.13 | .50 |
| Dist. of Columbia | 1.08 | −.62 | 1.01 | −1.63 |
| Idaho | 1.77 | .07 | .07 | .00 |
| Illinois | 1.00 | −.70 | −.06 | −.64 |
| Indiana | 1.15 | −.55 | −.21 | −.34 |
| Iowa | .95 | −.75 | .16 | −.91 |
| Kansas | 1.72 | .02 | .02 | .00 |
| Maine | .83 | −.87 | −.01 | −.86 |
| Maryland | 2.34 | −.64 | .05 | .59 |
| Massachusetts | .86 | −.84 | .05 | −.89 |
| Michigan | .63 | −1.07 | −.19 | −.88 |
| Minnesota | 1.68 | −.02 | .08 | −.10 |
| Missouri | 1.12 | −.58 | .06 | −.64 |
| Montana | 1.10 | −.60 | .02 | −.62 |
| Nebraska | 1.73 | .03 | .30 | −.27 |
| Nevada | 6.94 | 5.24 | .29 | 4.95 |
| New Hampshire | 1.64 | −.06 | −.04 | −.02 |
| New Jersey | 1.90 | .20 | −.10 | .30 |
| New Mexico | 3.89 | 2.19 | .22 | 1.97 |
| New York | .98 | −.72 | .12 | −.84 |
| North Dakota | 1.30 | −.40 | .40 | −.80 |
| Ohio | .95 | −.75 | −.13 | −.62 |
| Oregon | 1.50 | −.20 | .05 | −.25 |
| Pennsylvania | .10 | −1.60 | −.26 | −1.34 |
| Rhode Island | −.09 | −1.79 | −.09 | −1.70 |
| South Dakota | 1.99 | .29 | .41 | −.12 |
| Utah | 3.44 | 1.74 | .12 | 1.62 |
| Vermont | 1.00 | −.70 | .02 | −.72 |
| Washington | 1.83 | .13 | .22 | −.09 |
| Wisconsin | 1.40 | −.30 | −.08 | −.22 |
| Wyoming | 1.50 | −.20 | −.25 | .05 |

* Source: See Table 5.

The South experienced more rapid non-agricultural employment growth than the nation. Its rates are above the national rates for seven of the eight major divisions. The South's rural out-migrants have provided the basis for the region's above-average growth.

## Regional Growth

The distribution of employment growth among states has been as dramatic as the change in employment composition. Average annual growth rates by state for 1950–62 are given in the first column of Table 6. These range from an increase of 6.94 percent per year in Nevada through a decline of 1.35 percent per year in West Virginia. Differentials between overall state growth rates and the overall national rate are given in the second column of Table 6. A negative differential indicates a below-average growth rate, and a positive differential indicates an above-average rate.

The frontier states with high population growth rates (Florida, Arizona, and Nevada, for example) also had high employment growth rates. The over-all relation between population and employment growth rates, however, is very slight. The coefficient of rank correlation between the two growth-rate series is only 0.178 and is not significant at a 1-percent confidence level. The lack of a close relation follows from relatively high employment increases in the South and other states with substantial rural out-migration and relatively low population increase. Each Southern state, except Kentucky and West Virginia, had a non-agricultural employment growth rate greater than the national average.

The coefficient of rank correlation between the urban in-migration rates given in Table 1 and the growth-rate differentials given in Table 6 is 0.847 and is significant at a 1-percent confidence level.[8] This is not surprising, since most non-agricultural jobs are located within urban areas. Given urban population increases, employment increases follow once adjustments are made for participation and unemployment rate changes. It is generally safe to state that urban population and non-agricultural employment increase or decline *pari passu*.

8. The state ranking for urban migration rates is identical to a ranking for urban population growth rates, and the growth-rate differential ranking is identical to a ranking of non-agricultural-employment growth rates. Therefore, the same 0.847 coefficient would be obtained if the two growth rate series were rank-correlated.

## Weight and Rate Effects

Growth is influenced by starting position. A state with a relative specialization in national rapid-growth industries has an advantage over a state specialized in slow-growth or declining industries. In 1950, more than 25 percent of West Virginia's total employment was provided by mining, contrasted with 2 percent for the nation as a whole. Mining is a declining industry, and West Virginia's heavy commitment has provided a severe impediment to growth. Growth in other sectors has not been adequate to offset its decline in mining employment.

The growth-rate differentials listed in the second column of Table 6 are separated into weight- and rate-parts to reflect the respective influences of initial position and competitive gain.[9]

If each division in state $k$ had grown at the division's national rate, the state's 1962 total non-agricultural employment would have been

$$\sum_{j=1}^{8} E^k_j \mu_j$$

where $E_j^k$ is the state's 1950 employment in division $j$, and $\mu_j = e^{12\beta_j}$ is a national growth multiplier derived from the division's annual growth rate, $\beta_j$.

A weight-part differential, $\lambda^k$, is defined as the difference between the aggregate growth rate that state $k$ would have achieved if its divisions had experienced national growth rates, and the aggregate national growth rate, $\beta$:

$$(8) \quad \lambda^k = Log_e (\sum_{j=1}^{8} w^k_j \mu_j)/12 - \beta$$

where $w_j^k = E_j^k/E^k$ is the proportion of $k$'s 1950 employment in division $j$. The sign of Equation (8) can be determined by contrasting $k$'s hypothetical and the national aggregate growth multipliers. The weight-part differential will take the sign of the expression

$$\sum_{j=1}^{8} w^k_j \mu_j - \sum_{i=1}^{8} w_j \mu_j = \sum_{j=1}^{8} (w^k_j - w_j) \mu_j$$

where $w_j$ are national division weights. If $k$ has a net weight differential toward the more rapidly growing sectors, its weight-part differen-

9. The weight and rate parts defined here are quite similar to the proportionality and differential shifts developed by H. S. Perloff, E. S. Dunn, E. E. Lampard, and R. F. Muth, *Regions, Resources, and Economic Growth* (Baltimore, 1960), pp. 70–74 *passim*.

tial will be positive.   If $k$'s net weight differential is toward the more slow-growing sectors, e.g., mining, manufacturing, it will be negative.

The positive weight parts in Table 6 for Florida and California result from their relative specialization in trade and service industries in 1950.   The District of Columbia's positive weight part results from its specialization in government.   The large negative figures for West Virginia and Kentucky result from their specialization in mining.   The negative figures for North Carolina, Connecticut, and Michigan result from a relative specialization in manufacturing.   The South as a whole had a negative weight part as a result of the importance of mining and manufacturing.

The rate-part differentials, $\xi^k$, given in Table 6 are the differences between the over-all differentials and the weight parts:

$$(9) \quad \xi^k = (\beta^k - \beta) - \lambda^k$$

where $\beta^k$ is state $k$'s actual growth rate.   The sign of Equation (9) can be determined by contrasting $k$'s hypothetical and actual growth multipliers.   The rate-part differential will take the sign of the expression

$$\sum_{j=1}^{8} w_j^k \mu_j^k - \sum_{j=1}^{8} w_j^k \mu_j = \sum_{j=1}^{8} (\mu_j^k - \mu_j) \, w_j^k$$

which is an average of sector growth-multiplier differentials weighted by state division-composition weights.

On the whole, the weight parts in Table 6 are not large relative to rate parts, and initial composition does not appear to provide a general explanation of growth-rate differentials.   A few patterns, however, are noticeable.   Weight parts are small parts of the total differentials in the frontier areas but are positive for every state with a growth-rate differential greater than 3 percent.   The frontier states are not traditional centers of manufacturing, and the absence of initial manufacturing reinforced their high growth rates.   Several of the mature-urban areas possess negative weight parts because of initial specialization in manufacturing and mining.   Competitively slow growth was further hindered by initial composition in these states.

No general pattern is discernible for weight parts in the South. The weight part is positive in five states, negative in six, and zero in two.   All thirteen of the Southern states had positive rate parts which give further evidence of their competitive gains.

## Regional Equalization

### Broad Specialization

The number of Americans engaged in agriculture declined as mass rural out-migration took place. Thus, differences in the degree of agricultural–non-agricultural specialization among areas declined, and in this sense the various regions of the United States became more alike. Other resource-oriented industries (for example, mining and lumbering) declined in either absolute or relative terms during the past decade, and thus shared agriculture's fate. The result was a further decline in regional specialization.

A broad measure of regional specialization is defined and evaluated for 1950 and 1962 in this section in order to gain insight into recent changes in regional specialization outside of agriculture. A state's national employment image is obtained by distributing its total employment for a given year among the eight major divisions on the basis of the national division weights for that year. These employment levels are then subtracted from the state's actual levels to obtain image deviations. A positive deviation for a division indicates relative specialization, i.e., a weight higher than the national. Similarly, a negative deviation indicates relative underspecialization. Specialization is always matched by underspecialization; the algebraic sum of the percentage deviations for a particular state must equal zero by construction. An algebraic sum therefore provides no information of interest.

One-half the sum of the absolute values of the division deviations is utilized to measure the deviation of a state from its national image. Specifically, the percent employment deviation for state $k$ in a given year, denoted by $d^k$, is

$$(10) \quad d^k = \frac{\sum\limits_{j=1}^{8} |E^k_j - w_j E^k|}{2E^k} \cdot 100$$

where, as above, $E^k_j$ is state $k$'s employment in division $j$; $E^k$ is its total employment; and $w_j$ is the proportion of national employment in division $j$. The absolute sum is divided by two because of the compensating nature of the deviation definition. If one employee more than the national image were employed in manufacturing, it follows that one less must be employed in some other division. The resultant absolute sum is two, but only one employee is involved.[10]

10. The same result would be achieved if total specialization, i.e., positive deviations, were divided by total employment.

**Table 7.** National Image Deviations: 1950 and 1962*
(Percents of Total Non-Agricultural Employment)

| | 1950 | 1962 | | 1950 | 1962 |
|---|---|---|---|---|---|
| South | 6.5 | 4.9 | Kansas | 14.3 | 11.7 |
| Alabama | 5.2 | 5.1 | Maine | 10.2 | 8.7 |
| Arkansas | 9.8 | 4.6 | Maryland | 3.7 | 4.3 |
| Georgia | 3.5 | 3.9 | Massachusetts | 7.9 | 7.4 |
| Kentucky | 11.8 | 6.6 | Michigan | 15.4 | 10.0 |
| Louisiana | 11.9 | 13.8 | Minnesota | 8.9 | 6.2 |
| Mississippi | 10.0 | 6.4 | Missouri | 6.7 | 4.1 |
| North Carolina | 11.2 | 12.1 | Montana | 23.2 | 18.6 |
| Oklahoma | 20.4 | 16.7 | Nebraska | 19.3 | 13.6 |
| South Carolina | 12.2 | 13.0 | Nevada | 30.0 | 29.8 |
| Tennessee | 3.4 | 3.7 | New Hampshire | 13.6 | 13.3 |
| Texas | 15.7 | 11.8 | New Jersey | 11.7 | 8.7 |
| Virginia | 7.0 | 5.6 | New Mexico | 28.2 | 24.3 |
| West Virginia | 22.7 | 11.9 | New York | 5.2 | 5.6 |
| Florida | 20.5 | 15.0 | North Dakota | 29.7 | 25.8 |
| Arizona | 24.0 | 15.7 | Ohio | 10.2 | 8.7 |
| California | 11.3 | 4.6 | Oregon | 5.2 | 5.8 |
| Colorado | 16.7 | 13.5 | Pennsylvania | 9.6 | 7.9 |
| Connecticut | 16.4 | 14.4 | Rhode Island | 15.6 | 9.8 |
| Delaware | 12.3 | 7.3 | South Dakota | 25.0 | 22.3 |
| Dist. of Columbia | 38.6 | 36.6 | Utah | 19.1 | 13.9 |
| Idaho | 18.3 | 13.8 | Vermont | 7.0 | 4.9 |
| Illinois | 5.2 | 4.9 | Washington | 9.5 | 5.4 |
| Indiana | 11.7 | 10.6 | Wisconsin | 8.6 | 7.2 |
| Iowa | 10.3 | 6.3 | Wyoming | 29.1 | 25.4 |

* Source: See Table 5.

Image deviations for the forty-nine state units for 1950 and 1962 are listed in Table 7. The changes between 1950 and 1960 are rather striking. Forty-one of the forty-nine state units recorded decline, i.e., became more like the national average. The eight exceptions recorded relatively small increases. The average of the forty-nine state deviations fell from 14.2 to 11.5 percent. One seldom finds such predominant moves in one direction. The declines reflect the widespread relative increases in the importance of government and service industries, the widespread relative decline of mining and transportation, and a more even distribution of manufacturing employment. The percentage growth of manufacturing employment was generally greater in the relatively non-industrial frontier and urbanizing-rural areas than in the traditionally industrial mature-urban areas. A rough indication of this is given by a rank correlation coefficient of −0.632 for state observations covering manufacturing employment growth rates and percentages of total employment in manufacturing in 1950.

In terms of broad specialization, at least, the various regions of the United States are becoming more alike.[11]

The implications of the decline in specialization are many. For example, one might hypothesize that the volume of interregional trade has increased less rapidly than income and employment in recent years.

The percentage deviation for the South as a whole fell from 6.5 in 1950 to 4.9 in 1962. Five Southern states (Georgia, Louisiana, North Carolina, South Carolina, and Tennessee) recorded increases. The deviations for the Southern states varied from 3.5 through 22.7 in 1950, and from 3.9 through 13.8 in 1962. Kentucky, with a deviation of 11.8 percent, was the nation's median state in 1950. Seven of the remaining Southern states were below the median, and five were above. Rhode Island, with a 9.8 deviation, was the median state in 1962. Seven Southern states were below the median, and six were above.

### Southern Income Behavior

The South has long experienced the lowest per-capita personal income levels in the United States. Per-capita personal income levels for 1950 and 1962 are given in Table 8. All thirteen Southern states were below the national average in both years. If the 1950 incomes are ranked for forty-eight states and the District of Columbia, Southern states occupy the eleven lowest positions. Only Texas and Virginia had higher incomes than one or more states outside of the South. The relative low-income position of the South was little changed by 1962. Again, every Southern state was below the national average. The ten lowest income positions were occupied by Southern states. Oklahoma managed to join the two above-mentioned states in that its income was above one state outside of the South.

Southern income levels generally grew more rapidly than the level

11. The values of the percentage deviations depend upon the sector classification used in the computations. The eight-division classification suppresses differences between components within the same division. In particular, individual manufacturing industries have exhibited widely different growth rates. A more detailed sector classification would result in larger values for the percentage deviations, but it is unlikely that disaggregation would reverse the general decline. The author and R. Stephen Rodd performed deviation computations for six Upper Midwest States for a thirty-nine-sector classification with a two-digit manufacturing break. Percentage deviations were larger than in the eight-sector computation, but in each instance they were lower in 1960 than in 1950. With very few exceptions, the deviations declined between pairs of successive years during the decade.

**Table 8.** Per-Capita Personal Income Levels: 1950 and 1962*

| | PERSONAL INCOME (Dollars per Capita) | | INCREASE | |
|---|---|---|---|---|
| | 1950 | 1962 | Dollars | Percent per Year |
| United States | 1,491 | 2,366 | 875 | 3.85 |
| Alabama | 867 | 1,567 | 700 | 4.93 |
| Arkansas | 805 | 1,504 | 699 | 5.21 |
| Georgia | 1,016 | 1,759 | 743 | 4.57 |
| Kentucky | 958 | 1,712 | 754 | 4.84 |
| Louisiana | 1,089 | 1,705 | 616 | 3.74 |
| Mississippi | 729 | 1,285 | 556 | 4.72 |
| North Carolina | 1,009 | 1,732 | 723 | 4.50 |
| Oklahoma | 1,133 | 1,905 | 772 | 4.33 |
| South Carolina | 881 | 1,545 | 664 | 4.68 |
| Tennessee | 995 | 1,702 | 707 | 4.47 |
| Texas | 1,340 | 2,013 | 673 | 3.39 |
| Virginia | 1,222 | 2,018 | 796 | 4.18 |
| West Virginia | 1,095 | 1,810 | 715 | 4.19 |

* Source: Department of Commerce, *Survey of Current Business.*

for the nation as a whole. The percentage growth rates listed in Table 8 show that eleven of the thirteen Southern states had percentage increases of per-capita personal income that exceeded the national average. However, the dollar increase for each Southern state was below the dollar increase for the nation as a whole. In relative terms, the South moved closer to the national average; in absolute terms, it fell further behind. The South became more like the nation as a whole in many important respects, but its income performance was rather sluggish.

Two major forces appear to operate upon the relative position of Southern per-capita income levels; one is an exhilarant and one is a depressant. Both are tied to the rural-urban migration process. The exhilarating effect results from the decreasing relative importance of the South's rural areas. Per-capita incomes in the South's rural areas are substantially below incomes in the region's urban areas. Rural out-migration, therefore, removes persons from the lowest end of the income scale and thus tends to increase the average. The effect is in the same direction whether income-earning rural out-migrants leave the region or move to employment in its urban area. In the former case, the out-migrant is no longer counted in the computation of average income levels. In the latter case, he is still counted, but earns a higher income.

The movement of large numbers of rural out-migrants to Southern cities seeking employment serves as a depressant to prevent the increase of Southern wages to levels realized in other parts of the nation. A fair proportion of the South's new employment has been attracted by below-average wage rates.

The two pressures will continue to operate in the future. Their net effect, however, may turn more in the direction of income equalization than was true during the past decade. Table 4 indicates a drop in percent of total population that is rural in the South from 44.9 in 1960 to 37.1 in 1970. A decline as substantial as this should have a considerable exhilarating force upon per capita income levels. The extrapolations also indicate a fall of the urban in-migration rate. Thus the relative downward[12] pressure of new labor force entrants may lessen.

## Some Implications of Recent Developments

### State of the Art

Large-scale regional research is underway at a number of centers throughout the United States. Smaller research efforts are very common. Research is being conducted without the aid of well-developed theoretical structures for analysis of the regional growth process. Theoretical methods are being developed along with empirical research. Empiricism of this nature has several drawbacks, but it has the advantage of a close correspondence between theory and factual experience. Many of the difficulties in the development of regional theory result from the high standards which scholars in this field set for themselves. In some branches of economics, theories are formulated in terms of a few aggregates or general concepts with little concern about quantitative verification. Regional theory requires methods that cover disaggregated variables and will stand quantitative tests.

Most currently available methods for regional analysis are of value for specific purposes. A recent trend has been toward the development of summary measures of historical growth. Examples are provided by the weight- and rate-part differentials and image deviations presented above. These and similar measures provide valuable information with which to begin regional analysis, but do not provide the wherewithal for forward-looking analyses of regional growth.

The general decline of specialization shown by the historical measures and other information serves to complicate explanations of

12. The word downward is used in a relative sense and means a lower rate of increase.

regional growth. There are fewer obvious regional differences upon which to hang theories of differential growth.

Classical location theory provided a classification of industries by principal locational factor. Industries were thus resource-oriented, transport-oriented, labor-oriented, market-oriented, or foot-loose. These classifications provide information of interest, though it is sometimes difficult to place specific industries within a specific category. These classifications, however, provide little insight into the nature of the regional growth process in light of the relative decline of resource-oriented industries, and the rapid growth of market-oriented and foot-loose industries developed during the past decade.

### Export-Base Analysis

The well-known export-base, or economic-base, analysis provides the outstanding example of a widely used method that contains unworkable assumptions. In somewhat simplified form the analysis runs as follows: Two types of industries are recognized, base and service. Activity levels for base industries depend upon demands external to the region under investigation. Activity levels in the region's service industries are determined by internal income and employment, often via a multiplier process. Once levels for the base industries are determined, levels for service industries follow easily from internal variables.

Manufacturing, mining, and agriculture generally have been treated as base industries. During the past decade these industries either declined or grew at below-average rates. Service industries were the dynamic growth industries. In export-base terms the recent past has been an epoch during which the tail wagged the dog. If export-base methods are used, one must explain changes in the multiplier over time.

### Supply Emphasis

Most existing theories of location and regional growth emphasize demands for employment at alternative locations. Export-base analysis, orientation analysis, comparative cost analysis, and regional input-output analysis are all occupied with the demand side of employment determination. The supply side, i.e., the force underlying the potential migration of people to jobs at particular locations, has been largely neglected in the main stream of regional analysis. The large-scale migration of the past decade points to the need for intensive analyses of the supply side.

# VI

# Trends in Population and Employment in the South from 1930 to 1960 and Their Economic Significance*

*By John L. Fulmer*

## I. Introduction

The South is no longer the nation's Economic Problem Number One, nor is it yet quite the nation's Economic Opportunity Number One; but surely the South is a region that is increasingly attracting the attention of business leaders, politicians, and others. All can agree, certainly, that it is casting off rapidly the shackles of the past, the ties of an agrarian economy and a provincial type of thinking. Perhaps all would not agree that the South is rapidly emerging as the

* In this report I have drawn heavily from the published works of numerous research scholars who have already blazed the trail in regional analysis. Where possible, credit has been given in the footnotes. Obviously, almost all government agencies are the source for the basic statistics obtained from published reports. For current data on non-agricultural employment, I wish to acknowledge especially the valuable assistance provided by Messrs. Brunswick Bagdon and Charles Bullock of the Regional Office, U.S. Bureau of Labor Statistics. Mr. Harold C. Phillips, U.S. Department of Agriculture, supplied similar data on agricultural employment. I am sincerely grateful to Mr. Howard G. Brunsman, Chief, Division of Population, Bureau of the Census, for assistance in providing data from the 1960 Census of Population along with other reports of the Census Bureau on population and employment.

Many persons at Georgia Institute of Technology assisted me in numerous ways with the statistical analysis or the final report. Dr. Walter S. Buckingham, Jr., Director, School of Industrial Management, and also his predecessor, Professor Maurice R. Brewster, arranged a lighter teaching load and provided a student assistant to help with the statistical analysis. The interest and aid of both contributed greatly to the progress of the study. I wish to acknowledge also with appreciation the help of Professor J. Carlton Brown, who assisted with the curve fitting and calculation of the growth rates.

fastest-growing region in the United States, exceeded perhaps only by the West Coast. The South,[1] as defined for the purposes of this symposium,[2] has had a yearly rate[3] of population increase from 1930 to 1960 which exceeded slightly the rate for the rest of the nation; the yearly rates of increase for total employment have risen neither as much nor as consistently as population; yet during 1950–60 these exceeded by a good margin the yearly growth rates of the rest of the country. The objectives of this paper are: (1) to trace trends in population for the region and its states, (2) to study impact of migration on population changes, (3) to analyze interrelationships between population and employment changes, and (4) to show economic significance of population and employment changes on the region's economy.

Development of necessary data for the problem assigned was a task of major proportions, especially in obtaining data of an acceptable degree of reliability for analysis of changes in total employment. Population data were readily available from the Census Bureau reports.[4] On the other hand, a colossal problem was encountered in assembling data on total employment with any degree of consistency and comparability. The data problem arose in connection with employment because there was no single source which provided data on the region's workers continuously for the entire period. There were four sources of employment which had to be pieced and fitted together as well as possible. The first source was the two different reports prepared on labor force and employment by the Census Bureau, appearing first in the Census of Population counts of occupations each decade, available by states and even smaller units; the second was the Census Bureau monthly estimates of labor force and employment, showing primarily national agricultural and non-agricultural employment. A third source was the Bureau of Labor Statistics estimates of employment and earnings appearing by states monthly since 1939. The fourth and last source readily available was the

1. The region as defined in this report includes Alabama, Arkansas, Florida, Georgia, Kentucky, Louisiana, Mississippi, North Carolina, South Carolina, Tennessee, Texas, Virginia, and West Virginia.

2. The data in this report as first prepared for the Conference at St. Petersburg, Florida, October 28, 1960, reflected estimates for the year, 1960. In the current revision, data for the 1960 Census of population and other data reflect more recent official estimates.

3. Yearly rates by decades or longer periods were computed by use of following formula: $\text{Log } Y = \text{Log } a + X \text{ Log } b$.

4. *Current Population Reports,* Series P-25, Numbers 139, 196, 208, 210, and 258.

U.S. Department of Agriculture estimates of agricultural employment, published regularly in *Farm Labor,* containing data on farm employment by states and by months, with a reasonably good series extending back to 1950.

The real difficulty in constructing a series of employment from 1930 to 1960 from these four sources is that no one source could be relied on for a continuous series on total employment, because there are important differences in definition and completeness between them. Ultimately it became necessary to abandon the idea of an annual series. Instead of a yearly series compounded with difficulties, we tried to make as complete as possible the occupational data from the Census of Population at ten-year intervals. But even this series had real data problems, and we ended up piecing and adjusting national totals with data from the 1930 Census of Population, the Bureau of Labor Statistics series, and the U.S. Department of Agriculture estimates of farm employment. Details of methodology used in developing employment data are given in a rather extensive appendix at the end of this paper. Although interesting in itself, we must dispense with a full discussion of methodology because of the technical nature of such an analysis and because of limitations of space.

## II. Population Growth

The method employed to calculate rates of change in population (and also expansion in employment) involved median decade growth rates in order to avoid statistical difficulties in comparing percentage increases from a base point greatly different in size. Yearly percentage increases were computed with a type of compound growth curve in order to allocate the change between decade intervals equally to each year in the period. The type of compound interest curve employed was: $\text{Log } Y = \text{Log } a + X \text{ Log } b$. One obvious advantage of this form of equation is that calculations can be made with the use of log tables directly by unsophisticated methods.

The yearly rates of population growth by this method for each of the thirteen states, and the two regions used in the comparisons, are given in Table 1. The data show that the South, compared to the rest of the nation,[5] performed quite well during the thirty-year period ending in 1960. Although the ratio of the South's yearly rate com-

5. Thirty-five states plus the District of Columbia, but excluding of course Alaska and Hawaii.

**Table 1.**  Trends in Decade Yearly Rates of Population Change in Southern States and Specified Regions, 1930–60*

| State or Region | YEARLY PERCENTAGE CHANGE[a] | | | |
|---|---|---|---|---|
| | 1930-40 | 1940-50 | 1950-60 | 1930-60 |
| Alabama | .75 | .73 | .75 | .78 |
| Arkansas | .50 | −.26 | −.63 | −.13 |
| Florida | 2.60 | 3.95 | 5.89 | 4.19 |
| Georgia | .70 | 1.01 | 1.39 | 1.03 |
| Kentucky | .92 | .29 | .27 | .50 |
| Louisiana | 1.19 | 1.08 | 1.91 | 1.43 |
| Mississippi | .82 | −.03 | .06 | .29 |
| North Carolina | 1.22 | 1.28 | 1.19 | 1.17 |
| South Carolina | .87 | 1.10 | 1.21 | 1.06 |
| Tennessee | 1.15 | 1.19 | .78 | 1.04 |
| Texas | .95 | 1.89 | 2.21 | 1.68 |
| Virginia | 1.15 | 1.83 | 2.02 | 1.66 |
| West Virginia | .96 | .52 | −.83 | .22 |
| Total 13 States | 1.03 | 1.25 | 1.56 | 1.28 |
| Rest of Nation[b] | .58 | 1.42 | 1.83 | 1.27 |
| Ratio of South to Rest of Nation | 1.78 | .88 | .85 | 1.01 |

* Source of basic data: See Appendix Table 1.
[a] Type: Log $Y = $ Log $a + X$ Log $b$.
[b] Thirty-five states plus the District of Columbia, but excluding Alaska and Hawaii.

pared to the other states showed a slight tendency to decline during 1950–60 relative to 1940–50, the region enjoyed a small advantage of 1 percent in population gain for the entire period. The backwash of migration from the depression years caused the yearly rates for 1930–40 to exceed the rate for the rest of the country by 78 percent. It was due entirely to the larger population growth of this period that the South had the greater population gain, for in the next two decades the region's rate was between 85 and 88 percent of the rate for the rest of the nation. The result is that the South's population ratio to all other states remained unchanged at 36.9 both in 1930 and 1960, although with some higher ratios for the other two decades. (See Appendix Table 1.)

Compared to that of the rest of the country, population growth among states of the South contain perhaps the greatest extremes. The region includes two of the nation's most rapidly[6] growing states

6. In actual numbers added, California led the states from 1950 to 1960, and even before. Percentage increases in the decade puts Florida in the lead, followed by Nevada, Arizona, and California. (This analysis does not include Alaska and Hawaii.)

(Florida and Texas), and the nation's two declining states. Population declines have persisted in Arkansas since 1942 and in West Virginia since 1951. Mississippi also declined from 1943 until late in the 1950's.

Aside from this broad generalization, the states of the region demonstrate a number of significant trends during the thirty-year period. Four states exceeded the yearly rate of increase for the region. They are Florida, Texas, Virginia, and Louisiana, in that order. Four other states, fractionally below the region's yearly rate, are North Carolina, South Carolina, Tennessee, and Georgia. Alabama shows a steady growth picture over the thirty-year period with a yearly gain of 0.78 percent; Kentucky had an irregular rate of growth with 0.5 percent. Mississippi and West Virginia had a yearly increase of around 0.25 percent, while Arkansas had a yearly decline of 0.13 percent.

From 1950 to 1960, while the yearly percentage increase was about 22 percent larger than for the thirty-year rate, the ranking of the states, although shuffled around a bit, remained in the same general relationships to each other. While Florida, Texas, Virginia, and Louisiana still led, in that order, Georgia moved up from eighth to fifth place, with North Carolina and Tennessee each moving down one or more places. West Virginia exchanged rank with Arkansas and became the lowest-ranking state in percentage change during the last ten years with a yearly decline of 0.83 percent. (See Table 1.)

In terms of actual population growth, we see the differences between states in an even more emphatic light. During the thirty-year period, the thirteen Southern states had a total population gain of 15,369,000; the rest of the nation had a growth of 41,537,000; the South's growth was thus 37 percent as large as the thirty-five other states plus the District of Columbia. Of the 15,000,000-plus growth which occurred in the South, Texas and Florida, in that order, accounted for almost 50 percent of the total gain for the region. If Virginia and Louisiana are added, the ratio becomes about two-thirds.

During the more recent 1950–60 decade, the South's growth was 6,959,000; the other states', 21,790,000, with the South's ratio being 31.9 percent (compared to 37 percent in the thirty-year period). But the concentration of growth in a few states was enlarged. Florida and Texas (note the change in order) accounted for 58.6 percent (but about 50 percent in the longer period), while Virginia and Louisiana added another 18.4 percent, making the total ratio 77.0. (See Table 2.)

Now looking at some of the reasons for state differences, we find that, with minor exceptions, the most rapidly growing states have the highest proportion of total population in Standard Metropolitan Statistical Areas.[7] The data are given in Appendix Table 4. The tabulation shows that West Virginia is the only state with a relatively large proportion of its population in SMSA's (37.7 percent in 1960) which had a small population gain from 1930–60 but a decrease since the 1950 census. Arkansas and Mississippi, the former a continuously shrinking state and the latter shrinking until 1955, have a very small population ratio in SMSA's. On the other hand, both Florida and Texas, with the highest ratio—about 65 percent each—had by far the largest population increases.[8]

We conclude from this section on population that the South appears to have excelled the rest of the nation in yearly rate of population increase during the thirty-year period by a very slight margin of .01 percent, with relatively less growth in the last two decades being slightly more than offset by the large depression growth. Florida and Texas have set the pace among the states of the region to such a great extent that these two states accounted for 48 percent of the South's increase from 1930–60, and 59 percent in the last decade. Virginia and Louisiana have percentage increases exceeding the region's composite. North Carolina, South Carolina, Tennessee, and Georgia have encouraging rates of growth, with Georgia's improvement especially noteworthy in the last decade. Alabama and particularly Kentucky have a mixed growth picture. The other three states, Arkansas, Mississippi, and West Virginia, lost population during one or more of the decades included in the study.

The most interesting aspect of the South's population change is the rapid decline in rural farm population since 1940, and the rather striking growth of urbanized areas. Urban population increase is and

7. The term "Standard Metropolitan Statistical Areas" will be referred to as SMSA's or the singular as SMSA, for the saving of space.

8. Although a detailed study of Standard Metropolitan Statistical Areas is beyond the scope of this paper, an interesting discussion of growth in Standard Metropolitan Areas (based on 1950 data), and some of the analytical reasons will be found in Donald J. Bogue, *Population Growth in Standard Metropolitan Areas 1900–1950, with an Explanatory Analysis of Urbanized Areas* (Washington, D.C.: Housing and Home Finance Agency, Dec. 1953). He has analyzed by linear regression methods five factors which one would presume affect growth of SMA's. These factors are rate of past growth, fertility, size of SMA, age of SMA, and industrial development. His results show that only the rate of "past growth can be thought of as a factor in metropolitan growth with nationwide generality. All the other factors either show no significant relationship or only a relationship in a particular regional context."

**Table 2.** Comparisons of Rates of Population Growth of States and Regions and Percentage of South's Growth Accounted for by Each State*

| State or Region | ACTUAL INCREASE (in Thousands) | | PERCENTAGE OF TOTAL INCREASE IN REGION | |
|---|---|---|---|---|
| | 1930-60 | 1950-60 | 1930-60 | 1950-60 |
| Alabama | 629 | 216 | 4.1 | 3.1 |
| Arkansas | −70 | −116 | −0.5 | −1.7 |
| Florida | 3,534 | 2,184 | 23.0 | 31.4 |
| Georgia | 1,048 | 510 | 6.8 | 7.3 |
| Kentucky | 419 | 82 | 2.7 | 1.2 |
| Louisiana | 1,154 | 560 | 7.5 | 8.0 |
| Mississippi | 178 | 14 | 1.2 | 0.2 |
| North Carolina | 1,404 | 511 | 9.1 | 7.3 |
| South Carolina | 648 | 272 | 4.2 | 3.9 |
| Tennessee | 952 | 268 | 6.2 | 3.9 |
| Texas | 3,799 | 1,894 | 24.7 | 27.2 |
| Virginia | 1,558 | 723 | 10.1 | 10.4 |
| West Virginia | 116 | −159 | 0.8 | −2.3 |
| Total 13 States | 15,369 | 6,959 | 100.0 | 100.0 |
| Rest of the Nation | 41,537 | 21,790 | 100.0 | 100.0 |

* Source: Appendix Table 1.

has been the dominant factor in Southern population growth for many decades; this is certainly true since 1930. Nothing shows this better than the strong positive relationship of the ratio of population in SMSA's to the percentage of population increase of states. (See Table 4 in the Appendix.)

## III. Migration Loss

Although significant differences exist between states in the natural rate of increase, the scope of this paper does not permit a detailed examination of rates of natural increase and their contribution to population increase of states. Migration changes are interesting in themselves in reflecting the underlying strength of economic development; for migration[9] change is a phenomenon of an economy of a certain level of development, where freedom of movement of people is not inhibited or prevented,[10] and where a flow of informa-

9. We use the term "Migration" for "Net Migration" as a measure of the continuous interchange of people between states and regions. If the dominant movement is out of the state, a net out-migration has occurred (or net migration loss), and vice versa. Yet in the text the term "Migration loss or gain" refers to the direction of the net movement.

10. Obviously, the Soviet Union and satellite Communistic countries are ignoring the very important impact on economic development of the flow of information and free movement of people.

tion[11] on jobs and living conditions occurs. The reason for movement of people by and large is knowledge of better job opportunities and the wisdom and energy to seek the human betterment available. Kuznets and Thomas state it somewhat more pointedly:

> . . . the distribution of a country's population at any given time may be viewed as a rough adjustment to the distribution of opportunities . . . The rapidity and magnitude of the differential impacts that accompany modern economic growth are such that the vital processes of birth and death can play but a minor role in adjusting population to economic opportunities in different parts of the country. They do not necessarily follow the directions required to maximize these adjustments; and if they do, their effect upon the age structure is so delayed that it cannot conceivably provide adult workers when and where they are needed. In consequence, it is migration that must provide the main mechanism of adjustment, and it is migration that must account for most of the population redistribution that can be viewed as an effect of economic growth.[12]

Detailed calculation of net migration losses or gains yearly for 1930–40 were computed by the Residual Method.[13] Data by states for the decades 1940–50 and 1950–60 were taken directly from Bureau of the Census, Current Population Reports, Series P-25, Nos. 72 and 247. The results of the migration calculations added indicate that the thirteen Southern states considered in this study had a total migration loss of 1,040,000 for the decade 1930 to 1940, representing 23 percent of the region's natural increase; from 1940 to 1950, the loss was almost double that during the previous decade, or 2,039,000, and the ratio rose to 29 percent of natural increase. During the decade from 1950 to 1960, a great improvement in the South's population balance sheet occurred when migration of persons dropped to 1,413,000, or 17 percent of natural increase. During the entire period from 1930

11. For an interesting discussion of the relation of information flow to migration, see Phillip Nelson, "Migration, Real Income and Information," *Journal of Regional Science*, I, No. 2 (Spring 1959), 42–62; also Herbert S. Parnes, *Research on Labor Mobility; An Appraisal of Research Findings in the United States* (Social Science Research Council, 1954), pp. 162 and 188.

12. Simon S. Kuznets and Dorothy S. Thomas (eds.), *Population Redistribution and Economic Growth, United States, 1870 to 1950* (Philadelphia: The American Philosophical Society, 1957), I, 2.

13. Described in detail by C. Horace Hamilton, "Population Pressure and Other Factors Affecting Rural-Urban Migration," in *Demographic Analysis*, eds. Joseph J. Spengler and Otis Dudley Duncan (Glencoe, Ill.: The Free Press, 1956), p. 419. Also Donald J. Bogue, *The Population of the United States* (Glencoe, Ill.: The Free Press, 1959), p. 397. The technical appendix attached outlines in detail the method of procedure employed by the Residual Method.

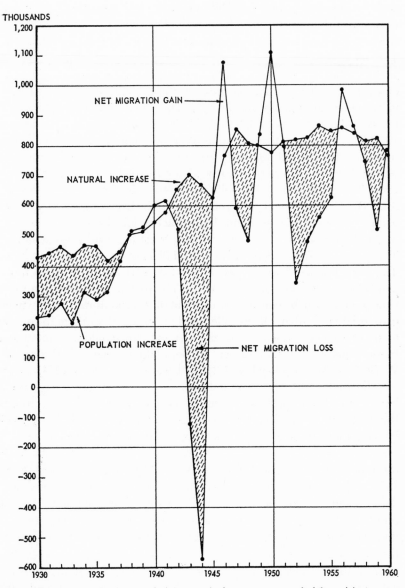

**Chart I.** Relationship of Natural Increase and Net Migration Change to Yearly Population Increase of 13 Southern States, 1930-60

to 1960, the region lost 4,492,000 of its natural increase, or about 23 percent. Although the decade 1940–50 showed the highest loss ratio, the trend in migration loss appears to be declining sharply. (See Table 3.)

The whole picture of migration changes relative to natural increase and the resulting population increase for the region in the aggregate is presented graphically in Chart I. The Chart shows five periods of heavy migration loss: 1930 to 1937, 1942–45, 1947–48, 1951–55, and 1958–59. We recognize peculiar situations dominating each of these periods. The period 1930–37, for example, was the great depression years. The loss averaged yearly about 200,000 but steadily became less. The great war of 1942–45 coincided with the second period we list. Heavy movement of troops overseas from Southern training camps was the dominant factor but attractive jobs in booming factories in the industrial Northeast and Middle West also had a great impact. The period 1947–48 again shows the influence of the postwar boom. The period 1951–55 is affected in the first part again by troop movements to the Korean Theater of War. The period 1958–59 was a recession period, which, coupled with shrinking agricultural employment, caused large numbers of unskilled and semi-skilled workers to migrate to other regions in search of employment. It should be noted that tremendous net out-migration of population occurred during the World War II period, when 1,241,000 were involved in 1944.

The periods of heavy migration loss are shown by the graph to have their counterparts by short periods of migration gain, though the numbers involved are not as large. We note 1938–41, 1946, 1949–50, and 1956–57 as such periods. Population gain from net in-migration occurred during 1938–41, when a combination of back-to-the-farm movement, beginning as early as 1930, was combined about 1939 with the beginning build-up of army camps and other related defense construction in the South. It is surprising, however, that the build-up of army training did not have a large impact. This tremendous flow of men into the area was probably offset in large part by the greater counter-movement out of the region to war factories. The gain of 1946 is explained by demobilization and the return of some veterans to their homes in the South. The years 1949 and 1950 represent in part the backwash of migrants from the 1948–49 recession, with a later rapid build-up in 1950 of troops in Southern training centers because of the Korean War episode. The net migration gains in 1956–57, though not tremendously large, are highly significant be-

**Table 3.** Relation of Net Migration Loss to Natural Increase by Decades From 1930 to 1960*

| State | MIGRATION LOSS IN THOUSANDS | | | PERCENTAGE OF NATURAL INCREASE LOST BY MIGRATION | | |
|---|---|---|---|---|---|---|
| | 1930-40 | 1940-50 | 1950-60 | 1930-40 | 1940-50 | 1950-60 |
| Alabama | 205 | 342 | 368 | 51 | 60 | 64 |
| Arkansas | 177 | 415 | 433 | 65 | 111 | 140 |
| Florida | −327ᵃ | −578 | −1,617 | −279 | −195 | −287 |
| Georgia | 208 | 290 | 214 | 50 | 48 | 30 |
| Kentucky | 132 | 366 | 390 | 36 | 79 | 81 |
| Louisiana | −13 | 147 | 50 | −5 | 32 | 8 |
| Mississippi | 151 | 433 | 434 | 47 | 101 | 100 |
| North Carolina | 148 | 258 | 328 | 27 | 34 | 40 |
| South Carolina | 136 | 230 | 222 | 46 | 51 | 46 |
| Tennessee | 34 | 143 | 273 | 10 | 28 | 50 |
| Texas | 103 | −73 | −114 | 15 | −6 | −6 |
| Virginia | −34 | −169 | −15 | −13 | −36 | −2 |
| West Virginia | 120 | 235 | 447 | 41 | 70 | 148 |
| Total | 1,040 | 2,039 | 1,413 | 23 | 29 | 17 |

* Source: Computed from Bureau of Census, *Current Population Report,* Series P-25, Nos. 72, 139, 196, and 247. Vital Statistics required for the period 1930–40 were obtained from issues of the *Statistical Abstract.*
ᵃ Minus shows gain in population from migration.

cause they may reflect the impact of an accelerating economic development in the South. The years ahead will be increasingly like the economic conditions of recent years in the South. Recent Census Bureau annual estimates of population already show strong evidence of this trend in most of the Southern States, particularly in Alabama, Georgia, North Carolina, South Carolina, and Tennessee.[14] Obviously, the South has not yet progressed to the point where it can employ all of its natural population increase plus additional job-seekers from outside. Some states are now providing an excess of jobs for out-migrants; others are close to it; some more states will do so in the next decade or two, while the remaining states, such as Arkansas and Mississippi, may be several decades reaching this desirable rate of economic development.

The differences in the status of migration between states, reflecting rates of economic development, are presented in Table 3. The table represents a number of distinct development trends according to the nature and size of the net migration trends, which as we discuss them

14. See Bureau of the Census, *Current Population Reports,* Series No. P-25, Nos. 72 and 247.

will tie-in closely with the population trends[15] discussed above. First, we detect a group of states which have attracted an inflow of migrants each decade during the thirty-year period. Such states as Florida and Virginia are clearly in this category, with Texas also (except for 1930–40). Secondly, there is the group of states with a moderate migration loss but with a trend down in the ratio of loss. This group is led by Louisiana, followed by South Carolina and Georgia. Third, North Carolina alone has a low migration-loss ratio but a distinct tendency for it to rise. This is surprising and may be attributed to the fact that North Carolina has maintained a fairly large agricultural economy throughout the period. Fourth, there is the group of states which have a high migration-loss ratio and also a trend up in the ratio. The states falling in this category are Alabama, Kentucky, and Tennessee. And fifth, and finally, is the group of states with migration loss exceeding 100 percent, representing a migration loss in excess of the natural increase. These states are the well-known, and frequently mentioned, Arkansas, Mississippi, and West Virginia. They not only have a high migration loss but a rate so high that it has caused an absolute decline in population. This trend for Arkansas is from 1930, for Mississippi from 1940, and for West Virginia from 1950. Not only do these three states have a high loss ratio but they have a rising one as well. To change the trend, therefore, will be like rolling back the tide.

## IV.  Interrelationships of Population and Employment Changes

The types of jobs, the rapidity at which economic activity is being generated, the conditions of work, pay scales, and numerous other conditions in a state become the balance against natural increase. If jobs and conditions associated therewith provide employment opportunities at a rate at least equal to the natural population increase, population growth over time may parallel the increase in the number of job opportunities available, depending upon the nature of economic progress in the area. The converse is true, of course, if economic growth is at a low rate, for some part or all of natural increase may be lost provided people recognize their plight, and also if there is communication from other parts of the country. From

15. A perfect correlation is obviously not possible because of the differences between states in natural rates of increase, which are quite large between such states as Kentucky and Florida at the low extreme and Louisiana and Mississippi at the top.

**Table 4.** Trends in Decade Yearly Rates of Change in Total Employment in 13 Southern States and Specified Regions, 1930–60*

| State or Region | YEARLY PERCENTAGE RATES OF CHANGE | | | |
|---|---|---|---|---|
| | 1930-40 | 1940-50 | 1950-60 | 1930-60 |
| Alabama | 0.47 | −0.42 | .87 | .31 |
| Arkansas | .00 | −0.03 | −.58 | −.21 |
| Florida | 3.08 | 3.88 | 5.55 | 4.14 |
| Georgia | .25 | .71 | 1.55 | .83 |
| Kentucky | .36 | .06 | .37 | .27 |
| Louisiana | 1.01 | 1.21 | 1.23 | 1.19 |
| Mississippi | .24 | .08 | −0.75 | −.14 |
| North Carolina | 1.25 | 1.52 | 1.30 | 1.34 |
| South Carolina | 1.07 | .78 | 1.35 | 1.07 |
| Tennessee | 1.25 | 1.31 | .80 | 1.12 |
| Texas | .61 | 2.76 | 1.74 | 1.71 |
| Virginia | 1.50 | 2.17 | 1.28 | 1.65 |
| West Virginia | 1.81 | .23 | −2.08 | −.01 |
| Total 13 States | .91 | 1.35 | 1.32 | 1.20 |
| Rest of the Nation | 1.06 | 2.04 | 1.16 | 1.42 |
| Ratio of South to Rest of the Nation | 0.85 | .66 | 1.14 | .84 |

* Source of basic data: See Appendix Table 2.

another point of view, some states achieve the very desirable condition where jobs are out-pacing natural increase, and opportunities[16] for employment and personal development act as magnets to draw employable persons and their families from other states. In the discussion which follows, we trace employment gains for the South as a prelude to an analysis of interrelationships between population growth and employment expansion.

The development of employment statistics for the thirteen states in this study has been referred to above and is explained in the Appendix. We conceive of employment in a very broad context, although keeping the Census Bureau national monthly estimates of employment and labor force as controls. Employment in the context as here used includes all persons fourteen years old or over working fifteen hours or more during the survey week. We include the military forces stationed in each state because they are employed for national protection. The Public Emergency workers of 1940 are included that year. They had jobs of a sort which provided a livelihood for their families, and emergency employment of the depression type is a factor in state migration-differences.

16. See Bogue, *Population of the United States*, p. 416, especially for a very interesting thesis relative to the impact of opportunities on migration and population growth.

In Table 4 are given the yearly percentage rates of total employment change in the thirteen states and two regions for decade intervals and also for the thirty-year period. It is seen that employment expansion in the South and the rest of the nation advanced by spurts, but in the latter more irregularly so. Yearly rates of expansion in the South increased in each decade, but the change from the 1940–50 to the 1950–60 decade was comparatively small. Employment in the rest of the nation almost doubled its yearly percentage rate of growth (1.06 to 2.04) from the decade 1930–40 to the war decade 1940–50. Because the South had a much less rapid rise in yearly percentage increase in employment during 1940–50, the region fell 34 percent below the rest of the nation in rates of employment expansion. But the sustained growth of the South into 1950–60 reversed the ratio between the yearly rates of growth in the two regions when the South forged ahead 14 percent, the rest of the nation falling back almost to the 1930–40 yearly percentage rate of employment expansion. For the entire thirty-year period, however, the South had a 16 percent less rapid expansion of employment yearly.

Among the states for 1930–60 we find almost the same categories of growth as for population, with minor exceptions. In the group of rapidly growing states are Florida, Texas, Virginia, North Carolina, and Louisiana, with the latter down one rank, compared to its population standing, and North Carolina up a place, from the second group of states. The next group of states, considerably below the rate of employment expansion for the region, includes Tennessee, South Carolina, and Georgia; Tennessee displaced South Carolina for the sixth rank in employment growth. The third and last group of states includes both the slowly growing states and also those with shrinking economies. Alabama and Kentucky are in the former category, while Arkansas, Mississippi, and West Virginia are in the latter. Compared to population growth, Mississippi's employment rank is down one place.

The comparisons for the 1950–60 decade show the shift recently in rates of employment expansion. Although several rearrangements in rankings of the states occurred, compared to the standings for 1930–60, those of most significance, we might note, are Georgia from eighth to third place; Tennessee from sixth to ninth; and West Virginia from eleventh rank to thirteenth. These changes mean simply that during 1950–60, Georgia has substantially accelerated its rate of employment expansion when this is compared to the over-all rate of growth during

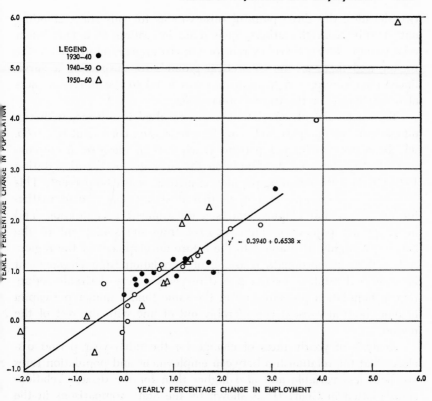

**Chart II.** Relationship of the Yearly Percentage Change in Employment to the Yearly Percentage Change in Population of 13 Southern States, Decade Rates from 1930 to 1960

1930–60, while both Tennessee and West Virginia have had a significant decline in the yearly rate of employment increase.

The cited comparisons for the period 1930–60 indicate a considerable degree of correlation between yearly percentage rates of change in population and the corresponding yearly percentage rates of change in employment. Chart II demonstrates that the relationship is a strong, positive one. In preparing the scattergram shown in Chart II, we have assumed for the purposes of the analysis that employment is the independent factor (and hence causative), although it might be the other way, with population considered as the independent factor —and it would not be difficult to find some good reasons for its treatment in that role. Because the Florida yearly rate of population growth consistently exceeded employment expansion during the last two decades, the three pairs of observations for this state, standing out sharply from the others, give some indication of a curvilinear relationship. Since Florida's rate of growth appears atypical for the region, and there are no theoretical grounds for suspecting a curvilinear relationship, a regression line was fitted to the thirty-six pairs of observations for the twelve other states.

The coefficient of correlation which resulted is +0.866, with significance at the one percent point. The regression coefficient is +0.65, which means that for a 1 percent yearly rate of increase of employment in the states of the South on the average for decades during 1930–60, the corresponding population increase was 0.65 percent. This is a highly interesting finding in that it shows partial confirmation for the thesis that employment is a determinant of migration, and hence of net population increase. Yet from the standpoint of the South it is highly favorable[17] to the future development of the region. A less than proportionate response of population from employment increase will produce over a period of years a very desirable reduction in population pressure and at the same time a higher per-capita income, both at present considerably out of line with the rest of the nation.

Analysis of yearly rates of change for the thirty-year period discloses that the relationship between employment and population rates are both less variable and also higher than for the decade relationships plotted in Chart II, as shown by the State comparisons in the tabulation following.

| State or Region | YEARLY PERCENT CHANGE, 1930-60 | | RATIO OF POPULATION TO EMPLOYMENT YEARLY PERCENT CHANGE |
|---|---|---|---|
| | Population | Employment | |
| Alabama | 0.78 | 0.31 | 2.51 |
| Arkansas | −0.13 | −0.21 | 0.62 |
| Florida | 4.19 | 4.14 | 1.01 |
| Georgia | 1.03 | 0.83 | 1.24 |
| Kentucky | 0.50 | 0.27 | 1.85 |
| Louisiana | 1.43 | 1.19 | 1.20 |
| Mississippi | .29 | −0.14 | −2.07 |
| North Carolina | 1.17 | 1.34 | .87 |
| South Carolina | 1.06 | 1.07 | .99 |
| Tennessee | 1.04 | 1.12 | .93 |
| Texas | 1.68 | 1.71 | .98 |
| Virginia | 1.66 | 1.65 | 1.01 |
| West Virginia | 0.22 | −0.01 | —— |
| Thirteeen States | 1.28 | 1.20 | 1.07 |
| Rest of the Nation | 1.27 | 1.42 | .89 |

17. It is noted that the slowly growing states, such as Arkansas and West Virginia, have either a yearly rate of population increase greater than employment or a decrease that is less than the decline in employment. The converse is true of the most rapidly growing states in general.

With the longer time-interval represented in the tabulation it would be expected that the normal relationship between rate of population increase and employment expansion would appear, especially for a geographic unit as large as a region. The rate of population increase in the South exceeded the rate of employment increase by 7 percent; in the rest of the nation, however, the rate of increase in employment exceeded the rate of increase in population by 11 percent. From what has been said in connection with the regression analysis, the ratio for the rest of the country is more nearly in line with what is expected of an area with a rising standard of living. For a region that must increase per capita income and reduce population pressure, the South will require for some decades in the future a rate of expansion in employment that exceeds by a good margin the rate of growth in population. The depression build-up of population in the South, followed by high birth rates during 1950–60, made the computed ratio for the thirty-year period considerably above normal.

In the case of states, the above comparisons contain some wide extremes in the ratio, from a ratio of 2.51 between population and employment rates for Alabama to 0.87 for North Carolina. The large minus 2.07 for Mississippi indicates only that employment decreased at a rate twice that of population increase. The actual rates show, however, that Mississippi's economy made little change in either direction. For all states, a ratio of 1.00 may be taken as a division point. States below this ratio had a favorable situation, on the average, during the thirty-year period; those with a ratio above 1.00 were unfavorable with respect to number of jobs to people. Note that the growth leaders—Texas and North Carolina—are in the former classification, while Alabama, Kentucky, Georgia, and Louisiana are in the latter category. Arkansas, Mississippi, and West Virginia, states with shrinking employment for a part or most of the thirty-year period, had a minus ratio.

### V. The Economic Significance of Population and Employment Trends

In general, the economic impacts of population growth and employment expansion appear in size of markets and their development, the pull of people to jobs by the route of migration, the nature and extent of employment, and many other aspects. In this paper we shall, however, examine a limited number of the consequences of employment changes to the economy of the South during the last three decades. More specifically, we shall analyze the effect of employment expansion on population pressure, population growth, and migration loss as factors in the rise of personal income payments, and the relationship of growth of cities to past and future growth of the region.

## A.   The Effect of Employment Expansion on Population Pressure

Population pressure may be defined as the ratio of people who have a pressing economic need to work[18] (not necessarily desiring work) to those actually employed. If a large number of people in need of employment are unable to find it, there is population pressure and consequently social unrest. Since it is impossible to determine accurately all those who need to work in a society at a particular time, we shall assume, for the purposes of this study, that it is some function of total population. Those actually at work will be our employment data discussed above. Therefore, a crude[19] measure of the population-pressure factor will be the ratio of population to total employment at the census dates. Table 5, according to the method described, contains the population pressure factors for all the states in the South plus the South as a region compared with the rest of the nation, for all three decades in our study. A low ratio of population to employment shows a low population pressure; conversely, a high ratio shows a high population pressure.

Comparisons of the regional totals given in Table 5 disclose that the South had, during the studied period, from 8 to 21 percent higher population pressure than the rest of the country. The rest of the country tended to reduce population pressure over the thirty-year period; but the South remained about constant. The rest of the country reached the lowest point, according to our method of calculations at decades, in 1950, before the high birth rates of the postwar era

18. All those who must work to feed and support dependents in accord with the acceptable standard of life. In our society, and perhaps even more so in some of the so-called "backward societies," many more need to work than want employment. A measure of all those wanting to work would be the total of the employed and the unemployed.

19. Crude because age distribution is not standardized.

**Table 5.** Trends in Crude Population Pressure Factor by States and Regions, by Decades from 1930 to 1960*

| State or Region | RATIO OF POPULATION TO TOTAL EMPLOYMENT | | | |
|---|---|---|---|---|
| | 1930 | 1940 | 1950 | 1960 |
| Alabama | 2.87 | 2.95 | 3.30 | 3.24 |
| Arkansas | 2.97 | 3.13 | 3.06 | 3.04 |
| Florida | 2.98 | 2.89 | 2.91 | 3.00 |
| Georgia | 2.67 | 2.80 | 2.88 | 2.84 |
| Kentucky | 2.95 | 3.10 | 3.19 | 3.16 |
| Louisiana | 2.88 | 2.91 | 2.94 | 3.13 |
| Mississippi | 2.86 | 3.03 | 3.00 | 3.25 |
| North Carolina | 2.75 | 2.74 | 2.68 | 2.65 |
| South Carolina | 2.80 | 2.74 | 2.83 | 2.79 |
| Tennessee | 2.91 | 2.88 | 2.85 | 2.85 |
| Texas | 2.86 | 2.96 | 2.71 | 2.84 |
| Virginia | 2.76 | 2.66 | 2.58 | 2.77 |
| West Virginia | 2.99 | 2.75 | 2.83 | 3.20 |
| Total 13 States | 2.85 | 2.88 | 2.86 | 2.92 |
| Rest of the Nation | 2.64 | 2.52 | 2.36 | 2.53 |

* Source: Appendix Tables 1 and 2.

had affected greatly the age distribution (and of course the labor force). The movement of the pressure factor against the South in 1940, when it was more favorable to the rest of the country, was due to the back-up of population on Southern farms during the depression '30's, exceeding the number of new jobs created. The rise of the pressure factor in both regions in 1960 is associated with the comparatively rapid rise in birth rates after the War.

The states included in the South had some widely different trends in population pressure during the thirty-year period. It is highly significant that of the most rapidly growing states, only Texas and Virginia had a fairly definite downward trend, except in 1960. Both Florida and Louisiana are above the regional average, with Louisiana having an upward trend. North Carolina has one of the lowest population-pressure factors and also a downward trend during the entire period. Other states with a favorable population pressure factor are Georgia and South Carolina.

Alabama, Kentucky, and Mississippi have the highest pressure factors with rising trends. Arkansas, a declining state, is generally below the former group and has been adjusting down its pressure factor since 1940. Arkansas, therefore, has made encouraging progress through the route of economic contraction in reducing its population pressure. On the other hand, West Virginia, a declining state in

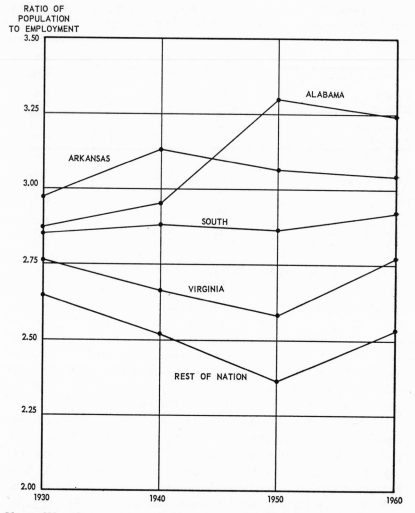

**Chart III.** Comparison of Trends in Crude Population Pressure Factor Between States and Regions, 1930-60

recent years, has suffered since 1940 a rise which became especially sharp from 1950 to 1960. The conclusion is that West Virginia is not maintaining jobs in relation to the population which insists upon remaining in the state, many of whom, it is understood, are displaced miners.

Chart III presents trends in population pressure for the two regions, and for three states which represent extremes in the population-pressure factor. The graph shows the South, despite recent phenomenal gains in employment, well above the rest of the nation in population pressure. This is so because the ratio at a moment reflects all employment trends in the past. A recent large gain in employment may be largely obscured by an unfavorable employment picture in the past. This is shown in particular by Alabama, which, despite some good gains in employment from 1950 to 1960, remains with the group of states having the highest population pressure. Alabama's ratio in 1960 is 28 percent above the rest of the nation and 11 percent above the ratio for the South. Note how rapidly Arkansas has improved the ratio since 1940. Virginia had for the given period the lowest population ratio of the Southern states; its population-pressure factor dropped rapidly from 1930 to 1950. From 1950 to 1960, in line with trends in the rest of the nation, it was rising. The heavy concentration of government workers and military personnel near Washington, D.C., many of whom are single, provides Virginia with one of the highly favorable population-to-employment ratios of the nation.

The conclusion from the analysis is that employment expansion in the rest of the country reduced population pressure from 1930 to 1960, though higher birth rates since the war have caused a minor reversal of the trend; the South held its own despite the rapid agricultural adjustment. The import of the finding for this country is that we have gained proportionately more employment than people, apparently with such sufficiently favorable employment opportunities that the general result has been, along with jobs providing a livelihood, continuous and progressive human development.

In this connection we should examine the relationship of a people's attitude, perhaps more correctly called its culture, to economic development. Under what conditions will population growth lead to a rise in the pressure factor, or, contrastingly, to progressive economic development, resulting in a decline in population pressure? It will depend basically on education and the standard of living. If the standard of living is high (including the educational level), the indication is that expansion in employment will exceed the rate of growth of population, while with a low standard of living, the converse seems to be true. This is the point Everett Hagen, of the Massachusetts Institute of Technology, makes with telling effect, I believe. Professor Benjamin Higgins, University of Texas, in his book, *Economic De-*

*velopment,* quotes Hagen's formulation of the Standard-of-Living thesis of economic development, as follows:

The Malthusian thesis suggests that as income rises, the rate of population growth will rise until it reaches the maximum biological growth rate of, say, 3 percent per year. Only by exceeding this maximum rate of population growth can growth in aggregate output beat population and continue to raise per capita income until it reaches a level high enough to induce new modes of behavior. Indeed, the forecast that population growth if not checked by deliberate action will prevent improvement in human welfare is the heart of the Malthusian message. But while the population of the West has grown, in not a single country has the expected rate of population growth occurred. There is no single case of continuing growth in aggregate output of even 1.5 percent per year, in which population growth has matched it and prevented continuing rise in per capita income. This fact, and not that of growth in world population, may be the fact of recent world history most important for population theory.

.   .   .   .   .   .   .   .   .   .   .   .   .

The tremendously important conclusion follows that technological progress, at any rate above a certain minimum rate, will cause a standard-of-living effect, i.e., will check population growth. First by raising per capita income, technological progress causes a fall in the death rate, and an accelerated rate of population growth. Then because the continuing technological progress holds per capita income above subsistence, the birth rate falls and with it the rate of population growth. Per capita income therefore rises further; the death rate falls further; and so on, until death and birth rates have reached their minimum levels.[20]

Fully interpreted, this thesis means that in the South and elsewhere in the world, economic development and reduced population pressure are acquired by first changing the attitudes and concepts of life of people through education and cultural advance. It will be recognized that this is a slow process but a demonstrably sure one. In the thirty-year period of our study, the South raised its educational level about two years of schooling. But along with improvement of the educational level, great things have happened to Southern thinking, which has been the most important factor altogether, despite the inflated claims of the earnest Chambers of Commerce, in getting the comparatively rapid economic progress we have discussed.

20. Higgins, *Economic Development* (New York: W. W. Norton, 1959), pp. 318-19.

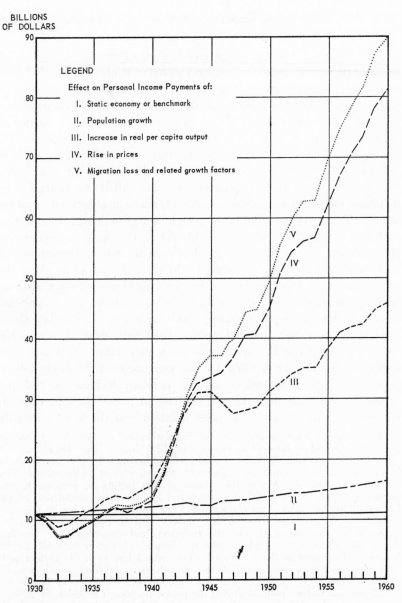

BILLIONS
OF DOLLARS

LEGEND

Effect on Personal Income Payments of:

I.  Static economy or benchmark

II.  Population growth

III.  Increase in real per capita output

IV.  Rise in prices

V.  Migration loss and related growth factors

**Chart IV.** Estimated Contribution of Specified Growth Factors to Total Personal Income Payments in 13 Southern States, 1930-60

## B.    Population Growth and Migration Loss as Factors in Personal Income Payments

Population growth is greatly desired by marked programmers because they take a given population increase as an equivalent change in the size of the market. Population growth as a factor in expectations of the future has been extolled by some prominent economists,[21] certainly by numerous marketing experts. Obviously, the optimism over population growth, particularly in this country, is based on the assumption that other factors contributing to market size, such as rise in productivity and price inflation, will accompany population growth,[22] or that lack of population increase will be accompanied by deflation and unfavorable business conditions. But a detailed examination of the actual contribution of population growth will demonstrate that it is not nearly so important directly as the optimism generated, although the indirect psychological effects are not to be minimized.

Chart IV has been constructed[23] in such a way as to show the net influence of the three major factors contributing to personal income payments from 1930 to 1960. These factors are population growth,[24] increase in productivity,[25] and rise in prices. The data show, if we take only the terminal points, 1930 and 1960, that personal income payments in the South rose from 10.9 billion dollars in 1930 to 80.7 billion dollars in 1960. Of this increase of 69.8 billion dollars, population growth accounted for 7.3 percent; increase in real per capita income, 42.3 percent; and the rise in prices, 50.4 percent. It will come as no surprise that price inflation was the largest contrib-

21. See for instance Joseph S. Davis, "Population and the American Economy, 1945–80," *Journal of Political Economy*, Vol. LXI, No. 3 (Oct. 1953), 384–85.

22. This arises from the habit of multiplying population by per capita income in current prices, which includes in composite the influence of all the other factors.

23. The estimated effect of the various growth factors on personal income payments, shown in Chart IV, was computed by successive cumulation of the factors: from the simplest calculation with only population varying to the most complex combination involving all four factors, that is, population growth, increase in real per capita income, rise in prices, and migration loss. The first line in the chart, for example, is the benchmark calculation with all growth factors held constant at the 1930 level. The second line from the bottom adds onto the benchmark the effect of the growth in population which actually occurred from 1930 to 1960. The top line, however, exceeds in height the actual personal income realized during the period because it includes, in addition to the effects of population growth; increase in real per capita income; and rise in prices; also the probable effect if all migrants had remained in the South, and the total rate of local growth had equaled the region's national rate of population increase.

24. Based on the Census Bureau annual estimates of population.

25. Inferred from rise in real per capita income.

utor, though gains in real per capita output was a close second among the factors. Yet it is surprising that population growth contributed only 7.3 percent in the thirty-year period, hardly more than one-sixth of the gain from the rise in productivity (real per capita income). Since the region kept 77 percent of its natural increase, the question is posed as to the impact of migration loss on personal income.

What then is the effect of the 23 percent migration loss during the period? If all these migrants had been retained and the South had grown at its natural rate of increase, personal income payments in 1960 would have been 90.1 billion dollars—9.4 billion, or 11.5 percent, higher than the personal income payments actually received. This means, of course, that the assumed higher population growth would have been accompanied by the same increases in productivity[26] and prices. The net effect of population is proportionate, or about 7.3 percent, because the accompanying factors would have caused an over-all 11.7 percent gain in total personal income payments, considering both the direct and indirect effects of the population growth from retained migration.

From these calculations we could depreciate the influence of population growth on a region's economic development. It would be a serious mistake to do so, however. The factor of expectations of the future, mentioned above, is vitally important in determining investments in housing, production capacity, and public buildings and roads. Wolff[27] has shown a high correlation between increments of population growth and relative increments of dwelling units constructed. He also found that "there is a definite correlation between the areas with in-migration and those that have strong housing markets." The impact of population growth on an economy through construction may be one of the key factors in economic development, not only through the multiplier effect generated from construction but also from the stimulative effects of land and real estate speculation. Supporting this view is a study by Professor Robert M. Williams, University of Cali-

26. Hoover and Ratchford make the point that the educational level of migrants lost from the South is significantly lower than that of in-migrants. See C. B. Hoover and B. U. Ratchford, *Economic Resources and Policies of the South* (New York: Macmillan Co., 1951), p. 38–39. This conclusion would argue against the assumption of equal productivity of migrants, and hence the gain in personal income from their retention would be somewhat less than the calculations show.

27. Reinhold P. Wolff, "The Role of National, Regional, and Local Factors in Postwar Housing Markets," *Papers and Proceedings of the Regional Science Association*, III (1957), 314–17.

fornia at Los Angeles, which shows the effect of migration on the economy of an area in California. He states that ". . . the experience of Southern California supports the view that large migration contributed substantially to business expansion. . . . Clearly the large influx of people created a boom in real estate activity and in residential construction. . . ."[28]

Migration brings an influx of mature individuals with skills and/or professional talents, and often with a limited amount of capital also. The effect on the volume of demand for the necessities of life and housing is immediate. Growth in population will definitely not have the same effect if it occurs through unskilled workers and families. This type of migration would probably be disadvantageous to economic development, because it would likely lead to a doubling-up in living areas, to sharing an already inadequate level of living, and to expansion of the welfare rolls.

In the observations made by Hoover and Ratchford,[29] we have seen that the South, in the interchange of migration, gains in quality of migrants over other regions. Where migrants constitute mainly the better-educated, professional classes, they not only generate economic growth directly through housing and other demands but also through leadership qualities. The other type of migrants, however, may have little effect, unless the economy is expanding from other causes. If the economy is not sufficiently strong to absorb them in the semi-skilled and other lower-quality jobs, this type of migration may result in building up population pressure.

The substance of the argument in summary is that the type of population growth, whether it occurs through migration or otherwise, determines whether the development impacts on the economy are beneficial or harmful. One type of population growth may lead to a rise in population pressure; another type will likely generate a more than proportionate growth in employment. In this latter context we are referring to the segments of population growth, such as skilled, professional, and similar types, who have a realizable demand[30] for houses, furnishings, and related durable goods, all necessary for the progressive generation of employment. Through the impact of expectations, a little population growth of this type becomes magnified as it moves

28. "Fluctuations in Urban Growth: Some Comparative Data and Analysis," *Papers and Proceedings of the Regional Science Association,* I (1955), E 13–14.
29. *Loc. cit.*
30. Through possession of a limited purchasing power directly, and reinforced by credit by virtue of professional ability and connections.

through the marketing stages to the consumer, particularly if the standard of living is high.

## C. The Rise of Cities as a Development Force in the South

The startling rise of cities in the South in the last couple of decades is an interesting phenomenon in itself, but it is of far greater significance to current and future economic development of the region. Using methods analogous to those employed by the Census Bureau in its classification of Standard Metropolitan Statistical Areas for the 1960 Census, we find that the thirteen Southern states had, in 1930, thirty-four SMSA's with 100,000 population or more; forty-two in 1940; fifty-three in 1950; and sixty-two in 1960. During the decade from 1930 to 1940, all SMSA's in the South[31] accounted for 52.2 percent of the region's growth; from 1940 to 1950, 83.5 percent; and 89.5 percent of the South's growth from 1950 to 1960. Thus it is seen that not only are urbanized areas growing in number and size, but they have determined to a large extent the growth of the region, especially since 1940.

According to Rody,[32] the tendency of the South to concentrate its growth around the larger urban centers is reminiscent of a similar trend in the United States from 1900 to 1930. Hitt supports this point of view in claiming that urbanization has been the dominant process for many decades. I quote directly from him:

Urbanization has been the dominant demographic process in the South for many decades. The shift of population toward urban residence in this most rural of the nation's regions has been in evidence since the beginning of the 19th century. Following generally the process in the nation, the rate of urbanization in the South has nevertheless lagged behind. However, the rapid acceleration of urban growth in the region during the first half of this century, notably since the first World War, has substantially narrowed the gap between the extent of urbanization in the region and that in the rest of the United States. Indeed, the momentum of urbanization in the South in recent years has attracted widespread interest and attention among scholars and laymen alike.[33]

While the rate of population growth in the South lagged that of the rest of the country during the last two decades, urban growth rates

31. Classified on the same basis as the 1960 Census.
32. Martin J. Rody, "Urban Growth and Development in Southeast 1930–50," *Journal of the American Institute of Planners*, XX–XXI (1954–55), 188.
33. Homer L. Hitt, "Population Movements in the Southern United States," *Scientific Monthly*, LXXXII–LXXXIII (May, 1956), 241.

**Table 6.** Trend in Average Size of Standard Metropolitan Areas in Thirteen Southern States and in the Rest of the Country, 1930–60*

| Year | Thirteen Southern States | Percent Increase | Rest of the Nation | Percent South is of Other States |
|---|---|---|---|---|
| 1930 | 165,400 | | 479,600 | 34.5 |
| 1940 | 200,500 | 21.2 | 502,200 | 39.9 |
| 1950 | 277,100 | 38.2 | 598,700 | 46.3 |
| 1960 | 303,150ª | 10.5 | 650,500ª | 47.0 |

* Source: Census of Population for 1930, 1940, 1950, and 1960; and Bogue, *Population Growth*, pp. 61–72 (for U.S. data, 1930).

ª Based on SMSA concept of 1960; other Census dates agree with SMA concept of 1950.

far exceeded those of SMSA's in the rest of the nation, as demonstrated by data presented in Table 6.

The data show that the SMA's in the South are outstripping the growth of SMA's in the rest of the nation both relatively and in percentage. In 1940 the 50 SMA's in the South were only 40 percent as large as 118 SMA's in the other states; and in 1960 the SMSA's were 47 percent as large.

In relation to the percentage increase, note that the growth of cities from 1940–50 was almost twice as great as from 1930–40. The ratio of the increase during 1950–60, however, was relatively slower, or 10.5 percent. This slower rate of increase was due, to a considerable extent, to the larger base from which the percentages were computed.

What is the economic relationship of growth of cities to the economic development of the South or of any other region? In economic development, the city possesses a number of advantages (and disadvantages).[34] The eminent British economist P. Sargant Florence lists the advantages as short transportation and communication to primary sources of supply and to related factories, and maximum advantage in combining the factors of production. On this latter point he is very explicit in stating that:

34. P. Sargant Florence, "Economic Efficiency in the Metropolis," *The Metropolis in Modern Life*, ed. Robert Moore Fisher (New York: Doubleday and Company, 1955), p. 90. The disadvantages given by Florence are traffic congestion, often long transport and communication, risk of mass unemployment from lack of diversification, scarcity of land, congestion at the center, long journey to work, high cost of living, high taxes, and lack of the rural amenities.

Economic organization and enterprise is largely a matter of bringing together the four productive factors of land, labor, management, and capital, in the most efficient proportions. Three of these classical four factors become easier to secure as concentration intensifies. The greater the population within the daily commuting radius, the greater is the available pool of skilled or unskilled labor and of managers from which to draw. For modern economic undertakings, capital is also required in large supply. To judge from evidence offered later, only the largest cities seem to provide a sufficiently pooled supply of capital available for financing industry.[35]

Apparently there are also conditions favoring especially the origin and development of small firms. Florence's data[36] demonstrate this. His studies of Standard Metropolitan Areas in the United States for the 1940 Census make the very significant point that the larger the city, the smaller the manufacturing plant. In the most populous cities, the percentage of all establishments that employ less than twenty workers was 66.4; in the less populous areas, the ratio was 55.4 percent. The reason for the higher proportion of small firms in larger cities he attributes to the external economies available to a cluster of small firms which large firms enjoy internally. This is obtained by linked specialized processes, services, or products on a fairly large scale, dependent upon close communication and the ability to obtain services, materials, and labor as required.

Significant to the accelerated growth of the region in the future is the recent emergence of a few moderately large-sized cities, that is, moderate by national standards as to size, which now provide factors, formerly seriously limiting to rapid progress, of leadership and finance. This is reflected by the rise of city complexes of 500,000 population or more. In 1930, the South had only one SMA over 500,000 population; in 1940, there were three; in 1950, six; and in 1960 there were thirteen SMSA's, of which four were cities of about 1,000,000, which it is believed magnify the South's prospects for future growth. It is the thesis of this paper that large cities[37] provide a powerful growth force through expert business leadership, professional and managerial talent, and financial requirements and conditions especially favorable to future economic progress through intercommunication of design and inventions. Bogue[38] has pointed out how migration distributes and redis-

35. *Ibid.*, p. 94.
36. *Ibid.*, p. 104.
37. For example, cities like Atlanta, New Orleans, Dallas, and Houston.
38. *The Population of the United States*, p. 417.

tributes specialists, experts, and managers to demand conditions which most profitably use their talents. Hallenbeck[39] finds a direct correlation between the ratio of a state's population urban and the proportion of its citizens listed in *Who's Who*. Florence emphasizes greatly the importance of the intercommunication of designs, inventions, and ideas to rapid economic progress. For three large metropolitan areas in the western world he shows that the proportion of such specialized personnel is in multiples of the areas' labor force. The three areas he has reference to are London, Paris, and New York, and I cite his data directly:

In 1931 Greater London contained 19.5 per cent of the employed population of Great Britain. But it held 52.7 per cent of all workers engaged in making scientific instruments and apparatus other than photographic and electrical. . . .

In 1946, the Department of the Seine (the metropolitan area with its center at Paris) contained 12.2 per cent of the employed population of France but held: 36 per cent of the engineers, 37 per cent of the industrial designers, 34 per cent of the technological workers, 37 per cent of the lab workers, and 32 per cent of the chemists.

The New York metropolitan area contained 11.2 per cent of the total employees in American manufacturing industries in 1947, but also held: 56.5 per cent of all workers employed in surgical manufactures and medical instruments, 32 per cent of all workers employed in making electrical measuring instruments, and 17.5 per cent of all workers employed in making mechanical measuring instruments.[40]

The manner in which a city of a million population dominates an area as large as a state is shown by some figures on the relative importance of Atlanta[41] in the economy of Georgia. No later than 1957 we find that with 24.7 percent of Georgia's population, Atlanta had a proportionately higher percentage of the state's economic activity in the following items: retail sales, 34.4 percent; wholesale trade, 65.7 percent; construction employment, 38.8 percent; employment in finance and related activities, 62.2 percent; and so on, with numerous other measures of the State's economic activity, including the professions, that were concentrated in Atlanta.

The South has long lagged in economic development for lack of

39. Wilbur C. Hallenbeck, *American Urban Communities* (New York: Harper and Brothers, 1951), p. 137.

40. *Op. cit.*, p. 106.

41. John L. Fulmer, "The Challenge of Economic Development in Georgia: Part III, Atlanta's Leadership," *The Atlanta Economic Review*, Vol. IX, No. 10, Oct. 1959, p. 8.

enough aggressive leaders, properly trained personnel, and adequate financing. Only since World War II has the nation realized the limiting nature of research in development. The South is only now awakening to the significance of this important concept, with the rise of a number of research centers in the region mostly university-sponsored. Yet a new day is dawning in another way: the dozen moderately sized urban centers, with some few larger cities at key points, now give the region the balance and the financial strength to meet the deficiencies of the recent past, and to make new demands on the growing research centers. The conclusion is that the region has now progressed to the point where it can find many of the answers to its problems from institutions and business leaders within the region.

## VI. Summary and Conclusions

During the period 1930–60, population growth in the South averaged slightly higher than in the rest of the country, although this surprising finding is primarily due to the considerably larger rate of population growth from 1930 to 1940, when there was a strong backwash of returning migrants to farms from the factories of the Northeast and Midwest. In the last two decades of the thirty-year period, however, the South's rate of growth lagged that of the other states by about 13 percent.

Migration, the escape outlet for lack of jobs, shows an irregular tendency to decline over the period; the decade 1940–50 interrupted the trend. While the percentage of migration loss for the thirty-year period was probably around 23 percent, it was down further to 17 percent in the 1950–60 decade, with further improvements in the loss ratio for 1960–70.

The yearly rate of expansion in total employment, while rising in surges more irregularly than population, had a very consistent gain relative to the rest of the country decade by decade throughout the period of the study. While population began the thirty-year period with a yearly rate of growth 78 percent greater than the rest of the country, the region's employment gains closed the final decade of the period 14 percent above that for the other states. For the entire period, however, the yearly expansion in employment was 16 percent less. The employment ratio for the last ten years of the period, 1950–60, is substantially better than the population ratio, or 114 percent compared to 85 percent for the rest of the nation. This gain in jobs relative to population growth represents an economic upsurge of the South compared to the rest of the country.

As the population and employment trends for the region as a whole were dominated by one decade in each case, likewise there occurred domination of growth rates among a few states. Five states in the fastest-growing category largely determined the population and employment course of the region. These states are Florida, Texas, Virginia, North Carolina, and Louisiana, which together accounted for approximately 75 percent of the region's growth in population and 80 percent of the employment gain during 1930–60. The concentration of growth is even greater because Florida and Texas are responsible for about 50 percent. At the other extreme are three states, Arkansas, Mississippi, and West Virginia, which have experienced an absolute decline in employment, mainly in the last decade. These three states are followed closely by Kentucky and Alabama, which have, however, low rates of growth.

The third group of states had a moderate growth rate somewhat below the region's composite; included in this group are South Carolina, Tennessee, and Georgia. During the 1950–60 decade, however, Georgia moved from eighth to fifth rank in population growth and from eighth to fourth rank in employment expansion. This was the most striking improvement in rank of any of the states.

Correlation analysis of the relationship between yearly rates of growth in population and expansion in total employment produced a highly significant positive $r$ of 0.87. The regression coefficient of 0.65 indicates that a 1 percent change in the yearly rate of expansion in employment is associated with 0.65 percent yearly percentage increase in population. Not only does this regression relationship show that population response to employment is somewhat insensitive, but it also predicts a progressive decline in the ratio of population to employment. This is very favorable to the outlook for Southern economic evolution because a more than proportionate rise in employment relative to population will produce a corresponding rise in the South's per capita income and standard of living.

The economic impacts of population and employment trends are shown in the effects on population pressure, personal income payments, and the growing importance of cities as generating forces in the South's development. The South has from 8 to 21 percent more people per job than does the rest of the country. Despite an encouraging surge forward in the yearly rates of employment expansion during the

1950–60 decade, the South's population-pressure factor rose two points in 1960 above 1930 because of the upsurge in births after World War II. Some states, however, have a comparatively low and declining population-pressure factor. They are North Carolina, Texas, and Tennessee. At the other extreme are Alabama, Kentucky, Louisiana, Mississippi, and West Virginia, which have not only the highest population ratio per job but also a rising population-pressure factor.

Despite the high value commonly attributed to population growth as a market factor, we found, ignoring all indirect effects, that population growth accounted for only 7.3 percent of the increase in personal income payments from 1930 to 1960. This rate compares to 42.3 percent due to the gain in productivity and 50.4 percent due to the rise in prices. If all migrants had been kept in the South, the direct and indirect effects on total personal income payments would have been 11.5 percent. However, it would be a mistake from these statistical ratios to play down population increase as a big factor in market development. Without population growth, business expectations become deflated and investment outlays slow to a walk, giving a stagnant economy. The conclusion is that psychological impacts of population growth, which assumes with it continuation of productivity gains and price increases of the past, are immeasurably more important than the direct effect of population growth, provided the consumers have not only a high, but a rising, standard of living.

Analysis of the impact of city growth on the South's economy shows that the region's SMSA's not only have dominated its population increase but also have been the center of forces pushing the area's development during the entire period of the study. In the decade 1930–40, these centers accounted for 52 percent of the region's population growth; from 1940–50, 84 percent; and from 1950–60, 90 percent. We infer from a relatively high employment ratio that the impacts on employment were proportionately greater. Because of economic advantages in organizing the factors of production, external economies from intrafirm relationships, the great concentration of business leadership, professional and special business services, and financial strength, the larger cities, not only in the South but throughout the world, are the magnets for business enterprise, and hence also for employment and population. They concentrate the critical forces in a unique way to determine rapid, progressive economic development up to an equilibrium point; and after this point of the maximum, a stable or downward trend of development begins. Might we possibly find here one of the causes of the ultimate decline of nations?

The South has made relatively more rapid progress in expanding employment during 1950–60 despite a still considerable agricultural adjustment. This augurs well for the future employment expansion of the South because it not only represents an accelerating development but is based on sound underlying forces. The first of these is the approaching end of agricultural adjustment, which will no longer absorb so much of the strength of expansion just to cover a retrenchment in one sector of the economy. Second, rising educational level and growth of mechanization are removing rapidly the provincialism of the past. Business leaders, politicians, and the man on the street are interested in economic development. It is one of the great issues in the South at present. The people are awake to its potentialities and are going to push hard at this new frontier. Third and most important of all, the South now has thirteen good-sized cities, from 500,000 to 1,000,000 population, scattered at strategic points. They are supported by about forty-nine more cities of 100,000 to 500,000 population, and these cities are interspersed relative to the dominant centers at economic locations throughout the region. These sixty-two city complexes have an efficiency in economic processes which are capable of generating economic growth at an accelerating rate during the decades of the future. Moreover, the larger centers are sufficiently strong to furnish now the finance, the business leadership, and the technical know-how to provide rapid employment expansion.

All of these factors promise to accelerate rates of employment expansion greater than the rate of population growth, thus gradually lowering the population-pressure factor to a level equal to the national ratio. The result will be progressive economic evolution in the South, with higher per capita incomes and rising living standards.

## Technical Appendix

### I. Concepts

#### A. Census of Population

*Census concept of gainfully employed in 1930.* In 1930 the compilations for gainfully employed[1] were defined so as to include all

---

1. *Fifteenth Census of the United States: 1930 Population, Vol. III, Parts 1 & 2* (Washington, D.C.: Bureau of the Census, U.S. Department of Commerce).

workers ten years old and over. The term "gainful workers" was a very broad one. It included all persons who usually followed a gainful occupation, even though they were not actually employed at the time the census was taken. New workers were excluded from the Census of 1930, but persons in institutions who reported a gainful occupation were included.

Unemployment data[2] were obtained from the Census of Unemployment for 1930. They were taken to coincide with Class A, "persons out of a job, able to work, and looking for a job."

*Census concept of the labor force: 1940 and 1950.* The labor force included all persons fourteen years old and over who were employed, unemployed, or in the armed forces during the census week. Employed included all those persons who worked, including paid workers and unpaid family workers, for fifteen hours or more during the census enumeration week. In 1940 the census enumeration week was the fixed period March 24 to 30, whereas in 1950 it was the shifting week which occurred just prior to the census enumerator's visit.

Unemployed persons were those persons fourteen years old and over who during the census week were either looking for work or would have been looking for work except that "(a) they were temporarily ill, (b) they expected to return to a job from which they had been laid off for an indefinite period, or (c) they believed no work was available in their community or in their line of work."[3]

*Incomparabilities.* The main incomparabilities exist between the 1930 concept of "gainful workers," and the 1940 and 1950 concepts of "labor force." In the case of "gainful workers" which despite corrections for the age classes ten to thirteen and the major category of unemployed, conceptual differences with "labor force" in 1940 and 1950 still exist. In general, the "gainful worker" concept is a loose one which depends upon the interviewee's general idea of whether he is gainfully employed, whereas the concept of 1940 and 1950 pins the interviewee down to a specific period and determines if fifteen or more hours of work was done in that period, or if the unemployment definition applied.

Other important differences derive from the fact that the 1930 Census included persons in institutions but excluded new workers. The 1940 and 1950 censuses excluded persons in institutions but included new workers who had just entered the labor force.

2. *Census of Unemployment, 1930, Part 1* (Washington, D.C.: Bureau of the Census, U.S. Department of Commerce).

3. *1950 Census of Population: Vol. II., Characteristics of the Population, Part I, United States Summary* (Washington, D.C.: Bureau of the Census, U.S. Department of Commerce).

## B. Monthly Estimates of Employment

Bureau of Labor Statistics concept of a monthly non-agricultural employment. I quote directly from the publication, *Employment and Earnings:*

Employment data for all except Federal Government refer to persons on establishment payrolls who received pay for any part of the pay period ending nearest the 15th of the month. For Federal Government establishments, current data generally refer to persons who receive pay for the last day of the month. The data exclude proprietors, the self-employed, unpaid family workers, farm workers and domestic workers in households. Salaried officers of corporations are included. Government employment covers only civilian employees; Federal military personnel are shown separately, but their number is excluded from total nonagricultural employment.

Persons on an establishment payroll who are on paid sick leave (when pay in received directly from the firm), paid holiday, or paid vacation, or who work during a part of the pay period and are unemployed or on strike during the rest of the period, are counted as employed. Persons are not counted as employed who are laid off, on leave without pay, or on strike for the entire period, or who are hired but do not report to work during the period.[4]

The BLS data are estimates, obtained through a joint reporting plan between the federal and state employment insurance agencies. The estimates depend upon reports submitted by 155,000 of the nation's 4,000,000 businesses. They are collected from these firms in a shuttle questionnaire form, with space available for data for the preceding twelve months. The reports cover about 16,000,000 workers. Estimates from state agencies are adjusted yearly to a benchmark estimate developed independently. For the 1947–54 period a special study of the relationship between estimates developed from state agency reports and the benchmark figures showed an average discrepancy[5] of only 0.5 percent. In only one year (1951) did the discrepancy go as high as 3.1 percent in construction, and as low as 0.04 percent in non-durables. Other discrepancies were: mining, 2.4 percent; service and miscellaneous, 2.3 percent; while all others varied from —0.6 to 0.7 percent.

*Agricultural Employment Since 1950.* Prior to the revisions which

4. *Employment and Earnings* (Washington, D.C.: U.S. Department of Labor), Vol. VI, No. 9, March, 1960, p. 5-E.

5. Walt R. Simmons and John P. Wymer, "Accuracy of BLS Current Estimates of Employment," *Monthly Labor Review,* LXXVIII (Dec., 1955), 1474–75.

occurred as a result of an intensive study of the 1954 Census of Agriculture, the employment concept[6] of the U.S. Department of Agriculture included as workers all farm operators performing one hour or more of work during the survey week, which was the last calendar week of the month. No limitations as to age were made, and nothing was said about criteria for hired workers.

Important revisions occurred after the study of the 1954 Census of Agriculture, as the department became more definitive in requiring unpaid family workers to perform fifteen or more hours of work in the survey week, in order to be counted as farm workers. There is no limitation as to age.[7] All hired workers doing one or more hours of work or chores during the survey week are included as hired workers. Farm operators are counted if they spent one hour or more on any farm work, chores, or the transaction of farm business during the survey week.[8] Mailed questionnaires are received from 20,000 to 25,000 farmers each month, reporting the number of workers. Data are adjusted to the 1954 Census of Agriculture benchmark.

The difference between this and the monthly concept of the Census is mainly the age factor and hired workers. Agriculture has no age limit on workers; hired workers are counted if they perform only one hour or more; farm operators if they do any work. Census limits farm workers to fourteen years of age or more and workers doing at least fifteen hours of work.

The Department of Agriculture gets mailed replies from 20,000 to 25,000 farms. The Census Bureau conducts interviews in 35,000 households. The mailed returns are subject to the usual mailed response bias. The Census surveys by direct interview are fairly free of bias but are subject to somewhat larger sampling error due to the fact that relatively fewer farms than the Department of Agriculture obtains would be included by the Census interviews.

Agriculture estimates that the age factor for children reaches a million to one and a quarter million workers during the summer. Persons working at more than one farm are counted in all cases by Agriculture but only once by the Census Bureau. In the harvest season this group may reach a quarter million workers. Persons working at both

6. *Farm Employment: Monthly, by States 1950–57; United States by Years, 1910–57–by Months, 140–57* (Washington, D.C.: United States Department of Agriculture), Statistical Bulletin No. 236, September 1958, p. 12.

7. However, in the January 1960 issue of *Farm Labor,* the Department of Agriculture limited its concept of unpaid family labor to that of the Census Bureau. Children under fourteen years of age and persons doing mostly non-farm work are excluded from the count of farm employment. But work by farm operators was broadened to include *any* farm work, chores, or business for their farms during the designated survey week.

8. However, see footnote 7 above for a broader concept recently for farm operators.

agricultural and non-agricultural jobs are counted as working on farms by Agriculture but on non-farms by the Census Bureau. This group may range from one-half to one million workers in different seasons of the year.

In 1950 the Department of Agriculture estimate was 32.2 percent higher than the Census Bureau estimate for the nation as a whole; in 1960 the agricultural estimates had narrowed the ratio somewhat but were still 24.4 percent higher.

*Concept of Bureau of Census monthly estimates of employment.* "The estimates are obtained by means of a sample survey of households, representing all persons in the continental United States except those living in institutions. . . . On the basis of responses to the Census Bureau interviewers all persons 14 years old and over in the sample households are classified as employed, unemployed, or not in the labor force for a calendar week ending nearest the 15th of the month (prior to July, 1955, for the calendar week containing the 8th of the month)."

The "employed are all persons who, during the survey week, were either (a) 'at work'—those who did any work for pay or profit, or those who worked without pay for 15 hours or more on a family farm or business; or (b) 'with a job but not at work.' "[9]

The unemployed are persons who did not work at all during the survey week and were looking for work. The total of employed and unemployed includes the civilian labor force. The Census Bureau includes all persons at work, or with a job, fourteen years old and older who worked fifteen hours or more during the week which included the fifteenth of the month. Estimates of wage and salary workers of the Bureau of Labor Statistics are based on reports from business establishments relative to workers on the payroll at the fifteenth of the month, except federal workers where payroll data are based on the end of the month. The BLS counts persons more than once who are on more than one payroll. There is no lower age-limitation for BLS estimates, but the Fair Labor Standards Act limits employment as a practical matter to fourteen years or above (in most states to sixteen years). On the other hand, Census estimates include proprietors, farm workers, the self-employed, unpaid family workers, and domestic service workers. BLS, like the U.S. Department of Agriculture, also does not set a minimum number of hours for workers during the survey week.

The tabulation in the table below shows that BLS estimates were from 9.5 percent to 17.1 percent lower than the Bureau of Census estimates. These differences are mainly due to BLS omissions of

9. *1957 Historical and Descriptive Supplement to Economic Indicators,* 85th Congress, 1st Session (Washington, D.C.: U.S. Government Printing Office, 1957), pp. 21–22.

domestic service workers, self-employed, unpaid family workers, and proprietors. Note the trend from 1940 to 1960.[10]

### Estimates of Non-agricultural Employment (000 omitted)*

| Year | Bureau of Census Estimates | Bureau of Labor Statistics Estimates | BSL Estimate as a percentage of Census Bureau Estimates |
|---|---|---|---|
| 1930 | 35,140 | 29,143 | 82.9 |
| 1935 | 32,150 | 26,792 | 83.3 |
| 1940 | 37,980 | 32,058 | 84.4 |
| 1945 | 44,240 | 40,037 | 90.5 |
| 1950 | 52,450 | 44,738 | 85.3 |
| 1955 | 56,225 | 50,056 | 89.0 |
| 1960 | 60,958 | 54,347 | 89.2 |

* Source: *1957 Historical and descriptive Supplement to Economic Indicators*, pp. 21 and 27; and *Economic Indicators*, June, 1963, pp. 10–13.

The U.S. Department of Agriculture monthly estimates of agricultural employment are, as noted above, much broader than the Census coverage. The following tabulation shows that for 1950, 1955, and 1960, the U.S. Department of Agriculture estimates with this broader concept were 24.4 percent to 32.2 per cent higher than the U.S. Bureau of the Census estimates:

| Year | Bureau of the Census Estimates | U. S. Dept. of Agriculture Estimates | Percent U. S. Dept. of Agriculture Estimate is of Census Estimates |
|---|---|---|---|
| | (000 of workers)* | | |
| 1950 | 7,507 | 9,926 | 132.2 |
| 1955 | 6,718 | 8,364 | 124.5 |
| 1960 | 5,723 | 7,118 | 124.4 |

* Source: *Farm Employment*, Statistical Bulletin No. 236, p. 15; *Farm Labor*, January, 1962, p. 6; *Economic Indicators*, June, 1963, pp. 10–13.

Compared to the 1950 Census of occupations, the agricultural employment estimate for the thirteen Southern states by the U.S. Department of Agriculture for 1950 was 32 percent higher. Similarly, the Bureau of Labor Statistics estimates of non-agricultural employment were 14.7 percent less than the 1950 Census of occupations. The differences are due primarily to the difference in the employment concepts governing the estimates. Another extenuating fact is that the agricultural employment as reported by the Department of Agriculture is derived from twelve monthly estimates. The Census of occupations, on the other hand, represents a count of agricultural em-

10. Beginning with the February, 1960, issue of *Economic Indicators*, the table and chart on page 11, entitled: "Employment, Unemployment, and Wages, Status of the Labor Force," drops the Department of Commerce (presumably the Census Bureau) as one of the sources of this information. Of the three original sources, only the Department of Labor and the council of Economic Advisors are listed as sources.

ployment during one week in April when farm work is not at its seasonal peak, nor on the other hand at the seasonal low, yet is short of the average. This difference between the methods of counting by the two organizations accounts for some of that 32-percent discrepancy but the unexplained difference due to the much broader coverage of the Department of Agriculture still remains large.

The conclusion therefore is that the agricultural concept is the broadest, the BLS the most limited, and the Census is in between.

## II. Methodology

*Adjustment for births for underregistration.* Birth statistics by states are reported as crude figures through 1950 without adjustment to allow for incompleteness of coverage. However, the National Office of Vital Statistics, Department of Health, Education and Welfare, by special studies established the incompleteness of reporting for the census years 1940 and 1950. For 1930 P. K. Whelpton has published estimates of incompleteness of registrations.[11] Beginning in 1951, all published data on births show an adjustment for underregistration. In order to compute natural increase, the underregistration ratios must be estimated for all intercensus years from 1930 to 1950. This was done by straight line interpolation. The ratios thus estimated were applied directly to reports of unadjusted births to inflate for incomplete reports.

No births were reported for Texas from 1930 to 1933. These were estimated by reversing the straight line extrapolations of the ratio of births to the total population for 1930 to 1933.

*Residual method of estimating net migration.* We have adopted the survivor-residual method described by Professor C. Horace Hamilton.[12] The formula is $P_1 - P_0 = B - D + M_1 - M_0$. Where $P_0$ and $P_1$ represent population at the beginning and the end of the period, $B$ stands for births; $D$ for deaths; $M_1$ represents in-migrants; $M_0$, out-migrants. To estimate migration the formula is written $M_1 - M_0 = P_1 - P_0 - B + D$.

Since the estimate is a residual, it inherits any errors in census enumeration of the vital statistics. Hamilton believes the error in estimating net migration is likely to be a small percentage of the total estimated.

In developing estimates for the Southern region on net migration, one additional step was necessary. Since yearly estimates of state population by the Census Bureau are as of July 1, the date was moved to January 1, by a simple averaging process, in order to get population

11. P. K. Whelpton, "The Completeness of Birth Registration in the U.S.," *Journal of the American Statistical Association,* Vol. XXIX, No. 186 (June, 1934), pp. 128–29.

12. "Population Pressure . . . ," *Demographic Analysis,* p. 419. See also Bogue, *The Population of the United States,* pp. 397 and 421.

changes simultaneous with vital statistics of births and deaths, which are on a calendar-year basis.

*Adjustment of data to Bureau of Census concept of employment in monthly estimates.* The Census of population for 1930 determined occupations on the basis of a rather broad concept of gainfully employed, discussed above. The 1940 count of occupations was based on the Census enumeration week of March 24 to 30 in 1940; in 1950, the count was based on the week prior to enumeration, which was generally some week in April. Seasonal factors in employment are consequently involved in the 1940 and 1950 censuses of occupations; other more serious problems are involved in 1930.

When the Census Bureau monthly estimates are combined and averaged for a yearly estimate, the seasonal factor is eliminated. Aside from seasonality, the Census of Population count of occupations and the Census Bureau sample estimates are roughly comparable.

The 1930, 1940, and 1950 Census data on occupations were adjusted to the Census Bureau annual estimates, which are published in several sources; but the author of this report relied primarily upon *Economic Indicators.*[13]

*1930 estimates of total employment by states.* The 1930 Census of Population was first adjusted for the 10–13-year-old workers. Then Class A unemployment[14] was deducted. Manufacturing employment was allocated from the national total to states on the basis of the 1929 and 1931 Census of Manufactures. The adjusted non-manufacturing[15] employment from the Census of population for 1930 was employed to allocate the respective national totals to states. Total farm population of the states served as the allocator of agricultural employment.[16] The three categories of employment as adjusted were added to produce total employment estimates by states.

*1940 estimates of total employment by states.* The BLS estimates of manufacturing and non-manufacturing employment by states for 1940 were used to allocate the respective national totals. The 1940 Census of farm population was used to allocate the national total of agricultural employment prepared by the Census Bureau. The total

13. *1957 Historical and Descriptive Supplement to Economic Indicators and Economic Indicators* (Washington, D.C.: U.S. Government Printing Office, 1957 and 1963).

14. Persons out of a job, able to work, and looking for a job.

15. Non-manufacturing is a term used for non-agricultural–non-manufacturing employment.

16. Regional control totals of agricultural employment for both 1930 and 1940, for use with farm population as an allocator, were based on the Census of Population regional total to the national total.

17. *Farm Employment*, Statistical Bulletin No. 236, p. 44. Data for years after 1956 came from current issues of *Farm Labor*. The Department of Agriculture data were not sufficiently detailed prior to 1950 to be employed as state allocators.

employment for each state was derived by adding the three categories. *1950 estimates of total employment by states.* BLS estimates of manufacturing and non-manufacturing by states for 1950 were employed to allocate the national totals to states. The U.S. Department of Agriculture estimates of farm employment[17] were the basis for allocating the national estimate of agricultural employment of the Census Bureau to states. State totals of employment were again obtained by summing the three categories as in 1930 and 1940.

*Methods employed to prepare 1960 estimates of employment.* State employment for manufacturing, non-manufacturing, and agricultural employment were derived by applying the 1960 percentages of national totals derived from the Bureau of Labor Statistics estimates of manufacturing and non-manufacturing and the U.S. Department of Agriculture estimates of agricultural employment to national totals for 1960 by the Bureau of the Census.

The figures shown in the text for total employment include the armed forces.

The 1940 figures also include public emergency workers. Thus we obtain a much broader concept than usually used for employment, but one we believe is more nearly consistent with the idea that population growth is in part at least a function of growth in total employment.

**Appendix Table 1.** Trends in Population by Decades 1930, 1940, 1950, and 1960* (The data are Census Bureau estimates as of July 1)

| State or Region | 1930 | 1940 | 1950 | 1960 | PERCENT CHANGE | | | |
|---|---|---|---|---|---|---|---|---|
| | | | | | 1930-40 | 1940-50 | 1950-60 | 1930-60 |
| Alabama | 2,647 | 2,845 | 3,060 | 3,276 | 7.5 | 7.6 | 7.1 | 23.8 |
| Arkansas | 1,859 | 1,955 | 1,905 | 1,789 | 5.2 | −2.6 | −6.1 | −3.8 |
| Florida | 1,471 | 1,915 | 2,821 | 5,005 | 30.2 | 47.3 | 77.4 | 240.2 |
| Georgia | 2,910 | 3,119 | 3,448 | 3,958 | 7.2 | 10.6 | 14.8 | 36.0 |
| Kentucky | 2,623 | 2,859 | 2,960 | 3,042 | 9.0 | 3.5 | 2.8 | 16.0 |
| Louisiana | 2,105 | 2,370 | 2,699 | 3,259 | 12.6 | 13.9 | 20.7 | 54.8 |
| Mississippi | 2,006 | 2,176 | 2,170 | 2,184 | 8.5 | −0.3 | 0.6 | 8.9 |
| North Carolina | 3,167 | 3,574 | 4,060 | 4,571 | 12.8 | 13.6 | 12.6 | 44.3 |
| South Carolina | 1,745 | 1,902 | 2,121 | 2,393 | 9.0 | 11.5 | 12.8 | 37.1 |
| Tennessee | 2,619 | 2,935 | 3,303 | 3,571 | 12.1 | 12.5 | 8.1 | 36.3 |
| Texas | 5,844 | 6,425 | 7,749 | 9,643 | 9.9 | 20.6 | 24.4 | 65.0 |
| Virginia | 2,427 | 2,720 | 3,262 | 3,985 | 12.1 | 19.9 | 22.2 | 64.2 |
| West Virginia | 1,733 | 1,907 | 2,008 | 1,849 | 10.0 | 5.3 | −7.9 | 6.7 |
| Total 13 States | 33,156 | 36,702 | 41,566 | 48,525 | 10.7 | 13.2 | 16.7 | 46.4 |
| Rest of the Nation | 89,921 | 95,252 | 109,668 | 131,458 | 5.9 | 15.1 | 19.9 | 46.2 |
| Percent of Rest of the Nation | 36.9 | 38.5 | 37.9 | 36.9 | 4.3 | −1.6 | −2.6 | 0 |

* Source: Census Bureau, *Current Population Reports*, Series P-25, Numbers 139, 196, 206, 210, and 258.

**Appendix Table 2.** Trends in Total Employment by Decades 1930, 1940, 1950, and 1960* In Thousands

| State or Region | 1930 | 1940 | 1950 | 1960 | PERCENT CHANGE 1930-40 | 1940-50 | 1950-60 | 1930-60 |
|---|---|---|---|---|---|---|---|---|
| Alabama | 922 | 966 | 928 | 1,012 | 4.8 | −4.0 | 9.1 | 9.8 |
| Arkansas | 625 | 625 | 623 | 588 | 0 | −0.3 | −5.6 | −5.9 |
| Florida | 493 | 663 | 970 | 1,666 | 34.5 | 46.3 | 71.8 | 237.9 |
| Georgia | 1,087 | 1,114 | 1,196 | 1,395 | 2.5 | 7.4 | 16.6 | 28.3 |
| Kentucky | 889 | 922 | 928 | 963 | 3.7 | 0.7 | 3.8 | 8.3 |
| Louisiana | 730 | 814 | 918 | 1,041 | 11.5 | 12.8 | 13.4 | 42.6 |
| Mississippi | 701 | 718 | 724 | 672 | 2.4 | 0.8 | −7.2 | −4.1 |
| North Carolina | 1,153 | 1,305 | 1,517 | 1,726 | 13.2 | 16.2 | 13.8 | 49.7 |
| South Carolina | 624 | 694 | 750 | 858 | 11.1 | 8.1 | 14.4 | 37.5 |
| Tennessee | 899 | 1,018 | 1,159 | 1,255 | 13.2 | 13.9 | 8.3 | 39.6 |
| Texas | 2,043 | 2,172 | 2,862 | 3,400 | 6.3 | 31.8 | 18.8 | 66.4 |
| Virginia | 880 | 1,021 | 1,266 | 1,438 | 16.0 | 24.0 | 13.6 | 63.4 |
| West Virginia | 579 | 693 | 709 | 577 | 19.7 | 2.3 | −18.6 | −0.3 |
| Total 13 States | 11,625 | 12,725 | 14,550 | 16,591 | 9.5 | 14.3 | 14.0 | 42.7 |
| Total Rest of Nation | 34,115 | 37,864 | 46,389 | 51,929 | 11.0 | 22.5 | 11.9 | 52.2 |

* Source: Basic calculations based on: (1) Census of Population, 1930, 1940, 1950, and 1960; (2) Bureau of Labor Statistics, *Employment and Earnings*, Annual Supplement Issues, and multilithed issues for states; (3) *Farm Employment*, Statistical Bulletin No. 236; and *Farm Labor*, February release annually—both publications by the U.S. Department of Agriculture.

**Appendix Table 3.** Comparisons of Rates of Employment Growth of States and Regions and Percentage of South's Growth Accounted for by Each State*

| State or Region | CHANGE IN EMPLOYMENT (000) 1930-60 | 1950-60 | PERCENTAGE OF TOTAL INCREASE IN REGION 1930-60 | 1950-60 |
|---|---|---|---|---|
| Alabama | 90 | 84 | 1.8 | 4.1 |
| Arkansas | −37 | −35 | −0.7 | −1.7 |
| Florida | 1,173 | 696 | 23.6 | 34.1 |
| Georgia | 308 | 199 | 6.2 | 9.8 |
| Kentucky | 74 | 35 | 1.5 | 1.7 |
| Louisiana | 311 | 123 | 6.3 | 6.0 |
| Mississippi | −29 | −52 | −0.6 | −2.5 |
| North Carolina | 573 | 209 | 11.5 | 10.2 |
| South Carolina | 234 | 108 | 4.7 | 5.3 |
| Tennessee | 356 | 96 | 7.2 | 4.7 |
| Texas | 1,357 | 538 | 27.3 | 26.4 |
| Virginia | 558 | 172 | 11.2 | 8.4 |
| West Virginia | −2 | −132 | — | −6.5 |
| Total 13 States | 4,966 | 2,041 | 100.00 | 100.00 |
| Rest of Nation | 17,814 | 5,540 | 100.00 | 100.00 |

* Source: Appendix Table 2

**Appendix Table 4.** Relation of Growth in Standard Metropolitan Statistical Areas to Population Increase in Thirteen Southern States 1950–60* (In Thousands)

| State | Total Population Increase 1950-60 | Population of Largest SMSA in 1960 | Percent Increase in Population 1950-60 | Ratio to 1960 Population of | | Percentage of Increase in Pop. Accounted for by Growth in SMSA's[a] | | |
|---|---|---|---|---|---|---|---|---|
| | | | | Largest SMSA | All SMSA's | 1930-40 | 1940-50 | 1950-60 |
| Alabama | 216 | 634.9 | 7.1 | 19.4 | 44.0 | 48.4 | 113.1 | 116.6 |
| Arkansas | −116 | 243.0 | −6.1 | 13.6 | 17.3 | 28.2 | b | b |
| Florida | 2,184 | 935.0 | 77.4 | 18.7 | 64.9 | 77.0 | 62.6 | 75.4 |
| Georgia | 510 | 1,017.2 | 14.8 | 25.7 | 47.9 | 77.2 | 103.1 | 99.4 |
| Kentucky | 82 | 725.2 | 2.8 | 23.8 | 28.2 | 17.5 | 122.0 | 331.0 |
| Louisiana | 560 | 836.3 | 20.7 | 25.7 | 49.0 | 44.2 | 87.8 | 68.2 |
| Mississippi | 14 | 187.0 | 0.6 | 8.6 | 8.6 | 12.6 | b | 320.0 |
| North Carolina | 511 | 272.0 | 12.6 | 6.0 | 24.5 | 24.4 | 33.9 | 43.5 |
| South Carolina | 272 | 260.8 | 12.8 | 10.9 | 28.7 | 34.6 | 59.4 | 45.1 |
| Tennessee | 268 | 627.0 | 8.1 | 17.6 | 47.0 | 49.6 | 86.4 | 104.5 |
| Texas | 1,894 | 1,243.2 | 24.4 | 12.9 | 64.7 | 90.2 | 105.7 | 94.8 |
| Virginia | 723 | 578.5 | 22.2 | 14.5 | 50.4 | 51.2 | 71.7 | 87.8 |
| West Virginia | −159 | 254.8 | −7.9 | 13.8 | 37.7 | 32.2 | 45.0 | b |
| Total 13 States | 6,959 | ... | 16.7 | ... | 45.0 | 52.2 | 83.5 | 89.5 |

* Source of basic data: Census of Population for 1940, 1950, and 1960.
a All data have been corrected to the 1960 SMSA concepts.
b State total shows a decrease; SMSA's show an increase.

# VII

# Income in the South Since 1929*

Frank A. Hanna

The purpose of this paper is to report on the changes in total and per capita personal incomes in the South since 1929 and to discern, as best I can, their economic significance. The sources of reliable data on state or regional incomes are but a few and are well known.[1] These estimates are in sufficient detail to permit a wide range of useful analyses. The concepts are consistent with those employed in constructing national estimates by month and by year as an integral part of the national economic accounts and, as a consequence, are widely known and generally understood. The amount of work required independently to estimate variants from these concepts is so great as to be prohibitive to the individual investigator.

* This paper was initially prepared for presentation to the October 1960 conference of the Inter-University Committee for Economic Research on the South. The new estimates of total and per capita personal income for 1960–62 and the revisions in the estimates for the years since 1950, which were available by August 1963, have been incorporated in the tables and the text of this version.

1. Since 1954 the state and regional estimates prepared by the National Income Division have been of personal income and are reconciled with the national estimates of this concept. See National Income Division, *Personal Income by States since 1929* (Washington, D. C., 1930), and the August issues of the *Survey of Current Business*. The concepts and reliability of these state estimates are also discussed in *The National Economic Accounts of the United States*, a Report by the National Accounts Review Committee of the National Bureau of Economic Research (New York, 1958), Chapter ix. The data for 1960–62 are the initial estimates for these years, and some improvement in them can be expected after they are revised to incorporate new and more detailed primary data which were unavailable at the time the estimates for these years were prepared. Unless specified otherwise, the income discussed in this paper will be personal income. For its relationship to other income concepts at a regional level, see Werner Hochwald, "Conceptual Issues of Regional Income Estimation," *Studies in Income and Wealth*, XXI (1957), 9–26. Some use also will be made of the Census Bureau distributions of money incomes by size.

**Table 1.** The South[a] Relative to the Continental United States[b] *

| Measure | Percentage of U.S. Total or Average |
|---|---|
| Land area, 1954: | |
| Total | 26.8 |
| In agriculture | 30.2 |
| Population, 1960: | |
| Total | 27.2 |
| Under 20 years of age | 29.1 |
| 20 to 64 years of age | 26.2 |
| 65 years and older | 24.3 |
| Urban | 22.1 |
| Rural | 39.0 |
| | |
| Manufacturing, average of 1929, 1939, 1947, and 1957: | |
| Number of employees | 16.9 |
| Payrolls | 13.5 |
| Average annual earnings of employees | 79.8 |
| Value added by manufacture | 15.2 |
| Ratio of payrolls to value added by manufacture | 88.9 |
| | |
| Personal income, average 1929-58: | |
| Total | 19.2 |
| Labor income | 18.5 |
| Proprietors' income | 24.8 |
| Property income | 15.5 |
| Transfer payments | 20.7 |
| | |
| Per capita personal income, average 1929-58 | 69.9 |
| | |
| Broad industrial sources of income, average of selected years:[c] | |
| Farm income | 32.6 |
| Federal government disbursements | 26.1 |
| State and local government disbursements | 18.9 |
| Private non-farm income | 17.4 |

* Sources: Area, population, and manufactures, *Statistical Abstract of the United States, 1959* and *ibid, 1962;* personal income, *Personal Income by States since 1929* and *Survey of Current Business,* August, 1962.

a The South, as used here, consists of thirteen states: Alabama, Arkansas, Florida, Georgia, Kentucky, Louisiana, Mississippi, North Carolina, South Carolina, Tennessee, Texas, Virginia, and West Virginia. It consists of the states in the Census Bureau's South region, i.e., the South Atlantic, East South Central, and West South Central divisions, other than Delaware, Maryland, Oklahoma and the District of Columbia. These are the states in the National Income Division's Southeast region plus Texas.

b Alaska and Hawaii are not included.

c The years are those for which data are available: 1929, 1933, 1940, 1946, 1950, 1955, and 1958.

### I. The Area

Since the data for states can be aggregated into a variety of regions, it seems worthwhile to pause for a moment to consider the area which I have been asked to consider and which will be called the South throughout this study. This area consists of the thirteen southeastern states bounded on the north and west by Virginia, West Virginia, Kentucky, Arkansas, and Texas. It also includes the Carolinas, Tennessee, Georgia, Alabama, Mississippi, Louisiana, and Florida. This area differs from the area designated as the South by the Census Bureau by excluding Delaware, Maryland, Oklahoma, and the District of Columbia. It includes Texas in addition to the states in the area now designated as the Southeast by the National Income Division.

The South, thus defined, includes slightly more than one-fourth of the land area and population of the Continental United States (Table 1).[2] The South can be described as more agricultural than many parts of the country. It contains 30 percent of the nation's agricultural land, 48 percent of those living on farms, and about one-third of the farm income. It has somewhat more than its proportionate share of persons under twenty years of age, a fact that has led it to be referred to as "the seed bed of the nation."[3] With about one-fourth of the nation's population, it has only one-sixth of the nation's manufacturing employees and produces slightly less than one-sixth of the total value added by manufacture in the United States.

The per capita incomes of the South are generally low, averaging over the past thirty years about 70 percent of the national average. To some extent, this is a consequence of the low incomes from farming and the disproportionately large numbers engaged in this pursuit. But farming is not a sufficient explanation of the low incomes in the South. Its manufacturing employees have average annual earnings which are only about 80 percent of the national average. A similar disparity in earnings also is found in other industrial segments. To some extent, the low levels of earnings reflect the prevalence of low-skill industries in the South and to some extent a disparity be-

2. Alaska and Hawaii are omitted primarily because of the lack of consonant data for all but a few periods and measures. These two new states are omitted also from the "Nonsouth," a designation used to describe the Continental United States outside the South.

3. C. B. Hoover and B. U. Ratchford, *The Economic Resources and Policies of the South* (New York, 1951), p. 26.

tween the earnings for a given occupation in the South and Non-south.[4]

## Significance of the South as a Category

The question may be asked whether the thirteen states in the South have relatively homogeneous income characteristics and, if they do, whether these characteristics differ substantially from those of the states in other parts of the country. An affirmative answer to both parts of this question would enable us to confine our analysis to the major attributes of the area as a single entity. A negative answer to the first part of the question would indicate that some attention should be accorded individual states or sub-areas in the South. A negative answer to the second part of the question would complicate our job by requiring more attention to small differences among detailed industries and components of income.

A rough answer to these questions can be obtained from an examination of the ranks of the states in the South with respect to their per capita incomes.[5] When the states are ranked from the lowest to the highest per capita incomes for 1919,[6] 1929, 1939, 1949, and 1958, all of the thirteen states in the South, with the single exception of Texas, have been counted among the thirteen lowest ranks for at least one of the five selected years. The four states which had a rank above thirteen during one of these selected years are West Virginia (ranks 9–15), Virginia (ranks 9–18), Florida (ranks 10–24), and Texas (ranks 15–24). The average rank of the states in the South deviated from the lowest possible average rank (7.0) by no more than 2.5 in any of the five selected years. This pattern of ranks is sufficient to show that the income characteristics of the South and Nonsouth differ significantly. Whether the characteristics of the states which attained ranks of 15 to 24 during at least one of the years differ significantly from the other states in the South depends in part on whether the state per capita incomes in this range are closely grouped or are fairly dispersed.

4. Frank A. Hanna, *State Income Differentials, 1919–1954* (Durham, N.C., 1959), Chapter v.

5. Per capita personal income for a state is the state's total personal income divided by its population. For interstate comparisons it provides a rough adjustment for the different numbers of inhabitants in the various states. In 1960, the populations of the states in the South ranged from 1.8 million inhabitants in Arkansas to 9.6 million inhabitants in Texas; in the Nonsouth, from .3 million inhabitants in Nevada to 16.8 million in New York.

6. The data for 1919 are from Maurice Leven, *Income Among the Various States, 1919, 1920, and 1921* (New York, 1925).

**Table 2.** Sources of Interstate Variation,[a] 1929–62, by Year*

| | Percentage of Total Interstate Variation | | |
|---|---|---|---|
| Year | Among States within South | Among States within Nonsouth | Between South and Nonsouth |
| 1929 | 2.1 | 42.6 | 55.3 |
| 1930 | 2.4 | 44.0 | 53.6 |
| 1931 | 2.5 | 46.3 | 51.2 |
| 1932 | 2.5 | 50.7 | 46.8 |
| 1933 | 2.3 | 54.8 | 42.9 |
| 1934 | 2.4 | 52.3 | 45.3 |
| 1935 | 2.8 | 40.6 | 56.6 |
| 1936 | 3.0 | 34.6 | 62.4 |
| 1937 | 3.7 | 39.1 | 57.9 |
| 1938 | 4.3 | 41.6 | 54.1 |
| 1939 | 4.4 | 39.5 | 56.1 |
| 1940 | 4.2 | 39.5 | 56.3 |
| 1941 | 3.7 | 38.1 | 58.2 |
| 1942 | 5.0 | 34.3 | 60.7 |
| 1943 | 6.2 | 34.4 | 59.4 |
| 1944 | 6.4 | 35.6 | 58.0 |
| 1945 | 6.5 | 34.9 | 58.6 |
| 1946 | 5.5 | 35.5 | 59.0 |
| 1947 | 6.5 | 29.4 | 64.1 |
| 1948 | 5.6 | 26.0 | 68.4 |
| 1949 | 10.6 | 28.5 | 60.9 |
| 1950 | 9.2 | 27.6 | 63.2 |
| 1951 | 8.4 | 26.2 | 65.4 |
| 1952 | 8.5 | 26.6 | 64.9 |
| 1953 | 7.4 | 28.9 | 63.7 |
| 1954 | 9.1 | 29.7 | 61.2 |
| 1955 | 7.7 | 34.2 | 58.1 |
| 1956 | 8.1 | 35.1 | 56.5 |
| 1957 | 9.0 | 33.1 | 57.5 |
| 1958 | 9.0 | 31.2 | 59.8 |
| 1959 | 8.3 | 34.5 | 57.2 |
| 1960 | 7.1 | 33.1 | 59.8 |
| 1961 | 4.4 | 39.4 | 56.2 |
| 1962 | 6.7 | 33.9 | 59.4 |

* Sources: 1929–49, *Personal Income by States Since 1929*; 1950–59, *Survey of Current Business*, August, 1962; 1960–62, *ibid.*, August, 1963.

[a] Variation is the sum of the squared deviations from the appropriate mean per capita income. The states were weighted by their midyear populations. The District of Columbia is excluded from these calculations.

Except for the three Depression years, 1932–34, more than one-half of the interstate variation in per capita incomes is attributable to the differences between the mean per capita incomes in the South and the Nonsouth (Table 2). This more precise measure of the significance of the South as an analytical category leaves no room for doubt. Moreover, the differences between mean per capita incomes, when measured in these absolute terms, have increased moderately during the past thirty years.

At the same time, the size of the absolute differences among the states in the South has been increasing faster than have the differences among all states. This is contrary to the tendency found among the states in the Nonsouth which, since 1934, have been becoming more alike and thus contributing a decreasing percentage of the total interstate variation. Even during recent years, when their contribution was the highest, the variation among states within the South has amounted to only 8 to 11 percent of the total interstate variation. Thus the failure to look behind the averages for the South at the behavior of individual states would, when measured against national totals, result in only a moderate loss of data. However, since it is the behavior of the South, and the states which compose it, with which this study is particularly concerned, these figures show the need for some attention to the behavior particular to one or more individual states within the South.[7] The fact that the interstate variation within the South has been an increasing proportion of all interstate variation, at least through 1958, emphasizes this need.

## II. Total and Per Capita Personal Income

During the three decades covered by this study, total income in the United States increased five-fold, from $86 billion in 1929 to $435 billion in 1962 (Table 3 and Chart I). In the South, the increases have been even greater, running over six-fold, from $13 billion in 1929 to $90 billion in 1962.

The period covered starts with the peak, or near peak, year of 1929. It was followed by the Great Depression of the early thirties, which was marked by decreases in income to about 55 percent of their 1929 levels. Since the trough of the Great Depression in 1932–33,[8] there have been prolonged increases in personal income, both in

7. I have made no attempt to compute the contribution of individual states to the variation within the South. An examination of charts showing the per capita incomes for each of the thirteen states in the South for the period 1929–58 indicates that principal contributors to this variation have been Florida, Texas, and Virginia, at the top, and Mississippi at the lower end of the scale. The first three states named have tended to pull ahead of the group, and Mississippi has tended to lag the other states.

8. In the South, 1932 was the trough of the Great Depression; in the Nonsouth, 1933.

**Table 3.** Personal Income, United States and the South, 1929–62*

| Year | PERSONAL INCOME (Billions of Dollars) | | South as a Percentage of the United States |
|------|---------------|-------|----------------------------|
| | United States | South | |
| 1929 | $86 | $13 | 15 |
| 1930 | 77 | 11 | 14 |
| 1931 | 66 | 10 | 15 |
| 1932 | 50 | 7 | 14 |
| 1933 | 47 | 7 | 16 |
| 1934 | 53 | 9 | 16 |
| 1935 | 60 | 10 | 16 |
| 1936 | 69 | 11 | 16 |
| 1937 | 74 | 12 | 16 |
| 1938 | 68 | 11 | 17 |
| 1939 | 73 | 12 | 17 |
| 1940 | 79 | 13 | 17 |
| 1941 | 96 | 17 | 18 |
| 1942 | 122 | 23 | 19 |
| 1943 | 148 | 29 | 20 |
| 1944 | 160 | 33 | 20 |
| 1945 | 165 | 34 | 20 |
| 1946 | 176 | 34 | 20 |
| 1947 | 189 | 37 | 19 |
| 1948 | 207 | 40 | 19 |
| 1949 | 205 | 41 | 20 |
| 1950 | 224 | 45 | 20 |
| 1951 | 251 | 51 | 20 |
| 1952 | 267 | 54 | 20 |
| 1953 | 281 | 56 | 20 |
| 1954 | 283 | 57 | 20 |
| 1955 | 305 | 62 | 20 |
| 1956 | 328 | 66 | 20 |
| 1957 | 347 | 70 | 20 |
| 1958 | 355 | 73 | 21 |
| 1959 | 379 | 78 | 21 |
| 1960 | 395 | 81 | 20 |
| 1961 | 410 | 85 | 21 |
| 1962 | 435 | 90 | 21 |

* Sources: 1929–49, *Personal Income by States Since 1929;* 1950–59, *Survey of Current Business,* August, 1962; 1960–62, *ibid.,* August, 1963.

the South and the Nation, marred only by the recession of 1937–38, and the even milder ones of 1949, 1954, 1958, and 1961. The most rapid increases were during 1940–45 and were associated with the Second World War. During this period, personal income just about doubled in the nation and grew even more rapidly in the South, to become by 1945 two-and-one-half times its 1940 size. Since 1945,

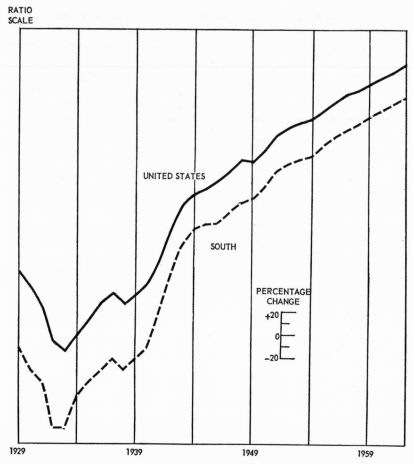

RATIO
SCALE

UNITED STATES

SOUTH

PERCENTAGE
CHANGE

+20
0
−20

1929          1939          1949          1959

**Chart I.** Personal Income, United States and the South, 1929-62
Source: Table 3

personal income both in the South and in the Nonsouth has continued
to increase at about the same rate, about 6 percent per year.[9] The
South has grown moderately, relative to the nation, during the upswing following the trough of the Great Depression and had increased
its share of the national total from around 14–16 percent during the
trough to 17 percent in 1938–40. During the war years, its share increased rapidly to about 20 percent, where it has remained since 1943.

9. This rate of increase is measured in current dollars, rather than in constant
dollars, and includes the effects of inflation as well as the growth of real income.
See below.

Since total income is measured in the current dollars of each year, these figures reflect the combined effects of inflation, growth of productivity, and growth in population. To obtain some knowledge of the direction of the differential growth in the productivity of the South and Nonsouth is, of course, the primary interest of a study of personal income. One of the commonly used measures of productivity changes is the change in real per capita income.[10] The best information now available is that the regional differentials in the changes in price levels are of inconsequential magnitude.[11] There is no net gain in the relative comparisons of the South and the Nonsouth if both are to be adjusted by the same price index. Consequently, the present analysis is based entirely on income in current dollars. The differences among states and regions in numbers of inhabitants and in population changes are both large and have important consequences for interregional comparisons. Personal income adjusted for the differences in the number of inhabitants, that is, per capita income, accordingly will be used extensively throughout this study.

### Changes in Per Capita Income

Since the population of the United States increased by 52 percent from 1929 to 1962, the changes in per capita income are smaller than those recorded for total income. In the United States, per capita incomes increased from a level of $703 in 1929 by somewhat more than three-fold to a level of $2,362 in 1962 (Table 4). Similar increases are noted for the Nonsouth. Since the low incomes which characterize the South are excluded in their computation, the per capita incomes for the Nonsouth exceed those of the United States by 10 to 15 percent. The largest increases during the period are recorded by the low per capita incomes of the South. From a level of $387 in 1929, they have increased by more than four-fold to a level of $1,794 in 1962.

### Relative Changes by Region

Although the population of the states in the South increased by only a slightly larger percentage, 53 instead of 52 percent, than did the population of the United States, the South had in both 1929

10. For example, see *The Midyear Economic Report of the President*, July, 1952, p. 2.

11. Abner Hurwitz and Carlyle P. Stallings, "Interregional Differentials in Per Capita Real Income Changes," *Studies in Income and Wealth*, XXI (1957), 195–265.

**Table 4.** Per Capita Personal Income, United States,[a] South and Nonsouth, 1929-62*

| Year | PER CAPITA PERSONAL INCOME (Dollars) | | | SOUTH AS A PERCENTAGE OF | |
|---|---|---|---|---|---|
| | United States | South | Nonsouth | United States | Nonsouth |
| 1929 | $703 | $387 | $820 | 55 | 47 |
| 1930 | 621 | 330 | 729 | 53 | 45 |
| 1931 | 526 | 286 | 617 | 54 | 46 |
| 1932 | 398 | 215 | 466 | 54 | 46 |
| 1933 | 373 | 215 | 432 | 58 | 50 |
| 1934 | 421 | 250 | 485 | 59 | 52 |
| 1935 | 470 | 275 | 543 | 59 | 51 |
| 1936 | 531 | 314 | 620 | 59 | 51 |
| 1937 | 570 | 341 | 657 | 60 | 52 |
| 1938 | 524 | 319 | 603 | 61 | 53 |
| 1939 | 553 | 335 | 637 | 61 | 53 |
| 1940 | 592 | 359 | 682 | 61 | 53 |
| 1941 | 716 | 451 | 822 | 63 | 55 |
| 1942 | 906 | 607 | 1,026 | 67 | 59 |
| 1943 | 1,099 | 757 | 1,238 | 69 | 61 |
| 1944 | 1,192 | 854 | 1,327 | 72 | 64 |
| 1945 | 1,231 | 891 | 1,366 | 72 | 65 |
| 1946 | 1,247 | 882 | 1,387 | 71 | 64 |
| 1947 | 1,313 | 929 | 1,461 | 71 | 64 |
| 1948 | 1,417 | 1,010 | 1,571 | 71 | 64 |
| 1949 | 1,378 | 1,007 | 1,517 | 73 | 66 |
| 1950 | 1,487 | 1,072 | 1,646 | 72 | 65 |
| 1951 | 1,646 | 1,189 | 1,823 | 72 | 65 |
| 1952 | 1,725 | 1,258 | 1,904 | 73 | 66 |
| 1953 | 1,785 | 1,297 | 1,971 | 73 | 66 |
| 1954 | 1,768 | 1,301 | 1,941 | 74 | 67 |
| 1955 | 1,863 | 1,386 | 2,041 | 74 | 68 |
| 1956 | 1,972 | 1,467 | 2,161 | 74 | 68 |
| 1957 | 2,044 | 1,519 | 2,243 | 74 | 68 |
| 1958 | 2,061 | 1,556 | 2,250 | 75 | 69 |
| 1959 | 2,160 | 1,635 | 2,356 | 76 | 69 |
| 1960 | 2,213 | 1,665 | 2,417 | 75 | 69 |
| 1961 | 2,264 | 1,725 | 2,465 | 76 | 70 |
| 1962 | 2,362 | 1,794 | 2,576 | 76 | 70 |

* Sources: 1929-53, *Personal Income by States since 1929*; 1954-59, *Survey of Current Business*, August, 1962; 1960-62, *ibid*, August, 1963.

a The District of Columbia is excluded in the calculation of the per capita incomes of both the United States and the Nonsouth.

and 1962 a larger share of the nation's inhabitants than it had of the nation's income. When its income is divided by the number of its inhabitants, the resultant per capita income in the South is found to be somewhat lower than that of the Nonsouth. One way of saying how much lower is to express the per capita incomes of the South as a percentage of those of either the entire United States or of the states in the Nonsouth. Both percentages are provided in Table 4. Neither of these sets of percentages appears to possess outstanding analytical advantages over the other. Since most comparisons based on total income, rather than per capita, can be made on the basis of national figures without loss of detail (the Nonsouth, in this case, is the complement of the South), most comparisons here will be made with the national data.

Since the differential movement of prices among regions is small enough to be ignored safely, if the per capita incomes of the South are expressed as percentage of the nation's per capita income, the resulting relative is free of both differences in number of inhabitants and changes in the price level. Their movement over time is effectively the same as that of relatives based on real per capita income.

The per capita income of the South as a percentage of the consonant figure for the United States has increased from 55 percent in 1929 to 76 percent in 1961–62. To a small extent these percentages are cyclically sensitive. With the onset of the Great Depression of the early thirties, the per capita income of the South decreased relative to that of the United States. This decrease perhaps is attributable to the great dependence of this area on income from agriculture, which at that time was not protected by price supports and subsidies of various kinds and was perhaps more cyclically sensitive than it is today. Subsequent changes in the per capita income relative, with the possible exception of the immediate postwar period starting in 1946, have tended to be contra-cyclical. Increases in the relatives are to be noted for the recession years, and decreases usually have marked the immediately preceding peak year. This behavior of the relatives would suggest that since the early thirties, at least, the incomes of the South are somewhat less sensitive to cyclical fluctuations than are those of the Nonsouth.

The growth of these relatives appears to be divided into three periods (Chart II). The first, from the peak-year 1929 to the peak years of 1938–40, was one of moderate growth, accounting for 6 of the 21 percentage points by which they increased during the period under study.[12] The war years, 1940–45, were a period of rapid growth, from a level of 61 to 72 percent of the national average. The nine-

12. The increase of 21 percentage points is measured from 1929 to 1959. This implicitly assumes that 1959 occupies about the same position as 1929 relative to cyclical fluctuations and to the trend line, an assumption that is tolerable only because of the near invariance of the relatives during recent years.

PERCENT OF U.S.
PER CAPITA INCOME

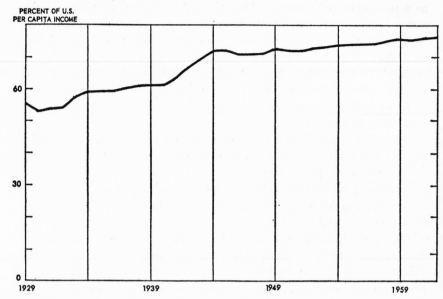

**Chart II.** Per Capita Income in the South as a Percentage of United States Per Capita Income, 1929-62
Source: Table 4

teen years since 1945 have been marked by an almost constant percentage level. Since 1945, the gross increase has amounted to four percentage points.

Apparently the readjustments following the Great Depression (minimum-wage laws, agricultural price supports, and the growth of old-age assistance and other transfers) and the great and rapid expansion of military expenditures and industrial production incident upon the war effort provided the stimulus for the bulk of the increase in the per capita income relatives. The period of full employment following the war has enabled the South to maintain these gains and to increase them slowly.

### Differential Growth of the States in the South

In general, most of the states in the South followed the same general pattern of cyclical responses and growth as was found for the South as a whole (Table 5). There was some decline in the state relatives during the downswing of the Great Depression, a moderate to sharp increase from the Depression low to around 1940, marked growth during the war years, and a slight increase since 1945. This pattern is clearest for the states with the lower per capita incomes among the states in the South—Mississippi, Alabama, the Carolinas, Georgia, and Tennessee. There are a few notable exceptions, however; West Virginia, for example, did not experience the war-time growth common to most of these states, achieved its highest relative in 1948, and has experienced less growth over the entire period. Virginia's relatives show the effects of its having become one of the "bedrooms of Washington" during the period of the federal government's most rapid growth, from around 1931 to 1943. Since that time its relatives have been influenced greatly by the relationship of the salary rates in the federal government to the general level of earnings. Texas' relatives have shown more pronounced contra-cyclical movements than the other states in the group. Florida, which missed much of the 1940–41 increase in incomes, experienced its peak relative in 1945, and suffered a greater relative decline in the immediate postwar period.

To facilitate interstate comparisons in the relative per capita incomes, the relatives have been plotted against a ratio scale (Chart III). Thus plotted, the slopes of the lines for the various states provide a visual indication of the percentage change in their relatives. Without the transformation to ratios it is difficult to compare the changes in Mississippi, whose relative fluctuated within the range of 31–53 percent, with those of Virginia, whose relatives are in the range of 61–86 percent. Even with this transformation it is difficult to distinguish visually cyclical from secular changes and thus to come to any firm conclusion about the relative growth of the states. Visually, the states with the more pronounced cyclical responses appear to have more rapid growth factors than states which are less affected by cyclical changes in the nation's economy.

One commonly used method of eliminating the effects of cyclical variation is to measure changes between years which have been selected as occupying about the same position with regard to the cycle, usually peak years. In view of the variety of cyclical responses in state income relatives, the selection of such years in a meaningful fashion is problematic at best. Should "peaks" refer to the state relatives or to the level of business activity in the state or the nation? To some extent, at least, it may be presumed that one of the reasons the states show varying responses to a change in the level of activity in the national economy is that each cycle differs with respect to the

**Table 5.** State$^a$ and Regional Relatives of United

| Year | South$^b$ | Ala-bama | Arkansas | Florida | Georgia | Ken-tucky | Louisi-ana |
|------|-------|------|----------|---------|---------|--------|------|
| 1929 | 55.1 | 46.1 | 43.4 | 74.1 | 49.8 | 55.6 | 59.0 |
| 1930 | 53.2 | 42.6 | 35.7 | 74.4 | 49.4 | 52.1 | 57.4 |
| 1931 | 54.4 | 42.0 | 39.5 | 74.7 | 48.4 | 54.6 | 60.1 |
| 1932 | 53.9 | 40.2 | 38.6 | 78.3 | 49.6 | 52.4 | 59.6 |
| 1933 | 57.7 | 44.0 | 41.3 | 75.7 | 54.4 | 54.7 | 60.3 |
| 1934 | 59.3 | 48.5 | 41.8 | 80.1 | 56.7 | 54.1 | 61.5 |
| 1935 | 58.6 | 45.6 | 42.6 | 77.8 | 56.6 | 55.5 | 60.6 |
| 1936 | 59.1 | 46.4 | 44.8 | 82.4 | 56.4 | 54.3 | 60.9 |
| 1937 | 59.8 | 45.7 | 43.1 | 93.1 | 54.3 | 58.3 | 60.7 |
| 1938 | 60.8 | 46.1 | 42.9 | 85.8 | 55.0 | 55.4 | 65.6 |
| 1939 | 60.6 | 45.0 | 43.5 | 87.4 | 55.8 | 54.5 | 64.2 |
| 1940 | 60.6 | 47.4 | 43.0 | 86.2 | 57.1 | 53.8 | 61.0 |
| 1941 | 62.9 | 52.2 | 47.0 | 83.0 | 59.0 | 54.5 | 62.4 |
| 1942 | 67.0 | 56.7 | 51.8 | 84.6 | 62.8 | 58.6 | 65.2 |
| 1943 | 68.9 | 59.1 | 49.1 | 89.4 | 65.8 | 62.5 | 71.1 |
| 1944 | 71.7 | 61.6 | 56.3 | 91.3 | 69.9 | 63.6 | 73.6 |
| 1945 | 72.4 | 63.2 | 58.5 | 93.3 | 71.5 | 64.3 | 72.3 |
| 1946 | 70.8 | 59.6 | 58.4 | 91.0 | 67.6 | 64.9 | 66.4 |
| 1947 | 70.7 | 60.3 | 54.6 | 86.8 | 67.2 | 64.6 | 67.0 |
| 1948 | 71.3 | 60.3 | 59.6 | 83.4 | 66.8 | 68.0 | 70.6 |
| 1949 | 73.1 | 58.6 | 56.4 | 87.0 | 67.4 | 66.6 | 76.6 |
| 1950 | 71.9 | 58.3 | 54.1 | 86.3 | 68.2 | 64.2 | 72.9 |
| 1951 | 72.1 | 59.8 | 54.9 | 83.4 | 69.2 | 68.0 | 71.1 |
| 1952 | 72.8 | 60.4 | 55.9 | 84.4 | 69.5 | 69.6 | 72.0 |
| 1953 | 72.5 | 60.6 | 55.6 | 85.8 | 69.3 | 69.9 | 72.4 |
| 1954 | 73.5 | 60.3 | 56.6 | 86.7 | 68.3 | 70.4 | 73.5 |
| 1955 | 74.3 | 64.2 | 58.2 | 88.9 | 71.4 | 69.5 | 72.7 |
| 1956 | 74.3 | 63.7 | 57.5 | 89.7 | 71.0 | 70.1 | 74.0 |
| 1957 | 74.2 | 64.7 | 56.0 | 89.3 | 69.2 | 69.8 | 76.4 |
| 1958 | 75.4 | 65.9 | 58.6 | 89.9 | 71.2 | 70.4 | 75.6 |
| 1959 | 75.6 | 65.9 | 61.3 | 90.6 | 72.0 | 70.0 | 74.5 |
| 1960 | 75.1 | 65.9 | 60.4 | 88.7 | 72.6 | 69.3 | 72.5 |
| 1961 | 76.1 | 65.6 | 63.4 | 86.8 | 72.2 | 72.1 | 72.5 |
| 1962 | 75.8 | 66.2 | 63.6 | 86.4 | 74.3 | 72.4 | 72.1 |

$^a$ Sources: 1929–49, *Survey of Current Business*, August, 1956; 1950–59, *ibid.*, August, 1962; 1960–62, *ibid.*, August, 1963.

## States Per Capita Personal Income, the South, 1929–62*

| Missis-sippi | North Carolina | South Carolina | Tennes-see | Texas | Virginia | West Virginia | Year |
|---|---|---|---|---|---|---|---|
| 40.5 | 47.5 | 38.4 | 53.6 | 68.0 | 61.9 | 65.7 | 1929 |
| 32.5 | 47.0 | 38.6 | 52.1 | 65.9 | 61.5 | 65.9 | 1930 |
| 32.9 | 46.9 | 38.6 | 52.0 | 65.4 | 69.6 | 67.7 | 1931 |
| 31.4 | 46.6 | 39.2 | 49.1 | 65.3 | 70.3 | 64.3 | 1932 |
| 34.9 | 55.2 | 46.4 | 54.4 | 67.5 | 75.5 | 69.3 | 1933 |
| 39.0 | 57.9 | 48.5 | 56.7 | 67.1 | 74.2 | 73.5 | 1934 |
| 37.1 | 57.0 | 47.9 | 55.1 | 67.4 | 73.1 | 71.4 | 1935 |
| 41.6 | 55.2 | 47.4 | 56.2 | 68.0 | 72.3 | 72.8 | 1936 |
| 38.3 | 56.0 | 46.6 | 57.2 | 71.2 | 72.8 | 72.6 | 1937 |
| 38.0 | 56.2 | 47.2 | 56.6 | 75.1 | 73.4 | 70.4 | 1938 |
| 36.9 | 56.8 | 49.1 | 55.4 | 73.6 | 75.9 | 69.6 | 1939 |
| 36.6 | 55.1 | 51.6 | 57.0 | 72.6 | 78.3 | 68.4 | 1940 |
| 43.5 | 59.2 | 54.5 | 60.2 | 72.9 | 80.8 | 68.8 | 1941 |
| 48.4 | 63.3 | 59.4 | 61.1 | 78.3 | 86.0 | 67.4 | 1942 |
| 47.9 | 62.7 | 58.0 | 65.1 | 84.5 | 76.1 | 67.0 | 1943 |
| 52.5 | 64.1 | 60.6 | 71.7 | 86.9 | 75.2 | 68.8 | 1944 |
| 50.8 | 66.5 | 60.2 | 73.1 | 85.2 | 76.7 | 72.1 | 1945 |
| 48.4 | 68.7 | 61.1 | 68.5 | 86.7 | 79.3 | 73.7 | 1946 |
| 50.3 | 67.9 | 59.2 | 66.6 | 85.7 | 76.1 | 78.2 | 1947 |
| 53.0 | 66.5 | 61.9 | 65.8 | 83.7 | 78.3 | 80.7 | 1948 |
| 48.3 | 66.5 | 60.6 | 66.9 | 92.8 | 79.7 | 76.8 | 1949 |
| 49.2 | 67.9 | 59.2 | 66.7 | 89.8 | 82.8 | 73.6 | 1950 |
| 48.1 | 67.6 | 63.4 | 65.5 | 88.1 | 84.5 | 74.0 | 1951 |
| 49.5 | 66.7 | 64.7 | 65.5 | 88.2 | 85.4 | 74.7 | 1952 |
| 49.6 | 65.5 | 63.8 | 68.1 | 86.6 | 83.0 | 73.1 | 1953 |
| 49.9 | 67.8 | 61.1 | 68.1 | 89.5 | 85.2 | 70.8 | 1954 |
| 53.3 | 68.9 | 61.5 | 68.1 | 88.2 | 84.2 | 72.7 | 1955 |
| 50.1 | 68.2 | 59.8 | 68.4 | 87.7 | 83.4 | 77.0 | 1956 |
| 48.4 | 65.7 | 59.1 | 68.4 | 88.6 | 81.6 | 79.9 | 1957 |
| 52.1 | 68.6 | 60.5 | 69.4 | 89.3 | 82.5 | 76.6 | 1958 |
| 53.2 | 69.0 | 61.3 | 69.7 | 88.7 | 82.9 | 75.6 | 1959 |
| 52.7 | 70.4 | 62.2 | 69.4 | 86.5 | 83.5 | 75.6 | 1960 |
| 54.7 | 72.2 | 63.5 | 71.5 | 86.7 | 83.5 | 76.3 | 1961 |
| 54.3 | 73.2 | 65.3 | 71.9 | 85.1 | 85.3 | 76.5 | 1962 |

a A state relative is the state's per capita personal income expressed as a percentage of that for the United States.

b Weighted by the midyear populations of each of the states.

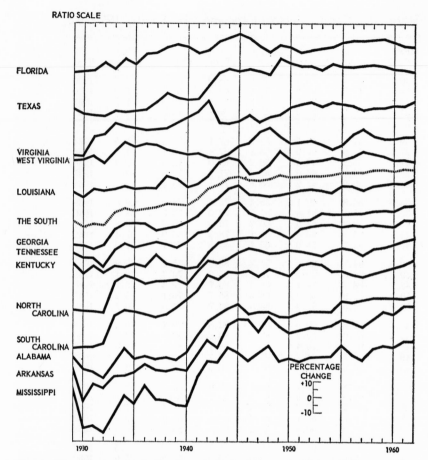

**Chart III.** State and Regional Relatives of United States Per Capita Income, 1929-62

Source: Table 5

intensity with which various industries are affected and that the states have different compositions of industry. It is doubtful that any selection of years would work uniformly well for all states in the South.[13]

13. This is a considerable body of evidence on the differential effects of cycles on industries. The work of the National Bureau of Economic Research, starting with Wesley Mitchell, *Business Cycles: The Problem and its Setting* (New York, 1927), deserves particular mention. Regarding the relationship between industrial composition and business cycles in the states, see Hanna, *op. cit.*, and the NBER occasional paper by George Borts, "Regional Cycles of Manufacturing Employment in the United States, 1914–1953," also published in *Journal of the American Statistical Association*, LV (March 1960), 151–211. The problems of measure-

**Table 6.** Annual Rates of Change in State Income Relatives between Fixed Pairs of Selected Years*

(Percentage Rate of Change)

| State | 1929-40 | 1940-45 | 1945-58 | 1958-62 |
|---|---|---|---|---|
| The South | .9 | 3.1 | .3 | .1 |
| Alabama | .3 | 5.9 | .3 | .1 |
| Arkansas | −.1 | 6.4 | ª | 2.1 |
| Florida | 1.4 | 1.6 | −.2 | −1.0 |
| Georgia | 1.3 | 4.6 | ª | 1.1 |
| Kentucky | −.3 | 3.6 | .1 | 1.7 |
| Louisiana | .3 | 4.3 | .3 | −1.2 |
| Mississippi | −.9 | 6.8 | ª | 1.0 |
| North Carolina | 1.6 | 3.8 | ª | 1.6 |
| South Carolina | 2.7 | 3.1 | ª | 1.9 |
| Tennessee | .6 | 5.1 | −.4 | .9 |
| Texas | .6 | 3.3 | .4 | −1.2 |
| Virginia | 2.2 | −.4 | .6 | .8 |
| West Virginia | .3 | 1.1 | .5 | ª |

* Source: Table 5.
ª Less than .05 percent.

If interest is confined to the question of the extent to which the states in the South follow the general pattern of the region as a whole, then the simple annual rates of change in relatives during the three periods, 1929–40, 1940–45, and 1945–59, will provide a rough indication. Such measures necessarily ignore some of the differential cyclical and irregular changes among the states. The effects of irregular forces on a state's income for a particular year can be quite large, especially if changes in agricultural prices are conceived in these terms. To identify these forces, even more to measure them and adjust for their effects for even a single state, is beyond the scope of this paper.

ment are discussed more fully in Hanna, "Relative Growth Among Regions," *Bulletin de L'Institut International de Statistique,* Vol. XXXVI, Book 4, pp. 143–58, where growth rates computed by alternative methods are given. Using regression methods to separate secular or persistent changes from cyclical and irregular ones, the following annual rates of growth were obtained for the 1929–54 period: South Carolina, 2.4 percent; Virginia, 1.9; North Carolina, 1.8; Georgia, 1.3; Florida, 1.0; Arkansas, .9; Texas, .9; and Louisiana, .7 percent. Only when farm income is excluded are significant trends discernible for Kentucky (.6), Tennessee and Alabama (.9 percent). Significant trends, over and above cyclical and irregular forces, were not found for West Virginia or Mississippi. The fact that during the years since 1945 the state relatives have tended to fluctuate within narrow limits and that cyclical fluctuations have been increasingly less severe would, perhaps, operate to reduce the effectiveness of the regression method if it were to be applied to the longer period, 1929–62.

**Table 7.** Interstate Dispersion of Per Capita Incomes,
United States, the South, and the Nonsouth, 1929–62*

| | STANDARD DEVIATIONS[a] | | | COEFFICIENTS OF VARIATION[b] | | |
|---|---|---|---|---|---|---|
| Year | United States | South | Nonsouth | United States | South | Nonsouth |
| 1929 | 259 | 72 | 198 | 36.9 | 18.7 | 24.2 |
| 1930 | 242 | 71 | 188 | 38.9 | 21.6 | 25.8 |
| 1931 | 208 | 63 | 166 | 39.5 | 22.0 | 26.9 |
| 1932 | 163 | 50 | 136 | 41.0 | 23.3 | 29.2 |
| 1933 | 147 | 43 | 127 | 39.4 | 19.8 | 29.5 |
| 1934 | 155 | 46 | 132 | 36.9 | 18.4 | 27.2 |
| 1935 | 158 | 51 | 118 | 33.7 | 18.5 | 21.8 |
| 1936 | 183 | 60 | 127 | 34.4 | 19.2 | 20.5 |
| 1937 | 186 | 68 | 136 | 32.6 | 19.9 | 20.8 |
| 1938 | 172 | 68 | 131 | 32.9 | 21.4 | 21.7 |
| 1939 | 183 | 73 | 135 | 33.1 | 21.8 | 21.2 |
| 1940 | 196 | 76 | 147 | 33.1 | 21.2 | 21.5 |
| 1941 | 219 | 79 | 160 | 30.6 | 17.6 | 19.5 |
| 1942 | 244 | 101 | 169 | 26.9 | 16.7 | 16.4 |
| 1943 | 283 | 131 | 197 | 25.8 | 17.3 | 15.9 |
| 1944 | 281 | 133 | 198 | 23.6 | 15.6 | 15.0 |
| 1945 | 279 | 133 | 195 | 22.7 | 14.9 | 14.3 |
| 1946 | 295 | 131 | 207 | 23.6 | 14.9 | 14.9 |
| 1947 | 297 | 144 | 190 | 22.6 | 15.5 | 13.0 |
| 1948 | 303 | 137 | 181 | 21.4 | 13.6 | 11.5 |
| 1949 | 291 | 181 | 182 | 21.2 | 18.0 | 12.0 |
| 1950 | 322 | 186 | 199 | 21.7 | 17.3 | 12.1 |
| 1951 | 351 | 192 | 212 | 21.4 | 16.2 | 11.6 |
| 1952 | 359 | 198 | 218 | 20.8 | 15.8 | 11.5 |
| 1953 | 377 | 196 | 238 | 21.1 | 15.1 | 12.1 |
| 1954 | 364 | 211 | 232 | 20.6 | 16.2 | 12.0 |
| 1955 | 382 | 203 | 262 | 20.5 | 14.7 | 12.8 |
| 1956 | 411 | 224 | 287 | 20.8 | 15.3 | 13.3 |
| 1957 | 425 | 244 | 289 | 20.8 | 16.1 | 12.9 |
| 1958 | 400 | 230 | 262 | 19.4 | 14.8 | 11.7 |
| 1959 | 425 | 234 | 292 | 19.7 | 14.4 | 12.4 |
| 1960 | 432 | 220 | 292 | 19.5 | 13.2 | 12.1 |
| 1961 | 439 | 177 | 323 | 19.4 | 10.3 | 13.1 |
| 1962 | 452 | 223 | 309 | 19.1 | 12.4 | 12.0 |

* Sources: 1929–49, *Survey of Current Business*, August, 1955; 1950–59; *ibid.*,
August, 1962; 1960–62, *ibid.*, August, 1963.
a The square root of the weighted average of the squared deviations from the
weighted mean of the states. The midyear populations of the states were used as
weights. The District of Columbia is excluded from these calculations.
b The standard deviation expressed as a percentage of the mean.

The simple average rates of change (Table 6) are useful mainly
in reading Table 5 and Chart III. For 1929–40, the rates among the
states vary significantly—and three states show declines during this
period. During the war period only one state, Virginia, shows a de-

crease, and this is a moderate one. In the postwar period all of the increases are moderate and only Tennessee shows a decrease. The patterns of increases noted for the South can, therefore, be said to be a meaningful average, at least during the war and postwar periods, though the effects of particular states are evident. Texas, with more than one-fifth of the income of the region, affects the weighted regional averages particularly.

### Interstate Dispersion

From the fact that the per capita income relatives have been increasing in the South, where incomes are below the United States average per capita income, it may be inferred that the relative interstate dispersion in the nation is decreasing. A measure of this interstate dispersion is provided in dollar terms by the standard deviation and in relative terms by the coefficient of variation (Table 7 and Chart IV).

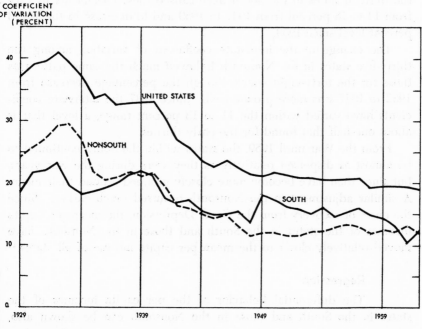

**Chart IV.** Interstate Coefficients of Variation for Per Capita Personal Income, 1929-62

Source: Table 7

For the United States as a whole, the interstate standard deviation has tended to increase with increasing income and to decrease with decreasing income but at a rate somewhat slower than that for income. Consequently, the interstate coefficient of variation has tended to increase with decreasing income and to decrease with increasing income. The interstate coefficient of variation reached a peak in 1932, decreased steadily to 1935, leveled off during 1936–40, decreased rapidly during the war years, and fluctuated within narrow limits around 21 percent during 1948–57; and it has decreased to 20 percent or below since then.

Among the thirteen states in the South, the tendency for the standard deviation to vary directly with average per capita income is somewhat weaker than that for the nation. Consequently, the changes in the interstate coefficient of variation in the South often are larger and sometimes in a direction opposite to that of the nation. During the war years, the interstate coefficients decreased from a level of around 19–21 percent to about 15 percent. The uneven rates of growth among the thirteen states in the South have caused these coefficients to vary from 14 to 18 percent from 1947 to 1959 and to decrease to the 10–13 percent level since 1959.

The change in the interstate coefficient of variation among the thirty-five states in the Nonsouth followed much the same pattern as those for the forty-eight states, though the percentage decrease from 1932 to 1947 was more pronounced. Since 1947 the interstate coefficients have varied within the 11 to 13 percent range, a level that is about one-half that found for the early thirties.

From the War until 1959, the states within the South continued to be almost as dispersed relatively as they were during the war years, but since then have become more closely grouped around their mean. A similar adjustment in the Nonsouth occurred much earlier. Since the onset of recovery from the Great Depression, the mean per capita incomes of the states in the South and those in the Nonsouth have moved relatively closer to the mean per capita income of all states.[14]

## Regression

The differential behavior of the per capita incomes of the states in the South and those in the Nonsouth can be shown also,

14. Because of the slow and consistent changes in state populations, the distributions of total variation (above, Table 2) lead to much the same conclusions without, however, the precision afforded by the coefficients of variation (Table 7).

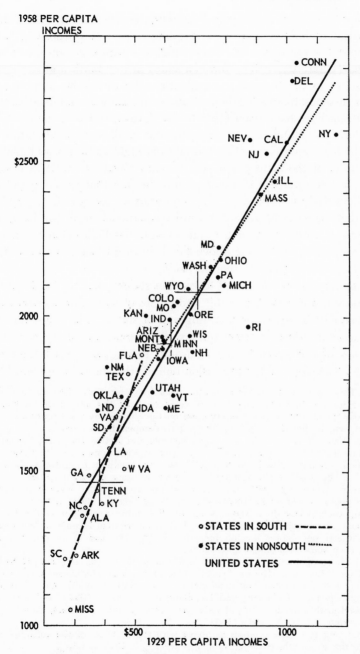

1958 PER CAPITA
INCOMES

$2500

2000

1500

1000

$500                    1000
1929 PER CAPITA INCOMES

o STATES IN SOUTH  ----
● STATES IN NONSOUTH ········
UNITED STATES  ———

**Chart V.** Regression of 1958 on 1929 State Per Capita Incomes

Sources: 1929, *Survey of Current Business*, August 1955; 1958, *ibid.*, August 1959.

perhaps with some net gain in clarity, by the use of still another statistical technique, that of regression. For this purpose, a single example, the regression of 1958 on 1929 per capita incomes, has been chosen (Chart V).[15] The thirteen states in the South and the thirty-five states in the Nonsouth are identified by distinctive symbols, the mean incomes for each group of states are shown, and least-squares regression lines have been fitted to the thirteen states in the South, to the thirty-five states in the Nonsouth, and to all forty-eight states.

The least-squares line fitted to all forty-eight states shows a marked regression of the state per capita incomes toward their 1958 mean.[16] The positive intercept of this line and the fact that its slope (1.7) is less than that of a line depicting proportional changes (3.9) indicates that there is some regression toward the national mean for 1958; that is, there is a tendency for the states below the 1929 mean to increase relatively more, and those above the 1929 mean to increase relatively less, than did the means themselves.[17]

The regression line for all forty-eight states is not too far from that for the states in the Nonsouth[18] and passes close to the intersection of 1929 and 1958 means for this subgroup of states. The regression line for the nation thus describes quite well the tendency of the per capita incomes of the states in the Nonsouth to regress toward their own mean. The slope of the regression line for the states in the South[19] is

15. This chart was prepared before data for later years became available. Except for the fact that any pair of years contains the effects of (unknown) irregular forces, they provide information on the changes over a twenty-nine–year period, which should be sufficiently long to dampen these effects.

16. Where $Y$ is the 1958 per capita income, and $X$ that for 1929, the regression line is: $Y^* = 858 + 1.7X$. The state per capita incomes used in these computations are unweighted; consequently, the means differ from those shown in Table 4. Because of the differential change in state populations between the two years, weighting would have required the use of some average population or the population of an intermediate year. Weighting the states is tantamount to treating each person in a state as having the state's mean per capita income, and none of the available weights would yield an average income which equaled the national per capita income for either year. The use of unweighted data treats each state as a single observation.

17. The expectation of regression is discussed in general terms in Harold E. Hotelling, "Review of Horace Secrist's The Triumph of Mediocrity in Business," Journal of the American Statistical Association, XXVIII (1933), 463–65, and in an exchange between Secrist and Hotelling, ibid., XXIX (1934), 196–200. It is discussed in the specific terms of state per capita incomes in Hanna, State Income Differentials, pp. 50–59 and 215–31.

18. Using the same symbols as above with the addition of the subscript $n$ to denote the Nonsouth, the regression line is: $Y^*_n = 1025 + 1.5X_n$.

19. Again, using the same symbols as above with the subscript $s$ to denote the South, the regression line is: $Y^*_s = 391 + 2.8X_s$.

much steeper, however, and indicates somewhat less of a tendency for these states to regress toward their own mean or toward those of the nation than is found in the Nonsouth. Alternatively, among the states in the South there was a tendency for their per capita incomes which were below their own mean in 1929 to increase relatively more than do those above their own mean, but this tendency is less pronounced than it is among the states of the Nonsouth. Moreover, all the states in the South (except Georgia) which were below their own mean in 1929 have lagged behind the relative increase indicated by the behavior of all states, while four of those above the mean of the South in 1929—Louisiana, Virginia, Texas, and Florida—experienced increases which equaled or exceeded those indicated by the national regression line.

This analysis singles out for special attention eight states in the South—Mississippi, South Carolina, Arkansas, Alabama, North Carolina, Kentucky, Tennessee and West Virginia—that had per capita incomes among the lowest in the nation in both 1929 and 1958 and which apparently have lagged behind the national patterns of differential growth. Having isolated these states, this type of analysis is powerless to pinpoint the factors associated with their distinctive behavior. The search for these factors will proceed first in terms of income components and then in terms of the major industrial sources of income.

### III. Changes in Income Components

The period since 1929 has seen personal income decline by 45 percent in the four years following the prewar peak in 1929, and then, with only a few halting steps, rise continuously over the next twenty-nine years (Table 8). From its Depression low in 1933, personal income had by 1962 grown nine-fold when measured in current dollars.

During these thirty years, transfer payments became a more important source of income, increasing from less than 2 percent to 4–6 percent of personal income. With the decline in unemployment, the share going to labor increased from around 60 percent to about 70 percent of personal income. Proprietors' income, more sensitive to price changes than other components, has varied within the range of 10 to 20 percent of personal income but has shown no distinctive trend. The share of property income, which was around 22 percent during 1929–33, declined steadily from 1934 to 1942, and has been in the 10–13 percent range since then.

To what extent has the South participated in these changes in the

**Table 8.** Personal Income and its Components, United States and Share of South, 1929–62*

| Year | Total Income | Labor Income | Propri-etors' Income | Property Income | Transfer Payments | | |
|------|-------|-------|-------|-------|-------|-------|-------|
| | | | | | Gross | Contri-butions | Net |
| United States (Billions of Dollars) | | | | | | | |
| 1929 | $85.7 | $50.9 | $14.8 | $18.7 | $1.5 | $.1 | $1.4 |
| 1930 | 76.8 | 46.6 | 11.5 | 17.2 | 1.5 | .1 | 1.4 |
| 1931 | 65.6 | 39.5 | 8.7 | 14.8 | 2.7 | .1 | 2.6 |
| 1932 | 50.0 | 30.8 | 5.3 | 11.9 | 2.2 | .1 | 2.0 |
| 1933 | 47.1 | 29.3 | 5.6 | 10.2 | 2.1 | .1 | 2.0 |
| 1934 | 53.5 | 34.1 | 7.0 | 10.4 | 2.2 | .2 | 2.0 |
| 1935 | 60.1 | 37.1 | 10.4 | 10.4 | 2.4 | .2 | 2.3 |
| 1936 | 68.4 | 42.4 | 10.5 | 12.2 | 3.5 | .2 | 3.3 |
| 1937 | 73.8 | 46.6 | 12.7 | 12.7 | 2.4 | .6 | 1.9 |
| 1938 | 68.4 | 43.4 | 11.1 | 11.6 | 2.8 | .6 | 2.3 |
| 1939 | 72.8 | 46.4 | 11.6 | 12.3 | 3.0 | .6 | 2.4 |
| 1940 | 78.5 | 50.3 | 13.0 | 12.7 | 3.1 | .7 | 2.5 |
| 1941 | 96.0 | 62.5 | 17.4 | 13.8 | 3.1 | .8 | 2.3 |
| 1942 | 122.4 | 81.8 | 23.9 | 14.6 | 3.1 | 1.1 | 2.0 |
| 1943 | 148.4 | 103.6 | 28.2 | 15.4 | 2.9 | 1.7 | 1.3 |
| 1944 | 160.1 | 112.7 | 29.6 | 16.2 | 3.5 | 1.9 | 1.7 |
| 1945 | 164.6 | 112.4 | 30.8 | 17.2 | 6.1 | 1.9 | 4.2 |
| 1946 | 175.7 | 111.5 | 35.3 | 19.6 | 11.3 | 1.9 | 9.4 |
| 1947 | 189.1 | 123.7 | 34.4 | 21.2 | 11.8 | 2.1 | 9.7 |
| 1948 | 207.4 | 136.5 | 38.4 | 23.4 | 11.3 | 2.1 | 9.1 |
| 1949 | 205.5 | 136.0 | 34.1 | 25.1 | 12.4 | 2.2 | 10.2 |
| 1950 | 225.5 | 148.9 | 36.1 | 28.3 | 15.0 | 2.9 | 12.1 |
| 1951 | 253.0 | 173.2 | 40.8 | 29.8 | 12.5 | 3.4 | 9.1 |
| 1952 | 269.1 | 187.6 | 40.9 | 31.2 | 13.1 | 3.7 | 10.4 |
| 1953 | 283.1 | 200.5 | 39.2 | 33.2 | 14.2 | 3.9 | 10.2 |
| 1954 | 285.3 | 199.3 | 39.2 | 35.3 | 16.2 | 4.6 | 11.6 |
| 1955 | 306.6 | 215.2 | 41.4 | 37.7 | 17.5 | 5.2 | 12.3 |
| 1956 | 330.4 | 233.2 | 43.7 | 40.5 | 18.8 | 5.8 | 13.0 |
| 1957 | 347.9 | 245.0 | 44.5 | 43.4 | 21.7 | 6.7 | 15.0 |
| 1958 | 356.3 | 246.0 | 46.6 | 44.7 | 26.1 | 6.9 | 19.1 |
| 1959 | 381.3 | 266.3 | 46.5 | 49.0 | 27.4 | 7.9 | 19.5 |
| 1960a | 397.0 | 278.4 | 46.1 | 52.2 | 29.4 | 9.2 | 20.2 |
| 1961a | 412.8 | 286.1 | 47.9 | 54.8 | 33.4 | 9.5 | 23.9 |
| 1962a | 437.4 | 305.0 | 49.6 | 58.3 | 34.6 | 10.1 | 24.5 |
| South's Share (Percentage of U.S.) | | | | | | | |
| 1929 | 15 | 14 | 24 | 10 | 16 | 16 | 16 |
| 1930 | 14 | 14 | 22 | 10 | 16 | 14 | 16 |
| 1931 | 15 | 14 | 24 | 10 | 19 | 14 | 19 |
| 1932 | 14 | 14 | 25 | 10 | 17 | 14 | 17 |
| 1933 | 15 | 15 | 29 | 10 | 15 | 13 | 16 |
| 1934 | 16 | 15 | 28 | 11 | 15 | 14 | 15 |
| 1935 | 16 | 15 | 25 | 11 | 13 | 13 | 13 |
| 1936 | 16 | 15 | 26 | 11 | 17 | 13 | 17 |
| 1937 | 16 | 15 | 26 | 12 | 14 | 15 | 14 |
| 1938 | 17 | 16 | 25 | 13 | 14 | 15 | 14 |

## Table 8 (continued)

| Year | Total Income | Labor Income | Propri-etors' Income | Property Income | Transfer Payments | | |
|------|------|------|------|------|------|------|------|
| | | | | | Gross | Contri-butions | Net |
| | South's Share (Percentage of U.S., continued) | | | | | | |
| 1939 | 17 | 16 | 25 | 13 | 14 | 15 | 13 |
| 1940 | 17 | 16 | 24 | 13 | 14 | 15 | 14 |
| 1941 | 18 | 17 | 24 | 13 | 16 | 16 | 16 |
| 1942 | 19 | 18 | 24 | 15 | 17 | 20 | 16 |
| 1943 | 20 | 19 | 24 | 15 | 18 | 25 | 8 |
| 1944 | 20 | 20 | 25 | 16 | 19 | 25 | 11 |
| 1945 | 20 | 20 | 24 | 16 | 20 | 25 | 18 |
| 1946 | 20 | 18 | 24 | 16 | 23 | 21 | 23 |
| 1947 | 19 | 18 | 25 | 16 | 23 | 20 | 24 |
| 1948 | 19 | 18 | 24 | 16 | 22 | 20 | 23 |
| 1949 | 20 | 19 | 26 | 17 | 23 | 20 | 24 |
| 1950 | 20 | 19 | 25 | 17 | 23 | 20 | 24 |
| 1951 | 20 | 19 | 25 | 17 | 23 | 21 | 24 |
| 1952 | 20 | 19 | 25 | 17 | 23 | 20 | 21 |
| 1953 | 20 | 19 | 25 | 17 | 22 | 20 | 23 |
| 1954 | 20 | 19 | 24 | 17 | 22 | 20 | 23 |
| 1955 | 20 | 19 | 26 | 17 | 22 | 20 | 22 |
| 1956 | 20 | 19 | 25 | 18 | 22 | 20 | 22 |
| 1957 | 20 | 20 | 24 | 18 | 22 | 20 | 22 |
| 1958 | 20 | 20 | 25 | 18 | 21 | 20 | 21 |
| 1959 | 20 | 20 | 25 | 18 | 21 | 20 | 22 |
| 1960 | 20 | 20 | 24 | 18 | 21 | 20 | 22 |
| 1961 | 20 | 20 | 25 | 18 | 21 | 20 | 22 |
| 1962 | 21 | 20 | 25 | 18 | 21 | 21 | 22 |

* Sources: 1929–49, *Personal Income by States Since 1929*; 1950–59, *Survey of Current Business*, August, 1962; 1960–62, *ibid.*, August, 1963.
a Alaska and Hawaii are not included.

nation's income and its components? One answer to this question can be obtained by expressing the income components received by residents of the South as a percentage of the consonant figure for the nation. When thus viewed, the more rapidly growing personal income of the South results in an increase of its share from around 14–15 percent during the downswing of the Great Depression to around 19–20 percent beginning with 1942. Its share of the nation's labor income is only a shade lower and has shown much the same growth. The heavy dependence of the South on farms as a source of income is reflected in the South's larger share of the nation's proprietors' income —about 25 percent. One obvious implication of the large and almost constant share of proprietors' income is that the income of the South fluctuates with the vagaries of this price-sensitive component. To this extent, the income of the South is affected disproportionately by the success or failure of the federal price and income support programs for its principal crops.

The South's share of the nation's property income, which has tended to be small, has grown steadily from around 10 percent in 1929–33 to 18 percent since 1956. The increasing share of the South may well be a part of the nationwide tendency toward a wider geographic distribution of this dwindling share of personal income.[20] However, in 1958 about one-third of the property income received in the South flowed to residents of two states, Texas and Florida.

Transfer payments are basically a two-way flow; the gross payments to the residents of a state or region must be balanced against the contribution of residents of the state or region to various social security funds. The difference between these two flows are the net transfer payments to the state or region. To some extent they are designed to be contra-cyclical, as in the case of unemployment compensation, but for other programs such as that for old age and survivors the payments may be expected to continue during good economic weather and bad. If the South's share of transfer payments is compared with the South's share of labor income, to which these payments are most directly related, its share, both on a gross basis and on a net basis, is larger than for labor income except for the years 1935, 1937–45, and those since 1958. The share the South has contributed to social security funds also has been as great or greater than its share of labor income except for the years 1933–36 and 1938–41. During three of the war years the South made about one-fourth of the contributions to these funds. There is little in these figures to support the notion that the observed increase in the income of the South was due in any appreciable measure to transfer payments.

The two outstanding facts in these data which help to explain the pattern of changes in the South are its heavy dependence upon agriculture, which since the war has not grown as rapidly as other components, and its increasing share of labor income. The rapid rise of the labor share during the early years of the war was followed by a precipitous decline in the immediate postwar years and a slow recovery thereafter. These changes are due in part to the fact that the pay of military personnel is attributed to the state in which they are stationed.

20. The interstate coefficient of variation for property income decreased from a high of 69 percent in 1933 to 33 percent in 1954. Hanna, *op. cit.*, pp. 108–9.

**Table 9.** Income Components and Composition of Income,
the South, 1929–62*

| Year | Total Personal Income | Labor Income | Propri- etors' Income | Property Income | Net Transfer Payments |
|---|---|---|---|---|---|
| | | Components (Billions of Dollars) | | | |
| 1929 | $12.7 | $7.0 | $3.6 | $2.0 | $.2 |
| 1930 | 11.0 | 6.4 | 2.5 | 1.8 | .2 |
| 1931 | 10.0 | 5.5 | 2.1 | 1.5 | .5 |
| 1932 | 7.2 | 4.3 | 1.3 | 1.2 | .4 |
| 1933 | 7.3 | 4.3 | 1.6 | 1.1 | .3 |
| 1934 | 8.6 | 5.1 | 2.0 | 1.1 | .3 |
| 1935 | 9.5 | 5.5 | 2.6 | 1.2 | .3 |
| 1936 | 11.0 | 6.3 | 2.7 | 1.4 | .6 |
| 1937 | 12.0 | 7.0 | 3.2 | 1.5 | .3 |
| 1938 | 11.4 | 6.7 | 2.8 | 1.5 | .3 |
| 1939 | 12.1 | 7.3 | 2.9 | 1.6 | .3 |
| 1940 | 13.2 | 8.0 | 3.2 | 1.6 | .3 |
| 1941 | 17.0 | 10.6 | 4.2 | 1.8 | .4 |
| 1942 | 23.2 | 15.1 | 5.8 | 2.1 | .3 |
| 1943 | 29.3 | 20.0 | 6.8 | 2.4 | .1 |
| 1944 | 32.6 | 22.4 | 7.4 | 2.6 | .2 |
| 1945 | 33.5 | 22.6 | 7.5 | 2.7 | .8 |
| 1946 | 34.4 | 20.5 | 8.5 | 3.2 | 2.1 |
| 1947 | 36.7 | 22.3 | 8.7 | 3.4 | 2.3 |
| 1948 | 40.3 | 25.0 | 9.3 | 3.8 | 2.1 |
| 1949 | 40.7 | 25.3 | 8.8 | 4.2 | 2.4 |
| 1950 | 44.6 | 28.0 | 8.9 | 4.7 | 2.9 |
| 1951 | 50.7 | 33.2 | 10.3 | 5.0 | 2.2 |
| 1952 | 54.2 | 36.5 | 10.1 | 5.3 | 2.2 |
| 1953 | 56.2 | 38.4 | 9.9 | 5.6 | 2.3 |
| 1954 | 56.5 | 38.3 | 9.5 | 6.1 | 2.6 |
| 1955 | 61.5 | 41.4 | 10.8 | 6.6 | 2.8 |
| 1956 | 66.4 | 45.4 | 10.8 | 7.2 | 2.9 |
| 1957 | 70.1 | 48.3 | 10.6 | 7.8 | 3.4 |
| 1958 | 72.8 | 49.2 | 11.7 | 8.0 | 4.1 |
| 1959 | 78.1 | 53.1 | 11.8 | 9.0 | 4.3 |
| 1960 | 80.8 | 55.3 | 11.3 | 9.6 | 4.4 |
| 1961 | 85.0 | 57.4 | 12.2 | 10.1 | 5.2 |
| 1962 | 90.4 | 61.8 | 12.4 | 10.7 | 5.4 |
| | | Composition (Percentage of Total) | | | |
| 1929 | | 55 | 28 | 15 | 2 |
| 1930 | | 59 | 23 | 16 | 2 |
| 1931 | | 57 | 22 | 16 | 5 |
| 1932 | | 60 | 18 | 17 | 5 |
| 1933 | | 59 | 22 | 15 | 4 |
| 1934 | | 60 | 23 | 13 | 4 |
| 1935 | | 58 | 27 | 12 | 3 |
| 1936 | | 58 | 24 | 13 | 5 |
| 1937 | | 58 | 27 | 13 | 2 |
| 1938 | | 59 | 25 | 13 | 3 |

**Table 9** (continued)

| Year | Labor Income | Propri- etors' Income | Property Income | Net Transfer Payments |
|---|---|---|---|---|
| | Composition (Percentage of Total, continued) | | | |
| 1939 | 60 | 24 | 13 | 3 |
| 1940 | 61 | 24 | 12 | 3 |
| 1941 | 62 | 25 | 11 | 3 |
| 1942 | 65 | 25 | 9 | 1 |
| 1943 | 68 | 23 | 8 | a |
| 1944 | 69 | 23 | 8 | 1 |
| 1945 | 67 | 22 | 8 | 1 |
| 1946 | 60 | 25 | 9 | 6 |
| 1947 | 61 | 24 | 9 | 6 |
| 1948 | 62 | 23 | 10 | 5 |
| 1949 | 62 | 22 | 10 | 6 |
| 1950 | 63 | 20 | 10 | 7 |
| 1951 | 65 | 20 | 10 | 4 |
| 1952 | 67 | 19 | 10 | 4 |
| 1953 | 68 | 18 | 10 | 4 |
| 1954 | 68 | 17 | 11 | 5 |
| 1955 | 67 | 18 | 11 | 4 |
| 1956 | 68 | 16 | 11 | 4 |
| 1957 | 69 | 15 | 11 | 5 |
| 1958 | 68 | 16 | 11 | 6 |
| 1959 | 68 | 15 | 12 | 6 |
| 1960 | 68 | 14 | 12 | 5 |
| 1961 | 68 | 14 | 12 | 6 |
| 1962 | 68 | 14 | 12 | 6 |

* Sources: 1929–49, *Personal Income by States Since 1929*; 1950–59, *Survey of Current Business*, August, 1962; 1960–62, *ibid.*, August 1963.

a Less than one-half of one percent.

Only in 1957 did the South's share of labor income again reach the level it enjoyed in 1944 and 1945.

## Composition of Income

When each of the components is expressed as a percentage of the total personal income for a region or state, the relative dependence of the region or state upon a particular component is highlighted (Table 9). Such data are unaffected by the relative importance of such components in other regions, which is not the case when dealing with the region's share of a national total. Within the region, the sum of the components equals the region's personal income; and when the components are expressed as percentages of the total per-

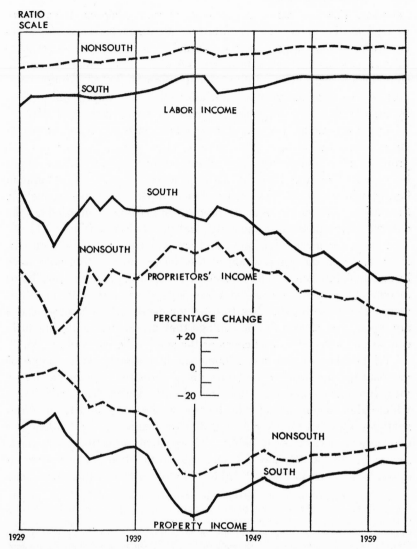

RATIO
SCALE

**Chart VI.** Composition of Personal Income, South and Nonsouth, 1929-62

Source: Table 10

sonal income, the sum of the percentages necessarily equals 100 percent. This last fact has unfortunate consequences for many comparisons, since a disproportionate increase in labor income, for example, means that the percentages for other components necessarily must decrease. For this reason the amounts of each component are shown as well as the percentage composition of income. When these peculiarities of the data on composition are kept in mind, however, useful comparisons can be made which reflect the differential changes in components over time. Interregional comparisons of income compositions for a single year are not affected to any appreciable extent by the fact that the sum of the percentages is forced to equal 100.

Labor income and net transfer payments have become increasingly larger sources of income in the South, while proprietors' income and property income have decreased in importance—changes which might be expected on the basis of data presented earlier. The national figures, which were the basis of previous comparisons, however, include the data for the South. A more precise comparison is afforded by the changes in composition in the South and the Nonsouth (Chart VI).

Except for levels of income and some narrowing of differentials, the changes in the composition of the South and the Nonsouth have been much the same. The Nonsouth is more dependent upon labor income and property income and less dependent upon proprietors' income than is the South. Net transfer payments in the Nonsouth also are equal to or exceed the percentage they are in the South, but little can be said about the significance of the small differences observed.

While labor income has become an increasingly large source of personal income in both the South and Nonsouth, a somewhat larger growth in this component is to be noted in the South. The percentages which labor income are of total income in the South and in the Nonsouth were closest together during the war years, but the tendency to converge started in about 1937.[21] The postwar adjustment was more severe in the South, and the changes of the two regions were in opposite direction in 1948–50 and in 1955; nevertheless, there was some

21. The national economic accounting procedures attribute military pay to the states in which the members of the armed forces are stationed, and beginning with 1940 there was a disproportionate increase in the military pay attributed to the South. Measured in percentages of all labor income, military pay in the South increased from around 1 percent during 1933–39 to more than 25 percent in 1944–45, then decreased to 4 percent in 1946, increased to 8 percent in 1953, and was 6 percent in 1958. The argument might be made that all or a part of such pay might better be attributed to the permanent home, rather than to the temporary military home, of service personnel, particularly since there is seldom an intention of changing place of residence, and intention is the usual test of residence. Even if such a position were adopted, military pay would then be roughly proportional to the numbers in military service, and it is doubtful that all of the observed tendency for the interregional differences in the labor-income percentages to become smaller would disappear. Certainly the 1937–39 moves in this direction would not be affected.

tendency for the labor income percentages to converge in the postwar period. The year-to-year changes in the percentages which property income were of personal income follow much the same pattern in the two regions. For this component also there has been a tendency for the decreasing percentages to converge.

The South has been and is much more dependent upon proprietors' income than is the Nonsouth. The evidence of a reduction in interregional differences in the relative importance of this component is difficult to assay in the face of very wide fluctuations, and any tentative conclusion wrung from these data is not very convincing. As a percentage of personal income, proprietors' income in the Nonsouth varied more from 1929 to 1937 and reached the trough a year later, increased more from 1937 to 1942, decreased less in 1943, and since 1943 has followed rather closely the changes in the South. In the Nonsouth, this component was relatively more important from 1941 to 1950 than it had been in 1929, and since 1950 it has been a larger percentage component than it was during the depressed years, 1931–34. In the South, on the other hand, proprietors' income was relatively more important in 1929 than in any year since then. Since 1953 it has been relatively less important than it was at the low point of the Depression in 1932. The observed reduction in interregional differences in this percentage component thus are traceable almost entirely to differential changes during 1937–43, the period when labor income became relatively more important in the South, rather than to a persistent trend that carried over into the postwar period.[22]

During the period under study, the composition of the personal income of the South has become more like that of the rest of the nation. The war mobilization period often obscures the real forces behind this movement. Sometimes, as in the case of labor income, the prewar trend continues in the postwar period. Property income has tended toward less regional concentration, and the South appears to have participated fully in this regional change. The reduced importance of proprietors' income is found both in and outside of the South, and while the major reduction in interregional dispersion occurred during the war period, the basic reduction in regional dispersion appears to stem from the growing importance of labor income as a consequence of a protracted period of full employment. During this period,

22. Many of the changes in the interstate coefficients of variation for proprietors' income apparently are attributable to the diverse movements of these coefficients for farm proprietors and non-farm proprietors during the 1929–54 period. Hanna, *op. cit.*, pp. 109–16.

**Table 10.** Personal Income and Composition of Income, Years*

| | Personal Income (Billions of Dollars) | | | | Labor Income | | | |
|---|---|---|---|---|---|---|---|---|
| State | 1933 | 1943 | 1953 | 1958 | 1933 | 1943 | 1953 | 1958 |
| The Nonsouth | $25.0 | $83.5 | $162.2 | $196.8 | 63 | 70 | 71 | 69 |
| The South | 7.3 | 29.3 | 56.2 | 72.8 | 59 | 68 | 68 | 68 |
| Alabama | .4 | 1.9 | 3.2 | 4.4 | 58 | 70 | 69 | 69 |
| Arkansas | .3 | 1.0 | 1.8 | 2.2 | 51 | 59 | 57 | 60 |
| Florida | .4 | 2.5 | 5.0 | 8.3 | 61 | 61 | 64 | 63 |
| Georgia | .6 | 2.4 | 4.5 | 5.7 | 61 | 69 | 69 | 70 |
| Kentucky | .6 | 1.9 | 3.6 | 4.3 | 58 | 64 | 68 | 66 |
| Louisiana | .5 | 2.0 | 3.7 | 4.9 | 62 | 70 | 68 | 70 |
| Mississippi | .3 | 1.2 | 1.9 | 2.3 | 47 | 53 | 56 | 60 |
| North Carolina | .7 | 2.5 | 4.9 | 6.3 | 56 | 67 | 67 | 66 |
| South Carolina | .3 | 1.3 | 2.5 | 2.9 | 61 | 72 | 71 | 70 |
| Tennessee | .6 | 2.1 | 4.1 | 5.0 | 59 | 66 | 68 | 68 |
| Texas | 1.5 | 6.5 | 13.0 | 17.0 | 57 | 65 | 68 | 67 |
| Virginia | .7 | 2.9 | 5.2 | 6.6 | 64 | 77 | 77 | 75 |
| West Virginia | .5 | 1.3 | 2.5 | 3.0 | 70 | 75 | 76 | 72 |

* Sources: 1933, 1943, and 1953, *Personal Income by States Since 1929*; 1958, *Survey of Current Business*, August, 1959.
a Transfer payments are net of social security contributions.

transfer payments have become an increasing source of income throughout the nation. As yet, interregional differences in transfer payments seem to be minor.[23]

## Differences Among States in the South

When the compositions of personal income of the thirteen states in the South are examined in the light of the findings for the region for a few selected years,[24] two facts stand out (Table 10). First,

23. In an intensive study based on three selected years, similar conclusions are reached by Howard G. Schaller, "Social Security Transfer Payments and Differences in State Per Capita Incomes, 1929, 1939, and 1949," *Review of Economics and Statistics*, XXXVII (February 1955), 83–89.

24. The years selected are 1933, the start of the upswing from the Great Depression and a period presumably containing most of the adjustments generated by the Great Depression; 1943, a peak period of the war mobilization effort; 1953, a decade after the war-time peak and near the end of the Korean affair; and 1958, the last year for which data were available when this section was

the South, the Nonsouth, and the States in the South, Selected

| COMPOSITION OF PERSONAL INCOME (Percentage of Total) | | | | | | | | | | | |
|---|---|---|---|---|---|---|---|---|---|---|---|
| Proprietor's Income | | | | Property Income | | | | Transfer Payments[a] | | | |
| 1933 | 1943 | 1953 | 1958 | 1933 | 1943 | 1953 | 1958 | 1933 | 1943 | 1953 | 1958 |
| 10 | 18 | 13 | 12 | 23 | 11 | 12 | 13 | 4 | 1 | 3 | 5 |
| 22 | 23 | 18 | 16 | 15 | 8 | 10 | 11 | 4 | [b] | 4 | 6 |
| 24 | 23 | 18 | 16 | 13 | 6 | 8 | 8 | 5 | [b] | 5 | 6 |
| 31 | 33 | 27 | 21 | 11 | 7 | 9 | 11 | 7 | 1 | 6 | 8 |
| 14 | 19 | 16 | 16 | 21 | 11 | 15 | 16 | 4 | [b] | 5 | 6 |
| 22 | 23 | 18 | 15 | 13 | 8 | 9 | 10 | 4 | [b] | 4 | 5 |
| 21 | 27 | 18 | 17 | 16 | 8 | 9 | 10 | 5 | 1 | 5 | 7 |
| 17 | 21 | 17 | 13 | 17 | 8 | 10 | 11 | 4 | 1 | 6 | 6 |
| 36 | 40 | 31 | 23 | 11 | 6 | 8 | 9 | 6 | 2 | 6 | 7 |
| 28 | 26 | 21 | 19 | 12 | 7 | 8 | 10 | 4 | 0 | 4 | 5 |
| 24 | 21 | 17 | 15 | 11 | 6 | 8 | 9 | 4 | 0 | 4 | 5 |
| 23 | 25 | 18 | 16 | 13 | 8 | 9 | 10 | 4 | 1 | 4 | 6 |
| 22 | 25 | 17 | 17 | 17 | 9 | 11 | 12 | 4 | 1 | 3 | 4 |
| 18 | 15 | 11 | 12 | 15 | 8 | 9 | 10 | 3 | [c] | 2 | 3 |
| 13 | 15 | 10 | 10 | 11 | 8 | 9 | 10 | 4 | 1 | 5 | 8 |

[b] Less than one-half of one percent.
[c] Social security contributions exceeded gross transfer payments.

the findings for the region typify most, if not all, of the states in the region. Secondly, there is within these patterns considerable interstate variation.

All of the states in the South, except Virginia and West Virginia for every selected year and an occasional state for one or two of the selected years, are less dependent upon labor income than is the average of the states in the Nonsouth. The dependence on proprietors' income is greater in the states in the South, again except for Virginia and West Virginia in 1953 and 1958, than in the Nonsouth as a whole. Property incomes play a less important role in personal income in the South than in the Nonsouth, except for Florida, where, for 1943 and later years, it is at least as important as in the Nonsouth.

prepared. An examination of state compositions for 1929, 1938, and 1948, as well as for those shown in Table 10, seem to indicate that the selected years show adequately both the essential trends and the interstate variations.

In spite of this apparent homogeneity of the region's composition of income, there is also considerable variation among the states. Labor income, for example, for 1933 varies from 47 percent in Mississippi to 70 percent in West Virginia, and for 1943 and 1953 it varies from 53–56 percent in Mississippi to 75–77 percent in Virginia and West Virginia. Proprietors' income tends to be a more important source in Mississippi and of less importance in West Virginia. As mentioned earlier, property income is a more important source of income in Florida than in the other states in the South. While the state differences in transfer payments are hard to discern in the face of much variation from one selected year to another, Mississippi and Arkansas appear to receive relatively more income in this form than do the other states in the South.

Do these data support the usual hypotheses concerning the relationship between income sources and level or growth of income? One such hypothesis is that proprietors' income, which is either cyclically sensitive or supported at minimum levels by various federal programs, usually is associated with low income-levels and small growth. Among the states with the lowest per capita incomes, two—Mississippi and Arkansas—have the highest percentages of income from this source. There seems to be some evidence that Mississippi, at least, is lagging the growth of the other states in the region (above, Chart III), but similar evidence is not found for Arkansas. The other state with but little growth—West Virginia—is less dependent upon proprietors' income than any other state in the region. While the data for Mississippi appear to be consistent with such an hypothesis, a single observation is scant support for it.

An alternative hypothesis, that a state's income grows as it becomes more dependent upon labor income, also is confronted with contradictory state data. Among the states with the most growth, Florida, Texas, and Virginia, there was an increase in the percentages labor income is of personal income, though this increase was smaller in Florida than in Mississippi. On the other hand, West Virginia, with a large and growing percentage of labor income, did not experience an outstanding growth in personal income. The fact that labor income showed increasing importance in most of the states in the region, and that with few exceptions most of them grew at about the same rate, is not inconsistent with this hypothesis. Neither is the fact that there was a somewhat slower growth of labor income in the Nonsouth, whose income also grew more slowly than that of the South.

But these facts provide little clue as the lines of causation or even as to the direction in which they run. It is just as plausible to hold that growing personal income is responsible for full employment and the consequent increase in the importance of labor income as it is to argue that growing dependence upon labor income leads to a growing personal income level.

Prima facie, such hypotheses are too simple and incomplete. Undoubtedly, the passage from a period of widespread unemployment to one of full employment will be accompanied by an increase in the share of labor income, at least in the short run. Presumably, the full employment of persons will also be accompanied by a fuller utilization, if not an expansion, of capital, so that the returns to property may be expected to rise also, though perhaps more slowly because of the longer time periods of the contracts relating to much of this type of income. Whether labor income or property incomes will increase more in the long run will depend in part on whether it is labor or capital that is most effectively shifted from the less economic uses to better ones. Even the period since 1933, which has been one of almost unbroken growth in personal income, is too short to provide a definitive answer to the conjectures. So far, labor income has shown a marked growth, while property income, after suffering a large decline, has tended to stabilize at a little less than three-fifths of its 1929 level.

## IV. Changes in Major Sources of Income

For a few selected years there are data for the personal income arising in four broad industrial categories: the private sector of the economy is further classified and shown separately for the farm and non-farm segments, and government disbursements are shown separately for the federal government and for state and local governments. For each of these four categories, the figures shown represent the sum of the principal components flowing from them to the residents of the various states or regions. Thus, income from farming consists of the sum of farm proprietors' income, farm labor income (i.e., farm wages plus farm "other labor" income), less the contributions to social security. Property income generated by farms, however, is treated as a part of the private non-farm income, a figure which is obtained by subtraction and thus includes all flows not specifically allocated elsewhere. The data for the governmental categories include wages and salaries, other labor income, interest, and transfer payments (less the social security contributions of government employees) disbursed to individuals. The allocation between federal government and state and local government is based on their ultimate disbursements (payrolls, interest payments, etc.) and thus are after some redistribution of governmental resources among levels of government via grants-in-aid from one governmental unit to another. The lack of an adequate statistical base for distributing dividends and other property incomes by industrial origin make further industrial classification impracticable.

While the few industrial categories are of uneven size, the differential changes among them are large enough to provide some insights into the interregional differences which have arisen since 1929 (Table 11). Private non-farm income, for example, exceeds the sum of the income from the other three categories in each of the selected years. The disbursements of the federal government have grown much more rapidly than the income from other major industrial categories, primarily as a consequence of defense expenditures, though they also have been affected by the increase in social security and other transfer

**Table 11.** Income by Broad Industrial Sources, the South and the Nonsouth, Selected Years*

| Year | FARM INCOME | | FEDERAL GOVERNMENT DISBURSEMENTS | | STATE & LOCAL GOVERNMENT DISBURSEMENTS | | PRIVATE NON-FARM INCOME | |
|---|---|---|---|---|---|---|---|---|
| | South | Nonsouth | South | Nonsouth | South | Nonsouth | South | Nonsouth |
| | (Billions of Dollars) | | | | | | | |
| 1929 | $2.5 | $4.8 | $.4 | $1.6 | $.6 | $3.4 | $9.3 | $63.1 |
| 1933 | 1.2 | 1.8 | .5 | 1.8 | .6 | 4.0 | 4.9 | 32.2 |
| 1940 | 1.9 | 3.7 | 1.3 | 4.2 | .8 | 4.9 | 9.2 | 52.5 |
| 1946 | 5.0 | 11.5 | 6.0 | 16.1 | 1.4 | 6.5 | 22.0 | 107.2 |
| 1950 | 5.0 | 11.0 | 6.2 | 16.6 | 2.6 | 11.0 | 30.8 | 142.4 |
| 1955 | 5.1 | 9.3 | 8.6 | 23.3 | 3.8 | 15.1 | 42.9 | 195.2 |
| 1958 | 5.3 | 11.6 | 10.3 | 30.1 | 5.3 | 19.8 | 52.0 | 222.0 |
| | Index Numbers (1929=100) | | | | | | | |
| 1929 | 100 | 100 | 100 | 100 | 100 | 100 | 100 | 100 |
| 1933 | 49 | 38 | 127 | 108 | 111 | 116 | 53 | 51 |
| 1940 | 76 | 78 | 326 | 253 | 139 | 144 | 99 | 83 |
| 1946 | 201 | 241 | 1527 | 978 | 234 | 190 | 238 | 170 |
| 1950 | 202 | 231 | 1585 | 1007 | 438 | 319 | 332 | 226 |
| 1955 | 203 | 196 | 2211 | 1416 | 656 | 440 | 463 | 309 |
| 1958 | 216 | 243 | 2628 | 1827 | 902 | 575 | 561 | 352 |

* Sources: 1929–55, *Personal Income by States Since 1929*; 1958, *Survey of Current Business*, August, 1959.

payments. Farm income has increased somewhat less than the income from other categories.

With the single exception of farm income, the increases in the South have been larger than those in the Nonsouth. Farm income in the Nonsouth declined somewhat more from 1929 to 1933, and has shown somewhat greater increases since 1933. In the South, farm income has been roughly double its 1929 level in each of the selected years since 1946. Compared with 1929, the increases in the South have been two-fifths to three-fifths greater than those in the Nonsouth, the largest increase being recorded for the private non-farm income category.

**Table 12.** South's Share of Broad Industrial Sources of Income, Selected Years*

(Percentages of National Totals)

| Year | Personal Income | Farm Income | Federal Government Disbursements | State & Local Government Disbursements | Private Non-farm Income |
|------|-----------------|-------------|----------------------------------|----------------------------------------|-------------------------|
| 1929 | 15 | 34 | 19 | 15 | 13 |
| 1933 | 15 | 40 | 22 | 14 | 13 |
| 1940 | 17 | 34 | 23 | 14 | 15 |
| 1946 | 20 | 30 | 27 | 17 | 17 |
| 1950 | 20 | 31 | 27 | 19 | 18 |
| 1955 | 20 | 35 | 28 | 20 | 18 |
| 1958 | 20 | 31 | 25 | 21 | 19 |

* Sources: 1929–55, *Personal Income by States Since 1929*; 1958, *Survey of Current Business*, August, 1959.

These interregional differentials in the rates of increase have changed appreciably the South's share of the nation's income in each category except farm income (Table 12). The cyclical fluctuations in farm income are so large that no distinct trend in the regional shares are discernible. The South's share of governmental expenditures has increased by approximately one-third, as has personal income, while its share of private non-farm income has increased by more than two-fifths. The fact that state and local government disbursements in the South have kept pace with federal government disbursements and with personal income would have more clear-cut significance had this development not been accompanied by a great expansion in federal grants-in-aid to state and local governments.[25]

25. One need mention only highways, airport development, and old-age-assistance programs to be reminded of the magnitude and extent of the expansion in

**Table 13.** Broad Industrial Composition of Income, the South and the Nonsouth, Selected Years*

(Percentage of Personal Income)

| Year | Farm Income | Federal Government Disbursements | State & Local Government Disbursements | Private Non-farm Income |
|------|-------------|-------------------|-------------------|-------------------|
| | | The South | | |
| 1929 | 20 | 3 | 5 | 73 |
| 1933 | 17 | 7 | 9 | 68 |
| 1940 | 14 | 10 | 6 | 70 |
| 1946 | 15 | 17 | 4 | 64 |
| 1950 | 11 | 14 | 6 | 69 |
| 1955 | 8 | 14 | 6 | 71 |
| 1958 | 7 | 14 | 7 | 71 |
| | | The Nonsouth | | |
| 1929 | 7 | 2 | 5 | 86 |
| 1933 | 5 | 4 | 10 | 81 |
| 1940 | 5 | 6 | 8 | 80 |
| 1946 | 8 | 11 | 5 | 76 |
| 1950 | 6 | 9 | 6 | 79 |
| 1955 | 4 | 10 | 6 | 80 |
| 1958 | 4 | 11 | 7 | 78 |

* Source: Table 11.

Another consequence of these differential changes has been the declining importance of farm income in the personal income of the South (Table 13). During 1955 and 1958, farm income, as a percentage of personal income, has been about one-half as important a source as it was in 1929 and 1933. A change in a similar direction, but of smaller magnitude, is to be noted also in the Nonsouth. On the other hand, the disbursements of the federal government have become a much more important part of the personal income of both regions. Private non-farm income, always a larger share of personal income in the Nonsouth than in the South, has declined slightly in importance in both regions. State and local government disbursements, thus viewed, have shown no appreciable change.

In terms of the broad industrial sources of income, examined in this section, the greater growth of income in the South, relative to the Nonsouth, would appear to be fairly general. The decline in the South's dependence upon farm income, which tends to be lower per

federal grants-in-aid. An assay of these developments, and the estimation of the proportion of the state and local government disbursements which is financed through non-federal tax and non-tax revenues, is beyond the scope of this paper.

person engaged, is accompanied by a somewhat more rapid growth in the income flowing from government and private non-farm pursuits.

## Income from Manufacturing

Since the search for new manufacturing industry consumes so much of the effort of regional, state, and local development agencies, it is worth a brief pause to review a few of the income effects of recent changes in this important industrial segment.[26] Although the data for manufacturing typically are more plentiful and in greater detail than for most industrial segments, they still do not provide information on the residences of the recipients of dividends paid out by corporations engaged wholly or chiefly in manufacturing. Consequently, the analysis is confined largely to earnings and proprietors' income.

**Table 14.** Income from Manufacturing as a Percentage of All Income Received by Persons for Participation in Current Production,[a] the South and the Nonsouth, Selected Years*

(Percentages of Income for Participation in Current Production)

| Year | MANUFACTURING INCOME | |
| | South | Nonsouth |
| --- | --- | --- |
| 1929 | 16 | 28 |
| 1940 | 17 | 28 |
| 1948 | 20 | 31 |
| 1958 | 23 | 32 |

* Sources: 1929, 1940, and 1948, *Personal Income by States Since 1929*; 1958, *Survey of Current Business*, August, 1959.

a Consists of wages and salaries, other labor income, and proprietors' income, exclusive of the earnings of military personnel.

Income from participation in manufacturing activity has been a growing share of the income from participation in all forms of current productive activity both in the South and the Nonsouth (Table 14). In the South it has increased from around 16 percent in 1929 to 23 percent in 1958 of all income from current productive activity, an increase of some 40 percent. In the Nonsouth, where manufacturing in 1929 accounted for more than one-fourth of all income from current productive activity, the growth has been of the order of 15 percent. Relatively, therefore, the South has recorded some overall gains.[27]

26. Detailed consideration of the changes in the industrial structure of the South and their consequences is beyond the subject of this paper.

27. Much the same kind of gain is shown by the differential increases in the

**Table 15.** Some Attributes of Manufacturing Income, the South and the Nonsouth, Selected Census Years*

| Census Year | SOUTH'S PERCENTAGE SHARE OF ALL MANUFACTURING | | AVERAGE ANNUAL EARNINGS FROM MANUFACTURING[a] (SOUTH AS A PERCENTAGE OF NONSOUTH) | PAYROLLS AS A PERCENTAGE OF VALUE ADDED | |
|---|---|---|---|---|---|
| | Employment | Payrolls | | South | Nonsouth |
| 1929 | 16 | 11 | 66 | 43 | 47 |
| 1939 | 17 | 12 | 67 | 47 | 53 |
| 1947 | 17 | 13 | 75 | 46 | 54 |
| 1954 | 17 | 14 | 76 | 50 | 58 |
| 1958 | 19 | 15 | 77 | 48 | 57 |

* Sources: *Census of Manufactures* for specified year.
[a] Average annual earnings were computed for each region by dividing total payrolls by the total number of employees. The average annual earnings thus computed for the South were then expressed as a percentage of the consonant earnings for the Nonsouth.

These gains show up in the South's increasing share of manufacturing employment and payrolls (Table 15). The percentage increases from 1929 to 1958 in the South's share has been about 22 percent for employment and 38 percent for payrolls. This differential growth implies some gain in average earnings relative to the Nonsouth. Manufacturing earnings per worker in the South in 1929 were about two-thirds those of the Nonsouth; since 1947 they have risen to about three-fourths the level in the Nonsouth.

These changes are difficult to interpret with confidence. The fact that manufacturing earnings in the South are lower than those in the Nonsouth would suggest that the South's manufacturing industries require relatively fewer skilled workmen, on the average, than those of the Nonsouth. The ratios of payrolls to value added for the two regions add some little support to this view. An intensive study of the manufacturing data for 1947 by states shows that this is the case for that year.[28] At the same time, there is also much evidence that earnings for a given skill are lower in the South.[29] As a consequence, there is some question as to whether the relative rise in the earnings levels of the South, as compared with the Nonsouth, indicates some convergence of earning rates for the same skills or some increase in

percentages of employed persons attached to manufacturing during the 1940 and 1950 census periods. In the South the increase was from 16 to 19 percent, an 18 percent gain; in the Nonsouth, from 26 to 28 percent, a 9 percent gain.

28. Hanna, *op. cit.*, pp. 150–58.
29. *Ibid.*, pp. 128, 142, 157, 162, *passim.*

the level of skills required by the South's manufacturing plants. The greater percentage increase in manufacturing employment in the South than in the ratio of its per-worker earnings relative to those of the Nonsouth suggests that the manufacturing industries which require a relatively less skilled labor force have grown as fast, if not faster, than those industries which require a relatively more highly skilled labor force.[30]

If this highly tentative interpretation is a correct reading of these fragmentary data, then much of the observed increase in the income of the South during the last three decades can be attributed to a migration from the underemployment on farms to somewhat fuller employment in relatively low-skill industries. This movement is still in progress and undoubtedly further increases in income can be attained in this way. Perhaps such a process will further narrow the gap between the per capita incomes of the South and the Nonsouth, but it can hardly be expected to close it. Low-skill industries may provide incomes superior to those from farming, but the income potential even of the low-skill industries can hardly be realized in the absence of competition by the more highly skilled industries for the more competent members of the labor force. Apparently such competition is needed to bring the South's earning rates for given occupations and industries up to the national average.

## V. Demographic Factors

Reliance on the observed relationships between income and various broad population groups, such as those by city size, race, sex, family size, and rates of population increase, often is compelled by the absence of data on more direct measures of the sources of income differentials, such as the occupation, education, age, and the attained skills of income recipients. For the most part the group characteristics reflect imperfectly factors which may be associated

30. Victor R. Fuchs, in "Changes in the Location of U.S. Manufacturing Since 1929 (an Interim Report)," a paper presented at a joint session of the American Economic Association and the Regional Science Association, December 28, 1958, provides tangential support for this interpretation. When the relative rates of national growth of the industries found in the states in the South are taken into account, the 1929–54 growth of manufacturing employment and value added relative to that of the nation is greater than when these differential industrial-growth rates are ignored. This would indicate that, on the average, the 1929 industries in the South were among those growing more slowly and that much of the overall growth in the South has been in these industries (which characterized the manufacturing segment of the South at the earlier date). He presents a similar finding for 1947–54.

more directly with income differentials in some economic sense.[31] As a consequence, the observed relationships with these group characteristics at best are tenuous, and seldom do they afford a reliable base for useful inferences.[32] In this paper an attempt is made to deal with the characteristics of recipients which are directly related to their contributions to production and income formation. The less direct and less reliable reflection of these characteristics provided by various grouping devices using demographic criteria largely are ignored.

In the estimation of national income and its personal income variant, the residents of the nation are considered the ultimate beneficiaries of all productive activity, rather than as a factor of production. The expenses incident to the training of workers and their maintenance in a state of good health thus are not considered "costs" of production. Similarly, activities incident to consumption, such as the preparation by the housewife of food for home consumption or the husband's shaving himself, are not considered a part of the nation's productive activity. Neither is the worker considered to be a "capital good" having some value.[33] For the most part, such concepts are essential to obtain meaningful totals from the flows of income and economic goods. They do, however, ignore the expenses incurred in raising and educating children who migrate early in their productive life from one region to another. To the extent that such a problem does arise at the national level, it is unlikely to be serious, and many of its

31. The distinction between economic and non-economic factors is difficult to delineate with precision. Conventions against the use of mixed groups (men and women, white and non-white, etc.) at a given task certainly is a fact of some economic significance, even though the convention may be based on prejudice rather than on any difference between aptitudes or performance. At the same time it is doubtful whether such conventions could long persist if the bank of available skills did not exceed greatly the demand for them. Thus, the existence of prejudicial conventions, and the income differentials associated with them, often can be viewed more fruitfully as a consequence of a maladjustment between the supply and demand for economic resources than as a factor generating the maladjustment.

32. Hanna, *op. cit.*, p. 214.

33. These principles are mentioned in *National Income, 1954 Edition* (Washington, D.C., 1955), pp. 37–38, and are treated more explicitly in Milton Gilbert, George Jaszi, Edward F. Denison, and Charles F. Schwartz, "Objectives of National Income Measurement," *Review of Economics and Statistics*, August, 1948. They are not followed rigorously in every instance, partly because of statistical difficulties and partly because of the adoption of a rule of thumb, "goods sold not for resale," to distinguish final from intermediate product. The furnishing of meals, medical care, and even housing without charge to employees is looked upon as a deductible business expense and not as income to the recipient when it can be shown that such expenses lead to increased product.

consequences can be controlled through immigration laws and similar devices.

It was mentioned earlier that the population of the South contained a disproportionately large number of persons under 20 years of age—enough, in fact, to lead it to be called the "seed bed of the nation." These are the age groups which typically have not yet entered the labor force. The existence of differential proportions among age groups affect interregional comparisons in two ways. First, to the extent that there are uncompensated expenses in the rearing and education of youthful persons to the point that they can become productive members of society, a region with an excess number of them receives no direct credit in the income estimates for this type of contribution to the nation's product. It must be recognized, however, that the failure of the young persons to migrate to areas where there was a greater demand for their skills might very well lead to a further disparity in regional incomes. The results of an attempt to measure the net effects of migration on regional incomes probably would depend more upon the assumptions made regarding economic alternatives than upon the magnitudes of relevant data. Secondly, the numbers of those who are too young to contribute to income generation enter the denominator of the per capita income computation. Thus a region with an excess proportion of persons in the lower age groups will have a per capita income that is lower relative to other areas. This effect can be eliminated by basing the interregional adjustments for population size on the numbers of persons in the productive ages.

Personal income can be adjusted for interregional differences in the populations which are twenty-one years old or older by computing income per adult. The interregional differences in income per adult are appreciably lower than those for income per capita, especially for the earlier years of the period under study (Table 16). Since the differences in the incomes per capita and per adult are proportional to the populations used in their computation, a measure of the reduction in the interregional differentials is provided by the final column of Table 16. Since the compositions of the populations in the South and Nonsouth are becoming more alike, the reduction in income differentials is smaller in the more recent years. When the disparity in the proportion of persons under twenty-one years old is removed, the interregional income differences are reduced by somewhat less than 10 percent.

**Table 16.** Income per Adult, by Region, Selected Years*

| Year | Personal Income Per Adult^a (Dollars) | | | Relatives of U.S. Personal Income (Percent) | | | | Persons 21 Years and Older as a Percentage of Total Population | | |
| | | | | Per capita | | Per adult | | | | |
| | U.S. | South | Nonsouth | South | Nonsouth | South | Nonsouth | South | Nonsouth | Percentage, South of Nonsouth |
|---|---|---|---|---|---|---|---|---|---|---|
| 1930 | $1,053 | $ 627 | $1,187 | 53 | 117 | 60 | 113 | 53 | 62 | 85 |
| 1940 | 935 | 627 | 1,037 | 60 | 115 | 67 | 111 | 57 | 66 | 87 |
| 1950 | 2,315 | 1,811 | 2,485 | 72 | 110 | 78 | 107 | 59 | 66 | 89 |
| 1957 | 3,375 | 2,679 | 3,612 | 74 | 110 | 79 | 107 | 56 | 62 | 91 |

* Sources: The personal income and per capita income figures are from table 4. The population data are from the *Statistical Abstract of the United States, 1931; ibid., 1944–45;* and *ibid., 1959.*

ª The personal income received by the residents of an area divided by the number of persons in the area who are twenty-one years old or older. The population figures for the census years are as of the census date, and as a consequence are not strictly comparable with per capita figures which are from Table 4, and which are based on populations as of July 1. The difference in the census period and July 1, however, would have a negligible effect on the relatives and on the percentage of the population which were twenty-one years old or older. The 1957 population figures relate to the civilian population.

While the interregional differentials in the age compositions of the populations have important policy implications for such issues as federal aid for education, their significance for income differentials should not be overestimated. To some extent, at least, the expenses connected with the raising of children are of the nature of a consumer expenditure that may be enjoyed much as a similar expenditure made for other purposes. The adjustments of the regional incomes to a per-adult basis is a sufficient one for most policy purposes; a further adjustment for the fact that those living in areas with an excess proportion of persons below productive ages are faced with additional expenditures for their care and education does not appear to be warranted. Such differences in regional expenditure patterns are to be found in housing, heating, cooling, and even in food. Such differences in expenditures, however, may follow but are unlikely to contribute much to the income level of an area. So far as I know, no one has yet shown that the proportions of young persons in the South have reached such magnitudes as might affect adversely the productivity of the adult population.

## VI. Distributions of Income by Size

Although interregional differences in the distributions of income by size tend to raise more questions than they answer, a study of this kind should mention, at least, the growing body of recent data relating to this interesting field.

There are two lines of development in the interregional comparisons of income distributions that are worthy of note. The first, following Kuznets, is concerned with the shares of the upper income groups.[34] These studies, based largely on income tax returns, have produced state estimates of the percentages of total income flowing, per person, to those in the top 0.5 percent, top 1 percent, and top 5 percent of the income scales for 1919, 1929, 1933, 1937, and 1953.[35] The other line of development is based on an extended use of sampling techniques by the Bureau of the Census to obtain regional distribu-

34. Simon Kuznets, *Shares of Upper Income Groups in Income and Savings* (New York, 1951).

35. These estimates are in unpublished dissertations by Hyman Menduke, "Shares of the Upper Income Groups in Income by States, 1919, 1929, 1933, and 1937" (University of Pennsylvania, 1952) and Seymour S. Goodman, "Income Inequality in States and Regions" (The Johns Hopkins University, 1960). The first covers the first four years mentioned; the latter extends the analysis to 1953. Both of these studies follow Kuznet's economic income variant reduced to a per-person basis, *op. cit.,* pp. xxxii-xxxiii.

**Table 17.**  Percent of Income Received by the Top 1-Percent* Group, Selected Years

| Region or State | 1953 | 1937 | 1933 | 1929 |
|---|---|---|---|---|
| The South | 6.8 | 12.8 | 12.5 | 12.7 |
| The Nonsouth | 6.1 | 12.1 | 11.3 | 12.5 |
| Alabama | 7.1 | 12.7 | 12.8 | 12.5 |
| Arkansas | 6.9 | 11.1 | 11.4 | 10.8 |
| Florida | 7.4 | 18.3 | 13.2 | 15.0 |
| Georgia | 6.9 | 13.6 | 13.2 | 13.4 |
| Kentucky | 6.7 | 12.2 | 13.6 | 14.0 |
| Lousiana | 7.4 | 13.2 | 11.7 | 12.3 |
| Mississippi | 7.0 | 12.0 | 11.5 | 11.0 |
| North Carolina | 7.0 | 12.5 | 12.6 | 13.0 |
| South Carolina | 5.9 | 10.5 | 11.0 | 13.0 |
| Tennessee | 6.9 | 13.2 | 13.8 | 14.4 |
| Texas | 7.6 | 14.1 | 12.5 | 12.8 |
| Virginia | 5.8 | 12.8 | 15.6 | 11.9 |
| West Virginia | 5.3 | 9.9 | 9.4 | 10.7 |
| *Memoranda:*<br>Position of states in Nonsouth with<br>respect to range of percentages in the<br>South (number of states)— | | | | |
| Below range | 5 | 11 | 9 | 13 |
| Above range | 2 | 1 | 1 | 6 |
| Within range | 28 | 23 | 25 | 16 |

* Sources: 1929, 1933, and 1937, unpublished dissertation by Hyman Menduke (University of Pennsylvania, 1952); 1953, unpublished dissertation by Seymour S. Goodman (The Johns Hopkins University, 1960). The regional averages are unweighted.

tions of money incomes among recipients and families on an annual basis. So far, the only analysis of these regional data that has come to my attention is that by Atkinson.[36] These approaches will be discussed in order.

### Upper Income Groups

The relatively low level of incomes in the South, coupled with the higher dollar incomes below which one did not have to file an income tax return, prevented the estimation of the income shares going to those below the top 1 percent group for all but five states for three of the four earlier years analyzed.[37] The war and postwar extension of the income tax to lower income levels and the rapid

36. Thomas R. Atkinson, "Money Income Distribution: South vs. Non-South," *Southern Economic Journal*, XXIII (July 1956), 15–27.

37. The five states in the South for which 1929 estimates could be prepared for the top 3 percent are Florida, Louisiana, Texas, Virginia, and West Virginia.

increase in current incomes have made it possible to estimate the 1953 share going to the top 5 percent group for all states. Comparisons over time, however, will have to be confined to the incomes of those in the upper 1 percent of the distributions.

Judged by these data, the distributions of income in the states in the South tend to be among those that are more unequally distributed (Table 17). The income per person reported on the return with the lowest income included in the top 1 percent of a state distribution is so low in many of the states in the South that it would not qualify the return to be included among the top 3 percent in some of the New England and Middle Atlantic states. The conclusion is inescapable, however, that the low incomes flowing to the residents of the South tend to be less equally distributed than are the larger incomes flowing to the residents of other areas.

The range of the percentages flowing to the top 1 percent groups in the states in the South is quite broad, though the largest state percentage within the region is a smaller multiple (1.4–1.8) of the lowest state percentage than are the multiples found for per capita income (1.8–2.2). Relative to the distribution of these percentages in other states, the range within the South was largest in 1953. This 1953 expansion of the relative range means that more of the states in the Nonsouth have percentages similar to those found in the South, and there are but a few states outside of the South which have percentages that are either higher or lower than that shown by some one of the Southern states.

The data from which these measures of inequality are derived are not in sufficient detail to permit the isolation of the industrial or occupational characteristics of those which comprise the top 1 percent of the income distribution. Goodman has found significant rank correlations (based on the 48 states) between the farm–non-farm ratio of labor and proprietors' incomes per worker to the percentages going to the top 1 percent for 1929, 1937, and 1953.[38] This would

38. The ratios are based on averages of 1930, 1940, and 1950. The rank correlations coefficients (Spearman's) are .3 for 1929 and 1937 and .4 for 1953. Similar significant rank correlations are found between the size of a state's population and inequality. I find it difficult to specify the economic significance of this finding. Some of the states in the South are among those having the larger populations, as are some of those in New England and the Middle Atlantic states which also have distributions which are among the more unequal ones. When military personnel stationed within a state is included in the state's population, the ranks for the states in the South range from 6 to 31, so that there are five states with larger populations, thirteen states within the range found in the South, and seventeen states with smaller populations.

**Table 18.** Percentage Decreases in the Percent of Income Received by the Top 1-Percent Group, 1929–53 and 1937–53*

| Region or State | 1929-53 | 1937-53 |
|---|---|---|
| The South | 46.7 | 47.1 |
| The Nonsouth | 51.1 | 49.5 |
| Alabama | 43.1 | 43.9 |
| Arkansas | 35.9 | 37.6 |
| Florida | 50.3 | 59.3 |
| Georgia | 48.9 | 49.4 |
| Kentucky | 52.4 | 45.3 |
| Louisiana | 39.9 | 44.3 |
| Mississippi | 37.3 | 41.9 |
| North Carolina | 46.5 | 44.3 |
| South Carolina | 54.4 | 44.0 |
| Tennessee | 51.8 | 47.8 |
| Texas | 40.7 | 46.1 |
| Virginia | 51.1 | 54.4 |
| West Virginia | 50.3 | 46.3 |

* Source: Table 17.

suggest that the heavy dependence for income upon agriculture, with its wide distribution of farms by size, accounts for much of the relatively unequal distribution of the low incomes in the South.

Kuznets found a marked reduction in the shares of income flowing to the upper income groups after about 1939.[39] To what extent have the states in the South participated in this trend? Have the fruits of the observed increase in income in the South gone chiefly to those occupational groups whose income levels typically are below the top levels or has a disproportionate share accrued to those already favorably situated? Has the observed decline in the relative importance of agriculture, and the increase in the shares going to labor and to property, resulted in some reduction in the inequality of the distribution in the South? Goodman's estimates for 1953 make possible tentative answers to these questions.

Whether the change in the shares going to the top 1 percent of the income distribution is measured from 1929 to 1953 or from 1937 to 1953, Goodman's estimates show a decrease for every state—the decreases averaging about 47 percent for each period. For the longer period, from 1929 to 1953, about half of the states in the South recorded decreases greater than the unweighted average of all states; about half, smaller ones (Table 18). For the shorter period, from

39. *Op. cit.*, Chapter ii.

1937 to 1953, only one-third of the states in the South reported decreases greater than the national average. During this period, however, only three of the states in the South—Arkansas, Florida, and Mississippi—experienced percentage decreases which departed from the average by more than three percentage points. In both periods, most of the states in the Nonsouth reported percentage decreases within the range of those reported by the thirteen states in the South.

These estimates would seem to indicate that the reduction in the inequality of the income distribution, at least as measured by the top 1 percent group, has been widespread, and that the South has participated in it to about the same extent as the Nonsouth.[40]

### Money Income

While the marked reduction in the share going to the upper income groups is a fact of some significance, more extensive data on the distribution of income are needed to reveal whether this reduction is the result of the declining relative importance of property incomes or the result of the fuller employment of an expanding labor force. Much of the property income accrues to those in the upper income groups, and some reduction in inequality may be expected to accompany the decline in its relative importance.[41] A similar reduction in the shares going to the upper income groups could result from a disproportionate increase in labor income per worker, whether through fuller employment (i.e., less unemployment or less underemployment) or increases in earnings rates, since such additional income swells the total and typically accrues to those below the upper income levels. This tendency is strengthened if at the same time

40. Goodman points out that "the manner of interpolation, in the estimation of the population represented on tax returns, in the handling of net capital gains . . . and in the use of income payments . . . as the income base" overstates the share of the top 1 percent for 1929 and 1937 relative to 1953 "by no more than one-fifth." On the other hand, "the change in the tax definition of income and the inclusion of the returns of fiduciaries" in the earlier years would operate "to understate the shares for the earlier years relative to those for 1953." He concluded that "the average relative decline in the shares of the top-1-percent group over either period cannot be less than 30 percent of their average level in 1929 and 1937." It is not known to what extent these factors affect the state estimates differentially, although some differences can be expected, due to differences in sources of income, industry mix, and occupational mix.

41. Goodman finds a highly significant rank correlation between the share of property income (averaged for 1929, 1937, and 1953) in a state's income and the share going to the top 1 percent in the state for 1929 and 1937, but not for 1953. In the latter year, the property income share of personal income was 12 percent, as compared with 22 percent in 1929 and 17 percent in 1937; and, as mentioned earlier, its interstate distribution was relatively less dispersed.

there is also an increase in the percent of the total population in the labor force.

Information on income obtained by interview methods typically understates all incomes, and the amount of understatement increases with income size. This reporting bias has been found to be sufficient to affect state average earnings per worker in a similar direction.[42] It can be expected to produce an income distribution that is biased in the direction of greater equality, the amount of distortion being somewhat larger in the states with the larger average incomes. Despite these biases, it nevertheless seems worthwhile to examine some of the available distributions for the light they throw on income inequality in the South.

The two distributions provided by the Bureau of the Census and chosen for examination are those for 1949 and 1958.[43] Both are recession years, though the recession characteristics of 1958 are much milder than those of 1949.[44] In part this choice is based on the desire to use data from the *1950 Census of Population,* both because it is the earliest year for which regional data are readily available and because, being based on a larger sample, more complete details are published. Similarly, the 1958 data are for the most recent year of recession. The distributions by individual recipients were chosen in preference to the family distributions because these are believed to reflect somewhat better the returns for individual economic effort.

The distribution among income recipients in the Southern region is less equal than that in the nation in both years ( Chart VII, panels A and B).[45] This pattern is consistent with the findings based on the upper income groups, although such a result was not necessary since

42. Hanna, *op. cit.,* pp. 120–23.
43. The *1950 Census of Population,* which contains the 1949 data, provides data by state, and these could be accumulated to obtain a distribution for the South as it is defined throughout most of this study. For 1958, however, regional data are available only for the Census regions. Consequently, this section deals only with the Southern region as defined by the Census, which also includes Delaware, Maryland, the District of Columbia, and Oklahoma, as well as the thirteen states which are the subject of this study.
44. Per capita income for 1949 was below that for 1948 in the nation and for all but five of the states outside the Southern region and three of the states in the Southern region. The 1958 per capita income for the nation was about the same as that for 1957, and declines were recorded only for West Virginia in the Southern region and for ten of the states elsewhere.
45. The United States was chosen as a basis for comparison as a matter of convenience. A comparison of the region composed of the ten states classified by H. W. Odum, *Southern Regions of the United States* (Chapel Hill, 1936), as the South with the remaining states is given in Atkinson, *op. cit.*

there are differences in the states included in the Southern region, and the Census data are confined to money income.

Since median money incomes in the Southern region are but 71 percent of those for the United States in 1949 and 74 for 1958,[46] the greater inequality in the Southern region reflects both the existence of a larger proportion of persons receiving very low incomes and the somewhat lower incomes of workers and proprietors throughout much of the income scale. The basic tables also show that there are relatively fewer persons in the South with incomes over $10,000. Individual money incomes in this region thus tend to be lower than those in the other regions throughout the entire income scale.

Comparisons of the distributions for 1949 and 1958 are affected by two changes in the treatment of the basic data. First, in the 1949 distributions, but not in the one for 1958, persons with losses are included in the lowest income class so that the use of the class midpoint to estimate the money income received by persons in the lowest class for 1949 overestimates its amount relative to 1958. For the latter year, persons with losses are shown separately and were estimated to have made no contribution, positive or negative, to the income total. Secondly, since the numbers of men and women included in the 1958 sample for the regions are "not available," it was assumed that the ratio of male to female income recipients was the same in the Southern region as in the nation. This assumption, which appears to underestimate the number of female recipients in the Southern region, may yield a median income that is higher and a distribution for the region that is more unequal than the use of possible alternatives.[47] The differences between the distributions for the two years are large, especially at the lower end of the scale (Chart VII, panels C and D). It is doubtful that these differences in treatment are responsible for more than a small fraction of the observed differences in the two sets of distributions.

The 1958 Lorenz curve for the Southern region is further from

46. These percentages do not differ greatly from those given in Table 5, 73 and 75 percent of the consonant national figure, for per capita personal income for the South.

47. These ratios for 1949 were 1.93 for the United States and 1.96 for the Southern region. The ratio in the 1958 sample is only 1.61 for the United States. Since the change in the ratio from 1949 to 1958 was much larger than the interregional difference in 1949 ratios, it did not seem feasible to base the combination of the two groups on 1949 data, even with some arbitrary adjustment. The reduction in this ratio, which is only slightly greater than the reduction in the ratios of males to females in the employed labor force for this period, may have contributed to the increase in inequality in the income distributions.

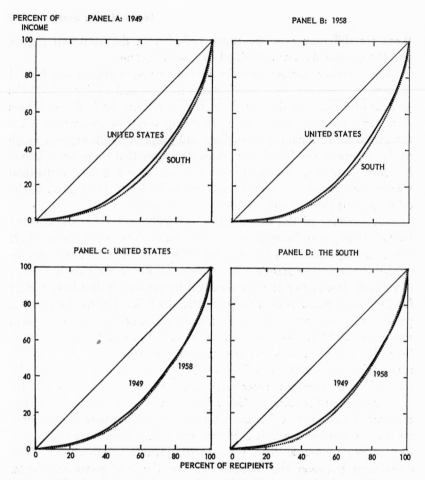

PERCENT OF INCOME   PANEL A: 1949

PANEL B: 1958

PANEL C: UNITED STATES

PANEL D: THE SOUTH

PERCENT OF RECIPIENTS

**Chart VII.** Lorenz Curves of the Distribution of Money Income Among Recipients, the United States and the Southern Region, 1949 and 1958

Sources: Estimated for 1949 from the 1950 *Census of Population,* vol. II, Characteristics of the Population, tables 138 and 162, and for 1958 from the Bureau of the Census, *Current Population Reports,* Series P-60, Consumer Income, No. 33, table 37. In estimating the income in each class, the class midpoints were used for all but the top, open-end class. For the open-end classes an estimated average income for the class was derived by averaging the per return amounts of adjusted gross income reported on returns in these income ranges in the 1955, 1956, and 1957 *Statistics of Income,* and rounding the result to the nearest $100. For 1949, the estimated average for those in the "$10,000 and over" class was thus estimated to be $18,700; for 1958, the average for those in the "$25,000 and over" class was estimated to be $47,000. In combining the 1958 distribution for male and female recipients in the Southern region, for which the numbers of male and female recipients in the distribution are "not available," it was assumed that the ratio of male to female recipients was the same as that reported for the United States.

the line of equal distribution at the lower end of the scale and closer to the line of equal distribution at the upper end of the scale than the one for 1949, crossing in the neighborhood of 85 percent of the recipients. Lorenz curves which cross are difficult to interpret satisfactorily. About the only statement that can be made with precision is that those in the upper 15 percent or so of the distribution received a smaller percentage of total income in 1958 than did the upper 15 percent in 1949. Above and below the point at which the lines cross, one has to work with segments and compare the slopes of the two curves. Neither the use of straight lines to connect the points provided by the data nor the smooth curves passing through these points provide a very satisfactory basis for comparisons within small segments of the curve. Indeed, it is not clear whether the segments to be compared should have terminals which have the same percentages of recipients, the same percentages of income, or should lie on a line perpendicular to the line of equal distribution. In part, the difficulty stems from the fact that the points for one curve do not correspond along either axis with the points for the other curve; in part, from the fact that we lack knowledge of the distributions of recipients within the classes in which the data are tabulated.

If, in the face of these difficulties, one may be permitted to hazard a guess, it would appear on the basis of the slopes of the two curves that recipients in the band from about 50–55 percent to around 80–90 percent received a somewhat greater share of the 1958 income than did the recipients in this band in 1949. If this guess is correct, it would seem to indicate that it was those in this area of the distribution that participated more fully in the fruits of the increases in total income in the Southern region. Those below and above this band perhaps experienced some increase in income, but the increases in their incomes were relatively smaller than the increase in total income.[48]

48. Of course, the persons in a specific percentage band in one year may not be the persons in that band in another year. While there is much stability in personal income, as has been shown in Horst Mendershauser, "Changes in Income Distribution During the Great Depression," *Studies in Income and Wealth*, Vol. VII, and Hanna, "The Accounting Period and the Distribution of Income," *ibid.*, Vol. IX, there are also many changes as persons enter the labor market, obtain experience, mature, or suffer declines in health, to mention only a few of the more common sources of income change. Moreover, the distributions relate to differing numbers of recipients. Consequently, it must be emphasized that the discussion here is concerned with groups whose members change rather than with individuals. Certainly, the percentage increase in the money income of a woman who shifted from an unpaid family worker on a farm to factory

The 1949 and 1958 distributions for the United States show much the same pattern as those for the Southern region. This similarity of change, whether it stems from the characteristics of the mild recession of 1958, from some quirk in the data, or from the actual situation being measured, increases the confidence with which one undertakes an interpretation of these curves. Basically, they seem to indicate the growth of the middle-income groups both in the nation and in the region, and although the income level of this group in the Southern region is somewhat below that found elsewhere, the income of the Southern region has improved sufficiently to make its effects evident in the region's patterns of consumption. The multiplication of modern homes, the increasing proportion of newer automobiles, the types and quality of the merchandise being offered in the stores, and other easily observed phenomena, perhaps are indicative of some of these changes.

The wide margins between the Lorenz curves for the United States and for the Southern region, particularly at the lower end of the distributions, are an area in which incomes in the region can be raised still further both through a shifting of its human resources from the low-income pursuits, such as agriculture, to more productive ones, and by obtaining for the industrial skills it now employs earning rates which are more nearly competitive with those found elsewhere.

---

employment, however meagre the pay, would be greater than the percentage increase in total income.

# VIII

# A Factor Analysis of Characteristics of the South*

*By Bernard M. Olsen and Gerald Garb*

Factor analysis is a body of methods by which a large number of variables can be analyzed on the basis of their intercorrelations.[1] By means of these methods a matrix (or table) of correlation coefficients ($r$'s) can be resolved into a factor matrix. For example, starting with values for twenty, thirty, fifty or more variables, the analysis can lead to a solution in which they are only five or six basic factors underlying the variables. The factor matrix shows the proportion of the variance of each variable accounted for by each factor. Thus for the $i^{th}$ variable, a four-factor solution would be represented as $a_{i1}^2 + a_{i2}^2 + a_{i3}^2 + a_{i4}^2 = h^2$, where $a_{i1}$ is called the loading (or correlation) of the $i^{th}$ variable on Factor One, etc., and $h^2$ is called the communality, or the part of the total variance of the $i^{th}$ variable accounted for by factors which are common to all variables. Generally, $h^2 < 1$, indicating the existence of one or more "specific" factors ($s^2$), that correlate with one variable only, and/or an error factor ($e^2$). Therefore, for each variable, $h^2 + s^2 + e^2 = 1$.

* The authors are indebted to Ernst W. Swanson and Donald W. Drews for their helpful comments. Appreciation is also due the North Carolina State Computing Center for the use of their IBM 650 and for the necessary programs.

1. The standard reference on factor analysis is L. L. Thurstone, *Multiple-Factor Analysis* (Chicago: The University of Chicago Press, 1947). Thurstone, who was a psychologist and psychometrician, introduced multiple-factor analysis in 1931. A more up-to-date treatment is Harry H. Harman, *Modern Factor Analysis* (Chicago: The University of Chicago Press, 1960). Included in Harman is a selected bibliography of 411 entries. For a somewhat less formal introduction to the subject, see R. B. Cattell, *Factor Analysis* (New York: Harper & Bros., 1952), and Benjamin Fruchter, *Introduction to Factor Analysis* (Princeton: D. Van Nostrand Co., Inc., 1954).

**Table 1.** Hypothetical Intercorrelations Among Four Variables

| Variable | Per Capita Income | Quality of Housing | Participation in Soil Conservation | Number of Workers in Agriculture |
|---|---|---|---|---|
| Per Capita Income | (1.00) | .80 | .96 | .60 |
| Quality of Housing | .80 | (1.00) | .60 | .00 |
| Participation in Soil Conservation | .96 | .60 | (1.00) | .80 |
| Number of Workers in Agriculture | .60 | .00 | .80 | (1.00) |

A simple example of the process begins with the intercorrelation of some variables as illustrated in Table 1. Assume that the four variables are: per capita income, quality of housing, adoption of soil conservation practices, and number of workers in agriculture. The value for each of these variables is found for the component segments of a region—for example, ten states. On the basis of these values, the variables are intercorrelated as displayed in Table 1; that is, when per capita income and the quality of housing are correlated, $r = .80$,

**Table 2.** Hypothetical Factor Matrix

| Variable | Factor I | Factor II | $h^2$ |
|---|---|---|---|
| Per Capita Income | .8 | .6 | 1.0 |
| Quality of Housing | 1.0 | .0 | 1.0 |
| Participation in Soil Conservation | .6 | .8 | 1.0 |
| Number of Workers in Agriculture | .0 | 1.0 | 1.0 |

and when per capita income and the number of agricultural workers are correlated, $r = .60$. Upon completion of the factor analysis, the results are those shown in Table 2.[2] This table demonstrates that the total variance of each of the four variables is accounted for by only two factors, e.g., Factor One accounts for 64 percent ($.8^2$) of the variance of per capita income, and Factor Two for the remaining 36 percent ($.6^2$). Mathematically the procedure is not especially difficult. The centroid method involves a laborious processing of the

2. This example is based upon Fruchter, *ibid.*, pp. 33–34. The reason this example is chosen is the unique simplicity of all values. Unfortunately, the second and fourth rows of the correlation matrix are the same numbers as the factor loadings in Table 2. It is only a coincidence that these numbers are identical.

correlation matrix (Table 1) in order to extract the first factor (column 1 of Table 2), and further computations on residuals for the extraction of each additional factor (such as column 2 of Table 2). As the number of variables is increased beyond a very few, the number of computations becomes prohibitive without the modern computer.

Factor analysis does not directly identify the factors. A factor is initially a blank entity. In an actual application of factor analysis it is the task of the analyst to determine what the factors signify. All that the technique will do is to suggest meaningful, complex associations. Identification of a factor is usually accomplished by considering only those variables that are the most highly loaded (have the highest numerical value) on each factor. The analyst must then apply his knowledge of his discipline and his analytical skills in an effort to arrive at the meaning of each factor that is being suggested by each corresponding pattern of highly loaded variables. In this example, the variables, per capita income and quality of housing, are highly loaded on Factor One; and the variables, participation in soil conservation and number of workers in agriculture, have high loadings on Factor Two. The figures in Table 2 indicate a high degree of association between per capita income and Factor One and between quality of housing and Factor One. On the basis of these associations,

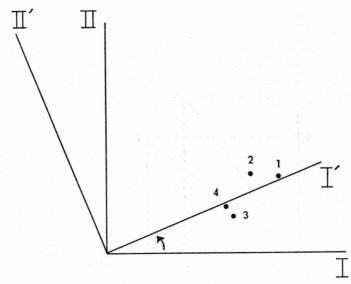

**Figure 1.**

what can Factor One signify? The answer to this question must be found by the analyst. In this highly simplified example, it might be inferred that Factor One indicates the presence of suburban development, and Factor Two indicates a highly developed agricultural sector. The first may be argued on the premise that per capita income and quality of housing vary directly with the degree of suburbanization. Similarly, the highly loaded variables suggest the nature of Factor Two.

In Figure 1 the example is expressed in geometrical terms. The two factors are the reference axes and the four variables are shown as vectors or points in the two-dimensional space. Although a geometrical treatment cannot go beyond three-dimensional space, the mathematical analysis holds for any number of dimensions (or factors). Figure 1 not only shows the vectors in terms of the reference axes, but also the relationship in two-dimensional space among the four vectors themselves, i.e., the "configuration." Since the configuration of the vectors is independent of the position of the reference axes, it is possible to shift or "rotate" the axes without altering the configuration. By so doing, it may be possible to simplify the problem of interpreting the factors. Figure 2 shows another hypothetical two-factor configuration. Before the rotation, the four points fell on both axes about evenly; after the rotation, the points have high loadings

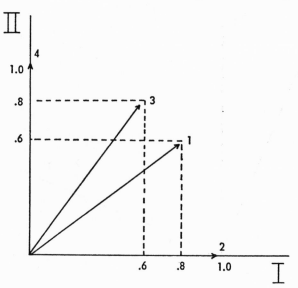

Figure 2.

on I' and very low or zero loadings on II'. Now the variables can be expressed, for the most part, in terms of only one factor.

Factor analysis has been used extensively in psychology and is being employed at an accelerating rate in other disciplines. However, this method of analysis has been largely ignored in economics. Actually, this is not very surprising, for two major reasons: lack of acquaintance or familarity with the technique and the difficulty of applying the method to much of economics.

The current trend to disaggregation in economics has intensified the problem of analyzing large numbers of variables simultaneously. This is particularly true in the study of economic growth, where analysts are casting their nets to include ever larger numbers of variables in a search for satisfactory explanations of the growth process. The conventional methods of searching for interrelationships among many variables are multiple-correlation analysis and intuition based upon observation. On the other hand, factor analysis is a method of organizing and analyzing even larger numbers of variables. Since the present stage of computer technology allows up to ninety variables to be employed simultaneously, a factor analysis can incorporate data and relationships that would necessarily have been put to one side on preconceived, intuitive grounds because of the limitations of other methods of analysis.

Since the purpose of factor analysis is to disclose relational patterns among variables as well as to suggest hypotheses about the subject on the basis of these patterns, another advantage becomes apparent. It is unnecessary to predetermine dependence and independence of variables at the outset. All of the quantitative characteristics are initially intercorrelated, and the factor loadings derived from the analysis simply represent degrees of association between these characteristics and the much smaller number of factors.

Another advantage of factor analysis is that while previously understood relationships are not lost, the larger number of variables that form into patterns of relationships increases the possibility of introducing novel hypotheses. That is, to discover for some population that consumption increased as income increased would hardly be a startling revelation. On the other hand, to discover in a region a high positive association between number of hospital beds and death rates suggests a paradox of better medical facilities joined with greater mortality. These considerations imply two things, that the validity of findings by factor analysis can be checked and reinforced by independently derived conclusions and that additional meaningful hypotheses are presented. In short, the whole range of ideas is broadened.

In comparison, multiple and partial correlation techniques are far less capable of establishing all of the associative properties of large numbers of variables. Cattell has termed partial correlation analysis used for the purpose of disclosing relations between many variables, "a patch-work factor analysis." If, at best, the same conclusions from a set of data can be derived with partial correlation, the process is discouragingly tedious and culminates in "a maze of uncertainties."[3]

One important area in economics that stands to profit from the application of factor analysis is the study of growth and development.[4] In this paper, the technique is employed for the purpose of delineating basic regional differences and similarities as a first step in accounting for regional differences in growth. Factor-analytic techniques are here applied to each of two regions and the results obtained are compared. The centroid method of factor extraction was employed, and the quartimax rotation was used to obtain the final factor loadings.

The data employed were characteristics of states in the Southeastern United States and of a selected number of high-income states. The characteristics were the forty-nine judged to be most closely related to economic growth and development, that number being the maximum capacity of the computer readily available. The one region was made up of ten states selected for their relatively high level of per capita income, industrialization, and technologically advanced agriculture, providing a "Standard Area" by which the level of development of the other region might be compared. The states selected for this purpose were California, Connecticut, Illinois, Massachusetts, Michigan, New Jersey, New York, Ohio, Pennsylvania, and Washington. The other region, called the "South," was composed of Alabama, Arkansas, Florida, Georgia, Kentucky, Louisiana, Mississippi, North Carolina, South Carolina, Tennessee, Texas, Virginia, and West Virginia. While there is disagreement about the regional homogeneity of this

3. R. B. Cattell, op. cit., p. 360.

4. Some use has been made of factor analysis for establishing regions rather than the nature of differences between regions. See for example; Brian J. L. Berry, "Basic Patterns of Economic Development," in N. Ginsburg (ed.), Atlas of Economic Development (Chicago: The University of Chicago Press, 1961); and Werner Hochwald and Mary Megee, "The Industrial Composition of the South and Its Bearing Upon the Economic Development of the Region," a paper delivered at the Second Annual Conference of the Inter-University Committee for Economic Research on the South, New Orleans, February 23, 1962.

group of states, there is no dispute over their lesser degree of productive attainment by measured comparison of per capita income with the Standard Area. So, despite the differences of opinion about inclusion or exclusion of certain states in the "South," the states included here form a region sufficiently homogeneous for the purpose of this analysis. With the ten high-income states as a standard for comparison, the purpose of this study is to discover what differences suggestive for the study of economic growth could be demonstrated in the patterns of relationship between the same variables in the Southeast.

One application that has been made of factor analysis to economic problems has been to define regions. It might be questioned why these two regions were not derived by this technique. This approach would be inappropriate for two reasons. First, if the region is defined by the characteristics incorporated in the factor analysis, reversing the process to argue that the regions are then different because of these characteristics is circular reasoning. Second, the development of regionalization by factor analysis has not progressed to the point where interpretation of differences has emerged.

## Characteristics

The economic, social, and demographic variables common to both regions that are used in the analysis are termed characteristics because they characterize the developmental condition of the region. The factors that emerge from the analyses of these characteristics indicate the significant elements of similarity and difference between the Standard Area and the South.

For the most part, census data were used for the forty-nine characteristics employed. The first consideration was to select those aggregate statistics that seemed to reflect salient social, psychological, traditional, and economic phenomena. The second consideration was to avoid obvious income linkage. That is, many of the economic statistics that are recorded for a region tend to be associated with levels of income. If existing economic analysis is correct, then an association of statistics of savings, investment, consumption, and similar characteristics for the purpose of measuring the present state of development in a region would lead to the revelation that a high level of income accompanies a high state of development. To avoid circularity and to try to discover some other elemental associations, characteristics were chosen that could suggest other interpretations for the development process than simply that of generating higher money income. It would have been desirable to include still other characteristics, but some do not exist and others could not be obtained in the time available.

The characteristics used in comparing economic development in the South with that of the Standard Area may be classified into two general categories. Any classification of such disparate characteristics is arbitrary in some degree, but for reference purposes the first category is termed demographic and the second economic.

### Characteristics

*Demographic:*

A.  Fertility Ratios[1]
    Death Rates[3]
    Infant Mortality Rates[19]
    Physician Rates[4]
    Hospital Beds[5]
    Negro Population[2]
    Selective Service Rejections, Medical[7]
    Selective Service Rejections, Mental[7]
    Selective Service Rejections, Medical and Mental[7]
    Urban Population[5]

B.  School Enrollment[21]
    Vocational Education[8]
    School Expenditures per Pupil[9]
    Ratio of School Expenditures to Income[22]
    Teachers' Salaries[20]
    Women in College[23]

C.  Quality of Housing[10]
    Charitable Collections[15]
    Public Assistance[15]

*Economic:*

A.  Per Capita Income[5]
    Wages in Manufacturing[16]
    Value Added by Manufacturing[5]
    Retail Sales and Service Receipts[6]

B.  Savings[11]
    Stock Ownership[5]
    Per Capita Investment in Manufacturing[5]
    Ratio of Manufacturing Investment to Income[6]
    Per Capita Value of Construction Contracts[5]
    Ratio of Construction Contracts to Income[6]

Per Capita Value of Industrial and Commercial Building[14]
Ratio of Industrial and Commercial Building to Income[15]
Per Capita Retail Sales[5]
Per Capita Service Receipts[5]
Per Capita Wholesale Sales[5]
Registration of Motor Vehicles[5]

C. Value of Land and Buildings per Farm[24]
Value of Land and Buildings per Acre[24]
Agricultural Use of Machine Fuel[25]
Workers in Agriculture[17]
Employees in Manufacturing[17]
Participation in Soil Conservation[18]
Electric Energy Capacity[12]
Registration of Commercial Vehicles[5]

D. Federal Tax Collections[6]
State Tax Collections[15]
Per Capita State Debt[5]

E. Retail and Service Proprietors[5]
Wholesale Proprietors[5]
Business Failures[13]

## Sources

U.S. Bureau of Census, *Census of Population 1960, U.S. Summary, General Population Characteristics*.

(1)  Number of children under 5 in ratio to number of women aged 15–49, 1960, Table 55, pp. 1–163.

(2)  Percentage of total population, 1960, pp. 1–164.

*U.S. Statistical Abstract for 1961.*

(3)  Per 1,000 population, 1960, Table 60.

(4)  Per 100,000 population, 1959, Table 76.

(5)  Per capita. Hospital Beds, 1959, Table 86; Urban Population, 1960, Table 12; Per Capita Income, 1959, Table 419; Value Added by Manufacturing, 1958, Table 1089; Stock Ownership, 1959, Table 615; Investment in Manufacturing, 1958, Table 1097; Value of Construction Contracts, 1959, Table 1052; Retail Sales, 1958, Table 1160; Service Receipts, 1958, Table 1174; Wholesale Sales, 1958, Table 1169; Motor Vehicles, 1960, Table 758; Commercial Vehicles, 1960, Table 758; State Debt, 1959, Table 541; Proprietors of Retail and Service Establishments, 1958, Tables 1159 and 1174; Proprietors of Wholesale Establishments, 1958, Table 1169.

(6)  In ratio to Personal Income. Retail Sales and Service Receipts, 1958, Tables 1160 and 1174; Manufacturing Invest-

ment, 1958, Table 1097; Value of Construction Contracts, 1959, Table 1052; Federal Tax Collections, 1959, Table 495.

(7) Percent of total examined, 1960, Table 335.

(8) Percent of total population aged 15–24, 1959, Table 177.

(9) Per pupil, 1958, Table 159.

(10) Percent of all sound houses with plumbing, 1960, Table 1067.

(11) Time deposits and savings capital in ratio to income, 1959, Tables 568 and 592.

(12) 1,000 kw. per capita, 1959, Table 706.

(13) Percent of concerns in business, 1960, Table 666.

U.S. Statistical Abstract for 1960.

(14) Per capita, 1959, Table 1035.

(15) In ratio to personal income. Charitable Collections, 1959, Table 394; Public Assistance, 1959, Table 382; Value of Industrial and Commercial Building Contracts, 1959, Table 1035; State Tax Collections, 1959, Table 528.

(16) Average hourly earnings, 1959, Table 288.

U. S. Statistical Abstract for 1960 and
U.S. Statistical Abstract for 1961.

(17) In ratio to total work force, 1959, Table 272, 1960, and Table 878, 1961.

(18) Cooperators' total area in ratio to total farm acreage, 1959, Table 821, 1960, and Table 846, 1961.

U.S. Department of Health, Education and Welfare, Vital Statistics of the United States, 1959, sec. 6.

(19) Deaths under 1 year per 1,000 live births, 1959, Table 6s, pp. 6–33.

U.S. Department of Health, Education and Welfare, Statistics of State School Systems, 1957–1958.

(20) Average annual salary, 1957–58, Table 40, p. 70.

(21) Percent of school-age population, 1957–58, Table 18, p. 40.

(22) In ratio to personal income, 1957–58, Table 44, p. 74.

U.S. Department of Health, Education and Welfare, Opening (Fall) Enrollment in Higher Education, 1960.

(23) Per female population aged 15–24, 1960, Table 18, p. 32.

U.S. Department of Commerce, 1959 Census of Agriculture, preliminary reports.

(24) Average value per acre and per farm.

(25) In ratio to total farm acreage, 1959.

The demographic variables were included to demonstrate the vitality of the population and to characterize social organization. The first set of variables, those listed under demographic category A, includes those that are usually termed vital statistics. The second component of the demographic data, designated B, reflects primarily the degree of education of the society. The C set is composed of associated variables indicating the welfare status of the region. The other major category of variables is termed economic. Of the economic variables there are five major components: first, the A set are those demonstrating the level of income of the region; the B group indicates resource allocation, or the proportion of income originating from specific sectors; those in C indicate proportions of agriculture and other sectors of the economy; those designated D reflect the level of governmental activity; and under E are listed those variables that suggest the development of entrepreneurship.

### Factor Identification

The value of factor analysis is that it permits one to discover the underlying associations and relationships implicit in a configuration of data. The implicit relationships emerge as high loadings, either positive or negative, appearing for each factor that is derived. In this case six factors emerged, as displayed in Table 3.

**Table 3.** Factors in the Standard Area and in the South

| Variables | COMMON FACTORS (LOADINGS x $10^{-4}$) | | | | | |
| | One | Two | Three | Four | Five | Six |
|---|---|---|---|---|---|---|
| | Standard Area | | | | | |
| 1. Per Capita Income | 7708 | 0416 | −3511 | −3058 | −1237 | −2165 |
| 2. Federal Tax Collections | 3234 | −5418 | 1640 | −1365 | 4817 | 4280 |
| 3. State Tax Collections | −3720 | 6358 | 7021 | −2318 | 2103 | −1087 |
| 4. Wages in Manufacturing | −0792 | 5099 | 1438 | 7341 | 1964 | 1856 |
| 5. Savings | 3165 | −3220 | 0763 | −8812 | 0397 | 0836 |
| 6. Stock Ownership | 5595 | −2525 | −4367 | −4260 | −1614 | −0813 |
| 7. Urban Population | 7327 | −2140 | −1221 | −2276 | −2882 | −4545 |
| 8. Fertility Ratios | −5181 | 2737 | 1237 | 5271 | −0991 | 1773 |
| 9. Death Rates | −1051 | −4232 | −0640 | −6722 | 1695 | 3602 |
| 10. Infant Mortality Rates | 4142 | −1887 | −1002 | 6635 | 4052 | −1058 |
| 11. Physician Rate | 3526 | −0510 | −0149 | −8816 | 0726 | −0945 |
| 12. Hospital Beds | 2683 | −6990 | −0440 | −6357 | 2733 | 0212 |
| 13. Quality of Housing | 5740 | 3338 | −3005 | −1649 | −2039 | −4663 |
| 14. Charitable Collections | −9347 | −0413 | −1706 | 0256 | 0831 | 3116 |
| 15. Public Assistance | −2274 | 4827 | 7733 | −2635 | −1235 | 2497 |
| 16. Selective Service Rejections, Medical | −1929 | 2555 | −1010 | −5306 | 0945 | 2201 |
| 17. Selective Service Rejections, Mental | 8548 | −1184 | −6205 | 0417 | −1740 | 1598 |
| 18. Selective Service Rejections, Medical & Mental | 1193 | −4600 | −3655 | −2093 | 4976 | −1903 |
| 19. Retail & Service Proprietors | 5943 | 2858 | 0486 | 1672 | 4009 | −1024 |
| 20. Wholesale Proprietors | 4529 | −0920 | 3287 | 1451 | 7290 | −0800 |

## Table 3 (continued)

| Variables | COMMON FACTORS (LOADINGS x 10⁻⁴) | | | | | |
|---|---|---|---|---|---|---|
| | One | Two | Three | Four | Five | Six |
| 21. Business Failures | 6826 | 4952 | 3255 | −0645 | 2929 | 1142 |
| 22. School Enrollment | 0297 | 9785 | −0743 | −1164 | −0846 | −0330 |
| 23. Vocational Education | −1689 | 7907 | 4562 | −1231 | 1431 | 3292 |
| 24. School Expenditures per Pupil | 7984 | −1509 | 0297 | −3448 | 2103 | −0670 |
| 25. Ratio of School Expenditures to Income | 0041 | 6483 | 4405 | 1900 | 3925 | 1244 |
| 26. Teachers' Salaries | 7938 | 3279 | 2289 | −0981 | 2479 | 0085 |
| 27. Women in College | 3018 | 3693 | 5701 | −1217 | −1590 | 3416 |
| 28. Negro Population | 3438 | −2240 | −2812 | 4586 | 3255 | 1021 |
| 29. Per Capita Investment in Manufacturing | −2971 | 0904 | −8136 | 0809 | 2404 | 1487 |
| 30. Ratio of Manufacturing Investment to Income | −2363 | −0395 | −4746 | 5274 | −2095 | 4948 |
| 31. Per Capita Value of Construction Contracts | 3234 | 8944 | 1623 | 1932 | −1230 | −1235 |
| 32. Ratio of Construction Contracts to Income | 1118 | 9276 | 1421 | 0639 | −1198 | 3921 |
| 33. Per Capita Value of Industrial & Commercial Building | 2616 | 1322 | −8332 | −1310 | −1393 | −2164 |
| 34. Ratio of Industrial & Commercial Building to Income | 1861 | 1960 | −8725 | −1346 | −2408 | −0592 |
| 35. Per Capita State Debt | 2705 | 3461 | 1739 | −7009 | 0520 | 2147 |
| 36. Value of Land & Buildings per Farm | 4023 | 5949 | 1241 | 2432 | −2721 | −1732 |
| 37. Value of Land & Buildings per Acre | 3595 | 0929 | −3988 | 0411 | −7955 | −3481 |
| 38. Agricultural Use of Machine Fuel | 1336 | −0177 | −4834 | −1511 | −1491 | −8194 |
| 39. Participation in Soil Conservation | −1611 | 1144 | −1216 | −6549 | −5228 | −1607 |
| 40. Value Added by Manufacturing | 0412 | −3350 | −9428 | 1043 | −3429 | 1855 |
| 41. Retail Sales & Service Receipts | 4090 | −0147 | 8856 | 1444 | −0740 | 2930 |
| 42. Per Capita Retail Sales | 7015 | 3282 | 0431 | −2211 | −2889 | −2886 |
| 43. Per Capita Service Receipts | 9020 | −2562 | 2353 | −0849 | 1356 | 4602 |
| 44. Per Capita Wholesale Sales | 6661 | −4080 | 2521 | −1647 | 3420 | 2484 |
| 45. Employees in Manufacturing | −2320 | −2012 | −8847 | −1043 | 1516 | −1150 |
| 46. Workers in Agriculture | −3000 | 4053 | 3949 | 6093 | 2900 | 3600 |
| 47. Electric Energy Capacity | −0888 | 6608 | 0682 | 1117 | −1233 | 8245 |
| 48. Registration of Motor Vehicles | −2825 | 9382 | −1647 | 1199 | 1428 | −0253 |
| 49. Registration of Commericial vehicles | −2458 | 8563 | 1373 | 2036 | 4665 | −2239 |
| South | | | | | | |
| 1. Per Capita Income | 8059 | −0958 | 2379 | −5482 | 0154 | −0721 |
| 2. Federal Tax Collections | 6528 | 2375 | 4378 | −1283 | −5430 | 0329 |
| 3. State Tax Collections | −0647 | 5541 | −0353 | 8141 | 1306 | 2463 |
| 4. Wages in Manufacturing | 4018 | −2010 | −1811 | 2608 | −5209 | −2468 |
| 5. Savings | 8242 | −2031 | 0599 | 1398 | 0457 | 1383 |
| 6. Stock Ownership | 5876 | 0496 | 2397 | −4980 | 4750 | 2004 |
| 7. Urban Population | 8769 | 4034 | −1710 | −0248 | −0594 | 0943 |
| 8. Fertility Ratios | −0863 | 1047 | −3043 | 7017 | −2354 | −1203 |
| 9. Death Rates | 0240 | 1364 | −1888 | 0659 | 1110 | 5307 |
| 10. Infant Mortality Rates | −1394 | −0004 | 0799 | 7265 | 1525 | −0199 |
| 11. Physician Rate | 9075 | −0549 | 0251 | −0011 | −1034 | 2483 |
| 12. Hospital Beds | −3036 | 2990 | 2408 | −1841 | −0310 | 7522 |

## Table 3 (continued)

| Variables | COMMON FACTORS (LOADINGS X $10^{-4}$) | | | | | |
| | One | Two | Three | Four | Five | Six |
|---|---|---|---|---|---|---|
| 13. Quality of Housing | 9591 | −2464 | 3267 | 0362 | 1735 | 0440 |
| 14. Charitable Collections | 4467 | 3592 | 5471 | 0578 | −2203 | −4943 |
| 15. Public Assistance | −1290 | 6287 | −2301 | 5108 | −2325 | 0872 |
| 16. Selective Service Rejections, Medical | 6583 | 1934 | −0280 | −6151 | 0694 | −0120 |
| 17. Selective Service Rejections, Mental | −3701 | 1439 | −1096 | 8910 | 5805 | −1605 |
| 18. Selective Service Rejections, Medical & Mental | −3780 | −1454 | 0772 | 4130 | 2329 | 4604 |
| 19. Retail & Service Proprietors | 5316 | 0055 | −6027 | −3073 | 0875 | −0534 |
| 20. Wholesale Proprietors | 4387 | 0235 | −3945 | 2238 | −5060 | −2915 |
| 21. Business Failures | 7060 | −1019 | 1143 | 1085 | 4316 | −1625 |
| 22. School Enrollment | 1790 | −1330 | −0743 | 0991 | 4887 | −0064 |
| 23. Vocational Education | −1118 | 1078 | −6584 | 4214 | 1286 | −1484 |
| 24. School Expenditures per Pupil | 7722 | 4621 | −0824 | 0080 | −1621 | −1544 |
| 25. Ratio of School Expenditures to Income | 0077 | 6655 | −2011 | 3258 | −0093 | −3983 |
| 26. Teachers' Salaries | 8695 | 2525 | 2907 | −1020 | 0177 | −1833 |
| 27. Women in College | 2494 | 0992 | −1147 | −2882 | −2951 | 3574 |
| 28. Negro Population | −2249 | 1097 | −0595 | 8683 | 0633 | −2307 |
| 29. Per Capita Investment in Manufacturing | −0415 | 6811 | 1803 | −6400 | −1367 | −0240 |
| 30. Ratio of Manufacturing Investment to Income | −1974 | 6161 | 2492 | −3407 | 0004 | 1954 |
| 31. Per Capita Value of Construction Contracts | 9543 | −0988 | −1145 | −0293 | −1125 | 2162 |
| 32. Ratio of Construction Contracts to Income | 7252 | 0551 | −2233 | 1288 | −1335 | 4609 |
| 33. Per Capita Value of Industrial & Commercial Building | 2405 | −0159 | −1176 | 2032 | −0807 | −6392 |
| 34. Ratio of Industrial & Commercial Building to Income | 2072 | 1353 | 1448 | 0906 | −0564 | −8035 |
| 35. Per Capita State Debt | 7045 | 3525 | 1992 | 1171 | −4231 | −0854 |
| 36. Value of Land & Buildings per Farm | 8882 | −0232 | −1426 | −0501 | 2487 | −2085 |
| 37. Value of Land & Buildings per Acre | 5979 | −3098 | 2076 | 3806 | 1690 | 0801 |
| 38. Agricultural Use of Machine Fuel | −1121 | −1029 | 1050 | 6084 | 0840 | 0874 |
| 39. Participation in Soil Conservation | −1007 | 5844 | −2794 | −0803 | 2577 | 0277 |
| 40. Value Added by Manufacturing | −2460 | 1385 | 7322 | −4285 | −0096 | −2914 |
| 41. Retail Sales & Service Receipts | 6099 | −0801 | −7234 | 1289 | 0381 | −0514 |
| 42. Per Capita Retail Sales | 9891 | 1243 | 0067 | −1931 | 3212 | −2458 |
| 43. Per Capita Service Receipts | 9935 | −2115 | 0065 | −1575 | 0545 | −0080 |
| 44. Per Capita Wholesale Sales | 6312 | 0887 | 2016 | −0687 | −5026 | −3661 |
| 45. Employees in Manufacturing | −2295 | 3384 | 2859 | 0673 | 5027 | −3914 |
| 46. Workers in Agriculture | −4078 | 3357 | −8007 | 1572 | −0236 | 1536 |
| 47. Electric Energy Capacity | −0230 | 0243 | 4511 | −3901 | −2362 | 1487 |
| 48. Registration of Motor Vehicles | 7672 | −2437 | −3923 | −1692 | −1107 | −3681 |
| 49. Registration of Commercial Vehicles | −1467 | 1674 | −7960 | 0991 | −2211 | −0217 |

Factor One was labelled "urbanization" because the associated characteristics indicated a pattern of urban living. The second factor in the Standard Area seemed to reflect the suburban development of recent years and was designated "suburbanization." Factor Two, in the South, was tentatively identified as a "capitalization" factor, where capital was defined in the broadest sense to include human capabilities. The third factor suggested the industrial origins of income for each region. The fourth factor in both regions was taken to represent the presence of a lower-income group of unskilled labor. Factor Five was different in the two regions, being identified as small business, commercial activity in the Standard Area, and as low-wage industry in the South.

The nature of factor analysis is such that the program will continue to extract factors as long as computations are made. As the analysis progresses, extracting Factors One, Two, Three, and so forth, ultimately factors begin to emerge that have such minimal loadings or so few high loadings that it becomes difficult to discover what factors are being suggested. The extent to which this process will go is to the end of selecting specific factors; that is, factors that are associated in a meaningful sense only with a specific variable. In this analysis, the machine computations were stopped after extracting the sixth factor. When the results were examined, it was discovered that the loadings that emerged on Factor Six were insufficient in both weight and number to permit identification.

## Unlike Factors

### Factor Two

Examination of the highly loaded variables discloses a marked difference between Factor Two in the Standard Area and Factor Two in the South. The explanation of Factor Two in the Standard Area that is consistent with the nature of the characteristics listed in Table 4 is the exodus to suburbia.

The highest positive loading of .98 is School Enrollment, a characteristic entirely appropriate to a suburban population. Of the other characteristics, the motor vehicle relationship is obvious; the ratio of construction contracts to income and to population would arise from the high rate of residential construction in suburban areas joined with a relatively high level of increase in public facilities such as schools, freeways, etc. The high loading on Registration of Commercial Vehicles, a characteristic that is most highly correlated with construction

**Table 4.** Factor Two in the Standard Area

| | |
|---|---|
| *Positive Loadings* | |
| School Enrollment | .9785 |
| Registration of Motor Vehicles | .9382 |
| Ratio of Construction Contracts to Income | .9276 |
| Per Capita Value of Construction Contracts | .8944 |
| Registration of Commercial Vehicles | .8563 |
| Vocational Education | .7907 |
| Electric Energy Capacity | .6608 |
| Ratio of School Expenditures to Income | .6483 |
| State Tax Collections | .6358 |
| Value of Land & Buildings per Farm | .5949 |
| Wages in Manufacturing | .5099 |
| *Negative Loadings* | |
| Hospital Beds | − .6990 |
| Federal Tax Collections | − .5418 |
| Selective Service Rejections, Medical & Mental | − .4550 |
| Death Rates | − .4232 |
| Per Capital Wholesale Sales | − .4080 |

contracts, is one that would reinforce the construction hypothesis. It is plausible to assume that migration into suburban regions would result in increased requirements for buses, construction contractors' vehicles, delivery trucks, and others, to maintain the expanding area of low-density population. Two other variables with reasonably high loadings are Vocational Education and Electric Energy Capacity, characteristics normally associated with the industrial complexes of large cities from which the suburbs spring. Also, another moderately high loading is Value of Land and Buildings per Farm, a result of suburban development and extension into formerly agricultural areas. Wages in Manufacturing would likely indicate the higher incomes in manufacturing that lead the factory worker to establish a home outside the city. Negative loadings include Hospital Beds and Federal Tax Collections; the former is a likely negative relationship, since hospitals are not usually located in suburban communities. Federal Tax Collections is a variable already adjusted for income, so it is probably negatively associated with any middle-income group with large numbers of children and other reasons for special deductions. Three other variables with very moderate negative loadings are Selective Service Rejections, Medical and Mental; Death Rates; and Per Capita Wholesale Sales. The first of these, Selective Service Rejections, Medical and Mental, might indicate the higher health standards of the suburban community, and the somewhat lesser tendency to psychoneurotic disqualifications and illiteracy, or at least the two in combination. Death Rates would obviously be lower in a younger group like that found in the suburbs, and Per Capita Wholesale Sales would not occur in suburban communities.

Before proceeding to an analysis of the other factors, let us extend our discussion of this factor in order to clarify further the general meaning of a factor. Consider the three most highly loaded characteristics on Factor Two in the Standard Area: (1) School Enrollment, (2) Registration of Motor Vehicles, and (3) Ratio of Construction Contracts to Income. When these characteristics are intercorrelated, the coefficients turn out to be $r_{12} = .80$, $r_{13} = .79$, and $r_{23} = .85$; in the South, the corresponding correlation coefficients are $r_{12} = .13$, $r_{13} = .29$, and $r_{23} = .60$. Now let us intercorrelate these characteristics with the highest negatively loaded characteristic in the Standard Area, Hospital Beds (4). In the Standard Area, $r_{14} = -.51$, $r_{24} = -.89$, and $r_{34} = -.77$; in the South, $r_{14} = -.23$, $r_{24} = -.60$, and $r_{34} = -.34$. It would be beyond the scope of this presentation to give a detailed technical treatment of how factor loadings are derived from correlation coefficients. As the foregoing illustration indicates, correlation coefficients are related to the factor loadings but they are not the same thing. The factor loadings are derived from the entire pattern of intercorrelated variables.

**Table 5.** Factor Two in the South

| | |
|---|---:|
| *Positive Loadings* | |
| Per Capita Investment in Manufacturing | .6811 |
| Ratio of School Expenditures to Income | .6655 |
| Public Assistance | .6287 |
| Ratio of Manufacturing Investment to Income | .6161 |
| Participation in Soil Conservation | .5844 |
| State Tax Collections | .5541 |
| School Expenditures per Pupil | .4621 |
| *Negative Loading* | |
| Value of Land & Buildings per Acre | − .3098 |

Factor Two in the South has been called the "capitalization factor." Capital here is defined in the broadest sense to include human capabilities. In the South (Table 5), the high loadings include items consistent with the hypothesis that Factor Two reflects capitalization of the region. The highest loading is Per Capita Investment in Manufacturing with a value of .68. Ratio of Manufacturing Investment to Income has a .62 loading. Both of these would be elements of the new growth of investment and hence the heavy allocation of income and resources to investment in manufacturing industries. The three

**Table 6.** Factor Five in the Standard Area

| | |
|---|---|
| *Positive Loadings* | |
| Wholesale Proprietors | .7290 |
| Selective Service Rejections, Medical & Mental | .4976 |
| Federal Tax Collections | .4817 |
| Registration of Commercial Vehicles | .4665 |
| Infant Mortality Rates | .4052 |
| Retail & Service Proprietors | .4009 |
| Ratio of School Expenditures to Income | .3925 |
| *Negative Loadings* | |
| Value of Land & Buildings per Acre | − .7955 |
| Participation in Soil Conservation | − .5228 |
| Value Added by Manufacturing | − .3429 |

variables, Participation in Soil Conservation, Public Assistance, and School Expenditures per Pupil, would indicate investment in land and in human resources. The negative loading on the Southern Factor Two is —.31 on Value of Land and Buildings per Acre. This value is so low as to be of little significance, and at best might only be influenced by extensive farming, since the counterpart item, Value of Land and Buildings per Farm, is —.02, or quite unrelated.

### Factor Five

Factor Five in the Standard Area suggests small business operations, commercialization, and perhaps entrepreneurship.

In Table 6, the highest positive loading is Wholesale Proprietors, .73. Other positive loadings include Federal Tax Collections, Registration of Commercial Vehicles, and Retail and Service Proprietors; all of these would be related to small business, commercial operations. Ratio of School Expenditures to Income, .39, is a small loading appropriate to the somewhat higher income that would be associated with this factor, but similar loadings of .40 on Infant Mortality Rates and .50 on the Selective Service Rejections, Medical and Mental, are characteristics not readily associated with the factor. The highest negative loading is Value of Land and Buildings per Acre in agriculture, and the other high negative loading is Participation in Soil Conservation. Both of these would be inversely related with small business enterprise, commercialization, and entrepreneurship.

Factor Five in the South (Table 7) is associated with low-wage, low-income manufacturing industries. The highest positive loading is Selective Service Rejections, Mental, .58, a characteristic that is likely to be associated with the mill village. Another high positive

**Table 7.** Factor Five in the South

| | |
|---|---|
| *Positive Loadings* | |
| Selective Service Rejections, Mental | .5805 |
| Employees in Manufacturing | .5027 |
| School Enrollment | .4887 |
| Stock Ownership | .4750 |
| Business Failures | .4316 |
| *Negative Loadings* | |
| Federal Tax Collections | − .5430 |
| Wages in Manufacturing | − .5209 |
| Wholesale Proprietors | − .5060 |
| Per Capita Wholesale Sales | − .5026 |
| Per Capita State Debt | − .4231 |

loading, .50, for Employees in Manufacturing, is self-evident, but the .49 loading for the measure of School Enrollment is not very clearly related. Stock Ownership may well be associated with owners of industries characterizing this factor, and Business Failures is a characteristic of this type of industry.

The negative loadings are on Federal Tax Collections, Wages in Manufacturing, Wholesale Proprietors, Per Capita Wholesale Sales, and Per Capita State Debt. Low-income industries do pay less federal tax, and because these industries tend to dispose of their product through agents located elsewhere, wholesale activities would not be associated with these firms. The negative measure of Per Capita State Debt may simply be evidence of the success of owners in limiting extension of state government operations.

### Like Factors

#### Factor One

Factor One is identified as "urbanization," a label immediately suggested by one variable. In both the Standard Area and in the South, Urban Population is a highly loaded variable (Table 8), being .73 in the Standard Area and .88 in the South. In both regions, the variable with the highest loading for Factor One is Per Capita Service Receipts, and this is typical of an urbanized population. The city is the locus of the greater portion of service production, and this would be accentuated in the urban centers of the South, leading to a somewhat higher loading on Factor One in the South than in the Standard Area. As for disposition of income to purchase retail goods, an activity that would also be associated with urban centers, the factor loading for Per Capita Retail Sales in the Standard Area is .70, and for the South the loading is .99. This indicates a closer association in the

**Table 8.** Factor One in the Standard Area and in the South

| Standard Area | | South | |
|---|---|---|---|
| *Positive Loadings* | | *Positive Loadings* | |
| Per Capita Service Receipts | .9020 | Per Capita Service Receipts | .9935 |
| Selective Service Rejections, | | Per Capita Retail Sales | .9891 |
| Mental | .8548 | Quality of Housing | .9591 |
| School Expenditures per Pupil | .7984 | Per Capita Value of Construction | |
| Teachers' Salaries | .7938 | Contracts | .9543 |
| Per Capita Income | .7708 | Physician Rate | .9075 |
| Urban Population | .7327 | Value of Land & Buildings per | |
| Per Capita Retail Sales | .7015 | Farm | .8882 |
| Business Failures | .6826 | Urban Population | .8769 |
| Per Capita Wholesale Sales | .6661 | Teachers' Salaries | .8695 |
| Retail & Service Proprietors | .5943 | Savings | .8242 |
| Quality of Housing | .5740 | Per Capita Income | .8059 |
| Stock Ownership | .5595 | School Expenditures per Pupil | .7722 |
| | | Registration of Motor Vehicles | .7672 |
| | | Ratio of Construction Contracts to | |
| | | Income | .7252 |
| | | Business Failures | .7060 |
| | | Per Capita State Debt | .7045 |
| *Negative Loadings* | | *Negative Loading* | |
| Charitable Collections | −.9347 | Workers in Agriculture | −.4078 |
| Fertility Ratios | −.5180 | | |

South of retail service provisions and urbanization. The same kind of association is true for Quality of Housing. Other highly loaded variables in the South that tend to be identified with urbanization are: Per Capita Value of Construction Contracts, probably implying more residential construction in the Southern cities and a greater rate of growth than in rural areas or in the Standard Area urban centers; Physician Rates, indicating larger proportions of physicians in Southern urban centers; and Value of Land and Buildings per Farm, suggesting that the presence of urban centers in Southern states tends to be highly associated with more productive Southern farms. As would be expected, Teachers' Salaries are highly related with Factor One in the South. In similar fashion, Savings, presumably because of higher incomes, are found to be highly associated with Factor One in the South, as is Per Capita Income for the same reason. School Expenditures per Pupil are similarly highly loaded. One difference between the South and the Standard Area is found in Registration of Motor Vehicles. The explanation is probably due to the difference in size of the urban centers in the Standard Area and the South, because the Standard Area cities are larger, traffic-bound complexes. The Ratio of Construction Contracts to Income (that is, the amount of income devoted to construction investment), tends, like the Per Capita Value of Construction Contracts, to be highly associated with Factor One in the South and undoubtedly for the same reason. Recent expansion of small Southern cities has entailed proportionately greater urban construction than in the larger, established metropolitan centers of the Standard Area. As is the case in the Standard Area, Business Failures are associated with Factor One; in the urban centers, there are heavy concentrations of small retail service establishments with their high probability of failure. Per Capita State Debt in the South is most highly correlated with school expenditures; these, in turn, are greatest in cities. Another reason for designating Factor One in the South as "urbanization" is the moderate negative loading on Workers in Agriculture, the percentage of the work force engaged in agriculture.

Factor One in the Standard Area also presents a pattern that may best be termed "urbanization." As in the South, Urban Population as a percentage of total population displays a high loading. Also as in the South, other characteristics customarily associated with urban living have significantly high values. These are School Expenditures per Pupil, Per Capita Service Receipts, Teachers' Salaries, Per Capita Income, Per Capita Retail Sales, Business Failures, and Quality of Housing. The high loadings that indicate differences between the Standard Area and the South are: Selective Service Rejections, Mental; Per Capita Wholesale Sales; Retail and Service Proprietors; and Stock Ownership. Mental test rejections for Selective Service may very well be the product of high-pressure living and other tensions encountered in life in the large metropolitan centers. High loadings for Per Capita Wholesale Sales also would appear to be consistent with a higher concentration of urban living; that is, a considerable source of income would tend to originate in the wholesale trade established in the largest cities. The loading on Retail and Service Proprietors is also consistent with urban characteristics. The remaining high loading of Stock Ownership is also typical of the Standard Area urban society. The two high negative loadings on Factor One in the Standard Area were Charitable Contributions and Fertility Ratios. The latter is consistent with all beliefs about urban birth rates, and the former demonstrates a fairly interesting pattern. In observation of the raw input data, it was discovered that Charitable Contributions, which are Community Chest and United Fund donations for the support of the Red Cross, Boy Scouts, YMCA's, and the like, tend to be fairly stable so that the higher the level of income, particularly per capita income, the lesser the proportion of income devoted to charitable contributions. In the large cities of the Standard Area, incomes are considerably higher than elsewhere, and a negative relationship between Charitable Contributions and urbanization may well be appropriate.

### Factor Three

Factor Three was assigned the same designation in both areas, "the industrial origins of income," signifying that a region is characterized by the types of economic activity that generate its income. Industry in this usage does not mean a specific type of industry like steel or chemicals, but rather division between primary, secondary, and tertiary industries as the term is used by Colin Clark. The variables (Table 9) indicate that in a region where value added by manufacturing is high, there are less retail sales and service receipts, and vice versa. In the case of the South, activity in agriculture is inversely related to Value Added by Manufacturing. After the signs of the factor loadings for the Standard Area are reversed, the largest loadings for both the Standard Area and the South are on the characteristic, Value Added by Manufacturing. In the Standard Area, this loading is accompanied by high loadings on Employees in Manufacturing

**Table 9.** Factor Three in the Standard Area and in the South

| Standard Area | | South | |
|---|---|---|---|
| *Positive Loadings* | | *Positive Loadings* | |
| Value Added by Manufacturing | .9428 | Value Added by Manufacturing | .7322 |
| Employees in Manufacturing | .8847 | Charitable Collections | .5471 |
| Ratio of Industrial & Commercial | | Electric Energy Capacity | .4511 |
| Building to Income | .8725 | Federal Tax Collections | .4378 |
| Per Capita Value of Industrial and | | | |
| Commercial Building | .8332 | | |
| Per Capita Investment in | | | |
| Manufacturing | .8136 | | |
| Selective Service Rejections, Mental | .6205 | | |
| *Negative Loadings* | | *Negative Loadings* | |
| Retail Sales and Service Receipts | − .8856 | Workers in Agriculture | − .8007 |
| Public Assistance | − .7733 | Registration of Commercial Vehicles | |
| State Tax Collections | − .7021 | | − .7960 |
| Women in College | − .5701 | Retail Sales & Service Receipts | − .7234 |
| Ratio of School Expenditures to | | Vocational Education | − .6584 |
| Income | − .4405 | Retail & Service Proprietors | − .6027 |
| Vocational Education | − .4562 | | |

and Per Capita Investment in Manufacturing. The three remaining high positive loadings for the Standard Area are Ratio of Industrial and Commercial Building to Income, Per Capita Value of Industrial and Commercial Building, and Selective Service Rejections, Mental. These suggest a high association between manufacturing activity and investment in industry and commerce in the Standard Area. The highest negative correlation in the Standard Area is for Retail Sales and Service Receipts. Two other relatively high negative loadings are Public Assistance and State Tax Collections. These negative relationships suggest that where an important source of income originates in manufacturing and is associated with considerable investment in similar types of production, then sources of income in retail sales and services and in activities providing welfare assistance at the local or state level tend to be less. Three educational variables, Women in College, Ratio of School Expenditures to Income, and Vocational Education, have relatively small negative loadings. Apparently, in those states of the Standard Area where income is generated by manufacturing, provision of welfare and education is less. Or, to put it another way, the areas in which education, welfare, and mental capability are least are those areas where manufacturing provides the principal source of income.

As mentioned above, the single high positive loading in the South for Factor Three is Value Added by Manufacturing. The other positive but relatively low loadings are Charitable Collections, Electric Energy Capacity, and Federal Tax Collections. This might suggest that, unlike the case of the Standard Area, those states in the South, where manufacturing contributes a large portion of income, are the rapidly growing, wealthy, higher-income states that can support higher charitable collections and pay more federal taxes. These are also the states that tend to have a somewhat greater Electric Energy Capacity. The high negative correlations in the South with Factor Three are Workers in Agriculture, Registration of Commercial Vehicles, and Retail Sales and Service Receipts. The latter relationship, Retail Sales and Service Receipts, as with Vocational Education, is similar to the relationships pointed out for the Standard Area. The one additional negative loading included for the South is Retail and Service Proprietors.

These relationships suggest that in the South the states with their greatest source of income in manufacturing also tend to be those with the lesser number of people in agriculture, which would be consonant with observation. Ownership of Commercial Vehicles also tends to

**Table 10.** Factor Four in the Standard Area and in the South

| Standard Area | | South | |
|---|---|---|---|
| *Positive Loadings* | | *Positive Loadings* | |
| Wages in Manufacturing | .7341 | Selective Service Rejections, | |
| Infant Mortality Rates | .6635 | Mental | .8910 |
| Workers in Agriculture | .6093 | Negro Population | .8683 |
| Ratio of Manufacturing Investment | | State Tax Collections | .8141 |
| to Income | .5274 | Infant Mortality Rates | .7265 |
| Fertility Ratios | .5271 | Fertility Ratios | .7017 |
| Negro Population | .4586 | Agricultural Use of Machine Fuel | .6084 |
| | | Public Assistance | .5108 |
| | | Vocational Education | .4214 |
| | | Selective Service Rejections, | |
| | | Medical & Mental | .4130 |
| *Negative Loadings* | | *Negative Loadings* | |
| Physician Rate | −.8816 | Per Capita Investment in | |
| Savings | −.8812 | Manufacturing | −.6400 |
| Per Capita State Debt | −.7099 | Selective Service Rejections, | |
| Death Rates | −.6772 | Medical | −.6151 |
| Participation in Soil Conservation | −.6549 | Per Capita Income | −.5482 |
| Hospital Beds | −.6357 | Stock Ownership | −.4980 |
| Selective Service Rejections, | | Value Added by Manufacturing | −.4285 |
| Medical | −.5306 | | |

be highly correlated with the number of Workers in Agriculture. The correlation of .65 suggests that Registration of Commercial Vehicles reflects to a considerable degree agricultural ownership of short-haul and pickup trucks. High negative loadings on Factor Three of Retail Sales and Service Receipts and Retail and Service Proprietors would suggest that these activities provide sources of income in lesser degree where manufacturing is the prime source of income. It is also likely that Vocational Education in the South tends to be agricultural vocational education, which would explain the high negative loading on Factor Three.

### Factor Four

Factor Four was interpreted to signify the presence of a low-income, unskilled labor force.

In the Standard Area (Table 10), the highest positive relationships are on Wages in Manufacturing, Infant Mortality Rates, Workers in Agriculture, Ratio of Manufacturing Investment to Income, Fertility Ratios, and Negro Population. The positive relationships between these variables and Factor Four suggest that where income originates in manufacturing, Infant Mortality Rates are high, as are Fertility

Ratios. There is a large proportion of the work force in agriculture somewhat associated with a Negro population. The negative loadings are those that would be inversely associated with a low standard of living: Physician Rate; Savings; Per Capita State Debt; Death Rates; Participation in Soil Conservation; Hospital Beds; and Selective Service Rejections, Medical. Here we have evidence of lesser accommodation for health facilities in the lower rates of physicians present in the community and in smaller provision of hospital beds. Death Rates are low, as are Selective Service Rejections, Medical. In modern communities, higher death rates tend to be associated with the presence of medical facilities; i.e., occupants of hospital beds are not usually robust. Medical Selective Service rejections have been discussed. The lack of participation in soil conservation programs would indicate an underdeveloped agriculture. Savings and Per Capita State Debt tend to be low when income is low.

Factor Four in the South (Table 10) has highest positive associations with Selective Service Rejections, Mental; Negro Population; Infant Mortality Rates; and State Tax Collections. Other high positive loadings are Fertility Ratios; Agricultural Use of Machine Fuel; Public Assistance; Vocational Education; and Selective Service Rejections, Medical and Mental. Since rejections for Selective Service on mental grounds are probably due in large part to illiteracy, this high association in conjunction with a high percentage of Negro population reinforces the selection of the factor designation. Infant Mortality Rates and Fertility Ratios are positively correlated with Negro Population in the South, as in the Standard Area. If minimum state services are to be provided, State Tax Collections will tend to be a high proportion of income when incomes are low. The variable, Agricultural Use of Machine Fuel, was included originally to indicate the mechanization of agriculture. In point of fact, it turned out to be not very highly correlated with any other variable, the highest correlation being a .49 with Employees in Manufacturing and a —.53 with Per Capita Investment in Manufacturing, so that this item best reflects an agricultural base to income. This base in the South is associated with low incomes and unskilled labor. Both Public Assistance and Vocational Education tend to be somewhat highly associated with low-income, unskilled labor. The correlation of urbanization and high income with Selective Service Rejections, Medical and Mental, is statistically significant and negative. Negative loadings on Factor Four in the South also indicate the presence of a low-income, unskilled labor force. The highest negative loading is Per Capita Investment in Manufacturing followed by Selective Service Rejections, Medical, and Per Capita Income. Stock Ownership has a moderate, negative loading on Factor Four, as has Value Added by Manufacturing. As developed in the explanation of Factor Five, lower Per Capita Investment in Manufacturing and Value Added by Manufacturing are typically associated with this class of worker in the South. Selective Service Rejections, Medical; Per Capita Income; and Stock Ownership, all tend to be positively associated with a higher-income, better-educated population.

## Conclusions

The factor analyses have disclosed broad patterns or underlying factors in the Standard Area and in the South. Because the selected variables are for the year 1960, the factors must be identified for that year only. To introduce the time element explicitly into the factor analysis, it would be necessary either to select variable data for a series of years and undertake a factor analysis for each of the years, or to analyze the increments of change between years. Nevertheless, it is possible to form hypotheses on the basis of the 1960 factors. This involves seeking out those broad economic and non-economic changes occurring prior to 1960 that appear to have promoted the patterns revealed by the analysis. In this way, dynamic elements are introduced and explanatory interpretations may be found for the differences in the two areas. The similarities in urbanization, the different interpretations placed on Factors Two and Five, and the similarities as well as the differences found in Factors Three and Four, all lead to some judgments about the state of development in the South compared with that of the Standard Area.

The similarities of Factor One in both areas vastly outweigh the differences, clearly suggesting that the same thing is being measured in both regions. The two most heavily loaded factors in the Standard Area are Factors One and Two, whereas in the South they are One and Four. Factor Two in the South has lower loadings and is not the same as Factor Two in the Standard Area; actually, the latter has no counterpart in the analysis of the South. Since Factor One, the urbanization factor, is important and quite similar both in the Standard Area and in the South, it cannot be used to explain major differences in the two areas; however, minor differences may be disclosed by analyzing relative variations within Factor One in both areas. On the other hand, Factor Two, suburbanization, is the most important factor in the

Standard Area, in terms of loadings, and is virtually absent in the South. There exists a whole literature relating urbanization to economic growth, yet suburbanization has not entered explicitly into this hypothesis. It is true that suburbanization is but one facet of urbanization; suburbs cannot exist without the *urbs*. Even so, suburbanization in contemporary U.S. society is significant for current growth because of its capacity for enlarging markets and increasing production of particular goods. Although the rapid growth of suburbs in the Standard Area during the period since World War II has been painfully obvious, especially to those involved in the process, this development has been insufficiently analyzed as an element contributing to the economic growth of the North compared with that of the South.

The development of suburbs can be looked upon as an expansion of markets, as a desire and a willingness to spend either saved or borrowed money in order to make the big leap away from concrete and congestion. It would require too much space, and it is really unnecessary, to itemize here the goods and services needed to raise from the cornfield a modern, middle-class suburb. Summarily, the process reduces to market growth and to the encouragement of producers to enlarge and improve their facilities to meet existing or anticipated market demands. This expansion of plant and equipment would then occur in the Standard Area, rather than in the South, for two major reasons: proximity to the market and the existence, in many cases, of businesses already well-established in the growing region.

Much of the industrial expansion that occurred in the South during the postwar period, such as the petroleum and petrochemical growth along the Gulf Coast, served national markets and upon completion required relatively few workers. In those industries in which larger numbers of workers were necessary (for example, textiles), wages have tended to be low. These developments have accentuated the disadvantage of the South in terms of relatively high-income, mass markets and all of the economic effects of such markets.

By comparison, Factor Two in the South exhibits the weaker impact on the region's growth of the attempt to provide means for future growth. The South has been striving to improve human resources and to increase manufacturing capital, but so far without the far-reaching consequences of expanding mass markets. This suggests that for the South a major problem is not only the amount of investment, but also the type of investment and distribution between investments for the long and the short term.

Factor Three is evidence of the lesser degree of contribution to income made by manufacturing in the South and the entrenched nature of manufacturing in the Standard Area. The array of characteristics, taken in conjunction with other factors, reinforces the suggestion by many that the highest standards of living are attained in association with development of service or tertiary industries. Factor Four simply indicates that the low-income, unskilled portion of the labor force tends to be linked with manufacturing in the Standard Area, and with agriculture in the South. Factor Five points up the retarding effect upon the South of dependence upon such low-income industries as poultry and textiles. In the Standard Area, there is demonstrated a greater degree of development of smaller-scale industrial and commercial establishments, which may disclose the existence of more aggressive entrepreneurs. These establishments may also serve as the training areas for entrepreneurship.

As stated in the beginning, the objective of this first analysis was to compare the characteristics of the two regions. Further application of factor analysis is planned to discover additional reasons for the differences in the regions as a means of explaining differential rates of growth. Its achievement will require development of techniques for introducing dynamic elements, deriving additional basic information, and incorporating qualitative data into the analysis. Further testing and analysis are expected to yield much more in the way of explaining change in the South.

# IX

# Interregional Income Flows
# and the South

*By Werner Hochwald*

## I. Southern Economic Development

The process of economic development can be viewed to start "within," focusing on the "internal" economic institutions as they motivate economic effort and innovation, or it may be viewed to start "without," focusing on "external" challenges to which the economy responds. In either case, the process depends on the way in which the growth of individual economic sectors is mutually reinforced for the economy as a whole.

The classical approach to this problem is expressed by the principle of comparative advantage. The optimum pattern of production and trade for each area is determined by comparing the domestic opportunity cost of producing a given commodity with the price at which this same commodity can be exported or imported. As the market grows, continuous adaptations to the resultant new opportunities for further specialization assure the balanced development of each economic sector, whether such sector be defined as a particular industry or a particular region in the world economy.

The rise of the great multilateral system of international trade and payments of the nineteenth and early twentieth centuries has stimulated a spectacular growth of productivity together with a widening of markets and thus has seemed to vindicate these great expectations of classical doctrine. Yet it has also left many "underdeveloped" countries with isolated export sectors of high productivity surrounded by relatively unchanging domestic economic backwardness. It is this apparent contradiction between the classical principle of comparative advantage and the spotty historical record of economic growth which has dominated recent discussions of economic development.[1]

Modern growth theory emphasizes the sequence of expansion by interrelated sectors rather than the classical assumptions of a competitive general equilibrium. It thus focuses on conditions which, at least temporarily, may prevent the beneficial workings of specialization in accordance with the classical doctrine of comparative advantage, such as structural disequilibria in factor markets; changes in resource endowments brought about by the very process of development; economies of scale; and complementarity in both producer and consumer demand. The imputation of resultant external economies to particular industries and firms may seriously affect the estimate of comparative advantage and support arguments for "balanced" or "planned" growth of interrelated sectors rather than specialization.

The relative merits of "foreign trade" as opposed to "balanced growth" depend on the strength of the forces governing market imperfections.[2] Though the extraordinary multitude and variety of these forces preclude attempts toward their exact measurement, any conceptualization of economic development is necessarily based on some estimate, explicit or implicit, of these forces. As the process of economic development thus conceived is expressed in terms of interrelated "sectors"—interrelated through "foreign" or "balanced" domestic trade—the analytic framework must be defined by sector aggregates and their interrelations.

Classical doctrine assumed perfect factor mobility within each country but restrictions to mobility across national boundaries; the most strategic sector aggregates were therefore "nations" related to each other through "foreign" trade. Modern growth theory generalizes the possibility of such restrictions, and sector aggregates are now defined in terms of any spatial combination of resources—a "region"; or any functional combination of productive agents—an "industry." It

1. For an excellent survey of the recent literature, see Hollis B. Chenery, "Comparative Advantage and Development Policy," *American Economic Review*, LI (March, 1961), 18–51.

2. The resistance to social change subsumed by economists under the category of "market imperfections" has been analyzed by Everett E. Hagen in his *On the Theory of Social Change* (Homewood, 1962). For a reformulation of classical theory see John M. Letiche, *Balance of Payments and Economic Growth* (New York, 1959). See also J. R. T. Hughes, "Foreign Trade and Balanced Growth: The Historical Framework," *American Economic Review*, XLIX (May, 1959), 330–37.

**Table 1.** U.S. Regional Income Per Capita 1880–1960*

| Region | 1880 | 1900 | 1920 | 1930 | 1940 | 1950 | 1960 |
|---|---|---|---|---|---|---|---|
| Continental United States | 100 | 100 | 100 | 100 | 100 | 100 | 100 |
| Far West | 211 | 163 | 135 | 131 | 132 | 120 | 119 |
| Middle Atlantic | 140 | 138 | 133 | 143 | 133 | 118 | 117 |
| New England | 141 | 133 | 124 | 129 | 127 | 109 | 111 |
| Great Lakes | 102 | 106 | 108 | 110 | 112 | 111 | 107 |
| Mountain | 166 | 145 | 102 | 86 | 89 | 96 | 95 |
| Plains | 90 | 97 | 87 | 82 | 81 | 94 | 93 |
| Southwest | 61 | 68 | 81 | 64 | 70 | 86 | 86 |
| South | 50 | 48 | 56 | 50 | 58 | 68 | 72 |

* Source: 1880–1920, estimates of Richard Easterlin published by Perloff *et al.* in *Regions, Resources, and Economic Growth*, p. 27; 1930–60, U.S. Office of Business Economics.

is the purpose of this paper to apply the notions of comparative advantage and economic development to the American South.

The South has been the most distinctive "region" in American history, a region well defined by a common economic and cultural background. The intense interest in its role within the American economy has produced a large number of data[3] and studies of which the present volume offers another illustration.

The South[4] has participated in the extraordinary rate of growth this country has witnessed over the last century, yet has retained its position as a region of relatively depressed per capita income even after the last generation has seen a marked tendency toward declining regional income differentials (Table 1). It is this characteristic of the South as a low-income region, low in relative if not in absolute terms, that has prompted the many studies to explain the apparent paradox of a region which is an integral part of the nation yet persists in maintaining large income differentials.

At the time of the Civil War, Southern per capita income was but half of the national average. It decreased even further in relative terms during the period of reconstruction, amounting to less than 48 percent of the nation at the turn of the century. Under the impetus of the First World War, the figure increased to 56 percent by 1920, only to fall back again to 50 percent at the onset of the Great Depres-

3. For a convenient summary of readily available data, see *Economic Characteristics of the Sixth Federal Reserve District* (Atlanta, 1958).
4. This paper, if not otherwise specified, follows the definition used by the U.S. Department of Commerce, which includes the following twelve states: Virginia, West Virginia, Kentucky, Tennessee, North Carolina, South Carolina, Georgia, Florida, Alabama, Mississippi, Louisiana, and Arkansas.

**Table 2.**  U.S. Regional Population 1870–1960*

| Region | 1870 | 1890 | 1910 | 1930 | 1940 | 1950 | 1960 |
|---|---|---|---|---|---|---|---|
| Continental United States | 100 | 100 | 100 | 100 | 100 | 100 | 100 |
| South | 29 | 26 | 24 | 22 | 23 | 23 | 22 |
| Middle Atlantic | 25 | 23 | 23 | 23 | 23 | 22 | 22 |
| Great Lakes | 23 | 21 | 20 | 21 | 20 | 20 | 20 |
| Far West | 1.6 | 3 | 5 | 7 | 8 | 10 | 11 |
| Plains | 10 | 14 | 13 | 11 | 10 | 9 | 8 |
| Southwest | 2 | 4 | 6 | 7 | 8 | 8 | 8 |
| New England | 9 | 8 | 7 | 7 | 6 | 6 | 6 |
| Mountain | 0.4 | 1 | 2 | 2 | 2 | 2 | 3 |

* Source: U.S. Bureau of the Census.

sion, when even absolute per capita income in the South was lower than it had been before the "roaring twenties." From then on, the South has seen a steady improvement in absolute as well as relative terms until the figure today stands at about 72 percent, still almost a third below the national average.

One explanation for these persistent income differentials is the high birth rate of many Southern low-income areas, which accounts for an age distribution of low labor-force participation. Even a high level of out-migration has thus been neutralized by a rapid natural increase in population, with the result that Southern income is shared by an unusually large percentage of children and retired workers outside the active labor force. Over the last hundred years, population of the South has almost quadrupled, though the region has had relatively little in-migration from abroad (Table 2). Yet even after adjusting for these differences in the regional age structure, Southern income per worker has remained far below the national average.[5]

Another obvious explanation of Southern income differentials is the industrial composition of the region.[6] Almost by definition, a

5. For a survey of recent trends, see John L. Fulmer, *Trends in Population and Employment in the South since 1930 and Their Economic Significance* (Atlanta, 1960). Population and migration projections for the South through 2020 have been prepared by James M. Henderson, "Some General Aspects of Regional Developments during the 1950–1960 Decade" (Paper prepared for Second Annual Conference, Inter-University Committee for Economic Research on the South, New Orleans, 1962). The most comprehensive survey of the subject has been directed by Simon Kuznets and Dorothy Swaine Thomas, *Population Redistribution and Economic Growth, United States 1870–1950* (Philadelphia, Vol. I, 1957; Vol. II, 1960).

6. The standard book on the industrial composition of the South has been written by Calvin B. Hoover and B. U. Ratchford, *Economic Resources and Policies of the South* (New York, 1951). A wealth of relevant materials and

low-income area has a high concentration of low-productivity industries. It has often been pointed out that the South, in spite of its remarkable population growth, has remained an essentially rural region with the lowest national rate of urbanization. Up to 1920 the South has increased its proportion of national primary employment, though its share of total employment, and of total primary output, has declined ever since the Civil War. Even in 1960, after substantial industrialization, the South's share of national employment in primary industries still amounted to 38 percent, far above the region's population share of 22 percent. This continued reliance on agriculture as a major source of employment and income is also shown by the fact that the South in 1960 still received 10 percent of its total personal income from farming, in contrast with the national average of 6 percent (Table 3).

Agriculture is not the only slow-growth industry with a dominant influence on Southern employment and income. In manufacturing, textiles illustrate another sector which has been declining nationally. In other regions, such local specialization in industries declining nationally has often been compensated by upward "differential" employment shifts[7] as new industries have been attracted by the resources released in the declining sectors of the local economy, which therefore has been expanding in certain employment sectors more rapidly than other regions. This upward differential effect has been strongest in areas of rapid industrialization, such as the Far West or the Great Lakes, where the growing metropolis has absorbed for many decades the rural population displaced by rapid strides in farm labor productivity.

The South, too, has seen, of course, many upward "differential" employment shifts. Its growth has been accomplished, as in so many "underdeveloped" areas, by absorbing a larger and larger share of

interpretation is contained in Harvey S. Perloff, Edgar S. Dunn, Eric E. Lampard, and Richard F. Muth, *Regions, Resources, and Economic Growth* (Baltimore, 1960), summarized and brought up to date by Harvey S. Perloff and Vera W. Dodds in *How a Region Grows* (New York, 1963). Special aspects of the problem have been treated in Otis Dudley Duncan, William Richard Scott, Stanley Lieberson, Beverly Davis Duncan, and Hal H. Winsborough, *Metropolis and Region* (Baltimore, 1960). See also Victor R. Fuchs, *Changes in the Location of Manufacturing in the United States since 1929* (New Haven, 1962). Many disciplines have contributed to *The Southern Appalachian Region: A Survey* (Lexington, 1962).

7. "Proportionality" and "differential" shifts are concepts used extensively by Perloff *et al., op. cit.*, pp. 70–74, to describe different aspects of regional economic growth.

**Table 3.** Industrial Origin of Personal Income 1960*

| Region | Farms Mining | Construction | Manufacturing | Trade | Finance Transportation Communication | Services | Government | Total |
|---|---|---|---|---|---|---|---|---|
| Continental United States | 6.0 | 6.6 | 29.6 | 19.5 | 12.9 | 13.4 | 12.0 | 100 |
| Far West | 5.2 | 7.6 | 25.0 | 20.0 | 13.0 | 15.2 | 14.0 | 100 |
| Middle Atlantic | 1.8 | 5.7 | 32.2 | 19.7 | 13.9 | 14.9 | 11.8 | 100 |
| New England | 1.7 | 5.8 | 37.9 | 18.1 | 11.6 | 14.5 | 10.4 | 100 |
| Great Lakes | 3.8 | 5.9 | 39.9 | 18.2 | 11.5 | 11.3 | 9.4 | 100 |
| Mountain | 13.6 | 9.2 | 14.8 | 20.4 | 15.0 | 12.4 | 14.6 | 100 |
| Plains | 13.7 | 7.3 | 21.4 | 20.9 | 13.9 | 12.0 | 10.8 | 100 |
| Southwest | 14.2 | 7.9 | 16.3 | 21.1 | 13.7 | 13.4 | 13.4 | 100 |
| South | 9.9 | 7.0 | 24.2 | 19.8 | 12.6 | 12.7 | 13.8 | 100 |

* Source: U.S. Office of Business Economics.

industries declining elsewhere. Food products, textiles, and apparel have been important throughout the region ever since the turn of the century. Tobacco products and furniture have become dominant in the Upper South, pulp and paper in the Lower South. Metal products have contributed to upward differential shifts in Alabama, Kentucky, and Tennessee. More recently, the decentralization of automobile assembly, rubber, chemical, and aerospace industries has accelerated Southern gains in nationally growing sectors. Yet in many areas of the South, unfavorable downward "proportionality" shifts due to the dominance of nationally declining industries, such as agriculture or textiles, even now still outweigh trends in the opposite direction.

The dominance of primary employment in farming and industries processing the products of agriculture, with relatively low labor productivity, accounts for average earnings in the South well below those prevalent in other parts of the nation. Such references to the industrial composition of the South, however, restate rather than explain the phenomenon of persistent income differentials which, in the succeeding sections of this paper, will be related to interregional income flows.

## II. Interregional Income Flows

Income accounts have become the most universal tool by which to understand the process of income determination and economic development. Information on the sources and uses of income helps to trace the sequence of expansion or contraction by interrelated sectors through the income circuit of the national economy. The direct sources are found in the industries paying for factor services, and estimates of regional income by industrial source have long been considered among the most valuable indicators of regional economic change. Yet income flows have no beginning and end; industrial sources can be pushed backward to the ultimate customers of the industries paying out income. These ultimate customers in turn are themselves income recipients, and income sources are therefore ultimately determined by the expenditure patterns of these same income recipients. This circular flow of income, in addition to the inter-industry effects just described, has a variety of dynamic multiplier effects depending on the speed with which income is spent and the rate of capital formation.

Interregional income flows focus attention on the points where these circular flows cross real or imaginary boundaries between the diverse geographic regions of the national economy. Income may be earned from the "export"[8] of commodities and services to other regions, "exports" which in turn call for many subsidiary local inputs by the direct "exporters" and thus create income through a whole hierarchy of industrial stages in the local economy. Again, as with all income flows, these inter-industry effects are reinforced by dynamic multipliers as local income recipients spend their incomes earned from sales to other regions, and new "export" markets encourage local capital formation as well as interregional capital flows.

On the other hand, there are "leakages" as the region "imports" commodities and services from outside. These "leakages" lead to income losses as local income recipients spend their money, directly or indirectly, "abroad" rather than at home. Yet analogous to the well-established principles of international trade, "imports" from other regions are essential to maintain "exports" and to close gaps in the interregional income circuit. The ultimate importance of "imports" for local income is measured, of course, not by their immediate "negative" impact on regional income receipts but rather by their contribution to local resource productivity and capital formation.

Interregional income flows thus may identify the extent to which a region has used its comparative advantage for growing with the national economy and, perhaps more importantly, for understanding changes in the region's comparative advantage as a result of structural transformation within the national economy. On the national level, the balance of international payments relates movements in the domestic income stream to the rest of the world. On the regional level, these relations tend to be larger and far more complex, as the region is by definition an "open" part of the national economy. At the same time, and for the same reason, these relations are far more difficult to measure, as few data are available to construct a regional balance of payments.

Even without a regional balance of payments, however, it may be useful to distinguish as carefully as possible among the several spatial and industrial components of regional income. Analogous to the national income accounts, regional product can be conceived as resulting from expenditures by local consumers, business, and government. In addition, the regional net balance of sales to and purchases from "foreigners" becomes a component of regional product. And anal-

8. "Exports" in quotes refer to sales of local industry to buyers located in other regions of the domestic economy.

ogous to the national balance of payments, this regional net balance in turn can be conceived as resulting from transactions on current, capital, and government accounts.

## III. Current Account

The South had its very beginnings as an export economy. Tobacco, rice, sugar, cotton, these were the export staples in which the South excelled and in which slave labor was both the major capital investment and an important intermediate product. Yet an export economy is likely to survive only if its supplies are elastic enough to adjust with changing export markets, a process facilitated by the growth of "residentiary industries" supplying the many demands derived from the export base and thus broadening the range of domestic resource allocation. Yet what stands out in the historical development of the South is its long hesitancy to expand the size of its own market.[9] At the time of the Civil War, New Orleans was the only Southern city ranking among the first fifteen in the United States. Locally oriented industries and services were conspicuously fewer in the South, on a per capita basis, than elsewhere. Only with the turn of the century did the South move toward some industrial diversification to meet more adequately growing local demands.

As long as export income is used primarily for investment "abroad" or imports of luxury consumer goods to satisfy the needs of a few high-income recipients, the region contributes little to the broadening of its own economic base and thus remains vulnerable to shifts in export demand. Foreign trade under these conditions does not transmit its full advantages to all sectors of the regional economy. The elasticity of local supplies is partly determined, of course, by the region's natural endowments, which are likely to have established its comparative advantage for the export products in the first place. Yet as the very essence of economic development is a change in the use of these natural endowments, the question turns to the characteristics of the export economy which facilitate or arrest more balanced growth. The importance of agricultural-production functions and land tenure in this context is a familiar theme; American history has often been discussed in terms of the striking contrast between the slave-operated plantation of the South and the general-purpose family farm of the North.

9. This thesis has been propounded with persuasive force by Douglass C. North, *The Economic Growth of the United States 1790–1860* (Englewood Cliffs, 1961), pp. 122–34.

**Table 4.** Median Income 1950 by Years of School Completed* (South as Percent of Non-South)

| Age | 8 Years of School Completed | | 12 Years of School Completed | | 16 Years of School Completed | |
|---|---|---|---|---|---|---|
| | White | Non-White | White | Non-White | White | Non-White |
| 14–17 | 101 | 84 | — | — | — | — |
| 18–19 | 85 | 68 | 91 | 76 | — | — |
| 20–21 | 84 | 81 | 81 | 73 | 120 | — |
| 22–24 | 78 | 69 | 91 | 62 | 103 | — |
| 25–29 | 84 | 69 | 94 | 72 | 101 | 86 |
| 30–34 | 82 | 71 | 96 | 75 | 101 | 84 |
| 35–44 | 79 | 70 | 97 | 78 | 99 | 86 |
| 45–54 | 78 | 66 | 96 | 74 | 98 | 83 |
| 55–64 | 73 | 57 | 91 | 70 | 96 | 79 |
| 65–74 | 70 | 50 | 86 | 49 | 97 | — |
| 75 and over | 85 | 48 | 84 | — | 98 | — |

* Source: U.S. Bureau of the Census.

Resultant differences in the distribution of export income may influence not only the demand for consumer goods but also, perhaps even more importantly, the demand for capital investment. Under the plantation system, with its marked inequality of incomes, the community was reluctant to spend public funds for education or research other than that immediately related to the staple export.[10]   In contrast, regions with a more equitable income distribution improved their comparative advantage through investment in human capital and thus raised the supply elasticities of a more highly skilled and more versatile labor force.   The persistence of educational differences, and their impact on Southern development, is illustrated by the 1950 Census data on median income (Table 4).   Southern workers with only elementary school training received considerably less than similar workers in other parts of the country, while regional income differentials disappeared for college graduates.[11]   Such an imbalance in educational investment may lead to the continued out-migration of abler workers attracted by opportunities outside the region.   Southern educators have for a long time complained of losing their college

10. For a case study, see William H. Nicholls, "Some Foundations of Economic Development in the Upper East Tennessee Valley 1850–1900," *Journal of Political Economy*, LXIV (October, 1956), 400–15.

11. Professor Burton A. Weisbrod has computed the present capital value of lifetime income and found substantially higher returns of educational investment in the South. This would appear to indicate the shortage of "human capital" in a developing economy.

**Table 5.** U.S. Regional Distribution of Manufacturing Labor Force and Value Added by Manufacture 1870–1950*

| Region | 1870 | | 1890 | | 1910 | | 1930 | | 1950 | |
|---|---|---|---|---|---|---|---|---|---|---|
| | Labor Force | Value Added | Labor Force | Value Added | Labor Force | Value Added | Labor Force | Value Added | Labor Force | Value Added |
| Continental United States | 100 | 100 | 100 | 100 | 100 | 100 | 100 | 100 | 100 | 100 |
| Northeast | 80 | 84 | 74 | 82 | 69 | 77 | 67 | 76 | 68 | 71 |
| West | 10 | 10 | 15 | 11 | 18 | 13 | 19 | 14 | 17 | 17 |
| South | 10 | 6 | 11 | 7 | 13 | 10 | 14 | 10 | 15 | 12 |

* Source: Kuznets and Thomas, *Population Redistribution*, Vol. I, Table M-8.

graduates; it could well be that a region with relatively low expenditures for education subsidizes the rest of the country, since its investment is too low for major innovations but "too high" for the limited local employment opportunities.

Data on the industrial composition of the South would indicate that the region has retained its position as an exporter of raw materials and an importer of finished goods or services until the recent past. As Table 3 shows, no other region of equal population density relies to the present day so heavily on primary industries as sources of personal income. Residents of the South received almost $11 billion in 1929, a post-World War I peak reached again only in 1940. Location coefficients of American industry suggest that Southern "exports" in the late twenties were concentrated in cotton, tobacco, coal, lumber, and textiles, while regional "imports" were high for most manufacturing industries and "invisible" services. Though the South at that time had only 20 percent of the total national labor force, it still employed 40 percent of all workers in U.S. resource industries. Value added by Southern manufacture in the late twenties was, as a percentage of total U.S. output, actually somewhat lower than it had been before World War I (Table 5). Similar conclusions emerge from a study of rail freight movements from and to the Southern District in 1929 (Table 7).

The large margin of error inherent in any estimate of interregional trade makes it difficult to come up with any precise statement about a net "export" or "import" balance of the South on current account in 1929. The evidence suggests that there may have been a slight excess of credits, including interest and dividends received from outside the region, though minor changes in the assumptions underlying these estimates would change the net "export" balance into a net "import" balance on current account, and the reliability of the estimates is so low that either result appears quite probable. The direct impact of any net current balance on Southern income therefore may have been small, though the gross interregional income flows have been a major determinant of the Southern industrial structure. The essential fact remains that Southern export industries were characterized by low per capita income in 1929 while most of the imports originated in "foreign" industries of much higher per capita productivity.

The continued reliance on "primary" exports of low labor productivity also suggests that the "indirect exports" of the South were relatively small. Each service or commodity "exported" depends on a large number of secondary industries from whom the "exporter" buys essential parts of the final "export" product. Indeed, it is this multiplier effect of inter-industry relations which explains the wide interest in regional "exports." For the nation as a whole, attempts have been made to trace either the complete reaction on all other industries of a single industry's exports[12] or the effect of all exports on each individual industry.[13] These attempts would indicate that for every dollar's worth of goods exported directly there is, roughly, another dollar's worth of goods indirectly exported through complementary reaction paths. This ratio will vary, of course, from industry to industry and from region to region. As mentioned before, the historical evidence would indicate that this ratio in the South, until the recent past, was far below the national average.

Over the last generation the South has experienced large "differential" employment shifts already referred to above.[14] These shifts have not only changed the over-all composition of Southern trade with the rest of the nation but also introduced a much more heterogenous industrial structure within the South, so that the analytical usefulness of an over-all Southern balance of trade may be questioned. The following picture emerges by 1960: Southern agriculture has become much more diversified, with a notable upward shift in livestock production. While the traditional staples of cotton and tobacco have remained major regional "exports" (either direct or "indirect," embodied in manufactured goods), farm imports into the region have shown a relative decline. Lumber and coal "exports" have remained important, though again with a shift from direct to indirect exports. Notable upward differential shifts in manufacturing have occurred in most states of the South, particularly in Florida, Kentucky, Tennessee, and Mississippi, with resultant net decreases in manufacturing "imports." Almost 90 percent of all tobacco goods are now manufactured in the South, and more than half of all American textiles come from this region. Lumber and furniture industries provide one quarter of the national output; chemicals and paper approach this ratio. Electrical machinery and precision instruments, almost non-existent before World War II, have increased eightfold their share of the national output (Table 6). Other striking upward shifts have oc-

12. Walter S. Salant and Beatrice N. Vaccara, *Import Liberalization and Employment* (Washington, 1961).

13. Marvin Hoffenberg, "Employment Resulting from U.S. Exports," *Monthly Labor Review*, LXV (December, 1947), 675–78.

14. See Table 13 as prepared by Edgar S. Dunn for Perloff and Dodds, *op. cit.*, pp. 78–79.

**Table 6.** Value Added by Southern Manufacture 1939, 1947, and 1958* (South as Percent of Continental United States)

|  | 1939 | 1947 | 1958 |
|---|---|---|---|
| All Manufacturing | 11.4 | 12.6 | 14.0 |
| Food | 10.1 | 12.1 | 14.5 |
| Tobacco | 70.0 | 72.1 | 87.2 |
| Textile | 34.5 | 35.6 | 56.1 |
| Apparel | 6.7 | 8.5 | 15.2 |
| Lumber | 32.0 | 32.4 | 25.1 |
| Furniture | 17.7 | 19.7 | 24.8 |
| Paper | 12.5 | 17.8 | 22.4 |
| Printing | 6.4 | 6.6 | 8.1 |
| Chemicals | 17.5 | 18.8 | 23.5 |
| Petroleum | 5.5 | 10.9 | 12.4 |
| Rubber | 0.1 | 0.1 | 7.7 |
| Leather | 4.3 | 5.8 | 8.7 |
| Stone | 13.2 | 14.9 | 15.8 |
| Primary Metal | 8.8 | 8.1 | 10.6 |
| Fabricated Metal | 5.4 | 5.6 | 8.0 |
| Machinery | 1.8 | 2.2 | 4.3 |
| Electrical Machinery | 0.1 | 2.3 | 7.8 |
| Transportation Equipment | 2.7 | 3.2 | 5.7 |
| Instruments | 0.4 | 0.1 | 3.0 |
| Miscellaneous | 2.5 | 2.3 | 5.8 |

* Source: U.S. Bureau of the Census.

curred in financial and professional services throughout the South, with tourist services standing out in Florida and Kentucky. Retirement income from outside the region has become another important credit among the "invisible" items in the Florida balance of payments.

Paucity of actual trade data again prevents any precise estimate of the net changes in the Southern balance of trade. While exports have grown, so, with a rising per capita income, have imports. What stands out are not changes in the net trade balance of the South but far-reaching shifts in the trade composition, with a relative decline of raw materials as a component of regional "exports." Residents of the South received a personal income of $65 billion in 1960, a six-fold increase over 1929. Rail freight tonnage shipped into and out of the South increased far less (Table 7), a fact explained in part by price increases and the general loss of rail freight to competing carriers, but more importantly by the shift from low-value raw materials to high-value finished goods in the interregional trade relations between the South and the rest of the nation. With the growth of Southern process and service industries, "indirect" exports and imports have increased; the resultant pattern of interregional income flows has become far

**Table 7.** Rail Freight Originating or Terminating in Southern District*† (Thousands of Tons)

| Freight | 1929 | | | 1940 | | | 1950 | | | 1959 | | |
|---|---|---|---|---|---|---|---|---|---|---|---|---|
| | Origin. | Term. | Net | Origin. | Term. | Net | Origin. | Term. | Net | Orgin. | Term. | Net |
| Products of Agriculture | 14865 | 16313 | −1448 | 10007 | 11887 | −1880 | 16104 | 18449 | −2345 | 15525 | 20345 | −4820 |
| Animals and Products | 1838 | 2013 | −175 | 1484 | 1675 | −191 | 1615 | 1784 | −169 | 1093 | 1445 | −352 |
| Products of Mines | 204705 | 98090 | +106615 | 183097 | 104692 | +78405 | 250795 | 134941 | +115854 | 260015 | 182998 | +77017 |
| Products of Forests | 29659 | 22817 | +6842 | 19666 | 31382 | −11716 | 32134 | 27532 | +4602 | 35229 | 35080 | +149 |
| Manufactures | 37284 | 40066 | −2782 | 35863 | 39863 | −4000 | 63614 | 69311 | −5697 | 74973 | 78332 | −3359 |
| Less than Carload | 7082 | 7077 | +5 | 2915 | 6562 | −3647 | 2479 | 2748 | −269 | 848 | 812 | +36 |

* Excludes Arkansas and Louisiana.
† Source: Interstate Commerce Commission.

more complex than a generation ago, indicating a less distinctive Southern region whose 1960 current account with the rest of the national economy exhibits a high degree of mutual interdependence with a large diversity of trade cross-currents.

## IV. Capital Account

Interregional income flows on current account affect regional capital formation in two ways. First, the industrial composition of the current account may reflect the import of capital goods which increase "domestic" productivity and in turn encourage "domestic" savings. Second, any net balance on current account may be financed by corresponding transactions on capital account in a way familiar from international trade analysis.

**Table 8.** Time Deposits and Construction Contracts 1929 and 1960* (South as Percent of Continental United States)

| Year | Personal Income | Time Deposits | Construction Contracts | Time Deposits/ Personal Income | Construction Contracts/ Personal Income |
|------|-----------------|---------------|------------------------|--------------------------------|-----------------------------------------|
| 1929 | 11.7 | 6.2 | 7.4 | 0.53 | 0.64 |
| 1960 | 15.6 | 8.5 | 19.1 | 0.55 | 1.22 |

* Source: U.S. Bureau of Business Economics, U.S. Comptroller of the Currency, F. W. Dodge Corporation.

As outlined above, the history of the South has been characterized by a relative lack of capital imports. Whatever capital formation took place before the Civil War was rather directly related to the export staple crops. With reconstruction and the beginnings of industrialization, the import of capital equipment increased; yet it appears that until the recent past, plant and equipment expenditures in the South remained below the national average while the primary resource industries were labor- rather than capital-intensive. In 1929, the value of construction contracts in the South amounted to but 7 percent of the national total (Table 8), though personal income approached 12 percent. Yet over the last generation this picture has been dramatically reversed, and Southern construction now runs ahead of the national average, amounting to more than 19 percent of the national total in 1960. A similar reversal has occurred for new plant and equipment expenditures, which now reach 17 percent of the national total (Table 9).

Though these capital expenditures can be estimated with reason-

**Table 9.**  Plant and Equipment Expenditures 1940 and 1959* (South as Percent of Continental United States)

| Year | Personal Income | Plant and Equipment | Plant and Equipment/ Personal Income |
|------|-----------------|---------------------|--------------------------------------|
| 1940 | 13.0 | 14.5 | 1.12 |
| 1959 | 15.8 | 17.5 | 1.11 |

* Source: U.S. Bureau of the Census.

able accuracy, it is much harder to establish their regional origin. As difficult and precarious as it is to measure interregional income flows on current account, these difficulties are compounded when it comes to an evaluation of capital flows. Assuming no major regional differentials in the national rate of savings, it would seem a plausible hypothesis that local capital expenditures below the national norm (computed as a function of income) would signify a net outflow on capital account, while an opposite ratio would suggest a net capital inflow. The testing of such a hypothesis is further complicated by the fact that the South—like most areas outside major capital markets—appears to have a net outflow on personal capital account and a net inflow on business capital account. Thus time deposits amount rather consistently to but half of the national average, again computed as a function of income, though the ratio of capital expenditures has changed greatly over the same period (Table 8). Similar conclusions are borne out by the interdistrict settlement fund net clearings of the Federal Reserve System. These clearings are influenced by Treasury transactions, and their proper interpretation is therefore beset with difficulties. Persistent net outflows from the Richmond, Atlanta, and Dallas Districts appear to indicate, though, the important role of the Chicago and New York money markets in financing the rapid growth of the Southern region, accommodating a net outflow of personal savings which were channeled back in the form of business and government funds. Personal income for the nation as a whole increased by 270 percent from 1941 to 1958. Over this same war and post-war period, the Atlanta and Dallas districts increased their income more than fivefold yet recorded a net outflow of more than $15 billion through the interdistrict settlement fund.[15] Still other evidence is provided by a recent survey which shows about three-fifths of all

15. Norman N. Bowsher, J. Dewey Daane, and Robert Einzig, "The Flows of Funds between Regions of the United States," *Journal of Finance,* XIII (March, 1958), 1–20.

funds used for industrial expansion in the Atlanta Federal Reserve District coming from outside the South. These figures would suggest sizeable and continued net credits on capital account.

## V. Government Account

The growth of the public sector has—whether by design or otherwise—led to a redistribution of income among persons, industries, and regions. Where the central government relies on the progressive income tax as its major source of revenue, and federal expenditures are distributed evenly, it is inevitable that low-income regions have a net inflow on government account. This impact is heightened if federal funds are spent more heavily in these areas, either as a deliberate social policy to alleviate distress and to speed up economic growth in the less developed regions of the nation, or as a by-product of other policies, such as the ready availability of unused resources for purposes of national defense.

Until a generation ago, the very smallness of the federal budget minimized the impact of the government account on the South. Since then, however, the federal government has become a major source of funds for Southern development.[16] Internal revenue receipts from the South have gone down as a percent of the national total, from over 17 percent in 1940 to 11 percent in 1960 (Table 10), a figure which overstates the federal tax incidence on the South by several percentage points because of the way alcohol and tobacco taxes are collected from manufacturers in North Carolina, Virginia, and Kentucky. Over this same time span, most federal expenditure programs in the South have been greatly expanded. In 1940, the South received about 16 percent of all federal aid; by 1960, this ratio had increased to almost 25 percent. Similar ratios hold for veterans' and other transfer payments, the most direct impact of federal payments on interregional income flows.[17] The Southern share of defense expenditures is smaller, about 14 percent, yet the Southern "space crescent" is receiving a very much larger share of total NASA expenditures.

16. Marshall R. Colberg, "The Effect of the Federal Government's Economic Policies upon the Economic Development of the South" (Mimeographed paper for the Second Annual Conference of the Inter-University Committee for Economic Research on the South, New Orleans, 1962).

17. Howard G. Schaller, "Social Security Transfer Payments and Differences in State Per Capita Incomes, 1929, 1939, and 1949," *Review of Economics and Statistics*, XXXVII (February, 1955), 83–89.

**Table 10.** Federal Receipts and Expenditures 1940 and 1960 * (South as Percent of Continental United States)

| Year | Personal Income | Internal Revenue Collections | Federal Aid | Veterans' Exp. | Defense Exp. | Internal Revenue/ Personal Income | Federal Aid/ Personal Income | Veterans' Exp./ Personal Income | Defense Exp./ Personal Income |
|---|---|---|---|---|---|---|---|---|---|
| 1940 | 13.0 | 17.4 | 16.4 | .... | .... | 1.35 | 1.26 | .... | .... |
| 1960 | 15.6 | 11.9 | 24.8 | 22.8 | 14.5 | 0.76 | 1.59 | 1.46 | 0.93 |

* Source: U.S. Bureau of Business Economics, U.S. Bureau of Internal Revenue, U.S. Social Security Administration, U.S. Department of Defense.

## VI. Factor Analysis

Still another approach to the analysis of interregional income flows is suggested by factor analysis. Correlations among a large number of observed data may help to disclose the aggregates of fundamental importance for the process of economic development. Factor analysis is a statistical technique to resolve a large set of variables linearly into a small number of strategic categories or "factors" by finding the correlations among all the variables. Thus far it has found its most extensive application in psychology and education to provide mathematical models for the explanation of human ability and behavior.[18] More recently, however, it has also been used to offer criteria for the delineation of "regions"[19] and to find similarities of industrial composition which might be condensed into basic development- or trade-patterns of a composite multi-index character.[20]

The variables refer to population, resources, and economic activities (Table 11); their 1960 scores for the South, as they relate to the national average, are shown in Table 12. The demographic data include population growth and density (Variables 1–4). Resources list, among others, value of farm real estate (Variables 5 and 6), road mileage and motor vehicle registrations (Variables 19 and 20), insurance and bank deposits per capita (Variables 12 and 13). Economic activities are sectored by major industry groups. State and local governments are recorded by per capita revenue (Variable 18) and expenditures (Variables 8–11). Construction contracts and electric energy produced are listed to indicate elements of growth (Variables 14–17). Employment and income per employee are entered for all major industries and two-digit subgroups of manufacturing (Variables 21–43). Average labor costs are computed per dollar of sales or

18. For a good survey and an extensive bibliography see Harry H. Harman, *Modern Factor Analysis* (Chicago, 1960).

19. Margaret J. Hagood, "An Examination of the Use of Factor Analysis in the Problem of Subregional Delineation," *Rural Sociology*, September, 1941. For a more general discussion, see Walter Isard, *Methods of Regional Analysis* (New York, 1960), pp. 293–305.

20. Brian J. L. Berry, "An Inductive Approach to the Regionalization of Economic Development," *Essays on Geography and Economic Development* (Chicago, 1960), pp. 78–107. The findings of this factor analysis have also been presented in Norton Ginsburg, *Atlas of Economic Development* (Chicago, 1961), pp. 110–19. For a factor analysis of urban patterns, see Leo F. Schnore, "The Statistical Measurement of Urbanization and Economic Development," *Land Economics*, XXXVII (August, 1961), 229–45. See also Christen T. Jonassen and Sherwood H. Peres, *Interrelationships of Dimensions of Community Systems* (Columbus, 1960).

**Table 11.** Seventy-Five Variables Used for the Factor Analysis

*Demographic*
1. Percent Increase in Population 1940–60[a]
2. Population Density[a]
3. Crude Birth Rate per 1,000 Population[a]
4. Death Rate per 1,000 Population[a]

*Agricultural*
5. Value of Farm Real Estate[b]
6. Percent of Tenant-Operated Farms[a]
7. Corn Yields per Acre[b]

*General Expenditures of State and Local Government per Capita*
8. Education[a]
9. Highways[a]
10. Public Welfare[a]
11. Health and Hospitals[a]

*Growth Indicators*
12. Insurance per Capita[c]
13. Bank Deposits per Capita[d]
14. Value of Construction Contracts per Capita[e]
15. Total Kilowatt Hours of Electric Energy Produced[f]
16. Per Capita Kilowatt Hours of Electric Energy Produced[f]
17. Percent Increase of Electric Energy Produced 1940–60[f]
18. State Revenue per Capita[a]
19. Road Mileage per Capita[g]
20. Motor Vehicle Registrations per Capita[g]

*Distribution of Employment*
21. Mining[h]
22. Contract Construction[h]
23. Manufacturing[h]
24. Transportation and Public Utilities[h]
25. Wholesale and Retail Trade[h]
26. Finance, Insurance, and Real Estate[h]
27. Services[h]
28. Government[h]

*Income*
29. Personal Income per Capita[i]
30. Share of United States Personal Income[i]
31. Average Teachers' Salary[j]
32. All Manufacturing Industries[a]
33. Food and Kindred Products[a]
34. Textile Mill Products[a]
35. Furniture and Fixtures[a]
36. Chemicals and Allied Products[a]
37. Fabricated Metal Products[a]
38. Apparel and Related Products[a]
39. Printing and Publishing Industries[a]
40. Stone, Clay, and Glass Products[a]
41. Machinery (except Electrical)[a]
42. Retail Trade[a]
43. Selected Services[a]

## Table 11 (continued)

*Value Added per Employee*
44. All Manufacturing Industries[a]
45. Food and Kindred Products[a]
46. Textile Mill Products[a]
47. Furniture and Fixtures[a]
48. Chemicals and Allied Products[a]
49. Fabricated Metal Products[a]
50. Apparel and Related Products[a]
51. Printing and Publishing Industries[a]
52. Stone, Clay, and Glass Products[a]
53. Machinery (except Electrical)[a]

*Sales per Employee*
54. Retail Trade[a]
55. Selected Services[a]

*Average Labor Cost per Dollar of Sales or Value Added*
56. Retail Trade[a]
57. Selected Services[a]
58. All Manufacturing Industries[a]
59. Food and Kindred Products[a]
60. Textile Mill Products[a]
61. Furniture and Fixtures[a]
62. Chemicals and Allied Products[a]
63. Apparel and Related Products[a]
64. Printing and Publishing Industries[a]
65. Stone, Clay, and Glass Products[a]
66. Machinery (except Electrical)[a]

*Location Quotients*
67. Food and Kindred Products[a]
68. Textile Mill Products[a]
69. Furniture and Fixtures Industry[a]
70. Chemicals and Allied Products[a]
71. Fabricated Metal Products[a]
72. Apparel and Related Products[a]
73. Printing and Publishing Industries[a]
74. Stone, Clay, and Glass Products[a]
75. Machinery (except Electrical)[a]

---

[a] U.S. Bureau of the Census.
[b] U.S. Department of Agriculture.
[c] Institute of Life Insurance.
[d] Board of Governors of the Federal Reserve System.
[e] F. W. Dodge Corporation.
[f] Federal Power Commission.
[g] U.S. Bureau of Public Roads.
[h] U.S. Bureau of Labor Statistics.
[i] U.S. Office of Business Economics.
[j] U.S. Office of Education.

**Table 12.** 1960 Standard Scores of 75 Variables

| Variables | Alabama | Arkansas | Florida | Georgia | Kentucky | Louisiana |
|---|---|---|---|---|---|---|
| 1 | −0.63 | −1.38 | 3.20 | −0.21 | −0.85 | 0.11 |
| 2 | −0.34 | −0.50 | −0.20 | −0.32 | −0.28 | −0.30 |
| 3 | 0.42 | −0.58 | −0.58 | −0.08 | −0.08 | 1.92 |
| 4 | −0.54 | 0.46 | 0.46 | −1.54 | 0.46 | −0.54 |
| 5 | 0.19 | −0.04 | 3.97 | 1.50 | −0.82 | 1.35 |
| 6 | 1.24 | 0.82 | −1.07 | 0.93 | 0.09 | 0.93 |
| 7 | −1.42 | −0.93 | −1.35 | −1.14 | 0.03 | −0.14 |
| 8 | −1.30 | −1.40 | −0.32 | −0.84 | −1.49 | 0.47 |
| 9 | −0.84 | −0.84 | −0.66 | −1.02 | −0.93 | 0.06 |
| 10 | −0.02 | 0.22 | −0.38 | 0.10 | −0.26 | 3.10 |
| 11 | −0.84 | −0.58 | 0.46 | 0.72 | −1.11 | −0.32 |
| 12 | −1.45 | −0.12 | −1.13 | 1.89 | 1.85 | −0.46 |
| 13 | −1.04 | −0.97 | −0.37 | −0.86 | −0.84 | −0.51 |
| 14 | −0.80 | −0.34 | −0.80 | −0.26 | 1.55 | −0.67 |
| 15 | 0.52 | −0.66 | 0.06 | −0.28 | 0.26 | −0.30 |
| 16 | 1.11 | −0.61 | −0.48 | −0.67 | 0.80 | −0.48 |
| 17 | −0.23 | 0.24 | 0.17 | −0.16 | 0.43 | −0.23 |
| 18 | −1.26 | −1.05 | −0.38 | −0.81 | −1.48 | 0.33 |
| 19 | −0.32 | 0.18 | −0.57 | −0.32 | −0.32 | −0.57 |
| 20 | 0.40 | −1.19 | 0.93 | 1.46 | 0.40 | 0.40 |
| 21 | −0.11 | −0.11 | −0.46 | −0.46 | 0.94 | 1.30 |
| 22 | 0.23 | 0.05 | −1.01 | 0.50 | −0.12 | −0.84 |
| 23 | −1.05 | 0.12 | 0.12 | −0.46 | 0.12 | 1.88 |
| 24 | −0.61 | 0.10 | 1.91 | −0.25 | −0.26 | 0.46 |
| 25 | −0.44 | −0.44 | 1.77 | 0.67 | −0.44 | −0.44 |
| 26 | −0.41 | −0.11 | 0.78 | −0.70 | −0.11 | −0.11 |
| 27 | 0.81 | 0.34 | −0.13 | 0.11 | −0.13 | 0.11 |
| 28 | −0.64 | 0.01 | 1.97 | −0.64 | 0.01 | 0.66 |
| 29 | −1.39 | −1.59 | −0.04 | −1.05 | −1.14 | −0.99 |
| 30 | −1.39 | −1.59 | −0.05 | −1.03 | −1.13 | −0.98 |
| 31 | −1.06 | −1.44 | 0.75 | −0.81 | −1.53 | 0.37 |
| 32 | −0.40 | −0.40 | −0.16 | −0.40 | −0.16 | −0.16 |
| 33 | −0.75 | −0.75 | −0.75 | −0.75 | 0.45 | −0.75 |
| 34 | 0.11 | 0.71 | −1.09 | 0.11 | 0.11 | −1.09 |
| 35 | 0.20 | 0.20 | 0.20 | 0.20 | 0.20 | 0.78 |
| 36 | −0.03 | 0.81 | −0.03 | −0.03 | 0.39 | 0.81 |
| 37 | −0.14 | −0.15 | −0.14 | −0.14 | 0.14 | −0.14 |
| 38 | −0.09 | −0.21 | 0.29 | 0.16 | 0.15 | 0.14 |
| 39 | −0.31 | −0.79 | −0.01 | 0.06 | 0.44 | −0.19 |
| 40 | −0.47 | −0.44 | −0.72 | −1.05 | −0.31 | 0.22 |
| 41 | −0.01 | −0.40 | −0.55 | −0.21 | 0.47 | 0.08 |
| 42 | −0.26 | −0.26 | −0.26 | −0.26 | −0.26 | −0.26 |
| 43 | −0.52 | −0.52 | −0.52 | −0.52 | −0.52 | −0.52 |
| 44 | −0.32 | −0.45 | −0.19 | −0.45 | 0.19 | 0.06 |
| 45 | −0.85 | −1.30 | −0.40 | −0.40 | 1.87 | 0.06 |
| 46 | 0.35 | 0.70 | −1.06 | −0.35 | 0.03 | −1.06 |
| 47 | 0.17 | −0.17 | 0.17 | 0.17 | 0.17 | 0.86 |
| 48 | 0.49 | 0.34 | 0.24 | −0.09 | 0.84 | 0.72 |
| 49 | 0.81 | 0.93 | −1.28 | 0.23 | 1.73 | 0.26 |
| 50 | 0.05 | −0.41 | 0.31 | 0.39 | 0.02 | 0.05 |
| 51 | 0.43 | −0.91 | 0.11 | 0.05 | −0.16 | 0.71 |
| 52 | 0.01 | −0.11 | −0.68 | −0.97 | −0.59 | 0.53 |
| 53 | −0.26 | 0.42 | −0.60 | 0.20 | 2.12 | −0.21 |
| 54 | −0.58 | −0.01 | −0.54 | −1.18 | 0.10 | −1.05 |
| 55 | −1.60 | −1.31 | −0.22 | −1.26 | −0.43 | −0.76 |
| 56 | −0.87 | −2.09 | 0.36 | −0.87 | −0.87 | 0.36 |
| 57 | 0.27 | −1.17 | −0.09 | 0.27 | −0.09 | 0.27 |

## Table 12 (continued)

| Variables | Alabama | Arkansas | Florida | Georgia | Kentucky | Louisiana |
|---|---|---|---|---|---|---|
| 58 | −0.19 | −0.47 | −0.61 | −0.19 | −1.73 | −1.31 |
| 59 | 0.37 | 0.16 | −0.88 | −1.09 | −2.34 | −0.88 |
| 60 | 0.07 | 0.42 | 0.61 | 0.61 | 0.99 | −1.27 |
| 61 | 0.41 | 0.71 | 0.41 | 0.24 | 0.41 | 0.28 |
| 62 | −0.13 | 0.63 | −0.05 | 0.29 | 0.04 | 0.21 |
| 63 | 0.19 | 0.69 | 0.33 | 0.10 | 0.51 | 0.46 |
| 64 | −0.72 | 0.34 | −0.08 | 0.13 | 0.77 | −0.82 |
| 65 | −0.43 | −0.33 | 0.08 | 0.19 | 0.50 | −0.33 |
| 66 | 0.46 | −0.53 | 0.30 | −0.21 | −0.79 | 0.51 |
| 67 | −0.41 | 0.11 | 0.19 | −0.16 | 0.02 | 0.17 |
| 68 | 0.67 | −0.26 | −0.44 | 1.87 | −0.38 | −0.48 |
| 69 | −0.41 | 3.47 | 0.88 | 0.14 | 0.26 | −0.57 |
| 70 | −0.18 | 0.34 | 0.84 | −0.25 | 0.47 | 2.05 |
| 71 | −0.14 | −0.15 | −0.14 | −0.15 | −0.14 | −0.14 |
| 72 | 0.69 | 1.05 | −0.20 | 1.90 | 0.84 | −0.29 |
| 73 | −0.78 | 0.02 | 1.51 | −0.17 | 0.24 | −0.22 |
| 74 | −0.02 | 0.47 | 0.78 | −0.14 | −0.16 | 0.35 |
| 75 | −0.63 | −0.83 | −0.74 | −0.64 | 1.15 | −0.74 |

| Variables | Miss. | N. C. | S. C. | Tenn. | Va. | W. Va. |
|---|---|---|---|---|---|---|
| 1 | −1.01 | −0.37 | −0.32 | −0.58 | 0.06 | −1.38 |
| 2 | −0.44 | −0.19 | −0.26 | −0.23 | −0.15 | −0.27 |
| 3 | 1.42 | −0.08 | 0.42 | −0.58 | −0.58 | −1.09 |
| 4 | 0.46 | −0.54 | −0.54 | 0.46 | −0.54 | 0.46 |
| 5 | 1.02 | 0.14 | −0.34 | −0.68 | 0.39 | −1.21 |
| 6 | 1.66 | 1.56 | 1.66 | 0.51 | −0.12 | −1.07 |
| 7 | −1.55 | 0.09 | −1.00 | −0.59 | 0.03 | 0.23 |
| 8 | −1.68 | −0.88 | −1.26 | −1.21 | −0.88 | −1 2ι |
| 9 | −0.75 | −1.11 | −1.29 | −0.70 | −0.30 | −1.20 |
| 10 | −0.14 | −0.86 | −0.98 | −0.74 | −1.70 | −0.38 |
| 11 | −0.71 | −0.71 | −0.58 | −0.45 | −0.45 | −1.11 |
| 12 | 1.15 | −0.94 | 0.29 | −0.56 | −0.30 | −0.22 |
| 13 | −1.10 | −1.12 | −1.42 | −0.57 | −0.68 | −0.91 |
| 14 | 0.88 | −0.83 | −0.80 | −0.53 | −0.82 | −0.58 |
| 15 | −0.82 | 0.24 | −0.39 | 1.46 | 0.16 | −0.08 |
| 16 | −1.29 | −0.11 | −0.21 | 2.53 | 0.01 | 1.30 |
| 17 | 1.20 | −0.16 | −0.11 | 0.06 | −0.03 | −0.34 |
| 18 | −1.17 | −1.34 | −1.54 | −1.30 | −1.32 | −1.18 |
| 19 | −0.32 | −0.57 | −0.32 | −0.32 | −1.57 | −0.57 |
| 20 | −1.19 | 0.93 | 0.93 | −0.13 | −0.13 | 1.46 |
| 21 | −0.11 | −0.81 | −0.81 | −0.46 | −0.11 | 3.40 |
| 22 | 0.23 | 1.30 | 1.30 | 0.59 | −0.03 | −0.03 |
| 23 | −1.05 | −1.05 | −2.22 | −1.05 | 0.12 | 1.29 |
| 24 | −0.25 | −0.97 | −1.33 | −0.25 | −0.25 | −1.33 |
| 25 | −1.54 | 0.44 | −0.44 | −0.44 | −0.44 | −1.54 |
| 26 | −1.00 | −0.70 | −1.00 | −0.11 | −0.41 | −0.70 |
| 27 | 1.05 | −0.83 | −0.13 | −0.36 | 0.34 | −0.60 |
| 28 | −0.64 | 0.01 | 0.01 | −0.64 | 0.66 | −1.29 |
| 29 | −1.97 | −1.21 | −1.57 | −1.12 | −0.42 | −0.85 |
| 30 | −1.95 | −1.18 | −1.59 | −1.13 | −0.41 | −0.88 |
| 31 | −2.02 | −0.60 | −1.40 | −1.08 | −0.64 | −0.88 |
| 32 | −0.40 | −0.40 | −0.40 | −0.40 | −0.40 | −0.16 |
| 33 | −0.75 | −0.75 | −0.75 | −0.75 | −0.75 | −0.75 |
| 34 | 0.11 | 0.11 | 0.71 | 0.11 | 0.71 | 0.11 |

## Table 12 (continued)

| Variables | Miss. | N. C. | S. C. | Tenn. | Va. | W. Va. |
|---|---|---|---|---|---|---|
| 35 | 0.20 | 0.20 | 0.20 | 0.20 | 0.20 | 0.20 |
| 36 | −0.46 | −0.03 | 0.39 | 0.39 | 0.39 | 0.81 |
| 37 | −0.15 | −0.14 | −0.14 | −0.14 | −0.14 | −0.14 |
| 38 | −0.15 | −0.03 | −0.11 | −0.14 | 0.05 | −0.06 |
| 39 | −1.04 | −0.49 | −0.40 | −0.06 | −0.43 | −0.58 |
| 40 | −5.10 | −1.39 | −0.93 | −0.31 | −0.67 | −0.01 |
| 41 | −0.27 | −0.40 | −0.49 | 0.12 | −0.23 | 0.23 |
| 42 | −0.26 | −0.26 | −0.26 | −0.26 | −0.26 | −0.26 |
| 43 | −0.52 | −0.52 | −0.52 | −0.52 | −0.52 | −0.52 |
| 44 | −0.57 | −0.45 | −0.45 | −0.32 | −0.19 | 0.06 |
| 45 | −1.76 | −0.85 | −1.30 | −0.40 | −0.85 | −0.85 |
| 46 | 0.35 | 0.35 | 0.70 | 0.70 | 0.70 | 0.35 |
| 47 | 0.17 | 0.17 | −0.17 | 0.17 | 0.52 | 0.52 |
| 48 | −0.01 | 0.02 | 0.35 | 0.06 | 0.12 | 0.46 |
| 49 | −1.28 | 0.28 | 0.87 | −0.30 | 0.38 | 1.16 |
| 50 | −0.45 | −0.07 | −0.23 | −0.21 | −0.23 | −0.45 |
| 51 | −1.21 | −0.52 | −0.41 | 0.03 | −0.73 | −0.69 |
| 52 | −4.10 | −1.50 | −0.47 | −0.32 | −0.02 | −1.00 |
| 53 | 0.05 | −0.21 | −0.52 | −0.11 | 0.05 | 0.05 |
| 54 | −0.57 | −0.91 | −1.23 | −1.07 | −1.61 | −0.78 |
| 55 | −1.54 | −1.62 | −1.46 | −1.32 | −1.19 | −0.60 |
| 56 | −2.09 | −0.87 | −0.87 | −0.87 | 0.36 | 0.36 |
| 57 | −0.81 | 0.27 | −0.09 | 1.36 | 1.36 | 0.99 |
| 58 | 0.37 | −0.61 | 0.09 | −0.33 | −0.89 | −0.61 |
| 59 | 2.03 | −0.46 | 1.83 | −0.05 | −0.26 | 0.58 |
| 60 | 0.92 | 0.61 | 0.61 | 0.45 | 0.42 | 0.45 |
| 61 | 0.11 | 0.33 | 0.58 | 0.41 | 0.11 | −0.01 |
| 62 | −0.13 | 0.55 | 0.55 | 0.97 | 0.46 | 0.55 |
| 63 | 0.88 | 0.42 | 0.51 | 0.46 | 0.69 | 1.10 |
| 64 | 0.45 | 0.13 | 0.13 | 0.02 | 0.56 | 0.34 |
| 65 | −4.68 | 0.70 | −0.33 | 0.08 | −0.64 | 1.53 |
| 66 | −0.11 | −0.01 | 0.25 | 0.41 | −0.11 | 0.36 |
| 67 | 4.46 | −0.47 | 4.02 | −0.29 | −0.27 | −0.51 |
| 68 | −0.09 | 3.20 | 4.61 | 0.23 | 0.59 | −0.40 |
| 69 | 1.41 | 3.15 | −0.30 | 0.74 | 2.01 | −0.66 |
| 70 | −0.13 | −0.34 | 1.02 | 2.41 | 1.87 | 3.48 |
| 71 | −0.15 | −0.15 | −0.15 | −0.14 | −0.15 | −0.14 |
| 72 | 3.79 | 0.30 | 1.33 | 1.18 | 0.56 | −0.54 |
| 73 | −0.82 | −0.82 | −1.03 | 0.04 | −0.21 | −0.73 |
| 74 | −1.01 | −0.53 | −0.32 | 0.03 | −0.19 | 3.47 |
| 75 | −0.74 | −0.78 | −0.83 | −0.46 | −0.88 | −0.58 |

value added, again broken down by major two-digit subgroups of manufacturing (Variables 56–66). Output data are listed separately, for manufacturing as value added (Variables 44–53), for trade and services as sales (Variables 54 and 55). Finally, location quotients have been obtained for all manufacturing subgroups of special importance to the South (Variables 67–75).

To correlate this wide variety of social and economic indices, the seventy-five variables have been resolved linearly in terms of a small

**Table 13.** 1960 Factor Values of 75 Variables

| | | | Factors | | | |
|---|---|---|---|---|---|---|
| Variables | 1 | 2 | 3 | 4 | 5 | 6 |
| 1 | −026 | 101 | 038 | 157 | 114 | −018 |
| 2 | 086 | 053 | 102 | −033 | −002 | 076 |
| 3 | −105 | −022 | −015 | 086 | 130 | 093 |
| 4 | 044 | −007 | 053 | −166 | −114 | −057 |
| 5 | 000 | −005 | −083 | 164 | 030 | 110 |
| 6 | −016 | −092 | −124 | 058 | 085 | 153 |
| 7 | 073 | 111 | 002 | 019 | 015 | −075 |
| 8 | −044 | 144 | −038 | 004 | 139 | 003 |
| 9 | −096 | 094 | 036 | −113 | 044 | 000 |
| 10 | −000 | 026 | −095 | −041 | 067 | −058 |
| 11 | 002 | 088 | 049 | −087 | −020 | 065 |
| 12 | 022 | 001 | 028 | −020 | −129 | 153 |
| 13 | 050 | 129 | 038 | −112 | −010 | 074 |
| 14 | −106 | 034 | 063 | −069 | −074 | 032 |
| 15 | 094 | 052 | −049 | 097 | −075 | 000 |
| 16 | −022 | 031 | −005 | 135 | −026 | −132 |
| 17 | −003 | 000 | 048 | 023 | 182 | 154 |
| 18 | −090 | 148 | −002 | −050 | −014 | 004 |
| 19 | −152 | 029 | −019 | −040 | −102 | 027 |
| 20 | 101 | 004 | −082 | 100 | −078 | −049 |
| 21 | −084 | −003 | −055 | 034 | 011 | −059 |
| 22 | 141 | −029 | 119 | −045 | −011 | 000 |
| 23 | −091 | 048 | −159 | 014 | −026 | −046 |
| 24 | −082 | −010 | −202 | −013 | 064 | 060 |
| 25 | 071 | 069 | −103 | −023 | 020 | 091 |
| 26 | −068 | 098 | 060 | 076 | −086 | −074 |
| 27 | −135 | −039 | −086 | 022 | 042 | 034 |
| 28 | −118 | 018 | −053 | 035 | 077 | 039 |
| 29 | 051 | 180 | 052 | −003 | 024 | 030 |
| 30 | 051 | 180 | 054 | −003 | 024 | 029 |
| 31 | 053 | 168 | 018 | 065 | 089 | 024 |
| 32 | 030 | 069 | −058 | −012 | −079 | 100 |
| 33 | 036 | 045 | −095 | −191 | −017 | 092 |
| 34 | 117 | 014 | 119 | 015 | −016 | 085 |
| 35 | 120 | −009 | −086 | −023 | −153 | −051 |
| 36 | 109 | −008 | −123 | 100 | −009 | 023 |
| 37 | −109 | −004 | −080 | −037 | −023 | −056 |
| 38 | 151 | 013 | −020 | −020 | 076 | −021 |
| 39 | 061 | 115 | −061 | 077 | −073 | 133 |
| 40 | 022 | 163 | −022 | 012 | 009 | −136 |
| 41 | 117 | −013 | −088 | −047 | 140 | −011 |
| 42 | −019 | 089 | 034 | 136 | −054 | −099 |
| 43 | 009 | 144 | 063 | 059 | −131 | 005 |
| 44 | 020 | 066 | −074 | 005 | −104 | 080 |
| 45 | 051 | 068 | −151 | −126 | 024 | 052 |
| 46 | 122 | 018 | 097 | 046 | −066 | 108 |
| 47 | 123 | 000 | −098 | 003 | −146 | 051 |
| 48 | 105 | −015 | −146 | 103 | −020 | 044 |
| 49 | 090 | −006 | −023 | 062 | 050 | 023 |
| 50 | 142 | 026 | −001 | −013 | 130 | 018 |
| 51 | 044 | 114 | −086 | 110 | −035 | 108 |
| 52 | −025 | 120 | −071 | 066 | 025 | −081 |
| 53 | 110 | −035 | −125 | −037 | 018 | 035 |
| 54 | −074 | 085 | −016 | −074 | −019 | −028 |
| 55 | 009 | 156 | −043 | −011 | −010 | 045 |

**Table 13.** (continued)

| Variables | Factors | | | | | |
|---|---|---|---|---|---|---|
| | 1 | 2 | 3 | 4 | 5 | 6 |
| 56 | 057 | 157 | 028 | 074 | −007 | −012 |
| 57 | 036 | 068 | 105 | 209 | −066 | −094 |
| 58 | 073 | 060 | 112 | −096 | 179 | 083 |
| 59 | −023 | −031 | 121 | −027 | −053 | 057 |
| 60 | 112 | −026 | 123 | −003 | −024 | 027 |
| 61 | 128 | −052 | −018 | −040 | 000 | −101 |
| 62 | 115 | −029 | 016 | 086 | 142 | −016 |
| 63 | 140 | −058 | −027 | −005 | 009 | −077 |
| 64 | 024 | 025 | −053 | 026 | −133 | 119 |
| 65 | 047 | 074 | 038 | −076 | −014 | −167 |
| 66 | 098 | −038 | −023 | −056 | 216 | −055 |
| 67 | 004 | −110 | −026 | 030 | −011 | 130 |
| 68 | 032 | −097 | 137 | 034 | −028 | 029 |
| 69 | 048 | −009 | 014 | −015 | −100 | −061 |
| 70 | 040 | −059 | −058 | 148 | 042 | −073 |
| 71 | −009 | −004 | −081 | −037 | −024 | −056 |
| 72 | 069 | −093 | 054 | 008 | −055 | 116 |
| 73 | 058 | 026 | −148 | −030 | −003 | −024 |
| 74 | 029 | −029 | −087 | −061 | 012 | −226 |
| 75 | 031 | 031 | −040 | −166 | −027 | −071 |

number of categories or "factors," with a limit set on six factors to be extracted from each data matrix.[21]

The 1960 factor values are shown in Table 13. The most important factor extracted from the 1960 data matrix relates primarily to construction[22] and manufacturing data; it confirms the general impression that manufacturing activities are of critical importance in explaining economic development. This first factor accounts for 21 percent of the total sum of squares in the data matrix of seventy-five variables. The second factor, accounting for 15 percent of the total, shows a close direct relationship with income per capita (Variables 29–31), trade and services (Variables 55 and 56), per capita bank deposits (Variable 13), and expenditures for education (Variable 8). The third factor, accounting for 7 percent, is strongly influenced by the textile

21. The factor analysis has been designed and directed by Professor Mary Megee, who will publish a detailed technical report on the statistical procedures and findings. See also Werner Hochwald and Mary Megee, "The Industrial Composition of the South and its Bearing upon the Economic Development of the Region" (Mimeographed paper for the Annual Conference of the Inter-University Committee for Economic Research on the South, New Orleans, 1962).

22. Note the interesting contrast between Value of Construction Contracts (Variable 14) and Employment in Contract Construction (Variable 22), indicating the importance of large construction contracts in non-metropolitan areas. Note also the heavy negative weight of the birth rate (Variable 3).

**Table 14.** 1960 Factor Values for 48 States

| States | Factors | | | | | |
|---|---|---|---|---|---|---|
| | 1 | 2 | 3 | 4 | 5 | 6 |
| 1 Alabama | 157 | −1794 | 255 | 898 | 67 | −199 |
| 2 Arizona | −943 | 468 | −389 | 328 | 2304 | −387 |
| 3 Arkansas | 125 | −2637 | 13 | 19 | −704 | 222 |
| 4 California | 1692 | 2488 | −376 | 1521 | 198 | −216 |
| 5 Colorado | −985 | 643 | −685 | −622 | 932 | −131 |
| 6 Connecticut | 2048 | 1938 | 1179 | −659 | −357 | 353 |
| 7 Delaware | 751 | 1599 | 1595 | 237 | 2984 | 1626 |
| 8 Florida | −94 | −179 | −835 | 966 | 595 | −219 |
| 9 Georgia | 572 | −1659 | 108 | 702 | −274 | 715 |
| 10 Idaho | −1772 | −126 | −1344 | 357 | 998 | −239 |
| 11 Illinois | 2286 | 2213 | −1265 | −284 | −1487 | 1468 |
| 12 Indiana | 940 | 108 | −456 | 431 | −345 | −343 |
| 13 Iowa | 20 | −156 | −1459 | −705 | −199 | −88 |
| 14 Kansas | −697 | −209 | −1989 | −762 | −371 | −838 |
| 15 Kentucky | 671 | −1229 | −967 | −112 | −804 | −36 |
| 16 Louisiana | −555 | −478 | −1651 | 1125 | 724 | −495 |
| 17 Maine | −795 | −1962 | 2397 | −1746 | 1721 | −1730 |
| 18 Maryland | 1075 | 405 | 333 | 756 | 69 | 242 |
| 19 Massachusetts | 1788 | 968 | 1187 | −797 | −235 | 125 |
| 20 Michigan | 1942 | 1254 | 230 | −185 | 335 | 341 |
| 21 Minnesota | 627 | 434 | −935 | −455 | 76 | 249 |
| 22 Mississippi | −549 | −4456 | 936 | 59 | −595 | 2365 |
| 23 Missouri | 648 | −29 | −910 | −190 | −16 | −350 |
| 24 Montana | −3822 | 556 | −180 | −252 | −629 | 310 |
| 25 Nebraska | −283 | −616 | −1731 | −230 | −439 | 572 |
| 26 Nevada | −4662 | 3693 | 2518 | 2442 | −1862 | −1162 |
| 27 New Hampshire | 541 | −430 | 2031 | −1635 | −321 | −386 |
| 28 New Jersey | 2181 | 1309 | 302 | 153 | −108 | 333 |
| 29 New Mexico | −3978 | 510 | 870 | 884 | 507 | 156 |
| 30 New York | 2623 | 2750 | 51 | −1151 | −400 | 1050 |
| 31 North Carolina | 881 | −2479 | 970 | 807 | −688 | −265 |
| 32 North Dakota | −4083 | −294 | −771 | −907 | −170 | 1038 |
| 33 Ohio | 1999 | 983 | 250 | 287 | −288 | −147 |
| 34 Oklahoma | −178 | 491 | −1352 | −603 | 358 | −226 |
| 35 Oregon | 993 | 1126 | 14 | −67 | −259 | −217 |
| 36 Pennsylvania | 1822 | 219 | 401 | −211 | −373 | −144 |
| 37 Rhode Island | 1053 | 11 | 1884 | −658 | 486 | 392 |
| 38 South Carolina | 697 | −2960 | 1246 | 1048 | −262 | 822 |
| 39 South Dakota | −3719 | 682 | −339 | −1317 | −55 | 995 |
| 40 Tennessee | 806 | −1629 | 400 | 984 | −425 | −666 |
| 41 Texas | 323 | −545 | −1155 | 1096 | 162 | 347 |
| 42 Utah | −1132 | 365 | −686 | 363 | 1416 | 31 |
| 43 Vermont | 294 | −426 | −50 | −3134 | −694 | −2074 |
| 44 Virginia | 567 | −1499 | 380 | 1254 | −439 | −305 |
| 45 Washington | 550 | 1738 | −725 | 786 | 234 | −1068 |
| 46 West Virginia | 726 | −1236 | −90 | 744 | −302 | −2028 |
| 47 Wisconsin | 1500 | 316 | 256 | −368 | −150 | −44 |
| 48 Wyoming | −4759 | 2106 | 536 | −1228 | −909 | 693 |

industry (Variable 68). The fourth factor, accounting for 6 percent, is closely related to farm values (Variable 5), energy production (Variable 16), and the chemical industry (Variable 70). The last two factors, each accounting for but 4 percent of the total sum of squares, give heavy weight to general growth indices, such as the birth rate (Variable 3) and percent increases of electric energy (Variable 17).

Perhaps the most interesting finding of the factor analysis is the distinct regional pattern which emerges from the individual factors whose values for forty-eight states are shown in Table 14. These patterns can be seen most clearly by dividing the states into quartiles based on factor scores on a map which indicates the lowest rank by a light color and moves to heavier shades with increasing scores.

Factor 1 (Map I) shows the manufacturing belt of the Northeast as well as California in the top quartile; New York ranks first with a factor value of 2623. The Upper South is well represented in the second quartile, joined by Minnesota and Missouri in the Midwest as well as Oregon on the West Coast. The leading states of the South are North Carolina and Tennessee, with factor values of 881 and 806. The Lower South makes up the third quartile, joined by Iowa and

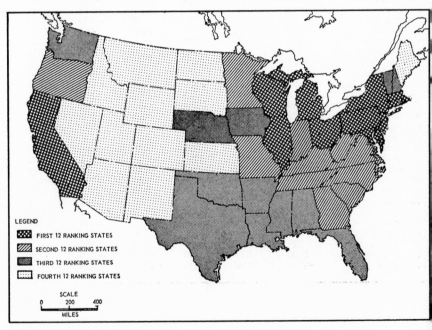

**Map I.** Factor 1 Quartiles for 48 States, 1960

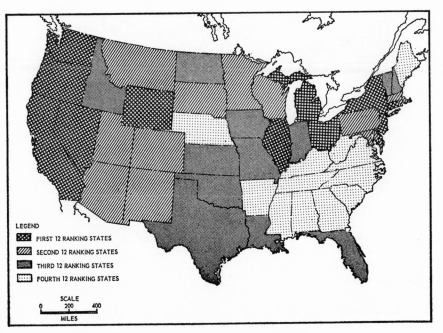

**Map II.** Factor 2 Quartiles for 48 States, 1960

Nebraska in the Midwest, New Hampshire and Vermont in the Northeast, as well as Washington on the West Coast. The Rocky Mountain states are at the bottom of the list, with the lowest factor values recorded for Nevada ($-4662$) and Wyoming ($-4759$).

Factor 2 (Map II) tells quite a different story. Services and other indices associated with Factor 2 rank highest in Nevada (3693), followed by states with high-income metropolitan centers, such as New York (2750), California (2488), and Illinois (2213). None of the Southern states appears in the second quartile, which rather shows a grouping of states with low population density, such as South Dakota (682), Colorado (643), Montana (556), New Mexico (510), and Arizona (468). Of the South, only Florida ($-179$) and Louisiana ($-478$) register in the third quartile, while all the remaining states of the region cluster at the bottom of the scale, with the lowest values of Factor 2 recorded for North Carolina ($-2479$), Arkansas ($-2637$), South Carolina ($-2960$), and Mississippi ($-4456$).

Factor 3 (Map III) shows the importance of textiles in the economic development of the South. Three Southern states appear in the

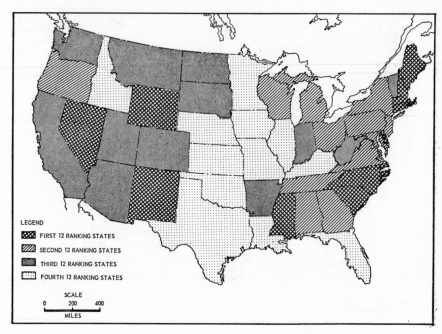

**Map III.** Factor 3 Quartiles for 48 States, 1960

top quartile, with South Carolina leading (1246); and most of the remaining states are recorded in the second quartile. Only Florida (−835), Kentucky (−967), and Louisiana (−1651) check at the lower end of the scale. Similarly, the South ranks high with Factor 4 (Map IV), influenced by farm values, per capita production of electric energy, and especially the chemical industry. As many as seven Southern states are grouped in the top quartile, with Virginia (1254) and Louisiana (1125) leading. All the remaining Southern states, except one, appear in the second quartile. The only exception is provided by Kentucky (−112) in the third quartile. The Northeast occupies the bottom rank in this category, with Vermont (−3134) taking the last place.

Of special interest for an understanding of interregional income flows appear the relations between Factor 1 and 2 (Figures 1 and 2), which reveal three distinct trade patterns within the United States. First, there are the "mature" states with high rankings on both, Factor 1 as well as Factor 2 (upper right corners of Figures 1 and 2): New York, California, Illinois, Connecticut, and New Jersey stand out in

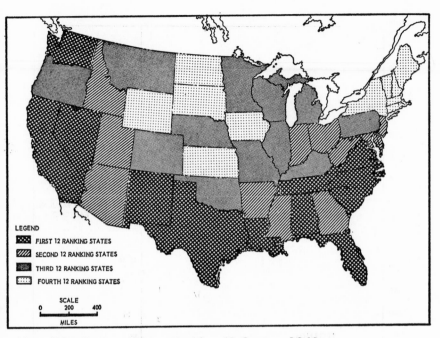

**Map IV.** Factor 4 Quartiles for 48 States, 1960

terms of manufacturing as well as other economic activities characteristic of metropolitan centers. Second, there are the states with low ratings for Factor 1 but high for Factor 2 (upper left corners of Figures 1 and 2): states with little manufacturing and low population density yet relatively high per capita income, like Nevada and Wyoming. These states have in common large service exports to the more industrialized parts of the country, whether these be government, tourist, or transportation services. Third, there are the states with low ratings for Factor 2 but relatively high scores on Factor 1 (lower right corners of Figures 1 and 2): states with limited local markets but large exports of manufactured goods. All the states of this last category are in the South, which has retained a remarkable homogeneity in these terms. Only Florida and Louisiana are slightly above the main cluster because of their relatively high Factor 2 ratings. At the other extreme, Mississippi appears well below the typical Southern position because of its exceedingly low rating on Factor 2.

These findings would support the hypothesis that the South has been essentially an export economy slow in developing its own mar-

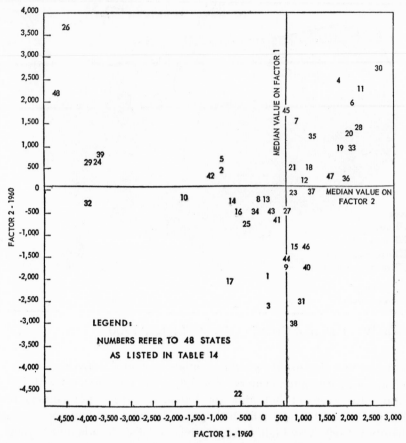

**Figure 1.** Factor 1 and 2 Relations for 48 States, 1960

kets, with relatively high rankings for manufacturing in general (Factor 1) as well as textiles (Factor 3) and chemicals (Factor 4) in particular, yet low rankings for the growth and welfare indices of Factor 2. They would suggest the persistence of a situation long familiar from the historical record of the South. Taken for a single year alone, however, they add little to our understanding of changes which may have occurred over the last generation in the role the South has been playing in the national economy.

To provide at least the beginning of a time series related to the 1960 cross-section data, a comparable factor analysis has been undertaken for 1940. The 1940 data matrix had 26 percent of the total sum

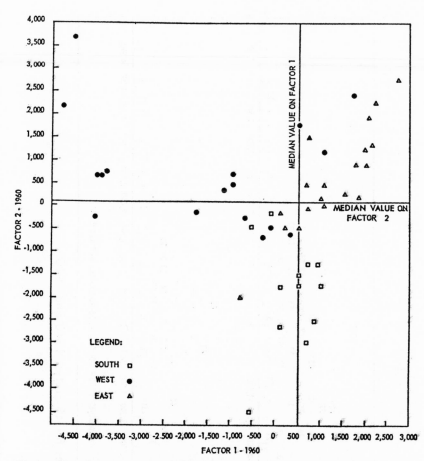

**Figure 2.** Factor 1 and 2 Relations for 3 Regions, 1960

of squares accounted for by Factor 1, in contrast to only 21 percent in 1960. Likewise, Factors 3, 4, and 5 all accounted for a higher percentage in 1940 than in 1960, reflecting the heavier weight of individual manufacturing industries a generation ago. Factor 2, on the other hand, counted only 11 percent in 1940, against 15 percent in 1960. These findings confirm the general impression that the relative importance of manufacturing in the explanation of over-all economic development has been decreasing. Just as the spectacular productivity increases in agriculture and mining have led to a continuous decline in the inputs of "primary" industries, so have output gains in manufacturing decreased the relative role of employment in the "sec-

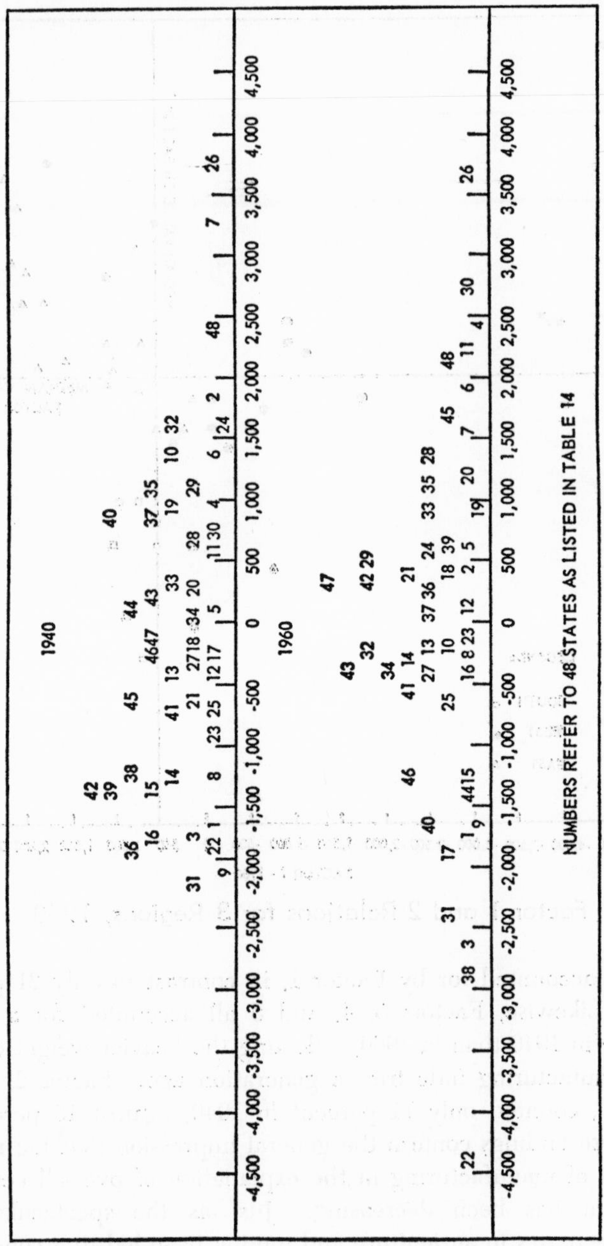

**Figure 3.** Factor 2 Values for 48 States, 1940 and 1960

ondary" industries. The result has been a marked advance throughout the national economy in the role of the "tertiary" trade and service sectors represented by Factor 2.

The implications of this shift for the South are twofold. First, as the South grows with the nation, a corresponding shift from primary and secondary to tertiary industries should be expected. Yet, second, if the South is to broaden its industrial composition and shed the past of a colonial export economy, its rate of shifting from Factor 1 to Factor 2 should surpass the nation just because its traditional characteristic has been such a sharp divergence of these two factors, whose persistence through 1960 has already been observed. The 1940 factor analysis suggests the following findings:

First, the dispersion of Factor 2 values among the states has increased rather than decreased over the last twenty years, ranging from —2200 (North Carolina) to +3600 (Nevada) in 1940 and from —4500 (Mississippi) to +3700 (again Nevada) in 1960 (Figure 3). This surprising result would appear to contradict the well-known narrowing of regional income differentials in the American economy. Yet it must be remembered that Factor 2 is weighted not only by welfare indices but also by the location of liquid-asset holdings and a wide variety of "tertiary" industries. The great spatial mobility of the American people has led to a new functional specialization among the states and resultant new interregional trade patterns, illustrated by the unique role Nevada and Florida play in the American economy.

Second, the heavy concentration of the South in the lowest quartile was much less marked in 1940 than in 1960. This, another surprising result, would appear to suggest a deterioration rather than an improvement of the South's relative position over the last two decades. Yet the 1940 data were influenced by depressed conditions in many farm and mining areas outside the South, explaining the low 1940 ranking of states like Pennsylvania (—1800), South Dakota (—1500), and Utah (—1400).

Third, and perhaps most importantly, there have been shifts within the Southern cluster at the lower end of the Factor 2 scale. In 1960, Mississippi held the place at the extreme lower end (—4456), followed by South Carolina (—2960), Arkansas (—2637), and North Carolina (—2479). In 1940, North Carolina held the bottom place (—2153), followed by Georgia (—2069), Mississippi (—1873), Arkansas (—1839) and Louisiana (—1789). These findings would suggest several substages of economic development within the South, moving from the simple trade pattern of exporting primary and low-value secondary goods to the complex mutual interchange among more highly developed regional economies. It is during the early stages of industrialization that the dichotomy between Factor 1 and 2 is largest, illustrated by Georgia and North Carolina in 1940, by Mississippi in 1960. As the economy matures, leading to a broadening of its industrial composition and concomitant demographic changes, areas move up on the Factor 2 scale and narrow their factor spread.

## VII. Summary

The general growth of the South as an integral part of the nation can be described in rather precise terms by data on aggregate regional income and its industrial sources. The role of interregional income-flows in bringing about (or retarding) this growth can be stated only in the most tentative way, however. It appears a plausible hypothesis that the South has a "favorable" balance of trade and thus receives a net inflow of income from other regions. Such inflows on current account are reinforced by credits on capital and government account from the more highly industrialized sections of the country, leading to a chain reaction of current income receipts from "exports," capital inflows to finance these "exports," and "domestic" capital formation out of local savings made possible by the larger income receipts. The South is thus described as a model of economic development in an open economy. The sketchy data presented above do not appear to contradict such a thesis but may permit two very general observations.

First, again in analogy to international trade doctrine, it is of but minor importance whether the interregional balance of trade is favorable per se. The important matter is the contribution of net income flows to regional resource development. An "unfavorable" balance contributes to regional growth as long as "imports" raise the productivity of regional resources and thus facilitate regional income growth. Conversely, a "favorable" balance may retard regional growth as long as the net "export" surplus reflects primarily an inability—or unwillingness—of the region to "import" capital goods, a situation typical of much of the Southern economy until the recent past and characteristic of many underdeveloped single-product economies. Thus the fundamental improvement in the economic position of the South is not due to a recent shift in the relative size of the "export" surplus—the data would indicate the persistence of such a surplus for a rather long period of time—but rather to a shift in the composition of this surplus.  Until a generation ago, the surplus reflected primarily large farm "exports" to other regions at prices which spelled low per capita incomes and limited "imports."  Today, the surplus persists in spite of much larger "imports" and reflects the sizeable income transfers from other regions on service and government account.  This situation encourages further capital inflows on private business account in a self-accelerating process of regional development.  For further testing and refinement of this hypothesis, better data on the sources and uses of regional funds by major transactor groups may carry a higher priority than data on interregional income flows.

Second, growth does not proceed evenly.  As the South grows, it will lose its homogeneity.  Differences within the region thus become more interesting than regional aggregates, and an analysis of intra-regional income flows may be more revealing than interregional esti-mates of doubtful validity.  The vagueness of the above presentation can therefore be explained, and perhaps excused, in terms of the vast netting-out implied in discussing a region which contains the state with the highest national growth rate (Florida) as well as states whose income has seriously lagged behind the nation (Arkansas, Mississippi, West Virginia).  Within the South, as suggested by the time series factor analysis, a wide diversity of growth patterns can be found in spite of the common historical background.  There are areas with a large net inflow on current as well as capital account, as illustrated by Florida.  There are areas with a large net inflow on current, yet a much smaller inflow on capital account, as illustrated by Arkansas.  There are areas with a net inflow on current and a net outflow on cap-ital account, as illustrated by rural pockets losing population.  There are areas with net outflows on current and net inflows on capital account, as illustrated by the countryside engulfed by the growing metropolis and industrialization.  There may even be areas with net outflows on both current and capital accounts, as illustrated by the depressed mining towns of West Virginia and Kentucky.

These situations are of varying stability, of course.  No community could endure net outflows on both current and capital accounts for long without bankruptcy, a fate not unknown to small areas passed by the stream of productivity growth.  There are wide variations in the direction of interregional income flows, therefore, not only over space but also over time.  Only a region as vast as the South viewed over the time span of a generation, netting out a multitude of spatial cross-currents as well as cyclical fluctuations, can be expected to show the stability claimed above.  Interregional income flows, among small areas as well as large regions, suggest the manifold ways in which spatial sub-sectors interact to overcome resource immobilities and thus to become integral parts of the nation.  Their analysis should serve as a useful tool to evaluate policy alternatives for regional economic development.

# PART THREE

## Introductory Summary

In the first paper in Part Three, Marshall Colberg observes that the passage of the Area Redevelopment Act has pushed the United States into rather intensive federal internal development activity on an area basis. He asserts that this Act, which was justified primarily on the basis of distressed coal-mining regions, now covers roughly one-third of the nation's counties. Further, the author notes that this wide coverage makes it more likely that large additional appropriations for federal loans and grants will be sought and that the program may well develop into one of substantial control of industrial location. He feels that both the price system and state and local subsidies will be relied upon less, and federal administrative discretion, loans, and subsidies relied upon more, in guiding the economic development of the United States. He looks with disfavor on these prospects.

Colberg notes that the redevelopment authority may not make loans to help finance the relocation of plants from non-distressed to distressed areas. This, he says, is inconsistent with the basic idea that the federal government is able to distinguish between and to improve the prevailing patterns. He feels that the taxpayer is subject to a type of blackmail, especially since help is given on an all-or-nothing basis. The facts that the commuting habits of people may affect an area's classification, and that selected distribution of races may benefit some places and not others; the uniqueness of aid on a geographic basis; and the large discretion given to an administrative agency under an untested (in fact unknown) type of program are disturbing. In particular, the author stresses the condition that per capita income in the South is approximately 70 percent of the nation's per capita income, while the South's share of depressed areas is scarcely greater, relatively speaking, than that of the non-South. Possibly Colberg's greatest concern centers on the thought that while natural forces may move plants from northern states to Southern, the ARA may tend to restrain this result. To put it mildly, Colberg prefers market forces to governmental controls as a general rule.

The theme of the Greenhut-Stewart paper is that space islands will arise under competitive market forces and, with their identification on regional levels, industrial development will take place. They use the paint industry and the South as empiric cornerstones for their theory, showing both the locational pattern in the industry and the basis for locating paint plants in the South. Along with Colberg, the writers lean towards the idea that if competitive market forces are maintained, a reasonable distribution of industry, based on principles of comparative advantage, must result. Whether or not, however, the development takes place as soon as might be the case under government planning, such as under ARA programs, is not considered. The subject paper is concerned chiefly with setting forth their location theory, using the paint industry and the South as vehicles for examining the theory, and studying the basis for regional economic development.

The authors contend that plant location in every industry is not exclusively cost-determined, and suggest that the paint industry illustrates a locational pattern strongly influenced by the geography of demand. In particular, they claim that different spatial price policies affect the choice of optimum location of manufacturing plants and note that national paint manufacturers follow the rough outlines of a uniform by zone delivered price policy, whereas local manufacturers generally price f.o.b. mill. Under the existing spatial price regime, local firms are induced to locate away from the plants of national firms, and in higher-price zones, maximizing phantom freight. Part of the paint market belongs to national firms, part (perhaps one-third) to smaller local firms.

Using data for the South on per capita income, population, and value added by paint-using industries, the authors find that sales in the South fell well below the area's sales potential. A "space island" may then exist in the South, offering the opportunity for increases in production and sales in the area.

The Ferguson paper uses the Arrow-Chenery-Minhas-Solow form of a constant-elasticity-of-substitution, linearly homogeneous production function to allocate fixed and working capital among the nine Census regions for each of the 20 two-digit S.I.C. industries. The NBER capital estimates prepared by Creamer and Borenstein are taken as the benchmark data.

Regional allocations are made in the following manner. First, the elasticity of substitution between labor and capital is estimated for each industry by means of cross-section (regional) data on value added per man-year and wages per man-year. Ferguson next observes that by using the ACMS function and the Creamer-Borenstein national capital estimates, one may infer regional capital magnitudes via the computed elasticity of substitution. He allocates fixed capital by this device, and allocates working capital according to the proportion which holds in each industry between regional and national compensation of employees. On the basis of this regional allocation of capital, regional capital-labor ratios, capital-value added ratios, and regional rates of gross quasi-rent are computed. These ratios and their rates of change are compared among Census regions. In addition, a weighted average of the three Southern regions is compared to the national average. Various statistical tests are performed in order to determine whether factors causing regional differences may be isolated.

Ferguson observes that the three Southern regions he worked with were second only to the Pacific West in the rate of growth of capital stock over the period 1954–58. He finds the rate of technological progress in the South to be greater than the national average. His study indicates that the South Atlantic is the fastest growing region in the South and that capital growth in the South has been especially rapid in the primary metals and miscellaneous industry and even more rapid yet in the textile, electric machinery, and instrument industries. In some contrast, the national average rate of gross quasi-rent either increased more or decreased less than the Southern average. Reasons for the different rates of growth are suggested.

In the final two papers, the South has been used to examine problems which probably are not unique to this particular area insofar as their origin or general impacts are concerned.

In the first of these, Robert Haveman examines the investment criteria used by the federal government as applied to "The Postwar Corps of Engineers Program in Ten Southern States." He describes the Corps program in the South, and discusses the several criteria based on the benefit-cost ratio which are used in evaluating government projects. The author then uses the alternative criteria as vehicles for determining the validity of projects by the Corps of Engineers in the South, and finally examines their probable impact on Southern economic development. Haveman concludes that a great number of projects have been constructed which would not have been constructed if economic efficiency had been the sole objective. On balance, however, despite misallocation, he ventures the opinion that Southern economic development has been aided through such elements as the encouragement (essentially indirect) of agricultural out-migration and the capital attraction which is present in various types of projects.

James Rinehart uses a sample of communities in the South to study rates of return on municipal subsidies to industry. He examines twenty-two firms in ten different localities. He concludes that "even on the basis of the assumption that subsidized firms are fly-by-night concerns (which is not even near the actual truth of the matter), under the present system of subsidization, industrial subsidy investments are still extremely profitable." He ends his paper with the caveat that his conclusions "are independent of a general acceptance of competitive subsidization of industry . . . [since his study was] strictly concerned with the profitability of industrial subsidization from the point of view of the local community." Rinehart was not concerned with the problem of economy-wide allocation (or misallocation) of resources.

# X

## Area Redevelopment and Related Federal Programs: Effects on the South

*By Marshall R. Colberg*

Southern economic development, like that of the rest of the nation and, indeed, much of the world, is affected by legislative, executive, and judicial actions of the federal government of the United States. Defense and space exploration stand out among these activities. However, I will confine the present paper to federal programs and policies which have their main effects on the costs of business firms and hence on Southern economic development. Greatest emphasis will be placed on the Area Redevelopment program and its consistency with other federal lending programs, with minimum wage legislation, and with other programs that are supposed to alleviate unemployment. The coverage will necessarily be incomplete even as to costs.

### Area Redevelopment Act

The Area Redevelopment program in which the Department of Commerce and other federal and state agencies are busily engaged was "sold" to the last Congress primarily as a way of relieving chronic unemployment in the coal mining areas. In the language used by Rutledge Vining at the 1961 Inter-University Committee conference, the "problem" perceived by certain legislators was considered to be reflected in the larger percentage and greater persistence of unemployment among coal miners than among most identifiable major groups of workers. On the assumption that the federal government should "do something," a reasonable "solution" might have been conceived in terms directly pertinent to unemployed coal miners, such as vocational retraining, subsidies to mobility, research to uncover new uses and new markets for coal, and reduction in union monopoly power. Instead, a far more costly and much less certain system of federal loans and subsidies to new industry of all kinds in "distressed areas" was instituted. Geographic coverage was made very wide in order to win the necessary political support, thus greatly blurring the distressed-area concept. The Area Redevelopment Act includes the following principal provisions:

(1) "Redevelopment areas" in which "substantial and persistent" unemployment exists are to be designated by the Secretary of Commerce primarily on the basis of a formula given in the law. In addition, rural redevelopment areas are to be designated. (Specifications for designating areas will be stated and examined later in the present paper.)

(2) Loans may be made by the federal government to public and private applicants to assist in financing within these areas the purchase or development of land and facilities for industrial or commercial use. A total of $100 million is authorized for rural redevelopment areas. Loans are for a maximum of twenty-five years and are not to exceed 65 percent of total cost, excluding all other federal aid.

(3) Another $100 million in loans is made available to state or political subdivisions or non-profit organizations representing any redevelopment area or part of an area, for the purchase or development of land for public facilities or for construction or improvement of public facilities. These loans are for a maximum of forty years at an interest rate equal to that paid by the federal government plus one-fourth of 1 percent. This interest rate is lower by one-fourth of 1 percent than the rate on the 25 year loans described in (2) above. Also the full cost of the public facilities can be financed by these loans.

(4) Grants to the extent of $75 million are authorized for land acquisition or development for public facilities and for the construction and improvement of public facilities. These grants are not to exceed the difference between the amount needed and the amount which can be met with other resources, including a loan under the Act.

(5) A redevelopment area must secure approval of an overall program for economic development before it becomes eligible for loans and grants.

(6) Occupational training and retraining may be assisted, where

needed, by means of contractual arrangements with public or private educational institutions. A total of $4.5 million is authorized for this purpose.

(7) A total of $10 million is provided for retraining subsistence payments to individuals residing in redevelopment areas and certified to be undertaking retraining.

(8) Other provisions relate to anti-pirating, amendment of the urban renewal provisions of the Housing Act of 1949, extension of federal wage fixing under the Davis-Bacon Act, research, amendment of the Small Business Investment Act of 1958, penalties, and administrative matters.

## Occupational Retraining

A major dilemma in connection with the retraining program is lack of information regarding the number of persons with particular skills needed in particular places. The Department of Labor has done relatively little to secure such information. A basic difficulty is that workers in any trade will seldom admit there is a relative shortage of labor in that trade. This is especially true when labor is organized and where the relative undersupply has been created by a deliberate policy of restricting membership through long apprenticeship or other means.

In competitive labor markets there are no absolute "shortages" of workers because wage rates equate the number demanded with the number supplied. The only measure of relative shortages is found in wage rates which appear to be above the long-run normal in the sense that they are out of line with wage rates in other occupations with a similar degree of training, hardship, constancy of employment, and the other factors detailed by Adam Smith nearly two hundred years ago. Detection of such shortages is a difficult empirical problem.

Success in a federal training and retraining program will require the discovery of specific places in which above-normal wage rates exist and appear likely to persist in view especially of demand factors that can be anticipated. Retraining may have to be accompanied by subsidies to permit workers to move to other parts of the country where suitable job opportunities may exist. However, opposition from labor groups already located in these non-depressed areas may be anticipated. In the rural South, especially, the concept of "retraining" is often not applicable. Instead, the need of a portion of the Negro population, particularly, may be for basic education in reading and writing as a preliminary to vocational training. The problem of preparing displaced agricultural workers to fill industrial jobs requiring a fair degree of skill appears to be particularly difficult. On the other hand, their non-union status should be helpful in the search for re-employment.

A basic defect of the Area Redevelopment Act is its coupling of vocational retraining with the distressed-area concept. If it is sound in principle for the federal government to aid chronically unemployed persons by means of retraining, the aid should not be restricted to residents of redevelopment areas. Relief given on a direct personal basis should not be geared to area characteristics. Indeed, similarly needy people, whatever their geographic location, should be afforded equal opportunities by the federal government. The theory underlying the retraining provisions of the Area Redevelopment Act is that chronically unemployed persons in coal mining and other hard-hit areas have very little chance of securing worthwhile local employment without extensive training in the skills currently in demand. However, much the same situation exists for unskilled individuals in relatively prosperous areas. There may, in fact, be greater returns from retraining in the *non*-redevelopment areas because migration by retrainees to other communities is less likely to be necessary. Actual use of newly acquired skills is more likely by those trained within the relatively prosperous areas.

There is some evidence that unemployed workers are less anxious to receive retraining than has been commonly assumed. In a pilot retraining program in Huntington, West Virginia, only about 10 percent of the unemployed workers applied for retraining.[1] This appears to support the view that much of the unemployment even in the most depressed areas is to a greater degree "cyclical" and to a lesser degree "structural" than is commonly assumed. That is, most of the unemployed expect to be called back to work or are at least very reluctant to retrain quickly for occupations that may pay lower wage rates than those for which they are already trained. It seems likely that this problem of worker disinterest will be less important in the more typical Southern states, where union organization has not created, as it has in West Virginia, so many monopolistic discrepancies between wage rates in alternative occupations for which an individual may readily qualify.

1. "Jobless Snub Chance to Learn New Skills," *Charlotte News* (Charlotte, North Carolina), Wednesday, December 27, 1961.

## Unemployment and Other Criteria for Eligibility

The framers of the Area Redevelopment Act set up different criteria for eligibility under sections 5(a) and 5(b) of the Act. For the most part, the provisions of 5(a) apply to the relatively concentrated labor market areas, while those of 5(b) are designed to bring in the poorer rural counties.

To qualify under section 5(a), current unemployment must be 6 percent or more and must both have averaged this rate and have exceeded the national average (1) by 50 percent for three of the four preceding calendar years, or (2) by 75 percent for two of the preceding three years, or (3) by 100 percent for one of the two preceding years. The formula attempts to give weight to both the volume and duration of unemployment. Like all such formulas, it is arbitrary and no more "correct" than any number of alternative formulas that might have been written into the law. Yet different selections of "distressed areas" will result from different formulas.

No attempt was made by Congress to set forth so specific a formula for qualification under section 5(b). This was left instead to administrative discretion. However, some "relevant factors" are set forth for qualification under section 5(b). These are: number of low-income farm families; proportion of such families; relationship of their income levels to general levels in the United States; extent of rural redevelopment projects previously located in an area by the Department of Agriculture; current and prospective employment opportunities; availability of manpower; extent of out-migration of population; and proportion of the population receiving public assistance. To the problem of deriving uniform criteria from this conglomeration of variables for urban and rural areas is added the legislative requirement that redevelopment projects be distributed widely among the states so that experience under a great variety of conditions may be obtained. This tends to give a political and experimental flavor to the whole program rather than to suggest a concentrated effort to improve conditions in the most distressed areas.

The Department of Agriculture and other agencies assisted the Area Redevelopment Administration in making section 5(b) criteria more explicit. As of July 23, 1961, the published criteria were:

(1) Areas of Low Income—where the average annual family income is less than one-third of the national average.

(2) Areas of Low Farm-Income—where the average annual income of farm families is less than 25 percent of the national average, excluding counties with metropolitan cities.

(3) Rural Development Counties—counties included in the Rural Areas Development Program of the Department of Agriculture, as of May 1, 1961.

(4) Areas of Low Production Farming—where there are 60 percent or more of Class VI commercial farms (as defined by the Bureau of the Census) among all commercial farms in the area.

(5) Indian Reservations—where there is substantial unemployment or underemployment, discounting seasonal or temporary factors; or where there are inadequate resources in terms of population support, or where individual family incomes are substantially below those of the non-Indian rural population in surrounding areas, and also below the level necessary to achieve a reasonable living standard; or where a high proportion of the Indian population is dependent wholly or partially on public and general assistance welfare programs.

(6) Very Small Areas of Substantial and Persistent Unemployment: Areas with a labor force of under 15,000 will be eligible if the approximate rate of unemployment, on the basis of the best available data, is currently 6 percent or more, and if the approximate annual average joblessness rate, on the basis of the best available data, has been substantially above the national average for the greater part of the preceding four calendar years, or 75 percent above the national average for two of the preceding three years, or 100 percent above the average for one of the preceding two years.[2]

In order to insure that *all* states in the nation be permitted to have redevelopment areas; the following administrative ruling was made on July 20, 1961:

"In any State *where no area shall* have otherwise qualified under the Act, an appropriate economic development area consisting of one or more counties may be designated (1) where the median annual income of families and unrelated individuals is lower than the median annual income in any other area with approximately the same population within the State or (2) where the unemployment in the county or counties is most severe within the State, or (3) where the Federally-aided assistance rates are among the highest in the State."[3]

2. *ARA Information Memo*, U.S. Department of Commerce, July 23, 1961.
3. *ARA Information Memo*, U.S. Department of Commerce, July 20, 1961.

## Appraisal of the Criteria

The last-mentioned "catch-all" criteria are the loosest of all. Under the wording used, it would be legally possible for a highly prosperous state to divide its territory into two parts of approximately equal population and to have the less prosperous half designated as a "redevelopment area." This is getting far away indeed from the original "distressed area" concept that motivated the legislation!

A more important and highly questionable criterion for eligibility as a redevelopment area is participation in the federal Rural Development Program as of May 1, 1961. This program, administered by the U.S. Department of Agriculture, involves community cooperation in a wide range of projects, utilizing all available agencies such as State Extension Services; the U.S. Small Business Administration; the Department of Health, Education, and Welfare; and others. This appears to be a useful, though low-powered, program for improving rural communities. However, the inclusion of nearly two hundred counties in the United States as redevelopment areas solely on the basis of the prior existence of such cooperative efforts is not consistent with the "distressed area" approach. This is particularly the case when a large number of Rural Development projects were added after the 1960 national election results were known and it was quite clear that there would be a distressed-areas Act. In Pennsylvania, nineteen counties were added to the Rural Development program subsequent to July 1960 but in time for automatic designation as redevelopment areas. In Texas, thirty-nine counties qualify for area redevelopment grants and loans solely on the basis of this type of cooperative rural action.[4] In Nebraska, twelve counties and, in Indiana, nine counties were qualified solely on the basis of this type of rural activity. It is clear that aggressive state and local action and political know-how, rather than comparative economic need, will in part determine the directions of federal subsidies to rural areas.

## Rules vs. Administrative Discretion

The eligibility criteria as a whole, under the Area Redevelopment Act, represent quite a typical compromise between rules and discretion in the exercise of federal control. In his famous article on rules versus discretion in monetary policy, Henry Simons favored

4. This has led to vigorous protests from businessmen who do not like to have Eastern Texas labelled a "distressed area." See: "East Texas Rejects 'Depressed' Label," *Industrial Development,* Vol. 130, No. 13, 1961.

definite, simple rules to govern the stock of money.[5]   A nod in this direction is made by Congress in the Area Redevelopment Act by the establishment of required percentages of unemployment for prescribed time periods.   However, in large part Congress allowed the administrators discretion in the *making* of rules and formulas governing eligibility.   This was especially the case with respect to rural redevelopment but also shows up in Section 5(a) where it is stated that designations should be made on "the basis of standards generally comparable" to those specified by means of unemployment formulas.   On the whole, the program is one which involves substantial administrative discretion in determining which areas shall be eligible, although it is carried out in the guise of a program which operates according to rules. In the matter of determining actual loans and grants, administrative discretion is complete.

A good deal of discretion on the part of statisticians derives from the inadequacy of unemployment data, especially for small labor markets.   Reporting is adequate only for persons covered by unemployment insurance, leaving the actual extent of joblessness on the part of other groups subject to estimation.   There is a strong temptation to statisticians to "make" unemployment average 6 percent or some other qualifying figure when administrative officials would like to see an area designated for redevelopment.   Adjacent counties in adjoining states are especially subject to unlike treatment, since different statisticians are in action at the state levels and different agencies are in charge of applying for redevelopment status.

### Extent of Geographic Coverage

The eligibility criteria which have been described are sufficiently loose to permit a large part of the United States to be classified as eligible for redevelopment.   As of November 13, 1961, there were 1,035 counties or parts of counties eligible.   The broad extent of coverage is evident when this figure is compared with the total of 3,099 counties in the entire country.[6]   Some exaggeration of the percentage of the nation's area covered by the federal redevelopment program is inherent in this comparison because Western states, where counties are usually large, have a smaller proportion of redevelopment counties than the rest of the country, despite inclusion of numerous Indian

5. "Rules versus Authorities in Monetary Policy," *Journal of Political Economy*, Vol. XLIV, No. 1, February 1936.
6. This figure includes 20 election districts in Alaska and 9 islands in Hawaii.

**Table 1.** The South's Share of Redevelopment Counties as of November 13, 1961*

| Southern States | Total No. of Counties | Redevelopment Counties[a] | Percentage of Redevelopment Counties |
|---|---|---|---|
| Alabama | 67 | 31 | 46% |
| Arkansas | 75 | 26 | 35 |
| Georgia | 159 | 64 | 40 |
| Florida | 67 | 11 | 16 |
| Kentucky | 120 | 67 | 56 |
| Louisiana | 64 | 18 | 28 |
| Mississippi | 82 | 53 | 65 |
| North Carolina | 100 | 31 | 31 |
| South Carolina | 46 | 23 | 50 |
| Tennessee | 95 | 40 | 42 |
| Texas | 254 | 48 | 19 |
| Virginia | 98 | 9 | 9 |
| West Virginia | 55 | 44 | 80 |
| Total South | 1,282 | 465 | 37 |
| Rest of Nation | 1,817 | 570 | 31 |
| United States | 3,099 | 1,035 | 33 |

* Source: Reports of the Area Redevelopment Administration.
a In a few cases, parts of counties are counted.

reservations. Nevertheless, it is clear that so much of the nation is now designated as "depressed" that the redevelopment program is not geared to attacking the type of structural unemployment that gave the program its original political motivation. It appears that either the program will have to be financed much more heavily, or the number of areas eligible for federal assistance will have to be sharply reduced. With available funds small in relation to the area to be "redeveloped," there is much danger that actual grants and loans will be made increasingly on political grounds.

The South's share of the nation's redevelopment counties, as of November 13, 1961, is shown in Table 1. Of the 1,282 counties in the thirteen Southern states, 465, or 37 percent, were eligible for federal assistance. In West Virginia, 80 percent of the counties were eligible; in Mississippi, 65 percent; and in Kentucky, 56 percent.

Of 1,817 counties in the non-South, 570, or 31 percent, were considered to be depressed. While this comparison suggests that the South has its full share of redevelopment areas, this is less obvious when the relative need of the region for economic development is considered. As one indicator of this need, per capita income in the South has in recent years averaged about 68 percent of that of the non-South.[7] The picture of the South's relative treatment under the Area Redevelopment program will not be clear until the region's actual share of grants, loans, and retraining allowances can be calculated. As indicated elsewhere in this paper, it is probable that Southern development will be hampered, relatively if not absolutely, by the program.

### Anti-Pirating Provisions

A great deal of discussion in the Congressional hearings on area redevelopment centered around the danger of "pirating" of plants by eligible areas aided by government subsidies. The resulting "anti-pirating clause" in the Area Redevelopment Act is not a model of clarity. It reads:

Such financial assistance shall not be extended . . . to assist establishments relocating from one area to another. The limitation . . . shall not be construed to prohibit assistance for the expansion of an existing business entity through the establishment of a new branch, affiliate, or subsidiary of such entity if the Secretary finds that the establishment of such branch, affiliate, or subsidiary will not result in an increase in unemployment in the area of original location or in any other area where such entity conducts business operations, unless the Secretary has reason to believe that such branch, affiliate, or subsidiary is being established with the intention of closing down the operations of the existing business entity in the area of its original location or in any other area where it conducts such operations.[8]

Congressional hearings relating to this provision revealed a typical concert of interest between political representatives of New England states and organized labor who want to block the relocation of firms to the South. A typical statement from the 1961 hearings before a Senate subcommittee is the following:

Mr. Bush (Senator from Connecticut): "We have lost a good many plants to the South, and only recently, the most recent one I think of is at Bristol, the Ingram Co., manufacturers of watches, has transferred a large part of their operations to the South because of what appear to

7. William H. Nicholls, *Southern Tradition and Regional Progress* (Chapel Hill: The University of North Carolina Press, 1960), p. 179.

Charles T. Taylor in a paper "Patterns of Regional Growth in the United States," delivered at the Conference on Area Development at Athens, Georgia, Jan. 9, 1962, states that, in 1960, per capita income in the Southeast was 72 percent of the national average. (The difference would be smaller, however, for the white population measured separately.)

8. Pub. Law 87-27, 87th Congress, S.1, May 1, 1961. Sec. 6(a).

be more economical, more competitive conditions that exist there that will enable them to become more competitive.

Now, in S.1 there is no real prohibition against the use of Federal funds in connection with relocating plants from one area to another, but in S.9 there is a prohibition which I will read to you. It is called the antipirating clause, and this is what it says: "Such financial assistance shall not be used for working capital, for the purchase of machinery or equipment, or to assist establishments relocating from one area to another."

My good friend the Chairman, has refused to accept that amendment. I have offered on the floor and in the debate which ensued he said he could not take it because he was afraid it would lose Southern support for his bill if that were put in there.[9]

Despite Southern opposition, the strong anti-pirating provision already quoted was written into the bill as finally enacted. Sufficient Southern support was secured to pass the whole bill through inclusion of low-income rural areas among those eligible for redevelopment assistance.

The emotional impact of relocation of plants, especially from one state to another, is indicated by the strong phrase "pirating" which is now commonly applied to the situation. The implication is that plants relocate entirely because of the vigorous promotional efforts of state and local authorities who may give tax concessions, free or low rent, or other inducements. While such activities are important, it is probable that most of the "pirating" is done by the more conventional forces of demand and supply. The impersonal forces of the market have fallen into low repute indeed in national political circles! The illusion that industry is attracted mainly through the vigorous efforts of development commissions and similar groups is promoted by these organizations, which like to take credit for locational decisions that would for the most part have been made anyway.

The natural forces of demand and cost work to move plants more often from the North to the South than vice versa. This is especially true in industries in which labor is strongly organized in the North and unorganized or weakly organized in the South. As a consequence, anti-pirating provisions are more likely to work against the South. It is interesting to note that the Area Redevelopment Administration may not make loans even to help finance the movement of a plant from a non-distressed area into a distressed area. This is inconsistent

9. Hearings Before a Subcommittee of the Committee on Banking and Currency, United States Senate, Eighty-Seventh Congress, First Session on S.1, S.6, S.9 and S.750, p. 378.

with the basic idea that the federal government is able to distinguish between areas that are sorely in need of additional industrial jobs and those that are not, and that it should "do something" about the problem.

It appears that not only are plants not to be helped to relocate, but they are to be helped *not* to move. The Administrator of the Area Redevelopment Act has recently publicized an application from a plant which "intends to move" if it does not receive a federal loan. This appears to be a particularly dangerous type of situation because it subjects the American taxpayers to a type of blackmail in the name of area redevelopment. In effect, the owners of plants in redevelopment areas (and these cover a substantial part of the country, as has been noted) can say they must be given federal aid "or else." Loans made on this basis are especially likely to be detrimental to the South. Low-cost capital provided by the Federal government becomes a particularly direct countermeasure to the comparative advantage which may have built up in another area.

The Department of Labor classifies relatively few major labor market areas as having "relatively low unemployment" and usually none as having "overall labor shortages." However, about 60 percent of such areas are designated as having "moderate unemployment" (3 to 5.9 percent of the labor force).[10] If federal intervention in plant location is sound in principle, it should not be improper to help finance the relocation of a plant from an area of moderate unemployment to one of substantial unemployment so long as the move does not bring down the classification of the area losing the plant to the level of those considered to be distressed.

### Area vs. Industry Relief

While foreign aid to underdeveloped nations has become commonplace, an internal program of economic relief on a geographic basis is unusual. Such a program does occur in the urban renewal program, however, and in the relatively weak rural redevelopment program recently renamed the Rural Areas Development Program. To some extent federal power projects, river and harbor work, and highway work also are of this nature. Typically, however, federal programs have been on an industry basis. Agricultural programs provide the outstanding example. Subsidies to shipbuilding, railroads,

10. *Supplement to Area Labor Market Trends,* August 1961, U.S. Dept. of Labor (Washington, D.C.).

airlines, and construction materials for veterans' housing are further examples. Price fixing during the 1930's in the bituminous coal industry and under N.R.A. codes, tariffs and quotas in international trade; enforcement of "fair trade" prices; gold, silver, and uranium purchases; and numerous other instances of federal action relating to price on an industry basis can be cited.

American economic history shows continual and often dramatic changes in the composition of output. Few of the largest industries in the nation, such as motor vehicles and equipment, aircraft and parts, organic chemicals, communication equipment, electrical machinery, or metal-working machinery, were of much importance in 1900. In well-diversified communities there is a good chance that declining employment opportunities in some industries will be offset by improving opportunities in other economic activities. Where this offset is incomplete, a moderate amount of out-migration may readily prevent serious unemployment. But where a geographic area is dominated by a single industry, declining employment in that activity is more likely to attract notice and to stimulate federal intervention. Coal mining and many types of agriculture are by nature specialized to certain geographical areas and tend to dominate the economies of these areas. To a lesser degree, this has also been true of the textile industry, although the recent boom in electronics has helped diversify many New England textile towns. Demands for government aid have been especially insistent in the area-dominating industries.

Areas receiving most of their income from a single economic source may, in a broad sense, be considered recipients of economic rent. When this is also true of most of the laboring force, as is the case with coal miners, the demand for relief is especially strong. Coal miners, who seldom have immediate alternative employment opportunities at so high an hourly wage, are especially reluctant to migrate. Quite understandably, they, and especially the more experienced among them, hope that an increase in the demand for coal or the establishment of new industries, along with work-sharing plans, will make out-migration unnecessary.

The low-income rural areas are also recipients of economic rent in the short run, but the low-income residents of these areas receive little economic rent, since any alternative employment is about equally unremunerative. Migration is more attractive to these than to the coal miners because a job secured by a low-income agricultural worker in another area is very likely to pay more per hour, rather than less.

Paradoxically, it appears that in general there is a better chance to attract new industry into low-income agricultural areas than into the declining coal-mining areas. Strong unionization tends to make the hourly wage rates of unemployed miners inflexible on the downside. A new industry must be able to utilize the abilities of former coal miners about as fully as do the coal mines if it is to pay the same hourly wage rates. Unless these skills are especially valuable to a new firm, the plant locator is likely to be able to find a more attractive area elsewhere.

Plants that locate in former coal-mining areas are especially likely to be heavy-capital-using in nature. In West Virginia, some $12 billion has been invested since the end of World War II for industrial expansion.[11] However, much of this investment is in chemical plants which employ much capital—both material and human—but not large numbers of ex-coal miners. Also, part of the investment is in machinery that directly replaces miners.[12] While government assistance under the Area Redevelopment Act is supposed to be rendered only when it will make "a substantial contribution to the permanent relief of unemployment," this is too subjective a criterion to prevent assistance to plants which use little of the type of labor that is actually in chronic surplus. This appears especially likely to be the case in the coal-mining regions, where even a modest increase in employment will be avidly sought and where political influence is at present strong.

The possibility of being misled by treating labor as homogeneous, and unemployment in the aggregate, for purposes of area redevelopment is illustrated by some data that I have compiled for the typical Deep South states—Mississippi, Alabama, Georgia, and South Carolina. As of November 13, 1961, in Mississippi 53 out of 82 counties were classified as redevelopment counties; in Alabama, 31 out of the 67 counties were so classified; in Georgia, 64 of the 159 counties were called redevelopment areas; in South Carolina, 23 of the 46 counties were eligible areas. Roughly half of the counties in the large areas covered by these four states are eligible for federal redevelopment assistance.

Without question, all of the designated redevelopment counties,

11. George Macesich and Charles Stewart, *Economic Change and Adjustment,* U.S. Chamber of Commerce, Washington, D.C., December 1961, p. 8.
12. Ernst W. Swanson, in a paper, "Appraising Economic Development Potentials: The General Case," presented at a Conference on Area Redevelopment at Athens, Georgia, Jan. 8–10, 1962, points out, however, that a community securing a highly automated plant may eventually have a reduction in unemployment through the rise in the needs for general business and public services.

and most of those not so designated, are greatly in need of additional industrial facilities and other new and expanded economic activities. However, an examination of the 1960 population census reveals an interesting fact. For each of the four states, the proportions of non-whites is much larger, on the average, in the redevelopment counties than in the other counties. In Mississippi redevelopment counties, the non-white population made up 50.8 percent of the total population, while in non-redevelopment counties the percentage of non-whites was 26.5. In Alabama, the redevelopment counties averaged 42.8 percent non-whites compared with 22.8 percent in non-designated counties. For Georgia, the redevelopment counties averaged 39.3 percent non-white population, while the other counties averaged 28.8 percent. In South Carolina, the redevelopment counties had a 49.8 percent non-white population compared with 33.5 percent in the remaining counties.

It is clear that unemployment and low family incomes among the colored population weigh heavily in the statistics used to secure federal designation of redevelopment areas in these Southern States. Yet, if federal loans and grants persuade some firms to locate plants in these "distressed areas," the additional jobs may well go mainly to the white residents. This will result both from the propensity of many employers to discriminate and from the general lack of education and skills of the Negro population. A peculiar type of discrimination on the part of the federal government against white residents of non-redevelopment counties will ensue to the extent that the whole program is effective. That is, white workers in redevelopment counties may be aided in securing industrial jobs because of the large number of impecunious Negroes in the same counties. Equal unemployment or equally low family incomes among the white population in other counties will not generate federal relief activity under the Area Redevelopment Act.

## Redevelopment Boundaries

Problems involved in defining an "industry" are well known to economists. This is one of the great difficulties in measuring concentration of manufacturing in a useful way and in enforcement of the antitrust laws. It is also central to the famous controversy between Harvard's Edward Chamberlin and the "Chicago school" over whether "monopolistic competition" is a legitimate addition to the older theories of pure competition and monopoly. Stigler and Friedman, especially, have maintained that "groups" within which competition between sellers of differentiated products is close, and between which competition is remote, cannot be distinguished sharply. Chamberlin had to make the distinction in order to arrive at long-run equilibrium for the monopolistic firm with only normal returns on investment.

In part, the difficulty of sharply defining "depressed industries" led to the "depressed area" concept. Unfortunately, there are also serious difficulties in delineating areas for purposes of unlike treatment in a federal economic program. Under the Area Redevelopment Act, boundaries for the most part follow county lines, and contiguous areas are usually designated in order to provide "redevelopment areas" of substantial size. While this may be the most "practical" way of designating areas, it is not theoretically right. Redevelopment area boundaries are not drawn on a basis actually related to the problem (unemployment) which is to be solved. Consequently, it is inevitable that many parts of redevelopment areas will have less unemployment than many parts of non-redevelopment areas.

Political boundaries such as those of counties are relevant when the activity in question, such as the taxing of property and expenditure of tax receipts, is actually confined to the same area.[13] Unemployment ratios do not follow county lines except by accident. Also, the practice of commuting to and from work by car or other means may, for example, make a new plant in the northern part of a county more important to residents of the southern part of the county abutting on the north than to actual residents in the county where the new plant locates.

In an attempt to minimize the inequities due to the commuting habits of American workers, the Area Redevelopment Administration prefers to group a number of counties into fairly large redevelopment areas. This tends to bring about a closer relationship between the individuals who will actually work in any new facilities that are created and those who were counted as unemployed members of the labor force. (Nearly perfect agreement between the two groups would be secured by treating the entire nation as a single area.) However, the "distressed area" concept tends to become more obscure as redevelopment areas are made larger, since a larger number of relatively prosperous sub-areas are inevitably included and made eligible for federal preferential treatment. The situation is rather similar to

13. O. D. Duncan, R. P. Cuzzort, and B. Duncan, *Statistical Geography* (Glencoe: The Free Press, 1961), p. 33. The authors examine numerous problems in analyzing areal data.

that of white workers receiving preferential treatment if they reside in counties with large numbers of low-income colored families.

A somewhat similar problem is involved in the all-or-nothing nature of the assistance that is being provided by the federal government under the Area Redevelopment program. If it is felt appropriate that the federal government "do something" about relatively severe unemployment on an area basis, the Act is open to criticism in the following respect: If it be assumed that measurement is correct and areas are properly delineated (although neither is the case), unemployment is *almost* as serious a problem in an area which nearly qualifies under the established criteria as in one that barely does qualify. If it is proper to subsidize the latter area to a certain extent, it is also proper to subsidize the former area to nearly that extent. Actually it will receive nothing. By the same token, it would be appropriate to help an area with extremely high unemployment much more than one that barely qualifies. While this may be accomplished administratively, there is no built-in rule to insure this.

In some states, at least, the Area Redevelopment Administration has permitted areas which fail to meet the unemployment criteria to be included in the program.[14] This sort of blurring of the eligibility criteria gets around the arbitrariness of the formulas, in a fashion, but does not change the all-or-nothing character of the government assistance. Instead, it is apt to result in the substitution of political influence for economic need. Areas which barely fail to meet the less rigidly defined economic and political criteria for eligibility are still completely excluded.

This is the same type of problem that has been recognized in connection with priorities systems for materials and equipment in periods of emergency control of production in the United States. Priorities tend to secure for holders the entire amount needed, while those without ratings are able to get none at all. Multiple priority ratings (and black market activities) help to alleviate this situation by channeling some materials to uses that do not qualify as the most important. An allocation system proved to be much more satisfactory than a priorities system for channeling critical materials during World

14. Letter to writer from Koder M. Collison, Director, State of Ohio department of Industrial and Economic Development. (Reproduced in *Industrial Development and Manufacturers Record*, Vol. 130, No. 13, p. 3 as a comment on the writer's article in the same magazine, entitled "Distressed Area Relief: Will it Work?", p. 6.

War II.[15] Under such a system, there can be fairly sensitive recognition of a great variety of needs for a material, and allotment can be made in rough accord with its marginal importance to various government objectives. No such sensitivity of allocation of federal funds is inherent in a system based on a "depressed" or "not-depressed" dichotomy.

By way of contrast, it is interesting to note that a competitive price system avoids the "all-or-nothing" problem. If the marginal value productivity of resource A exceeds that of resource B, both will be employed, although A will receive the greater remuneration. If commodities C and D are both demanded by consumers, both will be produced as long as the market price is sufficiently high in relation to the appropriate cost. Cessation of production occurs only when it is not privately (and socially) desirable to continue to turn out the product because of the evaluation of required resources compared with evaluation of the product. In contrast, the shut-down point for government assistance under the redevelopment program, where "employment" is the product being sought, has no similar economic significance but is the result of arbitrary formulas or administrative judgment. Similarly, the strength of the "demand" (for jobs) does not exert an automatic upward force on the amount that the government will attempt to supply. (As already stated, however, it is possible to administer the program in such a way as to conform partially on this score.)

### Small Business Administration

An onlooker at Congressional hearings on proposed distressed-area legislation might well have gained the impression that hard-to-get private loans would be the only alternative open to firms in such areas if the Area Redevelopment program were not enacted into law. The well-established and much larger lending activity of the Small Business Administration was not stressed by proponents of area redevelopment. Yet most of the firms that may seek government loans qualify in size for this assistance. In general, relatively small size is much better as an eligibility criterion than that of location in a designated area in the same way that a vocational retraining program which is open to any unemployed person is superior to one which is open only to those in redevelopment areas. A program stressing

15. M. R. Colberg, "Priorities, Allocations, and Limitations," *Southern Economic Journal*, Vol. XVIII, No. 2, p. 150.

redevelopment loans, with its substantial administrative machinery, cannot easily be justified when such a large federal lending program as the SBA was already well established. This is especially true when the SBA is quite anxious to make loans in order to demonstrate its social productivity.[16]

During the six months ended June 30, 1961, the Small Business Administration approved 3,068 business loans for over $154 million. The accumulated total since the start of operations in 1953 was about $1.2 billion. These loans are made both directly and in participation with banks. "Special consideration" is supposed to be given to loan applications to aid rural development.

A rapidly growing segment of the SBA activity consists of the Small Business Investment Company program which it assists. These private companies were authorized by Congress in 1958 to promote the flow of equity capital and long-term loans to small business firms. The SBIC's are selected and licensed by the Small Business Administration. Upon licensing, the companies become eligible for financial assistance from the SBA and for tax benefits. The bulk of the funds of the SBIC's comes from sale of stock to the public and from bank loans. Assistance in original financing is given by the Small Business Administration through the purchase of subordinated debenture loans. Also, SBA loans may be made to a Small Business Investment Company after it has begun operations.

The actual and potential importance of SBIC's is indicated by the 298 licenses active as of June 30, 1961, and the 225 additional proposals on hand. Potential capital in the entire group for financing small business is estimated by SBA at over $854 million.

Somewhat less progress has been made so far in still another Small Business Administration activity—the assisting of state and local development companies. As of June 30, 1961, seven loans had been made to state development companies and 118 to local development companies. In the case of the state companies, SBA can match the borrowings from all other sources. SBA loans to local development companies are made for the benefit of identifiable small firms, and such loans may also be made through State Development Companies. There is no limit to the number of such loans which may be applied for. The development company must have some equity to invest in

16. The new administrator of the SBA in the *16th Semi-Annual Report, Small Business Administration*, Jan.-June, 1961, p. 1, stresses the new record in loans established during the first six months of 1961. Other SBA data are taken from this report.

a project, and the SBA attempts to secure local bank participation. Several thousand local development companies are actual or potential borrowers from the Small Business Administration.

The SBA development company loans are at 5 percent or 5½ percent except in "areas of substantial unemployment" designated by the Department of Labor. In such areas, they are made at 4 percent—the same rate currently charged by the Area Redevelopment Administration. This provision appears to be detrimental to the South. Most of the redevelopment areas in the South are rural areas with low per capita incomes. "Areas of substantial unemployment" (6 percent or more) are usually in industrial areas in the North or far West. It is interesting to note that this is a distressed-area loan program based on easier criteria of eligibility than the Area Redevelopment program, since "persistence" of unemployment in an area is not necessary as a condition for 4 percent federal loans. Relaxed restrictions as to the size of eligible firms are also in force in areas of substantial unemployment. Firms may be up to 25 percent larger than the usual standard for a "small" business. (For example, this maximum is usually 250 employees for a manufacturing firm and $1 million in sales for a retail firm.) When the ample loan program of the Small Business Administration is considered, it becomes especially hard to see why an area redevelopment program should also be in force. The facilities of SBA are utilized in checking loan applications for soundness, prospects for repayment, and similar matters. Area Redevelopment loans are supposed to be made only after it has been demonstrated that credit is not available from private lenders or other federal agencies on reasonable terms. However, since the SBA must find that applications from private borrowers are of fairly good quality, it seems likely that most of these would be approved for SBA loans in the absence of an Area Redevelopment program.

### Local Initiative in Area Redevelopment

Sponsors of federal area redevelopment have continually emphasized the important role of the areas themselves in their effort. One device to increase such participation is the requirement that "an overall economic development program" be prepared by an area organization, approved by a State Development Commission or similar agency, and approved by the Area Redevelopment Administration. The latter agency has been approving preliminary plans at a wholesale rate in order to make areas eligible for federal redevelopment assistance.

It is probable that most of these OEDP's are no more than perfunctory descriptions of the areas, their resources, present economic activities and problems, and aspirations. Nevertheless, it is disturbing that *planning* is considered to be vital to area redevelopment. While it is unquestionably wise for communities to plan carefully the spending of tax revenues for *public* projects, there is the implication that areas should be able to plan in some detail the nature of *private* investment which is appropriate. Requests for financial assistance are supposed to be "consistent with the approved overall economic development program of the area." This means that area plans will usually be made so broad as to be virtually meaningless. If plans are specific there is risk that assistance to an excellent sort of enterprise not in the plan will be blocked. In general, the area redevelopers seem to be overimpressed with the possibility of effective planning.[17] For example, it is stated that the analysis of an area "should lead to estimates of additional jobs needed over the next decade."[18] Such long range projections are largely nonsense. Labor statisticians have great difficulty in measuring how many people in an area actually desire to be members of the labor force at the *present* time, let alone in the 1970's.

So long as we rely mainly upon private enterprise, the exact location of most new plants cannot be anticipated. A prospective firm may have a dozen or more sites under active consideration and is likely, in fact, to conceal the identity of the place selected as long as possible in order to prevent the bidding-up of land prices. Cooperative local action can make community facilities more attractive to industry, but the "price system" constitutes the master plan that guides most relocation decisions.

In spite of official insistence that the Area Redevelopment Program relies mainly on local action, there is some evidence that local efforts which are not part of the federal plan are unwelcome. *Financial Assistance Guidelines* issued in November 1961 by the Area Redevelopment Administration states:

17. The same is true of many American economists. For example, C. E. Bishop, in a paper presented at a Conference on Area Development at Athens, Georgia, Jan. 8–10, 1962, "Planning for Economic Growth," states: "Planning lies at the very heart of an economic development program."

18. *The Overall Economic Development Program*, U.S. Department of Commerce, Area Redevelopment Administration, p. 8.

. . . It is common practice for the various localities to compete with each other by offering various concessions. Many such concessions reduce the ability to repay a Federal loan for a public facility, since they have the effect of reducing local revenues or the local ability to repay a loan from user charges. Examples of such concessions are free sites, free water or sewage, and exemptions from local taxes.

Where such concessions have been offered and the applicant requests a Federal grant on the grounds that it cannot afford to repay a loan it is clear that the Federal grant would have the effect of subsidizing maximum concessions. Therefore ARA will review carefully all requests for grants for financial assistance to provide public facilities for industries which have been attracted to the area on the basis of significant concessions. Only in exceptional situations will grants for more than 75 per cent of the total cost of facilities be approved, and in most cases ARA will expect grants to amount to less than 50 percent of the total cost where such concessions are a factor.

Since it is most improbable that an apparent lack of tax revenue to repay a loan can properly be traced to local subsidies to attract industry, this administrative provision seems to serve as a threat that vigorous local promotional efforts are liable to be punishable by a reduction of federal grants. The redevelopment administrator, rather than depending primarily on local efforts, seems in this regulation to frown on really vigorous local efforts in the neediest communities.[19] In general, the Southern states have been more active than others in the local promotion of economic development.

19. J. M. Buchanan and J. E. Moes, in a communication entitled "A Regional Countermeasure to National Wage Determination," *American Economic Review,* Vol. L, No. 3, p. 434, point out that "in political federalism, conflicts between the national government and the state or regional government units seem certain to occur." They illustrate how one governmental unit may take steps to offset or negate the effects of policy measures taken by an overlapping jurisdiction. The observation applies to the case in point but in a direction that the writers would not applaud.

# XI

# Economic Theory, Regional Industrial Development, and the Paint Industry

*By Melvin L. Greenhut and Charles T. Stewart, Jr.*

Throughout the history of location economics, there has been a tendency to adhere to the cost approach alone.[1] This tendency is evidenced in both pure and applied theories, but especially in the applied field.

Possibly August Lösch[2] was the first really to combine demand and cost into a pure theory of location. His contribution is surprising, for he was not concerned with location processes in a capitalistic society, but rather with analyzing the location process in a broader context. The first integrations of demand and cost in location theory, as in price theory, might have been expected to flow from the pens of economists steeped in the traditions of capitalism, hoping to apply location theory to capitalistic processes. For, as we shall see, the institutional forces in capitalism, in the form of various price practices over space, rearrange the profit values that may be found in different places and thereby make demand as well as cost a location factor.

Those closest to the passing scene too often, however, visualize it out of focus or fail to note it altogether. Thus past theories tend to

1. J. H. Von Thünen, *Der Isolierte Staat in Beziehung auf Landwirtschaft und National Ökonomie* (3rd ed.; Berlin: Schumacher Zarchlin, 1875); A. Weber, "Reine Theorie des Standorts," *Über den Standort der Industrien* (Tübingen, 1909), Part I; A. Linke, *Die Lederindustria Erzeugende und Verarbeitende* (Tübingen, 1913); L. Dechesnes, *La Localization des Diverses Productions* (Brûxelles: Les Éditions Comptables, Commercials et Financières, 1945); D. C. Hague and P. K. Newman, *Costs in Alternative Locations: The Clothing Industry* (Cambridge: Cambridge University Press, 1952); W. Isard and V. Whitney, *Atomic Power* (New York: The Blakiston Co., 1952).

2. *Die räumliche Ordnung der Wirtschaft* (Jena: Gustav Fischer, 1944).

influence present practices long after the time and circumstance appropriate for their application has passed. Present-day location theory is still strongly influenced by contributions stemming from Von Thünen and Weber. Although references to demand (locational interdependence) and cost appear frequently in present literature,[3] it seems that cost is emphasized to the exclusion of demand influences in empirical studies of location.[4]

The forces of location vary from industry to industry, of course; in some instances, the demand element is quite obscure and insignificant. Where time of delivery is unimportant, close contact with buyers unnecessary, transport cost on the finished product slight, and an equalizing delivered price system in use, the location emphasis is properly placed on the cost factors of production. But opposite situations occur, where demand elements need emphasis. Their recognition is vital if sound forecasts and recommendations on future industrial locations are to be made.

Demand as well as cost factors have dominated some plant locations, demonstrating that the Marshallian scissors are operative here as elsewhere in theory. It has been shown that the demand factor in location economics has many interdependent facets, such as the elasticity of demand, the degree of competition in location that prevails in the industry, the degree of competition from substitutable products at the various locations, and the homogeneity or heterogeneity of the firms belonging to the industry. Imperfections such as the importance to sales of time of delivery, personal contacts, and custom or habit are also part of the demand factor. Finally, the shape of the marginal cost curve and the height of freight cost have been noted to influence the extent to which the demand factor may dominate a given location.[5]

There is perhaps no easier way to understand this factor in general

3. E. M. Hoover, *Location of Economic Activity* (New York: McGraw-Hill, 1948), Chapter iv; M. L. Greenhut, "Integrating the Leading Theories of Plant Location," *Southern Economic Journal*, XVIII (1952), pp. 526–38, and *Plant Location in Theory and in Practice* (Chapel Hill: The University of North Carolina Press, 1956), Chapters vi, xi, and xii, henceforth *Plant Location*; W. Isard, *Location and Space Economy* ("Regional Science Studies," No. I [New York: Wiley and Sons in conjunction with the Technology Press, 1956]), Chapter vii.

4. E.g., J. Airov, *The Location of the Synthetic-Fiber Industry* ("Regional Science Studies," No. II [New York: Wiley and Sons in conjunction with the Technology Press, 1959]) uses what is essentially a cost approach in his otherwise encyclopedic effort.

5. See M. L. Greenhut, "Games, Capitalism and General Location Theory," *The Manchester School*, January, 1957, pp. 61–88.

terms than to observe how different price systems in space help to determine the plant location. To prepare for our main interest in this paper, namely how location and economic theory may help uncover regional space islands which offer new plant-location opportunities, and to do this specifically with respect to the paint industry and the South, we first will summarize the way that different price systems in space influence the location of manufacturing activity. This examination of spatial price systems causes our theory to differ sharply from the location models traditionally followed, for it indicates that location is not determinable by reference to cost alone but involves elements of demand. In the second section, we introduce certain key statistics and information about the paint industry, showing that it is dispersed in an areal (not point-formed) market pattern. We will see that it follows on pragmatic grounds, if nothing else, that the traditional cost models of location theory are inadequate and, in fact, irrelevant.

The third section of this paper carries forward from this theoretical-empirical foundation. By reference to surveys of paint-plant locations in Florida and Virginia, we acquire further indication of the two-sidedness of industrial location. And last of all, our final sections discuss an approach to help evaluate the economic potential of different locations and to estimate the paint-industry potential in the South.

## I. Price Systems in Space

### A. The Equalizing Delivered Price System

Under a system of uniform price quotations throughout the country, or, at least, uniform over significantly large areas, firms are able to sell to distant buyers regardless of location and without limit in so far as prices are concerned. Under this system, any firm seeking a plant site visualizes a vast market area at its command regardless of where this plant site is situated. With sales potential in effect a constant, the matter of location boils down to finding the best cost site for achieving the particular sales distribution visualized by company officials.

In practice, a heavy concentration of firms tends to arise at places where population is centered, near the center of the whole market, provided that production costs there are satisfactory. There is greater agglomeration of firms than would take place with basing point and other systems allowing prices to vary spatially. This extra agglomeration, enabling firms to sell advantageously to all points in the market and, in this way, to share national prominence with other firms, causes some distortion. The malallocation is, in practice, confined to a greater use of transportation than otherwise would be employed. Since freight costs usually are low when the constant price policy is followed, transportation is a cheap resource to the industry in question, and the distortion over space tends to be insignificant.

### B. The Single Basing Point System

We find that under the single basing point system large firms tend to concentrate at the base point, generally selling over the whole of the market area. In contrast, small firms which, by definition, do not plan or seek sales to large market areas, do well in locating at a distance from the base point. They tend, in fact, to locate toward the peripheries of the market, though not so far away from the central site as would equivalent-sized firms under the f.o.b. price system.[6]

Given the firm's intended size, under basing point pricing it locates at the place where costs are least. Thus, for example, when a firm selects a certain sales total, it will look for that site which offers the given sum at lowest net cost. Under the basing point system, this computation involves subtracting from total production-and-procurement-cost the difference between freight cost from the base point to each buyer and freight costs from the actual plant site to the buyer. This means that if production-and-procurement-costs are equal everywhere, and if the firm's feasible production capacity is limited, the firm will tend to locate at a place which maximizes phantom freight. On the other hand, if costs are unequal, it will accept a smaller phantom freight, provided further that this is indicated by the cost pattern in the market. In a broad sense, the same results are true for the large plant.

In sum, there arises a tendency under the single basing point system for large firms to concentrate at the base point. Many small firms seeking a large sales potential in order to grow large are sucked in towards this center. Undue use of transportation facilities results, and only a change in industrial relations between sellers and buyers, making proximity advantageous, would offset the distortion of location that one finds under this form of pricing. Unlike the equalizing delivered price system, where the "location distortion" reflects a relatively unimportant wasting of transport facilities, the present case requires a harsher judgment.

6. See Greenhut, *Plant Location*, Appendix V.

## C. The Multiple Basing Point System

The pattern of location forces begins to change somewhat with the multiple-basing point system, for, in this case, demand and not only cost is a factor in industrial location. We may recall this process quite simply by observing that competition in price and location take hold at a distance when new base points are created. This competition has the effect of squeezing market areas into different shapes and magnitudes so that the demand potential from area to area may vary. Accordingly, size of markets, i.e., the demand factor, might be the chief variable in the location process. Once the area of location is given, cost will steer the firm to its particular site, unless other demand variables, such as the need for close contact, are assumed to be relevant.

It is manifest that the multiple-basing point system reduces the amount of distortion found under the single basing point system. Nonetheless, within each base point area, the same location pattern develops, *ceteris paribus*, as under the single base point system.

## D. Other Price Systems

Such other price systems as the plenary price system, where all plant sites become base points and each plant absorbs freight if desiring sales at points nearer to the location of a competitor; or the straight f.o.b. mill price, where each plant prices f.o.b. plus freight from its mill without absorbing freight; or any variant between the two, such as sporadic freight absorption or an equalizing delivered price over a zone with freight additions to more distant zones—all allow the magnitude of effective demand to vary from area to area. Unlike, say, the basing point system, where demand may enter into the location scheme only if close physical contact with selected consumers is of importance, present cases permit the elasticity of the demand curve to be a location factor, for certain curves induce firms to locate at a distance from each other and to monopolize market segments, whereas others do not.[7]

F.o.b. mill pricing and all close variants modify the geography of market potentials open to an industry. The upshot is that within certain well-defined limits of price differentials, any plant locator tends to visualize different areas over the economic landscape. Sometimes these overlap, but usually they are sufficiently distinct and bounded

7. *Ibid.,* Chapter vi.

because of competition, population, or consumer concentrations and topographical features. Accordingly, whereas the firm may sell its wares over much of any given area regardless of its location in that area, sales to other market areas often prove sharply limited, if not impossible. Where pricing and location are competitive, the firm and the industry will find cost *or* demand as the leading variable in the process of location.

## II. The Paint Industry in General

In order to understand plant location, one must look beyond cost and inquire into the price practices of the industry over space. This kind of examination, when applied to the paint industry, readily uncovers the two-sidedness that we claim is part of location theory.

We note in the paint industry a fairly wide dispersion of firms. This, along with other key characteristics to be summarized, serve in support of our theme.

The major paint producers (i.e., national concerns such as du Pont, Glidden, Sherwin-Williams, and Pittsburgh Paint) sometimes fabricate a special line in their non-main plants for sale in newly developed areas while continuing to produce the basic line for this and other markets at their original (or main) plants. In effect, the freight saving involved under basic-line branch-plant production is not always enough to compensate for the storage and inventory costs ordinarily associated with fabrication by large batches, which is required to keep production costs at economic levels. In the usual case, therefore, the national concern temporarily leaves the specialty field to small firms, and waits for the growth of regional markets before opening up its branch plant.

Batch production is associated with long-distance shipments. It is especially when continuous branch production of a basic line is possible that new branches will be created. However, the relative ubiquitousness of raw-material supplies and the openings to small firms for special-line production allow a large number of plants and producers to exist in the industry, with estimates of their total running as high as 1,591 separate plants in 1958. This raw-material condition, combined with the comparatively small cost of shipping materials and products, creates substantial price similarity among zones, to the point where, within given zones, large firms pursue identical delivered prices while small firms price f.o.b. mill. But before we devote attention solely to branch-plant locations and to such an intricate empirical matter as price practices in the paint industry, we must stay with more general data. This broad coverage is the objective of the next remarks.

## A. Selected Statistical Data

Over 594 million gallons of paint, varnish, and lacquer valued at $1,589,300,000 were sold in 1958.[8]   Most significantly, the overwhelming part of the total output in this industry was concentrated in 15 states.   Seven states, all (except California) in the North Central and Eastern part of the United States, accounted for about 71 percent of the total value of shipments in the country in 1958.[9]

It is suggested that the concentration of paint production in the designated states conforms to the spatial distribution of demand in the United States, with the absence of equalized delivered prices over the nation and the frequency of competitive location patterns tending to support this contention.   Indeed, since the single-basing point system is outlawed by recent interpretations of the anti-trust statutes, and since alternative market areas exist, the theoretical requirement of cost alone is further denied.   In its place, the likelihood of demand exercising a vital, if not the lead, role in location decisions must be considered.

By way of further preliminary thoughts, we might observe here that the concentration of paint manufacture in the industrial and population centers of the nation suggests its orientation to markets. This condition, for example, prevails in Florida to the extent that approximately 70 percent of the paint produced in Florida is manufactured in the Miami and Tampa areas.[10]   But whether this pattern results from demand considerations or some other factor cannot yet be answered.

Employment levels in the industry suggest the changing pattern of location.   For the period 1947 to 1954, employment rose from 53,412 to 56,580.   During the same period, a modest decline in employment occurred in the Middle Atlantic States and New England.   All other areas showed increases.   Among the states, dramatic rates of growth in employment occurred in Florida (80 percent), Texas (45 percent), and California (18 percent).   These patterns generally conformed to

8. See the National Paint, Varnish, and Lacquer Association's *Statistical Handbook* (1960 ed.; Washington, D.C.), p. 3.

9. *Ibid*, p. 12.   See also U.S. Department of Commerce, *Fifteen Leading Paint Producing States, 1954 Census of Manufacturers* (Washington, D.C.), pp. 28E–5.

10. Florida Development Commission, *"Illustrative Florida Marketing Studies,"* Report 115, April 1959, Table 3, p. 40.

**Table 1.** Trade and Industrial Products Shipments, Selected Areas, 1958*

| State | Per Capita Shipments | Per Capita Trade Sales Products Shipments | Per Capita Industrial Products Shipments | Trade/ Industrial Ratio |
|---|---|---|---|---|
| New Jersey | $32.83 | $16.82 | $16.01 | 1.05 |
| Illinois | 25.26 | 16.29 | 8.97 | 1.82 |
| Missouri | 12.93 | 9.66 | 3.27 | 2.95 |
| Ohio | 16.39 | 8.70 | 7.69 | 1.13 |
| Michigan | 13.29 | 3.17 | 10.12 | 0.31 |
| Kentucky | 12.85 | 7.77 | 5.08 | 1.53 |
| California | 11.48 | 7.35 | 4.13 | 1.78 |
| Pennsylvania | 10.27 | 5.27 | 5.00 | 1.05 |
| Maryland | 9.72 | 7.50 | 2.22 | 3.38 |
| Massachusetts | 7.91 | 5.37 | 2.54 | 2.11 |
| Georgia | 7.29 | 5.32 | 1.97 | 2.70 |
| Wisconsin | 6.62 | 4.21 | 2.41 | 1.75 |
| New York | 6.48 | 4.05 | 2.43 | 1.67 |
| Texas | 6.08 | 4.45 | 1.63 | 2.73 |
| Minnesota | 5.31 | 3.91 | 1.40 | 2.79 |
| Indiana | 4.79 | 3.19 | 1.60 | 1.99 |
| Washington | 3.08 | 2.50 | 0.58 | 4.31 |
| Oregon | 2.98 | 2.20 | 0.78 | 2.82 |
| Florida | 2.94 | 2.60 | 0.34 | 7.88 |
| North Carolina | 2.74 | 0.91 | 1.83 | 0.50 |
| Connecticut | 1.77 | 0.90 | 0.87 | 1.03 |
| Virginia | 1.35 | 0.78 | 0.57 | 1.37 |
| United States | 8.72 | 5.11 | 3.61 | 1.42 |

* Source: National Paint, Varnish, and Lacquer Association, *Statistical Handbook*, 1960, Table 18, p. 12.

population shifts during the same period. By 1958, employment, at 57,034, was little above that of 1954. It continued to decline in New England and the Middle Atlantic, and also in the West North Central States.[11]

Another measure of market quality is per capita sales. The table above shows the per capita value of shipments by representative states for 1958. The value of shipments is used for lack of geographical detail on sales by state. The dollar figures would have to be increased by one-third to approximate per capita sales at wholesale prices.

Paint products are classified into industrial products and trade-sales products. The latter are primarily for household and other domestic uses. Although this classification is not exhaustive, products excluded from Table 1 and classified as "miscellaneous paint products" and

11. *Statistical Handbook* (1960 ed.), Table 9, p. 7; *Statistical Handbook* (1957 ed.), Table 5, p. 10.

"paints, etc. not specified by kind" account for less than 10 percent of the industry total.

Trade-sales products and industrial products have different markets and might therefore be expected to differ in geographical pattern of production. For trade-sales products, population and population growth are two indices of the geography of demand, as they affect maintenance and new construction of residential property and allied service facilities. For industrial products, the location of paint-using industries is a better index, perhaps, than population. We find that the seven states leading in paint production account for 66 percent of trade-sales shipments, but 78 percent of industrial shipments, reflecting perhaps in part the fact that paint-using industry is more highly concentrated geographically than population.

The share of total paint-production accounted for by trade-sales products, formerly two-thirds of the total, has been declining, but is still over half. Further suggestion that plant location is influenced by a demand component is provided by the fact that there exists a number of less-industrialized states with significant production of trade-sales products but inconsequential output of industrial paint products. There are just two states in which per capita industrial products shipments exceed trade-sales products shipments, both by a wide margin: Michigan, with its motor vehicle industry, and North Carolina, with its furniture industry.

## B. Some Price-Policy History

In the paint, varnish, and lacquer industry, equalized stepped-zone price systems have been generally followed. It was noted years ago that sellers typically priced uniformly within certain zones and increased prices by zones as a function of distance.[12] For example, uniform delivered prices were found within each zone in the marketing of linseed oil, though some slight difference may have existed between sellers in base price and in zone differentials. For this product, the North Central States, including Minnesota, the largest linseed-oil-producing state, were designated as Zone 1.

In the sale of paint materials, such as white lead, the typical practice was to sell on consignment through retailers. Prices were left to vary on a zone basis. Areas nearest a warehouse or manufacturing point were designated as par zones or freight-free zones.

12. TNEC, *Economic Concentration and Corporate Power* (Washington, 1940), pp. 314, 315.

The pricing of prepared paints lacked the uniformity evidenced in linseed oil and white lead because of the large number of independent, small sellers. Nonetheless, there was a noticeable uniformity in pricing among the large manufacturers who distributed on a national scale. These firms used a four-zone price system. Zone 1 comprised most of the Northeast and was called the base zone. Prices in Zone 2 ranged from four to six cents a gallon higher while, in Zone 3, they were eight to twelve cents higher and, in Zone 4, thirteen to eighteen cents higher than in the base zone.

Among medium-size producers who operated regionally, the customary practice was to quote f.o.b. destination prices with full freight allowed if the purchaser arranged for transportation. Alternatively, f.o.b. plant pricing was used with freight prepaid. Among smaller plants, there was but little effort to equalize delivered costs.

### C. Present Price Practices

Today there are no price data available through sources such as the TNEC. The Federal Trade Commission has not made a study of price practices in the industry, and the National Paint, Varnish, and Lacquer Trade Association disclaims the compilation of such figures. Therefore, the only data available are those provided by individual companies, and, unfortunately, these are generally provided on a confidential basis.

Available evidence suggests that the four-zone price system on certain prepared paints is still followed, at least roughly, today, and that uniform zone prices increasing from zone to zone are also widely used. Uniform pricing by zones is especially prevalent for practically all of the raw materials used in the industry.

### 1. Finished Products

Major producers generally follow a series of stepped zones in pricing their products. On certain paints produced in batches and shipped long distances, remnants of the old four-zone pricing system are discernible. For other products, three zones with stepped prices for more distant markets are employed. It is generally agreed that the major producers in the industry not only follow similar delivered price-zone systems but charge nearly identical prices in comparable product lines.

In contrast, the small independents adhere chiefly to an f.o.b. price system, with sales being limited to more proximate points in reflection of the need for fast service and the existence of many small independents throughout the country.[13] Significantly, the paint-product lines of small companies vary from those of the large producers. The chief difference is that small independents tend to carry a low-price line. Thus, between large and small producers there exists a noticeable differential in delivered price which may or may not reflect a differential in quality. For trade-sales products in particular, this price differential may be required to counter the brand-name and advertising advantages of the nationally-known manufacturers.

The market for trade-sales products comes closer to being a single market than that for industrial paint products, which is in fact a number of highly specialized markets. Product differentiation therefore is more significant in industrial products than in trade-sales products, and this force promotes dispersion by small independents. More generally, the existence of "product islands" is another recognition of the locational influence of demand, as we find a different geography of markets for some specialized products, affecting plant location directly as well as indirectly, through differences in the identity and location pattern of competitors.

## 2. Raw Materials

About 1,200 raw materials are used in the industry, 2,000 intermediate materials (dryers, thinners, and resins), and some 1,700 formulas, each requiring different components. The final products are packaged in volumes ranging from carloads to small tubes. Because of large variations in sizes and components, a large part of total costs is tied up in raw materials.

Raw materials are generally received on a freight-equalized basis. Thus, solvent oils are received by one company in all of its plants at identical costs even though the points of origin may vary. Tung oil per pound is equalized from a few scattered production points. Pigments, such as titanium dioxide and extenders,[14] are obtainable at many places, with each origin-source pricing similarly by zones around

13. According to one small-company official, his company disguises its higher price on long-distance shipments through the discount it offers. In this way, the company maintains distant sales. Another argues that distant sales are impractical because dealers in such places require a larger discount to handle the line of a small company. This extra discount, when added to the already larger discount exacted because of small size, leaves little for the producer on sales to distant markets. The sales area of the small firm, he claims, is very limited.

14. Some extenders, such as magnesium silicate, are priced f.o.b. mine plus freight.

the supply point. Glycerine is said to be sold generally throughout the country on a zone-equalized delivered basis. This is also said to hold true for linseed oil, mineral spirits, hydrocarbons, soya oil, and China wood oil. Because of these practices, raw-material-cost differences tend to be quite small.

Freight-absorption practices discriminate in favor of distant buyers. Though the value added per man-hour may differ regionally, the discrepancies are quite small, except for isolated instances; consequently we find that unit sales potential rather than unit profit on sales appears therefore to be the significant variable in determining plant location (see p. 400 for detailed explanation).

### D. Price Practices in the Paint, Varnish, and Lacquer Industry: Location Theory and the Empirical Model

Traditional location theory suggests that cost is the main variable factor in plant location, and this is true when: (1) a national uniform equalizing delivered price system prevails, or (2) a single basing point system exists, or (3) a non-competitive location-price policy is pursued (i.e., where all firms locate side by side and adopt identical price schedules). Significantly, any price system predicated on a single base zone with stepped-up zone rates over distance is comparable to the single base point system. Accordingly, the large company seeks to minimize its cost throughout the whole market, while smaller independents tend to be willing to locate in higher-priced zones, taking advantage of the gains of phantom freight differentials.

If the national concern produces and distributes its products from a group of alternative plants rather than from just one main plant, the picture takes on the characteristics of a plenary or nondiscriminatory f.o.b. mill price system. Advantage then exists in locating new plants at places distant from old plants, as leading companies and small independents each trade for position at sites within developing markets. With raw materials shipped on a discriminatory price basis, and cost differences therefore slight, the tendency develops for production to spread out and be divided among more plants and firms. The narrowing of cost differences over space increases the influence of demand and tends to make it the chief location variable in the industry.

## III. Location Patterns in Two Southern States

### A. Florida

The paint-industry market has developed rapidly in Florida in recent years, with a trade-sales increase of 50 percent and an industrial-sales increase of 25 percent between 1954 and 1957.[15]   In 1954, when Florida had 2.14 percent of the United States population, trade sales in Florida already accounted for 2.69 percent of the national total, reflecting its relatively large residential construction and tourist activities.   Industrial sales in the state, on the other hand, accounted for only 0.42 percent of the national total, reflecting the comparatively limited industrial development in the state.

Florida paint production has been expanding even more rapidly than the Florida paint market; between 1954 and 1958, value of shipments increased nearly threefold, from $4.8 to $13.8 million; population increase was 32 percent.   Although total production rose more rapidly than total sales within the state, it still accounted for well under half of the state's paint purchases.   In terms of value of shipments, Florida paint manufacturers in 1958 accounted for 1.36 percent of total U.S. trade-sales products and 0.25 percent of industrial products.   Thus Florida paint production per capita remained far below the U.S. average, although its consumption of trade products per capita exceeded the U.S. average.

Most of the paint plants in Florida are located in the developed counties of the state, with such cities as Miami, Jacksonville, and Tampa accounting for most of the plants and output.   Since industrial sales are so small relative to the nation, it may be conjectured that the paint manufacturers of Florida use retail outlets much more than is customary in the nation.   The low ratio of industrial-products output to trade-sales output in Florida suggests that a slight expansion of industrial activity could induce a significant increase in industrial paint-products output.   The Florida industrial paint-products potential is said to be vast; it is argued that the industrial growth of the state will alone raise industrial sales from 13.7 percent of total paint sales in Florida to 18.9 over the period from 1957–70 at the same time that trade sales will be increasing around 80 percent.[16]

For industrial paint alone, the forecasted growth is 116 percent over 1957.   This computation incidentally is based on the assumption that Florida industries will consume the same ratio of paint to value added as will their non-Florida counterparts.   It includes an estimate of paint consumption by the industries which use paint heavily (e.g., lumber and wood products), and it utilizes an estimate of the growth of these paint-using industries in Florida.

15. Florida Development Commission, *op. cit.*, p. 39.
16. *Ibid.*, pp. 44, 45.

Trade sales were estimated to grow by over $16 million, essentially on the basis of an anticipated increase in population of three million persons. Moreover, the final estimate gives special consideration to the extra-heavy construction activity in the state. Finally, the fact that a large sales potential, as yet unexploited, exists in rural areas was recognized, and influenced the estimate. We shortly will find in considering "our proposed paint-location form" that, as with the estimates for Florida, particular state data (such as the state's industrial complex) must be made part of the calculation process in order to yield meaningful results.

## B. Virginia

There were nine respondents in Virginia of twelve firms surveyed by questionnaire. Of these, six were interviewed personally. In general, their story is this:

All believed they located in Virginia for personal reasons. The economic fact, however, is that a legitimate business opportunity existed in an area where the individual chose to live; and, profits and uncertainties being as they are, one could hardly call any of these locations uneconomic.

In each case, the reporting firm prices f.o.b. mill, though one firm did propose that really it used a stepped-up zone rate system rather than a price pattern over space that was roughly proportional to distance. In each case, they claimed that national concerns followed delivered price systems and that generally their own product was lower-priced or a specialty item. In the overwhelming number of cases (considering the large number of raw materials used per firm), the belief was that raw materials were received on a zoned price basis, that there was no advantage in shifting locations fifty or one hundred miles nearer to any raw-material source. The prevailing opinion was that possibly a slightly higher price was paid on some raw materials compared to that paid by firms located in New Jersey, a slightly lower price than that paid by counterpart firms in North Carolina, and the same general price as that paid by firms in Kentucky; in any case, whatever difference might exist, it was without doubt small.

Sales to the local city markets were estimated to run around 30 percent of total sales, with a fairly regular drop in sales as distance increased. In most cases, nearly all sales (e.g., 95 percent of the total sold by the company) were said to take place within a two-hundred-mile radius of the plant. Competition for markets within the local community and up to a fifty-mile radius was said to be confined gen-

erally to national concerns, especially since practically every company
official interviewed believed his product was substantially different
from that of the other small paint-plants located nearby in Virginia or
surrounding states.   In fact, even national concerns were said to compete indirectly—not directly, since uninformed customers may buy
the paint of the national concern despite the fact that the local product
was better *designed* for the use planned by the would-be customer.
Market inroads by other small concerns were therefore said not to
exist as a general rule, except as distances lengthened and a plant of
similar type "could be found in the region."  (How different the economics of capitalism in space, where each becomes a spatial oligopo-
list, from the large-city economics where one might try to argue for
monopolistic or pure competition and ignore the chain-linking of
markets!)

Typical of Virginia was the case of a small manufacturer whose
product and price were so different from those of national companies
that in effect the markets taken over by each were considered to be
discontinuous.  Whatever competition existed within the spokesman's
city for *his kind of product* was confined to that of a small company
located some two hundred miles away in Virginia and some small companies located a state or two distant in opposite directions.  The inroads
of these concerns totaled about 50 percent, it was believed; but the
respondent's sales in the more distant market (e.g., at a one-hundred-
and even two-hundred-mile radius) remained important per square
mile compared to the more proximate areas because of the comparative uniqueness of the paint and overall product use.  Thus the local
picture alone could not be stressed.

Another plant, located at a point not too distant from the one referred to in the previous paragraph, was not in competition at all with
this plant, nor, for that matter, with others located at greater distances
in Virginia.  Its competition came from far-away firms in other states,
producing specialty items which catered to an industrial activity found
rather extensively in this part of the country.  This firm tended to
dominate the local market (up to the fifty-mile radius); market-sharing
was generally limited to customer demands so specialistic that a distant
firm, admittedly possessed of greater experience in the particular line,
might be able to handle a particular order more economically than
the subject company.  That small companies have a job to do which
they are able to handle better than large companies is accepted talk
in the industry.

## IV. Industrial Development Potential (The Paint Industry)

The location theory developed herein points to a varying sales potential and cost pattern as one looks across the economic landscape. In particular, we find from evidence recorded here (and some that has not been detailed) that in the paint industry, delivered price systems on raw materials extend over wide zones, similarity in labor productivity prevails, and only small capital investment per plant is required. These data signify an industry type in which the demand (locational interdependence) factor, more generally than not, is the chief variable of location.

By estimating the sales potential at alternative places, one approximates a measure of the economic feasibility of a location in the paint industry. This conclusion was reached partly on *a priori* grounds, partly as a result of interviews with more than 50 paint company officials (of both small and national concerns), and checked by three different sets of questionnaires mailed to more than 150 other firms with an approximate 40 percent rate of response.

A sales potential form which we used in gathering information and which is applied in the last section of this paper towards the end of identifying the space island in the South (i.e. the market potential in the South) recognized that the demand for paint products is partly filled by national concerns and partly by small concerns. Usually the small firms produce lower-priced items and specialty products, and practically always price f.o.b. mill rather than delivered price by zones. Given this practice, part of the total paint market belongs to national concerns; part remains for small companies. Because both raw materials and final products are priced under similar zone rate schedules, a correspondence exists between the level of production costs and the umbrella under which the prices of small concerns are set. It follows that the difference between the final good prices of national concerns and of costs is similar from place to place and hence *particular* price and cost data may generally be ignored. Accordingly, our sales-potential form ignores such price and cost data, letting approximate statistics on the division of local markets between national and local concerns serve as the basis for estimation, thereby achieving needed simplification. Precise information about price zones, raw-material-buying points, and sales distribution among large and small concerns is tightly held and frequently unavailable. Inquiry into such sources as the Dun and Bradstreet library, and the National Paint, Varnish, and Lacquer Association, and visits to individuals revealed either that there is no known record of how much is sold by national and small concerns or that this information was, and will continue to be, tightly held. In addition to our questionnaires, letters were written to others asking their opinion. Finally, census data were studied. With some regularity, suggestive possibly of normality rather than happenstance, the sales total was divided on a 2–1 basis between national and small companies, as defined in the sales-potential form we ultimately used. Unfortunately, the replies received are too inadequate and rough to be really meaningful, much less scientifically established.[17] Agencies or companies with knowledge of objectives (including particular product-lines and types) may use a specific and more reliable figure than the 2–1 statistic proposed or, by using a value restricted, say, to a particular product line, avoid any reference to small or to national concerns, as the case may be.

Our general sales-potential form used the basic statistic that $950.00 worth of *all kinds* of paint, varnish, and lacquer are sold *throughout the United States* per hundred persons. Manifestly, an agency in a particular state may use a different statistic which considers the income, climate, population, rate of economic growth, and other factors appropriate to that state. We have already seen that trade sales in Florida are more than six times the industrial sales. Clearly a Florida group using our sales-potential form would have to employ a ratio quite different from the average for the U.S. ratio. Moreover, recognition might be given here to forecasted industrial growth, particularly of paint-consuming industries. Our sales-potential form, we repeat, complies with location theory and the described characteristics of the industry. It focuses attention on the demand factor, though, to be sure, unique conditions of cost from place to place are not to be ignored.

### V.  The Paint Industry Potential of the South: A Case Example

In estimating the sales potential of a region or state, adjustment must be made to account for regional or state differences in in-

17. More information is needed, for instance, on areas with different population patterns from those of Virginia and Florida, to determine the effects of population agglomeration or dispersion on the area of markets and the division of sales by local small manufacturers between local and more distant markets. More information is needed on the Atlantic and Midwest regions in order to ascertain the influence of the great concentrations of paint production in New Jersey in the East and the great concentration in Illinois (including lesser concentrations in Cleveland, Detroit, St. Louis, and Kansas City) on the division of sales between national and small local companies.

come and industry. Since we shall use 1954 census data here, and since our case-interest area, the South (defined here to include only the South Atlantic and East South Central States), had an income level at that time approximately 76 percent of the national average,[18] we use $7.10 as our average sales potential per person.

We ignore the national/small-concern ratio in this example, since we are not concerned with establishing the market potential for a particular type of firm. But we do not ignore the industrial complex of the region. Fortunately for simplicity in computation, the value added ratio of 1–5 for the South compared to the nation in *selected paint-using industries*[19] and the population ratio of 1–5 (33 million persons in the defined area compared to 165 million persons in the U.S. at that time) are the same; thus the 3.1 to 2.1 U.S. ratio between household and industrial sales may hold true for the subject area. Because our selected industry- and population-ratios are identical, we are able to take sales potential per person, multiply by population, round the result to yield the sales potential in the South. Other results follow simply, and are recorded without further discussion in Table 2.

**Table 2.** Sales Total and Potential in the South, 1954*

|  | Sales Total[a] | Sales Potential | Difference |
|---|---|---|---|
| Trade Sales | $105,000,000 | $139,500,000 | $34,500,000 |
| Industry Sales | 64,000,000 | 94,500,000 | 30,500,000 |
| Total | 169,000,000 | 234,000,000 | 65,000,000 |

* Figures of current production and sales by southern plants are rounded.
[a] *Statistical Handbook* (1957 ed.; Washington, D.C.), Table 12, p. 18.

The use of average data would suggest that the sales potential and the actual dollars worth of sales should be closer, especially since there was such a high identity in the subject region and the nation at large in so far as concerns the *selected paint-using industries'* output and the relative populations. How may we account for the discrepancy?

(1) The most obvious culprit is the assumption inherent to our

18. Estimated from U.S. Department of Commerce, *U.S. Income and Output* (Washington, D.C., 1958), Table II-9, p. 159.
19. The industries used are Lumber and Wood Products, Furniture and Fixtures, Fabricated Metal Products, Machinery (except electrical), and Electrical Machinery, with the relevant data having been derived from the U.S. Bureau of the Census, *Census of Manufacturers* (Washington, D.C., 1954), Parts I and II.

computation that sales per person may be proportional to income. In fact, it may be the case that the income elasticity of demand is much greater than one on sales of paint, varnish and lacquer.

(2) Related to the above is the assumption that trade and industry sales-potentials are unaffected by types of housing and factories. But homes and factories in the South may tend to use less paint, given any population and income level.

(3) Finally, and most notably, we must observe that the difference may reflect a state of underdevelopment of capacity in the region, and, related thereto, a rather high level of prices which via elastic demand encourages the use of substitutes.

If explanations (1) or (2) do not hold, but rather (3) does, it is manifest that a "space island" exists in the South in the paint industry and that, in turn, we may anticipate a relatively large expansion of paint production as well as sales in the South in the years to come.

To predict accurately the location potential of a given place, the general (average) information used here to develop our theme that demand is a vital factor in location economics[20] which not only should be considered in theory but may be applied in practice, could be modified by the use of more specialized information.[21]  In any case, we suggest that the outline for determining the feasibility of a given site has been recorded, and assert that it complies with general economic theory by recognizing the importance of demand as well as cost in economic relations.   Finally, we observe that industrial development commissions must devise systems which recognize and comply with demand and/or cost differences, as the case may be, if they are seeking to determine "the space-island potentials" that may prevail in their areas.

20. In seeking to uncover the demand potential over a large region or area, such as the South, we are utilizing one side of the demand factor of location (let us call it the area demand factor of location).  In many ways, this side of demand was included in Weber's theory of location (see M. L. Greenhut, "Integrating the Leading Theories of Plant Location," *Sou. Ec. Journ.*, XVIII, pp. 526–38) and has been included in many empirical studies (e.g. see Airov, *op. cit.*).  The other side of demand, namely the locational interdependence component, has most often been ignored in empirical as well as theoretical works in location economics; this component, which we may call the site demand factor of location, relates back to our effort to separate the sales potential of large and small firms, as described in Section IV.  Its influence on plant location is especially manifest under the f.o.b. price system or some variant thereof (see Section II).

21. Specialized information could relate to type of construction in the area, the price practices that are followed, and other forces (as described in Sections III and IV) which influence the type of sales and type of sellers.

# XII

## The Elasticity of Substitution and Regional Estimates of Capital and Capital Ratios in American Manufacturing Industry, 1954-1958*

*By C. E. Ferguson*

### I. Introduction

Regional estimates of capital are very important and become progressively more important as the industrial classification becomes progressively more narrow. With periodic estimates at hand of capital at the regional level, capital-value added ratios, capital-labor ratios, gross quasi-rents, and rates of capital accumulation may be readily estimated. The obvious significance of these magnitudes for analyses of intra- and interregional growth, output, and employment patterns obviates further comment. In this light it is somewhat surprising that there has been only one attempt to estimate capital stocks by regions; and that study was restricted to estimates for the Middle Atlantic, South Atlantic, and East South Central states.[1]

There are many ways of making regional capital estimates, but most of these are impracticable. For example, one might use the techniques of Creamer and Borenstein.[2] It seems, however, that this method is

* The study resulting in this publication was begun while the author held a grant from the Inter-Universities Committee for Economic Research on the South. Further work was done under a Ford Foundation Faculty Fellowship. Finally, computational and related expenses were met by funds from the Duke University Council on Research and from a Social Science Research Council Auxiliary Research Award. The usual *caveat* applies.

1. Lowell E. Gallaway, "Regional Capital Estimates by Industry," *Southern Economic Journal*, XXIX (July, 1962), 21–25.

2. Daniel Creamer, Sergei Dobrovolsky, and Israel Borenstein, *Capital in Manufacturing and Mining* (Princeton: Princeton University Press, 1960).

doomed to failure because so many important corporations have plants located in more than one census region. Alternatively, the two-digit industry capital estimates of Creamer and Borenstein may be allocated among the census regions. There must be an infinite number of ways of doing this because any method of apportionment is necessarily arbitrary. Nonetheless, the fact that all methods are arbitrary does not imply that some are not superior to others; this holds true even though the bases of selection are not themselves logically pure.

For example, Gallaway made his regional allocations by means of the linearly homogeneous version of the Cobb-Douglas "production function." Approximately the same method is adopted here to allocate the Creamer-Borenstein estimates among the nine census regions for each of the 20 two-digit American manufacturing industries. The procedure differs in detail from that of Gallaway; but the most crucial departure lies in our use of the ACMS production function.[3] In essence, this means that our estimates are based upon different sets of computed industry parameters.

The theoretical structure and estimation method are developed in Section II. Section III presents the data sources and the basic statistical results, while Section IV shows the associated estimates of the capital-value added ratios, the capital-labor ratios, and gross quasi-rents by region and industry. Section V presents various comparisons among the three Southern regions and between weighted Southern averages and the corresponding national averages. Finally, Section VI contains some concluding remarks.

## II. Theoretical Framework

### A. Production Functions

The notion of a production function is both old and important in economic literature. Most economists are well acquainted with functions such as

(1)  $y = f(x_1, x_2, \ldots, x_n)$,

where $y$ is the physical quantity of output of a single commodity and the $x_i$'s are the physical quantities of inputs. This equation, when given specific form, describes the processes and conditions of production. But of even greater interest, the isoquant map derived from (1) shows the various possibilities of substitution among inputs in produc-

3. Kenneth Arrow, Hollis B. Chenery, Bagicha Minhas, and Robert M. Solow, "Capital-Labor Substitution and Economic Efficiency," *Review of Economics and Statistics*, XLIII (Aug., 1961), 225–50.

ing given quantities of the commodity. This is, of course, the heart of the matter; a production function is a catalogue of different input combinations that may be used to produce the same output.

Production functions such as (1), and the related "transformation functions" for multi-product plants, also establish the basis of micro-economic distribution theory. The first partial derivatives of (1) are the marginal products of the inputs. Given the type of market in which the firm operates, almost every interesting characteristic of microeconomic functional distribution may be determined, including the change in relative input shares consequent to a change in relative input prices. Furthermore, if the market is perfectly competitive and if "unusual" restrictions are not placed on (1), the Clark-Wicksteed theorem obtains: in a position of long-run competitive equilibrium, rewarding each input according to its marginal product precisely exhausts the total product. One might also wish to add that the Clark-Wicksteed theorem holds for *all* acceptable forms of (1), only degenerating into the trivial Euler's theorem when (1) is linearly homogeneous.

Specific forms of (1) have been the subject of extensive statistical research. The results have generally been good, especially in agricultural studies. The limited scope of this production function, however, limits also the scope of its interest and applicability. Thus we proceed to a higher level of generality and to types of production functions that are also familiar. For example, we may write

$$(2) \quad Q_i = Q_i(X_1, X_2), \qquad\qquad (i = 1, 2)$$

where the $Q_i$ represents the physical quantities of two broad classes of goods, and $X_1$ and $X_2$ are the physical quantities of inputs of two generalized, homogeneous productive agents.

Production functions such as those shown in equation (2) are not susceptible of empirical testing. Yet they are conceivable and conceptually important, for they establish the production side of our simplest general equilibrium models. The two equations show the possibilities both of factor substitution in producing one commodity and of intercommodity substitution in a fully employed economy. Equations such as (2) also establish the foundations of the neoclassical theory of aggregate (functional) distribution. Again, the partial derivatives are the marginal products, and competitive imputations exhaust the product when the economy attains a position of long-run equilibrium. Finally, (2) does not have to be given any special form;

the elasticity of substitution may be a constant or a variable and may take any non-negative value.

In light of the economic significance of capital-labor substitution, we should ideally like to specialize (2) so as to obtain statistically testable equations of the form

(3) $Q = Q(C, L)$,

or

(4) $Q_i = Q_i(C_i, L_i)$,

where $Q$ is aggregate physical output, $C$ is the physical quantity of capital, and $L$ is the physical quantity of labor resources used. The subscript $i$ in (4) restricts the function to apply (say) to an SIC two-digit industry. If data were available for either (3) or (4), the mathematical form of the function would not be constrained, except for the signs of the first and second partial derivatives.

Unfortunately, it is not possible to obtain data on $Q$ and $C$, $Q_i$ and $C_i$. Consequently, there arises a question of great current interest. Can the variables in (3) and (4) be redefined and yet have the resulting equations meet two criteria: (a) they must retain their character as a *production* function showing the possibilities of technical substitution between capital and labor; and (b) they must be testable by means of available data.

These considerations led to the modification of (3) and (4) to

(5) $V = F(K, L)$,

and

(6) $V_i = F_i(K_i, L_i)$,

where $V$ is national income at factor cost and $K$ is a dollar value of capital available (used?) in the economy. Correspondingly, $V_i$ is value added by an industry and $K_i$ is the dollar value of capital in that industry.

The definitions of $L$ and $L_i$ do not have to change because man-hour or man-year data are available. But there is one important change that must be made: (5) and (6) *must be* linearly homogeneous because the accounting identity forces value added precisely to equal the compensation of employees and the property return. Or stated somewhat differently, the property return is, by definition, value added minus the compensation of employees. The product is exhausted (by definition) whether an equilibrium position is attained or not.

Perhaps the first attempt at statistical implementation of (6) was made by Cobb and Douglas,[4] and there have subsequently been many studies using the famous Cobb-Douglas function. Careful analysis, however, has led many economists to reject the Cobb-Douglas equation as a *production* function.[5] In particular, Phelps-Brown made the following observations: (a) when fitted to time-series data, the Cobb-Douglas function can only describe the relations between the historical rates of growth of labor, capital, and product; the coefficients of the function do not measure marginal productivities; (b) when fitted to cross-section data, the coefficients do have an analytical meaning in that they show what the distributive shares will be; but in this case there is a simpler explanation involving the limited divergencies of labor earnings and profit returns from one industry to another; (c) in neither case is it a production function.[6]

Among the objectionable features of the Cobb-Douglas function is the property that, whether in a linearly homogeneous form or not, the function implies constant relative factor shares. That is, an equation of the form

(7) $V = AK^a L_c^b$,    $a, b > 0$

always yields an elasticity of substitution equal to unity (whether *or not* $a + b = 1$). To remedy this defect, while retaining the necessary linear homogeneity of the production function, ACMS developed a general class of functions characterized by a *constant*, but not necessarily unitary, elasticity of substitution. It is with this function that we are primarily concerned.

### B. The Elasticity of Substitution and the ACMS Function

The production function proposed by ACMS is

(8) $V = \gamma[\delta K^{-\rho} + (1-\delta)L^{-\rho}]^{-\frac{1}{\rho}}$,

where $V$ is value added in a two-digit industry; $K$ is the Creamer-Borenstein estimate of fixed capital expressed in 1954 prices; $L$ is man-years of employee time; and $\gamma$, $\delta$, and $\rho$ are constants that

4. C. W. Cobb and P. H. Douglas, "A Theory of Production," *American Economic Review*, Papers and Proceedings, XVIII (Mar., 1928).

5. For example, see Horst Mendershausen, "On the Significance of Professor Douglas' Production Function," *Econometrica*, VI (Apr., 1938), 143–53; and E. H. Phelps-Brown, "The Meaning of the Fitted Cobb-Douglas Function," *Quarterly Journal of Economics*, LXXI (Nov., 1957), 546–60.

6. *Op. cit.*, p. 551 and p. 556.

ACMS call the efficiency, distribution, and substitution parameters respectively. The semi-aggregate production function so postulated is linearly homogeneous in the two generalized inputs $K$ and $L$; and it is characterized by a constant elasticity of substitution.

It is this elasticity that is crucial because it provides the fundamental parameter to be used in allocating fixed capital among the census regions. We might begin by recalling that the elasticity of substitution ($\sigma$) is, by definition,

$$(9) \qquad \sigma = \frac{d\left(\frac{K}{L}\right)}{ds} \cdot \frac{s}{\left(\frac{K}{L}\right)} \,,$$

where $s$, the marginal rate of technical substitution, is the ratio of the marginal product of labor to that of capital. In equilibrium the marginal rate of technical substitution must equal the factor-price ratio. Hence for an equilibrium situation, the elasticity of substitution is the proportional change in the capital-labor ratio resulting from a given proportional change in the factor-price ratio.

For the ACMS function (8), the marginal products of labor and capital are, after simplifying,

$$(10) \qquad MP_L = \frac{\delta V}{\delta L} = \gamma(1-\delta)L^{-\rho-1}[\delta K^{-\rho} + (1-\delta)L^{-\rho}]^{-\frac{1}{\rho}-1}$$

and

$$(11) \qquad MP_K = \frac{\delta V}{\delta K} = \gamma\delta K^{-\rho-1}[\delta K^{-\rho} + (1-\delta)L^{-\rho}]^{-\frac{1}{\rho}-1} \,.$$

The ratio of the marginal products, or the marginal rate of technical substitution is, therefore,

$$(12) \qquad s = \frac{MP_L}{MP_K} = \frac{(1-\delta)}{\delta}\left(\frac{L}{K}\right)^{-\rho-1} = \frac{(1-\delta)}{\delta}\left(\frac{K}{L}\right)^{1+\rho} \,.$$

To obtain the elasticity of substitution, one must first obtain the derivative of $s$ with respect to the capital-labor ratio:

$$(13) \qquad \frac{ds}{d\left(\frac{K}{L}\right)} = \frac{(1+\rho)(1-\delta)}{\delta}\left(\frac{K}{L}\right)^{\rho} \,.$$

Inverting (13) yields the derivative of the capital-labor ratio with respect to the marginal rate of technical substitution:

(14)
$$\frac{d\left(\frac{K}{L}\right)}{ds} = \frac{\delta}{(1+\rho)(1-\delta)} \left(\frac{K}{L}\right)^{-\rho} .$$

Finally multiplying (14) by the ratio of the marginal rate of technical substitution to the capital-labor ratio,

(15)
$$\frac{(1-\delta)\left(\frac{K}{L}\right)^{1+\rho}}{\delta\left(\frac{K}{L}\right)} = \frac{s}{\left(\frac{K}{L}\right)}$$

yields the elasticity of substitution:

(16)
$$\sigma = \frac{\delta\left(\frac{K}{L}\right)^{-\rho}}{(1+\rho)(1-\delta)} \cdot \frac{(1-\delta)\left(\frac{K}{L}\right)^{1+\rho}}{\delta\left(\frac{K}{L}\right)} = \frac{1}{1+\rho} .$$

Since $\rho$ is a constant by assumption, the elasticity of substitution must be a constant also.

A statistical model for estimating the elasticity of substitution cannot be derived directly from (16). As a matter of fact, we must take a rather circuitous route to find it. First, observe that by factoring $L$ from the right-hand side of (8) and dividing both sides by $L$, we may write[7]

(17)
$$v = \gamma[\delta\left(\frac{K}{L}\right)^{-\rho} + (1-\delta)]^{-\frac{1}{\rho}},$$

where $v = \frac{V}{L}$ is value added per man-year.

Next, raise both sides of (17) to the $\rho$-th power and transfer $\gamma$ from the right-hand to the left-hand side:

(18)
$$v^{\rho}\gamma^{-\rho} = [\delta\left(\frac{K}{L}\right)^{-\rho} + (1-\delta)]^{-1}$$

Assuming that the functional distribution of income is governed by marginal productivity, the product wage rate $(w)$ is precisely the marginal product of labor as given in equation (10):

7. Note that in factoring $L$ from the right-hand side of (8), we are in fact removing $L^{-\rho}$ from the bracketed expression. But since this expression is raised to the $-\frac{1}{\rho}$ power, we have $L^{-\rho\left(-\frac{1}{\rho}\right)} = L^{\frac{\rho}{\rho}} = L$ when it is removed.

(19)    $w = \dfrac{\delta V}{\delta L} = \gamma(1-\delta)L^{-\rho-1}[\delta K^{-\rho} + (1-\delta)L^{-\rho}]^{-\frac{1}{\rho}-1}$

$\qquad\qquad = \gamma(1-\delta)[\delta\left(\dfrac{K}{L}\right)^{-\rho} + (1-\delta)]^{-\frac{1}{\rho}-1}$

Substituting (17) in (19), one obtains

(20)    $w = v(1-\delta)[\delta\left(\dfrac{K}{L}\right)^{-\rho} + (1-\delta)]^{-1}$ .

Then substituting (18) in (20) yields

(21)    $w = \gamma^{-\rho}(1-\delta)\,v^{1+\rho}$ ,

or by transforming,

(22)    $v^{1+\rho} = \gamma^{\rho}(1-\delta)^{-1}w.$

Taking the logarithm of (22), we obtain

(23)    $log\ v = \dfrac{1}{1+\rho}\ log\ [\gamma^{\rho}(1-\delta)^{-1}]\ + \dfrac{1}{1+\rho}log\ w.$

The first expression on the right-hand side of (23) is the product of two constants since $\rho$, $\gamma$, and $\delta$ are themselves constants. The second term is a constant multiplied by the product wage rate. Thus (23) is linear in the logarithms of $v$ and $w$.

Since data covering value added per man-year and average wages per man-year are readily available for two-digit industries, one may estimate the parameters of (23) from its statistical counterpart:

(24)    $y = a + bx + u,$

where $y = log\ v$, $x = log\ w$, $u$ is the error term, and $a = \dfrac{1}{1+\rho}\ log[\gamma^{\rho}(1-\delta)^{-1}]$

and $b = \dfrac{1}{1+\rho}$ are parameters to be estimated by the least-squares

regression. Since $\sigma = \dfrac{1}{1+\rho}$, (24) is a statistical model for estimating

the elasticity of substitution between labor and capital.[8]

8. It is clear that in equations (19)–(23), w is the *product* wage rate. However, in estimating the parameters of (24), the regional average annual money wage was used because regional value-added price indexes are simply not available. Therefore, the estimates of *a* in (24) are not accurate; but this is not material since the intercept is not used in further calculation. A more important matter is the *necessary* assumption that the value-added price for a two-digit

## C. *Regional Capital Estimates*

In order to apportion fixed capital among the census regions by means of (8), it is necessary to obtain numerical values for the parameters $\rho$, $\gamma$, and $\delta$. The regression estimate of the elasticity of substitution is crucial. Assuming that $b$ is a valid representation of $\sigma$, one can obtain an estimate of $\rho = \dfrac{1}{b} - 1$ for each industry. A knowledge of $\rho$ enables one to make industry estimates of the other parameters and ultimately to allocate fixed capital among the census regions.[9]

Let $r$ represent the rate of gross quasi-rent. From (8), (10), (11), and the marginal productivity assumption,

$$(25) \qquad \frac{wL}{rK} = \left( \frac{\delta V}{\delta L} \cdot L \right) \div \left( \frac{\delta V}{\delta K} \cdot K \right) = \frac{1-\delta}{\delta} \cdot \left( \frac{K}{L} \right)^{\rho} .$$

Values of $V$ and $wL$ are readily available for each industry and each region. From the accounting identity

$$(26) \qquad\qquad V \equiv wL + rK,$$

one may obtain an industry value of $rK$. Furthermore, using the Creamer-Borenstein estimate of fixed capital by industry, $\dfrac{K}{L}$ is known.

Finally, using the industry estimate of $\rho$ based on regression (24), (25) may be solved for an industry value of $\delta$:

$$(27) \qquad\qquad \frac{1-\delta}{\delta} = \frac{wL}{rK} \left( \frac{K}{L} \right)^{-\rho} .$$

Since the right-hand side of (27) is a constant, the solution for $\delta$ is simple.

Let us now turn to $\gamma$, whose estimation presents one with an

---

industry is the same in every region. Under this assumption, using money wage rates only affects the intercept estimate. If value-added prices differ regionally, however, the slope estimate will be somewhat distorted.

9. There is a difficult problem associated with the estimation procedure in equations (25)–(33). If each region is regarded as operating on the same ACMS production function, the existence of regional differences in the wage rate implies that the regions are operating at points on the function that are not simply scale multiples of one another (i.e., all points do not lie on a ray from the origin). Thus the aggregates of $V$, $K$, and $L$ for all regions will yield a point that is not on the function. Yet the estimation procedure must assume that it does; hence an aggregation bias is introduced in the estimates in equations (25), (32), and (33).

embarrassment of riches. Other things being equal, since $\gamma$ is an "efficiency" parameter, it would be desirable to let it vary among regions within each industry. To this end, consider (8) a regional production function for a stipulated two-digit industry. Solving (18) for the capital-labor ratio, one obtains

$$(28) \qquad \left(\frac{K}{L}\right)^{-\rho} = \frac{\gamma^{\rho}v^{-\rho}-(1-\delta)}{\delta} \quad .$$

From the distribution equation (25),

$$(29) \qquad \left(\frac{K}{L}\right)^{-\rho} = \left(\frac{1-\delta}{\delta}\right)\cdot\frac{rK}{wL}\cdot$$

Eliminating $\left(\frac{K}{L}\right)^{-\rho}$ from (28) and (29), one may solve for $\gamma$ in terms of known magnitudes:

$$(30) \qquad \gamma = v\left[(1-\delta)\frac{V}{wL}\right]^{\frac{1}{\rho}} \quad .$$

Since $v$, $V$, and $wL$ change from one census region to another, so will the estimates of $\gamma$.

Regional values of $\gamma$ were estimated for a few industries and fixed capital allocated accordingly. However, in these cases, the "efficiency" parameter was too efficient; nonsense results were obtained.[10] In all cases the bulk of industrial fixed capital was allocated to regions other than those representing the American industrial heartland, namely the Middle Atlantic and East North Central regions. For example, the values of $\gamma$ obtained from (30) being used, the East South Central region was found to have a larger volume of fixed capital in the Primary Metals industry than the East North Central region. Since this type of result is untenable, we proceeded under the assumption that all three parameters are identical among the nine regions (although, of course, they vary from one industry to another).[11]

From (23) and the statistical estimate of $a$ in (24), one could estimate $\gamma$ by

10. These nonsense results may very well be attributable to the aggregation bias noted in footnote 9 above.

11. ACMS tested and rejected the hypothesis that all three parameters are identical for different nations. *Op. cit.*, p. 235. While the assumption of constancy is undesirable, it would seem to be less objectionable when applied to regions within an economy than when applied to different economies.

(31) $$\gamma = \left[ (1-\delta)(10)^{a(1+\rho)} \right]^{\frac{1}{\rho}} .$$

However, using (31) simply reinforces the errors of estimation already contained in $\rho$ and $\delta$. Therefore, we used an industry value of $\gamma$ obtained by a straightforward solution of (8):

(32) $$\gamma = V[\delta K^{-\rho} + (1-\rho)L^{-\rho}]^{\frac{1}{\rho}}.$$

Thus in our estimates, $\gamma$ actually functions as a parameter to deflate $V$ uniformly rather than as a parameter to indicate relative efficiency.

With the industry estimates of $\rho$, $\delta$, and $\gamma$ from equations (24), (25), and (32), respectively, one may immediately proceed to regional capital estimates. Letting the first subscript represent the industry and the second subscript the region, it follows from (8) that

(33) $$K_{ij} = \left[ \frac{\left( \frac{V_{ij}}{\gamma_i} \right)^{-\rho_i} - (1-\delta_i)L_{ij}^{-\rho_i}}{\delta_i} \right]^{-\frac{1}{\rho_i}}$$

for $i = 20, 21, \ldots , 39$ and $j = NE, MA, \ldots , P$.

### III. Statistical Results

#### A. Data and Sources

Regional allocation of fixed capital by means of (33) requires regional and industry totals for the following: value added, compensation of employees, and number of employees. All these data were obtained from the *Census of Manufactures* for 1954 and 1958. In addition to the *Census* data, however, one must use the Creamer-Borenstein estimates of fixed capital by industry in order to estimate $\delta$ and $\gamma$. To this end, the Creamer-Borenstein estimates for 1953 in 1929 prices[12] were first expressed in 1954 prices by using the National Income Division's implicit price deflator for producers' durable goods.[13] Net investment per industry in 1954 was added to these figures to obtain an estimate of fixed capital by industry in 1954 (end-year figures).

The data adjustments involved in obtaining net investment should be noted, inasmuch as the procedure was applied to the years 1955–58, as well as to 1954. Gross investment in plant and equipment by

12. *Op. cit.*, pp. 270–72.
13. Department of Commerce, *U.S. Income and Output*, Table VII-2, pp. 220–21.

two-digit industry is available for each year either from the *Census of Manufactures* or from the *Annual Survey of Manufactures*. Depreciation by two-digit industry for the corporate sector is available from National Income Division data.[14] Non-corporate depreciation, however, is given only for the manufacturing sector as a whole.[15]

The method suggested by Gallaway was used to allocate non-corporate depreciation among the twenty industries.[16] Assuming that the ratio of non-corporate to corporate depreciation is identical to the ratio of non-corporate to corporate value added,[17] non-corporate depreciation by industry may be estimated by the following formula:

$$(34) \qquad D_i^n = \left[ \frac{\sum\limits_{i=20}^{39} D_i^n}{\sum\limits_{i=20}^{39} \frac{V_i^n}{V_i^c} \cdot D_i^c} \right] \cdot \frac{V_i^n}{V_i^c} \cdot D_i^c,$$

where $D_i$ and $V_i$ represent depreciation and value added in the $i$-th industry and the $n$ and $c$ superscripts designate non-corporate and corporate sectors respectively. Equation (34) shows non-corporate depreciation as the same fraction of corporate depreciation as non-corporate value added is of corporate value added. The expression in brackets is a correction factor required to make $\Sigma D_i^n = D^n$.

The accumulation of fixed capital on an industry, but *not* a regional, basis from 1954 to 1958 was accomplished in the following manner. Fixed capital in 1955 equals fixed capital in 1954 expressed in 1955 prices[18] plus *net* investment in 1955. Estimates for 1956, 1957, and 1958 were obtained serially in the same way.

To obtain regional estimates of total capital-value added and total capital-labor ratios, as well as gross quasi-rent, it is necessary to allocate working capital among the census regions. This could have been done by using total industry capital in estimating $\delta$ and $\gamma$. Equation (33) would then have allocated total capital. This method seemed undesirable, however, because the regression estimates of $\rho$ and the regional allocations are based upon values added rather than upon values of shipments. The inter-business payments subtracted from

14. *Ibid.*, Table VI-18, p. 216; and July issues of *Survey of Current Business*.
15. *Ibid.*, Table VI-19, p. 217; and July issues of *Survey of Current Business*.
16. *Op. cit.*, p. 25.
17. Corporate and non-corporate value added by industry is obtainable from the *Census of Manufactures* and from the *Annual Survey* volumes.
18. The implicit price deflator for producers durable equipment was used in each year.

the value of shipments to obtain value added represent a substantial portion of the working capital of a firm. Furthermore, another important item, inventory, does not enter the calculations. Hence (33) was used to allocate fixed capital only, while working capital was allocated on a share basis.

In particular, the Creamer-Borenstein estimates of working capital in 1953 at 1929 prices were expressed in 1954 prices, using the implicit price deflator for (all) durable goods.[19] It was then assumed that working capital increases annually *pari passu* with fixed capital. That is, working capital per industry was augmented each year by an amount such that the 1953 fixed capital-working capital ratio, expressed in 1954 prices, remained constant. This is admittedly a rough estimation technique. However, Creamer and Borenstein found that the fixed capital-output and the working capital-output ratios moved together very closely, changing only five percent in nineteen years.[20] Thus over a relatively short span of time this assumption probably does not seriously distort reality.

Finally, the regional allocation of working capital was accomplished in a simple way. Since the data do reflect one significant use of working capital, the classical "advances to workers," it was assumed that working capital per region bears the same ratio to total working capital as compensation of employees per region bears to total compensation of employees. Using obvious notation:

$$(35) \qquad K_{ij}^{W} = \frac{(wL)_{ij}}{(wL)_i} \cdot K_i^{W} .$$

Table 1 contains the 1954 and 1958 current-dollar estimates of fixed, working, and total capital by industry, obtained from the Creamer-Borenstein 1953 estimates by the procedures just described. The regional allocations are subsequently shown in Table 3.

### B. The Elasticity of Substitution

The elasticity of substitution was estimated by means of regression (24) for the 20 two-digit industries for 1954 and 1958. That is, using data from the (usually) nine census regions as observations, least-squares estimates of $b$ were obtained. These estimates, together with their associated correlation coefficients and levels of significance, are shown in Table 2.

A few words of explanation are necessary before the results are

19. *U.S. Income and Output*, Table VII-7, p. 225.
20. *Op. cit.*, p. 91.

**Table 1.** Fixed, Working, and Total Capital, by Industry, in Millions of Current Dollars, 1954 and 1958*

| Industry[a] | 1954 | | | 1958 | | |
|---|---|---|---|---|---|---|
| | K^F | K^w | K | K^F | K^w | K |
| 20—Food & Related Products | $7,998 | $11,820 | $19,818 | $10,045 | $14,846 | $24,891 |
| 21—Tobacco | 218 | 3,051 | 3,269 | 319 | 4,460 | 4,779 |
| 22—Textile Products | 3,860 | 5,396 | 9,256 | 4,378 | 6,121 | 10,499 |
| 23—Apparel & Related Products | 633 | 3,914 | 4,547 | 789 | 5,374 | 6,163 |
| 24—Lumber & Lumber Products | 2,551 | 1,593 | 4,144 | 3,193 | 1,994 | 5,187 |
| 25—Furniture & Fixtures | 588 | 1,158 | 1,746 | 789 | 1,553 | 2,342 |
| 26—Pulp, Paper, & Allied Products | 3,939 | 2,091 | 6,030 | 6,178 | 3,280 | 9,458 |
| 27—Printing & Publishing | 2,317 | 2,491 | 4,808 | 3,190 | 3,430 | 6,620 |
| 28—Chemicals | 10,833 | 6,951 | 17,784 | 13,396 | 8,595 | 21,991 |
| 29—Petroleum & Coal | 14,672 | 7,557 | 22,229 | 14,819 | 7,633 | 22,452 |
| 30—Rubber & Rubber Products | 916 | 1,847 | 2,763 | 1,155 | 2,328 | 3,483 |
| 31—Leather & Leather Goods | 288 | 1,132 | 1,420 | 340 | 1,337 | 1,677 |
| 32—Stone, Clay & Glass | 2,633 | 2,196 | 4,829 | 4,289 | 3,576 | 7,865 |
| 33—Primary Metals | 11,141 | 5,878 | 17,019 | 14,943 | 7,884 | 22,827 |
| 34—Fabricated Metals Products | 3,340 | 4,871 | 8,211 | 4,589 | 6,693 | 11,282 |
| 35—Machinery, ex. Elec. | 5,593 | 9,375 | 14,968 | 6,951 | 11,652 | 18,603 |
| 36—Electrical Machinery | 2,794 | 6,966 | 9,760 | 3,510 | 8,752 | 12,262 |
| 37—Transportation Equipment | 7,591 | 9,807 | 17,398 | 9,860 | 12,738 | 22,598 |
| 38—Instruments | 855 | 1,754 | 2,609 | 1,008 | 2,069 | 3,077 |
| 39—Miscellaneous | 3,291 | 2,627 | 5,918 | 4,086 | 3,261 | 7,347 |

* Source: Computed from Creamer and Borenstein, *op. cit.*, pp. 270–72.
[a] All subsequent tables show industry by numerical designation only.

**Table 2.** Elasticity of Substitution, Correlation Coefficients, and Significance, by Industry, 1954 and 1958

| Industry | 1954 | | | | | 1958 | | | | |
|---|---|---|---|---|---|---|---|---|---|---|
| | $\hat{\sigma}=b$ | Signifi-cance[a] | Inter-val[b] | r | Signif-icance[c] | $\hat{\sigma}=b$ | Signifi-cance[a] | Inter-val[b] | r | Signif-icance[c] |
| 20 | 0.82 | .001 | >0 | .74 | .02 | 0.88 | .001 | >0 | .87 | .01 |
| 21 | 2.27 | .02 | >1 | .73 | .05 | 3.08 | .001 | >1 | .96 | .001 |
| 22 | 1.24 | .02 | >1 | .94 | .001 | 1.67 | .02 | >0 | .55 | ... |
| 23 | 1.02 | .001 | >1 | .99 | .001 | 1.14 | .05 | >1 | .99 | .001 |
| 24 | 1.06 | .05 | >1 | .99 | .001 | 1.05 | .001 | >0 | .99 | .001 |
| 25 | 1.04 | .001 | >0 | .97 | .001 | 0.91 | .001 | >0 | .98 | .001 |
| 26 | 1.10 | ... | ... | .30 | ... | 2.72 | .05 | >1 | .85 | .01 |
| 27 | 1.01 | .001 | >0 | .90 | .01 | 0.93 | .001 | >0 | .90 | .001 |
| 28 | 0.90 | .10 | >0 | .34 | ... | 2.11 | .001 | >0 | .72 | .05 |
| 29 | 1.46[d] | .05 | >0 | .41 | ... | f | ... | ... | ... | ... |
| 30 | 1.55[e] | .05 | >0 | .46 | ... | 1.28 | .05 | >0 | .44 | ... |
| 31 | 1.04 | .001 | >0 | .86 | .01 | 0.87 | .001 | >0 | .80 | .01 |
| 32 | 0.70 | .02 | >0 | .48 | ... | 0.61 | .05 | >0 | .44 | ... |
| 33 | 1.20 | .10 | >0 | .34 | ... | 1.37 | .02 | >0 | .51 | ... |
| 34 | 0.65 | .01 | 0<b<1 | .76 | .02 | 1.05 | .001 | >0 | .85 | .01 |
| 35 | 1.25 | .001 | >0 | .78 | .02 | 0.63 | .01 | >0 | .68 | .05 |
| 36 | 0.89 | .001 | >0 | .75 | .02 | 0.26[g] | ... | ... | .27 | ... |
| 37 | 0.81 | .05 | >0 | .34 | ... | 1.40 | .001 | >0 | .73 | .05 |
| 38 | 1.21 | .001 | >0 | .78 | .02 | 0.35[h] | ... | ... | .33 | ... |
| 39 | 1.41 | .001 | >1 | .96 | .001 | 0.29 | ... | ... | .29 | ... |

[a] One-tail test, significance given if $P \leqq .10$.

[b] ">0" means statistically different from zero but not from one. ">1" means statistically significant and significantly greater than unity. "0<b<1" means statistically significant and significantly different from both zero and one.

[c] Two-tail test, significance given if $P \leqq .10$.

[d] Omitting ESC.

[e] Omitting WNC.

[f] A positive regression coefficient could not be obtained. Therefore, the presumption is that the industry is characterized by fixed-proportions production.

[g] Omitting ESC.

[h] Omitting SA.

summarized. By its very definition, the elasticity of substitution is non-negative; however, statistical estimates of it may be less than zero. In the first place, $b$ may be negative because the data do not conform suitably to the theoretical model. Secondly, if the theoretical model is suitable but the elasticity of substitution is in fact zero or thereabout, a negative estimate may be the result of statistical error (i.e., a random sample from a population in which $b = 0$ would yield a negative $b$ of value $x$ with probability $y$). In our original regressions, five $b$'s were negative, those for Industries 29 and 30 in 1954 and for Industries 29, 36, and 38 in 1958. In all but one case, Industry 29 in 1958, a positive value of $b$ was obtained by omitting one region from the regression. This was done, with the results shown in Table 2.

In the exceptional case, however, a positive value of $b$ could not be obtained. The negative $b$ itself was very small in absolute value, so it was assumed that $b = 0$. Zero elasticity of substitution implies a fixed-proportions production function. That this situation is not incompatible with the ACMS function may be seen by noting that $b = 0$ implies $\rho \to \infty$. Substituting the latter expression in (8) yields a fixed-proportions function. Furthermore, substituting $\rho = \infty$ in (29), one finds that $\delta = 1$. Finally, using these two values in (32), the estimate of $\gamma$ is simply

$$(36) \qquad \gamma = \frac{V}{K} \ .$$

From (33) it follows that when $b = 0$,

$$(37) \qquad K_{ij} = \frac{V_{ij}}{\gamma_i} \ .$$

Fixed capital for Industry 29 in 1958 was allocated on the basis of (37).

Another preliminary point concerns the column labelled "Interval." Suppose a particular value of $b$ is such that one accepts both the alternative hypotheses that $b > 0$ and $b < 1$. This situation is indicated by the expression "$0 < b < 1$," and such an industry is said to be "inelastic" in the sense that its elasticity of substitution is less that unity. On the other hand, if one accepts the alternative hypothesis $b > 1$, the corresponding entry is "$b > 1$." Such an industry is "elastic." Finally, if one rejects the null hypothesis $b = 0$ but cannot reject the hypothesis $b = 1$, the entry is "$b > 0$."

The expression "$b > 0$" therefore means that the elasticity of substitution is not *statistically* different from unity. However, "$b > 0$" may occur either because the true value of $b$ is very close to unity or because $s_b$ (the standard error of the regression coefficient) is relatively large. The latter is very likely when the number of observations is small, as is unavoidably true in this study. There were many cases in which $b$ was substantially different from unity but in which $s_b$ was so large that there was not a statistically significant difference. As extreme examples, "$b > 0$" was as low as 0.70 in one industry and as high as 2.11 in another. We should certainly not be tempted to infer unitary elasticity of substitution in either of these industries; nor should we be so tempted in several other industries for which "$b > 0$" was found.

Let us turn now to Table 2. Despite the meager number of observations, the statistical results are rather good. The correlation coefficient ($r$) was significant in thirteen of twenty industries in 1954 and in twelve industries in 1958. The regression coefficients were even more significant. Only one $b$ was not statistically significant in 1954, while four failed the significance test in 1958.

The regression coefficient, our estimate of the elasticity of substitution, ranged quite widely in value, from the assumed absolute inelasticity in Industry 29 in 1958 to 3.08 in Industry 21 in 1958. Six industries appeared to be inelastic in 1954, although only one of these was statistically inelastic ($0 < b < 1$). On the other hand, nine industries seemed to be elastic, and four of the $b$'s were significantly greater than one. In total, fourteen of the 20 industries failed to yield elasticity coefficients that were statistically different from unity. However, fifteen coefficients were appreciably different from unity, a fact of economic, if not statistical, significance.

In 1958 only three coefficients were statistically greater than unity, and none was statistically inelastic. However, eight industries had coefficients that were less than one, while another eight had coefficients that were substantially greater than unity. Thus, especially in light of the remarks in the penultimate paragraph, it seems reasonable to conclude that the ACMS production function provides a more suitable theoretical model than does the unit-elastic Cobb-Douglas function.

## C. Comparison with Other Studies

There have been three other studies reporting elasticities of substitution based upon the ACMS function. The first of these was by Jora Minasian.[21] He correlated the wage share with the wage rate; however, the regression coefficient (with sign changed) is the elasticity of substitution. Using states as the units of observation, Minasian found elasticities for fourteen two-digit industries for 1957. Considering the different period and the different units of observation, his results are amazingly close to my 1958 estimates. Only in the Electrical Machinery industry is there a material difference, and this is probably attributable to my truncated regression. The levels of significance that Minasian obtained, however, are much lower than the levels shown in Table 2.[22] Some reasons for this are given below.

The ACMS study contained estimates for twenty-four ISIC three-digit industries for 1954.[23] Using nations as the units of observation, ACMS obtained highly significant results, the least correlation coefficient being approximately 0.80. In all but one industry the regression coefficient was less than unity, and in sixteen of the twenty-four cases, it was significantly less. These results are in sharp contrast to mine, for as one may see in Table 2, well over half of the $b$'s are greater than unity.

Finally, I obtained elasticity coefficients for 129 cases representing 61 four-digit industries in 11 two-digit groups covering the census years 1947, 1954, and 1958.[24] I used both regions and states as units of observation. The use of regions gave more significant results, but, even then, the levels of significance were generally less than those shown here. In particular, 30 percent of the $b$'s and 50 percent of the $r$'s were not significant ($P \le 0.10$). On the other hand, the significant $b$'s depicted elasticity and inelasticity more clearly. Twenty-two percent of the significant $b$'s indicated elastic industries and 19 percent inelastic ones. As would be expected, however, the grouping pattern by two-digit classification showed elasticity (inelasticity) in the same industries as do the coefficients in Table 2.

An overall comparison of results points out a general weakness of the ACMS function. The more homogeneous the units of observation and the industries studied, the poorer are the statistical results. Two-digit regressions are more significant than four-digit regressions,

21. Jora R. Minasian, "Elasticities of Substitution and Constant-Output Demand Curves for Labor," *Journal of Political Economy*, LXIX (June, 1961), 261–70.
22. *Ibid.*, p. 267.
23. *Op. cit.*, p. 227.
24. C. E. Ferguson, "Cross-Section Production Functions and the Elasticity of Substitution in American Manufacturing Industry," *Review of Economics and Statistics*, August, 1963.

**Table 3.** Fixed, Working, and Total Capital, by Industry and by Region, in Millions of Current Dollars, 1954 and 1958

| | NEW ENGLAND | | | | | |
|---|---|---|---|---|---|---|
| | 1954 | | | 1958 | | |
| Industry | $K^F$ | $K^W$ | K | $K^F$ | $K^W$ | K |
| 20 | $275.3 | $570.7 | $846.0 | $370.8 | $697.8 | $1068.6 |
| 21[a] | 0.6 | 23.9 | 24.5 | 0.8 | 34.3 | 35.1 |
| 22[b] | 841.9 | 993.1 | 1835.0 | 557.9 | 936.5 | 1494.4 |
| 23 | 43.9 | 277.4 | 321.3 | 53.3 | 393.9 | 447.2 |
| 24 | 67.7 | 79.9 | 147.6 | 107.3 | 99.1 | 206.4 |
| 25 | 29.4 | 67.0 | 96.4 | 37.0 | 83.2 | 120.2 |
| 26 | 376.2 | 265.9 | 642.1 | 629.8 | 416.2 | 1046.0 |
| 27 | 116.6 | 170.9 | 287.5 | 180.2 | 234.6 | 414.8 |
| 28 | 422.0 | 250.4 | 672.4 | 378.1 | 316.3 | 694.4 |
| 29 | 149.0 | 111.9 | 260.9 | 149.8 | 93.1 | 242.9 |
| 30[c] | 139.7 | 313.8 | 453.5 | 159.2 | 378.8 | 538.0 |
| 31 | 73.5 | 354.2 | 427.7 | 96.2 | 430.4 | 526.6 |
| 32 | 94.4 | 108.0 | 202.4 | 155.7 | 173.8 | 329.5 |
| 33 | 456.9 | 275.5 | 732.4 | 526.4 | 384.7 | 911.1 |
| 34 | 239.4 | 409.0 | 648.4 | 320.4 | 562.9 | 883.3 |
| 35 | 523.6 | 1020.7 | 1544.3 | 588.9 | 1221.1 | 1810.0 |
| 36 | 311.9 | 806.9 | 1118.8 | 339.6 | 847.2 | 1186.8 |
| 37 | 322.7 | 506.1 | 828.8 | 486.4 | 784.7 | 1271.1 |
| 38[d] | 87.4 | 209.5 | 296.9 | 125.2 | 263.6 | 388.8 |
| 39[e] | 417.8 | 411.9 | 829.7 | 556.3 | 426.9 | 983.2 |

| | MIDDLE ATLANTIC | | | | | |
|---|---|---|---|---|---|---|
| 20 | $1779.5 | $2485.0 | $4264.5 | $2124.5 | $3006.3 | $5130.8 |
| 21[a] | 18.8 | 623.4 | 642.2 | 17.7 | 681.5 | 699.2 |
| 22[b] | 1406.7 | 1298.8 | 2705.5 | 970.1 | 1348.5 | 2318.6 |
| 23 | 388.5 | 2189.7 | 2578.2 | 484.5 | 2832.7 | 3317.2 |
| 24 | 115.2 | 96.1 | 211.3 | 223.4 | 124.6 | 348.0 |
| 25 | 138.6 | 248.7 | 387.3 | 179.5 | 327.8 | 507.3 |
| 26 | 748.6 | 501.7 | 1250.3 | 1236.4 | 758.0 | 1994.4 |
| 27 | 963.2 | 834.4 | 1797.6 | 1291.7 | 1131.9 | 2423.6 |
| 28 | 1126.6 | 1853.1 | 2979.7 | 3586.0 | 2323.2 | 5909.2 |
| 29 | 2416.7 | 1695.7 | 4112.4 | 1798.1 | 1322.8 | 3120.9 |
| 30[c] | 133.6 | 269.3 | 402.9 | 185.2 | 431.8 | 617.0 |
| 31 | 71.1 | 331.3 | 402.4 | 85.9 | 394.7 | 480.6 |
| 32 | 687.9 | 627.2 | 1315.1 | 930.5 | 914.4 | 1844.9 |
| 33 | 2866.8 | 1813.5 | 4680.3 | 3780.3 | 2384.1 | 6164.4 |
| 34 | 803.6 | 1201.6 | 2005.2 | 1077.1 | 1615.0 | 2692.1 |
| 35 | 1212.3 | 2045.6 | 3257.9 | 1442.5 | 2656.7 | 4099.2 |
| 36 | 1044.9 | 2467.2 | 3512.1 | 1033.8 | 2712.2 | 3746.0 |
| 37 | 1208.3 | 1543.7 | 2752.0 | 1300.3 | 1723.5 | 3023.8 |
| 38[d] | 454.3 | 902.3 | 1356.6 | 485.2 | 1015.8 | 1501.0 |
| 39[e] | 1159.8 | 933.7 | 2093.5 | 1176.9 | 935.6 | 2112.5 |

**Table 3.** (continued)

| Industry | EAST NORTH CENTRAL | | | | | |
|---|---|---|---|---|---|---|
| | 1954 | | | 1958 | | |
| | $K^F$ | $K^W$ | K | $K^F$ | $K^W$ | K |
| 20 | 2180.3 | 3007.6 | 5187.9 | 2610.0 | 3649.2 | 6259.2 |
| 21[a] | 7.0 | 155.1 | 162.1 | 7.9 | 193.1 | 201.0 |
| 22[b] | 300.6 | 224.1 | 524.7 | 243.8 | 280.3 | 524.1 |
| 23 | 63.6 | 386.8 | 450.4 | 77.2 | 483.1 | 560.3 |
| 24 | 241.1 | 178.6 | 419.7 | 348.7 | 219.9 | 568.6 |
| 25 | 223.3 | 391.2 | 614.5 | 285.1 | 447.7 | 732.8 |
| 26 | 935.3 | 567.2 | 1502.5 | 1195.2 | 865.4 | 2060.6 |
| 27 | 634.1 | 706.7 | 1340.8 | 802.3 | 918.6 | 1720.9 |
| 28 | 3493.6 | 1627.9 | 5121.5 | 3012.1 | 1955.4 | 4967.5 |
| 29 | 3623.1 | 1740.9 | 5364.0 | 3113.7 | 1521.3 | 4635.0 |
| 30[c] | 314.9 | 856.3 | 1171.2 | 420.3 | 984.7 | 1405.0 |
| 31 | 65.0 | 202.2 | 267.2 | 70.1 | 221.4 | 291.5 |
| 32 | 802.0 | 672.4 | 1474.4 | 1231.8 | 1030.6 | 2262.4 |
| 33 | 4645.5 | 2463.2 | 7108.7 | 5682.5 | 3109.4 | 8791.9 |
| 34 | 1447.0 | 2052.6 | 3499.6 | 1796.3 | 2588.2 | 4384.5 |
| 35 | 2861.9 | 4634.2 | 7496.1 | 3359.9 | 5164.2 | 8524.1 |
| 36 | 1022.6 | 2612.9 | 3635.5 | 1314.0 | 3268.0 | 4582.0 |
| 37 | 3580.2 | 4123.5 | 7703.7 | 4296.8 | 4602.2 | 8899.0 |
| 38[d] | 171.2 | 375.1 | 546.3 | 201.4 | 427.0 | 628.4 |
| 39[e] | 1166.6 | 838.9 | 2005.5 | 744.2 | 558.6 | 1302.8 |

| Industry | WEST NORTH CENTRAL | | | | | |
|---|---|---|---|---|---|---|
| 20 | 938.7 | 1629.4 | 2568.1 | 1239.1 | 2041.3 | 3280.4 |
| 21[a] | — | — | — | — | — | — |
| 22[b] | 30.7 | 36.0 | 66.7 | — | — | — |
| 23 | 22.3 | 163.8 | 186.1 | 0.1 | 210.1 | 210.2 |
| 24 | 77.0 | 62.1 | 139.1 | 130.6 | 78.4 | 209.0 |
| 25 | 25.0 | 49.6 | 74.6 | 18.4 | 62.3 | 80.7 |
| 26 | 263.4 | 122.3 | 385.7 | 364.5 | 161.0 | 525.5 |
| 27 | 155.5 | 198.2 | 353.7 | 204.9 | 266.9 | 471.8 |
| 28 | 705.3 | 358.0 | 1063.3 | 758.3 | 416.9 | 1175.2 |
| 29 | 562.7 | 313.8 | 876.5 | 896.8 | 371.7 | 1268.5 |
| 30[c] | 51.6 | 52.3 | 103.9 | 60.4 | 80.1 | 140.5 |
| 31 | 32.0 | 109.1 | 141.1 | 35.5 | 123.3 | 158.8 |
| 32 | 223.9 | 147.5 | 371.4 | 428.3 | 241.7 | 670.0 |
| 33 | 185.9 | 123.2 | 309.1 | 321.4 | 182.9 | 504.3 |
| 34 | 160.3 | 229.8 | 390.1 | 286.4 | 344.7 | 631.1 |
| 35 | 277.8 | 510.3 | 788.1 | 470.0 | 756.2 | 1226.2 |
| 36 | 93.8 | 288.2 | 382.0 | 156.1 | 372.8 | 528.9 |
| 37 | 592.5 | 620.5 | 1213.0 | 716.4 | 849.6 | 1566.0 |
| 38[d] | 67.5 | 107.6 | 175.1 | 55.4 | 123.1 | 178.5 |
| 39[e] | — | — | — | 207.8 | 184.9 | 392.7 |

**Table 3.** (continued)

| | SOUTH ATLANTIC | | | | | |
|---|---|---|---|---|---|---|
| | 1954 | | | 1958 | | |
| Industry | $K^F$ | $K^W$ | $K$ | $K^F$ | $K^W$ | $K$ |
| 20 | 615.7 | 1086.4 | 1702.1 | 829.8 | 1432.6 | 2262.4 |
| 21[a] | 147.1 | 1770.7 | 1917.8 | 230.5 | 2809.4 | 3039.9 |
| 22[b] | 943.2 | 2333.4 | 3276.6 | 2291.1 | 2958.3 | 5249.4 |
| 23 | 37.9 | 358.3 | 396.2 | 64.5 | 577.7 | 642.2 |
| 24 | 141.0 | 221.5 | 362.5 | 166.0 | 278.0 | 444.0 |
| 25 | 66.8 | 185.2 | 252.0 | 113.7 | 286.1 | 399.8 |
| 26 | 624.3 | 235.7 | 860.0 | 975.3 | 403.1 | 1378.4 |
| 27 | 126.3 | 171.2 | 297.5 | 195.1 | 262.0 | 457.1 |
| 28 | 1729.2 | 1103.8 | 2833.0 | 1926.2 | 1389.2 | 3315.2 |
| 29 | 445.2 | 231.9 | 677.1 | 485.4 | 180.9 | 666.3 |
| 30[c] | 30.3 | 65.8 | 96.1 | 43.0 | 101.0 | 144.0 |
| 31 | 9.2 | 45.1 | 54.3 | 10.5 | 54.8 | 65.3 |
| 32 | 213.6 | 232.3 | 445.9 | 401.8 | 409.8 | 811.6 |
| 33 | 883.6 | 337.3 | 1220.9 | 1286.6 | 529.8 | 1816.4 |
| 34 | 154.2 | 221.9 | 376.1 | 203.1 | 350.0 | 553.7 |
| 35 | 75.5 | 204.0 | 279.5 | 170.6 | 325.6 | 495.7 |
| 36 | 83.8 | 227.2 | 311.0 | 173.1 | 389.5 | 562.6 |
| 37 | 433.7 | 535.0 | 968.7 | 527.7 | 794.9 | 1322.6 |
| 38[d] | 6.4 | 25.7 | 32.1 | 41.5 | 37.0 | 78.5 |
| 39[e] | 83.6 | 90.1 | 173.7 | 249.3 | 188.5 | 437.8 |

| | EAST SOUTH CENTRAL | | | | | |
|---|---|---|---|---|---|---|
| 20 | 371.9 | 501.4 | 873.3 | 473.7 | 685.9 | 1159.6 |
| 21[a] | 43.8 | 440.4 | 484.2 | 61.38 | 703.8 | 765.2 |
| 22[b] | 212.5 | 386.1 | 598.6 | 218.1 | 457.9 | 676.0 |
| 23 | 17.5 | 193.5 | 211.0 | 29.7 | 352.0 | 381.7 |
| 24 | 94.8 | 128.3 | 223.1 | 97.3 | 162.1 | 259.4 |
| 25 | 16.1 | 56.0 | 71.1 | 32.2 | 88.7 | 120.9 |
| 26 | 208.6 | 97.2 | 305.8 | 383.8 | 167.9 | 551.7 |
| 27 | 48.0 | 65.3 | 113.3 | 71.2 | 96.0 | 167.2 |
| 28 | 888.5 | 589.2 | 1477.7 | 957.5 | 719.4 | 1676.9 |
| 29 | 653.0 | 164.5 | 817.5 | 275.5 | 94.6 | 370.1 |
| 30[c] | 101.2 | 87.4 | 188.6 | 95.2 | 91.0 | 186.2 |
| 31 | 14.5 | 37.4 | 51.9 | 20.1 | 51.9 | 72.0 |
| 32 | 95.2 | 83.7 | 178.9 | 191.2 | 156.6 | 347.8 |
| 33 | 559.3 | 271.1 | 830.4 | 1006.1 | 407.6 | 1413.7 |
| 34 | 110.0 | 163.6 | 273.6 | 145.2 | 240.9 | 386.1 |
| 35 | 92.4 | 163.1 | 255.5 | 133.3 | 209.7 | 343.0 |
| 36 | 38.7 | 97.6 | 136.3 | 143.1 | 244.2 | 387.3 |
| 37 | 70.1 | 126.3 | 196.4 | 117.8 | 273.9 | 391.7 |
| 38[d] | 5.6 | 18.5 | 24.1 | 7.5 | 18.4 | 25.9 |
| 39[e] | 42.9 | 49.0 | 91.9 | 63.2 | 50.2 | 113.4 |

**Table 3.** (continued)

| Industry | West South Central | | | | | |
|---|---|---|---|---|---|---|
| | 1954 | | | 1958 | | |
| | K^F | K^W | K | K^F | K^W | K |
| 20 | 494.7 | 770.3 | 1265.0 | 621.1 | 1003.6 | 1624.7 |
| 21[a] | 0.4 | 25.1 | 25.5 | 0.7 | 36.6 | 37.3 |
| 22[b] | 36.8 | 64.9 | 101.7 | 34.3 | 66.1 | 100.4 |
| 23 | 11.4 | 108.9 | 119.3 | 19.1 | 189.2 | 208.3 |
| 24 | 85.4 | 119.2 | 204.6 | 116.3 | 150.1 | 266.4 |
| 25 | 19.2 | 49.3 | 68.5 | 29.7 | 72.8 | 102.5 |
| 26 | 267.3 | 115.4 | 382.7 | 469.0 | 196.5 | 665.5 |
| 27 | 74.9 | 93.6 | 168.5 | 108.5 | 136.5 | 245.0 |
| 28 | 1619.9 | 591.1 | 2211.0 | 1778.9 | 792.4 | 2571.3 |
| 29 | 4421.9 | 2302.7 | 6724.6 | 5424.1 | 2836.5 | 8260.6 |
| 30[c] | 50.9 | 28.1 | 79.0 | 57.6 | 48.0 | 105.6 |
| 31 | 3.3 | 16.7 | 20.0 | 4.8 | 20.9 | 25.7 |
| 32 | 190.6 | 108.9 | 299.5 | 328.1 | 217.1 | 545.2 |
| 33 | 406.5 | 166.1 | 572.6 | 725.8 | 226.3 | 952.1 |
| 34 | 91.7 | 142.3 | 234.0 | 173.1 | 267.1 | 440.2 |
| 35 | 215.9 | 267.2 | 483.1 | 299.5 | 406.7 | 706.2 |
| 36 | 22.6 | 50.5 | 73.1 | 48.5 | 108.5 | 157.0 |
| 37 | 168.3 | 419.3 | 587.6 | 401.0 | 656.0 | 1057.0 |
| 38[d] | 9.6 | 15.0 | 24.6 | 23.8 | 37.4 | 61.2 |
| 39[e] | 74.5 | 70.2 | 144.7 | 81.9 | 45.6 | 127.5 |

| Industry | Mountain | | | | | |
|---|---|---|---|---|---|---|
| 20 | 175.5 | 301.8 | 477.3 | 262.1 | 412.7 | 674.8 |
| 21[a] | — | — | — | — | — | — |
| 22[b] | 1.0 | 2.0 | 3.0 | 0.9 | 1.8 | 2.7 |
| 23 | 1.3 | 12.5 | 13.8 | 2.8 | 23.1 | 25.9 |
| 24 | 162.6 | 84.4 | 247.0 | 171.8 | 112.3 | 284.1 |
| 25 | 3.1 | 6.6 | 9.7 | 6.9 | 14.0 | 20.9 |
| 26 | 19.0 | 6.1 | 25.1 | 69.3 | 15.4 | 84.7 |
| 27 | 31.5 | 40.2 | 71.7 | 51.1 | 62.1 | 113.2 |
| 28 | 194.9 | 137.7 | 332.6 | 136.4 | 98.0 | 234.4 |
| 29 | 662.5 | 242.2 | 904.7 | 606.5 | 255.7 | 862.2 |
| 30[c] | — | — | — | — | — | — |
| 31 | 10.1 | 9.6 | 19.7 | 8.0 | 11.4 | 19.4 |
| 32 | 63.5 | 35.8 | 99.3 | 126.4 | 85.1 | 211.5 |
| 33 | 362.0 | 136.0 | 498.0 | 509.1 | 213.7 | 722.8 |
| 34 | 16.8 | 31.2 | 48.0 | 36.6 | 63.6 | 100.2 |
| 35 | 20.6 | 41.5 | 62.1 | 64.6 | 99.0 | 163.6 |
| 36 | 1.7 | 6.5 | 8.2 | 15.0 | 42.0 | 57.0 |
| 37 | 20.6 | 42.6 | 63.2 | 96.8 | 85.3 | 182.1 |
| 38[d] | 1.4 | 4.5 | 5.9 | — | — | — |
| 39[e] | — | — | — | 99.1 | 131.4 | 230.5 |

**Table 3.** (continued)

| | PACIFIC | | | | | |
| | 1954 | | | 1958 | | |
| Industry | $K^F$ | $K^W$ | K | $K^F$ | $K^W$ | K |
|---|---|---|---|---|---|---|
| 20 | 1164.4 | 1467.5 | 2631.9 | 1513.9 | 1916.6 | 3430.5 |
| 21[a] | 0.2 | 12.0 | 12.2 | .02 | 1.3 | 1.3 |
| 22[b] | 86.0 | 57.5 | 143.5 | 61.8 | 71.6 | 133.4 |
| 23 | 46.8 | 223.1 | 269.9 | 57.8 | 312.2 | 370.0 |
| 24 | 1566.2 | 622.9 | 2189.1 | 1831.6 | 769.5 | 2601.1 |
| 25 | 66.6 | 104.4 | 171.0 | 86.5 | 170.4 | 256.9 |
| 26 | 495.8 | 179.6 | 675.4 | 854.7 | 296.5 | 1151.2 |
| 27 | 166.6 | 210.5 | 377.1 | 285.0 | 321.4 | 606.4 |
| 28 | 653.1 | 439.8 | 1092.9 | 862.5 | 584.4 | 1446.9 |
| 29 | 1737.7 | 753.3 | 2491.0 | 2069.1 | 956.4 | 3025.5 |
| 30[c] | 93.4 | 174.0 | 267.4 | 134.1 | 212.6 | 346.7 |
| 31 | 9.4 | 26.4 | 35.8 | 8.9 | 28.2 | 37.1 |
| 32 | 261.8 | 180.2 | 442.0 | 495.2 | 346.9 | 842.1 |
| 33 | 774.2 | 292.1 | 1066.3 | 1104.8 | 445.5 | 1550.3 |
| 34 | 317.0 | 419.1 | 736.1 | 550.2 | 660.6 | 1210.8 |
| 35 | 313.0 | 488.4 | 801.4 | 421.7 | 813.3 | 1235.0 |
| 36 | 161.5 | 409.0 | 570.5 | 286.8 | 767.6 | 1054.4 |
| 37 | 1194.4 | 1889.9 | 3084.3 | 1916.8 | 2967.9 | 4884.7 |
| 38[d] | 51.4 | 95.9 | 147.3 | 68.0 | 146.7 | 214.7 |
| 39[e] | 345.4 | 233.3 | 578.7 | 907.3 | 739.3 | 1646.6 |

[a] Data for ENC and WNC combined; figures for ENC apply to the two areas collectively. The same applies to M and P.

[b] Data for ENC and WNC combined in 1958; figures for ENC apply to the two areas collectively in that year.

[c] Data for M and P combined; figures for P apply to the two areas collectively.

[d] Data for M and P combined in 1958; figures for P apply to the two areas collectively in that year.

[e] Data for ENC and WNC, M and P combined in 1954; figures for ENC and P apply to the areas collectively in that year.

and the regressions become progressively better as the units of observation change from states to regions to nations. This fact may be explained by economic, as well as statistical, arguments.[25]

## D. Regional Capital Estimates

With the methods described above, the current dollar values of capital for each industry were allocated among the nine census regions for the years 1954 and 1958. The results are shown in Table 3, where $K^F$, $K^W$, and K denote fixed capital, working capital, and total capital, respectively. The estimates contained in Table 3 were

25. See *ibid*.

**Table 4.** Estimated Average Annual Growth Rates of Capital, by Industry and Region, 1954–58 (In Percentages)

| Indus-try | US | NE | MA | ENC | WNC | SA | ESC | WSC | M | P |
|---|---|---|---|---|---|---|---|---|---|---|
| | | | | | | Region | | | | |
| 20[a] | 6.4 | 6.6 | 5.1 | 5.2 | 6.9 | 8.23 | 8.2 | 7.1 | 10.3 | 7.6 |
| 21[a] | 11.6 | 10.8 | 2.2 | 6.0 | ... | 14.6 | 14.5 | 11.6 | ... | −22.3 |
| 22[b] | 3.4 | −4.6 | −3.6 | −2.8 | ... | 15.1 | 3.2 | −0.3 | −2.5 | −1.8 |
| 23 | 8.9 | 9.8 | 7.2 | 6.1 | 3.2 | 15.5 | 20.2 | 18.7 | 21.9 | 9.3 |
| 24 | 6.3 | 10.0 | 16.2 | 8.9 | 12.6 | 5.6 | 4.1 | 7.6 | 3.8 | 4.7 |
| 25 | 8.5 | 6.2 | 7.8 | 4.8 | 2.0 | 14.7 | 17.5 | 12.4 | 28.9 | 12.6 |
| 26 | 14.2 | 15.2 | 14.9 | 9.3 | 9.1 | 15.1 | 20.1 | 18.5 | 59.4 | 17.6 |
| 27 | 9.4 | 11.1 | 8.7 | 7.1 | 8.4 | 13.4 | 11.9 | 11.4 | 14.5 | 15.2 |
| 28 | 5.9 | 0.8 | 24.6 | −0.7 | 2.6 | 4.3 | 3.4 | 4.1 | −7.4 | 8.1 |
| 29 | 0.3 | −1.7 | −6.3 | −3.4 | 11.2 | −0.4 | −13.7 | 5.7 | −1.2 | 5.4 |
| 30[c] | 5.6 | 4.7 | 13.3 | 5.0 | 8.8 | 12.5 | −0.3 | 8.4 | ... | 7.4 |
| 31 | 4.5 | 5.8 | 4.9 | 2.3 | 3.1 | 5.1 | 9.7 | 7.1 | −0.4 | 0.9 |
| 32 | 15.7 | 15.7 | 10.1 | 13.4 | 20.1 | 20.5 | 23.6 | 20.5 | 28.3 | 22.6 |
| 33 | 8.5 | 6.1 | 7.9 | 5.9 | 15.8 | 12.2 | 17.6 | 16.6 | 11.3 | 11.4 |
| 34 | 9.3 | 9.1 | 8.6 | 6.3 | 15.4 | 11.8 | 10.3 | 22.0 | 27.2 | 16.1 |
| 35 | 6.1 | 4.3 | 6.5 | 3.4 | 13.9 | 19.3 | 8.6 | 11.6 | 40.9 | 13.5 |
| 36 | 6.4 | 1.5 | 1.7 | 6.5 | 9.6 | 20.2 | 46.0 | 28.7 | 148.8 | 21.2 |
| 37 | 7.5 | 13.3 | 2.5 | 3.9 | 7.3 | 9.1 | 24.9 | 20.0 | 47.0 | 14.6 |
| 38[c] | 4.5 | 7.7 | 2.7 | 3.8 | 0.5 | 36.1 | 1.9 | 37.2 | ... | 10.0 |
| 39[a] | 6.0 | 4.6 | 0.2 | −3.9 | ... | 38.0 | 5.9 | −3.0 | ... | 56.1 |

[a] Data reported for combined areas. Figures for ENC and P refer, respectively, to ENC and WNC, M and P.
[b] Data reported for combined areas. Figure for ENC refers to ENC and WNC.
[c] Data reported for combined areas. Figure for P refers to M and P.

converted into estimated average annual growth rates for total capital, the results appearing in Table 4.

It is quite apparent that the Southern and Western regions enjoyed the most rapid growth. In particular, the South Atlantic, Mountain, and Pacific areas are foremost, with the West and East South Central regions following closely behind. Beyond this, however, few generalizations are possible. The most rapidly growing regions experienced highly diversified growth. In other words, these regions did not grow most rapidly because of relative specialization in the most rapidly growing industries. Indeed, except for Tobacco, the most rapidly growing industries tended to be regionally diversified.

Two rank correlation tests were performed, but they do not offer conclusive evidence. First, the average annual rates of regional growth were correlated with 1954 regional sizes of capital stock. The results are shown in the first column of Table 5. This test offers fairly definite evidence that Gibrat's Law does not govern regional rates of capital accumulation. There appears to be a marked tendency

**Table 5.** Coefficients of Rank Correlation Between Average Annual Rates of Regional Capital Growth and Regional Size and Regional Rates of Gross Quasi-Rent

| Industry | Size | Rate of Quasi-Rent |
|---|---|---|
| 20 | −0.44444 | +0.22222 |
| 21 | +0.42857 | +0.42857 |
| 22 | 0 | +0.57143 |
| 23 | −0.38889 | +0.50000 |
| 24 | −0.38889 | −0.05556 |
| 25 | −0.33333 | +0.22222 |
| 26 | −0.66667 | +0.44444 |
| 27 | −0.38889 | +0.11111 |
| 28 | +0.44444 | +0.38889 |
| 29 | +0.11111 | +0.38889 |
| 30 | −0.21429 | +0.07143 |
| 31 | +0.16667 | +0.11111 |
| 32 | −0.55556 | +0.50000 |
| 33 | −0.33333 | +0.16667 |
| 34 | −0.61111 | +0.05556 |
| 35 | −0.61111 | +0.16667 |
| 36 | −0.72222 | 0 |
| 37 | −0.72222 | −0.44444 |
| 38 | −0.35714 | +0.14286 |
| 39 | −0.33333 | +0.14286 |

for smaller regions to grow more rapidly than larger ones. However, this is not universally true. There are some positive coefficients, and some of the negative ones are not statistically significant.

Secondly, the average annual rates of regional growth were correlated with 1954 regional rates of gross quasi-rent (taken from Table 6). All but two of the rank correlation coefficients were positive, indicating that regional capital formation is somewhat responsive to rates of regional quasi-rent. On the other hand, most of the coefficients are small and are not statistically significant at the 0.10 level.

Over the postwar years, regions with smaller initial capital stocks and larger initial rates of gross quasi-rent have tended to grow somewhat more rapidly than their opposites. But size and "profitability" alone cannot account entirely for the rates and patterns of regional capital formation.[26] Entrepreneurial motivations other than immediate profitability doubtless influence investment decisions and hence the location of congealed investment.

26. Regional capital size and regional rates of gross quasi-rent are themselves highly correlated; either one yields relatively good rank correlations with the rate of regional growth. However, the partial rank correlation coefficients (rate of growth on size, after allowing for the effect of quasi-rent, and *vice versa*) are very small, and none is statistically different from zero.

**Table 6.** Ratios of Fixed and Total Capital to Value Added, Labor and Gross Quasi-Rents, by Industry and Region, 1954 and 1958

20—FOOD AND RELATED PRODUCTS

| Region | 1954 | | | | | 1958 | | | | |
|---|---|---|---|---|---|---|---|---|---|---|
| | $K^F/V$ | $K^F/L$ | K/V | K/L | r | $K^F/V$ | $K^F/L$ | K/V | K/L | r |
| US | .60 | 4.86 | 1.48 | 12.03 | .36 | .57 | 5.91 | 1.42 | 14.65 | .40 |
| NE | .50 | 3.28 | 1.52 | 10.07 | .30 | .50 | 4.35 | 1.44 | 12.54 | .36 |
| MA | .63 | 5.46 | 1.50 | 13.08 | .36 | .60 | 6.54 | 1.40 | 15.80 | .40 |
| ENC | .63 | 5.56 | 1.50 | 13.23 | .36 | .60 | 6.78 | 1.45 | 16.27 | .39 |
| WNC | .56 | 4.33 | 1.54 | 11.83 | .32 | .56 | 5.68 | 1.48 | 15.03 | .36 |
| SA | .50 | 3.31 | 1.38 | 9.15 | .39 | .48 | 4.03 | 1.32 | 10.99 | .44 |
| ESC | .58 | 4.59 | 1.36 | 10.78 | .44 | .54 | 5.25 | 1.33 | 12.86 | .45 |
| WSC | .54 | 3.90 | 1.37 | 9.96 | .41 | .51 | 4.55 | 1.33 | 11.91 | .44 |
| M | .54 | 3.99 | 1.47 | 10.85 | .35 | .54 | 5.29 | 1.40 | 13.62 | .40 |
| P | .66 | 6.13 | 1.49 | 13.85 | .38 | .63 | 7.43 | 1.43 | 16.84 | .42 |

21—TOBACCO

| Region | 1954 | | | | | 1958 | | | | |
|---|---|---|---|---|---|---|---|---|---|---|
| | $K^F/V$ | $K^F/L$ | K/V | K/L | r | $K^F/V$ | $K^F/L$ | K/V | K/L | r |
| US | .22 | 2.29 | 3.31 | 34.41 | .22 | .23 | 3.78 | 3.38 | 56.58 | .23 |
| NE | .15 | .67 | 6.13 | 27.22 | .08 | .16 | 1.01 | 6.90 | 44.21 | .08 |
| MA | .16 | .85 | 5.49 | 29.19 | .10 | .16 | 1.14 | 6.32 | 45.12 | .09 |
| NC | .19 | 1.40 | 4.45 | 32.42 | .14 | .20 | 2.10 | 5.01 | 53.51 | .14 |
| SA | .23 | 2.72 | 2.98 | 35.51 | .26 | .23 | 4.48 | 3.06 | 59.12 | .27 |
| ESC | .24 | 3.65 | 2.68 | 40.35 | .30 | .24 | 5.10 | 2.97 | 63.55 | .28 |
| WSC | .10 | .40 | 6.12 | 25.10 | .08 | .14 | .76 | 7.24 | 40.72 | .07 |
| W | .13 | .40 | 8.13 | 24.40 | .04 | .10 | .47 | 6.37 | 30.23 | .08 |

22—TEXTILES

| Region | 1954 | | | | | 1958 | | | | |
|---|---|---|---|---|---|---|---|---|---|---|
| | $K^F/V$ | $K^F/L$ | K/V | K/L | r | $K^F/V$ | $K^F/L$ | K/V | K/L | r |
| US | .81 | 3.72 | 1.95 | 8.93 | .19 | .90 | 4.86 | 2.16 | 11.64 | .18 |
| NE | 1.00 | 5.01 | 2.17 | 10.92 | .16 | .79 | 4.50 | 2.12 | 12.05 | .17 |
| MA | 1.18 | 6.60 | 2.28 | 12.70 | .17 | .91 | 5.71 | 2.18 | 13.66 | .18 |
| ENC | 1.38 | 8.35 | 2.41 | 14.58 | .18 | 1.04 | 7.27 | 2.24 | 15.63 | .19 |
| WNC[a] | .95 | 4.39 | 2.06 | 9.53 | .18 | — | — | — | — | — |
| SA | .47 | 1.88 | 1.63 | 6.53 | .21 | .97 | 4.80 | 2.21 | 10.99 | .18 |
| ESC | .62 | 2.39 | 1.76 | 6.73 | .21 | .60 | 2.83 | 1.85 | 8.78 | .22 |
| WSC | .65 | 2.63 | 1.78 | 7.26 | .20 | .63 | 3.08 | 1.84 | 9.01 | .23 |
| M | .67 | 2.50 | 2.00 | 8.50 | .13 | .61 | 2.94 | 1.84 | 8.82 | .20 |
| P | 1.51 | 10.75 | 2.52 | 17.94 | .17 | 1.06 | 7.47 | 2.28 | 16.13 | .18 |

23—APPAREL AND RELATED PRODUCTS

| Region | 1954 | | | | | 1958 | | | | |
|---|---|---|---|---|---|---|---|---|---|---|
| | $K^F/V$ | $K^F/L$ | K/V | K/L | r | $K^F/V$ | $K^F/L$ | K/V | K/L | r |
| US | .12 | .53 | .88 | 3.82 | .43 | .13 | .67 | 1.03 | 5.22 | .39 |
| NE | .12 | .50 | .89 | 3.69 | .42 | .12 | .61 | 1.04 | 5.08 | .37 |
| MA | .13 | .63 | .90 | 4.19 | .42 | .15 | .84 | 1.03 | 5.76 | .40 |
| ENC | .13 | .57 | .91 | 4.06 | .40 | .15 | .80 | 1.06 | 5.80 | .37 |
| WNC | .11 | .43 | .88 | 3.58 | .42 | .00 | .00 | .90 | 4.35 | .45 |
| SA | .08 | .28 | .85 | 2.93 | .44 | .10 | .43 | 1.00 | 4.26 | .40 |
| ESC | .07 | .21 | .82 | 2.57 | .47 | .08 | .29 | 1.02 | 3.75 | .36 |
| WSC | .08 | .27 | .83 | 2.84 | .46 | .09 | .38 | 1.02 | 4.17 | .37 |
| M | .08 | .26 | .84 | 2.76 | .46 | .11 | .52 | 1.04 | 4.81 | .37 |
| P | .15 | .75 | .86 | 4.35 | .42 | .16 | .92 | 1.02 | 5.88 | .42 |

## Table 6. (continued)

### 24—LUMBER AND WOOD PRODUCTS

| | 1954 | | | | | 1958 | | | | |
|---|---|---|---|---|---|---|---|---|---|---|
| Region | $K^F/V$ | $K^F/L$ | $K/V$ | $K/L$ | r | $K^F/V$ | $K^F/L$ | $K/V$ | $K/L$ | r |
| US | .80 | 3.95 | 1.30 | 6.41 | .30 | 1.01 | 5.49 | 1.63 | 8.92 | .23 |
| NE | .46 | 1.83 | 1.01 | 3.98 | .33 | .72 | 3.59 | 1.38 | 6.90 | .25 |
| MA | .64 | 3.03 | 1.16 | 5.56 | .31 | 1.05 | 6.61 | 1.63 | 10.30 | .26 |
| ENC | .71 | 3.65 | 1.23 | 6.36 | .30 | .99 | 6.03 | 1.61 | 9.83 | .23 |
| WNC | .65 | 3.21 | 1.18 | 5.80 | .31 | 1.00 | 6.08 | 1.59 | 9.73 | .25 |
| SA | .33 | 1.04 | .84 | 2.69 | .45 | .38 | 1.35 | 1.03 | 3.60 | .35 |
| ESC | .36 | 1.25 | .86 | 2.94 | .40 | .39 | 1.39 | 1.05 | 3.71 | .33 |
| WSC | .38 | 1.33 | .91 | 3.20 | .39 | .50 | 2.02 | 1.14 | 4.62 | .32 |
| M | .94 | 6.02 | 1.44 | 9.15 | .28 | 1.04 | 6.51 | 1.72 | 10.77 | .19 |
| P | 1.19 | 8.75 | 1.66 | 12.23 | .26 | 1.47 | 11.38 | 2.08 | 16.16 | .19 |

### 25—FURNITURE AND FIXTURES

| | 1954 | | | | | 1958 | | | | |
|---|---|---|---|---|---|---|---|---|---|---|
| Region | $K^F/V$ | $K^F/L$ | $K/V$ | $K/L$ | r | $K^F/V$ | $K^F/L$ | $K/V$ | $K/L$ | r |
| US | .30 | .49 | .89 | 1.46 | .44 | .34 | 2.27 | 1.00 | 6.74 | .41 |
| NE | .27 | .43 | .89 | 1.40 | .40 | .31 | 1.99 | 1.01 | 6.46 | .37 |
| MA | .32 | .54 | .90 | 1.51 | .45 | .37 | 2.65 | 1.04 | 7.48 | .38 |
| ENC | .34 | .55 | .94 | 1.52 | .41 | .41 | 3.21 | 1.06 | 8.25 | .40 |
| WNC | .30 | .49 | .91 | 1.46 | .42 | .20 | 1.39 | .88 | 6.12 | .45 |
| SA | .21 | .35 | .79 | 1.32 | .51 | .26 | 1.43 | .90 | 5.04 | .47 |
| ESC | .18 | .28 | .81 | 1.23 | .42 | .24 | 1.31 | .91 | 4.90 | .44 |
| WSC | .22 | .38 | .79 | 1.34 | .52 | .27 | 1.51 | .91 | 5.20 | .46 |
| M | .28 | .44 | .87 | 1.39 | .45 | .34 | 2.35 | 1.04 | 7.11 | .36 |
| P | .36 | .61 | .93 | 1.57 | .43 | .35 | 2.67 | 1.03 | 7.94 | .38 |

### 26—PULP, PAPER, AND PRODUCTS

| | 1954 | | | | | 1958 | | | | |
|---|---|---|---|---|---|---|---|---|---|---|
| Region | $K^F/V$ | $K^F/L$ | $K/V$ | $K/L$ | r | $K^F/V$ | $K^F/L$ | $K/V$ | $K/L$ | r |
| US | .86 | 7.43 | 1.32 | 11.38 | .39 | 1.08 | 11.12 | 1.66 | 17.03 | .31 |
| NE | .73 | 5.37 | 1.24 | 9.17 | .37 | .98 | 8.84 | 1.63 | 14.69 | .27 |
| MA | .76 | 5.85 | 1.27 | 9.77 | .36 | 1.01 | 9.35 | 1.63 | 15.09 | .29 |
| ENC | .82 | 6.78 | 1.31 | 10.89 | .36 | .86 | 8.42 | 1.48 | 14.52 | .32 |
| WNC | .92 | 8.50 | 1.35 | 12.44 | .40 | 1.18 | 12.74 | 1.70 | 18.37 | .33 |
| SA | .97 | 9.91 | 1.35 | 13.65 | .45 | 1.23 | 13.82 | 1.73 | 19.53 | .33 |
| ESC | .89 | 8.02 | 1.30 | 11.76 | .43 | 1.20 | 13.23 | 1.73 | 19.02 | .32 |
| WSC | .93 | 8.91 | 1.34 | 12.76 | .43 | 1.25 | 14.49 | 1.78 | 20.56 | .31 |
| M | 1.08 | 9.50 | 1.43 | 12.55 | .44 | 1.71 | 31.60 | 2.08 | 38.62 | .33 |
| P | 1.06 | 11.53 | 1.44 | 15.71 | .41 | 1.38 | 18.09 | 1.86 | 24.36 | .32 |

### 27—PRINTING AND PUBLISHING

| | 1954 | | | | | 1958 | | | | |
|---|---|---|---|---|---|---|---|---|---|---|
| Region | $K^F/V$ | $K^F/L$ | $K/V$ | $K/L$ | r | $K^F/V$ | $K^F/L$ | $K/V$ | $K/L$ | r |
| US | .37 | 2.88 | .77 | 5.98 | .55 | .40 | 3.69 | .84 | 7.66 | .52 |
| NE | .29 | 1.94 | .72 | 4.79 | .52 | .35 | 2.88 | .80 | 6.64 | .51 |
| MA | .43 | 3.78 | .81 | 7.05 | .56 | .46 | 4.78 | .87 | 8.97 | .54 |
| ENC | .37 | 2.91 | .78 | 6.15 | .51 | .40 | 3.63 | .85 | 7.79 | .48 |
| WNC | .32 | 2.22 | .72 | 5.05 | .57 | .34 | 2.78 | .78 | 6.40 | .54 |
| SA | .30 | 2.03 | .71 | 4.80 | .56 | .33 | 2.67 | .78 | 6.26 | .53 |
| ESC | .30 | 2.00 | .71 | 4.72 | .57 | .33 | 2.58 | .77 | 6.05 | .55 |
| WSC | .31 | 2.08 | .69 | 4.68 | .65 | .33 | 2.66 | .75 | 6.00 | .60 |
| M | .31 | 2.10 | .70 | 4.78 | .61 | .35 | 2.86 | .77 | 6.34 | .58 |
| P | .33 | 2.56 | .74 | 5.00 | .64 | .40 | 3.67 | .85 | 7.82 | .49 |

**Table 6.** (continued)

| Region | 1954 | | | | | 1958 | | | | |
|---|---|---|---|---|---|---|---|---|---|---|
| | $K^F/V$ | $K^F/L$ | $K/V$ | $K/L$ | r | $K^F/V$ | $K^F/L$ | $K/V$ | $K/L$ | r |

### 28—CHEMICALS

| Region | $K^F/V$ | $K^F/L$ | $K/V$ | $K/L$ | r | $K^F/V$ | $K^F/L$ | $K/V$ | $K/L$ | r |
|---|---|---|---|---|---|---|---|---|---|---|
| US | 1.15 | 14.66 | 1.88 | 24.06 | .34 | 1.09 | 19.16 | 1.79 | 31.45 | .38 |
| NE | 1.27 | 15.07 | 2.02 | 24.01 | .31 | .98 | 13.98 | 1.80 | 25.68 | .35 |
| MA | .45 | 5.78 | 1.19 | 15.28 | .54 | 1.09 | 19.12 | 1.79 | 31.51 | .38 |
| ENC | 1.62 | 21.05 | 2.37 | 30.85 | .27 | 1.09 | 19.36 | 1.80 | 31.92 | .37 |
| WNC | 1.33 | 17.63 | 2.01 | 26.58 | .33 | 1.13 | 21.28 | 1.75 | 32.98 | .41 |
| SA | 1.22 | 13.72 | 2.00 | 22.48 | .31 | 1.02 | 15.88 | 1.76 | 27.34 | .37 |
| ESC | 1.22 | 13.67 | 2.02 | 22.73 | .47 | 1.03 | 16.05 | 1.80 | 28.11 | .36 |
| WSC | 1.55 | 26.56 | 2.11 | 36.25 | .34 | 1.24 | 29.92 | 1.80 | 43.24 | .41 |
| M | 1.23 | 13.92 | 2.09 | 23.75 | .27 | 1.04 | 16.82 | 1.79 | 28.90 | .36 |
| P | 1.17 | 14.84 | 1.95 | 24.84 | .31 | 1.09 | 19.24 | 1.83 | 32.27 | .36 |

### 29—PETROLEUM AND COAL

| Region | $K^F/V$ | $K^F/L$ | $K/V$ | $K/L$ | r | $K^F/V$ | $K^F/L$ | $K/V$ | $K/L$ | r |
|---|---|---|---|---|---|---|---|---|---|---|
| US | 5.68 | 67.93 | 8.61 | 102.91 | .07 | 5.88 | 82.71 | 8.92 | 125.31 | .06 |
| NE | 4.78 | 49.66 | 8.36 | 86.97 | .06 | 5.89 | 63.88 | 9.55 | 103.58 | .05 |
| MA | 4.90 | 49.32 | 8.34 | 83.93 | .06 | 5.88 | 57.74 | 10.21 | 100.22 | .04 |
| ENC | 5.83 | 72.46 | 8.63 | 107.28 | .07 | 5.88 | 88.32 | 8.76 | 131.47 | .07 |
| WNC | 5.34 | 62.52 | 8.32 | 97.39 | .07 | 5.88 | 96.91 | 8.32 | 137.08 | .08 |
| SA | 5.81 | 63.60 | 8.84 | 96.73 | .06 | 5.89 | 101.25 | 8.08 | 138.99 | .08 |
| ESC | 7.12 | 130.60 | 8.91 | 163.50 | .08 | 5.88 | 103.77 | 7.90 | 139.40 | .09 |
| WSC | 5.69 | 69.09 | 8.65 | 105.07 | .07 | 5.88 | 82.99 | 8.96 | 126.38 | .06 |
| M | 6.47 | 94.64 | 8.83 | 129.24 | .07 | 5.88 | 99.49 | 8.37 | 141.44 | .08 |
| P | 6.14 | 82.75 | 8.80 | 118.62 | .07 | 5.88 | 92.67 | 8.60 | 135.50 | .07 |

### 30—RUBBER PRODUCTS

| Region | $K^F/V$ | $K^F/L$ | $K/V$ | $K/L$ | r | $K^F/V$ | $K^F/L$ | $K/V$ | $K/L$ | r |
|---|---|---|---|---|---|---|---|---|---|---|
| US | .48 | 3.72 | 1.45 | 11.34 | .31 | .35 | 3.32 | 1.06 | 10.01 | .45 |
| NE | .43 | 3.10 | 1.40 | 10.08 | .32 | .31 | 2.59 | 1.03 | 8.76 | .45 |
| MA | .47 | 3.61 | 1.40 | 10.89 | .33 | .31 | 2.72 | 1.05 | 9.07 | .44 |
| ENC | .41 | 2.89 | 1.53 | 10.74 | .23 | .33 | 3.06 | 1.12 | 10.23 | .38 |
| WNC | .65 | 6.45 | 1.30 | 12.99 | .48 | .43 | 5.00 | 1.00 | 11.62 | .58 |
| SA | .41 | 2.75 | 1.28 | 8.74 | .39 | .29 | 2.40 | .98 | 8.05 | .50 |
| ESC | .77 | 8.43 | 1.44 | 15.72 | .43 | .52 | 7.26 | 1.01 | 14.20 | .63 |
| WSC | .90 | 12.73 | 1.40 | 19.75 | .51 | .53 | 7.67 | .97 | 14.06 | .69 |
| W | .51 | 4.25 | 1.45 | 12.15 | .31 | .40 | 4.40 | 1.04 | 11.39 | .50 |

### 31—LEATHER AND LEATHER GOODS

| Region | $K^F/V$ | $K^F/L$ | $K/V$ | $K/L$ | r | $K^F/V$ | $K^F/L$ | $K/V$ | $K/L$ | r |
|---|---|---|---|---|---|---|---|---|---|---|
| US | .18 | .81 | .87 | 3.98 | .43 | .18 | .97 | .88 | 4.80 | .45 |
| NE | .15 | .67 | .90 | 3.89 | .36 | .17 | .89 | .92 | 4.85 | .39 |
| MA | .16 | .69 | .89 | 3.91 | .38 | .16 | .83 | .90 | 4.66 | .40 |
| ENC | .21 | 1.10 | .87 | 4.52 | .46 | .21 | 1.33 | .89 | 5.53 | .47 |
| WNC | .18 | .82 | .77 | 3.62 | .59 | .18 | .97 | .79 | 4.32 | .60 |
| SA | .15 | .61 | .86 | 3.62 | .40 | .14 | .66 | .88 | 4.12 | .42 |
| ESC | .20 | 1.04 | .72 | 3.71 | .73 | .21 | 1.25 | .74 | 4.48 | .73 |
| WSC | .12 | .47 | .73 | 2.86 | .61 | .14 | .66 | .75 | 3.52 | .63 |
| M | .55 | 5.05 | 1.06 | 9.85 | .50 | .41 | 3.63 | .99 | 8.81 | .51 |
| P | .24 | 1.34 | .93 | 5.11 | .41 | .22 | 1.40 | .92 | 5.84 | .43 |

**Table 6.** (continued)

|  | 32—Stone, Clay, and Glass | | | | | | | | | |
|---|---|---|---|---|---|---|---|---|---|---|
|  | 1954 | | | | | 1958 | | | | |
| Region | $K^F/V$ | $K^F/L$ | K/V | K/L | r | $K^F/V$ | $K^F/L$ | K/V | K/L | r |
| US | .69 | 1.36 | 1.26 | 2.49 | .39 | .78 | 7.74 | 1.42 | 14.20 | .37 |
| NE | .59 | .99 | 1.27 | 2.13 | .32 | .69 | 6.07 | 1.46 | 12.85 | .30 |
| MA | .67 | 1.24 | 1.27 | 2.37 | .36 | .73 | 6.84 | 1.44 | 13.56 | .34 |
| ENC | .70 | 1.35 | 1.28 | 2.49 | .38 | .78 | 8.07 | 1.44 | 14.81 | .36 |
| WNC | .78 | 1.72 | 1.30 | 2.86 | .42 | .94 | 11.52 | 1.47 | 18.02 | .42 |
| SA | .55 | 1.04 | 1.16 | 2.18 | .40 | .65 | 5.39 | 1.32 | 10.89 | .39 |
| ESC | .60 | 1.29 | 1.13 | 2.42 | .47 | .72 | 6.80 | 1.32 | 12.36 | .43 |
| WSC | .79 | 1.99 | 1.24 | 3.12 | .49 | .81 | 8.64 | 1.35 | 14.36 | .45 |
| M | .84 | 1.98 | 1.31 | 3.10 | .44 | .86 | 9.74 | 1.44 | 16.29 | .40 |
| P | .78 | 1.65 | 1.32 | 2.78 | .40 | .88 | 10.13 | 1.49 | 17.22 | .37 |

|  | 33—Primary Metals | | | | | | | | | |
|---|---|---|---|---|---|---|---|---|---|---|
| US | 1.19 | 9.97 | 1.82 | 15.24 | .25 | 1.28 | 13.63 | 1.96 | 20.82 | .24 |
| NE | 1.09 | 8.46 | 1.75 | 13.56 | .25 | 1.00 | 8.89 | 1.74 | 15.38 | .24 |
| MA | 1.08 | 8.21 | 1.76 | 13.41 | .23 | 1.15 | 11.37 | 1.88 | 18.54 | .22 |
| ENC | 1.20 | 10.23 | 1.84 | 15.66 | .24 | 1.26 | 13.41 | 1.96 | 20.75 | .23 |
| WNC | 1.02 | 7.44 | 1.70 | 12.36 | .24 | 1.17 | 11.72 | 1.84 | 18.39 | .25 |
| SA | 1.38 | 13.80 | 1.91 | 19.07 | .28 | 1.46 | 17.48 | 2.06 | 24.67 | .25 |
| ESC | 1.19 | 9.99 | 1.77 | 14.83 | .28 | 1.46 | 17.43 | 2.05 | 24.49 | .26 |
| WSC | 1.32 | 12.32 | 1.86 | 17.35 | .29 | 1.64 | 21.94 | 2.15 | 28.79 | .27 |
| M | 1.37 | 13.41 | 1.88 | 18.44 | .30 | 1.48 | 18.06 | 2.11 | 25.64 | .24 |
| P | 1.41 | 14.34 | 1.94 | 19.75 | .28 | 1.49 | 18.12 | 2.09 | 25.42 | .25 |

|  | 34—Fabricated Metal Products | | | | | | | | | |
|---|---|---|---|---|---|---|---|---|---|---|
| US | .44 | 3.28 | 1.08 | 8.06 | .39 | .49 | 4.34 | 1.20 | 10.66 | .35 |
| NE | .38 | 2.57 | 1.04 | 6.97 | .39 | .42 | 3.34 | 1.15 | 9.20 | .35 |
| MA | .43 | 3.15 | 1.07 | 7.86 | .39 | .48 | 4.20 | 1.19 | 10.49 | .35 |
| ENC | .46 | 3.56 | 1.11 | 8.60 | .37 | .50 | 4.58 | 1.22 | 11.17 | .34 |
| WNC | .44 | 3.27 | 1.06 | 7.96 | .41 | .54 | 5.19 | 1.19 | 11.44 | .40 |
| SA | .41 | 2.91 | 1.00 | 7.10 | .47 | .41 | 3.27 | 1.12 | 8.88 | .38 |
| ESC | .40 | 2.75 | .99 | 6.84 | .47 | .42 | 3.38 | 1.12 | 8.99 | .39 |
| WSC | .41 | 2.87 | 1.04 | 7.31 | .42 | .45 | 3.82 | 1.15 | 9.71 | .38 |
| M | .37 | 2.40 | 1.06 | 6.86 | .36 | .44 | 3.61 | 1.20 | 9.89 | .32 |
| P | .48 | 3.82 | 1.12 | 8.87 | .38 | .57 | 5.69 | 1.25 | 12.52 | .36 |

|  | 35—Machinery, Except Electrical | | | | | | | | | |
|---|---|---|---|---|---|---|---|---|---|---|
| US | .45 | 3.63 | 1.21 | 9.71 | .34 | .56 | 5.16 | 1.50 | 13.80 | .27 |
| NE | .40 | 2.93 | 1.18 | 8.63 | .34 | .48 | 3.92 | 1.48 | 12.06 | .25 |
| MA | .45 | 3.56 | 1.20 | 9.55 | .35 | .53 | 4.67 | 1.51 | 13.28 | .26 |
| ENC | .47 | 3.93 | 1.24 | 10.28 | .33 | .61 | 5.86 | 1.54 | 14.86 | .27 |
| WNC | .41 | 3.02 | 1.15 | 8.57 | .37 | .56 | 5.08 | 1.45 | 13.26 | .30 |
| SA | .31 | 1.94 | 1.15 | 7.17 | .31 | .47 | 3.77 | 1.36 | 10.95 | .32 |
| ESC | .41 | 3.08 | 1.14 | 8.52 | .39 | .55 | 4.91 | 1.40 | 12.62 | 33 |
| WSC | .52 | 4.69 | 1.17 | 10.50 | .44 | .61 | 5.86 | 1.43 | 13.82 | .34 |
| M | .37 | 2.58 | 1.13 | 7.76 | .36 | .59 | 5.55 | 1.49 | 14.06 | .29 |
| P | .48 | 4.01 | 1.23 | 10.27 | .35 | .49 | 4.79 | 1.44 | 14.04 | .28 |

## Table 6. (continued)

| | 36—ELECTRICAL MACHINERY | | | | | | | | | |
|---|---|---|---|---|---|---|---|---|---|---|
| | 1954 | | | | | 1958 | | | | |
| Region | $K^F/V$ | $K^F/L$ | K/V | K/L | r | $K^F/V$ | $K^F/L$ | K/V | K/L | r |
| US | .38 | 2.91 | 1.32 | 10.18 | .35 | .34 | 3.13 | 1.18 | 10.93 | .39 |
| NE | .35 | 2.58 | 1.26 | 9.25 | .38 | .34 | 2.87 | 1.18 | 10.02 | .39 |
| MA | .39 | 3.14 | 1.32 | 10.55 | .36 | .34 | 3.02 | 1.22 | 10.93 | .35 |
| ENC | .38 | 2.91 | 1.34 | 10.36 | .34 | .34 | 3.18 | 1.18 | 11.07 | .39 |
| WNC | .33 | 2.29 | 1.35 | 9.32 | .31 | .34 | 3.00 | 1.14 | 10.15 | .42 |
| SA | .35 | 2.54 | 1.30 | 9.42 | .36 | .34 | 3.41 | 1.10 | 11.08 | .47 |
| ESC | .34 | 2.42 | 1.18 | 8.52 | .44 | .34 | 4.14 | .91 | 11.19 | .69 |
| WSC | 1.12 | 2.83 | 3.62 | 9.14 | .43 | .34 | 3.18 | 1.09 | 10.29 | .47 |
| M | .29 | 1.70 | 1.30 | 8.20 | .30 | .34 | 2.81 | 1.28 | 10.68 | .31 |
| P | .28 | 2.94 | 1.34 | 10.37 | .34 | .34 | 3.21 | 1.24 | 11.81 | .34 |

| | 37—TRANSPORTATION EQUIPMENT | | | | | | | | | |
|---|---|---|---|---|---|---|---|---|---|---|
| US | .55 | 4.45 | 1.25 | 10.20 | .32 | .65 | 6.33 | 1.48 | 14.51 | .27 |
| NE | .48 | 3.51 | 1.21 | 9.01 | .31 | .55 | 4.87 | 1.43 | 12.74 | .25 |
| MA | .55 | 4.58 | 1.26 | 10.42 | .32 | .63 | 6.18 | 1.47 | 14.38 | .27 |
| ENC | .59 | 5.04 | 1.26 | 10.85 | .34 | .72 | 7.66 | 1.49 | 15.86 | .30 |
| WNC | .59 | 5.24 | 1.21 | 10.73 | .39 | .65 | 6.41 | 1.42 | 14.01 | .32 |
| SA | .54 | 4.43 | 1.21 | 9.89 | .36 | .56 | 5.03 | 1.40 | 12.60 | .28 |
| ESC | .40 | 2.70 | 1.13 | 7.55 | .34 | .41 | 3.04 | 1.35 | 10.10 | .24 |
| WSC | .36 | 2.21 | 1.26 | 7.73 | .19 | .55 | 4.83 | 1.44 | 12.72 | .25 |
| M | .41 | 2.94 | 1.26 | 9.03 | .24 | .83 | 9.82 | 1.56 | 18.48 | .30 |
| P | .49 | 3.76 | 1.26 | 9.70 | .27 | .60 | 5.67 | 1.53 | 14.45 | .21 |

| | 38—INSTRUMENTS | | | | | | | | | |
|---|---|---|---|---|---|---|---|---|---|---|
| US | .40 | 3.13 | 1.23 | 9.56 | .36 | .35 | 3.40 | 1.06 | 10.38 | .43 |
| NE | .34 | 2.36 | 1.16 | 8.02 | .38 | .34 | 2.91 | 1.05 | 9.05 | .44 |
| MA | .42 | 3.47 | 1.26 | 10.36 | .34 | .34 | 3.60 | 1.05 | 11.14 | .44 |
| ENC | .37 | 2.81 | 1.19 | 8.96 | .37 | .34 | 3.17 | 1.05 | 9.90 | .43 |
| WNC | .48 | 3.97 | 1.24 | 10.30 | .39 | .34 | 3.05 | 1.09 | 9.83 | .39 |
| SA | .24 | 1.28 | 1.18 | 6.42 | .30 | .34 | 5.67 | .64 | 10.73 | 1.20 |
| ESC | .28 | 1.87 | 1.22 | 8.03 | .29 | .34 | 2.51 | 1.16 | 8.67 | .32 |
| WSC | .42 | 3.20 | 1.07 | 8.20 | .52 | .34 | 3.44 | .87 | 8.85 | .69 |
| M[b] | .27 | 1.40 | 1.13 | 5.90 | .36 | — | — | — | — | — |
| P | .43 | 3.67 | 1.23 | 10.52 | .37 | .34 | 3.39 | 1.07 | 10.71 | .41 |

| | 39—MISCELLANEOUS | | | | | | | | | |
|---|---|---|---|---|---|---|---|---|---|---|
| US | .74 | 4.73 | 1.32 | 8.50 | .31 | .86 | 7.15 | 1.55 | 12.86 | .26 |
| NE | .61 | 3.51 | 1.21 | 6.97 | .32 | .86 | 6.33 | 1.52 | 11.19 | .28 |
| MA | .73 | 4.68 | 1.31 | 8.44 | .31 | .86 | 6.55 | 1.54 | 11.75 | .26 |
| ENC | .80 | 5.53 | 1.38 | 9.50 | .30 | .86 | 7.46 | 1.50 | 13.05 | .29 |
| WNC[c] | — | — | — | — | — | .86 | 5.92 | 1.62 | 11.18 | .20 |
| SA | .56 | 3.10 | 1.17 | 6.43 | .33 | .86 | 7.27 | 1.51 | 12.76 | .29 |
| ESC | .56 | 3.06 | 1.19 | 6.56 | .30 | .86 | 5.71 | 1.54 | 10.25 | .26 |
| WSC | .69 | 3.73 | 1.35 | 7.24 | .25 | .86 | 8.06 | 1.34 | 12.54 | .43 |
| M[c] | — | — | — | — | — | .86 | 5.21 | 2.00 | 12.12 | .05 |
| P | .85 | 6.17 | 1.43 | 10.33 | .29 | .86 | 9.63 | 1.56 | 17.47 | .20 |

[a] See footnote 2, Table 3.
[b] See footnote 4, Table 3.
[c] See footnote 5, Table 3.

Regional diversification of investment is attractive for several reasons. Producers of soft goods and of some hard goods may diversify regionally to alleviate the effects of localized recessions. Furthermore, regional diversification offers the opportunity to move into less unionized and typically "looser" labor markets; it offers at least a potential future saving in transportation cost; moving into certain regions frequently enables new firms to operate for a few years without the fixed cost of state and local property taxes and, perhaps, without the fixed cost of rent or its equivalent. In addition to these reasons, postwar shifts in the concentration of population (e.g., shifts to California and Florida) have been accompanied by relative shifts in regional capital formation because businesses follow markets, and markets are where consumers are. Many other arguments for regional capital diversification can, of course, be adduced. About the only explanation that seems to have no relevance is the older (and naive) forms of the economic base theory.[27]

## IV. Ratios and Quasi-Rents

### A. Statistical Results

Table 6 was prepared by utilizing the estimates in Table 3 and the readily available census data covering employment and value added by industry and region. This table presents the following estimates for 1954 and 1958, by two-digit industry and by region: the ratio of fixed capital to value added ($K^F/V$), the ratio of fixed capital to all employees ($K^F/L$), the ratio of total capital to value added ($K/V$), the ratio of total capital to all employees ($K/L$), and the rates gross quasi-rent, or the non-labor component of value added divided by total capital ($r = \dfrac{V - wL}{K}$). The units of measurement are arbitrary but consistent. The capital-value added ratios represent millions of dollars of capital (total or fixed) divided by millions of dollars of value added. The capital-labor ratios are millions of dollars of capital divided by thousands of man-years of labor-time of all employees.

The results correspond rather closely to aggregate results obtained by others and to what one should "expect" on grounds of economic theory. Using the national average, the total capital-value added

27. See, for example, C. E. Ferguson, "A Statistical Study of Urbanization," *Social Forces*, XXXVII (Oct., 1958), 19–26; and *idem*, "Statics, Dynamics, and the Economic Base," in R. W. Pfouts, ed., *Techniques of Urban Economic Analysis* (West Trenton: Chandler-Davis Co., 1960), pp. 325–40.

ratio exceeded two in only two industries, Tobacco and Petroleum. It was between one and two in fourteen industries, and it was less than one in the remaining four. Similarly, the fixed capital-value added ratio was greater than one, on a national average, in only three of the twenty industries. On balance, these results correspond to those of Kuznets and others.[28]

With only a few exceptions for "regional" industries such as Tobacco, Pulp and Paper, and Petroleum, the capital-labor ratios were greatest in the Middle Atlantic, East North Central, and Pacific areas. More to the point, perhaps, there was a strong positive rank correlation between the capital-labor ratio and the average regional wage rate in each industry for both census years. In like manner, except for the "regional" industries just mentioned, there was a marked negative rank correlation between the capital-value added ratio and the rate of gross quasi-rent.[29]

Finally, one might notice that in both 1954 and 1958 the three "Southern" regions had the highest rates of gross quasi-rent. In both years, seventeen of the twenty industries yielded the highest rates of gross quasi-rent in one or more of these three regions, the East and West South Central areas dominating. In light of the continuing decline in the minimum amortization period for new investment and the postwar relative concentration of investment in these regions, one might expect rates of regional capital growth to show a very strong positive rank correlation with regional rates of *net* quasi-rent.

## B. Some Effects of Diversified Regional Growth

One of the chief features of the postwar American industrial economy has been the aggregate substitution of "capital" for "workers." This substitution is shown more dramatically if the ratio of capital to "production workers" is taken; however, the general tendency is nonetheless apparent. The national averages of the ratios for 1954 and 1958 are shown in Table 7, together with the coefficients of variations for each of the years.[30]

28. See, especially, Simon Kuznets, *Capital in the American Economy: Its Formation and Financing* (Princeton: Princeton University Press, 1961), pp. 80–81. Also see Evsey D. Domar, "The Capital-Output Ratio in the United States: Its Variation and Stability," in F. A. Lutz and D. A. Hague, eds., *The Theory of Capital* (London: Macmillan, 1961), pp. 101–2.

29. The two sets of rank correlation coefficients just discussed are not shown here but are available from the author upon request.

30. The coefficient of variation V is the standard deviation divided by the mean of the series.

**Table 7.** The Average Ratios and Their Coefficient of Variation, 1954 and 1958*

| | $K^F/V$ | | | |
|---|---|---|---|---|
| Industry | Average | | V | |
| | 1954 | 1958 | 1954 | 1958 |
| 20 | .5711 | .5511 | .1019 | .0923 |
| 21 | .1714 | .1757 | .3002 | .2862 |
| 22 | .9367 | .8263 | .3886 | .2358 |
| 23 | .1056 | .1067 | .2724 | .4591 |
| 24 | .6289 | .8378 | .4605 | .4372 |
| 25 | .2756 | .3056 | .2238 | .2226 |
| 26 | .9067 | 1.2000 | .1344 | .2076 |
| 27 | .3289 | .3656 | .1355 | .1232 |
| 28 | 1.2289 | 1.0789 | .2696 | .0703 |
| 29 | 5.7867 | 5.8822 | .1279 | .0007 |
| 30 | .5688 | .3900 | .3253 | .2463 |
| 31 | .2178 | .2044 | .5959 | .4043 |
| 32 | .7000 | .7844 | .1481 | .1225 |
| 33 | 1.2289 | 1.3456 | .1191 | .1549 |
| 34 | .4200 | .4700 | .0859 | .1208 |
| 35 | .4244 | .5433 | .1491 | .1004 |
| 36 | .4367 | .3400 | .5910 | 0 |
| 37 | .4900 | .6111 | .1732 | .1939 |
| 38 | .3611 | .3400 | .2315 | 0 |
| 39 | .5333 | .8600 | .2157 | 0 |
| | $K^F/L$ | | | |
| 20 | 4.5056 | 5.5444 | .2256 | .2110 |
| 21 | 1.4414 | 2.1514 | .8789 | .8739 |
| 22 | 4.9444 | 4.8250 | .6217 | .3873 |
| 23 | .4333 | .5322 | .4411 | .5552 |
| 24 | 3.3456 | 4.9956 | .7666 | .6526 |
| 25 | .4522 | 2.0567 | .2340 | .3370 |
| 26 | 8.2633 | 14.5089 | .2414 | .4910 |
| 27 | 2.4022 | 3.1678 | .2516 | .2299 |
| 28 | 15.8044 | 19.0722 | .3614 | .2438 |
| 29 | 74.9600 | 87.4467 | .3393 | .1887 |
| 30 | 5.5263 | 4.3875 | .6380 | .4806 |
| 31 | 1.3100 | 1.2911 | 1.0908 | .7119 |
| 32 | 1.4722 | 8.1333 | .2565 | .2517 |
| 33 | 10.9111 | 15.3800 | .2403 | .2738 |
| 34 | 3.0333 | 4.1200 | .1521 | .2112 |
| 35 | 3.3044 | 4.9344 | .2517 | .1535 |
| 36 | 2.5944 | 3.2022 | .1668 | .1240 |
| 37 | 3.8233 | 5.9456 | .2801 | .3256 |
| 38 | 2.6700 | 3.4675 | .3725 | .2750 |
| 39 | 3.3089 | 6.9044 | .3715 | .1979 |

* Source: Computed from Table 6.

**Table 7.** (continued)

| Industry | K/V | | V | |
|---|---|---|---|---|
| | Average | | V | |
| | 1954 | 1958 | 1954 | 1958 |
| 20 | 1.4589 | 1.3978 | .0477 | .0420 |
| 21 | 5.1400 | 5.4100 | .3742 | .3285 |
| 22 | 2.0678 | 2.0700 | .1482 | .0934 |
| 23 | .8644 | 1.0144 | .0371 | .0455 |
| 24 | 1.1433 | 1.4700 | .2412 | .2382 |
| 25 | .8700 | .9756 | .0605 | .0752 |
| 26 | 1.3367 | 1.7356 | .0499 | .0966 |
| 27 | .7311 | .8022 | .0540 | .0539 |
| 28 | 1.9733 | 1.7911 | .1613 | .0132 |
| 29 | 8.6311 | 8.7500 | .0273 | .0842 |
| 30 | 1.4000 | 1.0250 | .0575 | .0464 |
| 31 | .8589 | .8644 | .1249 | .0987 |
| 32 | 1.2533 | 1.4144 | .0529 | .0466 |
| 33 | 1.8233 | 1.9867 | .0448 | .0704 |
| 34 | 1.0544 | 1.1767 | .0414 | .0380 |
| 35 | 1.1767 | 1.4556 | .0335 | .0384 |
| 36 | 1.5567 | 1.1489 | .4982 | .0951 |
| 37 | 1.2289 | 1.4544 | .0360 | .0450 |
| 38 | 1.1867 | .9975 | .0506 | .1663 |
| 39 | 1.0044 | 1.5700 | .1016 | .1133 |

| | K/L | | | |
|---|---|---|---|---|
| 20 | 11.4222 | 13.9844 | .1450 | .1485 |
| 21 | 30.5986 | 48.0657 | .1908 | .2383 |
| 22 | 10.5211 | 11.8838 | .3718 | .2531 |
| 23 | 3.4411 | 4.8733 | .1975 | .1640 |
| 24 | 5.7678 | 8.4022 | .5512 | .4886 |
| 25 | 1.4156 | 6.5000 | .0773 | .1961 |
| 26 | 12.0778 | 20.5289 | .1650 | .3652 |
| 27 | 5.3133 | 6.9189 | .1574 | .1489 |
| 28 | 25.1967 | 31.3278 | .2312 | .1635 |
| 29 | 109.8589 | 128.2289 | .2249 | .1218 |
| 30 | 12.6325 | 10.9225 | .2820 | .2137 |
| 31 | 4.5656 | 5.1256 | .4551 | .3022 |
| 32 | 2.6056 | 14.4844 | .1433 | .1625 |
| 33 | 16.0478 | 22.4522 | .1687 | .1947 |
| 34 | 7.5967 | 10.2544 | .1005 | .1217 |
| 35 | 9.0278 | 13.2167 | .1313 | .0399 |
| 36 | 9.4589 | 10.8022 | .0874 | .0532 |
| 37 | 9.4344 | 13.9267 | .1284 | .3969 |
| 38 | 8.5233 | 9.8600 | .1973 | .0955 |
| 39 | 6.1633 | 12.4789 | .2479 | .1659 |

* Source: Computed from Table 6.

**Table 7.**  (continued)

|  | r | | | |
|---|---|---|---|---|
| Industry | Average | | V | |
|  | 1954 | 1958 | 1954 | 1958 |
| 20 | .3678 | .4067 | .1175 | .0825 |
| 21 | .1428 | .1443 | .6929 | .6387 |
| 22 | .1789 | .1938 | .1437 | .1101 |
| 23 | .4344 | .3900 | .0553 | .0769 |
| 24 | .3367 | .2633 | .1867 | .2223 |
| 25 | .4456 | .4122 | .0959 | .1035 |
| 26 | .4056 | .3133 | .0864 | .0658 |
| 27 | .5656 | .5356 | .0766 | .0730 |
| 28 | .3500 | .3744 | .2646 | .0584 |
| 29 | .0678 | .0689 | .0984 | .2345 |
| 30 | .3750 | .5213 | .2526 | .2002 |
| 31 | .4933 | .5089 | .2548 | .2341 |
| 32 | .4089 | .3844 | .1303 | .1228 |
| 33 | .2656 | .2456 | .0962 | .0614 |
| 34 | .4067 | .3633 | .0991 | .0715 |
| 35 | .3600 | .2933 | .1049 | .1078 |
| 36 | .3622 | .4256 | .1330 | .2664 |
| 37 | .3067 | .2689 | .2049 | .1294 |
| 38 | .3689 | .5400 | .1800 | .5321 |
| 39 | .3000 | .2511 | .0861 | .4490 |

**Table 8.**  Changes in the National Average Ratios, 1954–58

|  | $\dfrac{K^F}{V}$ | $\dfrac{K^F}{L}$ | $\dfrac{K}{V}$ | $\dfrac{K}{L}$ |
|---|---|---|---|---|
| Declines | 7 | 3 | 5 | 1 |
| Increases | 13 | 17 | 15 | 19 |

**Table 9.**  Changes in the Coefficients of Variations of the Ratios, 1954–58

|  | $\dfrac{K^F}{V}$ | $\dfrac{K^F}{L}$ | $\dfrac{K}{V}$ | $\dfrac{K}{L}$ | r |
|---|---|---|---|---|---|
| Declines | 15 | 14 | 11 | 12 | 12 |
| Increases | 5 | 6 | 9 | 8 | 8 |

Tables 8 and 9 present the results in more compact form. Table 8 shows the number of industries in which the national average of the ratios increased and decreased. It is notable that in only two rapidly growing industries, Chemicals and Electrical Machinery, have the ratios declined; and these declines are probably attributable to inter-temporal shifts in the industry product mix.

The results are somewhat different, however, when changes in the coefficients of variation are observed. Under the assumption that "production functions" are uniform among regions, the trends in regional capital formation noted above indicate that the coefficients of variation should decrease, especially the coefficient of variation associated with $r$. While the declines outnumbered the increases in each of the five categories, the evidence is not overwhelming. Yet a majority of the increases are concentrated in five industries: Apparel, Furniture, Pulp and Paper, Primary Metals, and Transportation Equipment. Each of these industries tends to be regionally centralized in one or more of the census regions. One plausible explanation for these increases is that while the capital stock in the non-specialized regions grew relative to that in the specialized ones, the industry

**Table 10.** Total Capital and its Growth, by Region, 1954–58*

| Region | Total Capital (in millions of current dollars) | | Average Annual Percentage Change |
|---|---|---|---|
| | 1954 | 1958 | |
| U.S. Total | $178506.5 | $225402.8 | 6.57 |
| SOUTH | 37725.9 | 52198.2 | 9.59 |
| SA | 16533.1 | 24142.9 | 11.51 |
| ESC | 7403.2 | 9795.8 | 8.08 |
| WSC | 13789.6 | 18259.5 | 8.11 |
| NORTH | 54923.6 | 66649.1 | 5.34 |
| NE | 12216.6 | 14598.4 | 4.88 |
| MA | 42707.0 | 52050.7 | 5.47 |
| MIDWEST | 65183.9 | 76519.9 | 4.35 |
| ENC | 55596.3 | 63301.6 | 3.47 |
| WNCª | 9587.6 | 13218.3 | 9.47 |
| WEST | 20673.1 | 30035.6 | 11.32 |
| Mᵇ | 2889.3 | 3990.0 | 9.53 |
| P | 17783.8 | 26045.6 | 11.62 |

* Source: Table 3.

ª WNC combined with ENC for Industries 21 and 39 in 1954 and for Industries 21 and 22 in 1958.

ᵇ M combined with P for Industries 21, 30, and 39 in 1954 and for Industries 21, 30, and 38 in 1958.

product mix became even more specialized in the opposite direction. For example, relatively manual automobile assembly plants have spread quite widely; nonetheless, the relatively capital-intensive manufacturing processes have remained in the Detroit area.

The discrepancies between actual and "expected" changes in the coefficients of variation are partially explained by regional shifts in industrial product mixes. Nonetheless, the relatively large number of V-increases, as shown in Table 9, appears to be the weakest link in the chain of capital and capital-ratio estimates made in this paper.

## V. Growth Patterns in the Southern Regions

### A. Changes in Total Capital and its Industrial Composition

Total capital in American manufacturing industry grew by some $47 billion from 1954 through 1958. For the nation as a whole,

**Table 11.** Average Annual Percentage Change in Total Capital, 1954–58, Southern Regions, Weighted Southern Average, and National Average*

| Industry | South Atlantic | East South Central | West South Central | Weighted Southern Average[a] | National Average |
|---|---|---|---|---|---|
| 20 | 8.2 | 8.2 | 7.1 | 7.8 | 6.4 |
| 21 | 14.6 | 14.5 | 11.6 | 14.5 | 11.6 |
| 22 | 15.1 | 3.2 | −0.3 | 12.9 | 3.4 |
| 23 | 15.5 | 20.2 | 18.7 | 17.4 | 8.9 |
| 24 | 5.6 | 4.1 | 7.6 | 5.7 | 6.3 |
| 25 | 14.7 | 17.5 | 12.4 | 14.8 | 8.5 |
| 26 | 15.1 | 20.1 | 18.5 | 16.9 | 14.2 |
| 27 | 13.4 | 11.9 | 11.4 | 12.5 | 9.4 |
| 28 | 4.3 | 3.4 | 4.1 | 4.0 | 5.9 |
| 29 | −0.4 | −13.7 | 5.7 | 3.3 | 0.3 |
| 30 | 12.5 | −0.3 | 8.4 | 5.0 | 5.6 |
| 31 | 5.1 | 9.7 | 7.1 | 7.3 | 4.5 |
| 32 | 20.5 | 23.6 | 20.5 | 21.1 | 15.7 |
| 33 | 12.2 | 17.6 | 16.6 | 14.9 | 8.5 |
| 34 | 11.8 | 10.3 | 22.0 | 14.0 | 9.3 |
| 35 | 19.3 | 8.6 | 11.6 | 13.0 | 6.1 |
| 36 | 20.2 | 46.0 | 28.7 | 28.1 | 6.4 |
| 37 | 9.1 | 24.9 | 20.0 | 14.5 | 7.5 |
| 38 | 36.1 | 1.9 | 37.2 | 26.3 | 4.5 |
| 39 | 38.0 | 5.9 | −3.0 | 16.3 | 6.0 |

* Source: Table 4.
[a] South Atlantic, East South Central, and West South Central components weighted by their respective 1954 quantities of total capital.

this represented an average annual growth rate slightly in excess of 6.5 percent. This average is not a very meaningful measure of central tendency, however, because of the great dispersion of regional values. That is, the various census regions had widely different annual average rates of capital growth.

The pattern of total capital growth is shown in Table 10. As noted above, one or more of the three Southern regions grew most rapidly in almost every industry. Nonetheless, because of "spotty" growth patterns among the Southern regions, the West (comprising the Mountain and Pacific areas) enjoyed the greatest average annual rate of growth. More specifically, the Pacific area led all others from the standpoint of growth, with the South Atlantic region a close second. From a broader view, the South and the West were the rapidly growing areas, the North and Midwest lagging considerably behind.

Table 11 gives a more detailed picture of capital growth. In this table, as in Tables 13–15, data for the three Southern regions are shown, together with a weighted average of the Southern regions and the national average. First, it is interesting to note that the weighted Southern average annual growth rate exceeded the national average in seventeen of twenty industries. Only in Lumber, Rubber, and Chemicals did the South lag behind, and the last two cases are largely attributable to slow growth or decline in the East South Central region. Furthermore, in seven of the twenty industries the average Southern rate was double that of the nation as a whole.

Second, a comparison of the three Southern regions shows that the South Atlantic had the highest growth rate in seven industries; the East South Central, in eight industries; and the West South Central, in only four (one industry tied between South Atlantic and East South Central). The rates of growth were fairly uniform among regions in about half of the industries and widely divergent in the other half.

**Table 12.** Average Rates of Regional Growth and their Variability*

| Region | Simple Average Growth Rate | Standard Deviation | Coefficient of Variation |
|---|---|---|---|
| South Atlantic | 14.55 | 9.2 | 0.63 |
| East South Central | 11.88 | 11.9 | 1.00 |
| West South Central | 13.30 | 9.4 | 0.71 |

* Source: Calculated from data in Table 11.

**Table 13.** Average Annual Percentage Change in the Capital-Value Added Ratio, 1954–58, Southern Regions, Weighted Southern Average, and National Average*

| Industry | South Atlantic | East South Central | West South Central | Weighted Southern Average[a] | National Average |
|---|---|---|---|---|---|
| 20 | −1.87 | −.55 | −.73 | −1.2 | −1.01 |
| 21 | .67 | 2.71 | 4.57 | 1.1 | .53 |
| 22 | 8.90 | 1.26 | .84 | 7.6 | 2.69 |
| 23 | 4.41 | 6.10 | 5.72 | 5.1 | 4.26 |
| 24 | 5.66 | 5.52 | 6.32 | 5.8 | 6.35 |
| 25 | 3.48 | 3.03 | 3.80 | 3.5 | 3.09 |
| 26 | 7.04 | 8.27 | 8.21 | 7.6 | 6.44 |
| 27 | 2.47 | 2.11 | 2.18 | 2.3 | 2.27 |
| 28 | −3.00 | −2.72 | −3.67 | −3.2 | −1.20 |
| 29 | −2.15 | −2.84 | .90 | .3 | .93 |
| 30 | −5.86 | −7.47 | −7.68 | −7.1 | −6.73 |
| 31 | .58 | .70 | .69 | .7 | .29 |
| 32 | 3.45 | 6.42 | 2.22 | 3.7 | 3.18 |
| 33 | 1.96 | 3.96 | 3.90 | 3.0 | 1.92 |
| 34 | 3.00 | 3.28 | 2.65 | 3.0 | 2.78 |
| 35 | 4.57 | 5.70 | 5.56 | 5.3 | 5.99 |
| 36 | −3.85 | −5.72 | −17.47 | −6.3 | −2.65 |
| 37 | 3.93 | 4.87 | 3.57 | 3.9 | 4.60 |
| 38 | −11.44 | −1.23 | −4.67 | −6.3 | −3.46 |
| 39 | 7.27 | 7.35 | −.19 | 4.9 | 4.35 |

* Source: Table 6.
a South Atlantic, East South Central, and West South Central components weighted by their respective 1954 figures for value added.

Interestingly enough, every industry in the "widely divergent" category is predominantly a producer of producers' goods, although some producers of industrial goods are not in this category.

Third, some calculations using the data in Table 11 enable one to determine the relative stability of inter-industrial growth. The relevant statistics are contained in Table 12, where the average growth rate, and the calculations based upon it, refer to a simple average of the growth rates for each industry. As readily seen in Table 12, the South Atlantic region enjoyed the most rapid rate of growth.[31] Furthermore, industrial capital growth in this region was somewhat more "balanced" inasmuch as the coefficient of variation is smaller than it is for the other two regions. The West South Central region was the second most rapidly growing one, and it was also the second most

31. Note that this measure of average annual growth is different from that in Table 10. However, the original ranking is invariant.

stable. These results indicate that the East South Central region not only had the lowest average annual rate of capital growth but also had the least diversified or balanced industrial growth.

### B. Changes in the Capital Ratios

The average annual percentage changes in the capital-value added ratios are shown in Table 13. A comparison of Southern and national averages is rather difficult in this case. On the one hand, to the extent that the South was originally "less mechanized," one might expect the Southern average to exceed that of the nation as a whole. But on the other hand, to the extent that capital investment embodies technological progress, one might expect the opposite result. In this respect, it is illuminating to observe that in the five industries recording a decline in the capital-value added ratio, the decline in the South

**Table 14.** Average Annual Percentage Change in the Capital-Labor Ratio, 1954–58, Southern Regions, Weighted Southern Average, and National Average*

| Industry | South Atlantic | East South Central | West South Central | Weighted Southern Average[a] | National Average |
|---|---|---|---|---|---|
| 20 | 5.03 | 4.62 | 4.90 | 4.9 | 5.45 |
| 21 | 16.62 | 14.38 | 15.56 | 16.1 | 16.11 |
| 22 | 17.08 | 7.62 | 6.03 | 15.5 | 7.59 |
| 23 | 11.35 | 11.48 | 11.60 | 11.4 | 9.16 |
| 24 | 8.46 | 6.55 | 11.10 | 8.6 | 9.79 |
| 25 | 70.46 | 74.59 | 72.02 | 71.5 | 90.41 |
| 26 | 10.77 | 15.43 | 12.78 | 12.2 | 12.41 |
| 27 | 7.61 | 7.05 | 7.05 | 7.3 | 7.42 |
| 28 | 5.41 | 5.92 | 4.82 | 5.3 | 7.68 |
| 29 | 10.92 | −3.69 | 5.07 | 4.7 | 5.44 |
| 30 | −1.97 | −2.42 | −7.20 | −3.2 | −2.93 |
| 31 | 3.45 | 5.19 | 5.77 | 4.6 | 5.15 |
| 32 | 99.89 | 102.69 | 90.07 | 97.4 | 117.57 |
| 33 | 7.34 | 16.29 | 16.49 | 12.3 | 9.15 |
| 34 | 6.27 | 7.86 | 8.21 | 7.3 | 8.07 |
| 35 | 13.18 | 12.03 | 7.91 | 10.4 | 10.53 |
| 36 | 4.41 | 7.84 | 3.15 | 5.2 | 1.84 |
| 37 | 6.85 | 8.44 | 16.14 | 10.0 | 10.56 |
| 38 | 16.78 | 1.99 | 1.98 | 7.7 | 2.15 |
| 39 | 24.61 | 14.06 | 18.30 | 20.1 | 12.82 |

* Source: Table 6.
[a] South Atlantic, East South Central, and West South Central components weighted by their respective 1954 figures for value added.

exceeded that of the nation. In these cases of definite technological progress, one is very tempted to infer that the rate of technological progress in the South was greater than the national average.

Interregional comparisons are even more difficult than Southern-national ones. Variations in the industrial product mix from one region to another virtually preclude meaningful comparisons.

Table 14 shows the average annual percentage change in the capital-labor ratio. In this case, a comparison of the weighted Southern average with the national average is very meaningful. In only five of the twenty industries did the Southern increase exceed the national average; and in each of these cases, the average annual rate of capital growth in the South far exceeded the corresponding national rate. In particular, the Southern rate was almost twice the national average in Industry 33, almost three times the national average in Industry 39, and more than four times the national average in Industries 22, 36, and 38.

In other words, on average the capital-labor ratio increased in the nation as a whole by more than in the Southern regions except in those industries whose capital growth was markedly greater in the South. Other things being equal, the capital-labor ratio may change for two reasons: either a change in relative factor prices causes a movement along a production function, or a biased technological change induces a corresponding change in the ratio. Generally, wage rates have increased relatively more in Southern regions than elsewhere. In the absence of specific evidence of a proportionately greater increase in the cost of capital in the Southern regions, it seems doubtful that a change in relative factor prices can account for differences in the observed changes of the capital-labor ratio. While the relative increase in labor costs doubtless explains the general increase in the capital-labor ratio, there is no such relative increase to account for the interregional differences in the rate of change. Similarly, it is very doubtful that technological progress has generally been more "capital-biased" in one region than in another.

In practically all cases it seems likely that the differential rates of change are attributable to changes in the composition of demand. As demand changes, so does the regional product mix within an industry. For example, over the 1954–58 period, there was a significant shift in demand from woven cotton fabrics (S.I.C. 2211) to woven synthetic fabrics (S.I.C. 2221). The weaving of synthetic fibers is much more capital-intensive than the weaving of cotton fiber. Furthermore,

**Table 15.** Average Annual Percentage Change in the Rate of Gross Quasi-Rent, 1954–58, Southern Regions, Weighted Southern Average, and National Average*

| Industry | South Atlantic | East South Central | West South Central | Weighted Southern Average[a] | National Average |
|---|---|---|---|---|---|
| 20 | 3.21 | .57 | 1.83 | 2.2 | 2.78 |
| 21 | .96 | −1.67 | −3.13 | .4 | 1.14 |
| 22 | −3.57 | 1.19 | 3.75 | −2.7 | −1.32 |
| 23 | −2.28 | −5.85 | −4.89 | −3.7 | −2.33 |
| 24 | −5.56 | −4.38 | −4.49 | −5.0 | −5.83 |
| 25 | −1.96 | 1.19 | −2.89 | −1.6 | −1.71 |
| 26 | −6.67 | −6.40 | −6.98 | −6.7 | −5.13 |
| 27 | −1.34 | −.88 | −1.92 | −1.4 | −1.36 |
| 28 | 4.84 | −5.85 | 5.15 | 2.5 | 2.94 |
| 29 | 8.33 | 3.13 | −3.57 | −1.9 | −3.57 |
| 30 | 7.05 | 11.63 | 8.82 | 9.8 | 11.29 |
| 31 | 1.25 | 0.00 | .82 | .7 | 1.16 |
| 32 | −.63 | −2.13 | −2.04 | −1.4 | −1.28 |
| 33 | −2.68 | −1.79 | −1.73 | −2.2 | −1.00 |
| 34 | −4.79 | −4.26 | −2.38 | −4.0 | −2.57 |
| 35 | −.81 | −3.85 | −5.68 | −3.9 | −5.15 |
| 36 | 7.64 | 14.21 | 2.33 | 8.6 | 2.86 |
| 37 | −5.56 | −7.35 | 7.90 | −1.2 | −3.91 |
| 38 | 75.00 | 2.59 | 8.17 | 32.9 | 4.86 |
| 39 | −3.03 | −3.33 | 18.00 | 4.3 | −4.03 |

* Source: Table 6.
a South Atlantic, East South Central, and West South Central components weighted by their respective 1954 quantities of total capital.

the production of both is concentrated in the South Atlantic region (2211 in North Carolina and 2221 in South Carolina). Hence one would expect a significant increase in the capital-labor ratio in the South Atlantic region, in South Carolina because of a relative increase in the production of a capital-intensive good and in North Carolina because of a relative decline in the production of a labor-intensive good. When the various four-digit shifts are aggregated, the two-digit results shown in Table 14 emerge.

The entries in Table 15 show the average annual percentage change in the rates of gross quasi-rent (i.e., changes in the ratio of gross property return to capital). While the gross return to property increased in almost every industry and region over the 1954–58 period, it very frequently did not increase as rapidly as the capital stock. Hence many of the entries are negative.

**Table 16.** Regional and National Comparisons of Average Annual Changes in Capital and in the Capital Ratios

| Comparisons | $\Delta K/K$ | | $\frac{\Delta K}{\bar{V}} / \frac{K}{\bar{V}}$ | | $\frac{\Delta K}{\bar{L}} / \frac{K}{\bar{L}}$ | | $\Delta r/r$ | |
|---|---|---|---|---|---|---|---|---|
| | Co-efficient | Signifi-cance | Co-efficient | Signifi-cance | Co-efficient | Signifi-cance | Co-efficient | Signifi-cance |
| Rank Correlation for Weighted Southern Average & National Average | 0.37895 | 0.0192 | 0.83158 | 0.0001 | 0.70526 | 0.0001 | 0.62105 | 0.0001 |
| Coefficient of Concordance among Three Southern Regions | 0.62239 | 0.02 | 0.82790 | 0.01 | 0.68588 | 0.01 | 0.62907 | 0.02 |
| Rank Correlation for Southern Regions: | | | | | | | | |
| South Atlantic and East South Central | 0.26316 | 0.11 | 0.67368 | 0.0001 | 0.43158 | 0.008 | 0.53684 | 0.001 |
| South Atlantic and West South Central | 0.36841 | 0.02 | 0.53684 | 0.001 | 0.45263 | 0.005 | 0.24211 | 0.14 |
| East South Central & West South Central | 0.55789 | 0.001 | 0.61053 | 0.0001 | 0.69474 | 0.0001 | 0.30526 | 0.06 |

In the bulk of the cases, the national average either increased by more or decreased by less than the Southern average. This is more or less to be expected in light of the relatively more rapid growth of capital in the South. The only notable exceptions occur in Industries 35–39, in which the Southern averages grew more rapidly than the national averages in both capital and rates of gross quasi-rent. This is partially explained by the relatively greater increase in the capital-value added ratio in the nation as a whole. But to some extent it must also be attributable to a changing composition of the industrial product mix.

Taking a simple average of the changes for each of the Southern regions, one finds that the South Atlantic enjoyed an average annual increase of three percent and the West South Central of one percent, while the East South Central recorded an average annual decrease of one percent. The positive averages for the South Atlantic and West South Central regions, however, are exclusively attributable to the exceptionally large increases in Industries 38 and 39 respectively. But even in the absence of these, there would be approximately no change in the average rate of gross quasi-rent. In any event, it is interesting to observe that, contrary to the national tendency, changes in the rate of gross quasi-rent varied directly with the growth of capital. That is, the South Atlantic region enjoyed the greatest rate of capital accumulation and the greatest increase in the average rate of gross quasi-rent. The West South Central was second in both categories, while the East South Central was last.

### C. Some Comparison Tests

Table 16 presents several non-parametric tests for consistency in the rates of change in capital and in the capital ratios. The first row shows the rank correlations, and their levels of significance, between the weighted average Southern changes and the average national changes. While the coefficient is relatively small in the case of capital growth, it is nonetheless highly significant. In the other cases, the coefficients are both relatively large and significant. Generally, this implies that changes in the Southern ratios were fairly consistent with the national changes from the standpoint of relative magnitude. For example, the industry ranking (by magnitude) of changes in the capital-value added ratio was about the same in the South as in the nation as a whole.[32]

32. This particular rank correlation is immediately obtainable from Table 13.

The second row of the table contains the coefficients of concordance,[33] and their levels of significance, for the three Southern regions. All of these are fairly large and significant. This means that there is not a statistically significant difference among the industry rankings of the three Southern regions. To supplement this finding, the final set of rows in Table 16 contains the pairwise rank correlation coefficients for the three regions. Some of these coefficients are small and not statistically significant. This means that there is little or no similarity between the rankings of the regions concerned for the change in question. On the other hand, some of the coefficients are clearly significant. Comparing the coefficients in each column, one sees that the East and West South Central regions are more alike from the standpoint of capital growth and the change in the capital-labor ratio, while the South Atlantic and the East South Central regions show greater similarity in ranking the changes in the capital-value added ratio and in the rates of gross quasi-rent.

## VI. Conclusion

As previously stated, national capital aggregates may be regionally allocated in an infinite number of ways. The basic justifications of the allocation presented here are (a) that the latest NBER capital data were used, and (b) that the currently most widely accepted semi-aggregate "production function" was utilized as the principal allocative device. Regardless of the justifications, however, any particular regional allocation of capital is a set of estimates not susceptible of statistical tests based upon probability theory.

---

To illustrate the point more clearly, however, note that for the Southern average, Industry 26 (tied with 22) recorded the greatest increase in the capital-value added ratio, while Industry 24 had the third greatest increase, etc. For the nation as a whole, Industry 26 scored the greatest increase, Industry 24 the second greatest, etc. It is this *consistency* of ranking that is reflected in a large and significant coefficient of rank correlation.

33. In simple rank correlation, one measures the relationship between two sets of rankings, e.g., rankings of the rate of capital growth in the South and in the nation as a whole. The coefficient of concordance is an extension of this concept. In this case, however, one measures, not the correlation between two sets of rankings, but the similarity of rankings by different "individuals," i.e., regions. As applied to the problem at hand, for each region there is an industry ranking according to (say) the magnitude of the rate of capital growth. The coefficient of concordance measures the similarity of these industry rankings among the three regions. If the coefficient were unity, the three sets of rankings would be identical; if zero, there would be absolutely no similarity. For a more complete discussion, see Maurice G. Kendall, *Rank Correlation Methods* (2d ed.; London, 1955), pp. 94–106.

Despite the objections that may be raised against any particular allocation, the estimated data and ratios have potentially great significance for regional studies, especially studies of regional industrial growth. To be sure, since these particular estimates are based upon a specific assumption concerning industry production functions, they may not be used to estimate the parameters of regional production functions. But any other uses of these data seem, at least a priori, to be plausible and statistically justifiable.

# XIII

## The Postwar Corps of Engineers Program in Ten Southern States: An Evaluation of Economic Efficiency

*By Robert Haveman*

In recent years, the existing investment criterion used by the Federal government has undergone substantial scrutiny in the work of professional economists.[1] These studies had as their goal a refinement of the objective efficiency criterion used by those Federal agencies concerned with the evaluation of investment opportunities.[2] Consequently, the proposed criteria built upon, modified and, in one case, abandoned completely the embryonic form of the existing criterion. Because of the indisputable superiority of the proposed criteria, this study will apply them to the postwar Corps of Engineers water resource projects in ten Southern states. Through this approach an attempt will be made to estimate the misallocation of Federal funds and national resources in this area caused by the application of the

1. Primarily Otto Eckstein, *Water Resources Development: The Economics of Project Evaluation* (Cambridge: Harvard University Press, 1958); Roland McKean, *Efficiency in Government Through Systems Analysis, with Emphasis on Water Resources Development* (New York: John Wiley and Sons, Inc., 1958); and John V. Krutilla and Otto Eckstein, *Multiple Purpose River Development: Studies in Applied Economics* (Baltimore: Johns Hopkins Press, 1958), to mention only the main contributors.

2. Because the U.S. Army Corps of Engineers and the Bureau of Reclamation were the agencies primarily concerned with such evaluation, these studies centered about water resources investment decisions. See Subcommittee on Evaluation Standards, *Proposed Practices for Economic Analysis of River Basin Projects*, Report to the Inter-Agency Committee on Water Resources, 1958; and Bureau of the Budget, *Circular A-47*, Executive Office of the President, Washington, D.C., 1958.

existing agency criterion.   The analysis will be presented in the four following stages: (1) a brief description of the Corps program in the South; (2) a discussion of the several criteria to be used in the evaluation, and the assumptions necessary in applying them; (3) the presentation of the evidence concerning the effect of the application of the proposed criteria on the projects; and (4) concluding remarks concerning the volume of misallocated resources and the probable impact of the program on Southern economic development.

### The Corps Program in the South

Since 1946, Federal government appropriations to the South[3] for flood control, navigation, and other water resource development have flowed primarily through the General Construction program of the U.S. Army Corps of Engineers.   As noted in Table 1, total new construction appropriations under this program amounted to over $7.5 billion during this period.   Of this amount, over $1.5 billion or 20

**Table 1.** Water Resource Construction Appropriations to Projects in the South under the General Construction Program of the Corps of Engineers, by State, in Absolute and Percentage Terms, 1946–62

| State or Region | GENERAL CONSTRUCTION APPROPRIATIONS[a] | | |
|---|---|---|---|
| | ($000) | % of U.S. | % of South |
| Alabama | $113,787 | 1.51 | 7.55 |
| Arkansas | 273,717 | 3.64 | 18.16 |
| Florida | 187,141 | 2.49 | 12.42 |
| Georgia | 178,380 | 2.37 | 11.84 |
| Kentucky | 327,278 | 4.35 | 21.72 |
| Louisiana | 113,415 | 1.51 | 7.53 |
| Mississippi | 6,580 | .09 | .44 |
| North Carolina | 58,465 | .78 | 3.88 |
| South Carolina | 87,011 | 1.16 | 5.77 |
| Tennessee | 161,179 | 2.14 | 10.70 |
| South | 1,506,953 | 20.04 | 100.00 |
| Non-South | 6,011,605 | 79.96 | |
| United States | 7,518,558 | 100.00 | |

a Data computed from information in the House Reports on the Senate-House Conference on each of the annual Civil Functions Appropriation Bills from 1946 through 1962. In each case the appropriation was allotted to the state in which the specific project was located. In the cases in which a project was physically in two or more states, the appropriation was divided equally among the states.

3. The ten states included in the study are Alabama, Arkansas, Florida, Georgia, Kentucky, Louisiana, Mississippi, North Carolina, South Carolina, and Tennessee.

percent of the total, was allocated to projects in the ten Southern states. This represents an average appropriation of nearly $50 per person in the South.

Also from Table 1, it is seen that the program strongly favored some states to the relative neglect of others. Arkansas, for example, received nearly $275 million for new project construction while Mississippi received but $6.6 million. The top two Southern states (Arkansas and Kentucky), with but 3 percent of the nation's population, received 8 percent of the total appropriation and 40 percent of Southern appropriations. On the other hand, the bottom pair (Mississippi and North Carolina) possess nearly 4 percent of the nation's population but received less than 1 percent of the national appropriation and but slightly more than 4 percent of Southern appropriations.[4] In the following study, it is the set of projects represented by the appropriation data in Table 1 that will be re-evaluated in terms of the goal of allocative efficiency.

## The Criteria for Project Choice

In the analysis of the "worthwhileness" of any long-lived capital purchase, the evaluation of the streams of costs and returns is a necessary element. However, the technique by which these streams are evaluated is in no wise universal. With each interpretation of the stipulated goal and with each definition of the constrained variable, a different and unique criterion emerges. Consequently, before we proceed to a description of the individual criteria applied in this study, let us look briefly at the general concept of allocative efficiency which is assumed to be the proper goal for the evaluation of Federal government investment opportunities.

4. It should be noted, however, that these data omit an offspring of the Corps General Construction Program, the Mississippi River and Tributaries Program, as well as the entire TVA program, both of which financed projects only in the South. If the appropriations to the Mississippi River Program were included in the above data, total new construction appropriations would be $8.25 billion, of which the South received $2.25 billion, or 27 percent of the total. The appropriations to Arkansas, Kentucky, Louisiana, Mississippi, and Tennessee would be increased to $404 million, $373 million, $399 million, $161 million, and $271 million respectively. Not only is the disparity of appropriations among states again evident but, more significantly, the South, as a whole, with 18 percent of the nation's population and 27 percent of the total appropriation, appears especially well-blessed. In per capita terms the average appropriation in the United States was about $50 as compared with $72 in the South.

## The Concept of Allocative Efficiency

Just as a corporation decision-maker calculates and compares the relative return on proposed capital projects and then chooses that set which will both maximize his stated goal (in this case, profits) and exhaust his (in all likelihood) constrained budget, so too must a governmental agency. However, because the government is a social institution, the concept of maximum profits loses its meaning, and a new goal must be sought. Consequently, in the following analysis, the goal of government investment spending will be taken to be the maximization of total social welfare. More specifically, because of the problems of measurement and interpersonal comparison of utility, this goal will be equated with the maximization of national income. As the constrained variable in this case is a social cost represented by the budget of the governmental unit, it is this value the return on which must be maximized. Therefore, the criteria used in the study are all designed to point to that set of projects which will maximize the expected increases in national income from any governmental expenditure (national cost).

## The Criteria

### The Benefit-Cost Ratio

At present, the criterion applied by the Corps of Engineers is known as the benefit-cost ratio, and takes the following form:

$$Z = \frac{\Sigma \dfrac{B}{(1+i)^t}}{K + \Sigma \dfrac{O}{(1+i)^t}} \quad ,$$

in which $B$ is the expected annual benefit in the form of additions to national income from a project; $i$ is the rate of interest used to discount the future streams of benefits and costs; $t$ is the estimated life of the project; $K$ is the fixed investment cost; and $O$ is the estimated annual operation-maintenance-and-repair costs.[5] Since 1946, the expected streams of benefits and costs have been evaluated by an interest rate equal to the average long-term government bond rate, which has fluctuated between 2.5 and 3 percent. The length of project life used for evaluation during this period has typically been 50 years. If, for any

5. It should be noted that this criterion implicitly postulates the entire "expenditure" of money—a concept embracing both capital expenditure and necessary operation-maintenance-and-repair costs—to be the prober budget constraint.

given project, the calculated benefit-cost ratio is greater than 1, the project becomes eligible for Congressional authorization.[6]

For several reasons, economists have found this approach and its application to be faulty. Among the major criticisms of the approach one finds statements concerning the inadequate definition of the goal and budget constraint, the inappropriate evaluation of the time factor, and the incomplete treatment of uncertain expectations. Based on these criticisms, several alternative approaches have been suggested. Because of their conceptual superiority, let us describe and analyze these suggestions and apply them to actual project data.

### The Interest-Rate Correction

This suggestion accepts the basic benefit-cost ratio as an adequate criterion for choice. Objection is raised, however, to the exceptionally low rate of interest used by the Corps to evaluate the future streams of benefits and costs. Rather than the long-term bond rate, this criterion proposes that a more appropriate estimate of the social (or opportunity) cost of capital be used. Because the budget committed to water-resource development is raised through the taxation of private citizens and therefore any particular public project is constructed and maintained at the expense of its private alternative, this approach contends that national income can only be maximized if funds committed to public projects earn at least as high a return as their value in the private sector.[7] Consequently, the traditional benefit-cost ratio criterion incorporating an interest rate of 4.5 percent, estimated to be the social cost of capital by William L. Miller,[8] and

6. In the law, no mention is made of the possible existence of a budget which is unable to cover all projects bearing a ratio greater than unity.

7. It should be noted that, if this concept is incorporated into the benefit-cost ratio criterion, the rate of return on all of the projects with a benefit-cost ratio greater than 1 will be larger than the measure of the social cost of capital which is used. Moreover, if the budget is sufficiently restricted, the social marginal productivity of water resource investment will be greater than the social cost of capital.

8. The opportunity cost of Federal investment was estimated by Eckstein for the year 1955 to be in the range of 5 or 6 percent. See Krutilla and Eckstein, *op. cit.*, pp. 78–130. Harberger, following a somewhat different tack, suggests the use of a rate of interest in this same range. See Arnold C. Harberger, "The Interest Rate in Cost-Benefit Analysis," in U. S. Congress, Joint Economic Committee, *Federal Expenditure Policy for Economic Growth and Stability*, Washington, November 5, 1957, pp. 239–41. Miller, using a revision of Eckstein's technique, estimated the social cost of capital to be between 4 and 4.5 percent. It is this revised estimate which is used in this test. See William L. Miller, "The Magnitude of the Discount Rate for Government Projects," *Southern Economic Journal* (April, 1962), pp. 348–56.

an estimated length of project life of fifty years forms the essence of this test.

Where $B$ represents the estimated annual stream of benefits, $O$ the estimated annual stream of operation-maintenance-and-repair costs, and $K$ the investment costs, the traditional form of the benefit-cost ratio expressed earlier can be redefined as:

$$Z = \frac{B}{O + A_{it}\, K} \quad ,$$

in which $A_{it}$ is the annual capital charge of both interest and amortization per dollar of investment costs. Given the rate of interest $(i)$ and the length of project life $(t)$, the numerical value of $A_{it}$ can be secured from a table, "Annuity whose Present Value is 1."[9]

### The Eckstein-Krutilla Proposal

Again, the traditional benefit-cost framework is preserved. However, in an attempt both to correct the deficiency of the interest rate concept used by the Corps and to preserve the "long-term perspective" of the resource development program, both the interest rate and the length of project life have been modified. Proposing use of the social cost of capital concept and accepting their estimate of this rate, Eckstein and Krutilla suggest that the expected benefit and cost streams be evaluated with a 5.5 percent rate of interest. In order to preserve the long-term perspective of the program, they suggest using a length of project life of one hundred years instead of fifty.[10]

### The Eckstein Proposal

Eckstein elsewhere argues that, because the program under consideration will provide its benefits to future generations, it is not at all certain that the cost of capital to the present generation is the correct evaluation. Assuming that, as a nation, we ". . . prefer rejection of present intertemporal preferences in favor of a redistribution of income towards future generations," he proposes using the social rate of time preference in place of the opportunity cost of capital. He defines the social rate of time preference as that rate which a majority of the populace would choose as a guide to long-term investment projects whose income streams will go to large masses of population

9. The numerical value of $A_{it}$ used in this test is .05060215.

10. Krutilla and Eckstein, *op. cit.* The numerical value of $A_{it}$ in this case is .05526132.

at a later date.[11] Rather arbitrarily, Eckstein estimates this rate to be approximately 2.5 percent and proposes that projects be evaluated by means of a benefit-cost ratio making use of this rate. However, to insure that the entire Corps program earns a rate of return equal to his estimate of the opportunity cost of the funds committed (see note 8), he recommends that no project displaying a benefit-cost ratio smaller than 1.4 be accepted. The length of project life in this test is again assumed to be fifty years.

### The McKean Proposal

Whereas each of the above criteria views the relevant budget constraint to be the total "expenditure of money" and consequently aims at the maximization of the present value of the future income stream created by this expenditure, the McKean proposal has a rather different point of view on both the concept of the budget and the quantity to be maximized. By assuming that the future national water-resources construction budget is invariate with regard to the volume of necessary operating expenses arising from already constructed projects, McKean views the relevant constraint to be only the capital budget $(K)$.[12] Moreover, he interprets the concept "maximum national present value" to mean the maximum growth of asset values throughout the period.[13]

With this definition of both the goal and the relevant budget constraint of the water-resource development program, McKean argues that the necessary criterion is the internal rate of return rather than the benefit-cost ratio.[14] By applying the recommendation by Har-

11. This rate is suggested by both Eckstein and Joe S. Bain. Eckstein, *op. cit.*, pp. 99–104; and Joe S. Bain, "Criteria for Undertaking Water-Resource Developments," *American Economic Review*, L (May, 1960), 315–16.

12. It should be noted here that McKean's argument for such a constraint is based on the judgment that both marketable (e.g., irrigation and power) and non-marketable (e.g., flood control) project benefits are, in some sense, current receipts available for reinvestment by the government. This judgment has been open to severe criticism. See Julius Margolis, "The Economic Evaluation of Federal Water Resource Development," *American Economic Review*, XLIX (March, 1959), 105; and John V. Krutilla, "Some Recent Developments in River Basin Planning and Evaluation," *Journal of Farm Economics*, XL (December, 1958), 1676.

13. This judgment is likewise doubtful. Is it true that the maximum growth of a water resource program is the desired goal of such a program?

14. The formulation for this test is: $A_{it} = \dfrac{B\text{-}O}{K}$ .

Taking $t$ to be fifty years, the value of the rate of return can be determined from a table, "Annuity whose Present Value is 1."

berger that no project bearing a rate of return below 6 percent should be constructed, the McKean proposal likewise separates the projects into two distinct groups.

### A Proposed Adjustment for Uncertainty

The adjustment for uncertain expectations proposed here, although far from a complete treatment, does focus attention on a phase of the problem which has thus far been neglected, i.e., the existence of disparate elements of uncertainty present in project costs and benefits.[15] Essentially, it is proposed that allowance for this disparity be made through the insertion of a dual premium into the proper interest rate in the discounting of future costs and benefits.

Before examining the proposal, however, let us state and defend some rather basic assumptions upon which it is founded. First, it is assumed that a single-valued criterion is suitable for the treatment of certain types of risk and uncertainty. In so far as the purpose of a criterion is to serve as a standard for choice between alternative proposals, it follows that the more valuables which a criterion serves to evaluate, the more helpful it will be in the decision-making process.

15. The uncertainties present in water-resource projects can, for analytical purposes, be separated into three categories: (1) uncertainties peculiar to the *concepts* in which all projects are evaluated, i.e., future costs and benefits; (2) uncertainties peculiar to particular *types* of projects; and (3) uncertainties peculiar to *individual* projects. It is the first of these types for which this analysis specifically accounts. The presumption that there exists a greater degree of uncertainty in the benefit concept than in the cost concept (which presumption forms the heart of this proposed treatment) has been noted and defended elsewhere. See Fred A. Seaton, "Federal Expenditures and Programs for the Development of Natural Resources," in U.S. Congress, Joint Economic Committee, *op. cit.,* p. 655 and Robert Dorfman, "Basic Economic and Technologic Concepts: A General Statement," in *Design of Water Resource Systems,* Arthur Maass, Maynard Hufschmidt *et al.* (Cambridge: Harvard University Press, 1962), p. 104. It should also be noted that the term uncertainty as used in this study includes both sides of the Knightian dichotomy, i.e., risk and true uncertainty. Because elements of both risk and true uncertainty are present and inseparable in each of the categories of uncertainties mentioned above, the general notion of uncertain expectations is the one applied. Consequently, when it is claimed that future benefits are more uncertain than future costs, it is equivalent to stating that the degree of credibility associated with the *expected* value of benefits is smaller than the degree of credibility associated with the *expected* value of future costs. See Frank Knight, *Risk, Uncertainty and Profit* (reissue) (London: 1948), pp. 225–31; Nicholas Georgescu-Roegen, "The Nature of Expectation and Uncertainty," in *Expectations, Uncertainty and Business Behavior,* ed. Mary Bowman (New York: Social Science Research Council, 1958); and Robert Haveman, "The Post-War Southern Federal Rivers and Harbors Program: An Analysis of Allocative Efficiency and Regional Impact" (Ph.D. dissertation, Dept. of Economics, Vanderbilt University, 1963).

To be eligible for inclusion in the criterion, however, a variable must be of a form common to all the alternatives. Although those uncertainties peculiar to various *types* of projects or peculiar to *individual* projects cannot be included in a unique criterion applied to all projects, that type of risk and uncertainty which is common to all projects, such as the difference in the degree of uncertainty between costs (in general) and benefits (in general), is eligible for inclusion. Second, it is assumed that the concept of "certainty equivalent" is the correct approach in making an allowance for uncertainty. Having been applied in most classical discussions of behavior under non-static conditions, especially in analyzing buyer's and seller's uncertain expectations toward future prices[16] and more recently in the analysis of private investment behavior,[17] it appears that this same approach is acceptable in the appraisal of government investment decisions. Finally, it is assumed that the degree of disutility is a positive function of the degree of uncertainty; that "[e]ntrepreneurs and consumers prefer as a rule more definite to less definite expectations."[18] Consequently, it is asserted that a representative government, as a reflector of the attitude of the populace, should, in its role as investor of public funds, treat uncertainty as something to be avoided rather than courted.

Based on the more uncertain nature of benefits as opposed to costs, the goal of this proposal is to attempt to reach a quasi-certainty equivalent figure for both estimated costs and benefits.[19] With the basic benefit-cost ratio accepted, it is proposed that a dual premium (discount) be incorporated into the appropriate interest rate used in the discounting of deferred effects. The higher of the two rates will be used in the discounting of expected benefits and the lower in the discounting of deferred costs.

The first of the two variables which determine the size of this net premium centers about the dual role played by the government as it

16. See Oscar Lange, *Price Flexibility and Employment* (Bloomington, Indiana: Principia Press, Inc., 1944), pp. 29–31; J. R. Hicks, *Value and Capital* (Oxford: Clarendon Press, 1946), p. 125; and Milton Friedman, "Discussion," *American Economic Review, Papers and Proceedings*, XL (May, 1950), 196.

17. See F. Modigliani and M. H. Miller, "The Cost of Capital, Corporation Finance and the Theory of Investment," *American Economic Review*, XLIII (June, 1958), 262.

18. Lange, *op. cit.*, p. 30. See also A. C. Pigou, *The Economics of Welfare* (London: Macmillan, 1948), p. 776.

19. The term quasi-certainty is used to avoid the misconception that this modification attempts to make allowance for all forms of uncertainty. This it does not do. Its goal is to treat only that type of uncertain expectation which is capable of being treated in a single-valued criterion, i.e., uncertainties related to all costs and benefits.

evaluates costs and benefits.  As it evaluates costs, the government plays the role of a *buyer:* a buyer of resources to construct, operate, and maintain its projects.  The certainty equivalent value for a buyer who finds greater uncertainty to be a disutility will be a value which is greater than the expected value with uncertainty.  As Lange states, ". . . buyers consider a price or cost expected with greater uncertainty as equivalent to a *higher* most probable price or cost expected with less uncertainty."[20]  To achieve this result by means of an interest-rate adjustment necessitates the injection of a *discount* into the appropriate base interest rate.

In its role as an analyzer and estimator of benefits, the government acts as a *seller.*  Its role here is like that of a large corporation whose stockholders are the taxpayers and whose revenue from operations is similar to benefits from investment projects.  Project benefits thus resemble sales, and as a producer of benefits, the government's role is that of a seller.  In the case of a seller who is faced with uncertain expectations, the certainty equivalent value will be less than the expected value under conditions of uncertainty.  "An increased dispersion will have the same effect as a reduction of the expected price, in cases where the individual plans to sell."[21]  Again, this directional change can be achieved through a modification of the appropriate base interest rate.  The modification in this case, however, will have to be the injection of a *premium* into the interest rate.  Consequently, to achieve a quasi-certainty equivalent for deferred costs and benefits we must adjust the two expected uncertain values in opposite directions.[22]  In order to approximate the quasi-certain values for both costs and benefits, we must discount deferred costs at a rate which is *smaller* than the beginning base rate and discount benefits at a rate which is *larger* than the original interest rate.

The second reason which will lead to a net premium is the presumption that benefits involve a greater degree of uncertainty than do costs.[23]  "As more definite expectations are preferred to less definite ones, the risk premium is the greater the greater the degree of uncertainty of the actual expectation."[24]  For our framework, this implies that the interest rate used to discount benefits will deviate positively from

20. Lange, *op. cit.,* p. 30.  Compare also J. R. Hicks, *op. cit.,* p. 125.

21. Hicks, *op. cit.,* p. 125.

22. Lange, *op. cit.,* p. 31.  "For sellers the risk premium is positive, for buyers it is negative.  By means of this device, uncertain . . . expectations can be reduced to certain ones."

23. See note 15.

24. Lange, *op. cit.,* p. 31.

the original appropriate rate more than the interest rate used to discount deferred costs will deviate negatively from this rate.[25] Thus, accepting the benefit-cost ratio as the proper general form of the criteria and working from a base interest rate of 4.5 percent taken to be the social cost of capital, a premium of 1 percent was added to the rate in the discounting of future benefits and a premium of 0.5 percent was subtracted from the base in the discounting of future costs. The net premium is, therefore, 1.5 percent.[26] Again, fifty years is taken to be the estimated length of project life.

## Application of the Criteria

At its most basic level, then, the study involves the application of these proposed criteria to the data of the projects already constructed or under construction in ten Southern states since 1946. All of the data is based upon substantial economic base studies as outlined in the Corps Manuals[27] and was obtained from the 11 district

25. It should be noted that the only other detailed treatment of uncertainty by means of an adjustment in the rate of interest, that of Eckstein, fails to consider both the need of including a discount in the rate used in evaluating costs and the existence of a substantial difference in the degree of uncertainty between costs and benefits. Eckstein, *op. cit.*, pp. 86–90. By the use of an interest rate *bloated* by the inclusion of a positive risk premium to discount both deferred benefits and costs, Eckstein is adjusting the concept of costs in the wrong direction: by the use of but a single interest rate, the intrinsic difference in the uncertain nature of expectations associated with costs and benefits is ignored. It is the argument of this paper that an allowance for risk and uncertainty can be approximated in a single-valued criterion only through a recognition of both of these factors.

26. For defense of the size of the premium or discount chosen, see Eckstein, *op. cit.*, pp. 89–90; and Miller, *op. cit.*, pp. 354–56. Because of the use of the dual rate of interest, the simpler formulation of the benefit-cost ratio as presented on p. 455 cannot be applied. In this case, the traditional form of the ratio must be used in which $B$, $O$, and $K$ are defined as above but where $i_1$ is the rate of interest used to evaluate the stream of costs and $i_2$ is the rate used to evaluate the stream of benefits, i.e.,

$$Z = \frac{\Sigma \frac{B}{(1+i_2)^t}}{K + \Sigma \frac{O}{(1+i_1)^t}} .$$

Given $i_1$ and $i_2$ and the length of project life, the factors by which $B$ and $O$ must be multiplied to yield their present value can be secured from a table, "Present Value of an Annuity." The value of the $B$ factor is 16.931518, and the value of the $O$ factor is 21.4821864. It should be noted that, in all of these tests, the interest rate is assumed constant for the entire seventeen-year period. For defense of this assumption, see Krutilla and Eckstein, *op. cit.*, pp. 119–20.

27. U.S. Army, Corps of Engineers, *Survey Investigations and Reports*, EM1120-2-101.

offices of the U.S. Army Corps of Engineers which are concerned with project evaluation in these states. Through these studies, estimates of future annual flows of benefits and operation-maintenance-and-repair costs, as well as estimates of total investment cost, were secured for each of the projects. It is this "raw material" to which the proposed efficiency criteria are applied in appraising the Corps program.

In order to illustrate the application of the tests described above, the Corps data for one of these projects will be presented and evaluated by each of the tests. The data used is that computed for the Beaver Reservoir project, located in northwest Arkansas. The project was a "new start" in 1959, and by 1962 it had received some $14.5 million in appropriations. At the time of the decision to construct the project, the Corps estimated that it would produce an annual stream of benefits $(B)$ of $3,614,000, and would require $1,182,000 annually in operation-maintenance-and-repair costs $(O)$ and $58,238,000 in original investment costs $(K)$. Given this set of data, the Corps applied its benefit-cost ratio to the project, using an interest rate of 2.5 percent and an estimated length of project life of fifty years. The resulting ratio which was presented to Congress was 1.1—quite acceptable under the law.

**Table 2.** Results of the Proposals When Applied to the Beaver Reservoir Project

| Criteria | Computed Value |
|---|---|
| A The Interest Rate Correction | .88 |
| B The Eckstein-Krutilla Proposal | .82 |
| C The Eckstein Proposal | 1.12 |
| D The McKean Proposal | .042 |
| E The Uncertainty Allowance Proposal | .73 |

By applying the five proposals to this same data, substantially different results appear. These results are presented in Table 2. In no case, it should be noticed, is the project found to be acceptable. Proposals A, B, and E each reject the project because it bears a benefit-cost ratio below 1, Proposal C rejects it because it bears a benefit-cost ratio below the cut-off minimum of 1.4, and Proposal D rejects it because its internal rate of return is below the cut-off minimum of 6 percent.

In performing such a re-evaluation, several necessary assumptions must be made. Because of the inability of economic science to measure the worth of certain phenomena, it should be noted that these "intangibles" are not included in the estimates of annual benefits or costs. Lives saved through flood control, the "costs" of increasing the size of the Federal government, and contributions of a project to the national defense effort are examples of such indirect benefits (costs) which cannot be measured in dollar terms. It is, therefore, assumed that these intangibles are non-existent. Also, it is assumed that the configuration of benefits and operating costs through time is as posited by the Corps, i.e., that the stream of values is constant and continuous and stops abruptly at the end of the estimated project life. Moreover, it is assumed that the projects are mutually exclusive and independent, i.e., that side calculations have already been made to determine the best combination of projects to be included in an entire river-basin program.[28] Finally, it is assumed that the Corps estimates of benefits and costs are accurate; that there is neither over- nor under-estimation of the values involved.[29]

### The Results of the Study

During the seventeen-year period from 1946 to 1962, 163 projects in the ten-state area received Federal appropriation. Of these 163 projects, 35 were still under construction at the close of fiscal year 1962. The total amount of Federal funds committed to these projects amounts to approximately $2,687,942,000.[30] For 9 of the 163 projects, no benefit-cost computations were performed by the Corps of Engineers,

28. When a project is started which is but an integral part of an entire river-basin program, the data for the entire program at the time the project is started are used to evaluate the project rather than the data of the project alone.

29. The doubtful quality of this assumption is well known and recognized. To simply assume that these estimates are accurate covers up a host of necessary assumptions made in calculating the estimated values: assumptions concerning price projections, population growth, future land use and value, future river tonnage, and future demand for power, to mention but a few. For example, one of the most significant sources of bias in the expected benefit stream enters because of the excessive inclusion of secondary or indirect benefits. Examples of such benefits include reduction of losses of wage payments because of the control of flooding and the increase of property values because of the increased activity caused by navigation improvements. Bias is also introduced by the use of rail rates instead of out-of-pocket rail *costs* in the estimation of navigation benefits. Elucidation of these and description of many more less significant, but also important, defects in the measurement procedure can be found in the following sources: Eckstein, *op. cit.*, pp. 110–258; Otto Eckstein, "Evaluation of Federal Expenditures for Water Resource Projects," in U.S. Congress, Joint Economic Committee, *op. cit.*, pp. 657–67; and Task Force on Water Resources and Power, Commission on Organization of the Executive Branch of the Government, *Report on Water Resources and Power* (Washington, 1955), I, 126–45; II, 294–99, 789–821, 935–53; III, 1275–99, 1317–95.

30. The concept of Federal funds committed is a rather hybrid quantity. It consists of the funds already appropriated to the 163 projects plus the latest estimate of the necessary appropriations needed to complete the projects yet under construction.

**Table 3.** Distribution of 147 Water-Resource Projects Constructed in Ten Southern States from 1946–62 by Benefit-Cost Ratio Presented by the Corps of Engineers to the Congress at the Time of Initial Appropriation[a]

| Benefit-Cost Ratio | Number of Projects | Federal Funds Committed ($000) | Percent of Total Federal Funds Committed |
|---|---|---|---|
| .60–.79 | 0 | | |
| .80–.99 | 3 | $95,970 | 3.62 |
| 1.00–1.19 | 36 | 786,339 | 29.74 |
| 1.20–1.39 | 26 | 361,375 | 13.67 |
| 1.40–1.59 | 24 | 317,093 | 11.99 |
| 1.60–1.79 | 16 | 326,066 | 12.34 |
| 1.80–1.99 | 7 | 50,492 | 1.91 |
| 2.00–2.49 | 16 | 527,768 | 19.96 |
| 2.50–2.99 | 5 | 17,890 | .68 |
| 3.00–4.99 | 11 | 147,885 | 5.59 |
| 5.00 or more | 3 | 13,123 | .50 |
| Total | 147 | $2,644,001 | 100.0 |

[a] The length of project life is assumed to be fifty years unless specifically stipulated to be less by the Corps.

as project justification was based on non-economic grounds. The committed Federal funds accounted for by these 9 projects is $9,339,-000. On 7 additional projects, benefit-cost records were not available from the Corps offices, nor could they be secured from the documents or hearings. The Federal funds committed by these projects totals $34,602,000. On the remaining 147 projects, the benefit-cost data were secured, and it is to these projects that the proposed efficiency criteria have been applied. The Federal funds committed by this group of projects total $2,644,001,000, or 98.4 percent of the total. The results of the application of these criteria are summarized, together with the original Corps evaluation, in Tables 3 through 8.

Table 3 presents the benefit-cost ratios which faced the Congress at the time that the initial appropriation was made on each of the projects, that is, at the time that each project was a "new start." It should be noted that even under the Corps' own concept of efficiency, three projects were constructed in which the national outlay exceeded the expected return. Also, it is significant that by far the largest concentration of projects, both in absolute number and in Federal funds committed, is located at the very bottom end of the distribution—the range which, even under the most liberal interpretation, is marginal.

**Table 4.** Distribution of 147 Water-Resource Projects Constructed in Ten Southern States from 1946–62 by Benefit-Cost Ratio When Future Streams Are Evaluated by a 4.5 Percent Rate of Interest[a]

| Benefit-Cost Ratio | Number of Projects | Federal Funds Committed ($000) | Percent of Total Federal Funds Committed |
|---|---|---|---|
| .60–.79 | 9 | $295,527 | 11.18 |
| .80–.99 | 38 | 822,616 | 31.11 |
| 1.00–1.19 | 33 | 277,009 | 10.48 |
| 1.20–1.39 | 23 | 520,679 | 19.69 |
| 1.40–1.59 | 9 | 151,749 | 5.74 |
| 1.60–1.79 | 10 | 314,496 | 11.89 |
| 1.80–1.99 | 2 | 3,346 | .13 |
| 2.00–2.49 | 10 | 185,271 | 6.25 |
| 2.50–2.99 | 3 | 74,216 | 2.81 |
| 3.00–4.99 | 8 | 9,644 | .36 |
| 5.00 or more | 2 | 9,448 | .36 |
| Total | 147 | $2,644,001 | 100.0 |

[a] See note, Table 3.

The weighted average benefit-cost ratio of the projects as evaluated by the Corps is 1.67.[31]

Table 4 presents the results secured from the application of the Interest Rate Correction (Proposal A). The effect of this re-evaluation is to shift the entire schedule of benefit-cost ratios downward substantially. Whereas the modal class is 1.00–1.19 in the Corps distribution, the modal class in this distribution decreases to the .80–.99 range. This is likewise reflected in the weighted average benefit-cost ratio which, for this distribution, is a meager 1.3. Of the 147 projects, 47 were found unacceptable, representing some 42 percent of the committed Federal funds.

Table 5 presents the distribution of projects when the length of project life is assumed to be one-hundred years to insure the long-range nature of the program, and the social cost of capital raised through taxes is accepted as the appropriate rate of interest and is estimated to be 5.5 percent by Eckstein-Krutilla (Proposal B). The effect of this test is more severe than the previous test. Of the 147

31. The formula used to compute the average is the following: $\overline{X}_w = \dfrac{\Sigma X \cdot w}{\Sigma w}$

in which $\overline{X}_w$ is the weighted arithmetic mean, $X$ is the benefit-cost ratio, and $w$ is the amount of Federal funds committed by a project.

**Table 5.** Distribution of 147 Water-Resource Projects Constructed in Ten Southern States from 1946–62 by Average Rate of When Future Streams Are Evaluated by a 5.5 Percent Rate of Interest[a]

| Benefit-Cost Ratio | Number of Projects | Federal Funds Committed ($000) | Percent of Total Federal Funds Committed |
|---|---|---|---|
| .60–.79 | 18 | $399,153 | 15.10 |
| .80–.99 | 42 | 761,017 | 28.77 |
| 1.00–1.19 | 35 | 642,210 | 24.29 |
| 1.20–1.39 | 12 | 179,245 | 6.78 |
| 1.40–1.59 | 9 | 110,322 | 4.17 |
| 1.60–1.79 | 8 | 293,475 | 11.10 |
| 1.80–1.99 | 6 | 93,813 | 3.55 |
| 2.00–2.49 | 6 | 143,583 | 5.43 |
| 2.50–2.99 | 3 | 7,549 | .29 |
| 3.00–4.99 | 6 | 4,186 | .16 |
| 5.00 or more | 2 | 9,448 | .36 |
| Total | 147 | $2,644,001 | 100.0 |

[a] The length of project life is assumed to be one hundred years unless specifically stipulated to be less by the Corps.

**Table 6.** Distribution of 147 Water-Resource Projects Constructed in Ten Southern States from 1946–62 by Benefit-Cost Ratio When Future Streams Are Evaluated by a 2.5 Percent Rate of Interest[a]

| Benefit-Cost Ratio | Number of Projects | Federal Funds Committed ($000) | Percent of Total Federal Funds Committed |
|---|---|---|---|
| .60–.79 | 0 | | |
| .80–.99 | 1 | $94,600 | 3.58 |
| 1.00–1.19 | 25 | 477,694 | 18.07 |
| 1.20–1.39 | 31 | 568,757 | 21.51 |
| 1.40–1.59 | 22 | 187,082 | 7.07 |
| 1.60–1.79 | 21 | 514,953 | 19.47 |
| 1.80–1.99 | 7 | 91,123 | 3.45 |
| 2.00–2.49 | 17 | 450,032 | 17.02 |
| 2.50–2.99 | 7 | 97,866 | 3.70 |
| 3.00–4.99 | 12 | 148,751 | 5.63 |
| 5.00 or more | 4 | 13,123 | .50 |
| Total | 147 | $2,644,001 | 100.0 |

[a] See note, Table 3.

projects accepted for construction, 60 fail to pass the efficiency requirement posed by Eckstein-Krutilla. Nearly 45 percent of the committed Federal funds belong in this category. This severity is also reflected in the weighted average benefit-cost ratio, which has declined to 1.2.

Table 6 presents the results necessary for the application of the criteria suggested by Eckstein (Proposal C). In applying this test, a low rate of interest (2.5 percent) was used to evaluate future streams of benefits and costs, and a cut-off benefit-cost ratio of 1.4 was applied to assure an adequate rate of return of 6 percent. From the table, then, it can be seen that 57 of the 147 projects, representing about 43 percent of total funds committed, fail to satisfy the standard posited by Eckstein.

Based upon the suggestion presented by McKean (Proposal D), Table 7 displays the 147 projects by the average rate of return. Again, the bulk of projects are seen to cluster at the lower end of the scale. The weighted average rate of return for the 147 projects is .0644. If the recommendation by Harberger were applied, that no project should be constructed which did not return at least 6 percent, 84 of the 147 projects should have been rejected, implying that nearly 60 percent of the total committed Federal funds have been allocated to projects failing to pass this test.

**Table 7.** Distribution of 147 Water-Resource Projects Constructed in Ten Southern States from 1946–62 by Average Rate of Return[a]

| Rate of Return | Number of Projects | Federal Funds Committed ($000) | Percent of Total Federal Funds Committed |
|---|---|---|---|
| .0200–.0299 | 8 | $142,786 | 5.40 |
| .0300–.0399 | 24 | 565,658 | 21.39 |
| .0400–.0499 | 27 | 451,244 | 17.07 |
| .0500–.0599 | 25 | 373,030 | 14.11 |
| .0600–.0699 | 14 | 377,531 | 14.38 |
| .0700–.0799 | 7 | 69,783 | 2.64 |
| .0800–.0899 | 8 | 105,099 | 3.97 |
| .0900–.0999 | 4 | 283,728 | 10.75 |
| .1000–.1499 | 18 | 246,059 | 9.31 |
| .1500–.1999 | 3 | 11,431 | .43 |
| .2000–.2999 | 3 | 4,371 | .17 |
| .3000 or more | 6 | 13,281 | .50 |
| Total | 147 | $2,644,001 | 100.0 |

[a] See note a, Table 3.

**Table 8.** Distribution of 147 Water-Resource Projects Constructed in Ten Southern States from 1946–62 by Benefit-Cost Ratio When Allowance for Uncertainty Is Made in the Criterion[a]

| Benefit-Cost Ratio | Number of Projects | Federal Funds Committed ($000) | Percent of Total Federal Funds Committed |
|---|---|---|---|
| .60–.79 | 33 | $806,581 | 30.51 |
| .80–.99 | 46 | 631,118 | 20.09 |
| 1.00–1.19 | 24 | 577,792 | 21.85 |
| 1.20–1.39 | 12 | 160,812 | 6.08 |
| 1.40–1.59 | 8 | 305,952 | 11.57 |
| 1.60–1.79 | 7 | 96,980 | 3.67 |
| 1.80–1.99 | 2 | 18,792 | .71 |
| 2.00–2.49 | 6 | 130,900 | 4.95 |
| 2.50–2.99 | 4 | 1,918 | .07 |
| 3.00–4.99 | 3 | 3,708 | .14 |
| 5.00 or more | 2 | 9,448 | .36 |
| Total | 147 | $2,644,001 | 100.0 |

[a] See note, Table 3.

When uncertainty is treated as disutility to the community and when allowance is made for this disutility in the rate of interest, the resulting benefit-cost configuration is as presented in Table 8 (Proposal E). The effect of the premium (discount) is clearly seen in the resulting distribution. Over one-half of both the number of projects and the Federal funds committed are excluded by this test. The weighted average benefit-cost ratio in this case falls to a minute 1.11.

In the re-evaluation process, then, each of the alternative efficiency criteria, all of which have as their objective the maximization of national income, rejected a significant proportion of the projects. When measured by Federal funds committed, the proportion varies from 42 percent in the case of the interest–rate correction test to 58 percent in the rate of return–Harberger proposal. For any given project, however, the results may be quite varied, i.e., and given project may be accepted by some of the tests and rejected by the others in any combination. Table 9 portrays in a crude way the degree of such inconsistency in the results of the tests.

In 107 of the 147 projects, complete consistency was achieved. Of these projects, 62 were accepted by all of the criteria and 45 were rejected by all. In the remaining 40, the answer given by the proposed criteria is not so neat, since individual projects are accepted by some and rejected by others. By percent of Federal funds committed, how-

**Table 9.** Distribution of Number of Rejections out of Five Tests for Each of 147 Water-Resource Projects Constructed in Ten Southern States from 1946–62

| Number of Rejections | Number of Projects | Federal Funds Committed ($000) | Percent of Total Federal Funds Committed |
|---|---|---|---|
| 0 | 62 | $1,109,944 | 41.98 |
| 1 | 6 | 196,299 | 7.42 |
| 2 | 16 | 168,830 | 6.39 |
| 3 | 10 | 36,612 | 1.38 |
| 4 | 8 | 23,971 | .91 |
| 5 | 45 | 1,108,345 | 41.98 |
| Total | 147 | $2,644,001 | 100.0 |

ever, the degree of consistency is somewhat more clear; 84 percent of the Federal funds committed were allocated to projects accepted or rejected by all of the criteria and only 16 percent were allocated to projects in which the answer was inconsistent.

The inconsistency present among the criteria is not limited, however, to the type pointed out above in which those projects on the margin can be placed on different sides of the acceptance-rejection line by different criteria. This type of inconsistency can occur simply because of the higher standard of justification required by some criteria as compared to others, i.e., some criteria may simply be willing to move further down a list of monotonically ranked projects than others. Such a situation is obviously present, but an inconsistency of a higher order is also worthy of note. When some projects accepted by criterion Z are rejected by criterion Y while some projects accepted by criterion Y are rejected by criterion Z, such higher-level inconsistency is present. This inconsistency appears as a disparity in the actual ranking of the projects and its extent is expressed in Table 10.

Thus, for example, in comparing the results of the Eckstein test with the results of the proposal by Krutilla-Eckstein, it is seen that a substantial overlap exists. Among the ninety projects accepted by the Eckstein test, there were six that were rejected by the Krutilla-Eckstein formulation (row C, column B). Conversely, of the eighty-seven projects accepted by Krutilla-Eckstein, four possessed benefit-cost ratios below 1.4 when evaluated at a 2.5 percent rate of interest and were, therefore, not acceptable under the Eckstein test (row B, column C).

**Table 10.** Degree of Inconsistency among the Six Criteria Caused by Non-Unique Ranking of Projects as Expressed in the Acceptance-Rejection Decisions

| Criteria | No. Rej. by A | No. Rej. by B | No. Rej. By C | No. Rej. By D' | No. Rej. By D | No. Rej. By E |
|---|---|---|---|---|---|---|
| No. Accepted by Interest-Rate Correction (A) | .. | 12 | 11 | 26 | 35 | 31 |
| No. Accepted by Eckstein-Krutilla Proposal (B) | 0 | .. | 4 | 13 | 24 | 19 |
| No. Accepted by Eckstein Proposal (C) | 1 | 6 | .. | 17 | 25 | 21 |
| No. with Rate of Return of 5.5% or more (D') | 0 | 0 | 1 | .. | 10 | 5 |
| No. with Rate of Return of 6% or more (D) | 1 | 0 | 1 | 0 | .. | 1 |
| No. Accepted by Uncertainty Allowance Proposal (E) | 0 | 0 | 0 | 0 | 8 | .. |

Table 10 yields yet another insight. In setting up his test, Eckstein realized that, because the ratio of operating costs to investment costs directly influenced the size of the benefit-cost ratio, the choice of a single value as a cut-off benefit-cost ratio would lead to the acceptance of some projects, namely those of low capital intensity, with a rate of return significantly below the desired rate; and the rejection of some, namely those of high capital intensity, with a rate of return above the desired rate. In defense of his method, however, he makes the following assertions: ". . . the marginal projects which would be undertaken under the proposed test would not represent a misallocation of capital into a use in which it is incapable of earning a satisfactory rate of return"[32]; ". . . an interest rate of 2½ per cent coupled with a ratio of 1.4 are combinations which will produce an average rate of return for the entire federal program of about 6 per-cent. . . ."[33]

Both of these statements appear rather untenable. The evidence in Table 10 rather effectively illustrates the costs involved in choosing a single benefit-cost ratio as a cut-off. Although the ratio chosen by Eckstein (1.4) aimed at yielding a rate of return of 6 percent, it, in fact, accepted twenty-five projects with a rate of return less than 6 percent (row C, column D), accepted seventeen projects with a rate

32. Eckstein, *op. cit.*, p. 101.
33. *Ibid.*, p. 104.

of return less than 5.5 percent (row C, column D'), and rejected one project with a rate greater than 6 percent (row D, column C). Consequently, in opposition to the first statement, it appears that marginal projects may well be accepted even if they do not yield a satisfactory rate of return. Of the projects accepted by the Eckstein test, for example, two had rates of return less than 4.5 percent.

As regards the second statement, there is no more reason for claiming that such a combination of interest rate and cut-off benefit-cost ratio will yield an average rate of return of 6 percent than claiming that the average return will be 7, 8, 9, or any other percent. The adoption of such a single benefit-cost ratio only assures that some projects bearing rates of return equal to or greater than the desired rate (6 percent in this case) will be rejected by the test while other projects bearing rates of return less than the desired rate will be accepted. The average rate of return of the entire Federal program depends, then, upon the ability of the average rate of return of those accepted projects with a rate of return greater than 6 percent to outweigh the average rate of return of those accepted projects with a rate of return less than 6 percent. Consequently, the two statements in defense of the Eckstein test appear quite unwarranted.

### Conclusion

From the evidence presented, one can hardly doubt that a great number of projects have been constructed which, if economic efficiency had been the sole objective, would not have been constructed. Although each of the above criteria has presented somewhat varied estimates of the misallocation of national resources (see Tables 4–8), it seems plausible that some acceptable estimate of the size of this misallocation is possible. Consequently, it will be assumed that any project that is rejected by three or more of the five tests should not have been constructed; that any project which is accepted by three or more of the five tests should have been constructed. For those projects in the latter category, it is presumed that national income is the greatest possible per dollar devoted to rivers-and-harbors development. For projects in the former category, the reverse is presumed true. According to this approach, then, it appears that 63 of the 147 projects representing $1,169,000,000 of committed Federal funds, or 44.2 percent of the total, are devoted to projects which should not have been undertaken: projects the construction of which has led to a misallocation of national resources and economic waste.

However, abstracting from this gross inefficiency present in the program, it seems likely that the goal of Southern economic development has, on balance, been aided by the program. In so far as the South's low-income problem stems from small-plot, labor-intensive agriculture, lack of capital, and substantial immobility of labor, several comments concerning the effect of this investment on Southern development are relevant.[34]

First, it seems quite likely that the flood-control aspect of the program which is aimed at the prevention of agricultural flooding may be of relatively little benefit to the cause of Southern growth. In so far as such river bed regulation accomplishes its goal, it is true that production, land values, and incomes will be supplemented. However, it appears rather doubtful that the increase in income will be sufficient to bring it into equality with the farmer's potential income off the farm. In so far as agricultural out-migration (and consequent plot consolidation) are thus retarded while farm productivity is not significantly increased, such an expenditure may not, in fact, be of positive aid to the forces for economic development.

On the other hand, the extensive use of reservoirs for both navigation and flood-control purposes may well provide a positive stimulus for agricultural out-migration. Because the area inundated by reservoir projects is mainly rural, out-migration at least from the flooded region, if not from agriculture itself, is stimulated. Also, because of such forced movement, the stagnancy of community life and values is, to some extent, disrupted, and the existence of these barriers to development is consequently decreased.

Third, the degree of capital attraction present in various types of expenditure appears important in light of the existence of severe capital scarcity in the Southern region. Basically, the difference in the degree of capital attraction is intrinsic in the division of expenditures into flood control and navigation development. Flood control expenditures, it appears, have as their goal the protection of *existing* wealth and, in so far as new capital accumulation does occur in flood-protected areas, it is not prima facie evidence that this development would not have otherwise taken place. The concept of protecting the already existing does not, however, appear to be present in the case of navigation improvements. Rather, the stimulation of trade and the provision of cheap transportation furnish the goal in this case. Also,

34. William H. Nicholls, *Southern Tradition and Regional Progress* (Chapel Hill: University of North Carolina Press, 1960), pp. 164–76.

because the receipt of Federal appropriation often bears the requirement that local interests construct new terminals, warehouses, and other facilities, this basic investment in navigation projects appears to possess a greater propensity to stimulate additional growth than does flood-control activity.

Finally, it should be pointed out that, because of the ineffectiveness of the present benefit-cost ratio technique in eliminating unproductive projects, the disproportionate allocation of funds between states and especially between the South and the rest of the nation which was noted earlier must be a result of forces other than economic efficiency. The list of prime candidates, it appears, must include both the concept of regional income equalization and the force of simple political manipulation.   To ignore, because of their nebulous character, either or both of these forces as determinants of allocation would constitute a gross oversimplification of the allocative process.[35]

35. See Robert de Roos and Arthur A. Maass, "The Lobby That Can't Be Licked," *Harper's*, August, 1949, p. 25; Arthur A. Maass, *Muddy Waters* (Cambridge: Harvard University Press, 1951); and Paul H. Douglas, *Economy in the National Government* (Chicago: University of Chicago Press, 1952).

# XIV

## Rates of Return on Municipal Subsidies to Industry*

*By James R. Rinehart*

Persistent regional un- and underemployment problems have been a constant threat to the growth of the overall national prosperity for many years. The character and extent of these problems range from open unemployment in the various coal and textile regions of the United States to a state of disguised unemployment, such as now exists on Southern farms.

Most communities with persistent un- and underemployment problems are reluctant to accept their predicament. Convinced that industrial development is the answer, many of these localities are forming industrial development committees and organizations with the purpose of attracting industry to their particular communities. Subsidies have become a common method employed by such localities in securing industrial development.

Opinions, however, vary widely as to what the procedure for attracting industry should be. Some areas merely advertise their cities and counties as desirable industrial location sites in manifold papers and brochures, providing any industrial prospect easy access to data and other information of the local area. Many localities go further and, in addition to the above, offer loans at little or no interest to the industrial prospect for the construction of a new plant; install parking lots and driveways; and allow city and county tax exemptions for

* This article is reprinted from *The Southern Economic Journal*, April 1963 (© 1963, Southern Economic Association). The writer is indebted to James M. Buchanan and John E. Moes for worthwhile remarks and suggestions.

periods of five to ten years. Other communities go a step beyond this and offer industrial prospects more direct and substantial forms of subsidies such as cash outlays, free sites on which to construct new buildings, and free buildings and equipment. There are variations, of course, and municipalities can be found which offer none, one, all of these inducements, or any combination thereof to any of its industrial prospects. Consequently, financial assistance rendered to industries by localities for purposes of industrial development varies from subsidies of little cost to those of relatively high cost.

Because of considerable opposition to the practice of granting these financial concessions to new industrial enterprises, based fundamentally on the premise that subsidizing localities usually experience undesirable monetary results, a case study approach to the problem was undertaken. In each instance the cost incurred in securing the establishment of the industrial plant and the income benefits received as a consequence were measured. Ten currently existing communities were studied, several of these localities having subsidized as many as five plants in recent years.[1] In each case the aggregate quantity of the subsidy investment was procured and was discounted to present worth. Similarly, the income benefits (i.e., incremental income arising from the plant payroll itself and the income multiplier effect) were estimated and also discounted back to present worth. Placing the perpetual annual value of the income benefits over the capitalized cost of the subsidy yields the per annum rate of return received on the subsidy investment. This rate of return is expressed in percentage terms. Using this procedure for each of the subsidy endeavors executed by the ten selected communities, the financial success of each subsidy project was determined.[2]

Such calculations would provide some grounds for evaluating the merit of locating subsidized plants. Without such empirical estimation, statements regarding results that may be obtained by subsidiza-

1. Because of the confidential nature of information relative to subsidies and payrolls, the names of the communities and the industrial firms involved are withheld.

2. This approach assumes that the subsidies are given for the purpose of increasing community incomes and that the increments in local income attributable to a new industry locating in the community because of subsidies represent the returns on the capitalized value of the subsidies themselves. Moreover, it should be emphasized that the rates of return resulting from the augmented local income stream are returns on "community" investment, treated as a unit, and because of individual disparities with respect to subsidy costs and income gains, "private" rates of return may not coincide.

tion amount to little more than partisan assertions by adversaries and proponents of this type of action.[3]

This study has been confined to the South, where subsidization at the local level has been widely practiced in recent years. Upon request, most Southern states furnished essential data pertaining to the industrial activities of many of the political subdivisions. On the basis of this information, the cities and communities presented in this report were selected. These localities were known to have engaged in some form of subsidization aimed at industrial development. Communities considered successful in industrial development have been included as well as communities thought to be unsuccessful (i.e., localities with subsidized plants which ceased production shortly after locating in the area and those which subsequently required additional financial assistance). Because for each of these communities a detailed analysis was required of the subsidies extended to each plant, the payrolls of each firm, the shifts in employment due to the locating of the newly subsidized plant, and the income multiplier effects, it appeared desirable to confine the study areas to towns and localities under ten thousand population. Moreover, subsidized plants locating in the selected areas prior to 1950 were usually not considered. It was felt that since most of the data on which this work is based could be obtained only through direct conversations with the people involved in the transactions, accurate information on subsidies extended earlier than a decade ago would be difficult to acquire. In any event, in many of the case studies, subsidization policy is of quite recent origin.

The significance of this work rests primarily upon information and material procured on personal visits to the selected areas of study. Most of the data were acquired from conversations with industrial development engineers, Chamber of Commerce and industrial committee managers, store owners and managers, local citizens, and state employment security officials. The remainder of the material was gathered from city, Chamber of Commerce, and industrial development corporation records, brochures and pamphlets; and state security employment records. Whenever possible, these data were checked against available records from newspapers and from official reports

3. I realize that all industrial firms may not be motivated by subsidies, as they currently exist, and in so far as the firms considered in this report located in the communities as a result of other factors, these rates of return are not meaningful. However, it is clear that subsidies can and do affect industrial locations in many instances, and that any community desiring new industrial capacity can acquire the same by providing adequate financial aid.

issued by the United States Department of Commerce and the Bureau of the Census. Additionally, several local people in each selected community were asked the same questions so that their answers could be checked against one another for the sake of accuracy.

## The Nature of Subsidies Provided on the Local Level

The term "subsidization of industry," as used in this study, includes financial concessions extended an industrial enterprise by a community in order to secure its establishment and not fully paid for by that firm. Such financial aid may be in the form of direct outlays (e.g., cash) and foregone income (e.g., tax-exemptions) or in connection with the accepting of elements of risk (e.g., providing credit at interest rates below the market rate).[4]

## Benefits Resulting From Subsidized Industrial Development

In this report benefits are classified in two divisions: (1) that part of the factory payroll which represents a new addition to community income and (2) the local multiplier effect.[5]

The most obvious gain emanating from the establishment of a new industrial enterprise is the plant payroll. With the disbursement of a new industrial payroll within the locality, total community income is

4. This approach does not include expenditures incurred in the construction of playgrounds, in the improvement of garbage collection, etc., which are done as a general measure, even before considering a specific firm, for the purpose of encouraging the location of new industrial enterprises.

5. These benefits will be treated wholly in terms of enhanced local incomes. Any non-pecuniary utilities (as well as disutilities) resulting from the location of an industrial firm will be excluded from consideration in this study, principally because of the complexities or impossibilities involved in making reliable measurements of such intangible elements.

It has been argued that no meaningful rates of return can be computed unless the sacrifice of leisure experienced by the people accepting the new factory jobs is taken into account as a cost. First of all, this is impossible quantitatively. Second, it is not at all clear that in the case of involuntary un- and underemployment, becoming occupied necessarily results in a sacrifice. It may be that many individuals live to work rather than work to live. In this event, becoming occupied may actually be considered as additional gain in itself rather than an offsetting disutility factor. Moreover, even if there are disutilities caused by foregone leisure, which do represent a cost, other non-pecuniary utility gains exist (e.g., increased recreational facilities attracted to the locality because of higher local incomes, more jobs at home which permit relatives to remain in or return to the locality rather than being forced to live in another undesirable community or commuting everyday to such a locality to work, etc.). To a considerable extent, one counterbalances the other. Consequently, computing rates of return on industrial subsidization solely in terms of money income seems to be quite appropriate.

directly increased. However, it must not be presumed that the entire payroll represents a net addition to local income. For the payroll only produces an initial increment in the aggregate income of the locality by an amount commensurate to the sum of wages disbursed by the plant minus the total income lost as a result. For example, part of the payroll is lost to the community when individuals shift from lower-paying occupations to higher-paying ones (the lower-paying jobs being subsequently eliminated), or when individuals commute from foreign communities to the subsidizing community in order to accept one of the newly created jobs. How much of the factory payroll represents a net addition to local income depends upon the amount of income ultimately lost to the community as changes in occupations occur.[6]

The second pecuniary gain considered in this report is the multiplier effect. Most industrial firms sought by means of subsidization are export-oriented, i.e., they produce primarily for markets outside the area in which the plant is located. There are other enterprises in the locality that produce goods and services mainly for the local market. These may be termed non-industrial activities, and include such endeavors as construction, retail trade, professional services (e.g., doctors, lawyers, and teachers), repair services, wholesale trade, finance and banking, insurance, real estate, rental services, local government, transportation, warehousing, utilities, communications, and other personal and business services. With the location of a manufacturing concern (i.e., export-oriented industry), the factory payroll provides a net addition to community income. When this increment in local income is spent, the demands for goods and services provided by the local non-industrial businesses are directly increased, causing incomes and employment to rise in the latter. Thus a direct relationship exists between increased employment (payroll) resulting from the establishment of a local export-oriented manufacturing concern and enhanced employment (income) in the local non-industrial enterprises. The effect of a change in local export-oriented industrial employment (and consequently payroll) upon community employment (and thus income) in the local non-industrial industries is termed the multiplier effect. The local multiplier is commonly looked at in this manner; however, for purposes of this study another important element is added. Frequently, the location of a subsidized industrial firm pro-

6. For further comment on this point, refer to J. R. Rinehart, "Rates of Return on Municipal Subsidies to Industry" (Doctoral dissertation, University of Virginia, 1962).

ducing presumably for the export market will directly cause other industries to locate in the area in order to supply productive inputs to the initial subsidized plant. For example, with the establishment of a broiler processing plant, local broiler output increases, chicken feed manufacturers open plants nearby, industrial concerns producing broiler-related equipment (e.g., automatic chicken feeders, incubators, and so forth) may move in, and numerous other income-producing endeavors take form. Local income created by these related industries is considered as a benefit resulting from the establishment of the subsidized plant in the same way as income accruing indirectly through the disbursement of part of the payroll within the local community. Hence, the multiplier in this study refers to the annual local disbursement of payroll resulting from a subsidized industrial enterprise divided into the permanent increment in local income resulting from the location of the subsidized industry.

In each selected community studied, an attempt was made to estimate the local multiplier, principally in terms of employment. The employment multiplier is a conservative approximation to the income multiplier. In that it is the intention of this author to weigh benefit estimates resulting from subsidization conservatively, and since local officials appear to be more familiar with variations in employment numbers than with changes in aggregate community incomes, an approach by means of the employment multiplier, as it relates to the case studies in question, was thought to offer a more reliable estimate.

## How Benefits Were Measured

Getting accurate payroll figures was a rather simple task. Local industrial development corporations and employment security offices keep very close tab on factory employment and payrolls in their local areas. In every community this writer visited, these figures were made readily available. Procuring reliable statistics of income losses (explained above) and income multiplier effects, however, was far more difficult.

In response to the author's questions, local employment security officers presented estimates of income losses and income multiplier effects that resulted from the location of new industrial enterprise. The income loss was calculated by first ascertaining the original occupations of the persons filling the newly created jobs. Because local employment offices usually handle the screening procedures for hiring new employees, thus receiving personal information on each potential employee, the former were familiar with these data. It was discovered that most of the new jobs were quickly taken by people from four major groups: (1) those who commute from outside the community in question, (2) those persons who live in the subsidizing community and who had previously commuted to localities outside the area to work, (3) those who were unemployed, and (4) those who came from underemployed positions on surrounding farms. The amount of subsidized payroll taken by the first two groups was, of course, considered an income loss and was subtracted from the total payroll.[7] All of the income received by the unemployed workers was counted as a real income benefit, since no income was foregone as they moved into employed positions. As for the fourth group, income loss was extremely low. It was discovered that most of the farmers remain on their farms after accepting factory employment. They work eight hours each day in the plant and keep their farms going concomitantly. In many cases, farm output expanded above that of previous times as farmers used factory payroll to acquire machinery, fertilizer, etc., thus making their farms more productive.

Although the pervasive nature of the income multiplier makes any attempt to compute it difficult, this difficulty was held to a minimum by purposely selecting small communities for the study. In these small communities, local employment officials were able to make what they felt to be fairly reliable estimates of increased employment in the non-industrial endeavors and auxiliary industries caused by the newly disbursed factory payrolls. On the basis of these employment data, together with wage and salary rates furnished by the local employment offices, estimates of the income multiplier were made.

The most burdensome task of this study was the acquiring of reliable estimates of the indirect effects resulting from the location of new industrial enterprise. Admittedly, these calculations are rough, but it should be stressed that the conclusions of this report do not hinge upon the income multiplier and the payroll loss appraisals. These elements are included primarily for the sake of completeness. The payroll is the important factor, and it is a known quantity in every case. Moreover, since the income multiplier and the payroll loss produce offsetting effects ($K$ being positive and $L$ negative),[8] one counterbalances the other. Even though the two forces may be

7. To the extent that the persons in the second group earn more income at the subsidized plant than they did previously, that amount is not subtracted from the total payroll.

8. See below for an explanation of $K$ and $L$.

unequal, the net effect is insignificant. The income multiplier can be eliminated in every instance with no appreciable effect upon the rates of return derived in this study.

It is significant to note that few actual data have been presented in the literature concerning income benefits and losses resulting from industrial subsidization, and this author feels that some data, even though less precise than one might desire, are better than none.

## Method of Computations

Rates of return are computed in order to establish a means of judging between alternative investment opportunities: specifically, whether to use the funds in question in such a manner as to earn the market rate of interest on the one hand (say 6 percent),[9] or to invest the funds in industrial subsidization at a rate of return which is to be estimated in this study on the other. In other words, is it worthwhile in terms of monetary gains for communities to subsidize the location of industrial firms?

For this study, a per annum rate of return (expressed as a percentage) is computed for each subsidy investment. Such a rate-of-return estimate serves as an indicator of the profitableness of the investment and permits direct comparisons of the rates of return

9. Since these resources employed in subsidizing industry have alternative uses, the returns on the alternative uses are the costs of employing the funds in industrial subsidization. Most of the subsidies extended new enterprise are paid for by the local taxpayer via the local government. Hence, the social cost of subsidizing such an industry is the rate of return foregone on the subsidy funds given up by the taxpayer.

Krutilla and Eckstein estimated the social cost of capital raised by the federal government through taxation and used in water resource development. Through an elaborate statistical procedure they were able to provide an estimate intended to reflect the social cost of the capital raised. Social cost of capital was defined in terms of the opportunities foregone in the private sector of the economy, either because of curtailed investment or because of curtailed consumption. Their estimate of the opportunity cost of raising capital in this manner was between 5 and 6 percent. See Krutilla and Eckstein, *Multiple Purpose River Development* (Baltimore: The Johns Hopkins Press, 1958).

Although not on a national level, our problem is essentially the same. In the first place, subsidizing industry is looked upon as an investment, as previously pointed out, just as federal funds used for water resource development are viewed as investments. Secondly, in that the paying for water resource development is done through the taxing apparatus of the federal government, the bulk of local subsidization is financed by money procured through local taxing powers. Therefore, it is the opinion of this writer that the two cases are similar enough to warrant the use of the same rate of interest as derived by Krutilla and Eckstein as the social cost of raising capital via local taxation for purposes of industrial subsidization. An interest rate of 6 percent is employed in this study for discounting purposes.

received on community industrial subsidization with rates of return acquired on alternative investment endeavors.

In order to determine an annual rate of return on any particular subsidy investment, the annual income benefits resulting from the investment must be divided by the present value of the investment. The following formula is utilized for this purpose:[10]

$$r = \frac{K[(P-L)-S_a]+S_a}{S_c} \cdot 100$$

In this formula the numerator expresses the annual income gain resulting from the subsidy, in which $K$ denotes the local income multiplier, $P$ refers to the annual payroll accruing to the community from the subsidized plant, $S_a$ represents the annual value of the subsidy, which is presumed to be paid to outsiders,[11] and $L$ signifies the income lost to the community as workers vacate permanently lower-paying occupations in exchange for higher-paying ones created by the advent of the subsidized plant. The letter $L$ also denotes income lost in another sense, i.e., when individuals who live outside the subsidizing community accept some of the factory jobs and when local citizens forego commuting jobs for subsidized plant positions at home. The denominator $S_c$ is the capitalized value of the subsidy, i.e., the present value of the investment. The end result of this formula multiplied by one hundred yields the annual rate of return on the capitalized value of the subsidy (investment) in percentage form.

The data collected from the selected communities can be fitted into this formula in every case for a rather accurate estimate of the rate of return. Only one slight complication, which is fundamentally methodological, occurs. Unlike the hypothetical example above, most

10. John E. Moes develops this formulation in a recent work that explores the feasibility of making use of industrial subsidization on the local level as a means of mitigating un- and underemployment in labor surplus regions. See John E. Moes, *Local Subsidies for Industry* (Chapel Hill: The University of North Carolina Press, 1962).

11. This factor enters into the formula only in that the actual paying out of the subsidy to the "foreign" industrial enterprise produces a negative multiplier effect, which must be accounted for in order to get a true estimate of the income benefit. This is the first $S_a$, which is included inside the brackets and multiplied by the income multiplier. Without the second $S_a$ the formula represents a net rate-of-return concept, i.e., a rate of return on investment over and above the market rate. By adding in again the $S_a$ (not affected by the multiplier), only the negative multiplier impact of the annual subsidy payment is taken into account, that being the difference between the aggregate amount of the first $S_a$ and the second $S_a$ (the first $S_a$ is the larger of the two in that it is multiplied by the income multiplier whereas the second is not).

subsidizing communities extend subsidies to industrial firms through numerous means, in varying amounts, and over different time periods. Moreover, the ensuing income streams vary greatly from year to year, sometimes with a cutoff date at the end of one year, sometimes at the end of five years, ten years, etc., even to perpetuity in others, the payroll and subsidy figures cannot be substituted directly into the formula. The non-constant and non-infinite income flows must first be converted into constant perpetual flows before substituting in the formula can be executed. A hypothetical example may suffice to elucidate this issue.

Suppose that a community extends a subsidy to an industrial firm in three separate annual installments, $100 at the beginning of the first year, $150 at the beginning of the second year, and $200 at the start of the third year. The income benefits resulting from the subsidized plant are constant at $500 annually for five years ($500 at the end of the first year, $500 at the end of the second year, and so forth), then the payroll ceases entirely. It is supposed that none of the payroll is lost to the community and that the income multiplier is 1.2. What is the rate of return on this subsidy investment?

Clearly, these figures cannot be placed directly in the formula to get an answer. Both the cost and benefit streams must be discounted to their present values by the market rate of interest (6 percent). Both present values must be spread out (again using a 6 percent rate of interest) in perpetual annual streams, which are equivalent in value to the present values of the *actual* respective benefit and cost streams. Discounting at a 6 percent rate of interest, the three subsidy payments ($100, $150, and $200) represent a present worth of $420. At the same interest rate, the present value of the income stream ($500 annually for five years) is $2,108. The $420 present value of the actual subsidy stream is equivalent to a perpetual annual flow of $25. Likewise, the $2,108 figure represents a $126 perpetual annual flow. Now, the rate of return may be computed by substituting in our formula. The rate of return in this case is 29 percent per annum.

$$r = \frac{K[(P-L) - S_a] + S_a}{S_c} \cdot 100 = \frac{1.2\,[(\$126 - 0) - \$25] + \$25}{\$420} \cdot 100$$

For each subsidized firm, rates of return are computed under three different circumstances. The first method of calculation (hereafter referred to as Case I), and the more realistic one,[12] considers the pay-

12. It is argued in this study that this appears to be a reasonable assumption, especially in those instances where the industrial building belongs to the municipality or to a local development corporation. Another occupant may be easily

roll resulting from the subsidized firm as a perpetual income stream. The amount of subsidy involved is the capitalized value of the total subsidization promised the enterprise. The second type of rate-of-return estimation (hereafter denoted as Case II) is based on the supposition that the firm ceases immediately to operate in the community (to be specific, at the end of 1961).[13] Rates of return are estimated using as the income benefit only the payroll disbursed in the community while the subsidized firm was there. Since many of the subsidies (e.g., tax subsidies, utility concessions, and risk subsidies) are actually paid to the firm over a number of years rather than in a lump-sum, the subsidized industrial enterprise leaving the community within a few years of becoming established does not collect the entire promised financial inducement. Consequently, the capitalized value of the subsidy received by the firm in this case is apt to be less than in Case I. The third case (hereafter specified as Case III) involves "the worst of all possible worlds." Again the firm is assumed to leave the community at the end of 1961. Only payroll paid to the locality during the firm's stay is relevant. In this case, the amount of subsidy incurred is frequently higher than the amount of subsidy actually promised the firm. For example, when a community constructs an industrial building for a newly locating firm under the conditions that the latter repays the cost of the project, exclusive of interest charges, a subsidy exists only in accordance with the amount of interest foregone. However, if the firm leaves and the community is unable to lease or sell the building, the *actual* cost incurred in locating this firm rises above that expected, since the community would be forced to pay for the building. The chance of this happening is remote, but calculating rates of return on the basis of such an assumption can be meaningful in that something can be said as to the profitableness of the subsidization endeavor under the most unfavorable circumstances. If the rates of return are positive in Case III, it may be maintained with certain assurance that industrial subsidization by individual localities is overwhelmingly profitable.

---

encouraged to move into the building, often on the remainder of the subsidy not collected by the vacating firm. Nevertheless, the author does realize that the possibility exists that upon the departure of a subsidized firm the community in question may be unable to locate successfully another industrial firm without further subsidization. In this event, only payroll disbursed while the subsidized firm was producing locally can be considered as an income benefit arising from the initial subsidization. This leads us to the additional computations of rates of return on industrial subsidization as delineated below.

13. These data were gathered in 1961.

## Table 1*

| Industrial Firm | Capitalized Cost of Subsidies Extended (in Dollars) | | | Annual Income Benefit Resulting from the subsidized plant, i.e., $K[(P-L)-S_a]+S_a$ | | | Annual Rate of Return (Percent) | | |
|---|---|---|---|---|---|---|---|---|---|
| | Case Iᵃ | Case IIᵇ | Case IIIᶜ | Case Iᵃ | Case IIᵇ | Case IIIᶜ | Case Iᵃ | Case IIᵇ | Case IIIᶜ |
| Firm A | $346,548 | $268,912 | $553,042 | $852,371 | $412,095 | $409,368 | 246 | 153 | 74 |
| Firm B | 129,906 | 68,059 | 216,097 | 404,097 | 121,144 | 119,723 | 311 | 178 | 55 |
| Firm C | 127,698 | 46,302 | 295,991 | 713,334 | 78,282 | 75,885 | 559 | 169 | 26 |
| Firm D | 28,647 | 20,698 | 54,740 | 431,297 | 205,267 | 205,149 | 1,506 | 992 | 375 |
| Firm E | 276,199 | 124,098 | 430,809 | 499,140 | 123,222 | 121,382 | 181 | 99 | 28 |
| Firm G | 105,781 | 38,136 | 142,599 | 91,651 | 26,517 | 25,891 | 87 | 70 | 18 |
| Firm H | 81,618 | 30,563 | 180,802 | 179,282 | 58,247 | 57,344 | 220 | 191 | 32 |
| Firm I | 49,361 | 24,563 | 100,694 | 508,375 | 163,419 | 163,012 | 1,030 | 665 | 162 |
| Firm J | 47,079 | 27,365 | 105,071 | 313,305 | 103,960 | 103,493 | 665 | 380 | 99 |
| Firm K | 153,088 | 33,533 | 173,204 | 739,475 | 153,950 | 152,274 | 483 | 459 | 88 |
| Firm M | 178,858 | 43,638 | 299,658 | 1,715,269 | 353,496 | 338,135 | 959 | 810 | 113 |
| Firm O | 136,861 | 31,522 | 286,700 | 190,894 | 48,388 | 40,733 | 139 | 154 | 14 |
| Firm P | 138,627 | 33,444 | 416,454 | 462,736 | 74,023 | 69,425 | 334 | 221 | 17 |
| Firm Q | 7,990 | 1,209 | 45,990 | 109,728 | 12,085 | 11,548 | 1,373 | 1,000 | 25 |
| Firm R | 60,502 | 39,276 | 133,742 | 675,260 | 290,232 | 289,325 | 1,116 | 739 | 216 |
| Firm S | 188,255 | 53,673 | 440,963 | 970,217 | 241,527 | 227,584 | 515 | 450 | 52 |
| Firm T | 7,721 | 5,921 | 58,638 | 632,729 | 212,849 | 212,532 | 8,195 | 3,595 | 362 |
| Firm V | 147,990 | — | 333,704 | 699,720 | — | 237,400 | 473 | — | 71 |
| Firm W | 65,948 | — | 112,429 | 224,209 | — | 23,413 | 340 | — | 21 |
| Firm X | 110,027 | — | 233,971 | 475,320 | — | 35,331 | 432 | — | 15 |
| Firm Y | 3,955 | — | 5,893 | 209,320 | — | 42,814 | 5,293 | — | 727 |
| Firm Z | 150,978 | — | 263,654 | 1,015,822 | — | 62,019 | 673 | — | 24 |

* It should be emphasized that the data from which these figures were derived were taken from actual, existing communities, which had subsidized the industrial firms in question. Hence, for reasons already indicated, the names of both the municipalities and the industrial firms are not listed.

ᵃ Rates of return on industrial subsidization assuming that the subsidization assures a perpetual annual payroll.

ᵇ Rates of return on industrial subsidization assuming that all subsidized plants close at the end of 1961.

ᶜ Rates of return on industrial subsidization assuming that all subsidized plants close at the end of 1961.

## The Rates of Return Presented

Twenty-two firms, located in ten different localities, were analyzed. Appropriate computations in deriving the capitalized cost of subsidies extended each plant, acquisition of the annual income benefits resulting from each subsidized plant, and procurement of the estimated per annum rate of return acquired by each community on all twenty-two subsidized endeavors under Case I, Case II, and Case III conditions were realized. (See Table 1.) On the basis of these data it was discovered that in every case the rate of return on the subsidy investment was well above the 6 percent per annum rate of return acquired on alternative investment projects. On the supposition that the subsidized payroll is a perpetual stream (Case I), of the twenty-two firms subsidized by the ten selected communities the *annual* rates of return ranged from a high of 8,195 percent to a low of 87 percent. (Again, refer to Table 1.) Four-fifths of the specified cases yielded rates of return in excess of 200 percent per annum, while one-fourth exceeded 1,000 percent per annum.

Even under the more stringent assumptions of Case II, the rates of return were exceedingly high. In this instance, of the twenty-two subsidized firms the annual rates of return ranged from a high of 3,595 percent to a low of 70 percent.

Many location experts have argued vehemently that it is a misrepresentation of the actual state of affairs to assume that the subsidized plant payroll is perpetual. On the contrary, so they argue, most subsidized plants are fly-by-night concerns, remaining in the community extending financial assistance only long enough to acquire the subsidy before departing for more profitable grounds. Advocates of this line of reasoning further conclude that localities practicing industrial subsidization are experiencing disastrous financial results. Evidence presented in Table 1 of this paper does not bear out the validity of this argument.

For each of the twenty-two subsidized firms considered in this study, the rate of return on the subsidy investment was computed on the assumption that the industrial plant leaves the community immediately. (This is Case III.) It was further assumed that each community was unable to secure the establishment of another industrial firm without additional subsidization, that the entire capitalized value of the subsidy was lost to the community, and that the income benefits were to cease immediately. Slightly less than half of the twenty-two firms had been in their new locations less than four years, with five of these having been established from only one to two years. Therefore, by assuming that these subsidized plants leave the locality immediately, they are actually being characterized as "fly-by-night concerns."[14] Despite the harshness of these assumptions, however, the rates of returns were still found to be greater than the 6 percent alternative rate of return. Under Case III conditions, the annual rates of return ranged from a high of 727 percent to a low of 14 percent, still an extremely profitable investment. (See Table 1.) In this instance, slightly less than three-fourths of the subsidized projects manifested an annual rate of return in excess of 25 percent.

The fundamental conclusions of this report may be briefly summarized as follows:

(1) With respect to the twenty-two subsidized firms considered in this study, the ten selected communities in every case experienced rates of return on the subsidies extended significantly above the 6 percent alternative rate of return assumed to be acquirable by the communities on alternative uses of the subsidy funds.

(2) Even on the basis of the assumption that subsidized firms are fly-by-night concerns (which is not even near the actual truth of the matter), under the present system of local subsidization, industrial subsidy investments are still extremely profitable.

## A Final Comment

Chaotic pockets of poverty are evident in many regions of the United States, especially in the South. Such localities are relentlessly attempting to combat such economic degradation through well-organized industrial development programs. Commonly, these programs make liberal use of financial subsidies as a means of inducing industrial firms to locate in specified communities. On the basis of the data contained in this report, it is evident that many localized surplus labor problems have been alleviated through the use of industrial subsidies, thus providing substantial rates of return in excess of returns acquirable on alternative investment endeavors. However, it should be stated that the conclusions of this report are independent

14. It should be kept in mind that these rate-of-return estimates are true only in those instances where the "worst of all possible worlds" is assumed to exist. Actually, the rates of return would be higher almost consistently even if the subsidized plant did leave permanently, because the bulk of these subsidies are paid to the firm only over a long period of time. Should the firm leave after operating in the locality for a short while, most of the subsidy is yet to be paid. This depicts the Case II situation. As indicated above, Case II rates of return are only slightly below rates of return in Case I.

of a general acceptance of competitive subsidization of industry. There are objections to industrial subsidization that must be adequately treated before complete acceptance of the thesis can be realized. This study is strictly concerned with the profitability of industrial subsidization from the point of view of the local community. Moreover, it should be re-emphasized that these rates of return are relevant only in those cases where the subsidy actually caused the industrial firm to locate in the subsidizing community.[15]

It is the sincere hope of this author that the findings of this study will instigate further research and inquiry into the relationships that exist between local industrial subsidization and ensuing enhancements of industrial payroll. In light of such irritating and perplexing events as economic losses resulting from widespread un- and underemployment, disutilities yielded by non-desired migration of people from un- and underemployed areas, and disadvantages of centralized industrial capacity in the case of military conflict, surely the pros and cons of local industrial subsidization should be afforded thorough consideration by future examiners in this area.

15. Refer once again to footnote 3 above.

# Index